Montgomery's
AUDITING

By

NORMAN J. LENHART, C.P.A.

and

PHILIP L. DEFLIESE, C.P.A.

Partners of
LYBRAND, ROSS BROS. & MONTGOMERY

EIGHTH EDITION

THE RONALD PRESS COMPANY   •   NEW YORK

Library of Congress Catalog Card Number: 57–9301

PRINTED IN THE UNITED STATES OF AMERICA

Dedicated to the memory of
ROBERT H. MONTGOMERY (1872-1953)
a beloved partner and a leader of his profession

PREFACE

This book's purpose, which has remained unchanged since the first edition in 1912, is to set forth the principles underlying the theory and practice of auditing. Through seven editions and over four decades it has been accepted as an authority in the field of accounting and auditing. Changes in accounting principles, auditing practices, and business and financial conditions have required extensive rewriting of the seventh edition, which was published in 1949. It is hoped that this book will continue to be helpful in promoting wider acceptance of good accounting principles by the business world and maintenance of high standards by the accounting profession. Although it is intended primarily for practicing certified public accountants, accounting and financial executives in business and industry should find it a valuable aid in their work. It should also be useful as a reference book to credit men, bankers, underwriters, financial analysts, labor unions, lawyers, the courts, and teachers and students of accounting and auditing.

A large part of the public accountant's practice consists of examination of financial statements for the purpose of expressing an opinion on their fairness of presentation and conformity with generally accepted accounting principles consistently applied. Accordingly, a substantial part of this book is devoted to generally accepted accounting principles, since a knowledge of them is indispensable to the auditor. Review and evaluation of his client's internal accounting control and internal check influence the selection and timing of auditing procedures which afford a reasonable basis for his opinion. The auditor also needs to be familiar with the best practice relating to form and content of financial statements. Wherever applicable, therefore, the chapters are presented under four captions: (1) accounting principles, (2) internal control, (3) auditing procedures, and (4) statement presentation.

This edition, like the previous editions, emphasizes auditing objectives, the coordination of the examination of related accounts, and the influence of the interdependence of the balance sheet and income statement upon accounting principles and auditing procedures.

Income taxes continue to become more complicated, and the disparity between tax principles and accounting principles has not substantially lessened. Continuing high tax rates accentuate this disparity to a point where net income is materially distorted unless proper allocation of tax expense is made. This edition contains a new chapter entitled "Taxes" which deals with many matters relating to accounting for income and other taxes.

The auditor's independent approach to the examination of financial statements has never discouraged him from serving his client in other capacities. His training, experience, and unbiased viewpoint enable him to serve his client by suggesting and implementing improvements in the day-to-day operation of the accounting and financial departments. While such services to management have long been rendered by the certified public accountant, their character and extent have broadened greatly during recent years. A chapter entitled "Management Services" appears for the first time in this edition to indicate areas other than auditing in which the independent certified public accountant may be helpful to his client.

One of the standards of field work approved and adopted by the American Institute of Certified Public Accountants in 1948 states:

> There is to be a proper study and evaluation of the existing internal control as a basis for reliance thereon and for the determination of the resultant extent of the tests to which auditing procedures are to be restricted.

Internal control with which the independent public accountant is concerned may be divided into two classes: (1) those designed to bring about the accurate and suitable recording and summarization of authorized financial transactions (internal accounting control) and (2) those designed to safeguard assets against defalcation or other similar irregularities (internal check). The distinction between these two classes of internal control, the independent certified public accountant's responsibilities with respect to each, and the resultant effect upon his selection and timing of auditing procedures are discussed and clarified in the book; the questions in the "Questionnaire for Evaluation of Internal Accounting Control and Internal Check" in the Appendix are divided into these two classes, and brief statements of the purposes of many of the controls listed are given. We believe that this approach should promote a better understanding of auditors' responsibilities, not only in the profession, but between auditors and their clients. Such understanding has already led to a substantial modification of traditional audit procedures relating to cash; these changes have been recognized in this edition.

In 1951 the American Institute of Certified Public Accountants issued a "Codification of Statements on Auditing Procedure" which states: "The ordinary examination incident to the issuance of an opinion respecting financial statements is not designed and cannot be relied losses from third parties may be based. Close cooperation between the public accountant and the bonding company is desirable in such examinations.

The public accountant is called on occasionally to testify in court as an expert witness. Such testimony may be required when fraud has been discovered and is to be proved, when there are facts to be established by accounting evidence, or when the public accountant's opinion is sought as to whether generally accepted accounting principles have been followed.

In the activities discussed in the preceding paragraphs the public accountant furnishes his services directly to his client. Even when independence is not expected, the public accountant should maintain his objectivity and integrity.

PUBLIC SERVICES.—The accounting profession has been called upon with increasing frequency to perform public services for which its individual members are peculiarly well qualified by training and experience. Public accountants are active in charitable and public welfare groups in their communities, and many take part in assisting or participating officially in state and local government operations. Others devote time to accounting education, as teachers or in an advisory capacity. Services of public accountants in the fiscal and procurement branches of the armed services during both World Wars are well known. Members of the profession have served on such governmental projects as studies of methods of simplification and promotion of economy in the federal government under former President Hoover and the study of the efficiency of the Internal Revenue Service and the adequacy of its staff. Committees of the American Institute of Certified Public Accountants have studied and reported upon improvements in the federal tax structure, and a group of certified public accountants has assisted the appropriations committees of Congress in studying budget requests. There have been noteworthy appointments of certified public accountants to important posts in the federal government having to do with financial or taxation problems. The profession has demonstrated its capacity and willingness to perform public services.

Classification of Audits.—The work of the independent public accountant in examining financial statements has long been referred to as an audit. Since the word "audit" is a general expression, there have been many attempts to classify the various activities of public accountants by more descriptive terms, such as "detailed audit," "complete audit," "continuous audit," "test audit," "protective audit," "balance sheet audit," and others. None of these expressions has proved satisfactory, and they are more and more falling into disuse.

It is logical to classify audits into two general divisions: (a) examinations of financial statements for the purpose of expressing a professional opinion whether they present fairly the financial position of a business at a given date and the results of its operations for a stated period, in conformity with generally accepted accounting principles consistently applied, and (b) examinations for various purposes, as a result of which it is not expected that the public accountant will state his opinion regarding the financial statements as a whole. The former examination is often referred to simply as an "examination of financial statements." It should be conducted in accordance with auditing standards described hereafter in this book.

CHAPTER 2

AUDITING STANDARDS

Introduction.—The evidence upon which the independent auditor bases his opinion concerning financial statements is developed through application of auditing *procedures* which in his judgment are appropriate in the circumstances. Such procedures are chosen and executed in accordance with generally accepted auditing *standards*. Adherence to these auditing standards is of such importance that the short-form report currently recommended by the American Institute of Certified Public Accountants requires the auditor to state whether his examination was made in accordance with generally accepted auditing standards.

Generally Accepted Auditing Standards.—The matter of setting forth "generally accepted auditing standards" has been under study by the Committee on Auditing Procedure of the American Institute of Certified Public Accountants over a period of years, and its first pronouncement on the subject was made in 1947. The most recent document was issued in August, 1954 under the title "Generally Accepted Auditing Standards—Their Significance and Scope." All practicing independent public accountants should be familiar with it. The following summary, which has been approved and adopted by the membership of the American Institute of Certified Public Accountants, is a fitting introduction to a consideration of the work of the practicing independent public accountant:

General Standards:
1. The examination is to be performed by a person or persons having adequate technical training and proficiency as an auditor.
2. In all matters relating to the assignment an independence in mental attitude is to be maintained by the auditor or auditors.
3. Due professional care is to be exercised in the performance of the examination and the preparation of the report.

Standards of Field Work:
1. The work is to be adequately planned and assistants, if any, are to be properly supervised.

2. There is to be a proper study and evaluation of the existing internal control as a basis for reliance thereon and for the determination of the resultant extent of the tests to which auditing procedures are to be restricted.

3. Sufficient competent evidential matter is to be obtained through inspection, observation, inquiries and confirmations to afford a reasonable basis for an opinion regarding the financial statements under examination.

Standards of Reporting:

1. The report shall state whether the financial statements are presented in accordance with generally accepted principles of accounting.

2. The report shall state whether such principles have been consistently observed in the current period in relation to the preceding period.

3. Informative disclosures in the financial statements are to be regarded as reasonably adequate unless otherwise stated in the report.

4. The report shall either contain an expression of opinion regarding the financial statements, taken as a whole, or an assertion to the effect that an opinion cannot be expressed. When an over-all opinion cannot be expressed, the reasons therefor should be stated. In all cases where an auditor's name is associated with financial statements the report should contain a clear-cut indication of the character of the auditor's examination, if any, and the degree of responsibility he is taking.

PERSONAL OR GENERAL STANDARDS.—These standards apply both to field work and to the report, and require that auditing procedures be applied with professional competence by properly trained persons. Generally accepted auditing procedures are those ordinarily employed by skilled accountants, and are described in such authoritative statements as those by the Committee on Auditing Procedure of the American Institute of Certified Public Accountants and the writings of recognized authorities in the field of accounting literature. Professional competence, and the ability to direct and supervise assistants, in the application of auditing procedures can be expected only from persons who, through education and experience in the field of auditing, have developed a level of judgment appropriate to the requirements of these exacting professional standards. Such judgment must be exercised without bias and with objective consideration of the facts; without this impartiality the auditor's findings might not be dependable, however excellent his training and technical proficiency. Finally, the competent and unbiased auditor must exercise due care in the performance of his work. In Chapter 3 the personal standards of the auditor are discussed in more detail.

STANDARDS OF FIELD WORK.—In the performance of field work the auditor must keep in mind considerations of materiality and relative risk. The exercise of due care implies greater attention to the more important items in the financial statements than to those of less importance. The risk of error may be greater in certain areas and under certain conditions of internal accounting control or internal check than in others.

In planning field work, timeliness and orderliness of application of auditing procedures are essential to due care in their performance. A knowledge of the system of internal accounting control, gained by independent review, is essential to proper planning. After testing the effectiveness of the system in practice, the auditor exercises judgment as to the extent to which auditing procedures must be applied in the circumstances.

The bulk of the auditor's work in obtaining information upon which he may base his opinion lies in the examination of accounting evidence. Internal evidence includes data available within the client's organization. External evidence includes that obtained by inspection or observation of physical assets, by confirmation from customers, creditors and other independent sources, and by specific inquiries. In his exercise of due care in the performance of field work the auditor should defer the final determination of the nature and extent of his auditing procedures until he has obtained an understanding of the available evidence and, of equal importance, formed some judgment as to its reliability. A general discussion of preparatory and administrative auditing procedures is given in Chapter 4, and in Chapter 5 the auditor's review and testing of internal control are covered.

STANDARDS OF REPORTING.—The primary responsibility for reporting on financial position and results of operations of a business concern rests with its management. Such reports of management are called financial statements, and usually include a balance sheet and statements of income and surplus. The auditor's report is the medium through which he expresses his opinion on financial statements prepared by management, based on his examination of such statements through auditing procedures.

To comply with the standards of reporting previously summarized, the auditor must first be familiar with the principles of accounting which have become generally accepted. He recognizes that there are principles which have had limited usage but which nevertheless are generally accepted, and he also knows that there are many variations in application of such principles to fit the wide variety of operating conditions which will be encountered. His determination whether "generally accepted accounting principles" have been followed requires the exercise of judgment based on the facts in each case.

Determination of consistency in application of accounting principles requires judgment as to whether a change is (a) the proper consequence of altered conditions, (b) a change to a procedure of definite preference in general practice from one not enjoying such preference, though both procedures may be acceptable, or (c) merely the choice, when two or more procedures are available, of an alternative dictated not by change in circumstances and with the possibility of ulterior motives.

Item 3 of "Standards of Reporting" requires in effect that if informative disclosures in the financial statements are not regarded as reasonably adequate, the auditor's report should so state. Informative disclosure may be inherent in the arrangement as well as the content of the financial statements, including the appended notes or explanations. Adequacy of disclosure involves consideration of the terminology used, sufficiency of explanatory or descriptive matter, and classifications in the financial statements. Questions of informative disclosure may arise in the presentation of such items as the following: the bases of stating investments, inventories, and plant; liens on assets; preferred stock dividend arrearages; restrictions on dividends; contingent liabilities; post-balance sheet date information.

Whenever the independent auditor permits his name to be associated with financial statements, his report should contain either (1) an expression of opinion regarding the financial statements taken as a whole (which opinion, under certain circumstances, may be qualified) or (2) the reasons why an over-all opinion cannot be expressed. The independent auditor will decline to express an opinion if (a) his examination has been so limited by restrictions or circumstances as not to afford him a basis for an informed opinion or (b) his reservations or exceptions with respect to the financial statements are of such extent that they preclude the expression of an opinion.

In Chapter 6 the auditor's professional standards applicable to reporting upon his examination are discussed and illustrated.

CHAPTER 3

QUALIFICATIONS AND RESPONSIBILITIES

Introduction.—The work of the public accountant calls for a specially trained person of the highest integrity and ability. The public accountant's responsibility to his client requires that, within limitations of the scope of the engagement, he conduct the examination and prepare the report with the care appropriate to his profession. This chapter discusses the personal characteristics of the public accountant, his qualifications, training and experience, and his relations with clients, fellow accountants, and the public.

Qualifications Desirable in the Public Accountant.—A useful member of the public accounting profession should have certain qualities, some equally necessary to success in any field, and others peculiarly essential to the public accountant.

HONESTY.—Honesty is an essential qualification of a public accountant. It means that under all circumstances he is conscientious and careful in his work; it means fearlessness in distinguishing the relative merits of two or more courses of action and in advocating his decision. Without scrupulous honesty in performing and in reporting on assignments at every level of responsibility, the public accountant cannot hope to measure up to the high requirements of his profession.

OBJECTIVE POINT OF VIEW.—The public accountant's viewpoint should be one of complete objectivity—detached, impersonal, and unprejudiced. This quality is related to the important attribute of independence, of which more will be said later, but it is as essential in the public accountant's work when independence is not required as it is when independence is a prerequisite.

CAPACITY FOR GROWTH.—New demands are constantly being thrust upon the public accountant, resulting from constant changes in the problems and conduct of business. Only by continual study and alertness can the public accountant keep abreast of these demands, and his ability to serve his clients will be limited only by his own capacity for growth.

ANALYTICAL ABILITY.—The auditor must be able to analyze problems encountered—whether of auditing procedure, application of accounting principles, or statement presentation—in such a way that the underlying facts may be logically stated and weighed. The weighing of facts presented involves exercise of judgment, the quality of which in turn depends in large part on the auditor's training and experience. When the problem is one of reporting, whether by way of statements, schedules, or descriptive matter, the auditor should endeavor to put himself in the place of those for whom his report is intended. Statements that may not be understood by those receiving them are unsatisfactory even though they may be free of material error. The auditor should be able to analyze and interpret the facts behind the figures and to arrange his conclusions so that they are intelligible to those to whom the report is directed.

CONSTRUCTIVE AND INTERPRETIVE ABILITY.—The auditor should be more than an analyst. Proper presentation of all the material facts in financial statements requires imagination and constructive thinking by company personnel who prepare them, and the public accountant may offer assistance to his client in drafting them. Problems of business and their solution by management are reflected in the accounts, and the meaning of accounting results often must be interpreted to management by accountants. The interpretation of accounting data to those not technically trained in their use requires constructive ability of a high order. The same qualities are essential when the auditor is faced with selection of appropriate auditing procedures.

ABILITY TO WRITE AND SPEAK.—Thorough training in the spoken and written use of the language by which thoughts must be conveyed is of great importance to the public accountant. No matter how competently he may execute auditing procedures, his usefulness is limited unless he can report adequately upon the results of his efforts, both orally and in writing. Skill in speaking and writing may be developed by participation in discussions in accountants' technical meetings and

by contributing articles to accounting publications. Those who do so benefit not only themselves but also their profession by contributing to the growing body of accounting literature.

PERSONAL ATTRIBUTES.—Self-reliance must be cultivated by the young auditor. He will not always be in a position to ask for advice or instructions. Many times he must work out his own solutions to puzzling problems. He may make mistakes to be corrected by his superiors, but unless he displays initiative he will fail to develop self-confidence which instills confidence in him by others.

The public accountant often corresponds or confers with others in arriving at decisions. It is important that his position be sound, but it is equally important that he be able to persuade others of its soundness. Accordingly, tactfulness, the nice discernment of what is appropriate to do or say in dealing with others without giving offense while firmly maintaining his position, is a valuable attribute of the public accountant.

A keen business sense is important to the auditor, not only in the conduct of his own affairs, but also in reviewing financial operations of clients and in counseling them with respect to their activities. Business sense, which means clear perception and reasoning as to the soundness of business transactions or policies, is frequently intuitive but, if it is not, it may be developed. Without it, an auditor's success will be restricted.

Education and Training.—The opportunities for education in public accounting are now abundant, thanks to the pioneering work of leaders of the profession many years ago. Most leading universities, in their schools of business administration or commerce, give courses leading to a degree with an accounting major and affording some preparation for the uniform CPA examination. In many universities graduate work in accounting is offered, leading to higher academic degrees. There are also a number of schools specializing in accounting which are accepted by certain states in which graduation from a school of accounting is a requisite for the CPA certificate. Many of these schools and colleges maintain evening courses and extension courses so that the ambitious may pursue their studies while employed during the day.

Public accounting firms recognize that academic education must be supplemented with directed on-the-job training, and their staffs appreciate the necessity for instruction of assistants in the course of their daily activities. Such training may be supplemented with periodic lectures on specific subjects, with general staff meetings in one office or for a group of offices, and with firm bulletins or articles in regular house organs on matters of current interest. A number of firms hold regular classes over extended periods for groups of new employees before assigning them to regular staff duties, as well as conducting advanced courses for staff members after one or more years of service.

In addition to thorough grounding in principles of accounting and auditing, the independent auditor's training should develop some knowledge of business and tax laws, familiarity with various accounting systems to enable him to recommend improvements in the client's accounting procedures that may provide more efficient operation and better internal control, and a knowledge of cost accounting and the various methods of arriving at costs.

Familiarity with Professional Publications.—The usual short-form report on examination of financial statements includes the sentence "Our examination was made in accordance with generally accepted auditing standards, and accordingly included such tests of the accounting records and such other auditing procedures as we considered necessary in the circumstances" and states that the financial statements are presented "in conformity with generally accepted accounting principles." The American Institute of Certified Public Accountants, through its appropriate committees, has issued a number of pronouncements to assist the independent auditor in arriving at the opinion expressed in his short-form report. The important publication "Generally Accepted Auditing Standards" was discussed in Chapter 2, and is elaborated upon in this chapter and in Chapters 4, 5, and 6. The public accountant should be familiar with the following publications of the Institute:

Restatement and Revision of Accounting Research Bulletins (Bulletin No. 43) and subsequent bulletins

Accounting Terminology Bulletin No. 1 (Review and Résumé) and subsequent bulletins

Codification of Statements on Auditing Procedure (Statements No. 1 through No. 24) and subsequent statements

Internal Control (1949)

Audits by Certified Public Accountants (1950)

Generally Accepted Auditing Standards—Their Significance and Scope (1954)

Accounting Trends and Techniques (an annual publication which analyzes and illustrates corporate reporting practices)

There are numerous other publications of the Institute and of the various state societies of certified public accountants which are available to the practitioner to assist him in meeting the growing demands of his profession.

Judgment.—The exercise of judgment involves choosing between two or more courses of action. The auditor makes a choice of auditing procedures to be applied in the circumstances and also exercises judgment as to the extent to which those procedures should be applied. He often must decide which of several generally accepted accounting principles is applicable in the circumstances and approve one of several alternatives in reviewing the form, content, and wording of financial statements. In his own report, he must exercise judgment in determining whether and to what extent explanations or exceptions are necessary, and sometimes must decide whether he can properly give any opinion at all.

The auditor must be sure that his judgments are based on evidential matter which he has examined through auditing procedures. Such evidence is weighed without bias in the light of the auditor's experience and his knowledge of the experience of others. Soundness of judgment will vary with the extent and quality of practical experience which the auditor can bring to bear on the problem.

All judgments are thought to be good judgments at the time they are made, and in the light of the information then available, they may be, but the exercise of judgment often implies a present estimate of the results of future events. Judgment, therefore, cannot be finally assayed until time has revealed the soundness of the estimate. A man of good judgment is one skilled in evaluating relevant data, with the knowledge and experience to weigh the probable consequences of action based on this appraisal, and one whose earlier judgments have proved sound.

State Recognition of Public Accountants.—Each of the states and Alaska, Hawaii, the Virgin Islands, Puerto Rico, and the District of Columbia have laws under which the public accountant who meets with certain educational and experience requirements and passes the required examination may call himself a "Certified Public Accountant." Everyone who intends to make public accountancy his life work should try to obtain this certificate. It indicates his compliance with state standards for the practice of his profession and makes him eligible to join one of the professional societies devoted to the interests of the profession. Accountants who have not qualified as certified public accountants are licensed in some states as public accountants, registered accountants, or registered public accountants.

Current Study of Educational and Experience Requirements for the CPA Certificate.—The educational and experience requirements referred to above as prerequisites for sitting for the CPA examination vary considerably among the states. Since 1952, the Commission on Standards of Education and Experience for Certified Public Accountants has been engaged in a study "to formulate standards of education and experience which are considered desirable prerequisites for state certification as a CPA."

The report of this Commission was published in August, 1956 and is expected to have important influence on standards of training for the accounting profession in the United States. The report recommends as a long-range goal substantially increased educational requirements for the CPA certificate, looking forward to establishment of professional academic programs at a postgraduate level. It anticipates that such programs may eventually be so effective that formal education may become the primary method of preparing for the profession. The Commission recognizes that practical experience advances the competence of a public accountant throughout his career. It believes that the CPA certificate may eventually come to be interpreted as a mark of competence, obtained through formal education, to enter the profession as a CPA. Recommendations are given for the gradual introduction of this new approach to professional accreditation. It will undoubtedly be some years before the major long-range recommendations in this report are accepted and put into effect.

State and National Societies of Certified Public Accountants.—Certified public accountants have organized into societies in all jurisdictions granting the certificate and into a national organization, the American Institute of Certified Public Accountants. The American Woman's Society of Certified Public Accountants is also an active body. Each CPA should affiliate with either his state society, the national organization, or both. State societies and the American Institute of Certified Public Accountants furnish educational opportunities for their members through technical meetings at which current problems are discussed. The Institute maintains a research department which is available for consultation on problems arising in members' practice. The Institute and the various state societies of certified public accountants also have numerous technical committees, appointed from specialists in their fields, from whom members may obtain advice. *The Journal of Accountancy,* published by the American Institute of Certified Public Accountants, is the leading technical publication of the profession, and a number of the state societies have periodicals which are of merit in their field. In providing forums for the exchange of ideas the Institute and state societies contribute to the growth of the profession. Through publications and activities of their committees they interpret the aims and needs of the profession to its members and to the public.

The Accounting Profession in Canada.—In Canada the accounting profession is controlled by provincial legislation, somewhat as is done by the various states in this country. The degree issued under these statutes in Canada, and which closely corresponds in stature to that of CPA, is Chartered Accountant. There are Institutes of Chartered Accountants in each Province, which are banded together to form the Canadian Institute of Chartered Accountants. As in this country, there are other organizations of practicing accountants chartered under provincial laws, one of which uses the initials CPA.

The Companies Act (Canada) and the similar provincial Acts require shareholders to appoint an "auditor" who may not be an officer or director, and who usually is a Chartered Accountant, to examine the financial statements and give his opinion on them. When the auditor performs this service, he is responsible primarily to the shareholders and his report is addressed to them. He may not be dismissed by the directors or officers nor may they curtail his statutory duties and responsibilities. In other respects and in relation to the many other services which a Chartered Accountant may perform, his status and his relationship to the director and officers are little different from those of his United States counterpart.

In the United States a person working for a private concern or for a public accounting firm may be called an auditor, and as such his duties may be quite varied. The members of an accounting firm or its employees, when engaged in an examination of financial statements with a view to issuing an opinion thereon, may be called auditors, but preferably would be called "independent (certified) public accountants."

Rules of Professional Conduct.—The American Institute of Certified Public Accountants has adopted formal procedures for disciplining its offending members. After specified steps of complaint, investigation, notice, and hearing before the trial board, a member may be admonished, suspended, or expelled. Among the acts making a member liable to such penalties are infringement of the by-laws of the Institute or any of the rules of professional conduct as approved by the Council of the Institute. Such rules of professional conduct, which supplement the disciplinary clauses of the by-laws, are comparable to the rules of professional conduct of other professions such as medicine and law. They are designed to promote the interests of the public and the group interest of the members of the profession. These rules are of such importance in reinforcing requirements of general standards for adequate training and efficiency, independence, and due care that they are reproduced here (as revised December, 1950):

(1) A firm or partnership, all the individual members of which are members of the Institute, may describe itself as "Members of the American Institute of Certified Public Accountants," but a firm or partnership,

not all the individual members of which are members of the Institute, or an individual practicing under a style denoting a partnership when in fact there be no partner or partners, or a corporation, or an individual or individuals practicing under a style denoting a corporate organization shall not use the designation "Members of the American Institute of Certified Public Accountants."

(2) A member shall not allow any person to practice in his name who is not in partnership with him or in his employ.

(3) Commissions, brokerage, or other participation in the fees or profits of professional work shall not be allowed directly or indirectly to the laity by a member.

Commissions, brokerage, or other participation in the fees, charges, or profits of work recommended or turned over to the laity as incident to services for clients shall not be accepted directly or indirectly by a member.

(4) A member shall not engage in any business or occupation conjointly with that of a public accountant, which is incompatible or inconsistent therewith.

(5) In expressing an opinion on representations in financial statements which he has examined, a member may be held guilty of an act discreditable to the profession if

(a) he fails to disclose a material fact known to him which is not disclosed in the financial statements but disclosure of which is necessary to make the financial statements not misleading; or

(b) he fails to report any material misstatement known to him to appear in the financial statement; or

(c) he is materially negligent in the conduct of his examination or in making his report thereon; or

(d) he fails to acquire sufficient information to warrant expression of an opinion, or his exceptions are sufficiently material to negative the expression of an opinion; or

(e) he fails to direct attention to any material departure from generally accepted accounting principles or to disclose any material omission of generally accepted auditing procedure applicable in the circumstances.

(6) A member shall not sign a report purporting to express his opinion as the result of examination of financial statements unless they have been examined by him, a member or an employee of his firm, a member of the Institute, a member of a similar association in a foreign country, or a certified public accountant of a state or territory of the United States or the District of Columbia.

(7) A member shall not directly or indirectly solicit clients by circulars or advertisements, nor by personal communication or interview, not warranted by existing personal relations, and he shall not encroach upon the practice of another public accountant. A member may furnish service to those who request it.

(8) Direct or indirect offer of employment shall not be made by a member to an employee of another public accountant without first informing such accountant. This rule shall not be construed so as to inhibit

negotiations with anyone who of his own initiative or in response to public advertisement shall apply to a member for employment.

(9) Professional service shall not be rendered or offered for a fee which shall be contingent upon the findings or results of such service. This rule does not apply to cases involving federal, state, or other taxes, in which the findings are those of the tax authorities and not those of the accountant. Fees to be fixed by courts or other public authorities, which are therefore of an indeterminate amount at the time when an engagement is undertaken, are not regarded as contingent fees within the meaning of this rule.

(10) A member shall not advertise his professional attainments or services:

    (a) The publication of what is technically known as a card is restricted to an announcement of the name, title (member of American Institute of Certified Public Accountants, CPA, or other professional affiliation or designation), class of service, and address of the person or firm, issued in connection with the announcement of change of address or personnel of firm, and shall not exceed two columns in width and three inches in depth if appearing in a newspaper, and not exceed one-quarter of a page if appearing in a magazine or similar publication.

    (b) A paid listing in a directory is restricted to the name, title, class of service, address and telephone number of the person or firm, and it shall not appear in bold type, box, or other form of display, or in a style which differentiates it from other listings in the same directory.

(11) A member shall not be an officer, director, stockholder, representative, or agent of any corporation engaged in the practice of public accounting in any state or territory of the United States or the District of Columbia.

(12) A member shall not permit his name to be used in conjunction with an estimate of earnings contingent upon future transactions in a manner which may lead to the belief that the member vouches for the accuracy of the forecast.

(13) A member shall not express his opinion on financial statements of any enterprise financed in whole or in part by public distribution of securities, if he owns or is committed to acquire a financial interest in the enterprise which is substantial either in relation to its capital or to his own personal fortune, or if a member of his immediate family owns or is committed to acquire a substantial interest in the enterprise. A member shall not express his opinion on financial statements which are used as a basis of credit if he owns or is committed to acquire a financial interest in the enterprise which is substantial either in relation to its capital or to his own personal fortune or if a member of his immediate family owns or is committed to acquire a substantial interest in the enterprise, unless in his report he discloses such interest.

(14) A member shall not make a competitive bid for professional engagements in any state, territory, or the District of Columbia, if such a bid would constitute a violation of any rule of the recognized society of certified public accountants or the official board of accountancy in that state, territory, or District.

(15) A member of the American Institute of Certified Public Accountants engaged in an occupation in which he renders services of a type commonly rendered by public accountants must observe the by-laws and rules of professional conduct of the Institute in the conduct of that occupation.

(16) A member shall not violate the confidential relationship between himself and his client.

Rule 5 has special importance because it describes acts referred to generally in the by-laws as those considered "discreditable to the profession." It supports the public accountant in his insistence upon an independent attitude, emphasizes the necessity for application of generally accepted accounting principles and for making his examination in accordance with generally accepted auditing procedures applicable in the circumstances, and is of great importance in determining the public accountant's responsibilities for his opinion on financial statements (see Chapter 6).

The Committee on Professional Ethics of the Institute reviews complaints and inquiries arising under the "Rules of Professional Conduct." Complaints are investigated and are usually discussed with the members complained against, and, where the circumstances warrant, the committee recommends to the Executive Committee of the Institute that offending members be summoned for trial. A large part of the work of the Committee on Professional Ethics consists of advice to members whether proposed actions are permissible under the "Rules of Professional Conduct."

Rules of professional conduct appear in the laws of some states and have been promulgated by many state boards of accountancy. Five states have adopted the American Institute "Rules of Professional Conduct." The remaining states generally have adopted the substance of the American Institute rules and some have adopted additional rules.

Independence of the Public Accountant.—The professional public accountant offers clients technical skill and knowledge based on training and experience, but when he is retained to examine and give his opinion on financial statements, the value of his work rests even more upon his disinterested and objective viewpoint. Such a viewpoint can be consistently maintained only if the public accountant is truly independent in his attitude. Independence is a reflection of honesty and integrity. It is an inward quality and not susceptible of objective determination or definition. Public accountants know that a reputation for independence and integrity is their principal asset, and they are impelled by enlightened self-interest, and supported by certain rules of professional conduct, to maintain independence at all cost. Further discussion of independence of certified public accountants appears in Chapter 25.

Responsibilities of the Public Accountant.—It may be said that the primary obligation of the public accountant is to himself. As a professional man of honesty and integrity, he must perform his tasks with that care and skill which will satisfy his own high standards. In accepting engagements from his clients, he is obligated to complete each assignment with the knowledge that his best efforts have been expended regardless of the size or relative importance of the task or of the monetary profit to him.

The legal requirements as to the degree of skill and care expected of the public accountant have been well expressed in the frequently quoted Cooley on Torts:[1]

Every man who offers his services to another and is employed assumes the duty to exercise in the employment such skill as he possesses with reasonable care and diligence. In all those employments where peculiar skill is requisite, if one offers his services, he is understood as holding himself out to the public as possessing the degree of skill commonly possessed by others in the same employment, and, if his pretensions are unfounded, he commits a species of fraud upon every man who employs him in reliance on his public profession. But no man, whether skilled or unskilled, undertakes that the task he assumes shall be performed successfully, and without fault or error. He undertakes for good faith and integrity, but not for infallibility, and he is liable to his employer for negligence, bad faith or dishonesty, but not for losses consequent upon mere errors of judgment.

The independent public accountant's responsibility for work of other public accountants who may be engaged to report upon examinations made in certain branches or subsidiaries of the client is discussed in Chapter 6.

RESPONSIBILITIES TO THIRD PARTIES.—The public accountant has a legal responsibility to parties who have relied on his reports, other than those by whom he was retained, but only when his negligence has been so gross as to result in failure to detect serious error or omission in financial statements. Mere negligence in the performance of his professional duties is not sufficient basis, ordinarily, to support a claim against the public accountant by third parties, but gross negligence may suffice to permit the inference of a fraud. A court has held the following:[2]

Accountants certifying a representation as true to knowledge of accountants when knowledge there is none, or making a reckless misstatement or an

[1] 4th Ed., Vol. 3, p. 335.
[2] 37 C.J.S., Fraud, Sec. 48, n. 90(2).

opinion based on grounds so flimsy as to lead to conclusion that there was no
genuine belief in its truth or refusing to see the obvious or failing to investigate the doubtful, if sufficiently gross, are liable to third persons injured in
their use of a certified balance sheet, even though there is lacking deliberate
or active fraud.

The determining of legal responsibilities of the public accountant
to third parties involves many complexities, and legal counsel should
always be sought when questions relating to such responsibilities arise.

In addition to his common-law liability, the independent public
accountant who examines financial statements for inclusion in statements filed with the Securities and Exchange Commission may be subject to statutory liability to third persons. This subject is discussed in
Chapter 25.

Responsibilities Not Assumed.

For Work Other Than Accounting.—The public accountant
has a full-time job in following the profession of accountancy. He is
not, and does not pretend to be, an engineer, an appraiser, or a lawyer.
His work brings him into contact with many kinds of documents,
stocks, bonds, notes, mortgages, checks, and the like, but he is not a
handwriting expert nor an expert in forged documents. He may make
suggestions to his client that the employment of members of other
professions or specialists such as insurance brokers or traffic experts
might be advisable, but the public accountant should not attempt to
give advice outside his own field.

For Illegal or Improper Transactions.—Although the public
accountant is not a lawyer, he is expected to be generally familiar with
laws governing business and rules of regulatory commissions affecting
the accounting of his clients. The auditor cannot, however, be responsible for a policing program to see that all government regulations are
followed. If, as a result of his tests, indications of what may be illegal
transactions appear, and legal counsel agrees that illegal acts are involved, the public accountant should so report to the board of directors,
or in extreme cases, to the stockholders. He should also receive written opinion from legal counsel as to the liabilities of his client because
of such transactions. If a substantial contingent liability is believed to
exist because of illegal acts, the public accountant should insist that
necessary reference to such liability be made in the financial statements, or qualify his opinion.

If the public accountant finds that improper payments have been
made, he should report them to the board of directors. If the board of

directors approves these payments, the public accountant should receive a certified copy of minutes covering the approval.

FOR DISCOVERY OF FRAUD.—The Committee on Auditing Procedure of the American Institute of Certified Public Accountants has stated the position of the profession in "Codification of Statements on Auditing Procedure" (p. 12) as follows:

The ordinary examination incident to the issuance of an opinion respecting financial statements is not designed *and cannot be relied upon* to disclose defalcations and other similar irregularities, although their discovery frequently results. In a well-organized concern reliance for the detection of such irregularities is placed principally upon the maintenance of an adequate system of accounting records with appropriate internal control. If an auditor were to attempt to discover defalcations and similar irregularities he would have to extend his work to a point where its cost would be prohibitive. It is generally recognized that good internal control and surety bonds provide protection much more cheaply. On the basis of his examination by tests and checks, made in the light of his review and tests of the system of internal control, the auditor relies upon the integrity of the client's organization unless circumstances are such as to arouse his suspicion, in which case he must extend his procedures to determine whether or not such suspicions are justified.

Bonding companies under their right of subrogation have a definite interest in the work of the public accountant as it relates to fraud, and The Surety Association of America has published a booklet entitled "Safeguards against Employee Dishonesty in Business" which indicates the attitude of this Association regarding the responsibility of public accountants for discovery of fraud:

The independent audit itself is an important deterrent against dishonesty as it increases the likelihood of discovery. The audit is conducted primarily to enable the expression of a professional opinion concerning financial position and operating results, and therefore is not designed and cannot be relied upon to disclose defalcations and other similar irregularities. Nevertheless, audits very often result in discovery of dishonest practices when they do occur.

The statement of the Auditing Procedure Committee of the American Institute of Certified Public Accountants previously quoted presumes that the examination is to be made in accordance with generally accepted auditing standards, including that requiring due professional care, and that the selection of tests and auditing procedures is made with the degree of skill commonly possessed by members of the profession. It is important to keep in mind that the auditor's primary responsibility is for a reasonable basis for his opinion on the financial statements under examination. His tests and auditing procedures are principally designed to assure him that generally accepted accounting principles have been consistently applied and that the account balances are combined to produce financial statements which are reasonably stated.

Such summarizations of figures, especially those which usually appear on the statement of income, are often composed of numerous detail account balances. While the tests that the auditor may make are intended to afford reasonable assurance that the statement of income is fairly presented, they are not ordinarily designed to insure that the details making up the relatively few totals appearing therein are precisely classified or that all types of losses or expenses are separately disclosed. A concern may suffer losses in many ways; management may be incompetent, sales policies may be ill-advised, costs may be higher than necessary, operating losses of various kinds may be suffered, and defalcations may be concealed through improper or unauthorized charges to cost or expense accounts. All such elements are reflected in the statement of income, but in order to state his opinion with respect to the operations of the year the auditor is not expected to segregate the various types of losses. This view is not new; it is similar to that expressed by nine prominent accounting firms in the well-known "Correspondence" with the New York Stock Exchange in 1933, when it was stated as to the income account, that "the essential point is to guard against any substantial over-statement of income, and this can be reasonably assured by the auditor satisfying himself of the correctness of the balance-sheets, at the beginning and end of the period covered by his examination and reviewing the important transactions during the year."

Auditing procedures followed by the public accountant are largely composed of tests, analyses, reconciliations, counts, and comparisons with independent sources of items appearing on the balance sheet. Accordingly, defalcations which are material and significant in the circumstances and which have not been concealed through charges to income are more likely to be disclosed through such procedures than those which have been concealed through improper charges to income. While the extent of tests should be dependent on the apparent quality of internal accounting control and internal check, nevertheless, under any dependence on tests and samplings, large areas of detailed transactions or balances will not be examined by the auditor. Errors may remain undetected; such errors may be innocent, or they may conceal a fraud. The American Institute has properly pointed out that if an auditor were to attempt to discover defalcations and similar irregularities he would have to extend his work to a point where its cost would be prohibitive.

However, an examination leading to an opinion on financial statements may disclose facts indicating the possibility of loss through defalcations and similar irregularities. The auditor should satisfy himself whether or not a potential loss is of such magnitude as to affect his opinion of the financial statements. He may well take into consideration the circumstances in which his suspicions were aroused. For example, peculations from an imprest fund would normally be expected to be of less consequence than those arising from "lapping" accounts receivable collections. In any event, the client should be fully advised of the situation. If the auditor has established to his own satisfaction that a probable loss is not so material as to affect his opinion, the client should decide whether to pursue the matter further. When the auditor has reason to believe that a material loss from defalcations or similar irregularities exists, he has no alternative than to request that the amount be reasonably determined. The decision, whether the initial determination is to be made by the client or by the auditor as an additional assignment, would, of course, be made by the client. If the determination is made by the client, the auditor should satisfy himself of its reasonableness by appropriate tests.

The public accountant should endeavor to make sure, *prior* to starting an examination, that his client understands what he may expect from the type of examination to be made as to the discovery of defalcations and other similar irregularities. If such understanding is not reached, a client may take the position, after a defalcation not discovered by the auditor comes to light, that he expected the examination to include detailed audit procedures which should have detected the particular defalcation. It should be pointed out in advance that the extent of the tests to which auditing procedures are to be restricted will be determined by the auditor after proper study and evaluation of existing internal accounting control and internal check. The auditor should also point out that, if the client so desires, additional or extended audit tests may be made which may give some additional assurance against irregularities remaining undetected, but that the results of such tests will be indicative but not conclusive. Even if extended tests are made, large areas would usually remain untested. It should always be made clear that the auditor is *never* an insurer. A client with a reasonably good system of internal accounting control and internal check and an understanding that the usual examination for the purpose of expressing an opinion cannot be relied upon to disclose defalcations, particularly those concealed in the statement of income, usually does not wish to incur the expense of an examination beyond that necessary under generally accepted auditing standards to the formation of the auditor's opinion. Many auditors believe it prudent to confirm in writing their understandings with their clients concerning discovery of defalcations and similar irregularities.

Too frequently the auditor makes extended tests of cash transactions, vouchers, etc., with a resulting higher audit fee, because he is unwilling to discuss with the client the limitations of an examination, made for the purpose of expressing an opinion on the financial statements, as to detection of defalcations and other similar irregularities and hopes such extended tests may afford him some protection against unreasonable claims for undetected irregularities. The authors believe that such higher fees are unjustified, because they result from work which can neither be depended upon to disclose defalcations nor to protect the auditor from claims by the client. The proper course is to make sure the client understands the auditor's responsibilities in advance of undertaking the engagement.

It should not be understood from the above discussion that the independent auditor in making an examination leading to an expression of opinion upon financial statements is indifferent to the possibility that fraud exists. He always has in mind, in framing his audit program and in reviewing the system of internal control, the possibility that the auditing procedures he follows to afford a reasonable basis for his opinion may detect fraud, if it exists at the time of his examination, and, more importantly, that they may deter fraud. These examinations over the years have uncovered many defalcations and peculations. There is no way of knowing how many potential cases of fraud have been prevented, either because of fear that fraud might be discovered by the auditor, or because the auditor has recommended procedures which made it difficult. The number must be large.

The Public Accountant and Surety Companies.—In spite of a good system of internal control, established and maintained by the management, which periodic examinations of the public accountants indicate is reasonably adequate and functioning as designed, defalcations may still occur. Any system of internal control must be tailored to the circumstances of the business and, especially in small or medium-sized companies, the cost of maintaining a system so elaborate as to amount to a guaranty against fraud would probably be out of proportion to the risk of loss through defalcation. Public accountants generally recommend, as an additional line of defense against fraud, coverage of all employees, or at least those occupying positions of trust, by fidelity bonds. Adequate fidelity bond coverage not only assures recovery of losses from discovered defalcations, but it also tends to discourage misappropriations. The underwriter often investigates the past record of bonded employees and, as a result of notification to the employer, tends to prevent the employment of persons of doubtful character. Employees may be deterred from theft knowing that bonding companies are much more likely to insist on prosecution than their employer.

In the past, a few bonding companies, under their rights of subrogation, have asserted claims against public accountants on the ground that all or part of the losses insured under a fidelity bond would not have occurred if the public accountant had made timely discovery of the theft. As has been stated many times, the auditing procedures in general use, which are designed to give the public accountant a sound basis for an opinion on financial statements, are not designed and cannot be relied upon to detect defalcations. If the public accountant is to be subjected to suits based on the theory that he is responsible for something which his examination was not intended to disclose, he might well conclude that he should protect himself by extending the scope of his examination beyond that which would ordinarily be necessary, and the resulting cost to his client would be excessive. Of course, any public accountant should be held responsible for an affirmatively dishonest act on his part, or the willful failure to follow those audit procedures generally accepted as necessary to the purpose of his examination.

Extension of audit procedures in an effort to disclose defalcations would not serve the best interests of either the public accountant or his client. Some years ago a committee of the American Institute of Certified Public Accountants explored the matter with representatives of a large number of surety companies, with the result that surety companies writing a substantial percentage of the fidelity bonds written in the United States signed a letter, addressed to the Institute, in which they stated that they would not assert claims against accountants when affirmatively dishonest or criminal acts or gross negligence on the part of accountants are not involved, and that claims would not be asserted unless, after a hearing of the matter by an impartial committee of three persons who are not accountants, such committee should conclude that the circumstances are such that the surety company might assert its claim.

CHAPTER 4

AUDITING PROCEDURES—PREPARATORY
AND ADMINISTRATIVE

Introduction.—This chapter presents a more detailed consideration of the auditing standards outlined in Chapter 2, particularly the standards of field work having to do with adequate planning and supervision, and with the nature and examination of accounting evidence.

Organization of the Public Accountant's Office.—Proper planning of an accounting engagement begins with proper organization of the public accountant's office and staff. In all human endeavor the more people required to accomplish a purpose the more exactly must the lines of responsibility and authority be defined. Requirements of modern far-flung business have fostered the growth of firms of accountants with hundreds of employees and many offices in this country and abroad. In such firms staff members are assigned to tasks for which they are fitted by temperament, training, and experience, and their work is supervised at each level by others of correspondingly higher capabilities. The levels are fewer, but the same principles are followed by the public accountant who works with but one assistant.

The personnel of a large firm is usually classified by level of responsibility and consists of partners, supervisors or managers, seniors, semi-seniors, and juniors. The firm will probably also employ men who are specialists in taxes, in government regulations such as those of the Securities and Exchange Commission, or in management services. There will also be a report department and an office staff of clerical assistants, file clerks, messengers, and telephone operators, and there may be branch offices under the supervision of resident partners or managers.

Every engagement should be under the general supervision of a partner or resident manager. A partner may take direct charge of some engagements and participate actively in the examination. Much of a partner's time is likely to be devoted to general guidance and review of audit programs and of the work of staff members, consideration of the proper treatment of debatable matters, consultation with clients, writing of reports and opinions, and administration of the office.

Supervisors or managers may take charge of several engagements simultaneously. They may do little of the field work, but they plan the work, check its progress, review the completed work, and review or prepare the report for a partner's consideration.

Seniors are qualified by training and experience to assume immediate charge of engagements in the field, to lay out and direct work for semi-seniors and juniors, to pass upon matters of practice or principle that arise in the course of an engagement, and to draft the report. For each engagement to which he is assigned, a senior is directly responsible either to a supervisor or a partner.

Semi-seniors are qualified to take charge of small and uncomplicated engagements or portions of larger engagements.

Juniors work under the supervision of seniors or semi-seniors and perform many of the detail tasks required.

Rotation of Personnel.—Many large accounting firms follow the practice, where possible, of rotating seniors and supervisors at suitable intervals among engagements. This policy is advantageous to clients since it periodically insures a fresh approach to their problems while maintaining the background of familiarity with them by the same firm. The varied experience received by the staff members is of value both to them as well as to the firm. Changing both the supervisor and senior on an engagement in the same year should be avoided.

Responsibility for Work of the Staff.—In the final analysis, the work for clients by the partners and the staff of a public accounting office is the joint responsibility of the firm as a whole. The particular responsibility for each engagement falls on the partner who has general supervision over the work. The field work is usually the responsibility of the supervisor to whom the engagement is assigned and he, in turn, delegates certain procedures to the senior and his assistants. At each of these levels of responsibility the individual in charge must review the work of his assistants.

Planning Field Work.

ARRANGEMENTS WITH CLIENTS.—It is imperative that proper arrangements be made with the client as part of the preparatory planning for an engagement. Unless uncertainties are settled before beginning the audit, embarrassment to either the auditor or the client may result.

Who Is the Client?—Uncertainty sometimes exists as to the client whom the public accountant is serving, to whom he is responsible, and who will pay the bill. Rather than the person whose financial statements are under examination, it may be a banker or a prospective lender or purchaser, a dissatisfied stockholder, a trustee in bankruptcy, petitioning creditors, a creditors' committee, a municipality, a congressional or an aldermanic committee, a state, or an investigating committee of the legislature. It is prudent, therefore, to determine in advance whom the public accountant is to regard as his principal.

Understanding of Purpose of Examination.—Most businessmen today understand the purposes and limitations of an audit leading to an opinion by a public accountant. Nevertheless there remain some who do not, and the public accountant should make sure he understands what the client expects, particularly on entering upon a new engagement. If the client expects the impossible, the auditor should explain why his expectations cannot be fulfilled. The client may expect an unqualified opinion on his financial statements, but the circumstances may make impossible certain procedures which are necessary if an opinion is to be expressed. The client may expect that the examination will be so detailed as to amount to a guaranty that defalcations will be discovered; the auditor should explain why such an examination is impracticable. On the other hand, unless the public accountant discusses the client's needs before starting the examination, he may assume that an opinion is required and undertake unnecessary procedures, only to find that the client has a different purpose in mind which does not require expression of an opinion.

With Whom Arrangements Are To Be Made.—For many years arrangements for an examination were usually made by a company official. More recently, to avoid any suggestion that the auditor's independence might be jeopardized, many companies, particularly those with securities listed on a national stock exchange, have adopted the practice of having shareholders approve the selection of the independent public accountant at the annual meeting. Sometimes a committee of the board of directors who are not officers of the company is appointed to select and make arrangements with the auditors. The choice of the committee is frequently submitted to stockholders for ratification.

Written Evidence of Arrangements.—Having reached an understanding with the client as to the purpose of the examination and who is to be responsible for the fee, it is prudent to confirm the arrangements in writing, usually by an exchange of letters.

The letter from the accounting firm may be in the form of a proposal to be accepted by the client. Although such letters cannot be standardized, following is an example of such a proposal:

(Name and address of company)

Dear Sirs:

We submit the following proposal for an examination of the financial statements of _____ Company for the year _____.

Our examination will be made in accordance with generally accepted auditing standards and will include all procedures which we consider necessary to enable us to express an opinion as to the fairness of presentation of the Company's financial statements.

In determining the extent of our test procedures, full consideration will be given to the apparent effectiveness of the system of internal accounting control and internal check and to the activities of the Company's internal auditors.

Our charges for these services will be based on the time of partners and staff members participating in the engagement, at our usual rates, plus out-of-pocket expenses.

Our examination, which will be for the purpose of expressing an opinion on the Company's financial statements, will be of the type stated by the American Institute of Certified Public Accountants as one which is not designed and cannot be relied upon to disclose defalcations and other similar irregularities, although if any exist, their discovery may result. Any suggestions for improving the system of internal accounting control or internal check which we believe feasible under the circumstances will be directed to the Controller's attention and, where appropriate, to the attention of the Audit Committee.

Very truly yours,

(Name of certified public accountants)

The letter may also include reference to preparation of federal and state income tax returns, Securities and Exchange Commission reports, and assistance in other fields. The addressee, who may be the board of directors, the president, or other appropriate company official, would be expected to reply accepting the proposal in appropriate terms.

When and Where Work Is To Be Done.—It is desirable that the appointment of independent public accountants to examine financial statements be made as early in the fiscal year as is possible. This permits the auditor to become familiar with the client's business, to be consulted during the year on accounting problems, and to plan to complete a substantial portion of his examination prior to the year end. In each of the chapters which has a section devoted to auditing procedures there will be indicated some of the work which normally can be accomplished in advance of the year end. Early appointment of the auditors facilitates the selection of locations and dates, if it is desirable that portions of the work at certain locations be done on a surprise basis.

Working conditions are just as important to the auditor's staff as to the client's personnel. But because the auditors are usually present for a comparatively limited time, adequate space and lighting, reasonable privacy, and proximity to books and records are not always provided. In the interest of efficient conduct of the examination, these matters should be discussed and proper arrangements made before the audit starts.

Use of Client's Staff.—The public accountant's auditing procedures may be described by such words as check, vouch, test, scrutinize, analyze, review, compare; but the materials with which he deals require clerical operations such as the preparation of trial balances, lists, schedules, obtaining from the files bank statements, vouchers, monthly statements, and tax returns, and sorting checks. The public accountant usually requests assistance of the client's staff in clerical operations in order to reduce expense to the client. The supervisor in charge of the engagement will usually arrange for this assistance as early in the year as possible.

PRELIMINARY REVIEW OF WORK TO BE DONE.—There are a number of general matters on which the auditor should be informed before beginning the examination.

Understanding the Type of Business.—During the auditor's early training he usually has an opportunity to become familiar with the general divisions of business—manufacturing, wholesaling, retailing, service, banking, and finance—and probably with some of the more specialized aspects of each. It is impossible, however, for any one auditor to have experience in every kind of enterprise, and engagements are sometimes accepted to examine financial statements of a business of which he has had no technical or special knowledge.

In any event, before beginning the examination the auditor should know how the business is conducted. No two organizations, even in the same field, are exactly alike, and the auditor should never hesitate to ask all questions necessary to obtain a complete understanding of the special features of the particular business under review. For example, if the client is a manufacturing company, he will want to know about its products, the methods of manufacture and distribution, its competitive position, selling and collection policies, and about many other features of the business. He should obtain an organization chart so that he may know the lines of authority of the personnel with whom he is to deal.

Location of Plants, Branches, and Subsidiaries.—It will often be found that the business of the client is handled at various locations. There may be several plants at which different products are manufactured. District sales branches may be established in various sections of the country, with local sales or service offices reporting to each district. When there are subsidiary companies, there may be similar dispersion of their operations at various geographical locations. The auditor should ascertain the location, function, and relative importance of each of the units of the company.

Inspection of Plants and Premises.—A tour of inspection of the client's major plants and offices is desirable before the audit procedures are started. The auditor then has an opportunity to confirm visually information gained orally about the plant, its products and manufacturing processes, and to meet many of the key personnel whose names he has seen on the organization chart. His later inquiry into accounting procedures will have more meaning if he has a background of knowledge of the physical conditions of receiving, storing, and requisitioning materials and products and the conditions under which the basic factory records are produced. A tour of the offices will acquaint the auditor with the principal locations of the accounting and related activities and with the size of the client's organization. After the inspection trip is completed, the knowledge gained should be summarized for later reference.

Review of Available Financial Statements.—An excellent starting point for any examination is a review of the balance sheets and statements of income for several past years and of preliminary or interim figures for the year or other period under review. This gives the auditor a good background of the financial history of the enterprise and may give him an indication of what are likely to be the relatively important matters requiring his consideration.

Review of Tax Returns.—The auditor should review tax returns and related correspondence for those years for which it is still possible for taxing authorities to assess additional taxes and should also review revenue agents' reports on previous examinations. Such review, in addition to furnishing valuable background information as to possible additional tax assessments, enables the auditor to determine if claims for refunds should be filed. It also permits him to plan his work so that he may readily perform such tax services as may be required.

OPENING TRIAL BALANCE.—In an initial engagement the auditor does not have the benefit of past knowledge of the company's affairs as a guide to whether accounting principles have been applied during the period under examination on a basis consistent with that of the prior period. The opening trial balance should therefore be reviewed and material items examined to determine whether they are stated on bases comparable with those of the period under review. If they are not, it is evident that even though the closing balances may be fairly stated, earnings for the period cannot be reported as on a basis consistent with that of the prior period. For example, if the inventory has been stated on one basis at the beginning of the period and on a materially different basis at the end of the period, the cost of sales for the period is obviously not computed on a basis consistent with that of the preceding year. Opening balances of prepayments and accrued expenses should be reviewed to determine the extent to which possible errors therein affect the income statement for the period under audit.

A comparison of the opening and closing trial balances may give the auditor an early clue as to asset and liability accounts that have been closed between balance sheet dates and may indicate other important changes in the accounts which require his consideration.

In an initial engagement the auditor should also review the composition of the balances of capital stock, surplus, long-term liabilities, reserves, allowances, investments in fixed assets and securities, and deferred charges at the beginning of the period. He is justified in limiting his examination for prior periods to a review or survey of the accounts without detailed examination, unless the results of his survey or analyses indicate the need for further investigation of accounting methods followed in the prior years. Such documents as the articles of incorporation, by-laws, and minutes of meetings of board of directors and stockholders should be reviewed.

If the accounts have been examined for prior periods by reputable independent certified public accountants, the auditor should read their reports and take cognizance of the information furnished. If he has sufficient confidence in the ability of the predecessor independent public accountants, he is warranted in reducing the scope of the review he would otherwise make of accounts and documents relating to prior periods. The extent to which the scope may be reduced will depend upon the circumstances of each engagement.

REVIEW OF RATIOS AND TRENDS.—A review of comparative figures, actual and budgeted, ratios, and trends assists the auditor in planning his examination. It focuses attention on the important relationships in the accounts and helps him to form an opinion of the integrity of the financial statements. Among the more important sales ratios which may be considered are gross profit, inventory and various items of expense. Balance sheet ratios often used include the current ratio, the ratio of cash and marketable securities to current liabilities, and the average collection period of accounts receivable. The inventory turnover figure (cost of sales divided by average inventory), when considered in conjunction with the gross profit ratio, may afford an indication of the effectiveness of inventory control.

When a comparison of ratios over a period of years discloses an unusual variation in the period under examination, the auditor should seek an explanation of the causes of the variation. Unusual fluctuations frequently are caused by changed operating or business conditions; however, they may be caused by a change in the application of accounting principles, or by errors or manipulations. Explanations obtained may lead the auditor to change his proposed plan of audit procedure.

Review of comparative figures and ratios often may uncover practices dictated by policies of the management as, for example, inconsistencies in providing allowances for depreciation, obsolescence, or depletion; purchases and sales of commodities on speculation; unusual credit losses owing to a change in credit policy; or fluctuation in maintenance expenses resulting from change in policy of capitalization of certain expenditures.

ANTICIPATION OF IMPORTANT QUESTIONS.—One of the purposes of the preliminary review of tentative financial statements, opening trial balance, prior audit reports, tax returns, and comparison of figures and ratios is to raise at an early stage of the engagement questions whose decision may require study and conferences with the client. Often the client is under pressure to release preliminary year-end figures before completion of the audit, and it is important to reach agreement on points of accounting principles or statement presentation before preliminary figures are released. Review of interim figures per books, supplemented by questions addressed to the controller as to changes in accounting policy during the year, ordinarily will identify major matters requiring clarification. This does not mean that any prescribed audit procedures should be omitted, but rather that those bearing on such matters will be given priority in the audit time schedule.

INQUIRY AS TO BASIC ACCOUNTING POLICIES.—The auditor must reach an opinion as to the consistency of application of generally accepted accounting principles. To accomplish this, he must first ascertain the client's accounting policies through inquiry and examination. Many companies, especially larger ones, have prepared manuals of accounting procedure, describing accounting policies; these manuals should be reviewed. Other companies have formally adopted by resolution of their boards of directors a statement of accounting policies which it intends to follow; this practice, unfortunately, is not widespread. Some of the more important policies of which the auditor should be informed are discussed below.

Cost of Inventories.—The general rule for pricing inventories is the lower of cost or market. But there are a number of permissible methods of determining both cost and market. These methods are discussed in Chapter 11. The auditor should ascertain the method or methods which have been adopted as the company's accounting policy. For example, the basis of costing of sales may be last-in—first-out, first-in—first-out, average, or specific lot; and production cost may include all or only part of manufacturing overhead.

Plant Additions, Repairs, and Replacements.—In practice, proper differentiation between plant additions, repairs, and replacements of plant is difficult. Consistent treatment of like items from year to year is essential and is difficult to attain unless precise regulations have been laid down. Some companies have a rule of thumb that items costing less than a specified amount shall be expensed, even though they may have a relatively long life. Others customarily charge off all additions to furniture and fixtures, capitalizing only the initial investment.

Depreciation of Fixed Assets and Amortization of Intangibles.—There are a number of acceptable methods of computing depreciation on fixed assets, and a number of variations in their application. Even wider variations are permissible in the amortization of intangible assets, especially those with no determinable life. The auditor must be informed of the company's accounting policy in these respects.

Prepaid Expenses and Deferred Charges.—The company should have an established accounting policy for handling certain types of expenditure which benefit income of both current and future operations. Frequently it is optional whether an item of expense be charged to operations of the year in which incurred or deferred, in whole or in part, to some future year or years. The policy adopted, assuming that choice is permissible, should be consistently followed.

Year-End Cutoff of Sales and Expenses.—The company may have adopted a policy of closing certain of its records, such as the sales book or the invoice register, a few days prior to the end of the fiscal year, to facilitate closing the books. If such early closing has no material effect upon the financial statement (and it seldom has), there is no objection to the practice, but it is one of which the auditor must have notice.

REVIEW OF ACCOUNTING PROCEDURES.—In his preparation for an examination the auditor must also review the client's accounting procedures because they provide the basic data for implementing company policies and because they must be considered in determining auditing procedures and techniques to be employed. Accounting procedures may be said to include the plan and methods by which financial transactions are classified and recorded in books of original entry and summarized in ledgers; such procedures range from the chart of accounts and accounting manuals to the methods used in summarizing accounting data. The purpose of an accounting procedure is to obtain a desired result as efficiently as possible. In itself, it cannot provide the necessary internal accounting control or internal check. For example, accounts payable transactions may be recorded in an accounts payable ledger or in a voucher record; either procedure may be accompanied by good or poor internal accounting control or internal check.

Before even a tentative audit program can be drafted, the auditor must have a fairly complete knowledge of major accounting procedures in use. Some of the alternatives which may be encountered are:

Control of cash and accounts receivable may be centered at the head office, or each branch or factory may maintain its own records of cash receipts and disbursements, and sales and collections.

Inventory control accounts, supported by perpetual inventory records and tied-in cost accounts may be maintained, or the accounting for inventory and cost of sales may depend on periodic physical inventories alone.

The cost system may be job, process, standard, or a combination of two or more of these.

Additions to and retirements from property accounts may be accumulated on job or work orders, or postings to classified accounts may be made directly from the underlying records.

Different accounting procedures for payment and distribution of invoices and payrolls.

Before beginning his examination, the public accountant should have knowledge of other features of the company's accounting procedures, but the above illustrates the kind of information required. It should be understood that accounting procedures affect mainly the *kind* of audit procedures or techniques to be followed; the *extent* to which audit procedures are applied depends on other considerations which are discussed later in this chapter.

The auditor's usual method of inquiring into accounting procedures is first to ask questions of those responsible for various sections of the work. He will customarily record, in narrative form, the various steps said to be taken in recording each of the major classes of transactions. Such narrative will usually be illustrated with copies of forms used, and possibly with a flow-chart indicating the origin, routing, and final disposition of the several copies.

During the course of his examination, the auditor will substantiate the information he has obtained, generally by selecting a number of transactions in each category and following them through the records. Such auditing methods ordinarily will determine whether described accounting procedures are actually in effect.

Audit Program.—Attempts in the past to devise a standard or all-purpose audit program for the guidance of the senior accountant in charge of an engagement have proven unsuccessful. Even though many audits have points of similarity, different problems are encountered, not only in different businesses and in different companies in the same business, but also in any one company from year to year.

An audit program designed for each engagement is a different matter. The authors believe that such programs are valuable because they

provide a guide in arranging and distributing the work,

provide a check against the possibility of omissions,

facilitate control and review by partners and supervisors, and

provide a record of work done.

After completion of the preparatory work thus far described, the senior in charge of an engagement is in a position to draft a tentative audit program. This tentative program, based on knowledge of the company's business, location of operating units, and accounting policies and procedures, may be revised after reviewing the system of internal accounting control and internal check. Further revisions may be required as tests indicate the degree of effectiveness of such internal controls and as the audit reveals areas which require further investigation. Even in recurring engagements, the audit program usually requires periodic revision either before the engagement is started or during the course of the examination to fit changed circumstances resulting from changes in accounting or internal accounting control procedures or in the character or volume of business.

Working Papers.—The public accountant should devote considerable thought to the preparation of working papers. They are instruments of his profession, produced anew for each examination. Every engagement presents an opportunity to demonstrate the auditor's sense of orderliness and his skill in preparing papers which competently record pertinent information about the material under audit and provide cross checks not only as to the records under review but also as to the auditor's own work.

The preparation and preservation of clear and effective working papers furnish the auditor and reviewer with the following:

1. Evidence of the extent of the auditor's examination and of the care exercised in its accomplishment;
2. The results of the evaluation of the internal accounting control and internal check;
3. The basis of conclusions and summarizations submitted in the report;
4. A source of information for the preparation of tax returns and reports to the Securities and Exchange Commission;
5. Historical data which later may be requested by the client; and
6. A starting point for subsequent examinations.

Contents of Working Papers.—Certain rules should be followed in the mechanical details of working paper preparation. Each sheet should be headed with the name of the client, the date of the examination, and the subject matter of the working paper. It should bear the date of preparation, and the names or initials of the staff members who prepared, checked, footed, extended, and reviewed the data. It should be clear, legible, and neat.

Trial Balance as a Basis for Audit Procedures.—The trial balance is usually among the first working papers prepared and may be used as an index of working papers. There are a number of ways of preparing the working paper trial balance, each of which has its advantages. Often the trial balance is prepared in a form that compares the current figures with those of the previous year end. It is usually taken off in balance sheet and income statement order, and amounts are grouped into subtotals to permit ready identification of trial balance amounts with those on financial statements. Post closing and auditor's adjustments are shown in additional columns and the adjusted trial balance may be cross-referenced to supporting working papers.

ANALYSES AND SCHEDULES.—The working papers reflect the performance of the procedures prescribed by the audit program. They will include analyses of certain accounts designed to summarize transactions during the period under review, logically classified so that the tie-in with related accounts is apparent. Such analyses will also indicate by appropriate notation the work of the auditor in his examination of the account. There will be a record of tests made and evidence examined, reconciliations, detailed trial balances supporting controlling accounts, and memoranda of data upon which opinion is formed as to the basis or adequacy of certain items, such as the basis of stating inventory, plant, or investments, or the apparent adequacy of valuation allowances or accruals. All symbols used to indicate tests made or other work done should be clearly explained in the working papers. All material to be presented in the text and schedules of the report should be clearly supported in the working papers.

Working paper files usually include a permanent file which, carried forward from year to year, contains relatively unchanging data such as the certificate of incorporation, by-laws, bond and note indentures, union agreements, important contracts, notes on accounting policies and procedures, organization, key personnel and location of plants, and continuing material such as extracts from minutes of board of directors' meetings.

DATA TO BE OMITTED.—The auditor should avoid the mere copying of the client's records. Copying is not substantiation. When the data are a part of the client's permanent record, a reference to the location may be sufficient for the working papers. If the auditor feels that he will have reason to refer to the data after leaving the client's office, he may request the client to prepare copies or have photostats made for his use. It should be borne in mind that working papers are a means to an end and not an end in themselves. They assist the auditor in forming an opinion on the financial statements and in the preparation and substantiation of his report. Preparation of working papers which go beyond these purposes should be avoided.

FILING OF WORKING PAPERS.—The primary purpose of careful filing and indexing of working papers is to facilitate ready reference when needed. This purpose applies during the course of the audit as well as after its completion. During the audit, the papers are usually arranged by subject matter in folders or loose-leaf binders with heavy separators and index tabs attached. Papers should be kept in the order in which they will be filed permanently.

Numerous methods of filing and indexing working papers for permanent storage are in use. Frequently the papers are arranged in the order of items on the balance sheet and income statement or the trial balance, numbering the sheets in order, and prefacing the set of papers thus filed with a carefully prepared index. Some auditors find it convenient to use the trial balance itself as an index, placing the numbers of the working papers opposite the trial balance items to which they apply. If the trial balance is thus used as a general index, a supplementary index, covering miscellaneous papers which cannot be directly identified with items on the trial balance, should be placed in the front of the set. Whatever the method used, the important thing is the ease with which data can be located after completion of the examination.

After arrangement in the desired order, working papers should be bound to minimize the possibility of loss, misplacement or disarrangement. In binding working papers it is desirable that a heavy backing be used and that the cover contain, in addition to the name of the accountant or firm responsible for the work included therein, such information as the name and address of the client, the character of the engagement, the date or period covered, and the names of the men engaged in the work. If the accounting firm files working papers numerically, the assigned file number should also be shown.

REVIEW OF WORKING PAPERS.—Working papers prepared by staff accountants should be reviewed critically by a principal or qualified delegate. In its findings and decision in the *Interstate Hosiery Mills, Inc.* case (promulgated March 18, 1939), the Securities and Exchange Commission expressed its views as follows:

> We think it is self-evident that the review upon which an accounting firm assumes responsibility for work done by subordinates must be more than a series of perfunctory questions as to the performance of particular items in an audit program. Nor should explanations of unusual items be accepted by a reviewer without support in detail from the working papers. As a matter of principle, a review should, it seems to us, be designed with two objectives in mind: First, to insure the integration of the original work papers with the financial statements; second, a searching analysis of the ultimate facts developed in the course of the actual audit.

The reviewer should determine that the examination of internal accounting control and internal check and the audit program, as finally decided upon, have been completed and that unusual items have been adequately explained. He should see that the working papers properly support the audit report and the financial statements. The extent of the review should be sufficient to determine that auditing procedures were adequate and permit an informed judgment as to the fairness and clarity of the financial statements.

STORAGE OF WORKING PAPERS.—Working papers of completed engagements should be filed alphabetically or if given a number, filed numerically in a fireproof cabinet or vault. For continuing engagements it is usually desirable to keep the latest two or three years' papers in the public accountant's office; thereafter they may be transferred to fireproof public storage vaults.

The storage of working papers of many clients over a number of years presents a difficult problem for the public accountant. Some have resorted to microfilming working papers after a certain period has elapsed; this reduces materially the necessary storage space, and preserves them permanently for later reference.

Other accountants believe that under reasonable limitations, old working papers may be destroyed at some point of time after the expiration of the applicable statute of limitations. This applies primarily to papers of nonhistorical importance. Working papers containing articles of incorporation, by-laws, historical data as to capital, surplus, and plant accounts, indentures, agreements, and audit programs are often retained permanently.

OWNERSHIP OF WORKING PAPERS.—Since working papers are produced by the public accountant from information contained in books and records of his client, there has sometimes arisen the question as to ownership of these working papers. Based upon at least one legal case (*Ipswich Mills v. Dillon,* 260 Mass. 453), it appears that papers originating in the client's office and loaned to the auditor belong to the client; working papers prepared by the public accountant supporting his report to the client belong to the public accountant.

Accounting Evidence.—As previously indicated, the bulk of the auditor's work in obtaining the facts upon which to base his opinion on financial statements consists of the examination of accounting evidence. In testing the validity of this evidence the auditor brings to bear his experience and judgment.

NATURE OF ACCOUNTING EVIDENCE.—In his examination of financial statements, the auditor finds that accounting evidence falls into two main categories: internal and external. Internal evidence includes data available within the client's organization, such as books of account, various subsidiary and detail records, collateral memoranda and documents incidental to and supporting the recorded transactions—including journal entries, checks, vouchers, invoices, bank statements, contracts, leases, correspondence, and minutes of meetings of directors and stockholders. External evidence is that which the auditor can obtain from sources other than the company records to corroborate the internal evidence. For example, he will confirm the existence of bank balances and securities in safekeeping by correspondence with the depositary or custodian; accounts receivable may be confirmed by customers; securities on hand and inventory quantities may be inspected; liabilities may be confirmed by creditors, and outstanding issues of capital stock may be confirmed by registrars and transfer agents.

ACCOUNTING PROCEDURES AND ACCOUNTING EVIDENCE.—The auditor's knowledge of the client's accounting procedures will assist him in determining the types of supporting evidence which may be available. Explanations of the way in which certain transactions are handled in the accounts and of the types and locations of the related records will usually be obtained through questioning the client's staff. Experience has shown that this is one of the auditor's more difficult tasks; clerks who are questioned are familiar with their own work, but frequently are unfamiliar with related work of others. They may supply him with information which they believe to be true but which is inaccurate. The auditor should be careful in his questioning to assure himself that he has tapped a dependable source of information.

EXAMINATION OF ACCOUNTING EVIDENCE.—The examination of supporting data should afford a reasonable basis for an opinion whether the evidence reflects and supports the related transaction as recorded in the books of account, and also whether such evidence appears to be genuine. While the auditor is not an insurer against forgeries, he should observe whether documents appear to be authenticated by signatures and approvals of authorized persons, and whether there has been any apparent alteration of dates, amounts, or approvals which would cast doubt on the genuineness of the documents. He should ask himself whether, in the light of all the circumstances, the transaction appears a reasonable one for the business under audit. The supporting data may often consist of schedules or computations such as those for tax accruals, bonus accruals, and certain types of inventories. Although it is important that the auditor check or test arithmetical computations, it is even more important that he understand and approve the basis of the calculation.

EXTENT OF EXAMINATION OF ACCOUNTING EVIDENCE.—The sections of this book which describe auditing procedures which may be appropriate in certain circumstances do not discuss the extent to which such procedures should be followed. The reason for applying a certain procedure has an important bearing on extent. For example, if the purpose is to ascertain whether a certain accounting procedure is followed as prescribed, the tracing of a very few transactions should furnish the necessary assurance. On the other hand, if the purpose is to determine that established company policy is being followed, e.g., that in distinguishing property additions from maintenance expenses, a greater number of transactions should be reviewed. If the purpose is to consider the effectiveness of the system of internal accounting control and internal check, a different approach will be made, as described in the following chapter.

TESTING THE ACCOUNTING FUNCTIONS.—The auditor wishes to satisfy himself that the accounting procedures and the methods of internal accounting control and internal check are functioning as described to him, and that they are producing proper account balances without serious error. These purposes are often accomplished by performing certain tests of the basic accounting functions such as those of receipts and disbursements, sales and customer billing, inventory flow, and the recording of liabilities and related entries. These tests are generally described in later chapters of this book, and the nature and extent of these tests depend upon circumstances and upon the exercise of judgment by the auditor. They may frequently be performed as part of the preliminary audit work prior to the balance sheet date.

MATERIALITY AND RELATIVE RISK.—Materiality and relative risk are also important in determining the extent of auditing procedures.

It is fundamental that there should be stronger grounds to sustain the auditor's opinion of relatively important items in the financial statements and those with possibilities of relatively material error than are required to sustain his opinion of items without these characteristics. Inventories of an industrial company are likely to vary from year to year and are of major importance because of their relative size and the complexity of their accounting problems, whereas inventories of public utility companies vary less from year to year, are usually not material in amount, and present fewer questions of accounting principle. On the other hand, plant accounts of public utility companies are important because of their relationship to the rate base, and the public accountant will usually consider that his examination of plant additions and retirements of a public utility company requires greater attention than similar procedures for an industrial company. Seldom is the importance and possibility of material error in prepaid items and deferred charges so great as to warrant extended audit procedures.

In planning and carrying out his examination, the auditor is constantly exercising judgment whether, under all of the circumstances, he is justified in curtailing some of the contemplated detailed procedures. He will do so only if he believes that there is but slight risk of material undetected error, which if discovered would affect his opinion of the financial statements. The auditor has a number of guides, based upon experience, which should lead to a sound decision. Examples of some of them are given below.

If a total is composed of a large number of small items, there is less risk of material error than when the total is composed of a few large items. This is pertinent when considering audit procedures for substantiation of the large numbers of small accounts receivable of a public utility company as compared with the relatively few large accounts receivable of a manufacturing company. Supply inventories of a manufacturing company are often composed of a large number of small cost items, and audit procedures usually can be safely curtailed for this portion of the inventory.

The financial soundness of a business has a bearing on the degree of risk the auditor may safely assume. There is less pressure on the successful concern to window-dress, to understate expenses or inflate sales, or to conceal liabilities. The auditor must consider that the newly organized business struggling for a foothold, or the established business fallen on hard times, may endeavor to postpone write-offs, adopt less conservative accounting policies, and conceal pledging of assets and creation of liabilities.

Finally, in his estimation of the permissible effect of relative risk on his audit procedures, the auditor will consider the plan and effectiveness of the company's system of internal accounting control and internal check. The relationship between the apparent effectiveness of such controls and the audit procedures of the public accountant is so important that the next chapter of this book is devoted entirely to that subject.

The doctrine of materiality and relative risk tends to promote efficiency in the conduct of an audit. It insists upon proper attention to the important and encourages the exercise of judgment in eliminating or minimizing the unimportant. The auditor may properly reduce the extent of auditing procedures if the item under examination is not of importance, because an undetected error would seldom affect materially the fairness of the financial statements or, if corrected, change the auditor's opinion.

TEST-CHECKING THE EVIDENCE.—Since an audit based upon an examination of all available records would be economically unfeasible if not impossible, the auditor relies upon sampling techniques. This test-checking is based on the mathematically founded assumption that an analysis of representative samples of a group of items will indicate the quality of the whole.

The application of these techniques has greatly influenced the present-day auditor's thinking about the extent of application of audit procedures. After thoroughly checking all the items in a representative sample, the auditor may assume, under the mathematical laws of probability, that the number of errors found in the sample will appear in the group as a whole in about the same proportion. The auditor, therefore, has justifiably reduced the extent of his detail examination by the use of the test-check or sampling method.

The basis of selection of the sample for test may vary. The auditor may check all items included in a selected period; he may check all the items over a certain minimum amount for a selected period; he may select a percentage of larger items and another percentage of smaller items; he may check a percentage of a total, either in dollars or number of items; or, in examining accounts filed alphabetically, he may select certain letters.

In recent years, some accountants have advocated the extension of statistical sampling techniques to auditing, believing that it is possible thereby to establish the minimum sampling required to attain results of specified accuracy. Although many articles have been published on the subject, there has not yet been any widespread adoption of statistical methods of sampling. The authors believe that statistical tools may be a valuable supplement to traditional auditing procedures, but emphasize the fact that in evaluating the reliability of accounting records, there is no substitute for an auditor's experience and judgment.

The bases of his audit tests should not be disclosed by the auditor to the client's employees in advance of performance of the work. If they are disclosed, the employees may take care that the samples selected for test are free from error, thus reducing the value of the sample.

The value of a test check as assurance to the auditor of the reliability of the records tested depends not only on judicious selection of items and careful check of each one selected, but also on proper consideration of errors or differences discovered. Errors disclosed may not be important in themselves, but since they result from a sampling, they are indicative of possible important inaccuracies in the total. The auditor's procedure with respect to such errors generally should be to:

(a) Recheck the work to ascertain that the differences or errors are as indicated;

(b) Satisfy himself whether the errors represent mere clerical mistakes, an attempt to hide an irregularity or defalcation, or an attempt to misstate financial statements;

(c) Discuss the differences with the client, and determine whether the tests are to be carried further by the auditor or by the client;

(d) Reach a conclusion whether the aggregate error or difference is of sufficient importance to require adjustment of the accounts.

Within the limitation of the review decided upon in any year, the auditor's inquiries and tests should be searching, and any deviation from prescribed policy or procedure, or from the client's professed routine of internal control, should be critically investigated. Records appearing too neat should be investigated to determine whether they represent original records rewritten with an ulterior motive. Any evidence of laxity on the part of any of the client's employees in matters of accounting or in the handling of moneys or other assets should be noted and called to the attention of a responsible official without undue delay.

Machine Bookkeeping.—The era of machine bookkeeping has progressed from the typewriter, the adding machine, and the calculator to punched card and electronic equipment. Electronic computers for scientific and engineering purposes have been in use for some years, and a number of companies have installed adaptations of this type of equipment to handle their general clerical work. There are numerous types of electronic equipment now available that have been designed for data processing, and the present-day auditor should be familiar at least with the principles of their operation.

Although the mechanics of auditing have to be adapted to machine bookkeeping, the fundamental purposes of auditing remain the same. Difficulties may arise in preserving a trail that can be audited, and the auditor will be forced to use his ingenuity in following information from the ultimate result back to original data. Internal accounting control will probably be affected, but it may not be weakened if proper division of duties is maintained; in fact, it may be strengthened since the mathematical accuracy of electronic machines is infinitely greater than that of human beings.

CHAPTER 5

INTERNAL CONTROL

Introduction.—The second of the "Standards of Field Work" (see Chapter 2) states, "There is to be a proper study and evaluation of the existing internal control as a basis for reliance thereon and for the determination of the resultant extent of the tests to which auditing procedures are to be restricted." The accounting profession has long recognized the importance of internal control both for the purpose of contributing to accuracy of the account balances and for the safeguarding of assets. The "Standard" quoted above gives formal recognition to the necessity for an understanding of the system of internal control in use, and to the fact that its nature and extent will affect the audit program. This chapter discusses internal control, some of the background of its impact on the work of the auditor, and the auditor's methods of investigating and test-checking its operation.

Description.—The following definition is taken from "Internal Control," a special report by the Auditing Procedure Committee of the American Institute of Certified Public Accountants:

> Internal control comprises the plan of organization and all of the coordinate methods and measures adopted within a business to safeguard its assets, check the accuracy and reliability of its accounting data, promote operational efficiency, and encourage adherence to prescribed managerial policies.

The committee stated that its definition "possibly is broader than the meaning sometimes attributed to the term" and that "a 'system' of internal control extends beyond those matters which relate directly to the functions of the accounting and financial departments." The authors agree that the term "internal control" as defined by the committee is very broad, and they believe that unless the *kind* of internal control under discussion is clarified, conclusions reached as to the independent auditor's responsibility in certain of the areas relating to it may be misunderstood. The general concept of internal control encompassed by the committee's definition may be classified into three areas; these are discussed in the following paragraphs.

INTERNAL ADMINISTRATIVE CONTROL.—Broadly, the prime responsibility of successful management is to operate a business at a profit. It must produce an acceptable product at lowest practicable cost; it must develop markets in which its products can be sold at proper prices; and, because pressure of competition, changes in customer demand and other factors cause obsolescence of product lines, it must develop new or improved products to replace those obsolete. To accomplish these objectives, management must, among other things, develop proper policies leading to efficient production, distribution, and research; implement these policies through proper personnel selection, training, and compensation; communicate the means of effecting its policies through instructions, procedure manuals, and conferences; and police performance through operating supervision and controls. For example, the personnel department may have methods, standards, and procedures designed to ensure the hiring, training, and retention of employees; time and motion studies may promote efficient use of labor; quality control may sustain a policy of selling only first-grade merchandise to customers; comparison shoppers may police a policy of maintaining competitive selling prices. In this book the "plan of organization and all of the coordinate methods and measures adopted within a business . . . . to promote operational efficiency and encourage adherence to prescribed managerial policies" are briefly described as "internal administrative control."

Internal administrative controls are distinguishable from the other two areas of internal control (i.e., internal accounting control and internal check, discussed below), because they originate in and are usually conducted by operating departments other than financial or accounting. Certain administrative controls may be based on data or information such as operating budgets and reports of expenditures for plant additions furnished by accounting or financial departments. On the other hand, internal administrative controls, especially those of a physical nature, may replace or supplement internal accounting control or internal check procedures. While there are borderline cases, it is usually not difficult to distinguish between internal administrative controls which do, and those which do not, enhance internal accounting control or internal check.

INTERNAL ACCOUNTING CONTROL.—Controls which "check the accuracy and reliability of accounting data" or, as the authors prefer to put it, controls which are designed to bring about accurate and suitable recording and summarization of authorized financial transactions, are logically described as "internal accounting controls." The responsibility for the installation, maintenance, and correction of faulty operation of such internal accounting controls is clearly that of the accounting (or financial) department. Equally clearly, such controls are of prime interest to the independent auditor who is to report on the fairness of the financial statements drawn from the records these controls are designed to protect. The auditor should, of course, consider whether seeming weaknesses in controls exercised through accounting means are compensated by physical, statistical or other forms of control or by close attention on the part of the owner or owners of a business.

INTERNAL CHECK.—Internal check may be described as those accounting procedures or statistical, physical, or other controls which *safeguard assets* against defalcations or other similar irregularities. To the extent that such controls may be exercised through accounting procedures, or by proper assignment of duties within the accounting department or between the accounting department and other operating departments which furnish data for recording financial transactions, the accounting department is responsible for their installation and maintenance. Some of the usual forms of internal check of a physical nature such as fences, gates, watchmen, and inspection of outgoing material or personnel, are ordinarily the responsibility of other operating departments.

Distinguishing Between Internal Accounting Control and Internal Check.—In the past little attention has been given to the differences between internal accounting control and internal check, both as to character and effect upon the auditor's procedures.

Internal accounting controls are usually present even in simple bookkeeping systems operated for small businesses. They spring from the desire of every honest and capable bookkeeper to follow generally accepted accounting principles, to avoid errors in his accounts, and to minimize the task of locating errors if present. As soon as the size of the business permits, there usually are adopted such procedures of accounting control as double-entry bookkeeping; controlling accounts for receivables, payables, and inventories; periodic trial balances; and cross-checking debits and credits on journal entries before posting. Book balances will be checked against outside sources when possible; for example, book balances of cash in banks will be reconciled with statements received from the bank, book inventories compared with physical counts, and possibly debtors' accounts circularized. As business grows and personnel is added, there is more necessity for official authorization and approval of book entries, and more employees are available among whom duties may be divided so that clerical accuracy is enhanced by double-check and cross-check. In addition, the bookkeeper's staff promotes accuracy by numbering and accounting for documents such as sales orders and sales invoices, purchase orders and vendors' invoices, receiving reports, checks, and numerous others. Such procedures are representative of internal accounting controls which are necessary or desirable to ensure accurate and suitable recording and summarization of authorized financial transactions; if there were no dishonesty to combat, convenience or efficient operation would be the sole criterion in assigning duties.

Unfortunately, experience teaches that not every bookkeeper is honest; neither is every workman, storekeeper, salesman, or other person who has access to business assets. It is therefore necessary to provide controls to safeguard assets from defalcations or other similar irregularities. Such controls are encompassed in the term "internal check." For example, duties of accounting and financial personnel may be assigned in such a way that not only is accuracy enhanced through internal accounting controls, but also the arrangements of such assignments provide deterrents to wrongful actions. These arrangements provide for independent performance of incompatible functions and are one of the most important tools of internal check.

Broadly, custodianship functions are incompatible with record-keeping for property; control account functions should be independent of related detail records; those who record and summarize financial transactions should be independent of other operating functions. Thus, the requirements of internal accounting control (to ensure the accurate and suitable recording of authorized financial transactions) are satisfied when the signer of a check has before him written evidence that the payments liquidate liabilities recorded by means of approved vouchers and that the data on the checks have been compared with the vouchers, and then cancels the request for payment by appropriate means. But internal check requires that the signer be independent of persons who prepare vouchers for approval, approve vouchers for payment, and prepare checks. A number of other procedures of internal check are frequently encountered. Among them are the independent accounting for prenumbered documents, independent surprise counts of cash and securities, and the use of protective paper and writing devices for checks. They have the common characteristic that they are not needed to ensure the accurate and suitable recording of authorized financial transactions by the honest bookkeeper, but are desirable only to deter or disclose defalcations or other similar irregularities.

In each chapter on auditing procedures a section is devoted to consideration of procedures of internal accounting control and procedures of internal check applicable to the subject matter of the chapter. It is not expected that all procedures listed will be present in any one business organization. The necessity for any specific internal control procedure will vary with the nature of the business and its circumstances. Some suggested procedures may be impractical, and alternative methods may be devised. Others may cost more than they are worth. Good judgment again plays its part in tailoring methods of internal accounting control and internal check to the needs of a specific business or organization.

Independence as Related to Internal Check.—The value of "independence" on the part of persons performing many of the procedures of internal check is based upon the assumption that an independent person will report to knowledgeable authority deliberate errors, falsification or improper use of documents, forgeries, or other irregularities coming to his attention. To be "independent" in this sense, the employee must be free to report such matters both from the standpoint of the duties assigned to him and that of his position in the line of organization. When there is such freedom, failure to report to proper authority should occur only if the independent employee is incompetent, or if there is collusion between employees presumed to be independent.

An employee may be considered functionally independent when his assigned duties include only functions which are compatible from the standpoint of internal check. For example, the function of listing incoming receipts would be incompatible with those of preparing the bank deposit, posting detailed customers' accounts receivable, or posting credits for cash received to general ledger accounts; the function of preparing invoices for payment is incompatible with those of approval for payment and cancellation of basic documents. In weighing independence, therefore, the first consideration is whether an employee's assigned duties are intrinsically incompatible.

The next consideration is the extent to which employees to whom compatible functions have been assigned are in fact independent from the standpoint of their position in the line of authority. In smaller organizations, incompatible functions may have been assigned to different employees, but if these persons report to a common chief who has hire-and-fire or disciplinary control over them, their functional independence may be impaired by their job dependence on their chief. In other words, the chief may be able to direct actions which result in fraud and to ignore its indications in the accounts when reported to him. In larger organizations, the extent to which functional independence is affected by the line of authority in which the function is placed may be difficult to appraise. Incompatible functions may be divided between subsections of accounting or financial departments, but their heads may report through intervening subchiefs to the head of the accounting or financial function. Since in the last analysis, all department heads report to the president, it could be argued that there can be no organizational independence at all. As this, in practice at least, is an absurdity, it follows that the line may be drawn at some point on the organization chart; it is not always easy to determine just where this is.

In succeeding chapters the functional division of duties which promotes independence in the performance of assigned duties is discussed in general terms. In practice, measurement of the effectiveness of the contribution of independence to internal check requires sound judgment by the auditor as to both the assignment of functions and the position of related personnel in the line of authority.

The Independent Auditor's Responsibility in Relation to Internal Control.

INTERNAL ADMINISTRATIVE CONTROL.—It seems clear that in making an examination of financial statements leading to an opinion on them the independent auditor is not expected to investigate and evaluate internal administrative control *as such*. It is not part of his responsibility to determine whether salesmen are making a reasonable number of calls per day, whether the truck maintenance department is adhering to job schedules, whether established criteria for hiring are being followed by the personnel department, whether experiments being conducted by the research department are in an area consistent with management policy, or whether administrative controls are present and are effective in providing the answers to a host of other questions arising from business operations.

The experienced independent auditor gains much knowledge of internal administrative controls during the course of his examination, especially those which may provide effective alternates for certain internal accounting controls or internal check procedures. Among these are such physical controls as watchmen and gates, and statistical records which may be kept by production, maintenance, sales, or other operating departments. There is no reason, of course, why he should not take into consideration the presence of acceptable alternative internal administrative controls when evaluating internal accounting control and internal check, and when appropriate he may suggest the use of such procedures. For the independent auditor, however, any review or evaluation of internal administrative control procedures is not a part of his responsibilities regarding internal accounting control and internal check.

Many accounting firms offer management advisory services to their clients which include recommendations for improvement of certain internal administrative controls. Many cost systems, for example, provide management controls in addition to the computation of current costs. Management services are not a part of the usual examination leading to a short-form report.

INTERNAL ACCOUNTING CONTROL.—Internal accounting control, as described in this book, is by definition designed, in the absence of dishonesty on the part of those who operate and administer it, to promote the accurate and suitable recording and summarization of authorized financial transactions. Thus, if generally accepted accounting principles have been consistently applied in recording properly controlled financial transactions by completely honest persons, financial statements prepared therefrom should present fairly financial position and results of operations. There is no question that the independent auditor is responsible for making an examination which will permit him to express a well-founded opinion as to whether financial statements are fair presentations. Accordingly, if the independent auditor charged with reaching an opinion finds poor internal accounting control, he has no alternative to making such examination as would supplement the absent controls with audit tests or over-all checks and comparisons. In practice, of course, any business using double-entry bookkeeping has the rudiments of internal accounting control, and most businesses' have reasonable accounting control even though it may be lacking in some particulars; it is seldom, if ever, necessary to apply *all possible* audit procedures for the *entire* period under review in any one examination. For this reason it is a generally accepted auditing standard that the auditor's examination should include investigation and evaluation of internal accounting control (see Chapter 2) on which to base his judgment whether and to what extent his audit procedures may be restricted.

For example, if the client made no proper review of the account classification to which voucher charges are initially assigned, the independent auditor would extend his examination of voucher charges, and if numerous errors of significant dollar amount were thus disclosed, he might well carry his tests further. If inventories are not controlled through perpetual detail records, currently checked by comparison with physical counts, he should probably broaden the scope of his physical tests when attending the annual physical inventory taken by the client, as compared with what would be appropriate if the client kept perpetual records which were periodically compared with physical counts.

The review of internal accounting control made as part of an examination for the purpose of rendering an opinion on financial statements differs in method and extent from a "systems examination" designed to reduce accounting costs or to improve periodic reporting. Nevertheless, suggestions for improvement in accounting controls will often result from such a review, and the auditor has a responsibility to report to his client wherein, in his opinion, the accounting controls are inadequate, in the circumstances, reasonably to assure the accurate and suitable recording and summarization of authorized financial transactions.

INTERNAL CHECK.—Internal check, as described in this book, is by definition an adjunct to internal accounting control and is designed to supplement the latter by furnishing means to safeguard assets against manipulations of dishonest employees concerned with the accounting functions of business. The position of the American Institute of Certified Public Accountants that the ordinary examination incident to the issuance of an opinion respecting financial statements is not designed and cannot be relied upon to disclose defalcations and other similar irregularities, and the public accountant's responsibility for discovery of fraud were discussed in Chapter 3. It is generally understood that the primary responsibility for the accuracy of records and for protection of its assets lies with the management to whom stockholders (owners) have delegated this responsibility. The Securities and Exchange Commission in a well-publicized decision (4 SEC 721) also stated its opinion that management has the fundamental and primary responsibility for the accuracy of financial statements. These opinions might be taken to imply that the independent auditor assumes no responsibility whatever for the discovery of defalcations; if this were so, the question might be raised why the auditor in making such an examination devotes *any* time and attention to investigating and evaluating internal check, as the term is used in this book.

As indicated in Chapter 3, however, the independent auditor is not indifferent to the possibility that fraud exists. On the contrary, his audit program is framed and his examination conducted in such a manner that material fraud, particularly one concealed in the balance sheet, is sought to be, and often is, discovered. In essence, the Institute's statement recognizes the fact that reasonable audit procedures applied with due care should more often than not disclose material errors in fairness of presentation of financial statements resulting from poor internal check; however, when fraud has been concealed through improper charges to the income account, even substantial extension of audit tests might not bring it to light. Extension of audit tests to complete coverage might not suffice when collusion is present. It is obviously impractical, in most examinations, to extend audit procedures to this extreme, because the cost would be out of proportion to possible benefits in the very great majority of cases. Clients generally appreciate this, and will agree to the existence of limitations on the auditor's responsibility for the discovery of defalcations; moreover, as further discussed in Codification,[1] good internal check and surety bonds provide reasonable protection against defalcations at much less cost.

This limitation of the auditor's responsibility in relation to fraud has its corresponding effect upon his responsibility in relation to internal check. While he makes somewhat the same investigation and evaluation of internal check as he does of internal accounting control, it does not follow that he must extend his audit program in the same manner or to the same extent that might be appropriate if the revealed weaknesses were those of internal accounting control. If internal check weaknesses are such that might permit abstraction of assets resulting in a corresponding difference between accounts and the actual assets on hand, the auditor might conclude that his counts and reconciliation of cash and inventories or confirmation of accounts receivable should be done at the balance sheet date, possibly with extended coverage, rather than at an interim date. However, if it appears that the weakness might permit concealing the defalcation through fraudulent entries buried in cost or expense accounts, even a complete detailed examination might not reveal the manipulations. Unless his suspicions are aroused by specific circumstances, the auditor need not unreasonably extend his examination, but may rely upon his understanding with the client and upon the more and more generally accepted position of the accounting profession that he cannot accept responsibility for discovery of defalcations and other similar irregularities.

The certified public accountant, as an expert in the field of accounting, believes he should assist management in the discharge of its responsibilities by reporting to proper persons serious weaknesses in internal check which, if not corrected, may lead to diversion of assets. His review and evaluation of internal check procedures are largely for the purpose of revealing and reporting such weaknesses. Although corrective measures are management's responsibility, the public ac-

[1] Codification of Statements on Auditing Procedure, pp. 11-13 (1951).

countant should be ready to offer constructive advice based on his experience.

The auditor's tests of internal accounting control will also indicate whether many of the prescribed procedures of internal check are being followed. For example, a review of vouchers initialed by those preparing and approving them will indicate whether employees stated to have been assigned to these functions have actually performed them. There are many types of internal check procedures, however, as when an independent person is stated to have custody of cash or securities, or to have been assigned to verification of numerical sequences or reconciliation of differences or balances, where there is no signature to show that the authorized person has in fact followed the prescribed procedure. Here the auditor must rely on inquiry and observation. When he finds that prescribed procedures of internal check are not being followed, he should report such failure to a responsible person in the client's organization.

Internal Control and the Controller.—The responsibility of management for maintaining an adequate and effective system of accounts, for properly recording transactions in the books of account, and for safeguarding the assets is usually assigned to the controller who implements this responsibility through the installation and proper maintenance of an adequate system of internal accounting control and internal check. The controller, who is an important member of management, shares in the formulation of business policies and is expected to interpret the results of past policies and to estimate the results of proposed policies. It is logical that he be responsible for the correct entry and summarization of data upon which many management decisions are based. He should remember that these are personal responsibilities as well as responsibilities of his office—in a famous fraud case the controller was convicted of complicity while two directors were acquitted. Controllers generally appreciate that the independent public accountants' emphasis on properly designed and executed systems of internal accounting control and internal check is in their interest and in the interest of the company.

Internal Control and the Internal Auditor.—The necessity for centrally controlled policing of internal accounting control and internal check procedures of large businesses has fostered the growth and importance of a group titled "internal auditors." This title probably was intended to distinguish this group from "outside auditors" or independent public accountants. While it is true that many of the procedures followed by internal auditors are patterned after those used by independent public accountants, the approach of each group is different.

The duty of the internal auditor is primarily to see that company accounting policy is followed. He is vitally interested in the cost of prescribed procedures and in their effect on customers and company personnel. The independent public accountant is interested primarily in the end results of accounting processes; the internal auditor, on the other hand, is interested primarily in the processes themselves. The public accountant will propose correction of errors disclosed by his examination; the internal auditor will try to prevent occurrence or recurrence of errors. The internal auditor properly approaches his work from the point of view of management and is not always expected to have the unbiased attitude of the independent public accountant.

Usually the internal auditor reports to the chief accounting officer of the company, but sometimes he reports to the president, or even to the board of directors. He should not report to the individual who is directly responsible for bookkeeping or accounting. The work assigned to the internal auditor usually includes auditing procedures such as physically testing inventories at factories and branches, confirming customers' accounts receivable and counting imprest funds at sales or division offices, and other testing, checking, analyzing, and reconciling at accounting centers. The internal auditor also acts as the direct representative of his chief in investigating and reporting whether prescribed accounting policies and internal accounting control and internal check procedures, methods, and routines are followed. He will also report whether he believes the methods of internal accounting control and internal check being followed are adequate for the purposes, and, like the independent public accountant, he may suggest improvements in them. His responsibilities often include investigation of company policy in other departments of the business—quite often as to credits and collections and general office management, and sometimes as to sales, advertising, and factory departments, especially as their activities produce records useful to the accounting department.

The internal auditors may be assigned certain functions or checking operations which require "independence." For example, it is not unusual for the internal auditors to be responsible for reconciliation of bank accounts. In the authors' opinion, however, it is generally undesirable to assign operating functions to internal auditors even where independence is required to enhance internal check. When proper internal check procedures are prescribed, internal auditors can best devote their efforts to policing them and to the prevention and discovery of collusion.

The Internal Auditor and the Public Accountant.—Even when good procedures of internal accounting control and internal check are maintained, the results are greatly strengthened by a well-operated internal auditing group. This is fully recognized by the independent public accountant, and in weighing the effectiveness of internal control he will give due consideration to the work of internal auditors. He will, of course, investigate procedures of the internal auditing group just as he investigates other features of internal control. He will review the program of the internal auditor to determine whether it is designed to reveal errors and minimize fraud, and he will assure himself that the internal auditors are following their prescribed program. This may be done by interview and by reviewing audit working papers and reports of the internal auditors.

The development of internal audit departments in companies of medium as well as large size has continued in recent years and is likely to have a major effect on the practice of public accounting. As the development of internal accounting controls decreased the detail checking required of the public accountant, so will the development of internal auditing further decrease such checking. This is a healthy trend, which will advance further the independent public accountant's position as an impartial advisor on matters of accounting principle and technique.

Method of Investigation.—In Chapter 4 reference was made to the review of accounting procedures necessary before drafting a tentative audit program. This review acquaints the auditor with the general methods followed in the day-to-day operation of the system of accounts, and the practices followed under the system. The auditor must also analyze the procedures to determine whether they provide a proper measure of internal accounting control and internal check; such analysis goes beyond a mere description of the procedures followed. Accounting procedures are designed to furnish internal accounting control (i.e., to promote proper recording and reporting of authorized financial transactions), but the auditor must determine whether this objective is being realized. He must also consider whether the procedures are accompanied by satisfactory internal check designed to safeguard assets.

A practical and useful device for investigating and recording the auditor's inquiries into a system of internal accounting control and internal check is the standard questionnaire, prepared for the use of staff members on all engagements. Such a questionnaire, designed by persons fully conversant with problems of internal control, makes available a large fund of accumulated experience and, perhaps more importantly, furnishes a basis for measuring the performance of the system under review. Questions can be framed so that a negative answer indicates a weakness in internal accounting control or internal check, which should be considered either for its possible effect on the audit program or for reporting to the client for consideration. An example of a questionnaire designed for evaluating internal accounting control and internal check is given in the Appendix to this book. It is believed that the principles of internal accounting control and internal check are similar in all types of business; the nomenclature of some businesses may be specialized, but it is usually translatable into conventional accounting terms. Some types of business may require supplementary questions to bring out specialized situations, and if so they may readily be added.

Such questionnaires must not be used as a substitute for thinking, and they should always be susceptible to revision to fit the needs of the client. Properly used, they provide information upon which the public accountant can exercise judgment to determine whether the system of internal accounting control and internal check is reasonably designed to produce accurate summaries of the transactions and to minimize opportunities for fraud.

Testing the System.—It is not enough that the auditor be familiar with the prescribed system of internal accounting control and internal check and consider it adequate in the circumstances; he must also satisfy himself whether this system is actually in effect. This is the chief purpose of the audit procedure of testing transactions for a period. Because of the nature of many of the prescribed routines, the auditor may determine whether they are in fact followed by retracing some of the steps taken by company employees. Certain clerks usually check the arithmetic of invoices, see that proper documents are attached and that they are properly approved. The auditor can best reach an opinion whether these duties are being performed by rechecking some of the invoices himself. The presence of previously undetected errors indicates that the work was not properly done in the first place. To determine that petty cash vouchers are handled as prescribed, the auditor should review some of them. To ascertain that receipts are deposited daily and intact, the auditor should compare, on a test basis, the record of incoming remittances with the daily deposits. In short, the auditor should arrange his audit program so that during the course of his work he has followed procedures which will give him reasonable assurance of the accuracy of the answers to his questions on the internal accounting control questionnaire. The nature of certain procedures of internal check, however, are such that the auditor must depend principally on inquiry and observation for substantiation of these answers.

CHAPTER 6

THE SHORT-FORM REPORT

Introduction.—When the independent public accountant states his opinion on financial statements, it is usually in what is generally referred to as a "short-form report" (sometimes called a "certificate"). This report briefly describes the scope of the examination and states the auditor's opinion. The auditing standards of reporting have been briefly stated in Chapter 2 and, since they relate to the short-form report, they are more fully discussed in the present chapter.

Standard Form of Short-Form Report.—A standard form of auditor's report was first recommended by the American Institute of Certified Public Accountants in 1933, and there have been several revisions in the intervening years. The latest revision, made in 1948, reads as follows:

We have examined the balance sheet of X Company as of December 31, 19___ and the related statement(s) of income and surplus for the year then ended. Our examination was made in accordance with generally accepted auditing standards, and accordingly included such tests of the accounting records and such other auditing procedures as we considered necessary in the circumstances.

In our opinion, the accompanying balance sheet and statement(s) of income and surplus present fairly the financial position of X Company at December 31, 19___, and the results of its operations for the year then ended, in conformity with generally accepted accounting principles applied on a basis consistent with that of the preceding year.

Some auditors use a one-paragraph short-form report in which the opinion is given first to emphasize its importance. This form is as follows:

In our opinion, the accompanying balance sheet and the related statements of income and surplus present fairly the financial position of The X Company at December 31, 19___ and the results of its operations for the year then ended, in conformity with generally accepted accounting principles applied on a basis consistent with that of the preceding year. Our examination was made in accordance with generally accepted auditing standards and accordingly included such tests of the accounting records and such other auditing procedures as we considered necessary in the circumstances.

The standard short-form report was devised for use in reporting on financial statements of business enterprises organized for profit. Appropriate forms of reporting for noncommercial, nonprofit organizations and other types of special reports are discussed later in this chapter.

It is not expected that any form of report can be used in every situation. The Institute's recommended short-form report is intended as a carefully worded framework upon which can be built an understandable report appropriate to the circumstances.

TITLE OF SHORT-FORM REPORT.—Independent public accountants usually refer to the short-form report upon their examination of financial statements as "Accountant's Report" or "Auditor's Opinion"; many minor variations are seen in practice. Prior to 1933 it was customary to refer to the accountant's report as a "certificate," because it frequently began with the words "We certify that . . . ." The word "certificate" implies testimony to a fact whereas the independent accountant's responsibility is to state his opinion on financial statements presented to him for examination. The word "certificate" is occasionally used today, but the authors believe that its use should be avoided, especially in printed reports distributed to stockholders.

CONTENTS OF SHORT-FORM REPORT.—The short-form report should be clear and concise; important limitations, exceptions, or explanations should be stated in a manner that precludes misunderstanding or unintended implications. If the report states that the examination was made in accordance with generally accepted auditing standards, details of the scope of the examination made in accordance with these standards need not be given. When such details are of interest, the auditor usually prepares a long-form report; this is the subject of Chapter 23.

Address of Report.—The auditor's report should be addressed to his client. The authors have already referred in Chapter 4 to the importance of determining, in advance of starting the engagement, the identity of the client and have also pointed out that the public accountant's liability to his client is not the same as to third parties. Company officers, acting for the corporation, often arrange details of the engagement with the public accountant, and the report is then addressed to the client company. When the independent public accountant is appointed by vote of the stockholders, or by the board of directors, the auditor's report is addressed to the body which has appointed him. When the financial statements are to be included in the company's annual report to stockholders, the auditor's report may be addressed to them, whether or not he is officially appointed by them.

Date of Statements and Report.—The financial statements under examination bear the date of the balance sheet and the period covered by the statements of income and surplus. The auditor's examination will necessarily continue for some time after the books are closed, so that the date of its conclusion will always be subsequent to the date of the statements. The auditor has responsibility for inquiry about, and reporting upon, events occurring subsequent to the balance sheet date which materially affect the financial statements. This responsibility is considered more fully in Chapter 7. The public accountant's report should not be dated before he has obtained all the data necessary for the proper formation of his opinion, and it should not be unduly delayed thereafter lest he be charged with knowledge of subsequent events which he could not have. Obviously he cannot have first-hand knowledge of developments occurring after the completion of his field work.

Incident to a discussion of "Events Subsequent to the Date of Financial Statements," the American Institute Committee on Auditing Procedure in Statement No. 25 (par. 18) recommended that the date of completion of the work in the client's office should normally be used as the date of the auditor's report.

Some auditors believe that when a long-form report is issued at a date later than that of the related short-form report, or a short-form report is reissued at a later date (and sometimes includes information obtained since the date of the original report), either the long-form report or the reissued short-form report should be dated, for example, "March 31, 19—, as of February 15, 19—," when the original short-form report was dated February 15, 19—. The authors believe that dating reports at a later date and indicating the completion of the field work by an "as of" date, have little significance to the reader of the report and financial statements, and that, in the preceding example, a long-form or a reissued short-form report should be dated February 15, 19——. The dating practices resulting from certain requirements under the Federal Securities Acts are discussed in Chapter 25.

Signature of Report.—The usual practice of accounting firms is to sign their reports with the firm name without reference to the partner in charge. Occasionally a governmental commission or bureau requires, in addition to the firm name, the signature of an individual member of the firm. Of course, these requirements should be observed.

Variations in the Standard Form of Report.—Apart from minor variations in wording which reflect preferences of individual accountants or firms, there are many circumstances (other than those causing explanations or exceptions) which require adjustment of the wording of the standard form. Some of these circumstances are described below.

IDENTIFICATION OF FINANCIAL STATEMENTS.—Financial statements are not always of a single company, or for a single year, nor do the fiscal years of all companies coincide with the calendar year. The report should identify the statements and the periods covered. If a report to stockholders or other published document includes financial statements or supporting schedules not covered by the independent public accountant's report, it is particularly important that the statements and schedules covered by his report be clearly identified therein by reference to titles, page numbers, or an accompanying index.

Comparative Financial Statements.—Frequently financial statements are presented in comparative form, usually for two years. Standard of Reporting No. 4, which states that "In all cases where an auditor's name is associated with financial statements the report should contain a clear-cut indication of the . . . . degree of responsibility he is taking," would seem to apply to the prior as well as to the current year. The opinion of the auditor may be worded to cover both balance sheets and both statements of income and surplus. If he has not examined the prior year, his report should clearly indicate that fact.

Some auditors believe that Standard of Reporting No. 4 does not require them to report on or even to refer to a previous examination and report on prior statements, and accordingly they word their report to cover only the current financial statements.

In general, it is not necessary for the company to repeat verbatim all the footnote data included in the prior year's financial statements.

Only such data relating to the prior year need be included as are necessary to proper understanding of such statements in comparison with those of the current year.

The American Institute Committee on Auditing Procedure is now considering a "Statement on the Auditing Procedure" which will include consideration of the application of Standard of Reporting No. 4 to the prior year in comparative statements.

Consolidated Financial Statements.—If the examination has covered a parent and its subsidiaries, the financial statements reported on will usually present the consolidated position and consolidated results of operations. The opening sentence of the short-form report must be worded to identify the company and indicate the degree of consolidation, the date of the balance sheet, and the period covered by the statements of income and surplus.

The usual heading of such statements is "The X Company and its subsidiary companies." When one or more subsidaries are not included in the consolidated statements, many auditors feel that the statements should then be headed "The X Company and its subsidiaries consolidated" or "consolidated subsidiaries."

Sole Proprietorships.—When an examination is made of financial statements of an enterprise conducted as a sole proprietorship, a problem of identification arises, because the business examined may be only one of the interests of the proprietor. The report should clearly indicate that it refers to statements of the business enterprise under examination, and not to all assets, liabilities, income, and expenses of the proprietor, as in the following example:

We have examined the balance sheet of

John Jones Company
(A sole proprietorship)

as of December 31, 19__ and the related statements of income and capital for the year then ended. Such statements are those of the business carried on under the name of John Jones Company and do not include other assets, liabilities, income and expenses of the proprietor.

SCOPE OF EXAMINATION.—The portion of the standard form of auditor's report which briefly describes the examination is referred to as the "scope" paragraph. Even though the examination is reported to have conformed with generally accepted auditing standards, this paragraph is sometimes expanded by adding comments on the extent of examination of such items as cash, receivables, inventories, depreciation, and plant additions.

An objection to the expansion of the scope paragraph of the short-form report under such circumstances is that the selection of certain auditing procedures for comment may provoke doubt or raise questions. The reader may wonder whether the mention of certain procedures implies that there is some undisclosed significance which should have a bearing on his understanding of the statements; he may believe the omission to mention other procedures implies that they were not followed, and that he is expected to weigh the importance of this omission. Public accountants agree that they must assume the responsibility for determining the scope of each examination. Because an expanded scope paragraph may, as stated above, be interpreted as an attempt to evade this responsibility, most public accountants believe that the present standard form of scope paragraph usually should not be so expanded.

Observation of physical inventories and confirmations of accounts receivable, however, present an exception to this general rule. The "Extensions of Auditing Procedures" approved by the American Institute of Certified Public Accountants in 1939, and incorporated in Statement on Auditing Procedure No. 26 and in the "Codification of Statements on Auditing Procedure" (1951), have stated that when such procedures have been omitted with respect to inventories or receivables as at the end of the period or year, even though the auditor may have satisfied himself by other methods, he should disclose such omission in the general scope section of his report. Illustrations of these disclosures are given later in this chapter.

Another exception is that under the Investment Company Act of 1940, the auditor is required to state the manner of substantiating investment securities.

RELIANCE UPON OTHER AUDITORS.—It is not unusual for two or more firms of independent public accountants to collaborate in the examination of a large company with geographically scattered branches or subsidiaries. Rule Six of the Rules of Professional Conduct (see Chapter 3) permits such collaboration between members of the American Institute of Certified Public Accountants, a member of a similar association in a foreign country, or a certified public accountant of a state or territory of the United States or the District of Columbia.

Having accepted an engagement to examine the financial statements of a company with branches or subsidiaries in various cities or countries, the independent public accountant may engage another auditor who is in good professional standing to make an examination of a subsidiary or branch. The second auditor may be the agent of the first, who may direct and review the examination, and pay the second auditor's fee.

Under these circumstances, the principal must be prepared to accept full responsibility for his agent's examination just as for that by his own staff. His report, in this case, should not mention that his opinion is based, in part, on an examination by another auditor acting as his agent.

Often the client may desire to retain other auditors to examine financial statements of domestic or foreign subsidiaries or branches, and the independent public accountant who is to report upon the consolidated financial statements usually will have no objection if requirements of Rule Six are met. If the auditor of the parent company does not wish to accept responsibility for the work of the other auditors, he should disclose in his report that he has not examined financial statements of certain subsidiaries or branches, but has received reports of other public accountants on their examinations of such statements, and that his opinion of the consolidated financial statements is based in part on such reports. He usually cannot, of his own knowledge, characterize such other public or professional accountants as "independent," and he should avoid any expression which may imply that he has such knowledge.

REPORTS ON CANADIAN COMPANIES.—Independent public accountants in the United States are sometimes called upon to report on their examination of a Canadian corporation, usually one which is a subsidiary of a domestic corporation. The Companies Acts of the Dominion of Canada and of all provinces except Ontario require that the auditor report that "the statements are in accordance with the books and that the auditor has obtained all the information and explanations he requires." The auditor in the United States who reports on a Canadian company will wish to comply with the laws under which it is incorporated, and the Canadian auditor who reports on the Canadian subsidiary of a United States company is required to do so. A form of auditor's report which combines such compliance with the approved American Institute form follows:

We have examined the balance sheet of X COMPANY, LTD. as of December 31, 19___, and the related statement of income and surplus for the year then ended and have obtained all the information and explanations we have required. Our examination was made in accordance with generally accepted auditing standards, and accordingly included such tests of the accounting records and such other auditing procedures as we considered necessary in the circumstances.

In our opinion, the accompanying financial statements are properly drawn up so as to exhibit, in conformity with generally accepted accounting principles applied on a basis consistent with that of the preceding year, a true and correct view of the state of the affairs of the company at December 31, 19___, and the results of its operations for the year then ended according to the best of our information and the explanations given to us and as shown by the books of the company.

This report may be used when the United States auditor has made the entire examination or is willing to accept the responsibility for any part of the examination which has been made by Canadian Chartered Accountants.

REPORTS ON A PARENT COMPANY.—Occasionally the public accountant is asked to report on the financial statements of a parent company not consolidated with either its domestic or foreign subsidiaries. When the operations of the subsidiaries are relatively minor, there is usually no objection to doing so without qualification. When the reverse is true, the auditor usually feels that single company statements of the parent do not fairly present its financial position and results of operations. Unless the subsidiaries are relatively large, footnote disclosure of their position and results of operations may be considered by the auditor to constitute fair presentation. In other cases he may consider such presentation inadequate and may insist that statements partly or fully consolidated be presented together with those of the parent company, and as required by Item 4 of "Standards of Reporting" (see Chapter 2) his opinion should also be given upon the consolidated financial statements. His opinion might read as follows:

In our opinion, the accompanying statements present fairly the financial position of X Company and the consolidated financial position of X Company and its subsidiaries at December 31, 19___, and the results of their operations for the year then ended, all in conformity with generally accepted accounting principles applied on a basis consistent with that of the preceding year.

When consolidated statements and parent company statements are presented in columnar form on the same page, it is desirable to indicate by footnote that they should be read together; and when they appear on different pages, a footnote to the parent company statements should state that the parent company statements should be read only in conjunction with the related consolidated statements.

As an alternative method, the parent company statements may be accompanied by those of the subsidiaries (as a group or individually). The scope paragraph of the auditor's report could be expanded or a separate paragraph added to recite the examination made of the subsidiaries, and the opinion paragraph might read as follows:

In our opinion, the accompanying balance sheet and related statements of income and earned surplus of the (Parent Company), when read in conjunction with the financial statements as of December 31, 19___ and for the year then ended of the (Subsidiary Company) referred to in the immediately preceding (scope) paragraph, present fairly the financial position of the (Parent Company) at December 31, 19___, and the results of its operations for the year then ended, in conformity with generally accepted accounting principles applied on a basis consistent with that of the preceding year.

The auditor's opinion on the financial statements of the subsidiary may be given separately or incorporated in his opinion relating to the parent company.

REPORTS ON COMPANIES UNDER REORGANIZATION.—When the auditor is called upon to report on financial statements of a company in process of reorganization under Chapter X of the Bankruptcy Act, a problem arises because substantial adjustments of assets and liabilities may result from the reorganization proceedings. His report should recite that the company has been operating under an order of a United States Court since a specified date and explain in pertinent detail the status of reorganization proceedings. The opinion paragraph may state that, in his opinion, the balance sheet presents fairly the assets and liabilities on the basis of accounting which has been consistently maintained by the company in accordance with generally accepted accounting principles, but that the assets and liabilities may be adjusted in the course of reorganization and consequently the position of the company is not at present determinable. A similar question might arise about the results of operations for the period.

The "Opinion" Paragraph.—The most important portion of the auditor's report is the paragraph in which he states his opinion on the financial statements which he has examined. His opinion should indicate whether he believes the financial statements present fairly the financial position and results of operations in conformity with generally accepted accounting principles applied on a basis consistent with that of the preceding period. In those instances where, because of insufficient scope of examination, disagreement as to application of accounting principle, or for other reasons, the auditor cannot express an opinion, he should state why he is unable to give an opinion on the statements as a whole.

It is not always understood that the auditor's report consists primarily of matters of opinion rather than statements of ascertained fact. The opinions are those of a trained professional acting without bias and with due care, but the auditor can seldom assert that the client's representations being reported upon are statements of fact. He may state as a matter of fact that he has made an examination of the financial statements of a company, but whether or not he has made an adequate examination under the circumstances is a matter of opinion. The auditor is not even safe in stating as a fact that he has examined the securities of a client and found them correct; for he cannot always be certain that the securities are the property of the company, that they are bona fide securities and not forgeries, or that the record to which he has checked the securities is correct. He may feel reasonably sure of these matters, but in the last analysis they are matters regarding which he should express an opinion rather than certain knowledge.

The phrase "in our opinion" should be made clearly applicable to all parts of the report which are intended as expressions of opinion. Violations of this rule are sometimes found in reports containing wording in addition to that of the standard form. Unless it is clear that the phrase "in our opinion" is applicable, such additional wording may be understood to be statements of fact rather than of opinion.

GENERALLY ACCEPTED ACCOUNTING PRINCIPLES.—The first standard of reporting is that the auditor's report shall state whether, in his opinion, the financial statements are presented in accordance with generally accepted accounting principles.

It is now generally agreed that the accounting principles referred to in the auditor's opinion are not those general principles which are defined as fundamental truths or comprehensive laws from which others are derived. The art of accounting may be based on such a body of fundamental concepts which are not affected by changes in business or economic conditions or political philosophies. But such principles would necessarily be so broad that they would be of little use as a yardstick in measuring comparability and consistency of financial statements. Over the years, in applying the more general and fundamental principles of accounting to situations arising in practice, many rules, conventions, and doctrines have been developed which authoritative writers, professional bodies, and practitioners of standing have agreed contribute to fair presentation of financial statements. Such rules, conventions, and doctrines are referred to in the standard short-form auditor's report as "generally accepted accounting principles."

Authority for Generally Accepted Accounting Principles.—There are many authorities to guide the public accountant as to the accounting principle which is applicable to a particular circumstance. He should be familiar with the extensive literature of accounting in which accounting principles are expounded and discussed, and he may refer to current published reports and prospectuses of corporations which are accompanied by the opinions of reputable accountants. In this book a section of each chapter dealing with the examination of items in financial statements indicates the accounting principles which are applicable.

Since 1938, the Committee on Accounting Procedure of the American Institute of Certified Public Accountants through its Accounting Research Bulletins has issued, from time to time, opinions on a number of accounting practices or procedures which were of interest at the time of issue. In 1953 the committee issued "Restatement and Revision of Accounting Research Bulletins" which amended, superseded, or withdrew certain bulletins no longer of current interest, and arranged the retained material by subjects rather than in the order of issuance. This bulletin is known as "Bulletin No. 43," and together with subsequent bulletins serves as a guide to generally accepted accounting principles on the subjects covered.

It should be said the committee has stated that its opinions and recommendations are directed primarily to accounting practices reflected in financial statements of business enterprises organized for profit. Therefore, such opinions and recommendations may not always be considered applicable to accounting problems or procedures of religious, charitable, scientific, educational, and similar nonprofit institutions, municipalities, professional firms, and the like.

The authority of Bulletin No. 43 (and subsequent bulletins) is stated in paragraph 8 of the introduction as follows:

> Except in cases in which formal adoption by the Institute membership has been asked and secured, the authority of opinions reached by the committee rests upon their general acceptability. The committee recognizes that in extraordinary cases fair presentation and justice to all parties at interest may require exceptional treatment. But the burden of justifying departure from accepted procedures, to the extent that they are evidenced in committee opinions, must be assumed by those who adopt another treatment.

The rules which were formally adopted by the membership of the Institute in 1934, and therefore are endowed with more authority than pronouncements of the committee, are six in number and are given as Chapter 1 of Bulletin No. 43. They deal with treatment of unrealized profit, charges to capital surplus, earned surplus prior to acquisition, treasury stock, notes or accounts receivable from officers, and donated capital stock.

The necessity for revision of previously issued bulletins of the committee illustrates the fact that accounting principles are constantly under review. It is not to be expected that there will ever be compiled one body of authoritative, exhaustive, and permanent accounting principles against which the auditor may weigh all of the practices he encounters. The reason is inherent in the nature of accounting, which must be readily adaptable to changes in business practices as well as to conditions under which business operates. The application of accounting principles to the infinite variety of business situations is a matter for judgment of the experienced accountant rather than for mechanical application of a set of fixed rules.

General Acceptance.—The choice of the qualifying phrase "generally accepted" instead of "sound" in describing accounting principles is based on two considerations: first, that an accounting principle which, after full discussion and development through experience, has been accepted by a majority of practicing accountants should be regarded as sound because of that acceptance, with the corollary that minority opinion, if any, should give way to the majority; second, that general acceptance is a fact which can be determined objectively and is accordingly more useful as a criterion of the propriety of an accounting principle than is its inherent soundness, which is necessarily a matter of opinion. When the Institute's Committee on Accounting Procedure states its opinion that a certain accounting rule is proper, most public accountants are willing to be bound by the majority decision of that committee as indicating general acceptance, even though some may consider an alternative to be sounder practice.

General acceptance does not necessarily mean general practice. For example, a number of accounting rules are acceptable in certain circumstances but are not widely used, or are used primarily in certain industries. There are, for example, about forty technical committees of the New York State Society of Certified Public Accountants which deal with problems peculiar to particular industries or businesses. A great deal of their work is advising practitioners of what, in their opinion, are the generally accepted principles of accounting to be applied in special situations.

Materiality.—The consideration of materiality is important to the auditor in his appraisal of whether financial statements are presented fairly in accordance with generally accepted accounting principles. The statements on which the independent public accountant gives his opinion are expressed in figures, as well as in words. The auditor may believe that the client has adopted an accounting principle, general acceptance of which is doubtful, or he may feel that the less desirable of alternative accounting principles has been used; but if the effect of the client's practice is not material in relation to the pertinent figures in the financial statements, there is usually no need for an exception in the auditor's report.

Bulletin No. 43 (par. 9 of the introduction) states with respect to materiality:

The committee contemplates that its opinions will have application only to items material and significant in the relative circumstances. It considers that items of little or no consequence may be dealt with as expediency may suggest. However, freedom to deal expediently with immaterial items should not extend to a group of items whose cumulative effect in any one financial statement may be material and significant.

CONSISTENCY OF APPLICATION OF ACCOUNTING PRINCIPLES.—The second standard of reporting is that the auditor's report shall state whether such generally accepted accounting principles have been consistently observed in the current period in relation to the preceding period. It should be remembered that the term "accounting principles" relates not only to the manner of recording of transactions, but also to their classification and presentation on financial statements.

For the very reason that the choice between alternative accounting principles is flexible, depending upon the client's judgment as concurred in by the independent accountant, consistency in application is of prime importance. It might make little difference in the total profits over a long period whether a long-term contractor computed his periodic profit and loss on a percentage-of-completion basis or completed contract basis. The two accounting principles might, however, produce markedly different results *by periods,* and if one method were followed in certain periods and the other in other periods, no sound comparison would be possible. The reader of the annual statements is entitled to know whether and to what extent apparent changes in operating results are due to changes in accounting practices. Another example of a change in the application of accounting principles resulting in an inconsistency is the change made by many companies in the costing of sales from the first-in, first-out basis to the last-in, first-out basis. Both bases are in accordance with generally accepted accounting principles, and decision as to which to use is a responsibility of management. Nevertheless, the effect of such a change upon the income statement in the year of change might be significant. Even though the independent auditor agrees with the propriety of such changes, they result in an "inconsistency" of application of accounting principles which he must recognize in giving his opinion.

A change in the application of accounting principles may stem from a change in operating conditions or other governing circumstances. Such changes cannot be termed "inconsistent," but nevertheless the auditor may feel that they require comment in the financial statements. In the absence of such comment the auditor may feel he should call attention to the change in his report, in order to facilitate reasonable interpretation of the statements.

A client may change from one accepted accounting principle to another without the justification of changed conditions and without apparent benefits, other than seemingly more favorable presentation of financial position or operating results. If the client insists upon making such a change, the independent public accountant is obliged to point out the inconsistent application of accounting principles where the effect of the change is material; he may wish to express his disapproval. When there has been an inconsistency in the selection or application of an accounting principle, whether or not the change is approved by the independent public accountant, the effect in dollars upon the comparability of financial statements, if material, should be indicated by footnote.

Consistency and Comparability.—Accounting Research Bulletin No. 43, Chapter 2, states, "It is necessary that prior-year figures shown for comparative purposes be in fact comparable with those shown for the most recent period, or that any exceptions to comparability be clearly brought out." Changes in classification which materially affect comparability of items in financial statements, whether in the balance sheet or the statement of income, should be disclosed in a footnote. It is not always necessary to indicate lack of consistency in the application of accounting principles in the auditor's report.

Statements may lack comparability even though consistency in application of accounting principles has been maintained. A subsidiary, consolidated at one date because it was controlled through majority stock ownership, may not be consolidated the following year because control was relinquished. There is no inconsistency of application of accounting principle, but attention may be called to the lack of comparability in a footnote.

On the other hand, if a subsidiary of material size is consolidated in one year and not consolidated in the succeeding year, when degree of control remains unchanged, an exception as to consistency in the application of accounting principles usually should be taken in the auditor's report. The test of materiality is applicable to questions of disclosure of inconsistencies and noncomparability. If the change, whether in accounting principles, their application, or merely of classification, does not materially affect comparability of financial statements of one year with those of the preceding year, the change need not be disclosed, unless the conditions are as cited below. Inconsistent application of an accounting principle may affect, or even destroy, proper comparability of financial statements. It is possible that a change may be instituted at a time when the effect of the change upon the current financial statements is small, but the effect in the future may be material. For example, the change from the Fifo to the Lifo basis of costing sales and inventory may be made when the effect in the year of change is negligible, but there may be reasonable certainty that the effect in the future will be material. Similarly, the effect in the current year of a change from the straight-line method of computing depreciation to the declining-balance method may not be material, but prospective large property additions or other conditions may indicate a major difference in the results of the two methods in the future. In this connection, Accounting Research Bulletin No. 44 (1954) says:

> When a change to the declining-balance method is made for general accounting purposes, and depreciation is a significant factor in the determination of net income, the change in method, including the effect thereof, should be disclosed in the year in which the change is made.

When the change has no material effect on the comparability of results of the current year with the preceding year, but may have material effect on comparability with some future year or years, it may seem unrealistic to mention the change in the year of change. But it would be equally unrealistic to delay mention of such change to the year in which the effect becomes material, when the change was in fact made several years previously. Better practice is to report the change in the year in which it is made, even though it has no material effect on the comparison of the results for that year with those of the next previous year. If the change in basis does not materially affect the comparability of the financial statements until in a later year, the auditor may suggest that attention be called by footnote in such later year to the effect and the amount (if determinable) of the change.

When a statement of income is prepared covering a period of years during any one of which a change has been made which affects the comparability of any of the years under report, disclosure of the change should be made in the report together with the effect of such change on the year of change and, if feasible, the effect upon the subsequent year or years.

Necessity for Expression of an Opinion.—The fourth standard of reporting, approved in substance by the membership of the Institute at the annual meeting in November, 1949, is worded as follows:

> The report shall either contain an expression of opinion regarding the financial statements, taken as a whole, or an assertion to the effect that an opinion cannot be expressed. When an over-all opinion cannot be expressed, the reason therefor should be stated. In all cases where an auditor's name is associated with financial statements the report should contain a clear-cut indication of the character of the auditor's examination, if any, and the degree of responsibility he is taking.

The application of this standard to the short-form report is considered in this chapter. Its implications when a long-form report is issued is discussed in Chapter 23.

When an auditor permits his name to be associated with financial statements, he must (1) express an unqualified opinion, (2) express a qualified opinion, or (3) disclaim an opinion on the financial statements as a whole and, if meaningful, he should add an opinion limited to certain items in the financial statements.

Financial statements ordinarily should not be submitted on an auditor's stationery unless he has made an examination and his report is included. If unaudited statements are presented on such stationery, it should be indicated clearly that no examination was made.

Qualifications and Disclosures in the Auditor's Report.—The auditor's report contains the following opinions which may require qualification or disclosure:

(a) That the examination was made in accordance with generally accepted auditing standards, and accordingly included such tests of the accounting records and such other auditing procedures as he considered necessary in the circumstances. (Although these phrases do not include the words "in our opinion," it is apparent that they are not statements of fact but represent the opinion of the auditor.)

(b) That the financial statements are presented fairly.

(c) That the financial statements are presented in conformity with generally accepted accounting principles.

(d) That such accounting principles have been applied on a basis consistent with that of the preceding year.

AUDITING STANDARDS.—Standard of Field Work No. 3 states:

Sufficient competent evidential matter is to be obtained through inspection, observation, inquiries and confirmations to afford a reasonable basis for an opinion regarding the financial statements under examination.

Two auditing procedures have special importance since they have been designated as "generally accepted" by the membership of the Institute at its 1939 annual meeting. These are the required observation of inventory-taking and confirmation of receivables when the related assets are material factors or represent a significant part of current assets or of total assets of a concern. "Codification of Statements on Auditing Procedure" (1951) includes a discussion of these two so-called "extended procedures" in some detail.

Certain types of debtors, such as U. S. Government departments and chain stores often indicate in reply to confirmation requests that their records do not readily permit reply. Usually the auditor is able to satisfy himself by other means as to the reliability of the records (see Chapter 10), in which case he should disclose the omission of confirmation procedures and state whether alternative procedures have been followed. When a significant portion of the assets is represented by receivables not susceptible of confirmation, specific qualification or even denial of opinion may be required.

In brief, therefore, failure to follow generally accepted auditing procedures with respect to material amounts of inventories and receivables as at the end of the period or year, for whatever reason, requires disclosure in the scope paragraph of the auditor's report. When alternative procedures have been followed which, in the opinion of the auditor, are sufficient to enable him to form an opinion, qualification as to the fairness of statement presentation in the opinion paragraph is not required. Statement on Auditing Procedure No. 26 (1956) again emphasizes the point made in the Codification that there are very few cases in which the "extended procedures" are not practicable and reasonable, and in which "other procedures" can be satisfactorily employed. In deciding upon the "other procedures" to be employed in these rare situations, the auditor must bear in mind that his is the burden of justifying the opinion expressed. When neither generally accepted auditing procedures nor acceptable alternatives have been followed, the auditor should specifically qualify his opinion, or deny an opinion on the statements as a whole, according to the circumstances.

Examples of disclosures in auditor's reports concerning the scope of examination are given below:

INVENTORY

. . . . Our examination was made in accordance with generally accepted auditing standards, and accordingly included such tests of the accounting records and such other auditing procedures as we considered necessary in the circumstances. It was not considered practicable and reasonable to substantiate the book inventory of work in process by physical inventory. However, we satisfied ourselves with respect to such inventories by means of other auditing procedures.

ACCOUNTS RECEIVABLE—U. S. GOVERNMENT

Our examination was made in accordance with generally accepted auditing standards, and accordingly included such tests of the accounting records and such other auditing procedures as we considered necessary in the circumstances. We did not consider it practicable and reasonable to confirm by direct correspondence amounts due from United States Government departments as to which we satisfied ourselves by means of other auditing procedures.

The client may request that one of these so-called "extended procedures" should not be followed by the auditor. In such a situation, the auditor should not assume the risk of an unqualified opinion. If a material misstatement of inventories or receivables later develops which probably would have been discovered had the auditor observed the inventory-taking or made a test confirmation of receivables, he would have difficulty in defending a claim asserted against him on the ground that he should have followed the so-called "extended procedures," qualified his opinion or refused to give an opinion because of the materiality of the amount involved. When the amount involved is not material and the auditor feels therefore that he can express an unqualified opinion, he would nevertheless be well advised to obtain a letter from his client relieving him of responsibility for any discrepancy which might have been discovered had he followed the so-called "extended procedures."

Occasionally an auditor may be unable to follow an auditing procedure (other than the so-called "extended procedures") which he believes necessary in the circumstances. Under such conditions, alternative procedures are usually not available, and if not, the auditor should either express a qualified opinion or disclaim an opinion on the statements taken as a whole.

FAIRNESS OF PRESENTATION.—When the auditor's examination has been limited in scope by circumstances (e.g., inability to observe inventories or confirm receivables, as discussed above) and alternative auditing procedures satisfactory to the auditor have not been followed, it is usually necessary to qualify the auditor's opinion as to the fairness of presentation of the financial statements. Illustrations of auditors' opinions under such circumstances follow:

(Partial opinion)

We have examined the balance sheet of X Manufacturing Corporation as of December 31, 1956 and the related statement(s) of income and surplus for the year then ended. We did not make an examination of the company's balance sheet at December 31, 1955, and accordingly we did not observe the inventory-taking as at the beginning of the year nor were we able to satisfy ourselves as to such inventory by other auditing procedures. In all other respects our examination was made in accordance with generally accepted auditing standards, and accordingly included such tests of the accounting records and such other auditing procedures as we considered necessary in the circumstances.

Because we did not observe the inventory-taking at the beginning of the year, we do not believe we have sufficient basis for an opinion concerning the cost of goods sold and the over-all results of operations for the year.

In our opinion, (a) the accompanying balance sheet presents fairly the financial position of X Manufacturing Corporation at December 31, 1956, and (b) the items of income, costs and expenses, other than cost of goods sold, included in the related statements of income and surplus for the year then ended are presented fairly, in conformity with generally accepted accounting principles applied on a basis consistent with that of the preceding year.

(Denial of opinion on statements as a whole)

We have examined the balance sheet of X Company, as of December 31, 1956 and the related statement(s) of income and surplus for the year then ended. We did not observe the taking of inventories as of December 31, 1955 or December 31, 1956, nor are the inventory records such that it is practicable for us to satisfy ourselves as to such inventories by alternative auditing procedures. In all other respects our examination was made in accordance with generally accepted auditing standards, and accordingly included such tests of the accounting records and such other auditing procedures as we considered necessary in the circumstances.

Because of the limitation in scope of our examination of inventories, we are unable to express an opinion as to the fairness with which the accompanying financial statements, taken as a whole, present financial position and results of operations. In all other material respects, in our opinion, the accompanying financial statements present fairly the assets (other than inventories) and liabilities of X Company, at December 31, 1956, and the income, costs (other than such costs as may be affected by inventories), and expenses for the year then ended, in conformity with generally accepted accounting principles applied on a basis consistent with that of the preceding year.

(Qualification of opinion as to fairness of presentation)

. . . . Our examination was made in accordance with generally accepted auditing standards, and accordingly included such tests of the accounting records and such other auditing procedures as we considered necessary in the circumstances, except that we did not examine the financial statements of a joint venture in which the company had a sixty per cent interest during the year ended December 31, 19___.

Except for such changes, if any, which might have been disclosed by an examination of the financial statements of the joint venture referred to in the preceding paragraph, in our opinion, the accompanying financial statements present fairly the financial position of the X Company at December 31, 19___, and the results of its operations for the year then ended. . . .

Even though the auditor's examination has been made in accordance with generally accepted auditing standards and he need take no exception in the scope paragraph, there may be circumstances which compel him to qualify with respect to fairness of presentation of the financial statements. Such circumstances arise when an uncertainty with respect to major items on the financial statements cannot be resolved at the date of the auditor's report. An example of a report under such a condition follows:

Except for the loss, if any, that may be sustained upon disposition of the nonoperating property, plant and equipment referred to in Note 1, in our opinion, the accompanying balance sheet and related statements of income and surplus present fairly the financial position. . . .

(Note 1 describes briefly the nature and book amount of the property stated to have been offered for sale and the uncertainty as to amount which may be realized therefrom.)

CONFORMITY WITH GENERALLY ACCEPTED ACCOUNTING PRINCIPLES.—Occasionally the independent auditor will disagree with his client as to the propriety of an accounting principle applied in the preparation of the financial statements under examination. Businessmen generally listen to sound arguments before the statements are prepared, and frequently, perhaps usually, it is possible to effect changes in the statements which will permit the auditor to give an unqualified opinion with respect to conformity with generally accepted accounting principles. When the disagreement cannot be resolved, and a qualification is necessary, it should appear in the auditor's report in clear and unequivocal language. There have been many instances, both as to application of principles in the accumulation of balances in the financial statements and in the classification and arrangement of such balances, which were the subject of necessary qualification by the independent accountant. Following are two illustrations:

(1)

As explained in Note 2 to the financial statements, during 19___, the Company incurred certain maintenance costs aggregating (indicate amount) which, pursuant to the order of the Public Service Commission, were deferred except for the purpose of computing federal income tax, and had the effect of reducing the current provision for that tax by (indicate amount). Under generally accepted accounting principles, such costs should have been charged to maintenance expense and, in our opinion, net income for 19___ and the balance of unappropriated earned surplus at December 31, 19___, as shown in the accompanying statements, are overstated by (indicate amount).

With the exception stated in the preceding paragraph, in our opinion, the accompanying balance sheet and related statements of income and earned surplus present fairly the financial position. . . .

(2)

Inventories of raw materials, work in process, finished goods and supplies were priced by the management at amounts approximately (indicate amount) less than would have resulted from the application of the generally accepted basis of the lower of cost or market, and accordingly net income for the year then ended was reduced by (indicate amount).

Except as to the basis of the inventory valuation and its effect upon net income, described in the preceding paragraph, in our opinion, the accompanying statements present fairly the financial position of the X Corporation at December 31, 19___ and the results of its operations for the year then ended. . . .

CONSISTENCY WITH PRIOR PERIOD.—When the effect of a change in application of an accounting principle materially affects the comparability of the balance sheet or statement of income, the auditor should note an exception to the application of generally accepted accounting principles on a consistent basis, regardless of the reason for making the change. Disclosure of the nature of the change is usually accompanied by an indication of the dollar effect of the change on the financial statements. The auditor should also indicate whether he agrees with the propriety of the change. The paragraph of the report dealing with this phase may be worded as follows:

In our opinion, the accompanying financial statements present fairly the financial position of X Corporation at December 31, 19___, and the results of its operations for the year then ended, in conformity with generally accepted accounting principles applied on a basis consistent (except as to the change described in Note 1, with which change we concur) with that of the preceding year.

(Note 1 to financial statements describes the nature of the change and the dollar amount of the effect on the comparability of the financial statements with those of the preceding year.)

Whenever the auditor disapproves of a change, his report should briefly describe his reasons for disapproval. It is likely, however, that when an auditor disapproves a change in application of accounting principles, he would also have reservations as to the fairness of presentation of the financial statements which would require qualification.

"Informative Disclosures" in Short-Form Reports.—Item 3 of "Standards of Reporting" states that "Informative disclosures in the financial statements are to be regarded as reasonably adequate unless otherwise stated in the report." Explanatory matter not conveniently included in the face of the financial statements themselves is usually presented in the form of "Notes" to the financial statements; the auditor's opinion relates to these notes as well as to the financial statements. When the auditor believes that neither the statements nor the accompanying notes disclose material information necessary to a fair presentation of financial position or results of operations, he should include such information in his report, usually in a paragraph between the "scope" and the "opinion" paragraphs.

When the question is merely one of location, the auditor should recommend inclusion of such explanations in the notes, although if the client requests inclusion in the auditor's report, the authors see no reason why the auditor should not accede to such a request.

Presumably after inclusion of the data in the auditor's report he will have no further reservations as to disclosure and the opinion paragraph of his report may state:

In our opinion, the accompanying balance sheet and statement of income and earned surplus, when read in conjunction with the explanation in the preceding paragraph, present fairly . . . . etc.

A somewhat specialized explanation is usually required to accompany financial statements of individual proprietorships or partnerships, because income taxes on the profits of such businesses are payable by the proprietor or partners, and usually do not appear on income statements of the business. It is usual therefore (except with respect to partnerships conducting banking or brokerage businesses) to include the explanation that the income statement does not include provision for federal and state income taxes on the proprietor's business and personal income, or that income credited to partners' accounts is subject to such taxes payable by the individual partners.

In succeeding chapters the authors describe generally in the sections dealing with "Statement Presentation" what, in their opinion, represents adequate disclosure.

The "Rules of Professional Conduct" adopted by the American Institute of Certified Public Accountants and most similar ethical codes which have been enacted into state law or which are used by state societies (see Chapter 3) usually require that the auditor's report disclose any absence of independence in his relationship with his client. The practical effect of this requirement is that most auditors in this country will not accept engagements leading toward expressions of opinions on financial statements of companies as to which they are not, in fact, independent. In the few instances when independence of relationship is absent, the auditor should disclose in his report the nature of his affiliation with his client.

Other Reporting Problems.

SPECIALIZED FIELDS AND INDUSTRIES.—The short-form report so far discussed in this chapter is appropriate when the related examination covers financial statements of commercial or industrial enterprises in business for profit. It is clear in such instances that the "financial statements" upon which the auditor reports are those which purport to show financial position and results of operations; there is no question that the auditor's work and his report should conform to generally accepted auditing standards, and he has a large body of authoritative literature and accepted accounting principles to guide him.

Some categories of industry in business for profit pose problems for the reporting accountant in that they must conform to special accounting requirements in reports filed with various governmental commissions, and these requirements may be reflected in financial statements upon which the independent public accountant is asked to report. Examples of these are public utility companies, railroads, banks, and insurance companies, in respect of which commission regulations may require or permit accounting which is at variance with the accounting principles deemed to be generally accepted by business at large. In the authors' opinion, generally accepted standards of reporting apply equally to all organizations in business for profit, including the requirement that the opinion state whether generally accepted accounting principles have been applied. It would not, therefore, be appropriate for the independent public accountant to limit his opinion as to compliance with generally accepted accounting principles by indicating that the principles applied are those authorized by the regulatory commission for that industry. His report should state whether, in his opinion, the financial statements fairly present financial position and results of operations in accordance with *generally accepted* accounting principles. Having done so, there is no objection to stating that the financial statements conform to the requirements of a regulatory body or the practices of a particular industry.

Another type of problem arises with respect to nonprofit organizations, such as municipalities, educational institutions, and hospitals, which may follow special accounting practices evolved and recommended by representative bodies in those fields. As indicated previously, "generally accepted accounting principles," as used in the short-form report, apply to business enterprises organized for profit. Accordingly, when the independent auditor is asked to report on *financial statements* of nonprofit organizations, and if the statements have been prepared in accordance with special practices promulgated by an authoritative body in that field which deviate in important respects from generally accepted accounting principles for business organizations, he should report that the statements have been prepared in accordance with generally accepted accounting principles for (universities, hospitals, etc.). However, in the authors' opinion the auditor's report or the statements themselves should include explanations of the character of the deviations from generally accepted accounting principles for business organizations.

CASH BASIS OR MODIFIED CASH BASIS ACCOUNTING.—Nonprofit organizations as well as smaller business organizations may employ cash basis accounting in the preparation of financial statements. In many instances such organizations have little or no inventory, fixed assets, or accrued income and expenses and may have fiscal years coinciding with a natural operating cycle so that income and expenses for such fiscal periods are closely matched. Where such conditions exist, cash basis financial statements may not differ materially from statements prepared on the accrual basis, and if they do not, the conventional short-form report may be given.

The application of cash basis accounting in many enterprises, whether nonprofit or business, would not produce financial statements that could be described as prepared on the basis of generally accepted accounting principles, and the independent auditor's report, therefore, could not properly so describe them. Further, a balance sheet or statement of income prepared on the basis of cash receipts and disbursements might not show financial position or results of operations, and if such is the case the auditor should not so report on them. The auditor's report upon his examination of a business or professional enterprise organized for profit, but keeping its accounts on the basis of cash receipts and disbursements, might appear as follows:

We have examined the balance sheet (cash basis) of the X Company as of December 31, 19— and the related statement of cash receipts and disbursements for the year then ended. Our examination was made in accordance with generally accepted auditing standards, and accordingly included such tests of the accounting records and such other auditing procedures as we considered necessary in the circumstances.

These statements have been prepared on the cash receipts and disbursements basis and therefore do not purport to present financial position and results of operations as they would have appeared had generally accepted accrual basis accounting principles been applied in their preparation.

In our opinion, the data set forth in the accompanying balance sheet (cash basis) at December 31, 19— and the related statement of cash receipts and disbursements for the year then ended have been fairly summarized on the basis indicated.

The same type of report would be appropriate for a nonprofit organization such as a club, religious, charitable, or fraternal organization keeping its accounts on a cash basis.

SPECIAL REPORTS.—*Reports on Other Than "Financial Statements."*—There are many types of statements, other than those of cash receipts and disbursements, on which the independent auditor may be asked to give his opinion, and which do not purport to present financial position or results of operations. The substance of those auditing standards entitled "General Standards" and "Standards of Field Work" (see Chapter 2) apply equally to the examination of such statements, but it is apparent that all of the "Standards of Reporting" would not apply to them. Accordingly, he is usually not expected to state an opinion whether generally accepted accounting principles have been consistently applied; he would, however, be expected to state whether, in his opinion, the statements fairly present what they purport to present. Examples are calculations of royalties, profit-sharing bonuses, rentals, and statements of cash and securities on hand.

Reports Prepared on Printed Forms.—Statements required to be prepared on printed forms, other than tax return forms, furnished by governmental agencies with which they are to be filed, may result in classifications or accounting treatments which, in the auditor's opinion, do not fairly present financial position or results of operations in conformity with generally accepted accounting principles. Also, such forms may contain a printed form of opinion or certification which the auditor feels he cannot sign because it does not conform to reporting standards discussed in this chapter, or because it may require assertions by him which are outside his functions and responsibilities as an independent auditor. Some forms can be adjusted by typing in additional captions or wording; others can be made acceptable only by complete revision. Whenever the printed forms call upon the accountant to make an assertion which he believes he is not justified in making, he has no alternative but to reword them or to submit his separately typed report. Use of separately typed statements and reports is recommended wherever the language of the printed forms does not conform in essential matters with professional standards.

Reports Required by Indentures.—Bond indentures and trust agreements frequently require special reports by the independent auditor or his opinion on statements which may vary somewhat from the usual form of financial statement. For example, the document may call for a presentation of "net income available for dividends" under a definition of such term which would not be appropriate for general purposes. It is considered proper for the accountant to submit opinions regarding such statements provided they are accompanied by statements prepared in conformity with generally accepted accounting principles together with his report, or appropriate references thereto.

Sometimes the auditor is required to express an opinion upon the company's compliance with certain covenants of the indenture or with the indenture as a whole. The scope of the regular examination of financial statements would not ordinarily permit him to give an opinion on compliance with all the provisions of an indenture. In some cases he may, by following additional procedures, be able to express an opinion on the company's compliance with certain sections of the indenture. In any event his report should be qualified when necessary. Some illustrations follow:

(1)

. . . . As prescribed by Section 7.08(1) of the (Indenture) we report to you that during the course of such examination we obtained no knowledge of any default existing during the year 19_ in the observance, performance or fulfillment of any of the terms and provisions contained in the aforesaid (Indenture). However, it should be understood that our examination was not directed primarily toward obtaining such knowledge.

(2)

During the course of our examination nothing came to our attention which indicated any action or nonaction by (client) in violation of the covenants contained in Sections 5.05 through 5.11 of Article Five of (Indenture). However, it should be understood that our examination was made primarily for the purpose of enabling us to give an opinion on the financial statements, and therefore would not necessarily include a direct investigation to determine that such covenants were fulfilled by (client).

When the auditor's procedures are adequate to cover the subject matter of specific covenants, and he considers himself qualified to pass upon such subject matter, his report may read as follows:

. . . . In the course of our examinations we have obtained no knowledge of any default by the Company, existing at the end of the fiscal year under review, in the observance, performance or fulfillment of the terms, provisions and conditions as set forth in Sections 2(a) and 9 of the (Indenture).

Reports Under SEC Practice.—Various reports by independent public accountants are required in connection with filings with the Securities and Exchange Commission under the securities acts it administers. These reports are described in Chapter 25.

CHAPTER 7

FINANCIAL STATEMENTS

Introduction.—When the independent public accountant refers to "financial statements," he usually has in mind those to which his examination is directed and on which he is expected to give his opinion. As such, they include at least a balance sheet at a given date and statements of income and surplus for a period, usually one year, then ended. Such statements may be of a single company, or of a parent company and one or more subsidiaries consolidated; the statement of income may be shown separately or combined with the statement of earned surplus, and there may be presented statements of one or more categories of capital surplus. In practice, there are many variations in form, title and descriptive wording of financial statements, and this chapter will discuss their preparation and presentation. Considerations applicable to consolidated financial statements are discussed in Chapter 21.

Nature of Financial Statements.—Neither the balance sheet at a given date nor a statement of income for a specified period can be presented, as some may believe, as the unvarying result of mathematical formulae. While financial statements are based on business transactions which are facts, and mathematics is employed as one of the tools of accounting, the reflection of the basic facts in financial statements involves the exercise of judgment in the application of accounting principles or conventions. The soundness of the judgments of company officials in the initial preparation of financial statements depends not only upon their competence but also upon their objectivity. The opinion of the independent certified public accountant on financial statements cross-checks both the competence and the objectivity with which the statements have been prepared.

Accounting Principles and Financial Statements.—The meaning of accounting principles has been discussed in Chapter 6, and principles applicable to specific balance sheet and income statement items are covered in the succeeding chapters. A number of rules of general application may be mentioned here, although it should be stressed that accounting principles, conventions, doctrines, and rules are not inflexible, but must be adapted to conditions of the business or other entity to which they are applied.

Unless otherwise stated, financial statements are presumed to be those of a going concern. Amounts on the balance sheet do not usually purport to represent liquidation values, present economic values, or replacement values. The conventional basis for stating fixed assets in use is cost less allowance for depreciation, even though such amount may differ substantially from either reproduction cost or realizable value. Certain debit balances subject to final disposition and applicable to future operations, such as prepaid items and deferred charges, are by convention classified as assets on the balance sheet, even though the amounts at which they are stated are seldom realizable in cash or available for payment of debts. Profits are accurately and definitely determinable only for the entire life of the business enterprise; the apportionment of profit by accounting periods is necessarily tentative at the close of each of such periods.

Conservatism in Financial Statements.—Conservatism in accounting prescribes that in applying judgment in selecting one of two or more generally accepted accounting principles applicable in the circumstances, one be selected which understates, rather than overstates, the assets and results of operations. Conservatism, as thus defined, has weight only in deciding between permissible alternatives. It cannot be invoked to sanction unwarranted or dishonest understatements.

Formerly, when emphasis was placed on the balance sheet, conservatism in accounting sometimes led to advocating that expenditures be charged against income when made, even though future periods might reasonably be expected to benefit from some part of the expenditure. The so-called conservative point of view was the basis for such practices as charging additions or improvements of plant and equipment to expense accounts; charging off discount on long-term debt at the time of sale of the securities; writing down inventories unduly in otherwise profitable years; and providing overgenerously for liabilities, direct or contingent. With increasing appreciation of the importance of the statement of income, there has been recognition that this "conservatism" usually relieves subsequent income statements of charges properly applicable to them, with the result that the income of future periods is overstated.

In the authors' opinion, experienced judgment plays a leading role in the application of the doctrine of conservatism to accounting problems. If it is obvious to an experienced accountant that a material item is a proper charge to fixed assets, good accounting practice does not sanction its charge to income. If experienced judgment indicates that a reasonable doubt exists as to its character, good accounting practice permits a charge to income rather than to fixed assets.

Responsibility for Financial Statements.—It should be clearly understood that owners or management are responsible for the financial statements; the auditor is responsible for his report and opinion. The following is quoted from "Codification of Statements on Auditing Procedure," issued by the American Institute of Certified Public Accountants in 1951:

Management has the direct responsibility for maintenance of an adequate and effective system of accounts, for proper recording of transactions in the books of account, and for safeguarding the assets. It is also charged with the primary responsibility to stockholders and to creditors for the substantial accuracy and adequacy of statements of position and operations. The transactions with which the accounting records have to do and the recording of those transactions in the books and accounts are matters within the direct or primary knowledge of the company; the independent auditor's knowledge of them is a secondary one, based on his examination. Accordingly, even though the *form* of the statements may show the influence of the accountant—it can do so only if the company accepts, and adopts, the form of disclosure advised by the accountant—the *substance* of the financial statements of necessity constitutes the representations of the company. The independent auditor's representations, therefore, are confined to and expressed in his report, or opinion, upon the statements. The pronouncements of the Institute to this effect have been given the added weight of general affirmation by the Securities and Exchange Commission.

The auditor may assist, advise, and persuade management with respect to form and content of financial statements, but he cannot compel management to accept his recommendations. The auditor can, and should, state in his report wherein he disagrees with the fairness of presentation of financial statements if he cannot persuade management to make changes he believes necessary. The auditor's duty to state exceptions in his report is often a compelling argument to bring about changes in accord with his views.

A few large corporations authorize their chief financial officer to sign their published statements, which are sometimes accompanied by a short report of this officer. This is sound practice and is recommended by the New York Stock Exchange. It emphasizes the responsibility of management for published financial statements and, by contrast, the responsibility of the independent public accountant for his opinion.

If financial statements reflect adjustments (usually as between periods or as to valuations) which have not been entered on the books, it is good practice for the auditor to secure the client's written approval of the financial statements so prepared. This approval often is obtained on a copy of the financial statements for the auditor's files.

However, an accountant might be engaged by a prospective purchaser of a business, by a creditor, or by the management or owners themselves to prepare from the books and accounts and all other available information financial statements which he believes fairly reflect the position and results. Such statements might not agree with the books and records in existence and might even reflect views not concurred in by the management. The auditor would then assume responsibility for such changes as are reflected in the statements prepared by him.

All-Purpose Financial Statements.—The auditor has no practicable method of restricting the use of financial statements on which he has submitted an opinion. Such financial statements are perhaps most commonly designed for inclusion in the company's annual report to stockholders, who will consider the data given in deciding whether to hold, increase, or sell their shares in the enterprise. They are often delivered, in compliance with agreements, to banks, insurance companies, or other holders of the company's note, bond, or preferred stock issues. The auditor should therefore urge that statements be in a form that meets the needs of most readers, including financial writers and analysts who will interpret the statements for investors and others. Statements so designed are sometimes termed "all-purpose financial statements," in contrast to statements prepared to meet special purposes.

There have been suggestions in the past that all-purpose financial statements be supplanted by, or at least supplemented with, a series of statements containing more detailed information of interest to special readers. The trend in recent years to furnish additional details in financial statements, in appended notes or schedules, as data in narrative portions of reports to stockholders, or in annual reports (Form 10-K) to the Securities and Exchange Commission, has apparently met the need, since such suggestions are now seldom heard.

The authors by no means suggest that progress in the development of more useful financial statements should cease. Management and independent public accountants will continue to strive for improvement in form and content of data furnished to stockholders. The usefulness of all-purpose statements, however, is too well established to warrant the substitution of other means of presenting the financial information to which stockholders and other readers are regularly entitled.

Financial Statements for Special Purposes.—It is not intended to imply that special-purpose financial statements should never be presented. For many years, independent public accountants have been reporting on special-purpose financial statements. Special-purpose statements offer the auditor an opportunity to exercise his imagination, ingenuity, and capabilities to suggest a statement which in form and substance most adequately gives the reader the information he should have. Some types of special-purpose statements are discussed below.

For Prospective Investors.—Financial statements containing information of special interest to prospective purchasers of a business or investors in its securities have been prepared by certified public accountants for many years. The Securities and Exchange Commission, under the Securities Act of 1933 (see Chapter 25) requires certain financial data in addition to that ordinarily given for annual reporting purposes to be included in prospectuses and registration statements for the information of prospective investors.

For Credit Grantors.—Banks, insurance companies, and others who lend money to corporations frequently require data amplifying or supplementing that contained in all-purpose financial statements. Often special forms are provided by the lender requesting the information he requires, much of which could not be shown in usual financial statements. Robert Morris Associates has prepared a booklet entitled "Financial Statements for Bank Credit Purposes" (1951) which indicates the kind of additional information this type of lender frequently desires.

Balance Sheets with Fixed Assets Stated for Special Purposes.—Balance sheets may be prepared in which fixed assets may be stated in amounts adjusted to indicate valuations significant to a special situation. For franchise tax purposes, fixed assets may be stated at appraised valuations; for companies in bankruptcy, at estimated liquidating values. The purpose of the statements and the basis of valuation should be clearly indicated.

CONDENSED STATEMENTS.—The auditor is sometimes asked to report his opinion on condensed financial statements. The propriety of doing so depends upon the degree of condensation. If the statements lack information essential to a proper understanding of the company's position or results of operation, the auditor cannot give an opinion without supplying the missing data in his report. It is not unusual, however, that statements first prepared for his examination and for internal use contain data which may reasonably be eliminated from published reports.

PRO FORMA FINANCIAL STATEMENTS.—Pro forma financial statements are those which purport to give effect to transactions actually consummated or expected to be consummated at a date subsequent to that of the date of the statements. Auditors consider it proper to submit their report and opinion on such statements only when the nature of the transactions to which effect is given is clearly described in the statements, and when satisfactory evidence of good faith, such as actual subsequent consummations or signed firm contracts, is available. The positions of the American Institute of Certified Public Accountants and of the Securities and Exchange Commission regarding certain types of pro forma statements are discussed in Chapter 25.

OTHER TYPES OF SPECIAL FINANCIAL STATEMENTS.—The auditor may be called upon to assist in the design or preparation of schedules supplementing the usual financial statements, desired by management for various administrative purposes.

The peculiar characteristics of municipalities, endowed institutions such as universities and hospitals, estates, and other fiduciaries require that they prepare statements of financial position in forms somewhat different from those for commercial and industrial undertakings.

Railroads, electric and telephone companies, other public utilities and holding companies which are under the supervision of federal commissions or state regulatory bodies use prescribed uniform classifications of accounts, and the arrangement of captions in financial statements of these companies also differs in noteworthy respects from that customarily used by commercial and industrial companies.

Bond indentures sometimes contain a provision that financial statements required to be filed with the trustee be prepared in a prescribed form in which grouping and classification may not conform with customary accounting practice. Financial statements prepared under such conditions should indicate that they have been prepared in that form solely to meet specific requirements of the bond indenture. It may be desirable to indicate wherein such statements differ from those which may have been prepared in accordance with generally accepted accounting principles.

Comparative Financial Statements.—Presentation of financial statements in annual reports to stockholders in comparative form has become quite general. This presentation is highly desirable, for the information obtainable from the study of balance sheets at the beginning and end of a period, or from a comparison of statements of income for two or more years, is often more illuminating than mere position at a date and the results of operation for one year. Comparative statements indicate whether the concern is showing progress and, to some extent, why.

Innovations in Financial Statements.—Corporation managements and their independent public accountants have a mutual interest in presenting understandable accounts of stewardship. The search for improved form and content of financial statements has been accelerated in recent years, and accounting literature continues to discuss the pioneering of certain corporations. Studies by public relations counsel have indicated that many stockholders do not understand common accounting terms.

There are countless possible variations of terminology and of form. Some of them are mentioned below.

TERMINOLOGY.—A statement which shows assets, liabilities, and stockholders' equity is most often called a "balance sheet," but frequently it is termed a statement of "financial position" or "financial condition," especially when not in the conventional form. The majority of companies continue to describe the results of operations for the period reported as the "statement of income," although an increasing number of them have adopted the expression "statement of earnings." The heading "profit and loss statement" seems to be decreasing in popularity. Although accumulated undistributed earnings continue to be described as "earned surplus," the recommendation of the Institute's Committee on Terminology that terms such as "retained earnings," "retained income," or other suitable variations be substituted has had wide acceptance, as has the suggestion that the term "capital surplus" be replaced by descriptions indicating its source.

FORM.—Most innovations in the form of balance sheet are aimed to avoid the impression that it is merely a bookkeeping statement whose principal virtue is that the total of one side equals the total of the other side. Sometimes the order of the items on the balance sheet is changed to emphasize that a corporation has an investment in various types of assets and debts which must be met from them, and that these net assets have come into being through investment by the stockholders plus earnings which they have permitted to remain in the business. Usually this type of balance sheet is accompanied by a "single-step" income statement which is described later in this chapter.

Previous editions of this book have advocated rounding out all figures on financial statements to the nearest dollar, or even the nearest hundred or thousand dollars. The showing of pennies imparts an unreal impression of exactitude, whereas in truth many important items on financial statements are estimates. Furthermore, statements so prepared are easier to read. A large portion of published reports to stockholders have now adopted this practice, the Securities and Exchange Commission has approved it, and the Internal Revenue Service permits the use of whole dollar amounts in income tax returns of individuals and corporations.

There is no objection to experimenting with the form of financial statements in an effort to make them understandable to more stockholders. In the opinion of the authors, most stockholders want to be told three things: the earnings per share of capital stock in the current year, the earnings per share in the preceding year, and the earnings per share that may be expected in the following year. Conventional financial statements will give the stockholders information on current and past earnings per share just as well as any of the newer forms; no form of financial statement predicts future earnings. Most reports to stockholders include a letter from the president giving supplemental information. Some companies hold regional meetings of stockholders during the year at different locations to give them an opportunity to raise questions with management. Supplementing and amplifying financial statements by these means is more effective in getting information to stockholders than are some of the innovations in statements that have been seen recently.

The Balance Sheet.

DEFINITION.—Strictly, "balance sheet" is a technical accounting term which, according to the Committee on Terminology of the American Institute of Certified Public Accountants, may be defined as:

A tabular statement or summary of balances (debit and credit) carried forward after an actual or constructive closing of books of account kept according to principles of accounting.

IMPORTANCE OF BALANCE SHEET.—The trend has continued toward emphasis on the importance of the income statement to an understanding by investors and others of the financial affairs of a corporation. It is said that the value of a business, and consequently of its assets, depends almost entirely on its earning power. Because of this feeling, there has been some tendency to belittle the balance sheet as a principal source of information, and to view accounting problems largely from the point of view of the income statement. It is not to be denied that earnings are of great interest, and it is important that the income statement be prepared on a basis that fairly presents the results of operations. Nevertheless, the balance sheet also provides information for the intelligent reader which, in some circumstances at least, may be of greater importance. Such significant relationships as those of total cash to total current liabilities, total cash to total current assets, accounts receivable to sales, inventories to sales and cost of sales and total current assets, fixed assets to long-term debt, and long-term debt to total capital stock and surplus—all these and others may convey valuable information which obviously could not be obtained from the income statement alone. While the investor properly desires earning power, he prefers earnings plus ample working capital to earnings plus insufficient working capital. For data as to working capital he looks to the balance sheet.

It is worth repeating that a balance sheet does not report facts so much as judgments or opinions based on facts. When an auditor speaks of the facts reported in a balance sheet, he usually means the descriptive matter, not the figures. For example, it may be a fact that notes receivable are due within one year, but it may not be a fact that they will be liquidated at their face amount. Their estimated value is indicated by giving consideration to an allowance for losses in collection, which allowance is not a matter of fact, but of opinion. The lower of cost or market is a factual description of a method of stating an inventory, but opinions may differ as to how either cost or market should be determined.

THE BALANCE SHEET AS RELATED TO FINANCIAL POSITION.—The independent public accountant states his opinion whether or not the financial statements (balance sheet, statements of income and surplus) fairly present the financial position of an enterprise at a specified date and the results of operations for a period. Question has been raised as to whether the balance sheet alone can give financial position at a specified date, or whether financial position has no meaning unless accompanied by income and surplus statements which help to explain the changes in financial position since the last balance sheet date. The question is raised practically when clients request the public accountant to report upon the balance sheet without statements of income or surplus, and to give an opinion whether such balance sheet fairly presents the company's financial position. In the past, many auditors have given such an opinion, and a number continue to do so, although the statement of income is now rarely omitted in published financial statements. Some auditors insist that a statement of financial position at a given date is meaningless unless there is an indication of the direction in which financial position has traveled; they insist that at least a summary of surplus be included with the balance sheet. Some auditors believe a statement of income is also necessary to a proper understanding of position.

The authors believe it highly desirable to furnish stockholders with statements of income and surplus. If a client insists that a balance sheet alone be furnished, the authors believe the auditor cannot reasonably refuse to give his opinion on it; if a summary of surplus is shown either on the balance sheet or as a supporting statement, the auditor should insist that full disclosure be made of any unusual or nonoperating items entering into the determination of the net income figure included in such summary.

At one time it was not unusual for short-term credit to be granted on the basis of the balance sheet alone. This practice is no longer prevalent; credit grantors expect their loans to be repaid as a result of profitable operations, and are equally interested in the statement of income.

CONTENT OF BALANCE SHEET.—A balance sheet has five main categories, as follows:

Name of the individual, business, or organization whose financial position it presents;

Date as at which the statement is presented;

Assets;

Liabilities; and

Capital.

A balance sheet usually has appended explanatory notes, and these are discussed later in this chapter.

It is important that the name of the company be given correctly in the balance sheet heading. If a company has been incorporated as "The Mammoth Manufacturing Company, Inc.," its name should appear in the balance sheet exactly so. Omitting "The" at the beginning, abbreviating the word "Company," or changing "Inc." to "Incorporated" are undesirable alterations. If the state of incorporation is not part of the name of the company, some consider it desirable to include this information in parentheses directly beneath the company's name, but this practice is not widely followed.

The Committee on Terminology of the American Institute of Certified Public Accountants in Bulletin No. 1 (Review and Résumé) has offered definitions for assets and liabilities which are reproduced here to clarify what the balance sheet contents represent. The term "asset," as used in balance sheets, means:

Something represented by a debit balance that is or would be properly carried forward upon a closing of books of account according to the rules or principles of accounting (provided such debit balance is not in effect a negative balance applicable to a liability), on the basis that it represents either a property right or value acquired, or an expenditure made which has created a property right or is properly applicable to the future. Thus, plant, accounts receivable, inventory, and a deferred charge are all assets in balance-sheet classification.

A liability is defined as:

Something represented by a credit balance that is or would be properly carried forward upon a closing of books of account according to the rules or principles of accounting, provided such credit balance is not in effect a negative balance applicable to an asset. Thus the word is used broadly to comprise not only items which constitute liabilities in the popular sense of debts or obligations (including provision for those that are unascertained), but also credit balances to be accounted for which do not involve the debtor and creditor relation. For example, capital stock and related or similar elements of proprietorship are balance-sheet liabilities in that they represent balances to be accounted for, though these are not liabilities in the ordinary sense of debts owed to legal creditors.

The committee stated that it did not consider the above definition inconsistent with the view that the balance sheet consists of an asset section, a liability section, and a proprietary or capital section.

Items included under these general captions of a balance sheet should be self-explanatory. Definitions of items usually so included, as well as comment on the preferred presentation on the balance sheet, are discussed in later chapters of this book.

Working Capital.—The working capital of a prospective borrower has always been of prime interest to grantors of credit. Working capital, sometimes called "net working capital," represents the excess of current assets over current liabilities. It identifies the relatively liquid portion of the total enterprise capital which provides a margin or buffer for meeting obligations within the ordinary operating cycle of the business. The average time intervening between the expenditure of cash for materials and services which are converted into inventory and later into trade receivables, and the time when such receivables are converted into cash, constitutes an operating cycle.

The operating cycle is generally less than one year, and since most financial statements are issued annually, the test usually applied to determine whether an asset should be included in current assets is whether it will normally be converted into cash within one year. When the operating cycle is greater than one year, as in the tobacco, distillery, and lumber industries, and in those which customarily sell goods on a long-term instalment basis, the test applied should be such longer period, often with an indication of the basis in a footnote to the statements.

The Committee on Accounting Procedure in Bulletin No. 43, Chapter 3, Section A, discusses the determination of working capital.

FORM OF BALANCE SHEET.—The problems involved in the determination and proper statement of assets, liabilities, and capital are difficult, and the purposes to be served require that careful attention be given to description, order, and arrangement. Professional independence may militate against complete uniformity or standardization of balance sheets, but reasonable adherence to commonly accepted standards should be maintained. Words in common use should be used in their common meaning. Selection of suitable technical words and terms should follow the practice of a majority of accountants.

The authors' concept of an ideal balance sheet is one which sets forth, in addition to the name of the issuer and the appropriate date,

1. The assets adequately described, stated at amounts determined in conformity with generally accepted accounting principles, and arranged in appropriate groups in the order of their availability for payment of obligations;
2. All known liabilities properly grouped in the order in which they will, or should, be discharged; and
3. The details of capital or, in the balance sheet of a corporation, of capital stock to which is added surplus adequately segregated and described, or from which is deducted a deficit from operations.

United States and Canadian balance sheets are usually prepared to show assets on the left side of the page, and liabilities and capital on the right side, with the total of the assets appearing as an amount equal to the total of liabilities and capital.

Assets, liabilities, and capital are generally grouped as follows:

ASSETS	LIABILITIES
Current assets	Current liabilities
Long-term investments	Long-term liabilities
Fixed assets	CAPITAL
Noncurrent prepaid expenses and deferred charges	Capital stock
Intangible assets	Other paid-in capital
	Retained earnings (or earned surplus)

Other captions may be necessary to designate groupings of balance sheet items.

Another form of balance sheet, often called "Statement of Financial Position," is used by some companies because it is believed to be more understandable to their stockholders. Although there are several variations, basically this form is as follows:

Current assets	$----------	
Less, Current liabilities	----------	$----------
Plant and property less depreciation		----------
Other assets and deferred charges		----------

Less, Long-term liabilities		----------
Net assets		$----------
Net assets are represented by:		
Capital stock	$----------	
Retained earnings	----------	$----------

Details of the principal captions may be given in the body of the statement, in accompanying schedules, or in footnotes.

A form of balance sheet used by public utility companies, whose systems of accounts are prescribed by various federal and state commissions, places fixed assets and investments first on the asset side, and capital first on the liability side.

VALUE.—The term "value" has been the subject of wide discussion throughout the years. It has been freely used in many ways, such as "value in use," "value in exchange," "liquidation value," "quoted value," "fair market value," "appraisal value," "book value," and many others.

In the abstract, "value" has been defined as the attributed worth of anything expressed in money and applied to a particular asset. Without qualification and clear definition, including specific and operationally feasible rules for measurement, the term has only subjective significance, and should not be confused with, even though often identified with and measured by, cost.

The expression is most frequently encountered, together with a qualifying adjective as in the above illustrations, as an explanation of the basis of stating certain assets carried on the balance sheet, or as in the phrase "book value" to indicate the net amount of assets per share of capital stock or applicable to a partnership interest. The use of the word "value" in these circumstances does not imply current worth, but refers to a particular method of quantitative determination. Except when quoting the basis of an appraiser's report when describing plant and property, the authors believe the use of the word "value" in describ-

ing the basis of carrying assets should be avoided. For example, marketable securities may be stated "at quoted market prices" rather than
"at market value."

The Committee on Terminology, in Accounting Terminology Bulletin No. 3, has suggested a definition of the term "book value" as applied
to individual items in books of account or in financial statements:

Book value signifies the amount at which an item is stated in accordance
with the accounting principles related to the item.

Using the word "value" in this sense, it may be said that balance
sheet values generally represent cost to the accounting unit or some
modification thereof; but sometimes they are determined in other ways,
as for instance on the basis of market price or cost of replacement, in
which case the basis should be indicated in financial statements.

In its discussion of this definition, the committee said:

Thus one might refer to the "book value" or "net book value" of fixed
assets, or the "book value of investments." More specific terms, however, can
be used in describing the kind of value at which individual items are stated;
as, for example, *cost less depreciation, lower of cost or current replacement
cost,* or *lower of cost or selling price.* Similarly the term *ledger balance* or a
term such as *the amount shown in published financial statements* would more
clearly and accurately convey an exact meaning. The committee believes that
any reference to a quantitative determination of a specific item can be more
clearly and specifically described by terms other than the general and relatively vague term *book value.*

The committee recommends that the use of the term *book value* in referring
to amounts at which individual items are stated in books of account or in
financial statements, be avoided, and that, instead, the basis of amounts intended to apply to individual items be described specifically and precisely.

The committee also discussed the use of the term "book value" in
various business arrangements such as partnership agreements, contracts
for the sale of a business interest, and wills and trusts. While the
meaning to be ascribed to the term is one of legal interpretation of the
document, it appears to depend upon the intention of the parties rather
than on any accounting definition of the term. Misunderstandings
can develop when there has been a change in circumstances between
the date of the agreement and the time it must be interpreted. The
committee concluded that:

Even in the absence of such changes, questions arise as to whether "book
value" was intended to mean literally amounts shown on ledger accounts or
amounts so shown after correction for (a) errors, (b) departures from consistently maintained practices of the enterprise, (c) departures from established practices of the type of organization, or (d) departures from generally
accepted accounting principles, or any combination of such corrections.

When the intent of the parties is not clear as to the use of the term "book value" in reference to owners' equity, the committee suggests the following definition:

> *Book value* is the amount shown on accounting records or related financial statements at or as of the date when the determination is made, after adjustments necessary to reflect (1) corrections of errors, and (2) the application of accounting practices which have been consistently followed.

The committee concluded that in view of the fact that the intent of the parties to arrangements involving sale or transfer of business interest should govern, and the foregoing definition may not reflect such intent, the term "book value" be avoided. Instead of this term, it recommended that any agreement involving the general concept of book value should contain a clearly defined understanding in specific and detailed terms, particularly as to such matters as are referred to above.

The Statement of Income.—This title, with minor variations, is customarily used to indicate the statement which, together with the statement of surplus, displays the results of operations for a specified period. Sometimes the title "Statement of Earnings" is used. The net income of a business enterprise can be determined with finality only for the period from its organization to its dissolution. The problem of accounting for income for an interim period is essentially that of proper allocation of revenues and expenses to the period. Satisfactory solution of this problem requires application of experienced judgment to ascertained facts, and a review of management's judgment by the independent public accountant is an important safeguard.

PURPOSES OF THE STATEMENT OF INCOME.—Owners and managers require frequent reports of accomplishment, and it is an important function of accounting to furnish data for periodic reports of results of operations. Such reports indicate the financial results of past policies and may point the way to new managerial decisions.

Accounting is based on what is known to have happened and reflects opinion on the basis of knowledge at the time statements are prepared. Statements of income, therefore, are historical, not prophetic; they purport only to be a historical record of income, expenses, profits, or losses during the period or periods to which they relate.

The statement of income, when read with the accompanying balance sheet, indicates the relation of earnings to capital employed. It reflects the operating history of a business, which is useful in estimating future possibilities, and is, therefore, important to both present and prospective stockholders.

ALL-INCLUSIVE VS. CURRENT OPERATING PERFORMANCE STATE-
MENT OF INCOME.—The Institute's Accounting Research Bulletin No.
43, Chapter 8, contains a full discussion of the position of (1) those
who believe that the most practically useful determination of net income
results from the inclusion of all items affecting the net increase in
proprietorship during the period except dividend distributions and
capital transactions, and (2) those who believe that the income statement should be designed to disclose what a company was able to earn
under the *operating conditions* of the period covered by the statement.
The income statement concept described in (1) above is usually referred
to as "all-inclusive," while (2) is called "current operating performance."

The Committee on Accounting Procedure has stated its opinion
that

. . . . there should be a general presumption that all items of profit and loss
recognized during the period are to be used in determining the figure reported
as net income. The only possible exception to this presumption relates to items
which in the aggregate are material in relation to the company's net income
and are clearly not identifiable with or do not result from the usual or typical
business operations of the period. Thus, only extraordinary items such as the
following may be excluded from the determination of net income for the
year, and they should be excluded when their inclusion would impair the
significance of net income so that misleading inferences might be drawn
therefrom:

    (a) Material charges or credits (other than ordinary adjustments of a
        recurring nature) specifically related to operations of prior years,
        such as the elimination of unused reserves provided in prior years
        and adjustments of income taxes for prior years;

    (b) Material charges or credits resulting from unusual sales of assets not
        acquired for resale and not of the type in which the company gen-
        erally deals;

    (c) Material losses of a type not usually insured against, such as those
        resulting from wars, riots, earthquakes and similar calamities or
        catastrophes except where such losses are a recurrent hazard of the
        business;

    (d) The write-off of a material amount of intangibles;

    (e) The write-off of material amounts of unamortized bond discount or
        premium and bond issue expenses at the time of retirement or
        refunding of the debt before maturity.

The following, however, should be excluded from the determination of net
income under all circumstances:

    (a) Adjustments resulting from transactions in the company's own capital
        stock;

    (b) Amounts transferred to and from accounts properly designated as sur-
        plus appropriations, such as charges and credits with respect to
        general purpose contingency reserves;

(c) Amounts deemed to represent excessive costs of fixed assets, and annual appropriations in contemplation of replacement of productive facilities at higher price levels; and

(d) Adjustments made pursuant to a quasi-reorganization.

The committee appears to intend that the surplus account be used very sparingly, and the burden of proof is on those who wish to make charges or credits thereto instead of to income for the period. Accordingly, there should be, in practice, relatively few statements of income prepared on the all-inclusive basis which would differ from those prepared on the current operating basis.

MATERIALITY AND THE STATEMENT OF INCOME.—Whether an item is material in the circumstances and therefore should be considered as excludable from net income is one of the troublesome questions arising in practice calling for the most experienced judgment for its solution. Most accountants would advocate the inclusion of an item (or an aggregate of items) representing less than 10 per cent of net income before taxes, and many would include an item (or an aggregate of items) up to 25 per cent of such net income. Some consider that net income of the year, especially if abnormally low, should not be the sole yardstick, but the amount of the unusual item should be compared with the average net income of several years. Others believe that the percentage criterion should be higher for a loss of a character usually deducted from income, such as loss on disposal of depreciable property, than would be required for items not so clearly related to operating results, such as write-off of intangibles (where otherwise proper) or elimination of an unused provision.

FORM OF THE STATEMENT OF INCOME.—Like the balance sheet, the statement of income may be prepared in a variety of forms and with considerable variation in terminology. Reasonable uniformity is desirable to facilitate comparison with other periods and other businesses, but form must be subordinated to clarity. A form of statement commonly used follows:

Gross sales less returns, allowances, cash discounts, and freight
Cost of sales
    Gross profit on sales
Selling expenses
General and administrative expenses
    Operating income
Other income:
  Interest and dividends
  Miscellaneous

Other deductions:
  Interest paid
  Miscellaneous
      Income before federal taxes on income
Provision for federal taxes on income
      Net income for the year

A form of income statement which has gained some acceptance recently is called the "single-step income statement," because it arranges all items of income first, totals them, lists all items of costs, losses, and expenses, including federal income taxes, and deducts the total of the latter from total income to arrive at net income without intervening balances. An illustration of this form follows:

Sales and other income:
  Gross sales, less returns, allowances, cash discounts, and freight
  Dividends and interest income
  Other income

Costs and expenses:
  Cost of goods sold including depreciation
  Selling expenses
  General and administrative expenses
  Interest on long-term debt
  Provision for federal taxes on income
      Net income for the year

Sometimes the deductions are arranged to show the total employment costs (wages and salaries, social security taxes, pensions, and other benefits) and total taxes (state, local, and miscellaneous, with federal income taxes shown separately). Proponents of this last form believe that it eliminates poorly described subtotals of doubtful significance. There can be no profit, in any final sense, until all income and all costs have been taken into account. The single-step statement indicates that no cost or expense has any priority over any other, although in this presentation, federal taxes on income are often deducted as a separate item.

Objections to the single-step statement are that the intermediate balances shown in the more conventional type of income statement, such as gross profit on sales, operating profit, and income before and after provision for federal income taxes, are of interest to most readers, and if not supplied, readers have to make their own calculations of them. It is also contended that much of the significance that should be attached to such items as the provisions for income tax or other liabilities and extraordinary losses is obscured when they are grouped with other costs and expenses.

UNIFORM TERMINOLOGY IN THE STATEMENT OF INCOME.—The multiple-step form of income statement leads to a description of the result of each addition or subtraction. This has contributed to lack of uniformity in published reports. The terms "gross income," "gross profits," "net profits," "net operating income," "profits," "revenues," and "earnings" have been used according to the preference of each writer. This lack of uniformity of terminology tends to obscure comparison of operating results of one company with those of another. One solution of the difficulty is to omit any description of intermediate balances and describe only the final figure of net income for the year.

The Committee on Terminology issued in March, 1955, its Bulletin No. 2 in which it discussed and defined the terms "proceeds," "revenue," "income and profit," and "earnings." The authors agree that it would be helpful if accountants and others would adopt uniform terminology, especially as the public seems to find it difficult to understand financial statements, and the use of the same terms with different meanings does not lessen the difficulty. It may be that the committee's bulletin will aid in establishing more uniformity in terminology.

There seems to be general agreement that the final figure should be called "net income."

FORM OF DISCLOSURE OF ITEMS EXCLUDED FROM STATEMENT OF INCOME.—When it has been determined that an item is properly excluded in determining "net income for the year," Accounting Research Bulletin No. 43, referred to above, strongly indicates as preferable the carrying of such charge or credit directly to the earned surplus (retained earnings) account with complete disclosure as to its nature and amount. A second method promulgated by the Securities and Exchange Commission in Regulation S-X, Rule 5.03, would show such item somewhat as follows:

Net income for the year .... $---------
   Add (or Deduct) Special item (describe) .... ---------
   Net income and special item (describe) .... $---------

The Institute's bulletin accepts the above form of presentation "provided that care is taken that the figure of net income is clearly and unequivocally designated so as not to be confused with the final figure in the income statement."

Such special charge or credit, whether in the surplus statement or as the last item in the statement of income, should reflect allocation of related federal income tax. See Chapter 22.

CONTENT OF THE STATEMENT OF INCOME.—Items entering into the income statement may be broadly classified as follows:

   1. *Sales and Other Revenue from Operating Sources.* This includes gross sales, which means all sales of goods, either delivered or to

which title has passed to the vendees, less allowances for returned goods or goods to be returned, trade, cash, quantity and similar discounts, and all allowances which, if known at time of invoicing, would have been deducted from the sales prices, such as allowances for price changes, damaged goods, and shortages. It also includes revenue from services of public utilities or similar enterprises.

2. *Income from Other Sources,* such as dividends and interest.

3. *Profits* arising from sale of fixed assets, and extraordinary income.

with the following deductions:

1. *Charges Against Sales and Other Revenue from Operating Sources,* such as cost of goods sold or of services rendered; inventory write-downs; allowances not properly deductible from sales; selling, general, and administrative expenses; depreciation and depletion (when not included in cost of goods sold); and any other charges and expenses properly chargeable to current operations.

2. *Other Deductions from Income,* such as interest on borrowed money and federal and state income taxes.

3. *Losses* arising from sale of fixed assets, and extraordinary charges.

Some general considerations of the content of the statement of income are discussed in the following paragraphs.

Disclosure of Amount of Sales.—The present trend of published financial statements is in the direction of fuller information. It is now unusual to find statements published which omit net sales and cost of sales from the statement of income. Both the Securities and Exchange Commission and the New York Stock Exchange have helped to bring this about through their requirements.

Disclosure of Depreciation.—The importance of the disclosure of the amount provided for depreciation has been stressed by the stock exchange, bankers, and others interested in more fully presenting the component parts of net income. Depreciation may be disclosed either by the inclusion of this charge among the costs and expenses with parenthetical indication of the amount, or by showing it under a separate caption. For example:

Cost of sales (including $---------- depreciation) .... $---------- or,
Cost of sales before depreciation (with depreciation stated as a separate item in caption below) .... $----------

Another method frequently used is to state the amount of depreciation included in the statement of income in a footnote. This method is convenient and usually preferable, especially when substantial amounts of depreciation are included in captions other than cost of sales (e.g., selling or general expenses).

In concerns such as public utilities, trading, or commercial companies, any of the above methods may be employed since the allowance for depreciation is generally identified in the expense accounts. In manufacturing concerns there are difficulties in determining the amount of depreciation to be disclosed. Depreciation is usually included in overhead which is distributed over a number of departments and products and finds its way ultimately into cost of sales through inventory accounts. To determine the amount of depreciation which is included as a part of the cost of merchandise sold may require an extensive and usually impractical, if not impossible, analysis of cost accounts. The auditor usually solves the problem by suggesting that the amount of depreciation charged to manufacturing costs and to expense accounts be taken as representing the amount charged to income. Obviously this method does not correctly state the depreciation charge which was recouped through sale of the goods in which depreciation was an element of cost. From a practical standpoint, in view of the indicated difficulty, if not impossibility, of determining the exact amount of depreciation included in cost of sales, it has become recognized practice to report the amount of depreciation charged in the statement of income as that which has been charged to manufacturing costs and to expense accounts, even when amounts of depreciation included in inventories at the beginning and end of the period vary sufficiently to affect depreciation included in cost of sales. Such practice also is acceptable to the Securities and Exchange Commission.

Disclosure of Extraordinary or Unusual Items.—When it has been determined that an item is extraordinary or unusual, either as to character or amount, but nevertheless should be included in the determination of "net income for the year," question arises as to its disclosure and position in the statement of income. In analyzing a statement of income as a basis for drawing conclusions as to future possibilities, the reader will wish to consider the probability of recurrence of the various items of income and expenses. For example, an increase in the amount of current operating income would have a different significance than would a gain on sale of capital assets. It is important, therefore, that statements of income for inclusion in annual reports to stockholders disclose clearly extraordinary items of income or expenses, or items recognized in the accounts of the current period which apply to a previous period. Such items should be similarly treated in both the all-inclusive and the current operating performance income statement. Depending on the circumstances, they may be included under "Other income" or "Other deductions," or if representing adjustments of prior year income taxes, stated separately under that caption. Alternatively, statements may be prepared to show income before and after such extraordinary items, somewhat as follows:

Net sales
Cost of sales
    Gross profit on sales
Selling, general, and administrative expenses
    Profit before other income and deductions
Other income
Other deductions
    Income before extraordinary item below and provision for federal
      income tax
Extraordinary item (describe)
    Income before provision for federal income tax
Provision for federal income tax
    Net income for the year

Occasionally it may be deemed most informative to allocate the addition to or reduction in current income tax attributable to an extraordinary item as illustrated below:

    Income before provision for federal income tax and extraordinary
      item
Provision for federal income tax on above income
    Income before provision for extraordinary item
Extraordinary item (less increase or decrease in current federal income tax
  provision attributable thereto)
    Net income for the year

Preparation of a statement of income which contains extraordinary or unusual items of varying materiality requires experienced and informed judgment to make reasonably clear to the reader the importance of these items in interpreting the results of operations.

It may be desirable to show current items of income or expenses of an unusual nature separately in the statement of income. A strike in a company's plant may entail extraordinary expenses for transporting nonstriking workers, hiring guards, and other expenses. While there is no question that the expenses are applicable to the year in which they occur, and strikes are now a normal hazard of business, it may be desirable to segregate these expenses if they are susceptible of reasonably accurate determination.

It is sometimes urged that inventory losses or gains be separately shown in the income statement, particularly when falling market prices necessitate a write-down of inventory on hand at the year end. Concerns which are willing to disclose an item of extraordinary inventory write-down are not always willing to disclose an extraordinary profit in a succeeding year which may result from this write-down. It is usually very difficult, as a practical matter, to distinguish all the factors contributing to normal operating profit or loss and to segregate those which may be considered extraordinary. In the authors' opinion, while unusual operating factors may properly be referred to in explanatory comments accompanying a statement of income, the auditor should be cautious in approving the expression of them separately in the income statement. If unusual operating income or expense items are reported below operating income, the statement should clearly indicate that the item of operating income is determined before such charges or credits.

Statements of Net Income for Bonus or Profit-Sharing Purposes.— For years many business concerns have paid bonuses to, or shared profits with, officers and other employees. A large number of companies have entered into contracts with officers and other employees which provide for sharing in the annual net income. Others, including many large corporations, have bonus plans under which a part of the annual net income is set aside to provide incentive compensation or bonus awards to officers and other employees; such bonus plans may provide that officers and other employees have no equity in the net income so set aside until awarded, and often that awards need not be made in the full amount set aside each year.

Such bonus or profit-sharing plans should define the net income upon which the amount to be set aside or paid is to be calculated. The starting amount in the determination of such defined net income may be stated in the plan or contract as the net income shown in the annual statement of income; or the kinds of income and deductions to be included in arriving at such net income may be listed. It is usually undesirable to rely on listing items of income and deductions to be included in computing net income for this purpose since it is impossible to foresee the kinds of extraordinary or infrequent income and expense that should be included in later computations.

Computations are simplified if the plan defines the base as income before taxes on income. If the plan does not so define the base, these taxes, computed on taxable income after deducting contributions to the plan, should be deducted by a corporation in determining net income for purposes of the plan. Plans of sole proprietorships and partnerships should specify whether income taxes assessed to the partners or sole proprietors, owners' salaries, and interest on capital are to be deducted in computing net income for purposes of the plan.

If the intent of bonus and profit-sharing plans is to divide net income between stockholders or owners and officers and other employees, say nine-tenths to stockholders and one-tenth to officers and employees, and the amount set aside for officers and other employees is deducted in arriving at net income upon which the one-tenth for such officers and other employees is computed, the result is that less than one-tenth of the net income will be allocated to this group. The deductibility of the amount set aside under a bonus or profit-sharing plan or contract in arriving at defined net income should be clearly indicated in the plan; in the absence of a specific provision, a number of court decisions have expressed the opinion that it would be unreasonable to deduct the amount so set aside in arriving at net income to be used in computing the amount under the bonus or profit-sharing plan. The authors agree with the opinion of the courts.

Many bonus and profit-sharing plans have defined corporate net income as net income determined in accordance with generally accepted accounting principles, shown in the annual statement of income as certified by the company's independent public accountants. This net income may not be a fair basis for the purpose if certain items are included in surplus rather than in income. For example, it would be unfair to exclude from net income the return of an unused portion of a provision for an estimated liability charged against a prior year's net income upon which a bonus plan or profit-sharing amount was computed even though, in the year of restoration, the amount materially distorted net income and therefore was credited directly to surplus. On the other hand, it might be unfair, when bonus or profit-sharing plans have been instituted recently, to charge or credit income for purposes of the plan with adjustments relating to years prior to the beginning of the plan, such as federal income tax assessments or refunds applicable to such prior years but reflected in current income.

A bonus or profit-sharing plan or agreement may seem clear when drawn up, but questions of interpretation may arise if material extraordinary items are charged or credited directly to surplus as recommended in Accounting Research Bulletin No. 43. Public accountants should urge their clients to submit to them drafts of proposed plans or agreements for suggestions for clarification of these accounting matters before the documents are executed.

Statements of Surplus.—Most accountants believe, and the short-form report implies, that results of operations for a period of time are disclosed by the statement of income together with statements of surplus, whether earned, paid-in, or otherwise designated. This is true because the operations of a business include extraordinary charges or credits, changes in capital structure, restatements of assets, dividend distributions, and other transactions reflected in one or more of the surplus accounts.

A combined statement of income and earned surplus is often used, and it has been approved by the Committee on Accounting Procedure in Accounting Research Bulletin No. 43, Chapter 2. It has the advantage of bringing the figure of net income for the year in close juxtaposition to items which may have been shown in the earned surplus statement as approved in Chapter 8 of the same bulletin. An example of this form (beginning with "Income before taxes on income") is:

> Income before taxes on income
> Provision for taxes on income:
>   Federal income tax
>   State income tax
>   Net income for the year
> Add, Earned surplus at beginning of year
> Deduct:
>   Dividends on capital stock
>   Excess of fire loss over proceeds of insurance carried, less related reduction in taxes on income
>   Earned surplus at close of year

A statement of any surplus other than earned surplus similarly includes the balance at the beginning of the period, a description of the additions and deductions, and the balance at the close of the period.

Explanatory Notes to Financial Statements.—It is one of the standards of reporting (Chapter 2) that there be adequate disclosure of material matters in financial statements, and if, in the opinion of the independent public accountant there is not, he should make adequate disclosure in his report. Rarely must the auditor insist on disclosure in his report. If the choice is one of location, the auditor should urge that disclosure be made in the financial statements rather than in his report, so that the company's representations may be complete.

There are several types of information which by custom or convenience are given in notes to financial statements. A note on the financial statements themselves often refers to the accompanying notes as an integral part of the financial statements. The authors believe that even without such reference, the accompanying notes are in fact part of the statements, but the precaution of such a reference is well taken. So far as is known, there has been no legal decision in which the point was an issue.

Notes to financial statements may be classified into the following types:

Restrictions and liens—Provisions of debt or preferred stock agreements may restrict the payment of dividends or require the maintenance of specified working capital; receivables may be pledged against borrowings; foreign currency amounts may not be realizable in U. S. currency.

Commitments of an unusual nature—Extraordinary plant expansion commitments may have been made or expansion programs authorized; bonus and stock option plans may be operative.

Contingencies—Descriptions of status of lawsuits, tax controversies, and liabilities of uncertain amount.

Changes in application of accounting principles—While disclosure of a change in the application of accounting principles is required in the opinion, the nature and effect of the change is ordinarily described in a note referred to in the opinion.

Events subsequent to the balance sheet date—as described in the next section.

Explanatory notes—Those needed by the reader to obtain a fair understanding of the statements, such as the bases on which assets are stated, underlying equity in net assets and net income of unconsolidated subsidiaries, or descriptions of accounting policies for depreciation and amortization, tax accounting (see Chapter 22), or pension plans.

A number of matters may appear with almost equal convenience on the face of the statements or in notes; for example, the basis of stating such assets as inventories, fixed assets, and investments; the amount of accrued unpaid preferred dividends, and similar items. Some financial statements have been issued in which much of the descriptive matter and details of balance sheet items was eliminated from the face of the statements and included in accompanying notes. Whether the purpose of simplifying the statements for the casual reader was furthered by this presentation may be debatable.

What constitutes adequate disclosure of material items in financial statements is considered under the heading "Statement Presentation" in succeeding chapters. The question whether the auditor should refer in his report to information contained in the various categories of notes listed above is discussed in Chapter 6.

Disclosure in Financial Statements of Events Subsequent to the Balance Sheet Date.—The auditor is necessarily present at the client's office for a certain period of time after the date of the balance sheet under examination, because the field work requires some time for its completion. During this period facts may come to his attention, either through ordinary auditing procedures customarily related to the post-balance-sheet period (cash cutoffs, review of subsequent collections, reading of minutes, etc.), or through discussions with management, which may require (a) adjustment of the year-end figures or (b) disclosure in a footnote or elsewhere in the financial statements. The independent auditor's responsibility for discovery of and reporting upon post-balance-sheet events is discussed in the Committee on Auditing Procedure Statement No. 25 (1954), which states that, in general, there are three types of subsequent events or transactions which are encountered in the period into which certain audit procedures extend; these are summarized as follows:

1. Subsequent events which affect directly the financial statements and should be recognized therein, as for example collection of receivables or settlement or determination of liabilities on a substantially different basis than previously anticipated.

2. Subsequent events which have no direct effect on and do not require adjustment of the financial statements of the prior period but disclosure of which may be advisable, as for example the sale of a large bond or capital stock issue with restrictive covenants, mergers, or acquisitions, or serious damage from fire, flood, or other casualty.

3. Subsequent events (sometimes more troublesome from the accounting viewpoint than the others) which usually do not require disclosure in financial statements, as for example nonaccounting matters such as war, management changes, product changes, strikes, unionization, marketing agreements, loss of important customers, etc. Disclosure of such events frequently creates doubt as to the reason therefor, and inferences drawn could be misleading as often as they are informative. The committee stated its belief that the auditor should confine disclosure to those matters essential to proper interpretation of the financial statements being presented.

Responsibility for ascertaining and disclosing material transactions or events subsequent to the date of the balance sheet rests with the management, although the auditor may learn of them through inquiry, inspection of minutes, or examination of financial statements for the year under review. Committee on Auditing Procedure Statement No. 25 states that to the extent the auditor has knowledge of post-balance-sheet events or transactions which may be significant, it is his duty either:

(a) To see that they are properly considered and, when deemed appropriate, given effect to by adjustment or annotation of the statements; or

(b) If, in his opinion, there is, in the financial statements, significant lack of compliance with any of the points covered in (a) above, to qualify his report or present therein appropriate information, depending upon the circumstances.

Special requirements for disclosure of subsequent events under the Securities Act of 1933 are discussed in Chapter 25.

CHAPTER 8

CASH

Introduction.—The volume of transactions in the cash account is greater than in any other; most of the activities of business are eventually reflected in this account. Since questions of valuation or judgment rarely affect determination of the amount of cash, it can be stated more precisely than most other accounts. Because it is the medium of exchange and because of its mobility, it is more susceptible to manipulation than other assets; consequently the safeguarding of cash through internal check procedures has been given considerable attention through the years.

The auditor's responsibility for the cash item on the balance sheet does not differ from his responsibility for other balance sheet items; he should exercise judgment, based on knowledge and experience, in selecting and applying appropriate auditing procedures that will enable him to form an opinion whether cash is fairly stated. Too many auditors continue to follow detailed auditing procedures requiring an undue expenditure of time in their examination of cash. Such detailed procedures may include not only checking bank reconciliations at one or more dates and making one or more independent reconciliations, but also examining cash receipts and disbursements and supporting vouchers for one or more months. It is the purpose of this chapter to indicate procedures for examination of cash and to guide the auditor in his selection and timing of these procedures.

ACCOUNTING PRINCIPLES

Cash on Hand and on Deposit.—This caption on a balance sheet should include only cash on hand and demand deposits in banks at the close of business on the balance sheet date.

The practice of including cash received after the close of the period and reducing accounts receivable correspondingly is not in accordance with the foregoing rule although it has been defended on the ground that such receipts were forwarded by debtors before the close of the period and represented cash in transit. Checks drawn prior to the balance sheet date, but held for later delivery to creditors, and checks drawn after, but dated prior to, the balance sheet date should not be treated as outstanding checks; they should be restored to the cash balance and to liabilities. These considerations are important when provisions of bond indentures, loan agreements, or preferred stock issues require that certain current ratios be maintained.

An exception to the general rule is that of organizations for charitable, religious, and similar purposes which usually operate on a budget, and more often than not disburse income in its entirety, and keep their books open after the year end for cash receipts and disbursements applicable to the fiscal year. The close relation of budgeted income and expense leads these organizations to force one to equal the other. They claim that the resulting statements present more fairly results of operations and financial position. Financial statements prepared on this basis should describe the policy followed and disclose the amounts involved. The auditor may consider it necessary to qualify his opinion with respect to such statements.

DISPOSITION OF OUTSTANDING CHECKS.—Checks should not be listed as outstanding on bank reconciliations indefinitely. A sound practice is to stop payment after a year has elapsed, return the amounts to cash, and credit a liability account. The liability account should be debited and income credited after the applicable statute of limitations has run, unless state laws provide for other disposition. Dividend checks may require special treatment, for the laws of some states make a distinction between the liability for uncashed dividend checks and for other uncashed checks.

CASH IN FOREIGN CURRENCIES.—Foreign currency on hand and on deposit in foreign countries should be translated at the rate of exchange in effect on the balance sheet date. Translations are usually at official rates, but when transactions have been settled during the period principally at free rates of exchange or when there are other indications that the free rate will be used in the future, that rate should be used.

Unrealized losses on translation are normally charged against operations. Unrealized gains on translation may be credited to income to the extent that they offset prior provisions for unrealized losses. If there have been no previous charges for unrealized losses, unrealized gains should not be taken into income.

RESTRICTED CASH.—Cash on a balance sheet is presumed to represent cash on hand or deposits in banks immediately available for any purpose. Cash balances which are restricted as to availability or purpose, when material, should be shown separately and properly described; they may be included in current assets or excluded therefrom, according to circumstances. The balance sheet presentation is discussed later in this chapter.

INTERNAL CONTROL

Internal Accounting Control.

CASH RECEIPTS.—Cash is usually received by mail in the form of checks, or it may be received in the form of currency or checks over the counter, through collectors or through outside salesmen. The initial step in the accounting control of cash receipts is to list them; collections by mail should be listed showing names and amounts; receipts over the counter may be listed on cash register tapes or counter sales slips recorded in the presence of customers; receipts from collectors or outside salesmen may be accompanied by listings when they are received through these channels. Such lists should be totaled, usually at least daily, and the totals should be compared with the corresponding totals of cash and checks received, the cash book totals, the deposit slip totals, and totals of credits to contra control accounts.

When receipts include items not suitable for immediate deposit, such as postdated checks or checks made out for an improper amount, and not included in the original listing, they should be controlled by separate listing.

Counter sales slips, cashier's receipts, and collector's receipts should be prenumbered, and the numerical sequence should be accounted for in detail.

Receipts should be recorded promptly and those at branch offices should be reported promptly to the main office. When receipts flow from a number of sources, such as departments, cash registers, vending machines, or ticket sellers, procedures should be adopted to insure the inclusion of receipts from all locations daily.

DISBURSEMENTS MADE BY CHECK.—A detailed listing should be made of disbursements by check, showing payees and amounts, and this listing should be totaled daily or at other regular intervals. The list may be in the form of entries in the cash book, a written tabulation, requests for checks to be issued, or an adding machine tape, perhaps supported by copies of checks issued. Totals of these lists should be compared with credits to cash control account in the general ledger and with debits to accounts payable or other control accounts. Transfers of funds between banks should be controlled through a clearing account to assure the recording of both sides of the transfer simultaneously.

Checks should be numbered and under numerical control, including spoiled checks and, if prenumbered, those unissued. When checks are signed, the signer should have written evidence that the payments liquidate liabilities represented by approved vouchers and that the data on the checks have been compared with such vouchers. The check signer should cancel the vouchers by appropriate means to prevent their use as support of duplicate payments.

Reconciliation of Bank Accounts.—Periodic reconciliations of bank accounts with book records are important elements of internal accounting control over bank deposits and disbursements by check. For internal accounting control purposes, such reconciliation may include the following:

(a) Reconciliation of the bank balance as shown by the bank statement with that shown by the books at the same date, which assures that the net increase or decrease in recorded cash reconciles with the net increase or decrease shown by the bank statement.

(b) Reconciliation of total debits and total credits for the period as shown by the bank statement with comparable totals shown by the books, which assures that there are no items of receipts and disbursements offsetting each other in the cash records which are not included in the bank statement and vice versa.

(c) Reconciliation of detailed items listed on the bank statement with detailed items recorded on the books during the period covered by the bank statement, which assures that recognition is given to all items recorded on the books, including offsetting items within receipts or within disbursements, and to all items recorded on the bank statement, including offsetting items in the debit or in the credit columns.

DISBURSEMENTS MADE IN CURRENCY.—Disbursements made in currency are normally for advances, freight bills and other petty expenditures, or wage and salary payments. Accounting control over such disbursements is best maintained when the funds from which they are paid are kept under the imprest system. Under this system, an appropriate amount of cash is set aside, disbursements from which are supported by properly approved vouchers signed by the recipient of the funds disbursed. At regular intervals, or when the fund nears exhaustion, vouchers with supporting documents are presented for reimbursement from general cash, at which time the vouchers should be canceled in some manner to prevent their use in support of a duplicate reimbursement. Imprest funds should be reconciled periodically with general ledger controls.

Disbursement in currency for payrolls should be made from a specially designated imprest fund, usually provided by a transfer from general cash of the net amount of each payroll. Cash and currency should be inserted in envelopes provided by the payroll office showing payee and amount of wages payable. When these envelopes have been prepared, the information on them should be compared with the approved payroll list. Signed receipts should be obtained from the employees when they are paid. Unclaimed envelopes should be reported and at regular intervals the currency therein should be deposited in a general bank account and unclaimed wages credited.

Internal Check.

CASH RECEIPTS.—Good internal check over cash receipts requires that persons who enter amounts in cash receipts books or prepare deposits for the bank should be independent of those who post the related credits to accounts receivable records and to general ledger accounts. Other independent persons should perform the functions of:

1. Preparing detail listings of cash receipts; and
2. Obtaining authenticated duplicate deposit slips from the banks and comparing them in totals and in detail with cash book entries and listings of cash receipts, and in totals only with entries in control account columns and with credits on bank statements.

Each day's cash receipts (other than authorized exclusions) should be deposited intact and without delay.

Deposit or collection items charged back by the bank as uncollectible should be delivered to an employee other than the one making the deposit or the accounts receivable bookkeeper. Such items should be investigated by someone who has no responsibility for cash receipts or entries in the cash books.

Cash items withheld from deposit for proper reasons should be reviewed by a responsible independent employee who should release them promptly for either deposit or return to payors. Such withheld items preferably should be under accounting control, but when that is not practicable they should be held by a person who does not prepare deposits or make entries in accounts receivable or general ledger accounts.

Cash receipts of branch offices should be deposited in a bank account segregated from disbursement accounts and subject to withdrawal only by the home office.

Banks should be instructed not to cash checks or money orders drawn to the order of the company; also, not to accept such checks for deposit in special accounts, such as for payrolls or petty cash.

DISBURSEMENTS MADE BY CHECK.—Checks should be protected against alteration by use of special paper and a protective writing device; also, by providing that amounts are inscribed prior to or at least simultaneously with comparison with approved vouchers.

Persons authorized to sign checks, manually or in facsimile, should not have duties which include preparing or approving vouchers, preparing checks, inserting check numbers, recording and accounting for sequence of check numbers, or custody of unnumbered checks.

When a mechanical check signer is used, the die should be in sole custody of the person authorized to use it and he should see that only authorized checks are signed by the die.

Checks should be drawn specifically to the order of the creditors being paid or to custodians of imprest funds being reimbursed. If these checks are paid by the bank without adequate endorsement, they should be returned and the bank requested to obtain proper endorsement. Checks should not be drawn payable to "cash" or to "bearer."

Signed checks should be kept in custody of the signer until mailed or delivered by himself or someone under his control. However, that person should be independent of any functions pertaining to cash receipts or payments, preparation of vouchers, preparation or distribution of payrolls, custody of cash funds, and general ledger posting.

Comparison of the totals of the lists of issued checks against the cash book and contra control accounts should be made by a person who does not prepare the lists, sign checks, or prepare and approve vouchers. Footings of the lists should be verified at the same time. An employee whose duties do not include signing checks or preparing lists of checks issued should be designated to account for transfers of funds between banks.

Signing or countersigning of checks in advance should be prohibited. The dangers of signing checks in advance are obvious, but often are ignored. Countersignatures are effective as an internal control procedure only when each signature is affixed after examination of checks, completed except for signatures, and accompanying vouchers. If this procedure is not prescribed, the affixing of one signature on a blank check requiring two signatures is particularly dangerous, for then the requirement of signature and countersignature implies a security that is not present. Furthermore, the second signer of the check might accept the first signature as indication of approval of the payment and examine the accompanying documents less carefully because of it.

Countersignatures affixed with proper understanding and discharge of assigned responsibility afford good internal check, but signature by one employee after examination of supporting vouchers offers much greater protection than countersignatures misused. Some countersignature procedures require that one of the signers, who is independent of the other signer, certify that the payments liquidate liabilities recorded by means of approved vouchers. If the second signer does not examine checks and supporting vouchers, but signs in reliance upon the first signature, such procedure offers little, if any, protection beyond that afforded by the first signature.

Reconciliation of Bank Accounts.—Effective internal check requires that the employee who reconciles bank balances with book balances have no regularly assigned cash receipts, cash disbursement, or voucher functions; that he obtain the bank statement directly from the bank; and that he make certain comparisons as part of the bank reconciliation procedure, such as comparison of paid checks and other debits and credits listed on the bank statement with entries on the books, examination of signatures and endorsements, reconciliation of bank transfers, and other procedures described later under "Auditing Procedures."

DISBURSEMENTS MADE IN CURRENCY.—The primary responsibility for each petty cash or other imprest fund should be placed in one person whose duties should not embrace other funds, cash receipts, approval of disbursement vouchers, reimbursement of the funds, or authorizing, recording, or posting distributions of the disbursements. Other negotiable assets should not be in the custody of persons responsible for cash funds. Accommodation checks cashed by the petty cash custodian should not be drawn to the order of the company.

An internal auditor or other independent employee should count petty cash funds at unannounced intervals. The composition of the funds at such times should be submitted to a responsible officer for review. Both the fund itself and the expenditures from it may be petty, but over a period of time misappropriations may be large if adequate safeguards are not maintained.

Unclaimed wages, both cash and checks, should be held by an employee whose duties are divorced from payroll preparation and who handles neither cash receipts nor petty cash; if unclaimed, they should be returned to general cash after a specified period.

AUDITING PROCEDURES

Objectives.—As more fully discussed in Chapter 3, the ordinary examination incident to the issuance of an opinion on financial statements is not designed and cannot be relied upon to disclose defalcations and other similar irregularities, although their discovery frequently results. Accordingly, the auditor's examination of cash should be sufficient to afford a reasonable basis for his opinion that cash in the balance sheet is stated fairly, but not necessarily precisely.

Information To Be Obtained in Advance.—As part of his preliminary review of the work to be done, the auditor will determine the approximate amounts and locations of all cash funds, bank accounts, and other negotiable assets. He should also inquire whether cash or securities in the possession of the company's custodian include property of other organizations, such as an employee's association, or company property not recorded on the books, such as unclaimed wages, employees' savings, and the like.

Internal Control.—The relation of internal accounting control and internal check to the auditor's program was generally discussed in Chapter 5. The scope of examination of cash at the balance sheet date should be determined by the auditor's opinion of the degree of excellence of internal accounting control and internal check. The auditor should investigate prescribed procedures of internal accounting control and internal check of cash, and make sufficient tests to afford a reasonable basis for an opinion as to whether they are being followed.

Extent of Coverage of Total Cash.—The item "Cash" may be composed of a substantial number of bank accounts used for general corporate purposes, and located at the general office, at branches, or at subsidiaries. In addition, petty cash funds are frequently made up of balance in banks as well as cash on hand; imprest funds such as those for payrolls, freight bills, dividends, and the like are also usually deposited in a bank account. In short, there may be a large number of bank accounts represented in the total of "Cash," of which relatively few may comprise a large percentage of the total.

The auditor should consider whether it is necessary to include all of the regular bank accounts in his examination. When internal accounting control and internal check procedures are good, and especially when the funds are regularly examined by a competent internal audit group of the client, in the authors' opinion it should not be necessary for the independent auditor to examine all of the relatively small accounts which represent an immaterial portion of total cash.

Generally, the auditor should not find it necessary to reconcile the "one-way" type of bank account, when receipts are deposited by a branch, plant, or selling office and withdrawals may be made only by central office transfer into a general bank account, and the account balance is kept to a nominal figure. Evaluation of the procedures, test of the adequacy of control by identification of selected transactions, and tracing transfers of deposits into general bank accounts normally should serve the purposes of the auditor.

Similarly, the auditor should not ordinarily find it necessary to reconcile all imprest bank accounts which may be used for payment of payrolls, dividends, customer refunds, branch office expenses, and the like. These accounts are limited to a nominal balance, and deposits are in amounts equal to the totals of checks drawn for purposes of the accounts. Usually, the auditor need only review procedures and determine whether or not adequate safeguards appear to be in effect; and as a part of such review, he may make tests of evidence supporting selected disbursements, such as payrolls, dividend lists, refund documents, and vouchers, and compare paid checks, as to serial number, date, and endorsement, with entries in original supporting documents.

Selection and Timing of Cash Examination Procedures.—The auditor has at his disposal certain basic procedures which he may wish to use in his examination of cash. They include:

1. Count of cash on hand
2. Examination of cash records
    (a) Reconciliation of cash per books with cash per banks,
    (b) Confirmation of bank balances,
    (c) Test of cash receipts and disbursements.

The auditor should decide the extent to which these basic procedures should be applied to cover the following two major areas of his examination: (1) test of procedures of internal accounting control and internal check to satisfy himself whether the prescribed procedures are being followed, and the application of auditing procedures considered necessary because of determined inadequate or missing controls, and (2) substantiation of cash balances at the balance sheet date. There may be no clear-cut distinction, in practice, between these major areas. For example, a cash reconciliation may be made for the dual purpose of testing whether the company's reconciliation procedures appear to have been properly followed, and of substantiating cash balances at the balance sheet date. Similarly, comparison of bank transfers may represent a test of company procedures; but, if accounting control or internal check is inadequate, such comparison may be employed at the year end to guard against kiting and possible misstatement of cash balances.

The auditor may combine the testing of internal control and supplementary auditing procedures (often referred to as a "procedural examination") with the substantiation of cash balances through reconciliation procedures. He may decide that it is proper to make some or all procedural tests well in advance of the close of the fiscal year, and he may believe it proper to perform some or all of the reconciliation procedures at a similarly advanced date.

For example, if he is satisfied that internal accounting controls and internal check are excellent, and are being followed, he should not extend his examination beyond that necessary to assure himself that the cash balances are fairly stated. When he finds, as he usually will, that many of the steps of internal control would be duplicated by the basic procedures listed above, he may decide to curtail them. If some features of internal accounting control are lacking, his examination should include tests to indicate whether such weaknesses have produced improper balances. If internal check weaknesses are serious, or if year-end balances may be misstated, by reason of weaknesses of internal accounting control, the auditor may well conclude that counts and reconciliations of cash balances should be made at the balance sheet date.

Since the purpose and timing of an audit procedure may vary with the particular circumstances, the authors believe that it is not desirable to outline steps which might be misunderstood to be a typical audit program for an examination of cash. In the sections which follow, audit procedures will be discussed which represent substantiation of both company procedures and of year-end balances, and many procedures will be included which would be employed only when internal accounting control and internal check are poor or lacking. Some of these procedures may be performed simultaneously and others at different times; the auditor may decide that most, or even all, of those selected may be applied prior to the year end.

The discussion of cash examination procedures will follow the order of the basic procedures listed at the beginning of this section.

COUNT OF CASH AND NEGOTIABLE ASSETS ON HAND.—Examination of cash funds and undeposited receipts should be coordinated with the examination or confirmation of other negotiable assets such as marketable securities, notes receivable, and collateral held as security on loans to others. If simultaneous physical examination of all negotiable assets on hand is not practicable, the auditor should establish control of all such assets so that a shortage in one group cannot be covered up by the use of other assets previously examined. Less active negotiable assets, such as reserve cash, notes receivable, and securities, may be counted in advance and placed under seal until completion of the count. It may be necessary occasionally to permit movement of assets so under seal; the auditor should control and record all such changes. If possible, the auditor should arrange to count cash funds and other negotiable assets at a time not disclosed in advance to the custodians. An unannounced count might lead to detection of shortages. The timing of preliminary work, before the close of the fiscal year, may be flexible and controlled by the auditor, thus affording opportunity for a surprise count, within limits. If there is reason to believe that a complete surprise is desirable, a second unannounced count might be made at a later date.

The auditor should not assume responsibility for custody of cash or negotiable assets, but he should insist upon continuous attendance by a representative of the client while these are being examined. After the count has been completed, the representative of the client should be given the opportunity to check it. Although it is frequently done, it is usually not necessary to obtain a receipt or acknowledgment from the custodian when funds are turned back to him. If for some reason a client's representative has not been present during the count, it is desirable to obtain a receipt from him after he has verified the count. When there is an overage or shortage in the fund, it is desirable to ask for a recheck and acknowledgment by the client representative.

Items making up cash funds and undeposited receipts are usually listed for convenience in localizing possible differences or errors in the count and for further examination. It is not normally necessary to count the contents of coin packages or all packages of currency notes. Checks are listed showing date, name or number of bank on which drawn, drawer, and amount; vouchers in the fund may be reviewed for validity, reasonableness, and approval; checks or vouchers not of recent date should be investigated.

All checks and undeposited receipts included in the cash count should be deposited intact on the same or the following day, and the auditor may wish to control this deposit until it reaches the bank. He may determine either from a subsequent bank statement or by inquiry from the bank whether any checks so deposited were subsequently charged back as uncollectible.

When individual cash funds are numerous, it is usually not necessary that all of them be examined by the auditor. The most significant funds should be counted and other funds may be counted on a test basis. Funds at distant branch offices or other locations may be confirmed in writing by letters addressed to managers or custodians, whenever it is impracticable to visit the locations. If they are significant in amount, and the auditor does not have a branch office in the vicinity, it may be desirable to employ a local public accountant to check them.

Totals of funds and negotiable assets counted or confirmed should be reconciled with general ledger controlling accounts as at the date of the examination.

EXAMINATION OF CASH RECORDS.—The following form offers a convenient control for the auditor's examination of cash records for a selected accounting period.

	Balance Nov. 30, 19—	Receipts	Disbursements	Balance Dec. 31, 19—
Per bank statement	$31,268	$42,687	$46,560	$27,395
Deposits in transit:				
November 30	1,000	1,000*		
December 31		2,000		2,000
Outstanding checks:				
November 30	3,917*		3,917*	
December 31			4,560	4,560*
Unrecorded charges and credits:				
Collection from customer on note credited by bank December 29, entered on books January 2......		2,078*		2,078*
Per books	$28,351	$41,609	$47,203	22,757
Audit adjusting entry #1:				
Collection of customer's note				2,078
Per books as adjusted				$24,835

* Indicates red figure.

The above form may be prepared by the auditor or it may be prepared by the client for the auditor's checking. It may be rearranged so as to cover a number of banks instead of one.

It will be noted that while the above form provides a summary of the reconciling items at the beginning and end of the month, the auditing procedures followed are usually confined to the month-end reconciliation. The reconciliation may consist of a review of the client's month-end reconciliation, a test of such reconciliation, or an initial (usually called an independent) reconciliation, depending upon considerations discussed above in the section on "Selection and Timing of Cash Examination Procedures." These procedures may be described as follows:

Review of Client's Reconciliation.—The steps taken in a review procedure would include:

1. Comparison of amounts on the reconciliation with original bank statements, cash books, and general ledger;
2. Proof of mathematical accuracy of the reconciliation; and
3. Obtaining bank statements for a subsequent period; comparing paid checks dated prior to the end of the period with checks listed as outstanding on the client's reconciliations; tracing transfers of funds to book debits and credits which should be recorded as at the same date; and substantiating other reconciling items by reference to supporting documents.

Test of Client's Reconciliation.—The auditor, in addition to making the review outlined above, makes tests of the steps taken by the client in the original reconciliation. Generally, the tests made will be selected from the steps described in the later section entitled "Independent Reconciliation of Bank Accounts."

Independent Reconciliation.—The auditor performs the initial reconciliation procedures, having received the bank statement and canceled checks directly from the bank. When the independent reconciliation is combined with procedural testing, the detailed steps outlined below would generally be followed. When procedural tests are made in another period, many of the steps may be appropriately curtailed or even eliminated.

Reference should be made to the following section entitled "Confirmation of Bank Balances" with regard to the desirability of obtaining confirmation of the balances from the banks.

INDEPENDENT RECONCILIATION OF BANK ACCOUNTS.—For purposes of the following discussion, it is assumed that the examination date is December 31, as in the illustrative form above, and that the auditor has decided to combine a procedural review for the month of December with substantiation of cash balances as at December 31, including an independent reconciliation by the auditor of cash per books and per bank statements. The procedures followed by the auditor may include the following steps, many, or even all of which, are those followed by the client in periodic reconciliations of bank accounts.

1. Obtain bank statement and paid checks directly from the bank for the period under examination and keep them under control until the reconciliation has been completed.
2. Prove the mathematical accuracy of the bank statement by footing deposits, footing paid checks, and determining that the sum of the

paid checks is equivalent to the amount of the opening balance plus deposits minus the closing balance.

3. Obtain client's reconciliation as at the close of the preceding period and compare book and bank balances shown on this reconciliation with the corresponding amounts shown by the books and the bank statement; substantiate outstanding checks at the close of the preceding period by examining paid checks returned by the bank in the current period; and substantiate deposits in transit and other reconciling items at the close of the preceding period by reference to the current bank statement, bank notifications of charges and credits, and other supporting documents.

4. Compare daily totals of recorded cash receipts shown in the cash book with daily deposits appearing in the bank statement.

5. If there are time lags between the receipt, recording, and depositing of collections, investigate those which appear unreasonable in the light of the company's normal practices. When receipts in currency are large and when receipts are not deposited daily, there may be opportunities for manipulation by "lapping"[1] of collections.

6. Compare paid checks returned with the bank statement with the disbursements record for check number, date, payee, and amount. This comparison will determine which checks have not cleared the bank during the period and that dates, payees, and amounts of disbursements as shown by the paid checks agree with those recorded in the disbursements record.

It is important that this comparison be made with a book of original entry (which may be a disbursements book, check register, check stub book, or file of check duplicates) rather than a summary record. If a summary record must be used, the auditor should assure himself that existing control procedures make such record reliable.

7. Examine transfers of funds within an organization, whether between banks, between divisions, or between affiliates. The examination should be made preferably from paid checks, bank advices, or bank statements to the cash records. The auditor should determine that each transaction represented as being a transfer is that in fact. He should determine that debits and credits representing transfers of cash are recorded

---

[1] The term "lapping" is used to describe a method of concealing a defalcation, wherein cash received from a customer is originally appropriated by the cashier; at a later date cash received from another customer is credited to the first customer's account and the second customer's account is credited still later by cash received from a third customer. This delay of credits continues until it is detected, the cash is restored, or it is covered up by credit to the proper customer and a fictitious charge to operating accounts.

in the same period and that the funds were deposited in the receiving bank. This work may disclose a defalcation concealed by "kiting."[2]

8. Account for all checks issued in the sequence between the first and the last checks drawn on the bank account during the period being examined.

9. Determine that other items in the reconciliation are proper and bona fide, bearing in mind particularly that a subsequent entry on the books which apparently offsets an item in the reconciliation is not necessarily proof of its correctness. It may merely transfer the item to some other account. Each adjusting entry, if material in amount, should be examined to determine its propriety. The propriety of reconciling items is not established merely by the fact that arithmetic reconciliation is effected by their inclusion.

10. Deposits in transit and outstanding checks revealed by the reconciliation should be substantiated later by comparison with a subsequent bank statement and accompanying paid checks. It is highly desirable that the auditor receive these documents directly from the bank. Checks outstanding which are not returned with the subsequent bank statement, if material in amount, should be substantiated by reference to properly approved vouchers or other available documents.

11. Items on the bank statement not accounted for in the above reconciliation procedures—such as debits or credits followed by offsetting entries of identical amounts, which appear to be, or the client claims are, bank errors and corrections not so coded—should be scrutinized to determine their exact nature. If information in the client's office is inadequate, the auditor should request clarification from the bank as to what they are. For example, if internal control procedures are inadequate, an entire deposit might be withdrawn from the bank by an unrecorded check subsequently destroyed when it is returned by the bank. The bank statement might then show an uncoded debit and credit in the same amount which might be claimed to represent a bank error and its correction.

In his examination of paid checks the auditor should note any seeming irregularities. He should investigate checks drawn to cash, to petty cash, to bearer, or to officers and employees other than for payroll. Questionable items should be traced to supporting documents, for a

---

[2] The term "kiting" is used to describe a method of concealing a shortage in a bank account by depositing in it, and not recording in cash receipts or disbursements, a check drawn on another bank; the unrecorded check may later be covered by drawing another unrecorded check on a bank other than the one on which the first check was drawn. The time required for the checks to clear through the banks may conceal the shortage for some time.

paid check in itself is not evidence of the propriety of a payment. Checks bearing second endorsements may deserve further attention. A second endorsement might indicate a fictitious payment of an invoice or payroll when the second endorsement is that of an employee involved in disbursement functions. Such items should be reviewed with a company officer. The auditor should determine that signatures on checks are apparently those of employees authorized to sign checks and review endorsements to see that they are in the name of the payee.

The auditor will find that some companies have arranged for additional bank service which saves time in reconciling bank accounts. The plan involves the use of a punched-card-type check in place of the regular check. No key punching by the client is required, and normally the checks can be prepared on the client's regular equipment. The bank provides for the key punching of paid checks and uses punched-card equipment for the sorting process. It returns the paid checks sorted into numerical sequence with a listing showing check number, amount, and a symbol indicating where, in the numerical sequence, checks are outstanding. The total of this listing is balanced with the total amount charged by the bank for the period and is so indicated on a reconciliation form showing opening balance, deposits, paid checks, and ending balance.

Another service which many banks have made available, when the punched-card system is not employed, is a check sorting service, in which checks are hand sorted into numerical sequence and balanced with total charges on the bank statement. If this service is available, the auditor may request it in order to reduce audit time consumed in the routine sorting of paid checks during his reconciliations at a location where it is not practicable to have client employees sort the checks under supervision of the auditor.

Block Proof Bank Account Reconciliation.—When the volume of check payments is considerable, some companies use a block proof reconciliation method instead of the regular method which has been discussed. The essence of this method is that the checks are not accounted for individually but in total for a group ("block"), representing either the checks issued during one or more days or a fixed number of checks in numerical sequence. These block totals are entered in a record as checks outstanding. When paid checks are returned by the bank, they are sorted and totaled by blocks and these totals are deducted from the related outstanding amounts. As of any reconciliation date the block remainder amounts are available but not a listing of individual checks supporting these amounts.

The most practical method of examining this type of record where check payments are so voluminous is by testing the accuracy of the block amounts outstanding. The auditor should obtain a statement and paid checks directly from the bank for a period deemed reasonable for clearance of most of the checks of the blocks to be tested. After applying paid items by blocks he may request an employee of the client who is independent of cash disbursement functions to prepare a list by check number and amount of unpaid items of selected blocks. This list, the total of which should agree with the block remainder amount, may be tested by review of the block files of paid checks. As part of the procedural review, tests may be made of the amounts of checks issued in selected blocks. A few of the blocks said to be closed may be tested in order to determine that all checks of the series are in the paid file.

Somewhat akin to the block proof method is the practice of issuing drafts in payment of obligations and disbursing cash from the bank account only once a day for the total of drafts accumulated daily at the bank. This scheme reduces the number of bank checks to a minimum and simplifies the reconciliation problem. Drafts payable issued but not presented to the bank for payment should be considered as outstanding checks and deducted from the amount of cash on deposit. In his review of internal accounting control and internal check, the auditor may confine his examination of paid drafts to selected days, as to which he should satisfy himself that they had been paid by the indicated bank check and were fully supported by appropriate evidence.

Confirmation of Bank Balances.—As a general rule, the auditor should confirm year-end balances of cash on deposit by direct correspondence with the banks even though all year-end reconciliations may not be reviewed or tested. When the client's bank reconciliation procedures are reviewed or tested, or an independent reconciliation made, at an interim date, confirmation of bank balances may or may not be obtained at that date, depending on the auditor's judgment as to its desirability in the circumstances.

Requests to banks for confirmation of bank balances and liabilities should be made on the Standard Bank Confirmation Form, which appears on page 139. This form is mailed to the bank in original and duplicate; the duplicate will be signed by the bank and returned to the auditor. It should be noted that the standard form makes no provision for reporting by the bank of securities or other items held in safekeeping, or as agent or trustee, or for collection for account of the company, or for obtaining a statement of the bank account. Accordingly, it is necessary to address a supplementary letter to the bank covering these items, or any others on which information is desired. An example of such a letter is as follows:

(Name and address of bank)

Dear Sirs:

Will you kindly furnish direct to our auditors, (name and address of auditors), in connection with their examination of our accounts as of the close of business December 31, 19___.

1. The information requested in the enclosed Standard Bank Confirmation Form;

2. Statement of any securities or other items for collection, and securities held by you in safekeeping or as agent or trustee for our account as of December 31, 19___; and

3. Statement of our account and the related paid checks for the period from January 1 to January ___, 19___, inclusive.

> Very truly yours,
> (Name of client)
> (Signature and title of officer)

As a practical matter, when it is not necessary to query the bank about items on hand for safekeeping or collection, the request for a bank statement may be added in the standard form either in the letter text at the top or added after Item 4 at the bottom.

TESTS OF RECEIPTS AND DISBURSEMENTS.—Limited tests of receipts and disbursements may be made as a part of the examination of internal accounting control and internal check procedures.

A number of tests that may be made are described in the following paragraphs. They may or may not be related to a period covered by the control form for examination of cash given on page 132.

Receipts.—Tests may be made of selected items of cash receipts by comparison of details of deposit slips with details of the cash receipts record. Duplicate deposit slips in the client's file can be tested for accuracy by requesting banks to authenticate deposit slips or permit examination of deposit slips in their files. However, it must be remembered that few banks compare amounts of individual checks with amounts listed on deposit slips. Since this step is not wholly conclusive, the auditor relies upon confirmation of accounts receivable as a better method of revealing any attempts at lapping. Lapping of collections is most effectively prevented by proper procedures of internal check. It may be detected by the auditor, but detection is difficult

STANDARD BANK CONFIRMATION FORM – 1953
Approved 1953 by
**AMERICAN INSTITUTE OF ACCOUNTANTS
NATIONAL ASSOCIATION OF BANK AUDITORS
AND COMPTROLLERS**

> **ORIGINAL**
> To be retained by Bank

_____ 19_____

Dear Sirs:

Your completion of the following report will be sincerely appreciated. IF THE ANSWER TO ANY ITEM IS "NONE", PLEASE SO STATE. Kindly mail it in the enclosed stamped, addressed envelope <u>direct</u> to the accountant named below.

Yours truly,

Report from

(Bank) _____

By _____
Authorized Signature

Bank customer should check here if confirmation of bank balances only (item 1) is desired. ☐

Bank should check whichever is applicable:
This report covers all accounts
1. with this office ☐ or
2. with this office and all other domestic offices ☐

(Name and Address
of Auditors)

Dear Sirs:

1. We hereby report that at the close of business on _____ 19__ our records showed the following balance(s) to the <u>credit</u> of _____

| AMOUNT | DESIGNATION OF ACCOUNT | REMARKS | |
		IS BALANCE SUBJECT TO WITH-DRAWAL BY CHECK?	DOES ACCOUNT BEAR INTEREST? GIVE RATE
$			

2. We further report that the above mentioned depositor was directly liable to us in respect of loans, acceptances, etc., at the close of business on that date in the total amount of $_____ , as follows:

| AMOUNT | DATE OF LOAN OR DISCOUNT | DUE DATE | INTEREST | | DESCRIPTION OF LIABILITY, COLLATERAL, LIENS, ENDORSERS, ETC. |
			RATE	PAID TO	
$					

3. Said depositor was contingently liable as endorser of notes discounted and/or as guarantor at the close of business on that date in the total amount of $_____ , as below:

AMOUNT	NAME OF MAKER	DATE OF NOTE	DUE DATE	REMARKS
$ ·				

4. Other direct or contingent liabilities, open letters of credit, and relative collateral, were

Yours truly,
(Bank) _____

Date _____ 19 __

By _____
Authorized Signature

If the space provided is inadequate, please enter totals hereon and attach a statement giving full details as called for by the above columnar headings.

unless all accounts receivable are confirmed, including those that have been paid between the examination date and the date confirmations are mailed.

Kiting of checks is also best controlled through proper internal check; it may be detected by comparison of items on authenticated deposit slips with cash book entries, although the authors believe that examination of bank transfers in connection with reconciliation procedures is more expedient.

During the time the auditor is in the client's office he may examine receipts of a few days and control them until they are deposited. Items in these deposits may later be traced to credits to accounts receivable through the cash receipts record to determine that the proper customers were credited and that there was no attempt to cover up lapping during this period.

The auditor may inquire as to bank procedures in charging back uncollectible deposit and collection items. Banks dealing with businesses that deposit a large number of checks often do not record on the bank statement dishonored checks included in deposits, but have a runner take the dishonored checks to the client each day and return with cash or a check to cover the aggregate amount of the dishonored paper. If this procedure is in use, the auditor may examine vouchers covering the replacement of items charged back during a period following the date of his examination, to assure himself that a shortage has not been covered by depositing fraudulent paper that would be returned after the date of the auditor's examination without record thereof appearing on the bank statement.

The auditor may inquire into cutoff procedures and determine whether it is the practice of the client to include in cash receipts of the period amounts that are not deposited until the following period. If the books have been held open to include receipts after the closing date and these receipts are significant in amount, the auditor should insist that cash be decreased and accounts receivable increased by these amounts.

Many banks in larger cities are offering a service which simplifies the problem of controlling cash receipts in businesses which receive large numbers of remittances through the mail. Under this plan the client advises its customers that remittances should be made payable to the company, but mailed directly to a post office box number at the servicing bank. The bank prepares a listing of all remittances received, records the deposit, and delivers two copies of the listing together with all remittance advices and correspondence to the client. This procedure is practical and time-saving and represents a substantial increase of control with greater assurance to the company and the auditor.

Disbursements.—Tests may be made of selected cash disbursement items by comparing paid checks with approved vouchers and other appropriate evidence of authorized expenditure. The items may be selected from payments examined in the course of reconciling bank accounts. In lieu of selecting payments for a specific period of time, it is preferable to examine a series of related transactions, for example, to review data supporting the various steps arising from certain requisitions for materials, including preparation of the purchase order, record of receipt of the material, approval of the voucher for payment, payment thereof, and recording the transactions in the accounts. Such an investigation has the advantage of giving the auditor an extensive insight into the system of internal control. With this selection process covering various kinds of transactions typical of the business, the number of items reviewed usually need not be large.

If the auditor finds that the client records as cash payments checks which are written and distributed after the closing date, he should determine whether significant amounts are involved. Comparison of the number of checks outstanding at the end of the period with the number outstanding on reconciliations at other dates may indicate whether the cash book had been held open in this fashion. If he is able to ascertain the number of the last check drawn on the last day of a period, he can tabulate the amounts of checks recorded subsequently before the cash book is closed. If checks drawn in the subsequent period are significant in amount, the auditor should insist that cash and accounts payable be increased by these amounts.

If it is not the client's practice to have new bank accounts approved by an executive body such as the board of directors, the auditor may suggest that such approvals are desirable. He should also look to the minutes for approval for discontinuing bank accounts. Final statements of bank accounts closed since the last examination should be reviewed to determine that dispositions of balances were proper.

Some auditors request confirmation by the bank of authorized signatures for client's checks. This may lead to disclosure that certain employees authorized to sign checks occupy positions, or perform functions, which make such authorization inconsistent with good internal control. Also, it may reveal that persons no longer employed by the client are still authorized to draw on its bank account.

Abbreviated Methods of Year-End Cash Substantiation.—When the auditor has made appropriate tests of cash transactions at an interim period, including such reconciliations of cash per books with bank statements as he deems necessary in the circumstances, and the tests indicate that good internal accounting control and internal check procedures have been followed by the client, he may limit his examination of general bank accounts at the balance sheet date to the following:

1. Review of client's reconciliation, as described on page 133. The bank statements for the subsequent period should be obtained directly from the bank by the auditor at a date shortly after the year end.

2. Comparison of balances shown on bank statements with confirmations received by the auditor direct from the bank.

3. Review of general ledger cash accounts and test-comparison thereof with corresponding amounts shown in cash receipts and cash disbursements records for the period following the auditor's preliminary examination of the cash procedures to determine that the changes in such accounts appear regular and normal.

A number of large corporations have such excellent systems of internal accounting control and internal check, including periodic examinations in considerable detail by an internal audit staff, that the independent auditor is justified in relying on even more abbreviated year-end procedures. Having made appropriate tests of cash transactions and balances at an interim date, he may be content to confine his procedures at the year end to items 2 and 3 above, or he may apply the abbreviated method suggested above to a few bank accounts and for the remaining accounts only compare independently confirmed bank balances with those in the client's cash reconciliations, and possibly review general ledger cash accounts from the date of the interim examination to the balance sheet date.

STATEMENT PRESENTATION

Description of Cash.—In classifying cash it is not necessary to distinguish between currency on hand, undeposited checks, cash in banks, or deposits at various locations, unless the balance sheet is being prepared for a special purpose. The description of cash in banks as "demand deposits in banks" has merit in that it removes any question of restrictions. The reader of a balance sheet has a right to assume, however, that the item "Cash" is realizable in the amount stated and is completely and immediately available for operation of the business and the payment of debts. The majority of published reports use the simple description "Cash."

Segregation of Restricted Cash.—Time deposits should be so shown. If cash on hand includes balances with trustees, such as those for sinking funds, or amounts earmarked by the management for the purchase of fixed assets or other specific purposes, the facts should be adequately disclosed on the balance sheet and proper classification made as between current and noncurrent assets.

Balances on deposit in foreign countries subject to exchange restrictions, if material in amount, should be shown separately rather than as an unidentified element of cash, and the restrictions should be clearly indicated.

Cash which is not immediately available, such as that restricted to use for other than current operations, designated for expenditure in the acquisition or construction of noncurrent assets, or segregated for the liquidation of long-term debt should be excluded from current assets. Restrictions are considered effective even though the funds are not actually set aside in special bank accounts if it is the clear intent of the company to observe them.

When a preferred stock sinking fund requires cash to be set aside in the ensuing twelve-month period, the effect of such provision on the net current asset position is sometimes shown by deducting the amount so required from free cash and including such sum below current assets under a caption such as "Cash equal to preferred stock sinking fund instalment due in . . . ."

Cash may be segregated in a bank account which clearly indicates that the client acts merely as trustee, the balance not being available for its own expenditures. Such an account may arise in connection with employee savings plans. There is no objection to offsetting this cash against the related liability provided all of the following conditions exist:

1. The trust status is indicated clearly on the books of the depositary;
2. The client's counsel is of the opinion that the account may be used only by the beneficiaries, who may look only to the trusteed assets for satisfaction of their claims thereon; and
3. The records and internal control of the trust assets are such as to insure that the trust relationship is respected and that the beneficiaries' interests are clearly recorded.

Amounts withheld from employees for payment of income and social security taxes, purchase of savings bonds and insurance, and like items require segregation from other cash only when these amounts are a substantial portion of the company's total cash and a reader of the balance sheet might be misled by failure to segregate.

Bank Overdrafts.—When there are two or more bank accounts, an overdraft in one may properly be offset by a balance in another bank if the balance used to offset an overdraft is actually free, and the company is not required to keep a minimum balance in consideration of a loan or for other reasons. That portion of an overdraft not offset by a free balance in another bank should be included in accounts payable. If an overdraft is actually the bank's way of making a temporary loan to the company, it should be shown among the liabilities.

CHAPTER 9

MARKETABLE SECURITIES

Introduction.—Marketable securities are those which are salable under ordinary circumstances with reasonable promptness. Securities of affiliates and subsidiaries, since they are held for the purpose of control rather than investment, are not classified as marketable securities, even though they may possess the characteristics of such securities.

Marketable securities form a significant part of the assets of investment companies, banks, insurance companies, and institutions. In commercial and industrial companies they usually represent investment of excess funds and ordinarily do not constitute a material portion of assets, nor does the income from them constitute a significant part of total income.

ACCOUNTING PRINCIPLES

Basis of Recording.—Marketable securities are usually recorded at cost. Cost includes expenses incident to acquisition such as brokerage commissions. Conversely, expenses of sale are deducted from the selling price in computing proceeds of sale. When marketable securities are received as gifts, as they often are by educational, religious, and charitable institutions, they should be recorded at their fair value at date of gift. Fair value is usually determined on the basis of market quotations, or, if market quotations are not available, by appraisals. When securities are adjusted to an estimated fair value in the course of a reorganization or quasi-reorganization, the adjusted amount is considered as cost.

When securities have been acquired in exchange for other securities as the result of a consolidation, merger, or other reorganization of the company in which an investment is held, or as the result of the exercise of conversion privileges contained in the terms under which a security was issued, cost is considered to be the cost of the security delivered in exchange, adjusted for any cash paid or received in effecting the exchange. If more than one security is received in an exchange, cost generally should be apportioned to each security in the ratio that its fair market value at time of exchange bears to the aggregate fair market value of all securities received. Such ratios may frequently be obtained from one of the published capital adjustments services. Exchanges other than those discussed above are usually tantamount to purchases and sales, and cost of the security received, accordingly, should be considered the equivalent of its value at the time of receipt.

It is not customary to adjust book amounts of securities to reflect fluctuations in market values. However, evidence of a permanent decline in value should be recognized in the accounts by means of a write-down or the establishment of an allowance for the decline. While the financial statements of many investment companies state securities at amounts based on market quotations, or management's appraisals of fair values, which in the aggregate may be in excess of or less than cost, it is not generally their practice to record unrealized net appreciation or depreciation in the books of account.

Security transactions may be recorded as at either the contract (trade) date or the agreed settlement date. The latter is used largely by stockbrokers and is the date to which the seller is usually entitled to interest accrued on bonds and to dividends declared on stock provided the record date for dividends is prior to the settlement date.

Sales of Holdings in Part.—There are three methods in general use for costing sales of part of an issue held; first-in, first-out, cost of the specific certificates delivered in the sale, and average cost. The average cost method has the merit of recognizing the fungible character of different lots of the same security and is considered preferable to the other two methods. The identified cost method, although permissible, is obviously not as objective as other methods and permits considerable variation in recognizing gain or loss at the option of the vendor. However, when applied consistently, any of the three methods of computing realized profits or losses is generally accepted accounting practice provided that, when profits and losses on investments significantly affect a company's income, the change in unrealized net appreciation or depreciation of investments during the period is clearly indicated. It should be noted that under present regulations of the Treasury Department, the average cost method may not be used for federal income tax purposes.

Amortization of Bond Premiums and Discounts.—When bonds are held as long-term investments for income, as they often are by insurance companies, trusts, institutions, and certain investment companies, premiums paid at the time of purchase are generally amortized by periodic charges against income received on these bonds, since the indicated loss which will be realized if the bonds are held to the redemption date is in effect a reduction of interest received. The premium is usually absorbed in the period between the date of acquisition and the earlier of maturity or optional call date.

Bonds purchased at a discount are not usually written up by periodic adjustments to the amount at which they are redeemable. Discount should be amortized only when the bonds are high grade and the discount represents an adjustment of interest rate rather than doubt as to the ultimate realizability of the obligation.

It is not customary for industrial companies to record amortization of premiums or discounts on bonds purchased as short-term investment of excess working capital, particularly when there is clearly no intent to hold such bonds to maturity.

Arrearages of Income.—The cost or other basis of bonds with interest in arrears at date of acquisition, or preferred stocks with arrearages of cumulative dividends, should be reduced upon receipt of these arrearages to give recognition to the fact that the original book amounts included an element of accrued income. Opinions differ as to what portion of this income should be credited to the book amount of the security. The indicated market value of the bonds or preferred stock, or the trend of such values at the time the income in arrears is received, may well be a factor to be considered, since if the original investment may be expected to be recovered without loss, a credit to income for the amount in arrears may be appropriate, but if a loss is likely, conservatism indicates that the asset account should be credited. Securities and Exchange Commission Regulation S-X states in paragraphs (d) and (f) of Rule 6.04, applying to management investment companies, the following:

(d) Dividends in arrears on preferred stock may not be treated as income in an amount which exceeds an amount arrived at by applying the stated dividend rate to the period during which the stock has been held. . . . . Any such dividends which are treated as income but which are applicable to periods prior to the current fiscal year shall be included under the caption ("other income").

(f) Due consideration shall be given to the propriety of treating, as income, interest received on bonds which were in default when acquired. Any such interest which may be treated as income shall not be treated as ordinary interest income in an amount in excess of the amount arrived at by applying the stated interest rate to the period of report, and any excess thereof shall be included under the caption ("other income") . . . .

Contingent Interest on Income Bonds.—When income bonds with interest payable only if earned are not owned for the entire period for which the interest is being paid, and such interest is material in relation to total income, income should be credited with that portion of the total interest received which corresponds with that part of the interest payment period for which the bonds were owned, and the asset account should be credited with the balance. Interest should be accrued on income bonds only if earnings of the debtor corporation are sufficient to indicate that the interest will be paid. In practice, contingent interest on income bonds is usually not material in relation to total income, and is generally taken into income on the date declared payable, even though the bonds may not have been owned for the entire interest payment period.

Stock Dividends.—When a dividend on common stock is received in shares of the same common stock, the effect is merely to increase the number of units of ownership without any increase in the stockholder's proportionate ownership in the issuing company or any effective divestment of property or rights on the part of the company. Under these circumstances no income is deemed to have accrued to the stockholder, and the cost of the original shares is apportioned between those shares and the new shares received.

When dividends are received on common stockholdings in the form of preferred shares of the issuing company and when other shares of the same or similar preferred stock are outstanding, it is the opinion of some that income has been received because the dividend gives a stockholder an interest different from that represented by his former holdings. While this treatment may have merit in certain circumstances, it is the authors' opinion that such stock dividends are so similar in characteristics to dividends received in stock of the same class as that held that it would generally be preferable to accord them the same accounting treatment and to apportion cost between the stock received and the original stock held rather than to credit the fair market value of the dividend to income. It should be noted that dividends paid in preferred shares to common stockholders when no preferred shares were previously outstanding do not result in a change in relative interest and such dividends should not be considered as income under any circumstances. Likewise, dividends paid in shares of a junior preferred stock to common stockholders when no junior preferred stock was previously outstanding should not be considered as income. As to the taxability of stock dividends the Internal Revenue Code of 1954 (Section 305) provides that, with certain minor exceptions, any distribution by a corporation of its own stock or of stock rights to shareholders on or after June 22, 1954, does not constitute taxable income to the recipients.

Dividends of shares of stock of one company received as the result of ownership of shares of another company, commonly termed "in kind" dividends, represent the receipt of property and are tantamount to the receipt of cash dividends. Accordingly, they should be credited to income at their fair market value, provided that they have been paid from accumulated earnings of the paying company. If these dividends are not paid from accumulated earnings, the cost of the shares on which the dividends are received is ordinarily apportioned between the original shares and the shares received as a dividend on the basis of their relative fair market values. When the shares are received as a dividend pursuant to a plan of liquidation or divestment, such as a "spin-off" of a subsidiary, an allocation of cost is usually made.

Stock Rights.—Considerations as to whether receipt of stock rights constitutes income should be the same as those in making such determination with respect to stock dividends discussed above.

Optional Dividends.—When a corporation which declares a dividend gives stockholders the option of taking stock or cash, some argue that, if the investor elects to take stock, the stock dividends should be considered as income in an amount equal to the cash which the stockholder would have received had he so elected. A stockholder who is given the option of taking a dividend in cash or in stock is being given a choice between obtaining funds (which he may consider as income on his present holdings) or increasing the number of his shareholdings (and perhaps by reason of other stockholders electing to take cash, increasing his equity) in the corporation. The authors see no good reason why the privilege of taking a certain amount of cash in lieu of stock should make it proper or desirable to consider that the unaccepted offer of cash gives the stock dividend a status different than that of an ordinary stock dividend. Furthermore, a corporation which gives the stockholder the choice of a cash dividend or a stock dividend usually makes the offer so that the choice of stock appears more advantageous to the stockholders. Ordinarily, a majority of the stockholders avail themselves of the opportunity of receiving stock. The result, therefore, is usually practically the same as if an ordinary stock dividend had been declared.

However, the Internal Revenue Code of 1954 [Section 305(b)(2)] provides that if the shareholder has the right to elect the medium of payment, the entire distribution may be taxable as a dividend, regardless of whether it is actually made, in whole or in part, in stock of the distributing corporation.

INTERNAL CONTROL

Internal Accounting Control.

AUTHORIZATION FOR TRANSACTIONS.—Authority for purchase, custody, sale, and modification or exchange of marketable securities should be clearly defined and should be exercised by officials designated by the directors or trustees. It is good procedure to require that changes in investments be authorized or approved in the minutes of meetings of directors or trustees.

RECORDS AND PROCEDURES.—A detailed record of each security should be maintained by the accounting department showing, in addition to the number of shares of stock and the principal amount of bonds and their cost or other basis, a complete and accurate description including certificate numbers. A detailed record of income receivable or accrued should also be maintained either as part of the foregoing record, or separately, and a check should be made periodically to ascertain whether all income receivable or accrued has been recorded.

The cost or other basis of marketable securities, as well as income receivable or accrued, as shown by detailed records, should be balanced periodically with general ledger control accounts. At least annually the accuracy of the detailed records should be verified by inspection of the securities or, if held by outside custodians, by confirmation. At regular intervals securities should be extended at market quotations, and the comparison of these amounts with book amounts should be reviewed by responsible officials.

The custodian should maintain a record of securities deposited or withdrawn. It is good accounting control for the custodian to receive or deliver securities only upon written instructions of authorized persons.

The private placement of substantial blocks of bonds or notes with insurance companies and similar institutional investors has been common in recent years. Such holdings are frequently represented by a few registered instruments, often in contract form. In practice these instruments may or may not have to be presented to the issuer or his agent for endorsement when partial repayments, such as sinking fund payments, are made. If no endorsement is required, the reduction in face amount should be recorded on the instrument by the custodian. In such circumstances it is good practice periodically to obtain from the issuers or their agents confirmation of the balances outstanding.

SECURITIES DEEMED WORTHLESS.—At times securities held are deemed to have little, if any, recoverable value and, therefore, are either written off the books, carried at a nominal amount, or a full allowance provided. These securities should be under accounting control, and they should be reviewed periodically as to possible increase in value until it is finally determined that no recovery is possible.

Internal Check.

ASSIGNMENT OF DUTIES.—The custodian of the securities, the securities bookkeeper, the general ledger bookkeeper, and the cashier should be independent of each other. Persons independent of all of the above should be assigned the functions of periodically inspecting the securities on hand and confirming those held by outside custodians, reconciling the total of detailed securities records with the general ledger control, comparing the custodian's record of securities deposited or withdrawn with accounting records of purchases and sales, and comparing investments at market prices with related book amounts. Independent persons should also be assigned the responsibility for approving modifications of securities, for authorizing the receipt and delivery of securities and the write-off of worthless investments, and for endorsing securities to make them negotiable. The custodian of securities should be informed of partial reductions in face amounts by persons independent of those maintaining detailed records of securities.

CUSTODY.—When marketable securities are kept in a safe deposit box or vault under the control of the company, it is desirable that access thereto require the presence of at least two designated officers or responsible employees. As stated above, officers or employees so designated should not participate in cash functions nor in the maintenance of accounting records including the detailed records of securities owned.

Securities should be registered in the name of the company or an accredited nominee. However, if circumstances make it necessary or expedient to register securities in the name of an individual, the certificates should be endorsed promptly and an assignment of income obtained.

Separation of bond coupons, warrants, and the like should be subject to the same general safeguards as withdrawals of securities.

Securities held as collateral or for accommodation should be kept under accounting control, and procedures for their deposit or withdrawal should be the same as for securities owned by the company.

When securities are held by an outside custodian such as a trust company, it is desirable that instructions given the custodian bear the approval of at least two responsible officials.

AUDITING PROCEDURES

Objectives.—The auditor should satisfy himself that marketable securities shown by the accounting records to be owned as at the date of the balance sheet were on hand as at that date, or if not on hand, were held by others for the account of the client. He should also determine that the cost or other basis at which the marketable securities are carried is in accordance with generally accepted accounting principles and that the description of marketable securities in the balance sheet is proper.

Simultaneous Examination.—When there is a possibility of substitution of one for the other, marketable securities owned or held as collateral or for safekeeping should be counted simultaneously with cash funds, undeposited receipts, notes receivable, and other negotiable paper.

Count of Securities.—When the portfolio of marketable securities is relatively large and active, as in banks, insurance companies, investment companies, and stock brokerage concerns, the count of securities will ordinarily be made at the balance sheet date. When the holdings of marketable securities are incidental to the principal business and are relatively small and inactive, the count may be made before or after the balance sheet date provided the auditor establishes and maintains control of the securities by arranging to have them placed under seal for the period between his count and the balance sheet date. If the internal check procedures are weak and the cashier has access to notes receivable and marketable securities, the auditor who is making a bank reconciliation at a cutoff date soon after the end of the fiscal period should count cash funds, undeposited receipts, notes receivable, marketable securities, and other negotiable paper at the same date in order to assure himself that there has been no substitution. Whenever the count of marketable securities is made at a date other than that of the balance sheet, the details of the items counted should be reconciled with the items shown by the records to have been owned at the date of the balance sheet.

The auditor should maintain control over marketable securities from the start of his count until the count has been completed and checked to the list of securities, and all exceptions have been investigated. When marketable securities are relatively few, inactive, and kept in one location, the auditor has no special problem of control; but when opposite conditions prevail, as in concerns whose principal assets are marketable securities, the auditor must exercise care not only in determining the most expeditious plan of count, but also in setting up his controls with the least inconvenience to the client. At the outset of the examination of marketable securities, especially if the examination is being made without prior notice to the client, the auditor should immediately ascertain the location of all marketable securities, establish controls at the various points necessary in order to see that any movements of securities are appropriately recorded, and determine the sequence of count of the various items.

All counts of marketable securities should be made in the presence of responsible officials or employees of the client. A list of marketable securities owned or held as collateral, or for safekeeping, as at the date of the count should be prepared from the security records by the client or the auditor. The count of securities on hand should be checked against this list, which should show adequate descriptions of the securities, including the aggregate principal amount of bonds and notes, the number of shares of stock, denomination of bonds or par value, if any, of stocks, maturity dates of bonds, and interest and preferred stock dividend rates. As previously stated, certificates of stock and registered bonds should ordinarily be in the name of the client or an accredited nominee but, if they are not, the certificates should be appropriately endorsed or should be accompanied by powers of attorney. When bonds have interest coupons attached, the auditor should make at least a test examination of these coupons to determine whether there is any indication that coupons not yet due have been detached. If coupons presently coming due do not accompany the bonds, the auditor should inquire as to their location, and should either inspect them, or confirm them with those by whom they are held. If coupons past due are attached, the auditor should determine why they have not been presented for payment. If interest is in default, the auditor should note this fact in his working papers and consider it in connection with his examination of accruals of income and carrying amounts of investments.

After groups of securities have been counted, they should be kept under the auditor's control until the count has been completed and all items on the list of securities have been examined or reconciled. If any

movement of securities is necessary before the count is completed, the
auditor should observe the withdrawal or deposit, determine the reason
for withdrawal, and record the transactions in the working papers.
Securities taken to be mailed to correspondents, brokers, transfer
agents, or others, but which were included with securities already counted
by the auditor, should be recorded by him and controlled until they
are turned over to the postal authorities if they are to be in transit
over the audit date. Securities received by the client through the mail
for a few days subsequent to the date of examination may also be
examined and a record made for convenience in substantiating items
in transit at the date of the audit.

Relatively inactive securities may be counted and placed under seal
in advance of the main count or placed under seal and counted after
more active items have been examined. When securities remain unchanged over several years, and the internal controls are not considered
strong, certificate numbers of representative items noted during the
count may be compared with certificate numbers of the same securities
as shown in working papers of the previous audit to determine whether
movements of securities have taken place without proper authorization
and record.

Usually it is unnecessary for the auditor to examine securities
deemed by the client to be worthless and no longer shown on the accounting records or carried at a nominal amount. The auditor should
determine what attempts have been made by the client to sell or otherwise dispose of such securities. If the client feels that a potential value
still exists, the auditor should recommend that they be kept under
accounting control.

The auditor is not qualified to assume responsibility for the genuineness or authenticity of certificates or instruments representing securities
investments. Certificates commonly encountered cover a wide variety
of shapes, colors, types of engraving or printing, and quality of paper,
and clever forgers have frequently succeeded in deceiving personnel of
financial institutions experienced in handling securities. Nevertheless,
the auditor should be alert to the possibility of spurious certificates.
Certificates which appear unusual and as to which the auditor is unable
to satisfy himself by examination of purchase documents, income records, or the like should be confirmed with the issuer or transfer agent.
Insurance companies and similar institutional investors frequently have
in their portfolios registered instruments in large denominations which
may be reduced below face amount by partial payments. The auditor
should request confirmation of the amount outstanding against such
instruments where it appears that they do not have to be presented to

the issuer or his agent for endorsement or reissue at the time a partial payment is received.

When examinations are being made of one or more of several accounts of trusts handled by the same trustee or in the same office, the auditor should count securities for all trust and other accounts at the same time. Similarly, if different auditors are employed to examine the several accounts, they should make their counts simultaneously. Otherwise, material shortages may be concealed by temporary transfers from accounts whose securities are not being counted. When the client is reluctant to permit the auditor to count the securities of other accounts, or is unwilling or unable to arrange for a simultaneous count by all auditors concerned, the auditor may identify securities owned by the client by accounting for certificate numbers of stocks and bonds. This, however, is extremely difficult and time-consuming when the portfolio is large and purchases and sales have been numerous.

The possibility of substitution should also be considered when the treasurer or other official of the client's organization in charge of securities may hold a similar position in a charitable, educational, or social organization. The auditor should not overlook the possibility of substitutions, especially when there are weaknesses in internal check procedures.

Confirmation of Securities Not on Hand.—Items on the list of marketable securities owned as at the audit date but not counted should be confirmed with those by whom held. These items will ordinarily include securities held by banks as collateral for loans or for safekeeping, securities with transfer agents, and, if the client is a stockbroker, items with other brokers on loans or awaiting delivery. The auditor should determine not only the location of these securities as at the examination date, but also why they are held by others. Confirmation requests, if prepared by the client, should be compared with the security records by the auditor, who should mail the requests on the date of the count or as soon thereafter as feasible, in envelopes bearing his name and address either printed thereon or corner stamped. If a reply does not confirm information furnished by the client, the auditor should investigate and obtain a full and satisfactory explanation of any reported differences. If no reply is received to initial requests for confirmation, second requests should be mailed and the items in question should be followed up until confirmations are received or the securities are otherwise accounted for satisfactorily.

In examining the accounts of financial organizations, contracts for the purchase or sale of securities on a when, as, and if issued basis should also be confirmed by the auditor.

Securities with Outside Custodians.—When outside custodians, such as trust companies, have custody of the client's entire portfolio, the custodian should be requested to furnish directly to the auditor a list of securities held for the client at the balance sheet date. The auditor should compare this list with the client's security records and account for any differences. If the custody of securities is under the control of any person or group of persons taking an active part in the management of the client, the auditor is not justified in relying solely on written confirmation from the custodian; he should employ auditing procedures outlined above for examination of marketable securities in the custody of the client.

Comparison of Count with Records.—If the list of securities owned or held as collateral or for safekeeping as at the date of the count is prepared by the client, the auditor should compare it in detail with the accounting records, both as to quantities and dollar amounts. After checking the addition of dollar amounts, the auditor should compare the total with the general ledger control account.

Examination of Security Records.—The auditor should determine that the accounting record of units and related dollar amounts of securities owned as at the beginning of the period under audit is in agreement with that shown in his working papers of the previous examination. Subsequent entries affecting either units or dollar amounts, or both, should be substantiated by reference to original documents, such as brokers' advices of purchases or sales, bank advices, notices or published services concerning conversion privileges, stock dividends, rights issued, exchanges, capital adjustments and calls, and the like, or by computation as in substantiating realized gains and losses and amortization of bond premiums. The auditor should also determine that security transactions have been approved by the board of directors or trustees or by officials designated by these boards. Security transactions should also be checked to or reconciled with related cash receipts and disbursements records. Usually all transactions should be substantiated, but a representative test check may suffice when the internal control procedures are satisfactory and apparently effective and the volume of transactions is relatively large, such as in banks and insurance companies.

Income from Securities.—By reference to published services for dividends and rights and by computation for bond interest, the auditor should satisfy himself that all income from securities, receivable or accrued, has been taken up on the accounting records. This examination should be made in detail unless the client's system of internal control is such that a test check is deemed adequate.

Examination of Balances Carried at Cost.—The auditor should satisfy himself that the costs at which securities are shown as at the balance sheet date are determined in accordance with generally accepted accounting principles.

Examination of Balances Carried at Market or Other Quotations.— Whether marketable securities are carried on the balance sheet at amounts based on market quotations or at cost with the amount at market quotations stated parenthetically or by footnote, the auditor should satisfy himself that the amount at market quotations is fairly stated. Market quotations usually represent last sale prices on the balance sheet date or, in the absence of sales, either the last bid price or the average of the last bid and offered prices. Sometimes, particularly for special purposes, other bases, such as sales within a range of dates proximate to the balance sheet date, may be used. It is the auditor's responsibility to form his opinion as to the propriety of the basis selected by the company. In addition, the auditor should check the accuracy of the company's calculation of investments at market quotations. Prices used by the client should be checked to published sources; if a published market price of a security is not available, the auditor should obtain direct confirmation of the price used by the client from brokers or other competent persons, preferably from more than one source, if possible. In checking market prices, it is preferable to refer to a publication other than that used by the client to guard against the possibility of obtaining incorrect prices because of typographical errors. In using published quotations for stocks, consideration must be given to the company's practice regarding the time of recording dividend income. Although such amounts are usually not significant enough to require adjustment, it may be necessary to add back a dividend to a quotation "ex-dividend" to obtain a fair comparison of market with book amount where it is the company's practice to take up dividend income at a date subsequent to the ex-dividend date. Footings and extensions involved in the determination of the total amount of investments at market quotations should be checked.

It should be recognized that the amount of securities at market quotations is merely an indication of value. Indication on a balance sheet of the amount at market quotations is not intended as assurance that the securities could necessarily be sold at indicated prices. When blocks of securities are large and available market quotations are for relatively small quantities, consideration should be given to the need for appropriate disclosure in the financial statements that amounts at market quotations should not be construed as representations of realizability, at such quotations, of the blocks of securities held.

Portfolios of investment companies occasionally contain securities for which market quotations are not available and which are included in the balance sheet at management's appraisals of fair value. The auditor should inquire into the basis for management's appraisals and, without assuming responsibility for such amounts, should endeavor to satisfy himself as to their reasonableness in light of known conditions.

When the amount of securities priced at market quotations is in excess of cost, the auditor should consider the necessity of indicating the amount of taxes or expenses which would be incurred if the securi-- ties were disposed of at the indicated amount to avoid any implication that the entire amount of unrealized gain would be an increment to surplus. Ordinarily, commissions, transfer taxes, and similar expenses are not of sufficient significance to require consideration. However, federal and state taxes on gains may be material in amount and, if they are, appropriate allowance or provision for them should be made as a reduction of indicated unrealized gain. It is not contemplated, however, that this rule should be applied to casual holdings of marketable securities by industrial companies.

When, as with insurance companies, it is required that marketable securities be stated in the balance sheet at amounts determined by regulatory authorities, the auditor should acquaint himself with the applicable regulations. The prices used by the company should be verified by reference to prescribed sources, and footings and extensions should be checked. The auditor should also satisfy himself that the difference between the cost of the securities and the prescribed amounts has been accounted for as required by the regulations.

Coordination of Examination with That of Related Accounts.—Other accounts which may advantageously be examined concurrently with the examination of marketable securities include:

Accrued interest receivable
Dividends receivable
Interest income
Dividend income
Gain or loss on disposal of securities.

STATEMENT PRESENTATION

Statement of Basis.—The basis on which marketable securities are carried in the balance sheet should be clearly indicated. Commercial and industrial companies generally carry marketable securities at cost, indicating the amount of the securities at market quotations in a parenthetical note in the balance sheet caption. However, when the securities are included in current assets and total cost exceeds the total amount at market quotations by a material amount, an allowance for the indicated shrinkage should be provided, particularly when there is evidence of a permanent decline in values. When an allowance is deemed necessary, it should be provided by charge to income.

When the original cost of high-grade securities purchased on a "yield basis" has been adjusted to reflect amortization of premium or accumulation of discount since acquisition, a question may arise as to the appropriate description of the basis in the balance sheet. A similar question may arise when arrearages of interest or preferred dividends which existed at the time of purchase have been applied to reduce cost when later received. In the opinion of the authors, it is not necessary to characterize the amounts resulting from such proper adjustments as other than "cost."

In financial statements of investment companies marketable securities may be stated either:

(a) At cost, with the amount of the securities at market quotations indicated parenthetically or otherwise, or

(b) At market quotations, with cost indicated parenthetically or otherwise.

So that the reader may have sufficient information for proper consideration of financial statements of an investment company, its balance sheet should be accompanied by a detailed list of investments. This list should show, as a minimum, name and class of security, number of shares of stock or principal amount of bonds, and individual amounts at market quotations to support the aggregate amount of securities at market quotations on the balance sheet.

In financial statements of companies such as dealers in securities where securities constitute so-called "stock in trade," securities on hand are frequently carried on the balance sheet at cost or market, whichever is lower. When securities are carried on this basis, the amount at market quotations should be indicated parenthetically or otherwise.

It is the general practice of stockbrokers, in their published balance sheets, to carry securities in investment and trading accounts, at amounts based on market quotations without disclosure of costs, and to reflect the liability in "short" positions (securities sold, but not yet purchased) without indication of proceeds of sale.

When the balance sheet includes securities stated at management's appraisals of fair value, the amount of such securities should be shown separately and described in language similar to "at fair value as estimated by management." If the aggregate of such amounts is material, but the auditor has no reason to question the soundness of such valuations, the auditor's opinion should be stated as based, in part, on management's valuations. If the auditor has reason to believe that management's estimates of fair values are not reasonable in light of known circumstances, he should consider the need for qualifying his opinion, or if, under such circumstances, the amount involved is so material as to impair the fairness of presentation of the financial statements, the auditor may decide he should not express his opinion on the statements as a whole.

The necessity for making appropriate allowance or provision for taxes which would be incurred upon realization of unrealized net appreciation, and for other material expenses of realization when the market amount of securities is indicated, has been previously discussed. Where such provision is considered necessary and securities are carried in the financial statements at amounts based on market quotations, the provision for these taxes and expenses should be shown on the liability side of the balance sheet or should be deducted from the indicated amount based on market quotations with disclosure that this deduction has been made. When the amount at market quotations is shown parenthetically or in a note to the financial statements, the amount of these taxes and expenses should be disclosed in the parenthetic reference or footnote.

Classification as Current or Noncurrent.—In the balance sheets of commercial and industrial companies marketable securities may be included with current assets even though there is no present intention of disposing of them within one year from the balance sheet date. However, if the securities are held for special purposes, such as for sinking fund requirements or for costs of proposed plant additions, and, therefore, are not part of the company's working capital, they should be separately shown among noncurrent assets with an appropriate indication of their intended use.

Balance sheets of investment companies, banks, and insurance companies do not customarily classify assets as current or noncurrent.

Other Considerations.—When marketable securities have been pledged or deposited, this fact should be disclosed on the balance sheet. The application of United States Government securities as an offset to accrued federal taxes on income is discussed in Chapter 16.

CHAPTER 10

RECEIVABLES

Introduction.—Receivables most frequently arise from sales of either merchandise or services, and represent claims against customers and others, generally collectible within the normal operating cycle of the business. Types of receivables generally encountered are those from customers on open account, notes or acceptances receivable, and unbilled or accrued receivables.

Notes and acceptances receivable are formal evidence of amounts receivable, perhaps more readily negotiable but not necessarily more collectible than receivables on open account. Acceptances are a means of extending credit to a buyer. They are drafts across the face of which the drawee (buyer) has written the word "Accepted," the date, and his signature, giving it the legal status of a promissory note. Notes and acceptances are often negotiable and may be sold at a discount to provide funds in advance of maturity date.

Unbilled or accrued receivables include items for which an invoice is expected to be sent later, or which are expected to be collected when due without formal invoicing, such as interest, rents, and royalties, estimated price adjustments under contracts with price redetermination clauses, claims resulting from termination of contracts, and expenditures under cost-plus-fixed-fee contracts.

Sales on the instalment plan frequently are made under a conditional bill of sale with the title retained by the seller until the price is fully paid. Serial notes in the amount of the sales price may be received, and the merchandise sold may be pledged against these notes.

ACCOUNTING PRINCIPLES

Items To Be Included.—Receivable balances from customers usually should include only charges for services performed or merchandise shipped on or before the balance sheet date and similarly should reflect only credits for payments received, allowances made, or merchandise returned on or before that date. Customers may authorize billing and request that merchandise be held for future delivery. Such billings properly may be recorded as receivables, provided the merchandise is excluded from inventory. With this exception, unfilled orders of trading or manufacturing concerns are not considered to be receivables even though the goods are on hand and may be regarded as awaiting delivery.

Accounts receivable are usually recorded when title to goods passes from the seller to the buyer; title ordinarily passes when merchandise is shipped to the customer. Exceptions are shipments f.o.b. destination when title does not pass until the buyer receives the merchandise, and shipments on drafts accompanied by bills of lading when title does not pass until the drafts are paid. It is, nevertheless, customary to record an account receivable at the time such merchandise is shipped. Special limitations on passing of title under instalment selling plans do not preclude recognition of the transaction by recording accounts receivable when the merchandise is shipped. The terms of contracts such as those covering long-term construction may provide for interim billings for work partially completed.

Other receivable balances should also include only charges and credits applicable up to the balance sheet date. These balances may represent income receivable such as interest, dividends, or rent, and miscellaneous receivables such as those from officers and employees, transportation companies, insurance companies, and miscellaneous debtors.

Accumulated costs and related fees under cost-plus-fixed-fee (CPFF) contracts are ordinarily considered as receivables even if not billed. The nature of CPFF contracts is such that the right to bill usually arises as soon as expenditures are made, and the principal reason for costs not being billed at a balance sheet date is the time required to assemble clerical data for billing purposes. A portion of the fixed fee generally accrues in proportion to the expenditures made.

Many companies doing business with government agencies have contracts which include a tentative selling price, subject to revision at one or more stages of completion. After a specified percentage of the contract has been completed or a specified quantity shipped, the government agency will review accumulated costs on the contract for the purpose of establishing a firm price or series of firm prices. The prices so determined may cover the entire contract or only the quantity shipped, with provision for redeterminations. Contracts usually stipulate that shipments prior to the determination of a fixed price are to be billed and paid for at the tentative selling price. After redetermination, additional billings or credit memoranda may be issued. The company may have billed its shipments during the period at tentative prices because either the required stage of completion of the contract had not been reached or price redetermination negotiations had not been completed. Under such circumstances, an adjustment to recorded sales and receivables may be justified at a balance sheet date to reflect estimated price changes that will result from the redetermination. Such an adjustment should be based on a careful review of applicable contracts, the company's cost experience, the status of current negotiations, and the results of previous negotiations of a similar nature, if any. Upward redetermination should not be recognized unless circumstances are such that upward adjustment is reasonably assured.

The termination of defense contracts by the government converts inventory into a claim receivable as of the effective date of termination. Upon termination, the contractor is not required to perform further services which are not directly reimbursable; it is therefore proper to accrue as part of the claim receivable the related profit on the terminated contract, provided the amount can be reasonably determined.

Accounting problems under government contracts are discussed in Chapter 11 of Accounting Research Bulletin No. 43.

Claims for tax refunds resulting from the carry-back provisions of the Internal Revenue Code may be classified as receivables if no technical complications are foreseen. If the amount recoverable cannot be definitely ascertained, the claim, with such contra allowance as seems reasonable may be recorded on the books. This entry should prevent claims from being overlooked and call attention to the running of the statute of limitations and the necessity for instituting suit if the limitation date is imminent.

Deductions from Receivables.—Receivable balances should be reflected at amounts not in excess of estimated net realizable amounts. Periodic adjustment to estimated realizable amounts is necessary so that costs or expenses will reflect losses or diminution of balances in the period to which they are applicable. Adjustment is made by means of allowances such as those for doubtful accounts, cash discounts, returns and adjustments, collection expenses, finance charges, disallowed costs on CPFF contracts, and loss on foreign exchange.

An allowance for doubtful accounts receivable should be provided if losses on receivables reasonably can be expected. It is not always possible to identify the particular accounts on which losses will occur, but it is reasonable to make an over-all allowance based on past experience and current conditions. Frequently this allowance is provided regularly in an amount representing a percentage of sales. Such a basis must be reviewed periodically, as the percentage employed may not reflect current conditions, especially in a period of abnormal business activity. Whether the allowance provided as a percentage of sales is too large or too small cannot be determined until the probable collectibility of the receivable balances has been determined from analysis and review of the accounts. When the percentage is based upon experience covering a long period of years, the balance of the allowance account will usually be relatively larger in prosperous times when bad debt losses are low, and relatively smaller in less prosperous periods. If no allowance based on a percentage of sales is set up regularly, it is customary to provide an allowance as at the balance sheet date in an amount determined after study of the estimated collectibility of receivable balances, both current and overdue, as indicated by an aging of the accounts and information regarding the debtors' ability to pay. Due consideration should be given to events after the close of the fiscal year which have a bearing on the collectibility of the accounts.

Uncollectible receivables should be excluded from both the asset account and the allowance for doubtful accounts receivable. Receivable balances written off in whole or in part, and subsequent collections thereon, if any, should ordinarily be debited or credited to the allowance account, if there is such an account, or to income, if there is not.

The right to repossess merchandise does not remove the probability of loss from bad debts on instalment accounts receivable balances. Much of the merchandise sold on the instalment plan, if repossessed, either has no resale value as is, or, if reconditioned, cannot be sold at a price sufficient to cover the unpaid account, cost of reconditioning, and reselling expense.

Accumulated costs under CPFF contracts are submitted to the government agency concerned for reimbursement, subject to audit. The audit may result in certain costs being suspended or disallowed as not being applicable to the contract. If it appears that certain items of cost may be disallowed upon audit, it is proper to reduce the receivable to its estimated net realizable value by means of an allowance for disallowed costs. As with doubtful accounts, the allowance for disallowed costs may be provided regularly in an amount representing a percentage of costs incurred.

Allowance should be made at the end of the fiscal period for any material amount of cash discounts which experience and the terms of sale indicate may be deducted by debtors in settlement of their accounts. When uniform discounts are the rule, provision may be made by application of an estimated over-all percentage to the receivable balances.

If it appears that unusual amounts of merchandise will be returned in the ensuing fiscal period, allowance for these returns should be set up to eliminate the profit previously taken when sales of this merchandise were recorded. Furthermore, consideration should be given to the necessity for an allowance covering possible rebates and adjustments because of price adjustments, defective materials, guaranties, or for other reasons.

It is not necessary to make allowance for routine collection expenses. Expenses of the collection department of a company with an instalment selling plan may be large enough to justify such an allowance. However, the finance charges which are added to sales prices of merchandise when instalment accounts receivable are booked usually include adequate provision for collection expenses. If these finance charges are apportioned, so that credits to income are related to collections on instalment receivables, the amount of finance charges deferred as at the balance sheet date can be considered as an allowance against the receivables, in lieu of a specific allowance for collection expenses.

Receivable balances which are to be settled in a foreign currency should be translated into United States dollars at appropriate rates of exchange in effect at the balance sheet date. Unrealized loss on translation should be charged to the income account, and unrealized gain usually should be credited to a reserve for foreign exchange adjustments. However, unrealized gain may be credited to income insofar as it arises from recovery of the exchange rate from a level to which the accounts receivable had been written down previously.

INTERNAL CONTROL

Internal Accounting Control.

RECORDING OF NOTES RECEIVABLE.—New or renewed notes receivable should be approved by a responsible official prior to acceptance. A detailed record of notes receivable should be maintained showing the name of the maker, amount of the note, maturity date, interest rate, and collateral, if any. The notes themselves and related collateral should be inspected periodically and compared with the detailed record. If notes are discounted, a record of discounted notes receivable should be kept to reflect the contingent liability.

ENDORSEMENTS OF PARTIAL PAYMENTS.—It is good practice to endorse partial payments on notes receivable so that the notes will show the reduction in the face amount.

RECORDING OF ACCOUNTS RECEIVABLE.—Sales orders and changes therein should be subject to approval before acceptance to ensure that orders are accepted only on terms and conditions set by the company and that sales are made only to approved credit risks. Posting of entries to individual accounts receivable should be made from original media (or copies) such as charge tickets, invoices, remittance advices, or shipping documents, all of which should be under numerical control to preclude errors of omission. The total of the individual accounts in the customers' ledger, as well as the total of the individual notes receivable, should be reconciled periodically with the respective general ledger controls.

PERIODIC STATEMENTS TO DEBTORS.—Statements of account should be sent regularly to all debtors, providing opportunity for customers to report differences. Such reports by customers also afford management an excellent check on the effectiveness of billing and collection procedures. If it is not the practice to send statements to all debtors, the same objectives may be partially accomplished by sending statements only to customers with delinquent balances.

AGING OF RECEIVABLES AND ITEMS WRITTEN OFF.—Aging schedules of unpaid receivable balances and delinquent notes receivable should be prepared periodically and reviewed by a responsible official. The review should include consideration of the allowance required for doubtful accounts. To prevent undue delay in the recording of credits, credit memoranda for returned mechandise, price adjustments, special discounts, or damage claims should be under numerical control and should be issued and recorded promptly upon receipt of proper authorization.

It is good internal accounting control to have payments of customers' credit balances and write-offs of uncollectible amounts approved by a responsible employee. Notes and accounts receivable which have been written off should be kept under accounting control and reviewed periodically by an informed person.

POSTDATED CHECKS.—Postdated checks may be kept under accounting control by use of a debit account with a contra credit account in the general ledger, or they may be kept under memorandum control by recording them in a tickler file or noting their receipt on the accounts receivable ledger.

Internal Check.

NOTES RECEIVABLE.—The custodian of notes and related collateral, the notes receivable bookkeeper, the general ledger bookkeeper, and the cashier should be independent of each other. Persons independent of all the above should be assigned the functions of inspecting periodically the notes and related collateral, reconciling the total of the individual amounts with the general ledger control account, and confirming the notes receivable. Independent persons should also be responsible for approving changes in terms of notes receivable, authorizing the release of collateral, and approving write-offs of uncollectible amounts. It is also a good internal check procedure to require more than one person to be present to obtain physical access to the notes receivable and collateral.

The credit department, usually responsible for approving new accounts and following up unpaid balances, should be independent of the sales department and the department which keeps the records of notes and accounts receivable.

ACCOUNTS RECEIVABLE.—The employee who posts the individual customers' accounts, the general ledger bookkeeper, and the cashier should be independent of each other. Persons independent of all the above should be responsible for reconciling periodically the total of the individual accounts with the control account, confirming the individual accounts, and preparing or checking aging schedules. It is good internal check to have statements compared with the receivable ledger and mailed by someone other than the receivable bookkeeper or cashier. If statements are not sent to certain debtors, this practice should be authorized by a responsible person and the reasons for not sending statements recorded.

Disputed items should be handled by someone other than the receivable bookkeeper or cashier, so that adjustments, if necessary, will originate with an employee outside the bookkeeping department. Credits to accounts receivable other than through cash, and payments of credit balances should be approved by an independent official.

Records of written-off accounts receivable should be maintained by persons independent of cash receipts function.

Postdated checks should be held by someone other than the accounts receivable bookkeeper.

AUDITING PROCEDURES

Objectives.—Procedures in auditing receivables should be sufficiently comprehensive to enable the auditor to form an opinion as to the authenticity and probable collectibility of receivable balances, and the propriety of the description and classification of these balances on the balance sheet; they should bring to his attention any contingent liability arising from the discount or sale of notes or accounts receivable.

Generally accepted procedures are indicated in the paragraphs which follow, but it is improbable that all of them will be necessary or desirable in any one examination.

Notes and Acceptances Receivable.—Procedures for examination of notes and acceptances receivable include inspection, confirmation by direct communication with the makers, and comparison of the total of individual notes with the general ledger balance. If the notes and acceptances receivable are negotiable or are customarily discounted, the inspection should be simultaneous with examination or count of cash funds, undeposited receipts, and other negotiable assets. The examination of less active items may well take place prior to the date of examination of other items provided they are placed under seal until that date.

In examining notes and acceptances, the auditor should make a record of names of makers, payees, acceptors, dates, amounts, interest rates, maturities, endorsements, and complete details of collateral, if such a record has not been supplied by the client. Ordinarily, each note and acceptance should be examined, but, if the volume on hand is very large and internal control procedures are reasonably complete and effective, a test by partial examination of the notes may be sufficient. If the notes are not available for the auditor's inspection because they are held by a bank or other agent for collection, discounted or sold with guaranty, or pledged as collateral, the auditor can usually obtain confirmation or acknowledgments by correspondence. It may be desirable to supplement the confirmation of notes and acceptances discounted or sold by review of cash receipts records, including duplicate deposit slips, bank notifications, and other evidences of discount or sale. Similar evidence may be examined if the inspection is not made until after the balance sheet date and some of the notes have been collected in the interim.

When notes have been renewed in full, no entry may appear on the books, although good practice indicates the advisability of entries reflecting such transactions. Renewal notes, whether the original notes were renewed in full or in part, should be available for the auditor's examination.

If internal accounting control is considered to be weak, a test of the records of receipt and disposition of notes and acceptances during the period under review should indicate the apparent effectiveness of such control. The extent of any such test should take into consideration the relative importance of these assets and the number and size of individual notes. If internal accounting control and internal check procedures are reasonably good, this examination of transactions during the period may be unnecessary.

Accounts Receivable.—Procedures for the examination of accounts receivable include, in addition to test confirmation by direct communication with the debtors, review and checking of controlling accounts, test-checking trial balances of individual accounts and aging analyses, and examination of related supporting evidence.

General ledger control account balances should be compared with totals of individual accounts receivable, and any discrepancies between the two should be investigated and appropriate adjustment should be made by the client. Trial balances of accounts receivable prepared by the client (often on adding machine tapes) should be checked to the individual ledger accounts in detail, or, if internal accounting control and internal check procedures are satisfactory, on a test basis. Trial balance footings should be checked to the extent deemed appropriate.

If internal accounting control is not considered satisfactory, general ledger control accounts of receivable balances may be reviewed for all or part of the period under examination to determine whether there are any entries unusual in amount or source. This procedure may be followed especially when it is not the practice to balance regularly the total of individual accounts with general ledger control accounts. In any such extended examination the auditor should not overlook the possibility that an entry unusual in amount or source may be made in a subsidiary record, such as the sales journal or cash receipts book, so that it would not appear as a separate item in the general ledger control account.

Receivables other than trade accounts, such as debit balances in accounts payable, claims, advances, prepayments, and deposits, should be examined by reference to the transactions as recorded in the accounts and to supporting evidence. The precise nature of these accounts should be determined for purposes of the scope of audit, the study of their collectibility, and their classification in the balance sheet. Confirmations should be obtained by direct communication with the debtors to the extent considered reasonable and practicable. Although these receivables may not be significant in amount, if they are not subject to satisfactory internal accounting control and internal check, they may require more extensive procedures than are necessary for trade receivables.

The auditor should determine that drafts out for collection are recorded in the accounts, either separately as drafts receivable or included in accounts receivable. In substantiating receivable balances from foreign debtors, the auditor cannot always employ the usual confirmation procedures, and therefore, the existence of drafts may help in substantiating these balances. The auditor should inquire of the banks with which the drafts were deposited for collection or from which loans or advances on account of foreign shipments have been obtained, whether any drafts have been pledged against loans or advances. Drafts in the hands of collection agents should be confirmed, and their status determined as of the balance sheet date.

Supporting Evidence.—Even though receivable balances are confirmed, it may be considered advisable to compare billings, shipping memoranda, or other data with recorded transactions in accounts receivable for some period on a test basis. Such tests for the last week or month of the fiscal year and the first week or month of the succeeding period may be made as a part of the examination of internal accounting control and also should help to determine that a proper sales cutoff has been made. Aside from unintentional errors, improper cutoffs may result from a desire to record sales in an improper period because of bonus arrangements, sales quotas, royalty agreements, or income taxes. Further reference to cutoff procedures will be found in Chapter 20. If merchandise is billed to customers and held for them, care must be exercised to exclude this merchandise from inventory and to determine that billing before delivery has been authorized by the customers.

Credit memoranda issued for a period after the close of the fiscal year usually should be examined to determine that sales for the period ended at the balance sheet date were not inflated, and that allowances for discounts, returns, and freight have been provided in appropriate amounts.

If it is found that consigned goods are treated as sales and included in receivable balances, with a resulting anticipation of profits, the unsold goods in the hands of consignees should be adjusted to the basis of like items in the merchandise inventory and reclassified as inventory. If the goods appear to be salable at a sufficient margin of profit, related accrued charges, such as freight paid by the consignor, may be added to the inventory costs.

If charges to receivable accounts are test-checked as a part of an examination of billings, the auditor should note whether discounts allowed, if any, are in agreement with the client's policies as indicated by price lists or sales contracts.

Sales contracts with selling agents and other agreements affecting receivables should be read. Various matters such as title to the accounts receivable, time of billings, method or time of payments, and special discounts, might escape the attention of the auditor unless he reviews these documents.

Receivables representing amounts due under government contracts should be carefully reviewed. An analysis of billed and unbilled charges by contracts should be prepared, and substantial items supported by reference to available source data. The auditor should review contract provisions and determine that billed and unbilled charges appear to be allowable under their terms. If accruals have been made for anticipated price changes under redetermination clauses, the auditor should satisfy himself that the adjustments cover all shipments to the balance sheet date. The investigation may include a review of cost records, possible unallowable costs, gross profit margins, estimates submitted at the time tentative selling prices were established, estimated completion costs, and settlements negotiated in connection with similar contracts.

Confirmation of Receivable Balances.—Confirmation of receivables by direct communication with debtors has been a generally accepted auditing procedure for many years. This position was restated in "Codification of Statements on Auditing Procedure," issued by the Committee on Auditing Procedure in 1951, as follows:

Where the independent certified public accountant intends to report over his signature on financial statements in which notes and accounts receivable are a significant factor, confirmation by direct communication with the debtors shall, where practicable and reasonable, be a part of generally accepted auditing procedures; the method, extent, and time of obtaining such confirmations in each engagement, and whether of all receivables or a part thereof, shall be determined by the independent certified public accountant as in other phases of procedure requiring the exercise of his judgment.

Confirmations may be requested of receivable balances as at the end of the fiscal period or as at a date within two or three months thereof, usually before the end of the period. Confirmation of receivable balances is as much a test of the effectiveness of the internal control procedures as it is of the existence and dollar amount of the accounts confirmed. If the confirmation requests relate to balances as at a date other than that of the balance sheet, and the procedure has revealed no significant irregularities, the auditor is justified in assuming that substantially the same conditions exist as at the date of the balance sheet, provided his review of internal control procedures and transactions in the intervening period gives no indication to the contrary.

Replies from debtors to requests for confirmation should reveal whether the receivable balances confirmed are substantially correct. They may reveal partial payments on notes receivable which may not have been endorsed thereon, as well as complete payments of fully paid notes which may not have been returned to the maker. The existence of collateral, if any, also may be disclosed. When monthly or other periodic statements are not sent to debtors, confirmation requests frequently disclose a variety of differences and exceptions which require consideration.

SELECTION OF ACCOUNTS FOR CONFIRMATION.—From his review of internal accounting control and internal check procedures, the auditor should decide whether all or only part of the accounts should be confirmed and, if the latter, the basis for selecting the accounts to be confirmed. Accounts receivable selected for confirmation usually should include a representative portion of both the dollar amount and the number of accounts; they may include all accounts with balances over a selected amount and a number of small accounts taken in numerical or alphabetical sequence, accounts with old unpaid items, and those written off during the period under review. The selection should exclude accounts when replies to requests for their confirmation cannot reasonably be expected, such as those with most government agencies, foreign concerns, and chain stores.

An experienced auditor will usually confirm accounts which appear unusual, such as accounts with even dollar balances when the sales prices would not ordinarily produce even amounts. The confirmation of receivable accounts with zero or credit balances should be considered. There is always the possibility, especially when internal accounting control and internal check procedures are weak, that a credit balance is incorrect. Confirmation of an account receivable should not be omitted merely because payment or other credit has been recorded since the confirmation date. Sometimes the client will request that accounts not selected by the auditor be included among those to be confirmed, usually in the hope that the confirmation request may speed up collection; the auditor may properly accede to such a request.

Accounts receivable as well as notes receivable, discounted or pledged, should be confirmed by those with whom discounted or pledged, so that any liability, contingent or otherwise, will be brought to the auditor's attention. Confirmation by those with whom discounted or pledged does not mean that the auditor should omit requesting confirmation from the debtors as well.

If the client does not wish statements or confirmation requests sent to certain debtors, the auditor should be satisfied that there is an adequate reason. The auditor may wish to employ alternative procedures to satisfy himself, insofar as may be possible, that these accounts are authentic and accurate in amount. As indicated in Chapter 6, in such a situation the auditor may not wish to assume the risk of giving an unqualified opinion.

CONFIRMATION PROCEDURES.—After having decided upon the selection of accounts for confirmation, in processing the statements the auditor should observe the following rules which are applicable to both the negative and the positive method of confirmation:

1. Names, addresses, and amounts shown on statements selected for confirmation should be compared with the debtors' accounts. Thereafter, the auditor must maintain control over statements selected for confirmation until he has mailed them.

2. Proof that the total of the debtors' accounts, from which selection has been made, agrees with the control account should be obtained through adding machine tapes of individual receivable balances, prepared by the auditor or prepared by the client and checked or test-checked by the auditor.

3. Requests for confirmation, together with postage-paid return envelopes addressed to the auditor, should be mailed in envelopes showing the address of the auditor as the return address, or, if there is objection to use of this address, the return address may be to the client at a post office box controlled by the auditor. If the latter procedure is used, instructions should be left with the post office to forward mail to the auditor after the box is surrendered.

4. All requests should be mailed by the auditor, but not in the client's mail room.

5. Undelivered requests returned by the post office should be investigated, corrected addresses obtained, and the requests remailed by the auditor.

THE NEGATIVE CONFIRMATION.—The negative method of confirmation is a request that the debtor communicate directly with the auditor if the statement balance is considered in any way incorrect. Such request is conveyed by a sticker affixed to the statement, by a rubber stamp impression, or by a special letter with or without a statement. The auditor should enclose a business reply envelope addressed to himself. This requires no postage and facilitates a reply. The auditor expects replies only when the debtor reports a difference; he may assume that no reply signifies the debtor's acceptance of the balance.

The negative method of confirmation is that most frequently used. Depending on the circumstances of the engagement, it may be supplemented by positive method confirmations, particularly of the larger balances.

It is important to impress upon the debtors the desirability or necessity of communicating directly with the auditors when discrepancies exist. If the auditor has reason to believe that the negative form of confirmation request will not receive consideration, he should not feel that he has complied with generally accepted auditing procedures by sending out this form of confirmation request.

If statements are not mailed at the time confirmations are requested, or if statements are not to be sent to debtors, a letter form of request may be sent. With appropriate changes of language, the form of positive confirmation reproduced on page 176 may be employed.

If statements are sent to debtors, the auditor may inscribe the statements by means of a rubber stamp or affix a sticker reading somewhat as follows:

PLEASE CHECK THIS STATEMENT

If it is not correct, please report all differences directly to our auditors,
(Name and Address of Auditors)

who are now making their periodic examination of our accounts.

If you do not report any exceptions, it will be assumed that the statement is correct.

Remittances should NOT be sent to the auditors.

This request is for information and not for payment. We thank you for your cooperation.

THE POSITIVE CONFIRMATION.—The positive method of confirmation is a request that the debtor reply directly to the auditor stating whether or not the amounts and other details shown on the statement or letter submitted for confirmation are correct. The request may be conveyed by a letter, or directly on the statement by means of a rubber stamp impression or an affixed sticker. To facilitate replies the auditor should enclose a stamped or a business reply envelope addressed to himself.

Because the form of the request specifically asks for a reply, the auditor may not assume that failure to reply to the request indicates that the debtor agrees with the reported balance. Second requests should be made and, if necessary, third requests by registered mail to obtain proof of delivery. If he fails to receive positive confirmation of a substantial number of accounts or material dollar amount of receivables, the auditor should employ supplementary auditing procedures, as described later.

The positive method of confirmation is not generally recommended, except when there are indications that there may be disputes, inaccuracies, or irregularities in the accounts, or when the receivable balance is of outstanding materiality or arises from sales to a few large customers. Receivables of stock brokerage houses are customarily confirmed by the positive method. This procedure conforms with Rule X-17A-5 of the Securities and Exchange Commission and identical Rule 532 of the Board of Governors of the New York Stock Exchange. It should be remembered that a favorable reply to a positive confirmation request is not always conclusive evidence that the unpaid receivable balance is correctly stated. Later examination of supporting evidence may disclose that the account was misstated at the date of the confirmation request.

Unless replies to positive confirmation requests are satisfactorily numerous, the auditor is in no better position to judge the reliability of the receivable balances after he has sent out the requests than he was before. Experience has shown that the percentage of replies received varies considerably with the type of customer, and the auditor must exercise his judgment in deciding whether the nature and extent of the response are satisfactory.

Responsibility for genuineness or authenticity of signatures on replies to confirmation requests cannot be accepted by the auditor. Not only will replies be received from debtor corporations signed by officers unknown to the auditor as such, but also from debtor individuals signed by persons as agents, trustees, or guardians whose authority is unknown to the auditor. The difficulties involved make it impractical and unreasonable for the auditor to determine the genuineness or authenticity of signatures. On bank, brokerage, and certain special engagements, when the signature on a reply does not agree with the name of the account, the auditor should determine whether the client has written evidence of the authority of the person signing the reply. When the client cannot produce such written evidence, the auditor should consider such accounts unconfirmed and mail second requests appropriately worded to obtain properly signed replies. It may be desirable in such engagements to have the client supplement the confirmation procedure by reviewing signatures for genuineness and authenticity.

Experience has shown that a form of positive request which requires of the recipient a minimum of effort will produce the greatest percentage of replies. The letter form of positive request is designed for use when no statements of account are to be mailed to debtors or when the requests are sent after statements have been mailed by the client. On receipt the debtor has only to sign his name in the space provided at the bottom of the letter, if the amount shown is in agreement with his records, and mail the letter in the return envelope provided. This letter form is illustrated as follows:

(Date)

(Name and address of debtor)

Dear Sirs:

In accordance with the request of our auditors, (name and address of auditors), we ask that you kindly confirm to them your indebtedness to us at (date) which, according to our records, amounted to (amount).

If the amount shown is in agreement with your records, please so indicate by signing in the space provided below and return this letter directly to our auditors in the enclosed envelope. Your prompt compliance will facilitate the examination of our accounts.

If the amount shown is not in agreement with your records, please inform our auditors directly what amount is shown by your records and, if possible, send them full details of differences.

Remittances should NOT be sent to the auditors.

Very truly yours,
(Name of client)

The above-stated amount is correct as at (date).

(Debtor of client)

....

(Title or position)

....

If statements of account prepared by the client are to be used as a basis for a positive confirmation request, they may be sent out in duplicate with an appropriately worded request (often imprinted on the statement with a rubber stamp) that the debtor acknowledge its correctness by returning the duplicate directly to the auditor, duly signed. A variation is the form of monthly statement in which the balance owing and the name of the debtor appear in two places, one of which is separated from the main body of the statement by perforations. The coupon may be torn off, signed by the debtor, and returned directly to the auditor.

If duplicate statements are not sent out, the auditor may affix to each statement a sticker similar to that shown in the following illustration:

IMPORTANT

In connection with the periodic examination of our records by our auditors, (name and address of auditors), we attach a statement of your account as shown by our books as at (date of statement).

PLEASE EXAMINE THIS STATEMENT

If *correct,* kindly sign below and return this slip direct to our auditors.

If *not correct,* please give details of differences direct to our auditors, using the enclosed stamped envelope.

Remittances should NOT be sent to the auditors.

Very truly yours,
(Name of client)

(Debtor of client)

Correct (sign here) ....

(Title or position)

....

EXCEPTIONS TO CONFIRMATION REQUESTS.—Exceptions reported in replies to confirmation requests should ordinarily be investigated by the auditor. The investigation of these exceptions by the auditor may consume more time than their significance warrants, and if they are not material in amount nor indicative of serious weakness, they properly may be turned over for investigation to a responsible employee of the client whose regular work does not involve the handling of, or accounting for, cash or receivables. The findings of this employee should be reviewed by the auditor who should obtain for his working paper file copies of any resulting correspondence with debtors. Many exceptions reported will ordinarily prove to be not discrepancies, but merely payments in transit or shipments not received at the confirmation date. Other exceptions reported, probably small in individual amounts, will result from disputes over allowances, discounts, shipping charges, or returned merchandise.

If the exceptions reported are significant in amount or numerous, the auditor's investigation may reveal serious weaknesses in internal accounting control procedures, such as delay in recording debtors' remittances, or a breakdown in billing procedures or in adjusting debtors' claims. Then the auditor will have to decide what further auditing procedures will be necessary to satisfy himself as to the fairness of the amounts at which the receivable balances are stated as at the balance sheet date.

Procedures in Lieu of Confirmation.—When replies to confirmation requests cannot reasonably be expected, as from government agencies, foreign concerns, and chain stores, or when the number and character of replies to positive confirmation requests are not satisfactory, the auditor should attempt to satisfy himself as to the receivable balances by other means.

When internal accounting control and internal check are reasonably good, procedures in lieu of confirmation include the examination of cash receipts and other records of subsequent payments, bank advices, shipping records, sales contracts, correspondence, and other documentary evidence. The examination of remittances and remittance advices as they are received appears to be the best alternative to confirmation, but if this procedure is not feasible, the comparison of remittance advices with recorded cash receipts should be a satisfactory method. Test comparisons should be made of the component items of deposits with the corresponding items of recorded cash receipts to determine whether they are identical.

When internal check is weak, it may be necessary to control incoming receipts for the period immediately after the balance sheet date until the receivables at that date have been substantially collected. Such control would include tracing the related credits to the detail accounts receivable records. The auditor should investigate any apparently past due or slow accounts.

Collectibility.—The collectibility of receivable balances should be reviewed to determine the amounts of allowances which appear reasonable to cover losses which have occurred, or are expected to occur, rebates which may have to be made, and cash or other discounts which can be expected to be taken by debtors in the settlement of their accounts. Receivable balances should be carried at their net estimated realizable amount. The auditor should satisfy himself not only that the gross amount is fairly stated, but also that proper reductions have been made by allowances. Approvals should be examined for notes and accounts receivable written off during the year.

The auditor should examine transactions affecting receivables subsequent to the balance sheet date, such as cash receipts, discounts allowed, rebates, returns, and write-offs, as these transactions or their absence may reveal abnormal conditions of collectibility at the balance sheet date. What occurs after the close of the fiscal period is the best proof of whether the receivable balances are actually what they purport to be.

Notes and acceptances receivable, past due or current, may themselves be indicative of doubtful collectibility when it is not the trade custom to take notes, when they have been taken for overdue accounts receivable, or when they represent renewals of matured notes or acceptances. If it is usual to obtain notes or acceptances from debtors of high credit standing, the collectibility of the notes should be considered the same as that of other receivables. The collectibility of notes against which collateral has been pledged may depend on the value of the collateral.

Receivable balances, especially those with items past due, should be reviewed with the credit manager to obtain information on which to base an opinion as to their collectibility. Files of correspondence with collection agents and debtors should also be examined, especially if explanations by the credit manager are unsatisfactory. Information required by the auditor for review with the credit manager can be obtained from aged trial balances or by scanning individual ledger accounts for items which appear to be overdue. If the volume of accounts is large and transactions are numerous, it is usually not practical for the auditor to scan the individual accounts except on a test basis. At least a partial aging of accounts can be made as a supplement to test-scanning.

If it is not the client's practice to age accounts receivable periodically, he may be requested to prepare an aged trial balance for purposes of the examination. When there are many accounts, a representative portion of them may be aged and the results regarded as typical of all the accounts. Aged trial balances prepared by the client should be test-checked by the auditor to the ledger detail.

Whether all or only a portion of the accounts are aged, the results obtained, to be of value, must be reviewed with due consideration of the client's policies and its past experience with respect to credit losses.

The following suggestions will be found useful for the auditor's study of aged trial balance data or review of individual accounts receivable:

1. If the terms of credit have been ignored habitually, the debtor's credit may be perfectly good, but the account should have special attention of the credit manager.

2. If payments are being made on account, but the balance is increasing, the time may be approaching when all payments will stop. An account of this sort deserves more attention than it generally receives. Salesmen relinquish accounts reluctantly, and they are not the best authorities on the ability of debtors to pay.

3. An old item in a running account or a bill partly paid, followed by others fully paid, may indicate an amount in dispute on which an allowance may have to be made. Also, it is possible that the item is open because the amount received in payment has been misappropriated. If the amount is substantial, or if the explanation

is not satisfactory, the auditor should examine correspondence or other data in support of the explanation offered.

4. If credit has been stopped and there have been no recent collections, the account may have been placed with attorneys for collection. If so, it is well to ask for the correspondence. If accounts are neglected, the debtors will not pay. So long as their money lasts, or so long as they desire to maintain their credit, debtors pay those who press them hardest.

5. If a debtor who has formerly paid cash begins to give notes, the auditor should determine whether sound reasons have been offered and that the change has been approved by someone in authority.

6. Many concerns assign old outstanding accounts to agencies for collection on a percentage-of-recovery basis. If this is the practice, the auditor may obtain information, by correspondence with the agency, of amounts collected, of accounts found worthless, and of the face amount and estimated realizable amount of those still held for collection.

7. The auditor should determine whether receivables from employees are permitted to run past payday without some collection, and should particularly inquire into amounts due from persons who have left the client's employ.

Receivables from affiliates, directors, officers, and employees should be reviewed to determine that they have been properly authorized and are actually what they purport to be. If they represent advances or loans, they should be segregated and described as such. It is good practice to review such receivable accounts even though they appear to have been settled before the balance sheet date. If there is any doubt as to the affiliate's or individual's resources, the auditor should look at transactions affecting these accounts after the end of the fiscal period to see if the advance or loan is again made. Past practice, when loans have been made over a long period of time, often throws light on the good faith of the apparent liquidation of a loan. The client should not feel that the disclosure of receivables from affiliates, directors, officers, and employees reflects on the integrity of these debtors. If the client objects to their disclosure, the auditor must decide whether further investigation of these receivables is necessary.

Time of Examination.—Whether the examination of receivable balances can be made as at a date prior to the date of the balance sheet will depend largely on the apparent effectiveness of internal accounting control and internal check procedures. Seasonal or other factors affecting the nature, number, and size of receivable balances as between the two dates should also be considered. When internal accounting control and internal check are satisfactory, the examination of receivable balances as at a date other than that of the balance sheet should prove advantageous not only to the auditor but also to the client, who thereby may reduce the volume of clerical work otherwise necessary immediately after the close of the fiscal period. In addition, more time is available both for the auditor and for the client to investigate any differences disclosed by the examination.

Many concerns having a large volume of accounts, such as utilities and department stores, have adopted the "cycle billing plan" in order to spread the work of posting, collecting, billing, and reviewing the accounts. Under this plan, the accounts are divided, usually alphabetically, into groups. Each group is billed on a different day of the month. Accounts receivable at the end of any month represent a composite of charges as billed on the various cycle dates during the month, if still unpaid, plus net charges accumulated subsequent to the various cycle dates. As a result, confirmation of the various groups is necessarily made as at the respective billing dates, and group totals are reconciled with month-end controlling account balances. In such businesses where the volume of operations is large and the receivables are homogeneous, receivables may be examined well in advance of the balance sheet date. That is to say, confirmation requests may be mailed; trial balances and aging schedules may be checked; and collectibility of the accounts may be reviewed as at the advanced date. The results of this interim examination, together with a general review of intervening transactions, should afford a reasonable basis for the auditor's opinion as at the balance sheet date.

A common procedure in the examination of receivables is to mail confirmation requests and reconcile subsidiary ledgers to general ledger control accounts at the advanced date and to review collectibility of the accounts and make appropriate test checks as at the balance sheet date.

Coordination of Examination with That of Related Accounts.— Other items appearing on the balance sheet or statement of income often substantiated, at least in part, concurrently with the examination of receivable balances include:

Notes and accounts receivable discounted
Contingent liabilities
Sales
Discounts
Provision for returns and allowances
Provision for doubtful accounts
Interest income
Payroll deductions.

Conversely, the auditor's examination of the above items may disclose certain receivables of which he might not otherwise be aware.

The auditor should consider the reasonableness of receivable balances in the light of the ratio of these balances to related items in the financial statements. If a client's statements have been examined for several years, the comparison of ratios developed in the current engagement with those of prior years may quickly put the auditor on notice that all is not as it should be. One such ratio is that of trade receivable balances at the balance sheet date to net sales on credit for the period; this may be expressed as the number of weeks' or months' net sales on credit represented by the balance of trade accounts receivable at the balance sheet date.

Written Representations by Client.—Occasionally the auditor may desire to obtain written representations from the client as to accounts receivable, similar in nature to those for inventories and liabilities. The major items which such written representations may cover are listed in "Codification of Statements on Auditing Procedure," issued in 1951 by the Committee on Auditing Procedure.

STATEMENT PRESENTATION

Statement presentation of receivables involves consideration of description, classification, and segregation. The minimum requirement is adequate and informative disclosure of the nature of the receivables and bases of the related allowances.

Description.—If only the term "accounts receivable" or "receivables" appears on the balance sheet among the current assets, the reader is justified in assuming that the amount so described is collectible from trade debtors (customers) of the company within the period customary for the trade or industry.

Separate description and identification may be appropriate for various kinds of trade receivables, such as notes and acceptances, instalment accounts, accounts pledged as collateral, accounts past due, and notes discounted.

Receivables from customers may be captioned in accordance with terminology customary in a particular trade or business; thus, the term premiums receivable may be used by insurance companies, rentals receivable by real estate owners, or commissions receivable by commission houses. Receivables should be described usually as "receivable from customers" rather than "due from customers" because at the balance sheet date open balances may be due, not yet due, or past due. If it is desirable to segregate unsecured notes from those against which collateral is held, the careless usage of the word "secured" should be avoided. Its use may be understood to mean that the collateral can be converted within a reasonable time into cash sufficient to satisfy the note. This may not be true. A so-called "secured" note may be worth no more than the realizable value of its collateral.

Whenever the amounts are significant there should be separate description and identification of certain trade and nontrade receivables, such as:

Amounts receivable from affiliated and subsidiary companies;
Receivables arising from sales to employees;
Amounts receivable from officers, directors, and stockholders;
Amounts receivable from transactions outside the ordinary course of the business;
Deposits, advances, interest, amounts recoverable for returned purchases, and claims;
Receivables from U. S. Government;
Unbilled amounts under cost-plus-fixed-fee contracts; and
Amounts receivable as a result of terminated contracts.

When various receivables from other than trade debtors are not sufficiently significant to be stated separately they may be grouped in one figure described as "Accounts Receivable Other," or under a similar caption.

Classification and Segregation.—Receivables arising from ordinary transactions of the business, which reasonably may be expected to be collected during the normal operating cycle, are classified on the balance sheet with current assets, usually immediately after cash or marketable securities, if any. Chapter 3, Section A, of Accounting Research Bulletin No. 43 sets forth certain principles governing the classification of assets and liabilities as current or noncurrent. It states in part:

A one-year time period is to be used as a basis for the segregation of current assets in cases where there are several operating cycles occurring within a year. However, where the period of the operating cycle is more than twelve months, as in, for instance, the tobacco, distillery, and lumber businesses, the longer period should be used. Where a particular business has no clearly defined operating cycle, the one-year rule should govern.

If the normal operating cycle of the business extends beyond a period of one year because of long credit terms, such as for instalment receivables, it is proper to classify the receivables as current assets; but such classification of receivables maturing more than one year from the date of the balance sheet is not proper if inventories long in process are the sole reason for extension of the normal operating cycle beyond a period of one year.

The Securities and Exchange Commission also has a rule (Rule 3.13) in Regulation S-X relating to such classification. Text of that rule is as follows:

> Items classed as current assets shall be generally realizable within one year. However, generally recognized trade practices may be followed with respect to the inclusion of items such as instalment receivables or inventories long in process, provided an appropriate explanation of the circumstances is made and, if practicable, an estimate is given of the amount not realizable within one year.

For statements prepared in accordance with Regulation S-X of the Securities and Exchange Commission, notes receivable and accounts receivable are shown separately, and accounts receivable are segregated as trade accounts receivable and other accounts receivable. For general-purpose statements such segregations are not always made.

Notes and acceptances receivable arising in the ordinary course of business may be combined in one amount. They frequently are shown in combination with accounts receivable under a common designation, such as notes and accounts receivable. Significant amounts of trade instalment notes or receivables should be stated separately.

In considering the statement presentation of notes receivable, the custom of the business under review should be kept in mind, since in some businesses notes are given by concerns of the highest standing, whereas in others notes may be considered an indication of weakness. Demand notes are not necessarily current because of being payable on demand, and care should be taken in classifying them, especially when interest, if any, is not being collected currently. In addition, other notes, even though not due, may not be current if the debtor has had financial reverses making prompt payment of the note unlikely. Interest accrued on notes receivable may be included with the face amount of the notes provided the caption so indicates.

Many contracts include a clause requiring the customer to make payments as the work progresses, permitting him to withhold a percentage of the total amount until the contract is completed and the product accepted. The portion of the contract price represented by the withheld percentage may not be readily collectible by the seller, even during the normal operating cycle of the business. The circumstances of each such account of material amount should be investigated to determine whether withheld percentages may be included as current assets.

Receivables from subsidiaries and affiliates, if significant in amount, should be stated separately. Collection of these accounts before the balance sheet is released does not justify deviation from this practice, for the reader of the statements should be informed of these amounts as at the balance sheet date. Whether receivables from subsidiaries and affiliates are current or noncurrent depends largely on the expectation of realizing them in cash. Even though arising from ordinary business transactions and even though the debtor company is financially sound, in effect they may be long-term advances.

Receivables from employees arising in the ordinary course of business are sometimes stated separately on the balance sheet, although opinions differ as to the necessity for this segregation. It is contended that employees are customers, even though they are granted special discounts, and that collection of their accounts often can be made more readily than of accounts of other customers. Unless receivables from employees represent a substantial portion of the total receivables from trade debtors, or unless special circumstances require disclosure, there seems to be little reason for segregating them.

Receivables from directors, officers, and principal stockholders, if significant in amount, whether arising in the ordinary course of business or whether collected subsequent to the balance sheet date, should be stated separately on the balance sheet. The distinction between these receivables and trade receivables rests on the possibility that the relations between debtor and creditor are such that affiliation or self-interest will influence prompt and full collection.

Credit balances in accounts receivable, if material in amount, should be classified as liabilities unless they can properly be offset against debit balances. Often they represent advances to be applied against unbilled orders and are in the nature of accounts payable. If significant in amount, they should appear among the liabilities, grouped separately as customers' credits. Similarly, debit balances in accounts payable that are not direct offsets to credit balances should be segregated for classification in the balance sheet as accounts receivable.

Receivables arising from transactions other than sales in the ordinary course of business may include advances to salesmen and others, loans to officers, claims against railroads, creditors, or some branch of the government. Not infrequently they include considerable amounts rarely settled in cash and representing charges to vendors for goods returned to them. Often deferred charges to operations, such as rents paid in advance and similar items, are included under the caption "Accounts Receivable" although in no sense of the word is this proper. Claims for tax refunds resulting from carry-back provisions of the Internal Revenue Code should be shown as current assets when collection is reasonably assured within the normal operating cycle of the business.

Receivables arising from subscriptions to capital stock should be stated separately since they are unlike other types of receivables. Some objections have been raised to showing subscriptions receivable as an asset, but, if the debtors are financially responsible and the amounts are apparently collectible, they represent a realizable asset. If, however, they are overdue and doubtful of collection; if there is no intention that they be called; if they are to be collected only out of dividends earned on the stock; or if there is any other contingency with respect to their collection, they may be treated as a deduction from capital stock subscribed in the capital section of the balance sheet.

Cash deposited as security when making bids for public work, to assure the faithful performance of contracts, for goods ordered in advance, or with public utility companies properly may be included in current assets if they are known to be repayable within the normal operating cycle of the business. Deposits made to secure options for the purchase of real estate or plant are not current assets, since generally the deposit becomes a part of the cost of purchase of a fixed asset or is forfeited if the transaction is not consummated. A cash deposit required by terms of a lease may be returnable, but the date of realization may be uncertain and often the company cannot depend upon the deposit as a fund available for purposes other than the special one for which it is made. A landlord holding a cash deposit as security under a lease may require the same or a larger amount upon renewal, or, if there is no renewal, the landlord may hold the deposit for several years, pending settlement of a claim for damages to the premises.

Receivables under cost-plus-fixed-fee contracts usually consist of items billed and costs accumulated but not yet billed. Since there is a difference in character between billed items and unbilled costs, distinction should be made between them on the balance sheet if the amounts involved are material. Advances received on CPFF contracts or progress payments received under other type contracts may be offset against the receivable when there is good reason to believe that the advances will be applied in payment of those receivables. The amount of the offset should be clearly disclosed. If the advance is considered to be equivalent to a revolving fund to be liquidated near the completion of the contract, it should be shown as a liability. Progress payments received as a result of expenditures made for inventory may be shown as a deduction from inventory, particularly when they create a lien against such inventory.

Claims under terminated contracts are usually classified with current assets, unless disagreements or other conditions indicate the possibility of an extended delay in collection. Termination claims of material amount should be separately captioned. Partial payments received against the claim should be deducted from the receivable; termination loans, on the other hand, represent liabilities to third parties, and should be classified with liabilities, with appropriate cross-references.

Receivables Pledged, Sold, or Discounted.—If receivables are pledged against loans, the amount pledged should be indicated in the description of the receivables and also in the description of the loan liability.

If receivables are sold under a guaranty of repurchase by the seller, any portion of the net proceeds withheld by the buyer should be shown as a receivable by the seller. The contingent liability associated with the guaranty of repurchase should be indicated in the balance sheet.

The total amount of receivables discounted may be shown among the assets of the balance sheet with a contra liability, which thereby discloses the contingent liability related to the items discounted. Other methods of presentation include indicating the contingent liability in a footnote to the balance sheet, or deducting the discounted items from the aggregate receivables leaving a net amount representing receivables not under discount.

When discounted items have been paid by the debtors after the balance sheet date, but before the financial statements have been released, it sometimes has been urged that there is no necessity to indicate the existence of discounted receivables as of the balance sheet date. The authors believe that the information about discounted receivables may be of significance to readers of the balance sheet. There is no objection to including on the balance sheet a notation that the discounted items were paid at maturity.

Sometimes loans are obtained by discounting bank acceptances which have been issued against pledge of customers' notes or acceptances; such transactions generally develop from sales in foreign countries. The company's foreign representative obtains a bank acceptance and deposits, as collateral, the notes received from customers. The company in turn discounts the acceptance. The face amount of the collateral will generally exceed the face amount of the acceptances. Collection of the customers' paper usually occurs before the bank acceptance becomes due. Opinions differ as to whether the amount of the unmatured bank acceptances discounted should be shown as a liability or as a deduction from the assets. The following summary illustrates a method of stating the transaction on the asset side of the balance sheet and sets forth the facts:

Customers' notes and acceptances assigned to bank:

Unmatured	$110,000.00
Already collected and proceeds held	100,000.00
	210,000.00
Less bank acceptances issued against above and discounted, but not yet due	200,000.00
Equity	$ 10,000.00

Allowances Deducted from Receivables.—Allowance for doubtful receivables should be deducted from the related asset, the asset being shown on the balance sheet either gross less the allowance, or net, preferably with the amount of the allowance indicated in the caption heading. If the asset is shown net, the fact that an allowance has been deducted should be indicated even if the amount of the allowance is not disclosed. It is not considered necessary to disclose the amounts of individual allowances if a combined allowance for doubtful notes and accounts receivable is deducted from the sum of the related asset amounts. Other allowances, such as those for cash discounts, collection costs, or decrease of profit because of expected returns of merchandise, should be shown similarly, and they may be combined in one amount with the allowance for doubtful receivables, provided this is indicated in the caption. Carrying or interest charges on instalment accounts receivable that have been deferred as unearned at the balance sheet date should be classified in the balance sheet as a deduction from the receivables, either directly from the instalment accounts or from the sum of the receivables as part of the total allowances.

CHAPTER 11

INVENTORIES

ACCOUNTING PRINCIPLES

Components of Inventories.—Inventories usually include only items of tangible personal property which will be sold or will enter into the production of items to be sold currently in the ordinary course of business. Inventories generally consist of finished stock (goods awaiting sale), work in process (goods being produced), and raw materials and supplies (goods which are to enter directly or indirectly into the production of finished goods).

The question of inventory inclusions and exclusions can usually be decided without difficulty on the basis of the above definition. Obviously, the nature of the business determines the designation of an item as inventory; for example, real estate held for sale might well be inventory to a real estate dealer or a building contractor, but would rarely be inventory to a manufacturer. Manufacturing and maintenance supplies are properly includible in inventory, as are spare parts for machinery which are chargeable to expense when used. In certain manufacturing businesses, the dividing line between inventories and short-lived plant equipment is very fine; although expenditures for tooling represent productive facilities, they may be consumed or become obsolete in a short time. In practice, assets of this nature may also be included in fixed assets or deferred charges. Supplies which are ultimately chargeable to selling, general, and administrative expenses, if inventoried at all, are classified preferably as deferred charges.

Public utility companies usually are engaged in continuous programs of construction and maintenance and the same inventory items are frequently used for both purposes. While the classification of the construction portion as a current inventory item may appear to be a violation of the principle set forth above, segregation is usually not feasible and probably not essential for the average public utility, and the only practical solution is disclosure. Certain manufacturing companies may have a similar problem.

The term "current" means a period of one year or the normal inventory turnover period (the average period of time between the acquisition of inventories and their sale in the ordinary course of business), whichever is greater. Thus, the accumulation of a substantial inventory of items in quantities greater than can be sold within one year, when the inventory turnover period is one year or less, ordinarily calls for segregation of a portion as a noncurrent asset. It should be borne in mind, however, that almost every inventory contains items or groups of items which have a slower turnover period than the inventory as a whole and, if not impaired in value, they may be considered to be a current asset. Spare parts or special sizes are frequently made up in quantities sufficient for several years' sales in order to achieve manufacturing economies; sometimes these inventories are valued under formulae which reflect probable realization.

Thus, in considering an inventory when the indications are that a portion will not be sold within a reasonable period of time, the accountant is primarily concerned with determining whether the slow-moving portion is properly valued; mere segregation of slow-moving inventory is not always adequate treatment.

CONSIDERATIONS OF TITLE.—Legal title to inventories, as to other assets on the balance sheet, may be the line of demarcation followed in determining the inclusion of specific items. This rule should not be followed blindly; it has its limitations as a satisfactory basis for settling doubtful cases and, under certain circumstances, may be disregarded. Customarily, purchases in transit are included in inventory and sales in transit are excluded, regardless of the status of title, although purchases in transit shipped f.o.b. the purchaser's plant may properly be excluded from inventory. For accounting purposes, the intent of the parties generally should govern, provided the treatment is consistent.

Following are examples of items that should be included in inventories, following the rule of legal title:

Goods in transit (shipped f.o.b. the vendor's shipping point on or prior to the balance sheet date) should be in the purchaser's inventory.

Consignments out (in the hands of the consignee) should be in the consignor's inventory.

Bailments (in the hands of the bailee) should be in the bailor's inventory.

Goods out on approval (in the hands of the prospective customer) should be in the seller's inventory.

Protective title to C.O.D. and certain types of export shipments remains with the seller until payment is made; the seller of goods on the instalment basis may also retain protective title. Shipments under these arrangements are customarily accounted for as sales by the seller before payment is made and title passes. The important consideration is not one of title, but whether the receivable is collectible.

Inventories Under Government Contracts.—Accumulated costs (inventories) under cost-plus-fixed-fee (CPFF) contracts are generally not included in inventories but in receivables, since the right to bill usually arises as soon as expenditures are made.

Fixed-price contracts with the government may provide for partial payments in advance of delivery, varying in amount up to 90 per cent of inventory costs accumulated under the contracts. Such contracts usually contain a clause stating that title to all inventory upon which partial payments have been made vests in the government. Under these circumstances, the inventory usually is stated in the balance sheet after deducting the amount of the partial payments, even though sales and cost of sales under the contract are not recorded until delivery. The partial payments are generally cleared by applying them against invoices submitted for completed products or billable services.

Progress Billings and Advances.—Sales are usually recorded and inventories relieved upon shipment of goods or passage of title to a customer. However, under long-term contracts, it is customary to bill the customer as the work progresses, under contract provisions which may call for the right of inspection or for architect's certificates; the contractor usually has performed all that he is required to perform to be entitled to the progress payment. Under these circumstances, when progress billings are made, it is accepted practice to record sales and relieve inventories if the company is on the percentage of completion basis, or to apply such progress payments as a reduction of inventories if it is on a completed contract basis.

If advance payments by customers represent primarily a loan or a deposit, it may be preferable to treat the advance payments as liabilities rather than as a reduction of inventories.

Valuation of Inventories.—The basic reasons for carrying an inventory in the accounts are to reflect properly the existence of an asset at the balance sheet date and to match appropriate costs of current and subsequent periods against revenues of such periods to determine realized income. At the balance sheet date, the amount assigned to inventory is the unallocated balance of costs applicable to goods still on hand, which will be charged against revenues of future periods.

LOWER OF COST OR MARKET, THE GENERAL RULE.—Accounting Research Bulletin No. 43, Chapter 4, states "the primary basis of accounting for inventories is cost . . ." but "a departure from the cost basis of pricing the inventory is required when the utility of the goods is no longer as great as its cost." The bulletin in continuing states that recognition of diminution in utility of goods in the inventory is accomplished by writing down such goods to market. The objective of properly matching costs against revenues to determine realized income for a period is ordinarily attained when the inventories at the beginning and end of the period are priced at cost. However, this result is attained only if the utility of the inventory items has not diminished since their acquisition. When loss of utility has occurred through damage, deterioration, obsolescence, changes in price levels or for other reasons, the amount of loss is chargeable to the revenues of the period in which it occurred. Measurement of such loss and its allocation to proper periods are accomplished by the application of the rule of pricing inventories at cost or market, whichever is lower, so that inventory items are carried forward at amounts not in excess of their useful value.

DETERMINATION OF COST.—In general, cost represents the direct and indirect expenditures for items purchased, produced, or in the course of production. The amounts at which items still on hand were carried in previous inventories are also considered to be cost. However, there are various methods of determining (1) what outlays are considered to represent cost of items purchased or produced, (2) the portion of cost that initially should be applied to inventories, and (3) the relationship between the cost of inventories and their movement under circumstances in which the identity of individual items is lost or disregarded. Depending upon the methods chosen and the trend of prices, the effects may vary widely under otherwise identical circumstances.

Cost of Purchases.—The cost of purchased articles is generally understood to be the purchase price plus transportation charges incurred for delivery to the purchaser. In addition, other costs, such as import duties, insurance, warehousing, and handling costs, may be proper additions to purchase price. All discounts except cash discounts should be deducted from the invoice price, since they represent nothing more than a mechanical device for arriving at the purchase price; similarly, rebates, such as those for quantity purchases, should be deducted. Cash discounts of 2 per cent or less are usually reflected in income as a credit to cost of sales or other income. They also may be applied properly as a reduction of inventory costs; if so treated, they reduce cost of sales in the statement of income when the inventory is sold.

The entire inventory of mercantile enterprises normally consists of purchased items. The problem of determining cost for inventory purposes may be a relatively simple one, based on records of the cost of items purchased and sold, or it may be more complex when based on the retail method discussed later.

Cost of Production.—As opposed to mercantile companies, manufacturers not only must account for purchased materials cost but also must determine the cost of finished and semifinished products including material, labor, and a reasonable allocation of manufacturing overhead. Because of the complexities of modern manufacturing processes, which frequently convert raw materials into products of a radically different nature or appearance, determination of cost requires an adequate but not necessarily a complicated cost system.

Material costs consist of the costs of purchased materials used and may include indirect expenses or minor materials which often are accounted for as overhead. Labor may consist only of the wages of employees directly engaged in production, or it also may include wages of certain indirect and supervisory personnel which alternatively may be accounted for as overhead. Material and labor costs are commonly recorded in direct association with items or groups of items produced.

Overhead represents those costs which are difficult or impracticable to associate directly with units of production. It usually includes indirect labor (wages of supervisory production personnel and of factory administrative personnel), indirect materials (supplies and other small items not usually accounted for individually), depreciation, normal scrap, maintenance, light, heat and power, certain taxes, and a host of various expenses of running a factory. Production engineering is commonly included in overhead, while engineering of an experimental nature may or may not be included. Production overhead should not include selling expenses, interest, general and administrative, or any other expenses that do not relate to production. Frequently items of overhead which vary with production, such as indirect labor and materials, social security taxes, vacation pay and pension costs, and power, are classified as variable overhead, and others, such as rent, insurance, and real estate taxes, are classified as fixed overhead. Overhead may be applied to unit cost of items of production in a number of ways, ranging from a simple percentage of direct labor to more complicated methods.

Methods of Finding Inventory Cost.—Practically every business enterprise maintains some records of its costs. It is recognized as a principle of good internal accounting control, as discussed later in this chapter, that a cost system adequate for the needs of the business should be maintained. Costs are usually determined by items or groups of items as they progress through the plant; they may be charged directly to the product or charged initially to departments or processes and redistributed.

1. *Actual cost.*—Actual cost systems fully absorb all production costs incurred and apply to inventory the allocable portion thereof. Since under this method, costs are not determinable until production has been

completed, it may be necessary to resort to estimates and to prior performance records to determine costs at intermediate stages of production. For example, if the period of process is long and complicated, it is difficult to relate the physical inventory to cost under an actual cost system, having only a record of charges and credits to a particular lot in process. For inventory cost purposes under such circumstances, costs by stages of completion have to be developed from historical or estimated analyses or from underlying job or process cost records. Overhead must be studied to develop a proper application to the inventory, although frequently in actual cost systems a standard or fixed rate of overhead is used.

2. *Standard cost.*—Under a standard cost system, costs are predetermined or estimated in advance of production. Standard material costs are usually computed from actual consumption data or from bills of material, standard labor costs from actual production records or from time studies, and standard overhead costs from estimated and actual overhead expenses applied to operations at normal capacity, all usually based on prices and wage rates current at the time the standards are set. Differences between actual and standard costs are usually accumulated in separate variance accounts.

For the purpose of inventory valuation, standard costs may be readily converted to actual cost by adding or subtracting the applicable variances. Customarily, the application of the variances is made on the basis of their percentage relationships to groups of items or to the inventory as a whole. The variances should be studied carefully to determine the percentage to be used in adjusting the standards; it may be appropriate to adjust standard costs for variances developed in the period in which the inventory was produced, or it may be preferable to adjust standard costs for variances developed over a more extended period.

On the other hand, if standard costs are realistically determined, they may be deemed to represent useful costs properly carried forward to the subsequent period and thus a proper basis for inventory cost. If the variances do not represent (1) differences between actual wage rates or actual material prices and the standards, or (2) differences between actual normal operations performed or actual normal usage of materials and the standards, it may be decided that unfavorable variances (debits) reflect inefficiencies or abnormalities of one kind or another which should be charged off rather than added to inventory cost. The criteria for realistic standards reflecting normal operations should not be theoretical goals, possibly never realizable; they should represent performance which may reasonably and practicably be attained under operating conditions expected to prevail during the ensuing period. Favorable variations (credits) representing the excess of standard over actual cost, if material, should be applied as a reduction of standard costs insofar as they relate to the inventory. The proper use of standard costs is a progressive and desirable method of determining cost for inventory purposes; it well exemplifies the principle of carrying forward only the useful cost of an inventory and may be helpful in determination of reproduction cost.

3. *The retail method.*—As the name implies, this method is used by retailers and others who maintain their inventories at resale prices; it represents essentially a method of book control of departmental merchandise stocks at their retail price amounts. The cost of the ending inventory is determined as follows:

1. To opening inventory, at cost and at retail, are added purchases at cost, including transportation, and at retail.
2. Markups are added to purchases at retail only, but markdowns are not deducted from purchases.
3. The difference between the total cost and the total retail above is known as the cumulative mark-on; the percentage of cumulative mark-on to total retail is then determined.
4. Ending inventory at retail is determined by deducting sales and markdowns from the aggregate of opening inventory and purchases at retail.
5. Ending inventory at retail is then reduced by the percentage of cumulative mark-on; the result is the amount of ending inventory.

Proper operation of this method results in inventories closely approximating the lower of cost or market since the percentage of cumulative mark-on is determined from the original marked retail plus markups, and is applied to retail after markdowns.

It is customary in retail merchandise accounting to make provision for shortages which will inevitably exist. This provision is usually based on a percentage of sales, and is deducted from the inventory at retail. When shortages are revealed by physical inventory, the provision is adjusted to the amount of the actual shortages.

The retail method does not take into consideration anticipated markdowns; markdowns are reflected in inventory only as they are actually given effect in lowered prices offered to the public. Since seldom, if ever, will all goods be sold at the marked price, some accountants propose that an additional reduction of the inventory should be made by means of a reserve to provide for expected later markdowns. Unless such reserves result in the proper application of the lower of cost or market rule, they are not considered to represent good practice; they are not presently recognized by the Treasury as an allowable deduction for tax purposes under any circumstances.

4. *Common products and by-products.*—Many manufacturing processes obtain more than one product from the same material, particularly in the chemical, oil, lumber, packing, leather, and canning industries. There are two acceptable methods of allocating cost in such instances: (1) on the basis of the relative values of the products obtained, and (2) on the basis of the relative estimated identifiable costs, with common costs spread on the basis of value of products obtained. The first method is more common and is an acceptable method of determining cost for inventory purposes, but it may not always produce realistic actual costs of each of the common products; this method should not be used to equalize profits on different items in a line of merchandise. To do so might produce erroneous information not only as to the relative profitability of various items in the line, but also as to the valuation of inventory and the results of operations.

When by-products do not represent more than a small part of the total production, the so-called "by-product" method of costing is practicable and reasonable. Under this method, no part of cost is allocated to by-products; they are valued immediately on production at net selling price, and the over-all product cost is correspondingly reduced. This reduced over-all cost is then allocated to the primary product or products.

5. *Overhead methods.*—In practice there is considerable variation in the application of overhead to inventories. On the one hand, it is generally accepted that all overhead should not be charged off as incurred, and on the other, rarely should all items of overhead be applied to inventories.

As stated previously, overhead may include all the indirect expenses which are necessary for production, but should exclude all selling expenses and any general and administrative expenses not related to production. In the application of overhead under an actual cost system, studies should be made to determine abnormal or unusual items, as well as those which do not relate to production, and to establish the relationship of operations during the period in which the inventory was produced to the normal level of operations. For example, abnormal scrap, unusually large repairs, or production at 50 per cent of capacity would usually require adjustment in the application of overhead to inventory.

Many enterprises, no matter what the type of cost system in use, adopt standard rates of overhead which are periodically revised. These rates are commonly applied to direct labor dollars or hours, machine hours, or some other acceptable basis for absorption, and are usually computed on the basis of normal operations of the plant. Usually such standard rates are preferable to redeterminations of actual rates which, over short periods of time, may fluctuate radically and abnormally. Overabsorbed overhead should be applied ratably as a reduction of inventory and cost of sales, while underabsorbed overhead is usually charged off unless there is some good reason for its application to inventories.

Under the direct cost method of applying overhead, only such overhead items as vary with production are applied to inventories; fixed overhead items are charged off as incurred. The advocates of this method claim that it results in more useful information to management since the income account on its face discloses the gross margin available for absorption of all fixed expenses and more clearly sets forth price, cost, and volume relationships.

The proponents of the direct cost method also claim as theoretical soundness for the method, the broad concept that those costs and expenses which are measured by time should be recognized in the income account in the period in which they are incurred, while only those costs and expenses which are directly associated with output should be deferred and matched against future sales revenue. This concept has been extended to include fixed manufacturing expenses which continue regardless of output; since they are deemed to be measured by time, they are charged to expense in the period in which they are incurred.

It appears that extension of this general concept as theoretical support of the direct cost method is unwarranted. Whether or not manufacturing costs and expenses should be applied to the income of the period in which incurred depends upon not whether such cost is fixed during the period irrespective of business activity but, rather, whether by its nature it must be absorbed by the income of that period because it represents either (1) expenditures from which only the current period is deemed to benefit in measurable degree or (2) a loss which is "over the dam." In the first category fall most of the selling, general, and administrative expenses; in the second, such factory costs as maintenance of idle plant, excessive labor costs such as those due to inefficiencies, breakdown, and green help, excessive waste and spoilage, strike costs, and inventory shrinkage. It does not seem logical to say that superintendents' salaries, depreciation, and factory office supplies, being fixed expenses, do not attach to the product but that floor sweepers' wages, machine repairs, and cutting oil, being variable expenses, do attach to the product.

For interim reports to management direct costing of inventory for certain types of industry or situation may have merit; the authors do not purport to discuss in this book the pros and cons of direct costing for this purpose. As indicated in Chapter 24, many accounting firms maintain departments which are equipped to aid management in developing such reports which will be most useful to them. For purposes of inventory valuation to be included in annual or other published statements, however, the authors believe that there is a presumption against the exclusion of reasonably determined overhead costs, and that when such costs are eliminated from interim internal statements, they should preferably be restored to inventory included in annual or published financial statements.

6. *Intracompany and intercompany profits in inventory.*—The element of unrealized intracompany or intercompany profits should be eliminated in the preparation of combined or consolidated financial statements. Such elimination of intracompany unrealized profits is sometimes accomplished by means of allowances established in the accounts of the selling branch or division; elimination of intercompany profits in inventory is discussed in Chapter 21. Products are sometimes sold to an unconsolidated subsidiary, often a foreign subsidiary, at prices above cost. The authors believe that the parent company should not report profits on such sales; since the subsidiary's inventory is not consolidated with that of the parent, such profits are usually eliminated by the establishment of an allowance on the parent company's books.

Methods of Relating Inventory Cost to Inventory Movement.—The purchase or production cost is frequently not the same for identical items in the inventory, and may be subject to constant change. It is usually not feasible or desirable to maintain in the accounts identification of the various items and their cost. Some method must be devised for relating cost to the movement of inventory through production and into cost of sales. Except when specific identification is possible, these methods may be said to involve different assumptions as to the flow of inventories which may or may not coincide with the physical flow of the inventories. Depending upon the method and upon changes in price levels, they may have widely different results.

1. *Specific identification.*—When custom or contract work is involved, there may be a direct relation between the physical identity of the product which the customer ultimately receives and the accounting

record thereof; in these instances it is desirable to use the method of specific identification. It is usually not good practice to attempt to maintain costs by specific identification in violation of the normal physical flow or when the identity of the various lots becomes lost because of commingling, as this may permit arbitrary selection of the lot with the most favorable cost.

2. *First-in, first-out.*—Accounting under the first-in, first-out (Fifo) method is based on the assumption that the goods first received or produced are the goods first used or sold; consequently, any inventory remaining on hand at the end of the period is priced at the latest cost of that quantity.

Although frequently the assumption of Fifo is in accordance with the actual flow of the inventories, the flow may be exactly the opposite; for example, bulky materials may be placed on a pile and the most recently received unit used first. When the turnover is rapid, it may make no particular difference whether Fifo, specific identification, or the average cost method is used, especially if averages are determined frequently.

3. *Average.*—The average cost of an inventory is determined by adding to quantities and costs of items in the opening inventory the purchases or production during a period, determining the average for each item or group of items and applying the average so developed to quantities in the inventory or to the quantities consumed or sold. Averages are usually determined monthly; more than one average may be used for identical items in different locations.

4. *Last-in, first-out.*—The basic theory underlying the Lifo method is that operations require maintenance of a certain minimum quantity of inventory at all times and that increases in the value of this basic inventory give rise to unrealized profit which should not be reflected in income. Accounting under the Lifo method further coincides with the assumption that current purchases are used for current sales, and that consequently the most recent purchases should be charged against the most recent sales; physical flow need not be in accord with this assumption.

The basic inventory is carried at the price at which it was originally acquired; the practical effect during a period of rising prices is to eliminate from inventory and charge to current income an amount approximately corresponding to what would otherwise be the increase in valuation of the basic inventory under most of the other methods of determining cost. Lifo is an accepted method; its use, however, may produce such markedly different results from the other methods that it is important that the reader of the financial statements understand its implications and effect.

There are several different methods of applying Lifo, among them being unit basis, dollar value, and retail Lifo.

a) Unit basis Lifo.—Under the unit method the inventory is segregated into natural groups or pools on the basis of similarity in type of goods, if purchased; or if manufactured, on the basis of similarity in factory processes through which they pass, in raw materials used, in style, in shape, or in use of finished product. Computations for each of these pools are made separately. The opening inventory for each pool for the year of adoption of Lifo is determined at cost, computed on the basis previously in use. All units contained in each pool are considered as having been acquired at the same time for the same price so that the unit price is obtained by dividing the inventory amount by the total number of units in the pool. The inventory valuation of units on hand at the end of the year, to the extent that the number of such units does not exceed the number on hand at the beginning of the year, is obtained by multiplying the number of such units by the average unit price at the beginning of the year. If the inventory at the end of the year is greater, the increment may be valued by one of the following methods: the actual cost of the goods purchased or produced during the year in the order of acquisition; the actual cost of the goods purchased or produced during the year in the reverse order of acquisition; or the average cost of the goods purchased or produced during the year.

Increments in inventory from year to year form successive "inventory layers." When inventory is decreased, the most recently added inventory layer is the first layer eliminated. This is in accordance with the theory that the last goods acquired are the first goods sold. If inventory is never reduced below the quantity on hand at the beginning of the year of Lifo adoption, the original unit cost prices remain frozen in inventory. Once inventory is liquidated and not replaced before the year end, the original cost is lost. Reacquisition is generally treated the same as any increase in inventory; contemplated reacquisition when there has been an involuntary liquidation is discussed later.

b) Dollar value Lifo.—The use of a natural physical unit of measurement is simple and desirable, but when a company manufactures or distributes a large variety of products which may change in character from year to year, the practical application of such method is impossible. The use of the dollar value of the inventory components (labor, material, overhead), rather than the physical units, as a yardstick for the measurement of changes in the inventory makes Lifo practical regardless of the complexity of the inventory.

Under dollar value Lifo, the valuation of the closing inventory of each pool at opening inventory prices is determined and compared with the valuation of the opening inventory to ascertain if there has been an increase or decrease in inventory. The valuation of the closing inventory at opening prices can be accomplished by repricing the entire inventory at such opening inventory prices or by converting the closing inventory at current prices to a closing inventory valued at opening prices through use of an index number developed from an inventory sample. A representative cross section of inventory is priced at both opening and closing prices and an index of change in price level is derived by dividing the valuation at closing prices by the valuation at opening prices. By applying this index number to the closing inventory valued at closing prices, the value of the closing inventory at opening prices can be computed.

If the closing inventory, stated at opening inventory prices, is less than the value of the opening inventory, the closing inventory so determined is the Lifo inventory. If there has been an increase in inventory, stated at opening inventory prices, the increment is restored to current prices by multiplying by an index number computed from (a) prices of first purchases during the year, (b) average prices during the year, or (c) prices of last purchases during the year, depending upon the method chosen for valuing the increment. The index number shows the upward or downward movement of (a), (b), or (c), above, as compared with prices at the beginning of the year. The increment, as adjusted by the index, is added to the opening Lifo inventory to determine the closing Lifo inventory. Computations for years after the year of election can be made with reference to the opening Lifo inventory of the year of election—the basic inventory—or through use of a cumulative index.

c) *Retail Lifo.*—The retail Lifo method is a dollar value method adopted for use in conjunction with the retail method of arriving at cost. For income tax purposes stores that do not qualify as department stores usually must compute the change-in-price-level index from their own data on prices and quantities. Retailers who qualify as department stores and specialty stores under certain circumstances may use published indices in place of self-computed indices. Under this method, an approved index number prepared by the Bureau of Labor Statistics is applied to departmental inventories, stated at retail, to arrive at the quantitative change in inventory. Increase or decrease in departmental inventories at the price level at the beginning of the year is thus computed. If there is an increase, it is recomputed at close-of-the-year prices by use of the index, and reduced to cost by a method similar to the retail method discussed above. The cost of the increase is then added to the Lifo inventory at the first of the year to obtain the Lifo valuation at the year's end.

d) Inventory pools under Lifo.—In any election of the Lifo method of inventory valuation, consideration must be given to the inventory pools to be used. Broad classifications permit the maintenance of substantially equivalent quantities of inventory on hand from year to year regardless of changes in quantity of various components of the inventory. Narrow classifications may lead to substantial liquidations of portions of the basic inventory despite increments in other portions and a consequent distortion of income. Broad classifications are generally more desirable because, with fewer categories of inventory, accounting work is simplified.

e) Provision for replacement of liquidated inventories.—Refund provisions of the Internal Revenue Code may be applicable to the excess replacement costs if inventories involuntarily liquidated in a taxable year ended prior to January 1, 1955, because of orders or directives of the federal government in connection with national preparedness, were replaced in a taxable year ended prior to January 1, 1956. It is good practice, whether or not allowable for tax purposes, to provide for the excess of current replacement costs of inventories which have been involuntarily liquidated over cost determined under Lifo, if the intention is to restore all or part of the quantities liquidated when materials become available. This practice produces results similar to those produced under the base stock method in that basic quantities are valued at basic prices. When making such provision, a company on the Lifo basis for federal income tax purposes should be sure that it is shown in its financial statements in such a way that it does not jeopardize the company's right to continue on the Lifo basis for federal income tax purposes.

f) Considerations on the adoption of Lifo.—Lifo has been adopted by many enterprises in which the price of basic raw materials determines the price of the finished product—such as processors of nonferrous metals, oil producers, and cotton textile manufacturers.

In recent years, many other companies have adopted Lifo because of the tax advantages to be gained when tax rates are high and costs are rising. Probably a great many more companies would have adopted it but for the requirement that inventories on this basis may not be written down to market for tax purposes should market ever be lower than cost on the Lifo basis. This requirement might more or less per-

manently deny a deduction for an inventory write-down that would
otherwise be allowable, and removes some of the incentive for the adoption of the Lifo method during a period of high prices. The use of Lifo
for tax purposes also requires that it be used in the taxpayer's annual
financial statements. Under the regulations, it is permissible to provide in the accounts an amount equal to any excess of Lifo inventories
over market, but as stated above, such a provision is not deductible for
tax purposes.

The tax considerations involved in changing to the Lifo method are
of utmost importance and should be studied carefully. Lifo should not
be adopted for purely theoretical reasons or solely for the sake of an
immediate tax saving.

5. *Other methods.*—The methods discussed above are generally accepted for the determination of inventory cost; in practice the public
accountant will sometimes encounter variants or combinations which
may or may not be substantially equivalent to the accepted methods.
One important consideration in weighing the acceptability of a method
is that it should eliminate discretionary charges or credits to income.
While the normal or base stock method, which has been in use for some
time in certain industries, closely resembles Lifo in certain respects, it
differs in others and is discussed later in this chapter.

DETERMINATION OF MARKET.—As stated previously in this chapter,
under the lower of cost or market rule inventories are carried forward at
amounts not in excess of cost, which may not exceed market. To determine market, first compare replacement or reproduction cost and net
realizable value, both of which are discussed below. If net realizable
value is the lower, that will be market. If replacement or reproduction
cost is the lower, that will represent market except that the inventory
should not be reduced below the point at which a normal profit may be
expected to be realized. "Normal profit" for this purpose is equivalent
to gross profit or gross margin. The following table illustrates the
application of the lower of cost or market rule:

	Illustration No.			
	1	2	3	4
Cost	$1.00*	$1.00	$1.00	$1.00
Replacement or reproduction cost	1.05	.98*	.99	.94
Net realizable value	1.25	1.15	.95*	1.20
Net realizable value less a normal profit	.99	.91	.75	.95*

* Represents the value to be used for inventory purposes.

Net realizable value and net realizable value less a normal profit were
determined as follows:

Selling price	$1.30	$1.20	$1.00	$1.25
Less cost of completion and disposal	.05	.05	.05	.05
Net realizable value	1.25	1.15	.95	1.20
Normal profit, less disposal costs deducted above	.26	.24	.20	.25
Net realizable value less normal profit	$ .99	$ .91	$ .75	$ .95

When net realizable value becomes the measure of market, it generally should not be further reduced by an allowance for an approximately normal profit margin. An illustration of an accepted departure is the use of the retail inventory method which carries forward marked-down items at an inventory price which, it is expected, will yield what may be called the normal margin of gross profit for that class of goods or that particular department. Other instances may be encountered in which it is good business and good accounting to write portions of an inventory down to a point that may yield an approximately normal margin of gross profit, even though replacement cost is not below actual cost. On the other hand, in some instances it may be unjustified to write down portions of an inventory below net realizable value, resulting merely in shifting profits from one period to the succeeding period.

In the application of the test of market it may be necessary to consider the course of prices after the balance sheet date in order to determine market at the balance sheet date. This does not mean, however, that losses which clearly belong in the subsequent period should be provided for.

Replacement or Reproduction Cost.—The term "replacement cost" is generally used in connection with items purchased, while reproduction cost is generally used in referring to the manufacture of a finished product. A retailer would replace his inventory. A manufacturer would replace his raw materials but would reproduce his finished product.

The term "replacement cost" contemplates buying in the open market; therefore, the elements of salability, desirability, quantities, and other factors are to be considered. It is important that the quotation at market should reflect the customary volume purchased at one time as well as the customary terms and manner in which purchased. It should include all costs necessary to bring the goods to their usual location, such as freight, duties, and other expenses incidental to acquisition.

Occasionally, situations may be encountered where there is no true replacement market. For example, large tobacco companies buy green tobacco leaf at the end of the growing season, but this leaf requires processing and aging of from eighteen months to three years before it can be used. The partly processed and aged tobacco cannot be purchased in quantities required to replace the leaf tobacco inventories of the larger companies, and dealer quotations for small quantities are not indicative of the replacement value of these inventories.

Reproduction cost means the actual expenses of reproducing the identical goods in the identical quantity and quality, irrespective of the advisability or desirability of duplicating them. In an advancing market, the sales value of the finished product may not rise in proportion to increased reproduction costs, and in a declining market the sales value of the finished product is sometimes below reproduction cost. Reproduction cost affords an important check on inventory prices, but there is always the possibility that net selling prices may be lower than reproduction cost.

Net Realizable Value.—Net realizable value may be determined, as shown in the table on page 205, by deducting reasonably predictable costs of completion and disposal from the estimated selling price. Costs of disposal should include all directly identifiable costs, such as packing, shipping, and salesmen's commissions.

Point of Normal Profit.—Theoretically, one would expect some disagreement in the determination of normal profit, but in practice this point can be established without too much difficulty by reference to performance over a recent period of time or to budget figures. If the normal margin of profit is overestimated, the effect will be an understatement of inventory and results of operations; there will probably be much less room for discretion and judgment in the computation of normal profit than in the initial determination of cost.

Application of Market to the Inventory.—There are two ways to apply the market test to the inventory: (1) to each item or to small groups, and (2) to large groups of items or to the whole inventory. For some years the former method was followed in theory but for many enterprises it was not practical. It is now generally recognized that either method may be used. Obviously, the item-by-item method may result in a lower inventory since market of many individual items may be lower than cost, and these differences are not offset (as in the group method) by the excess of market over cost of other items. The best practice in the application of market continues to be the recognition of the logical groups or classifications of individual items into which the inventories in the particular business naturally fall. Treasury Department regulations provide that the lower of cost or market value be applied to each article in the inventory for tax purposes, but in practice this requirement is not insisted upon when it is obviously not practical.

Purchase Commitments.—Losses on unhedged firm purchase commitments for goods for inventories should be provided for. Accounting Research Bulletin No. 43, Chapter 4, indicates that such losses, "measured in the same way as are inventory losses, should, if material, be recognized in the accounts and the amounts thereof separately disclosed in the income statement." It is impossible to measure purchase commitment losses unless the inventories together with the commitments are compared with firm and probable sales orders. Frequently, the initiation of such studies leads to the cancellation of purchase commitments at smaller losses than would result from purchasing, processing, and selling the materials. Purchase commitments may be outstanding for obsolete or unsalable merchandise, delivery of which has been delayed because management did not wish to recognize the loss.

Excess and Unsalable Materials.—Inventories should consist substantially of quantities which are expected to be sold or consumed in a reasonable period of time. Purchase commitments should be considered in connection with the existence and extent of excess inventories. Unless the excess inventory is expected to be disposed of over a reasonable period of time, the problem becomes one primarily of valuation and may be very difficult; transfer of excess inventory to noncurrent assets may be required.

Inclusion of an item in the inventory implies that it is expected to be salable. If its condition is such that there is no real demand for it, or if it has become obsolete or spoiled, the inventory may require revaluation to a reduced amount which, it is expected, can be realized.

OTHER METHODS OF INVENTORY VALUATION.—There are other accepted methods of inventory valuation which may result in inventories stated below or in excess of the lower of cost or market basis.

Normal or Base Stock.—This method, which is in accordance with generally accepted accounting principles, has long been used by certain companies engaged in processing basic raw materials, although its use for federal income tax purposes has been denied by the Treasury and the courts. However, the Lifo provisions of the tax law represent, to a degree, a substitute for the normal or base stock procedure.

Both normal or base stock and Lifo methods have as their primary objective elimination from income of so-called "inventory profits and losses" resulting from changing price levels.

The normal or base stock method differs from Lifo in several respects. Under the normal or base stock method a basic normal inventory, required at all times for normal operation, is fixed as to quantity and price. Increases above such fixed quantity, if not resulting from increase in plant capacity or change in process, are ordinarily considered as reflecting management's appraisal of future markets, availability of materials, or other conditions and, therefore, are reasonably priced under one of the more conventional cost bases or at market, if market is lower. Under the Lifo method, such increases are priced at the price level obtaining when the increase occurred, and the most recent increase is considered the first to be sold when quantities decline.

Under the normal or base stock method, if quantities are reduced below those considered normal or basic, and such reduction does not result from a change in capacity or process, a provision for replacement of base stock is made in an amount measured by the difference between the basic fixed price and the then current market price applied to the reduction in quantities. When the items are replaced, they are carried at the basic fixed price, and the difference between such price and the amounts paid is offset against the provision to the extent applicable.

Conditions which may make the use of the normal or base stock method desirable are:

Necessity for keeping on hand substantial quantities of homogeneous raw materials;

Large raw material content in cost of the finished product;

Quick reaction of selling prices of finished product to fluctuations in the replacement cost of raw materials;

Relatively large investment in inventories;

Relatively slow manufacturing or treating processes.

Selling Prices.—While the valuation of inventories in excess of cost may seem to violate the rule against anticipation of profits, inventories sometimes may be stated at selling prices. Accounting Research Bulletin No. 43, Chapter 4, states:

. . . . precious metals having a fixed monetary value with no substantial cost of marketing may be stated at such monetary value; any other exceptions must be justifiable by inability to determine appropriate approximate costs, immediate marketability at quoted market price, and the characteristic of unit interchangeability. Where goods are stated above cost this fact should be fully disclosed.

Although the practice is accepted when the above conditions are met, the trend in current years appears to be toward the more conventional methods of valuation.

The selling prices to be used as a basis for inventory valuations should be computed after deducting estimated costs of completion and disposal. In the authors' opinion, mere difficulty of determining approximate cost is the least persuasive of the justifications for this method. The primary justification for the method is the consideration that the inventory is immediately marketable at quoted market prices.

INVENTORY ALLOWANCES AND RESERVES.—Such items fall into two classes: (1) those that reduce the inventory to a generally accepted basis (allowances), and (2) those that reduce the inventory below a generally accepted basis or provide for general contingencies, such as future declines in prices (reserves). Allowances are usually resorted to as a matter of mechanics because it may be inconvenient or even impracticable to reduce the inventory accounts in detail. Reserves should not be charged against income but should be regarded as appropriations of surplus and should not be shown as a reduction of inventories in the balance sheet.

There may be probable losses in an inventory which are not revealed by a physical inventory or which may have occurred since inventory-taking when physical inventories are taken prior to the balance sheet date, and consideration should be given to establishing an allowance for these losses. Frequently, such an allowance can be projected from experience or otherwise reasonably estimated to provide for physical shortages since the date of the physical inventory, scrap or spoiled work not reported, and other similar factors.

Provision for excess cost of replacement of liquidated inventories under the Lifo method has been discussed on page 203.

RELATION OF COMMODITY FUTURES TO INVENTORIES.—In certain industries manufacturers may sell and buy futures on commodity exchanges to hedge their purchase and sales orders against losses from fluctuations in market prices of raw materials. Futures are generally bought to hedge the price of raw materials required for goods sold for future delivery; futures are generally sold to hedge purchases and commitments to purchase raw materials. While futures are usually contracts for the purchase and sale of stated quantities at specified prices and dates of delivery, they are customarily closed out prior to maturity, in order to avoid physical delivery of materials involved; settlements are made through the commodity exchange for the gain or loss at the time they are closed.

If futures contracts are for the same commodities, not necessarily the identical grades as those carried in the inventories, and are entered into as part of a plan designed to decrease operating risks, they may be accounted for in conjunction with cost of materials. Realized gains may be credited and realized losses may be charged to cost of sales.

Unrealized profits or losses on futures purchased as protection against sales commitments or on sales of futures made as protection against commitments to purchase raw materials are usually not recognized in the accounts, but the facts may be stated in the footnote.

If the futures contracts are entered into for a purpose other than for hedging inventory risks, they should be accounted for separately from inventories, and profits and losses therefrom should be reflected as other income or other deductions. Unrealized profits should not be taken up in the accounts as such. Unrealized losses should be recognized in the same way as those on regular purchase commitments.

Consistency.—As previously indicated, the different methods of valuing inventories may have widely different effects and within the method adopted there is frequently a large area of judgment and discretion. This does not mean that management may or should adopt annually the method or the interpretation that best pleases it; it means that the inventory methods most advantageous and suitable to the enterprise should be followed consistently from year to year if the statement of income is to present fairly the results of operations.

On the other hand, every business will make some changes from year to year in striving to improve its determination of inventories, and such changes should not be judged inconsistent by the public accountant unless they constitute a real change with material effect in the current period or an anticipated material effect in succeeding periods. For example, a change from the first-in, first-out method to the average cost method may have material results; the effect of a change in the treatment of certain overhead items may not be material. Changes which represent material inconsistencies or which affect the comparability of the financial statements in a material way should be disclosed, as set forth in the last paragraph of this chapter.

INTERNAL CONTROL

Internal Accounting Control.—Adequate internal accounting control of inventories embodies the following:

1. Control of receipts and shipments,
2. Control of consumption and production,
3. An adequate cost system,
4. Perpetual inventory records, and
5. Periodic counts of inventories.

In the following pages the discussion is from the point of view of a manufacturing enterprise; however, this discussion is generally applicable to the usual aspects of internal accounting control of other enterprises. The particular procedure or its form is unimportant; the achievement of the control itself, which may frequently be accomplished in different ways, is important. The allied subjects of internal accounting control of purchases and payrolls are discussed in Chapter 20.

CONTROL OF RECEIPTS AND SHIPMENTS.—Responsibility for the receipt of all incoming materials should be centralized in one department. Receiving department procedures should normally include the following: (a) inspection of all receipts as to quantity, condition, and proper identification; (b) preparation of appropriate receiving documents; (c) the prompt transfer of control over materials received to the authorized recipients; and (d) maintenance of documentary files which will identify and aid in verifying all receipts.

Numerical control should be maintained for all receiving documents. The receiving document should ordinarily include identification of the vendor, date of receipt, quantity and identification of the materials received, any exceptions to the condition of the material received, and the signature, initials, or other identification of the employee checking the receipt. Since the receiving document may be the basis for a claim against the vendor or carrier, it is considered advisable to have all receipts rechecked by a second employee when exceptions are substantial.

The type of receiving report to be used for the control of receipts of material will be influenced by the type of materials normally received, and the frequency, value, and quantity of receipts. Under normal circumstances, the flow and use of the receiving report will require an original and several copies. The original should be retained in the receiving department as a permanent record of the receipt, preferably bound in numerical sequence following the chronological order of receipt; numerical control will aid in simplifying the inventory cutoff on receipts. One copy should accompany the material to stores where the storekeeper may make an additional check of the material prior to signing a receipt therefor. This copy will usually be the basis of an entry on his stores inventory cards. Either the storekeeper's or another copy should go to the accounting department as evidence of receipt in support of the recording and eventual payment of the vendor's invoice, although, to avoid the loss of cash discounts, it is customary to pay invoices of responsible vendors prior to the receipt or final inspection of materials. Another copy should go to the purchasing department. This copy provides information for any follow-up required and also may be posted to the purchasing department's record of commitments. Another copy should go to the traffic department to be used in examination of freight bills and as supporting evidence for any claims against carriers for merchandise damaged in transit. The distribution procedure should be followed consistently even when the material has been rejected and returned to the vendor.

All shipments out of the plant should be covered by an authorized shipping advice or material release. In addition to the approved shipping advice, a customer's invoice checked for quantities, prices, extensions, and terms, a stock requisition, and a packing slip are usually required for documentary support of the shipment. Simultaneous preparation of these papers provides the simplest and most reliable means of correlating the separate phases of the transactions. All shipping advices should have accounting department approval as assurance that billing of the shipment has been effected. The material requisition, similarly approved, is retained by the storekeeper in support of the issuance of material to the shipping department whose representative signs the requisition acknowledging receipt. The shipping department should attach to its copy of the shipping advice all other evidence of shipment such as bills of lading, copies of freight bills, and trucking bills. The details of the records kept relating to routing, carriers, and other pertinent shipping data will depend on whether the traffic department operates independently or within the shipping department's scope of authority. It is important that established procedures are not circumvented on the pretense of expediting shipments, and that the procedures apply to all types of shipments, including sales to employees, scrap and waste sales, sales of equipment, and no-charge shipments.

CONTROL OF CONSUMPTION AND PRODUCTION.—Proper operation of the receiving and shipping departments may be thought of as the first steps in providing control over the flow of materials from and to the outside. If management is to control the materials within the plant, and if it is to receive reports of current operating results, procedures should be established governing consumption of raw materials, transfers between processes, and production of finished goods. Materials issued from stores should be supported by requisitions approved by authorized employees with receipt of the materials acknowledged by recipients. Normally, one copy of the requisition is retained by the storekeeper and one or more copies forwarded to the accounting department. Practices as to controlling work in process vary greatly; the accounting department should be informed of the quantities of finished goods produced and of transfers from one major process to another; often it has been found desirable to use requisitions for transfers throughout the plant.

AN ADEQUATE COST SYSTEM.—Good internal accounting control presupposes an adequate cost system for the determination of the current entries in inventory controlling accounts as well as for the determination of the cost of individual items or groups of items produced. The cost system should be tied in with the general books of account, in order that adequate monthly or other interim financial statements may be produced and that accurate perpetual records may be maintained. An adequate cost system will be susceptible of periodic adjustment to market, directly or through an allowance if market is lower than cost. The type of cost system in use will depend on the needs of the business; simplicity should be the keynote, for an overcomplicated system may bog down from its own weight. From the point of view of control, there is much to be said for a standard or similar cost system which involves a budgetary principle or which predetermines costs. Some of the advantages of predetermined costs are as follows:

1. Prompt pricing of physical inventories, since costs do not have to be computed therefor;
2. Current control over production costs through study of variances;
3. Better understanding of production through studies for the purpose of setting standards.

Some cost systems introduce a hidden factor of conservatism, to allow for shrinkages and other production losses, and such a factor may be deliberately overestimated, so that physical inventories are frequently in excess of the book controls. While it is undoubtedly good practice to be conservative in interim financial statements, better control will be obtained if estimates are made as accurately as possible and any provisions for conservatism are reflected in allowance accounts pending year-end adjustment.

PERPETUAL INVENTORY RECORDS.—Many manufacturing and merchandising concerns have found it advantageous to maintain perpetual inventory records. They may include details of quantities and dollar amounts for each item or group of items in the inventory. The department maintaining the perpetual inventory records (frequently the accounting department) must be informed of all receipts, withdrawals, and adjustments. From a control standpoint, perpetual inventory records offer these important advantages:

1. They facilitate physical inventories. Frequently, periodic counts during the year are a satisfactory substitute for a complete physical inventory at one time. Furthermore, if complete physical inventories are taken, the differences between them and the general ledger accounts can be localized and may be investigated without a costly restudy of the entire inventory to ascertain the cause of the difference. The perpetual inventory records may be extended at the end of any month for comparison with general ledger balances.

2. They provide information essential to adequate purchasing and production controls and related sales policies. Purchasing policies are dependent largely on requirements of the production program. Good production planning in turn requires the maintenance of production materials at a level high enough to assure efficient manufacture and low enough to avoid overinvestment. A perpetual record also is useful in determining the adequacy of finished stock to meet customers' requirements and in the detection of overstocks.

PHYSICAL INVENTORIES.—Good internal control requires the taking of a physical inventory at least annually; the term "physical inventory" includes not only physical counting but also translation of the count into dollars. A complete count of the inventory of a company, plant, or department may be made at one time while operations are suspended or, if perpetual inventory records are maintained and other conditions are satisfactory, periodic counts of selected items may be made during the year covering all items in the inventory at least once. Sometimes both types of inventory-taking are employed. Since the two methods involve somewhat different techniques, they will be discussed separately. A physical inventory is not a substitute for book figures, but rather a complementary control device to check their accuracy and to provide for their correction. Physical checks frequently will not be in exact agreement with the records, for it is to be expected that differences will arise from spoilage, obsolescence, and shrinkage not previously recognized, and from errors in recording.

Inventories Taken at One Time.—A complete inventory at one time is a large undertaking and requires the cooperation of the production personnel, since it usually means shutting down the plant and physically rearranging the inventory to facilitate counting. Frequently, inventories are taken during the vacation period for factory employees, when production may be stopped, or at a time when inventories are at a low level. Physical inventories may also be taken at the year end or at a convenient month end prior to the balance sheet date.

Since it is essential that responsibility be placed upon someone with authority, it is usually desirable to have one of the top production men responsible for rearranging the stock and making available employees who are familiar with it. It is frequently the practice for production personnel to count the inventories as they are rearranged, particularly when rearrangement is equivalent to a count; counts should be checked.

An almost invariable requirement for a good physical inventory is the preparation in advance of a written program which can be clearly understood by the average employee, and which should include instructions pertaining to:

1. Good physical arrangement as a means of simplifying the count;
2. Proper identification and description of stock;
3. Segregation or proper notation of slow-moving, obsolete, or damaged goods, and inventory belonging to others;
4. Control, preferably numerical, of inventory tags or sheets;
5. Practices to be followed in the verification of individual counts; and
6. Practices to be followed in obtaining a proper cutoff of receipts and shipments.

In addition to the above, which relate to the counting of the inventory, the accounting department should be instructed as to:

1. Summarization of quantities;
2. Pricing; and
3. Check of summarization and pricing, including extensions and footings.

Special attention may be required for consignments in or out, goods in transit, and goods in warehouses or in branches.

It is important that the forms used in the inventory-taking be simple enough to be understood by the employees for whose use they are intended. Requirements vary, but experience with previous inventories should be drawn upon and applied to the design of forms which will facilitate inventory-taking. It is usually desirable and sometimes imperative that the forms on which the initial count is recorded be numerically controlled.

The counting and pricing of inventories and the preparation of summaries should be supervised to determine that the prescribed procedures are adequate and are being followed. A competent internal audit staff can be utilized to advantage in performing this policing function. When there is no internal audit staff, other responsible personnel should be assigned to this task.

The mechanics of counting will vary. Seldom, if ever, can all individual items in an inventory be seen and counted; they are frequently in the packages or cartons in which they were purchased or they may be located in bins in large numbers or in large stockpiles which physically cannot be weighed or counted. The only rule which can be laid down is that a reasonable number of items should be counted; some packages should be opened, and some items inspected, particularly if there are any unusual circumstances.

Differences between physical and book inventories should be investigated, and the possibility of leakage or pilferage should be considered. However, the books may be right and the count wrong, and adjustments should not be made without investigation.

Inventories Taken Periodically Throughout the Year.—As stated previously, when good perpetual records are maintained and other circumstances are favorable, physical counts may be made periodically throughout the year, covering all items at least once in a year. When this is done, the perpetual records are priced, extended, and summarized for comparison with general ledger accounts, at or near the end of the fiscal year. Procedures employed in making periodic counts during the year differ from those when inventories are taken at one time. Rather than enlisting production personnel to rearrange and count all the stock in the plant, counts are usually made by relatively small groups of employees who soon become expert and possibly spend a large part of their time counting inventories.

There are in practice two major problems frequently encountered which must be overcome if good periodic counts are to be made:

1. A good cutoff must be obtained by arranging that perpetual records are posted promptly and accurately, otherwise the counts will result in apparent differences which are actually delays in recording.
2. The physical arrangement of the inventory to be counted must correspond with the perpetual records.

Generally speaking, unless the results of periodic counts are uniformly good, these counts should be relied upon not as a substitute for, but as a complement to, a complete inventory at one time. Employees making periodic counts usually should not know what quantities are shown on the perpetual records; this eliminates the obvious tendency to report as a count quantities indicated on the perpetual record.

OTHER FEATURES OF INTERNAL ACCOUNTING CONTROL.—While the major aspects of internal accounting control have been discussed in the preceding sections, there are others which may be important, depending upon the size and character of the enterprise.

Approval of Adjustments.—Inventory adjustments should not be recorded without the written approval of a responsible official. Significant discrepancies between physical and book amounts should be promptly investigated and the causes determined. Inadequacies in the cost system, laxity in conformance to procedures covering the receipt, storage and issuance of the materials, theft, and errors in recording are among the possible causes. Equally as important as the detection and correction of errors are the steps taken by management to avoid the recurrence of similar discrepancies. Adjustments made during the year and following the annual inventory should be set forth clearly in special inventory adjustment accounts and adequately described in the internal reports, thereby providing management with concrete evidence as to the effectiveness or ineffectiveness of inventory control procedures.

Reporting of Slow-Moving, Obsolete, Overstocked, and Damaged Items.—An important requirement of a properly functioning inventory system is the current reporting of items which do not move in the usual course of business, for whatever reason. These reports should originate with storekeepers and with those responsible for work in process and finished goods; they should be required at specified intervals so that recognition can be given to the facts, and recurrence prevented, rather than relying upon the annual inventory, at which time it may be too late for preventive measures.

Inventories Not on Premises.—Inventories not on the premises normally include consignments out, inventories in hands of suppliers, in warehouses, with finishers, and in branches. These classifications of inventory should be carried in separate accounts and should be supported by perpetual records. Additional control procedures may include monthly inventory reports, confirmation, and periodic physical tests. Controls of receipts and shipments should be similar to those discussed earlier in this chapter, even though the shipments may be on memorandum only. Materials in public warehouses should also be supported by warehouse receipts which may be compared currently with the accounting records. To avoid possible duplication, special attention should be given to goods in transit.

Inventories Belonging to Others.—All inventory belonging to others should be clearly identified, physically segregated, and its count scheduled as part of the physical inventory procedure. If the amount is significant and the activity frequent, a perpetual record should be maintained with documentary support for all entries. Records of accountability for the property of others should be carefully maintained, particularly if there is commingling with owned inventory.

Defective Work, Scrap, and Waste.—Good production control requires a system of inspection whereby defective work may be detected promptly to prevent further accumulation of costs in completing a substandard or defective product. If such defective items can be utilized in some other manner or can be sold as seconds, they may be returned to stock. If not, they should be segregated and quantity control should be maintained pending disposition. Similar control should be exercised over scrap and waste materials. It is important to have proper supervision of the weighing and grading of scrap, as well as of the price received therefor.

Items Charged Off, But Physically on Hand.—Frequently, certain types of supplies, such as small tools, are charged to expense as purchased. These items should be under physical control and those unissued subjected to the same requisitioning and inventorying procedures (for quantity control) as other inventories. Items of doubtful value written off, but on hand, should also be under physical control.

Returnable Containers.—Returnable containers in which the company's product is shipped may be treated either as current assets subject to inventory adjustment, or as fixed assets depreciated over their estimated useful life. Containers on hand should be checked physically in the same way as other inventories. Physical tests should include inspection of the containers to determine their potential usefulness. Some companies continue to include containers shipped to customers with those on hand, setting up memorandum accounts indicating their location. The quantity of containers represented by such memorandum accounts should be added to those on hand in determining the total quantity for inventory purposes. In some instances the seller may permit its customers to return containers on a freight collect basis or may have to expend a substantial amount for cleaning and reconditioning returned containers before they can be reused. When the estimated amount for freight, cleaning, and reconditioning of containers in the hands of customers is material, the containers may be valued on a reduced basis or a provision made for the amount of the estimated expenses.

Production Control.—The requirements of management to control inventories and purchase commitments in relation to sales volume should be based upon a correlation of inventory records and purchase commitment records, usually maintained by the purchasing department, with records of sales orders from the sales department. The avoidance of excessive, unbalanced, and obsolete inventories frequently depends upon maintenance of good production control records which too often are merely collateral records not tied in with the accounts. Various other devices are helpful, such as the use of maximum and minimum stock levels, special studies of rates of turnover, and analyses of inventory balances to determine the number of months' supply on hand. Frequently, other production control devices may be tied in with the accounting records so that their functioning is more or less automatic and subject to test.

Internal Check.—Controls which may be established for safeguarding inventories from misappropriation or theft are primarily of a physical nature. The construction of walls or fences with limited entrances into the plant, the maintenance of locked storerooms, and the use of plant guards are examples of security measures. Accounting procedures may be designed so that, in addition to providing internal accounting control, they will supplement the physical controls established.

CONTROL OF RECEIPTS AND SHIPMENTS.—It is desirable that receiving reports and shipping advices be prenumbered by the printer. To assure that all movements into and out of the plant are recorded and to reduce the opportunities for improper diversion of assets, all receiving reports and shipping advices should be accounted for by persons independent of the stores function and the maintenance of perpetual inventory records. Control of the forms should include the filing of voided forms.

PERPETUAL INVENTORY RECORDS.—Good internal check requires that the perpetual inventory records be maintained by someone independent of custodianship of physical inventories. Under such circumstances, the records serve as a check on the storekeepers. Awareness by the custodian of the existence of an independently maintained record tends to prevent laxity in conforming to established procedures and to discourage theft or misuse of inventories. Often, the accounting department maintains the perpetual inventory records.

The responsibility for comparing physical inventory counts with perpetual inventory records and with related general ledger control accounts should be assigned to someone independent of the custodianship of inventories and the maintenance of perpetual inventory records. The same requirements of independence should apply to those who investigate and correct significant differences between physical and book inventories and to those who approve adjustments to perpetual inventory records and related general ledger control accounts. A competent internal audit staff can be utilized to advantage in the performance of these functions.

PHYSICAL INVENTORIES.—It is important that persons independent of custodianship of inventory and maintenance of the perpetual inventory records participate in the taking of the physical inventory. When the size of the organization permits, the second count of inventory items, the determination of inventory procedures, and the preparation of the written instructions should all be performed by persons with such independence. The check of the clerical work of summarizing and pricing should be done by employees who did not perform the original work. Maintenance of numerical control over original inventory tags and sheets and confirmation of inventory quantities held by outsiders are functions frequently handled by an internal audit staff.

PHYSICAL PROTECTION AND INSURANCE COVERAGE.—Inventories are generally exposed to certain physical risks such as fire, theft, floods, weather, and spoilage, some or all of which may be insurable. However, the first line of protection is proper physical handling, storage, and guarding, the requirements of which vary greatly.

Unless the company desires to assume the risks of fire and theft, such risks should be covered adequately by insurance, whereas other risks may or may not be covered depending upon circumstances. Proper internal control requires periodic analysis and reporting to management of amounts and insurance coverage of inventories in various locations. All policies in effect should be inspected periodically as to renewal dates. When there are co-insurance clauses, the total coverage should be maintained at least at the level required by such policies to insure the greatest return in the event of loss. The maintenance of perpetual inventory records may be of great assistance in proving loss, particularly partial loss.

AUDITING PROCEDURES

Objectives.—Inventories are often the largest current asset; their valuation may require considerable judgment and discretion. Although the public accountant does not assume the responsibilities of an appraiser or stocktaker, the application of appropriate auditing procedures will usually furnish him with a basis for a well-founded opinion on the inventories. Generally, such auditing procedures include a review and tests of the system of internal accounting control and internal check, analysis of inventory accounts, observation and tests of physical inventories when practicable and reasonable, and examination of physical inventory records, including tests of the quantities and pricing.

Review of Internal Control and Other Preparatory Considerations. —The system of internal accounting control and internal check is of considerable importance in determining the scope of the auditor's examination of inventories. For example, an adequate cost system makes it possible to localize the differences between physical and book inventories in terms of the various controlling accounts; perpetual inventory records make possible further localization of such differences in terms of individual items or groups of items. On the other hand, if the cost system or perpetual record is inadequate the auditor may need to make extensive analyses and investigations to determine reasons for material inventory differences. Absence of good internal accounting control would usually call for a more intensive review of transactions between inventory-taking and the balance sheet date than otherwise might be necessary; and absence of either good internal accounting control or internal check might lead the auditor to conclude that the physical inventory must be taken at the balance sheet date. In initial engagements considerable time should be devoted in advance of the physical inventory, if possible, in becoming familiar with the client's accounting procedures and internal control, and in studying the business and its products.

VISIT TO PLANTS.—After a general discussion of the client's accounts, the auditor's next step on an initial engagement might well be a visit to one or more of the principal plants or other places of business to obtain a visual impression of the manufacturing, warehousing, or retailing processes. It is usually helpful to have a preview of the products to be inventoried, and, when reviewing the system of internal control, to have some knowledge of the physical attributes of the product and how it is made.

PROCEDURES IN REVIEWING INTERNAL CONTROL.—The more important features of a good system of internal accounting control and internal check for inventories have been set forth earlier in this chapter, and Chapter 20 contains a discussion of internal control of purchases, expenses, and payrolls, of which a large part usually relates to cost of production.

It is usually not difficult to establish through inquiry what features of internal accounting control and internal check of inventories are nominally in force. The auditor can get reasonable assurance whether such features are actually being followed by tracing selected recorded transactions through the various routines from purchase commitment to final sale, observing also, as the audit tests suggested herein are made, whether transactions are handled in accordance with instructions. It is desirable for the auditor to have constantly in mind the manufacturing processes and related factory records during his review and to refresh his understanding thereof by physical inspection; only then can he avoid misunderstandings that result from too much work at a desk and too little in the field.

A review of previous physical inventory summaries may give the auditor a good conception of what the inventories comprise, where they are located, and how they are valued. Inquiry into previous inventory adjustments may furnish clues as to weaknesses in inventory control and may be helpful in shaping the audit program.

PLANS FOR PHYSICAL INVENTORIES.—The primary responsibility for a good inventory is the client's, and clearly written instructions are an important first step. The auditor should review and criticize constructively the client's written instructions for the physical inventory or, if the client does not have instructions, suggest that they be prepared. It may be desirable for the controller or other accounting executives to hold instructional meetings with those who are to be in charge of taking physical inventories, in order that they may have a thorough understanding of the instructions as written. This procedure not only serves to expedite the taking of the inventory but also clarifies many points that cannot be spelled out in the instructions.

In planning for the observation of inventory-taking, the auditor should consider manpower requirements and the timing of the inventories at the various locations. Manpower requirements are maximum when a complete physical inventory is taken at one time, whereas they are minimum when only periodic counts are made. When the client's internal auditing staff participates in taking the physical inventory, the independent auditor may reduce his tests and thus relieve his manpower problem.

Analysis of Inventory Accounts.—Occasionally, in conjunction with his review of the system of internal control, the auditor may prepare or review analyses of inventory accounts for the period or for part of the period since the beginning of the year. These analyses may show by departments the charges to cost of production and the cost of finished or semifinished items transferred. Entries in support of labor and material costs may be reviewed and traced to original data; factory overhead may be reviewed and tested and tied in with analyses of other accounts, such as depreciation allowances, tax accruals, and the like. Credits to inventory may be traced to cost of sales or to charges to other departments or to other accounts, and the basis of such credits examined. Entries of an unusual nature should be scrutinized. The extent of the auditor's tests will be governed by his examination of purchases and payrolls (discussed in Chapter 20), by the extent of his examination of the physical inventory, by whether or not it is an initial engagement, and by the apparent effectiveness of the system of internal accounting control.

The auditor customarily will analyze the various inventory allowance and reserve accounts, since analyses of these accounts will frequently give him information as to important matters of valuation.

Observation of Taking of Physical Inventories.—Generally accepted auditing procedures for many years have required that, whenever practicable and reasonable, the auditor should be present at and observe the physical inventory-taking. As set forth in the preceding pages of this chapter, physical inventory-taking means either a count of the whole or sections of the inventory at one time, or periodic counts when perpetual records are maintained, or a combination of the two procedures.

PRIMARY OBJECTIVE.—The primary objective of the auditor's observation of inventory-taking is to determine, insofar as he reasonably can, whether an accurate inventory is being taken. The auditor is not a stocktaker and he cannot be expected to be an expert appraiser of inventory quality, quantities, or condition. While his test counts are usually relatively limited, there may be instances in which, because of poor internal accounting control or internal check, lack of responsible employees, or special request, the auditor checks a substantial part or all of the inventory quantities. It may not be necessary for the auditor to visit all branches every year to observe the taking of physical inventories if control is good and the inventories are well supervised or periodically tested by internal auditors or others.

INVENTORIES TAKEN AT ONE TIME.—In order to satisfy himself as to the effectiveness of the methods of inventory-taking, the auditor should make the following observations or tests:

1. Physical arrangement. The auditor should first make a general, brief inspection of the premises. Experience will tell him whether the arrangement of stock is such that a good count is possible or probable. If the arrangement is extremely poor, he should ask that the stock be rearranged.

2. Identification and description. The auditor should inspect some items of the stock, determine the source of the description, see that proper differentiation is made for the various stages of work in process, and check his findings with production personnel. Conflicting answers to his questions may cause doubt whether the client's employees taking the inventory are actually familiar with it.

3. Segregation or notation of slow-moving, obsolete, or damaged goods. Frequently such items can be recognized by the auditor, or his inquiries and review of perpetual records may reveal their existence.

4. Control of tags or sheets. The auditor should determine that each inventory count team is charged with a sequence of prenumbered tags and that each team is required to turn in those unused or spoiled. He should inquire whether an employee accounts for all tags at the completion of the inventory. He should observe

whether items have been properly tagged or marked to avoid duplication or omissions.

5. Practices in verifying individual counts. The auditor should observe some of the counts, noting whether quantities and descriptions are being carefully entered on the tags or inventory sheets. The auditor will usually make a certain number of counts of his own, including some items of substantial value; in the event that differences between the limited test counts which the auditor makes and the counts by client's employees indicate laxness, the auditor may insist upon recounts of the entire section in which the unsatisfactory condition exists. When inventory sheets are used instead of tags, he may select some items from the sheets to count on the floor, and trace some items on the floor to the inventory sheets. It is not reasonable to expect that many original cartons or packages be broken open or that an unreasonable amount of inspection be made of items not easily accessible, but when the auditor suspects that the inventory is not well taken he should take all steps which he believes necessary to insure a reasonably accurate count.

6. Practices in obtaining proper cutoff. At the time of inventory-taking the auditor may visit the receiving and shipping departments, noting the last receiving and shipping document numbers, and seeing that each department has been informed that no receipts after and no shipments before the cutoff should be included in inventory. It is frequently desirable for receiving and shipping departments to earmark materials which should not be included in the inventory. The auditor can usually make a subsequent check of the records of these departments after the inventory, and compare the last receiving and shipping numbers with accounting department records. Manufacturing operations should be suspended for the physical inventory; if they are not, unusual care must be taken to control the movement of inventory.

The auditor should make notations of his counts of certain items and of other data to be checked further when he receives the finished inventory records. He may request and retain control of duplicate inventory tag stubs or sheets which he will test to the physical inventory records. If he does not receive duplicate count records, he may note items from the original counts to be checked to inventory summaries. In his review of internal accounting control the auditor will determine the procedures followed in inventorying goods on the premises belonging to others, such as consignments in, bailments, goods on approval, and goods held for repair; when the physical inventory is being taken, the auditor should be satisfied that these items are properly identified, that employees are aware of the nature of the items, and that they are properly recorded as the property of others. The auditor can later make such tests of accounting or other records as will give him further assurance that the property of others is properly recorded.

INVENTORIES TAKEN PERIODICALLY THROUGHOUT THE YEAR.— The auditor's observation of periodic counts is largely directed toward determining whether the methods are satisfactory. He should observe the group making the counts and follow as many of the audit procedures, outlined above for inventories taken at one time, as are practicable. He should consider whether procedures followed in taking the counts conform to those outlined previously under the section on internal accounting control and review the differences between counts and perpetual records. The following factors may justify belief that perpetual records properly reflect inventory quantities: absence of substantial differences over a period of time and of difficulties in cutoff of receipts, shipments, and transfers between departments; careful counts made by experienced employees; correlation of records with physical arrangement of stock; and reasonable identification of stock without physical rearrangement.

DIFFICULT INVENTORIES.—Certain types of material, by their nature, may present difficulties in determining quantities on hand. Examples of such materials include logs in a river, piles of coal, or piles of scrap metal. Measurement of a pile of metal may prove unsatisfactory because the pile may have sunk into the ground to an unknown depth, the metals may be of varying weights precluding the use of an average, or the pile may be of uneven density. Under these circumstances, the auditor may be guided by the client's system of handling receipts and disbursements from the piles. The client may use a pile rotation system, whereby the metal is taken from a specified pile until it is exhausted, at which time errors, if any, in the book records will be disclosed. Meanwhile, metal received is placed on other piles. If the pile rotation system has proved satisfactory, the auditor may feel that he can rely to some extent on the book records. On the other hand, if amounts involved are of sufficient materiality, the auditor may suggest that an expert be brought in to assist in the inventory-taking.

ALTERNATIVE PROCEDURES WHEN OBSERVATION OF PHYSICAL INVENTORIES IS NOT PRACTICABLE OR REASONABLE.—If no physical inventory is or can be taken by the client or if the auditor cannot be present at the inventory-taking, the auditor may or may not be able to form an opinion as to the reasonableness of inventory quantities by the application of alternative procedures. Such alternative procedures are summarized into two basic categories on the next page.

1. The establishment of other physical evidence which may be tantamount to physical observation; or
2. The establishment of the validity of the inventories through further
   examination of the accounting evidence.

The first category could be applied, for example, when the auditor
has been engaged to examine financial statements after the physical
inventory has been taken. Physical tests made subsequently may be a
satisfactory substitute for observation of the inventory-taking. The
auditor may also examine written procedures prescribed for the inventory-taking, review the original tags or sheets, and make suitable tests
of the compilation.

Government requirements may prohibit shutdown and interruption
of production for inventory purposes. When, for this or any other
reason, work in process inventory cannot be taken in the customary
way, the auditor may have to exercise his ingenuity in finding a reasonable substitute. Quantity records maintained for labor bonus purposes
may be priced and extended and the total compared with the control
account; records of finished production may be examined after the
inventory date to determine quantities produced. Such procedures may
offer a satisfactory basis for an opinion.

Even though it was not practicable and reasonable for the auditor to
be present and observe the inventory-taking at the close of the period, if,
through his examination of the accounts and the system of internal
control, he is satisfied that inventories are fairly stated, he may express
this opinion, disclosing, however, that the taking of the physical inventory was not observed and that he has satisfied himself by means of
other auditing procedures. On the other hand, there may be no practicable substitute for observation of inventory-taking, and the auditor
may express a qualified opinion, or no opinion, depending on the materiality of the inventory.

In an initial engagement, the auditor usually has not been present
at the taking of the physical inventory at the previous year end. This
inventory is one of the factors in determining the cost of sales for the
current year. If reputable independent public accountants had expressed an unqualified opinion on the statements of the preceding year,
the auditor may accept this opinion and perhaps merely review the
inventory sheets. If no examination had been made for the preceding
year, the auditor may expand substantially his tests of accounting evidence in order to establish the validity of the inventories. If the auditor is unable to form an opinion as to the opening inventory, he may
wish to qualify his opinion with respect to the opening inventory and
the results of operations for the year.

Examination of the Physical Inventory Records.—Some time necessarily will elapse between taking and summarizing the inventory. Usually the client will make his own investigation of inventory differences, although the auditor may wish to do so concurrently; satisfactory explanations of differences between book and physical inventory may be the most important part of his examination. In testing quantities and pricing of inventory summaries, the auditor will be guided by the evidence as to whether the client has already made careful and competent checks; the fact that employees have indicated by their initials that certain steps have been taken is assuring, but it is of even greater assurance to find as the result of test checks that the work was accurate. In examining inventories compiled by accounting machines, the auditor should not assume that their mechanical accuracy is necessarily any greater than that of those compiled by hand. It is true that errors by the machines themselves may be rare, but they do occur, and the operators of the machines may have made errors which were not detected by rechecking. Usually the auditor should concentrate on larger items, scanning certain footings and extensions and checking others exactly. He should determine that items included in, and excluded from, inventories are properly treated and that inventories are valued in accordance with generally accepted accounting principles consistently observed.

QUANTITIES.

1. Tests are usually made to provide reasonable assurance that only tags used for the physical counts are included in the physical inventory summaries.

2. The auditor should check his record of counts and test-check original count sheets or tags to inventory summaries; conversions and summarizations of units should also be checked.

3. If perpetual records are maintained, the auditor should test-check quantities thereto and review differences.

4. Quantities should be compared with those in previous inventories on a test basis; this comparison may indicate some slow-moving items.

5. Perpetual records should be reviewed for further indications of slow-moving items. If the client does not maintain perpetual records, the auditor may examine purchase orders or production orders to determine how recently certain items of inventory were acquired.

6. The auditor should test the observance of cutoff and the inclusion of in-transit items.

7. Stock held by others, such as that in public warehouses, on consignment, or in hands of processors should be substantiated by direct confirmation in writing from the custodians; in addition, the auditor may desire, because of the size of the inventory or because the con-

firmation is not satisfactory, to have a physical inventory taken, applying the same procedures as if the stock were located in a company ware-house. The confirmation might be considered unsatisfactory if the holder is not believed responsible in relation to the amount of the inventory which he holds, or the holder may, as public warehouses customarily do, only confirm that he has possession of certain packages bearing a description of the contents but without representation as to the contents. While negotiable warehouse receipts are usually trust-worthy, withdrawals are not always noted on these receipts, and it is often advisable to request direct confirmation by letter.

PRICING.

1. The auditor will have reviewed and tested the client's cost sys-tem in connection with his review of internal control and analyses of inventory accounts. He should make sufficient tests to be satisfied that costs to be applied to inventories are fair and in accordance with generally accepted accounting principles. In examining an inventory of purchased items these tests will include reference to current invoices or purchase contracts.

2. The auditor should test-check the application of prices to inven-tory quantities, extensions, footings, and summarizations.

3. Pricing of obsolete, slow-moving, scrap, and damaged stock should be reviewed to determine that it is not in excess of net realizable amount.

4. The auditor should review and test the determination of market prices. Tests similar to the following may be made to determine whether market is lower than cost.

Inventory prices may be compared with the net realizable value (estimated selling prices less cost of completion and disposal) of indi-vidual or major groups of products. If inventories are priced at mar-ket, however, they should not be stated at less than net realizable value reduced by an allowance for an approximately normal profit margin. Consequently, the auditor need not determine the amount of inventory at reproduction or replacement costs when there is acceptable evidence that individual or groups of products, priced at cost, will be sold at prices which will yield normal profit margins. Acceptable evidence may consist of current and expected selling prices and sales orders as related to current costs.

Replacement costs may be test-checked by reference to cost records, current invoices, or purchase contracts. Reproduction costs may be test-checked by cost records supplemented by conferences with produc-tion and accounting employees.

Retail Inventories.—When a retail method of inventory account-ing is used, the physical inventory is priced at retail and the totals are compared with the book inventory. Unusual shortages may require investigation to determine whether the retail method is functioning properly or excessive stealing is taking place. The auditor will also review and make selected tests of the retail method computations out-lined in the "Accounting Principles" section of this chapter.

Employment of Experts.—In special circumstances the auditor may suggest calling in an independent expert to determine, for example, the value of an inventory of precious stones.

SPECIAL CONSIDERATIONS AS TO WORK IN PROCESS.—The examina-tion of work in process inventories frequently involves troublesome pricing problems.

As indicated previously, sometimes there is difficulty in identifying work in process with the accounting records, even though a complete inventory is taken at one time. This difficulty is most pronounced when (1) the physical nature of the work in process is such that it is not easy to identify, such as when it does not take on the aspects of the finished product until or shortly prior to completion, or (2) good process costs are not maintained, because the product is manufactured on a custom basis and costs vary from lot to lot, or simply because of a poor cost system. There is no set formula to prescribe in such in-stances, and the auditor must relate the physical evidence to the records as best he can, or rely upon comprehensive tests of the accounting records.

Furthermore, work in process inventories may not be taken phys-ically; they may be taken physically at some time other than when raw materials and finished stock are taken; or they may be taken at one time while the balance of inventory is counted on a cycle basis through-out the year. Under these circumstances the auditor should take par-ticular care to determine, through study of the internal accounting control and through tests of transactions, that proper credits have been made to work in process both for production transferred to finished stock and for shipments directly from work in process to customers, since unrecorded transfers may result in a misstatement of the inven-tory. Unless controls over relief of work in process are good, the auditor may insist that the entire inventory be taken at one time or undertake comprehensive tests of the records, which tests may or may not give satisfactory results; in such tests the auditor may be well advised to refer not only to the conventional accounting records but to such records as those of the production control or other departments which record the physical movement of inventories.

General Considerations and Over-All Tests.—In the application of various detailed tests, the auditor should not lose perspective; he should consider the inventory as a whole. He should beware of any increase in inventories without a corresponding increase in sales, or of a lower turnover which may indicate overproduction or sales resistance on the part of customers. He may analyze differences in the rate of gross profit during the year and between current and past years, since discrepancies may be the result of errors in recording inventory transactions. Occasionally purchase or production records in terms of units can be correlated with opening inventories, sales, and closing inventories; major discrepancies in this correlation should be investigated.

Purchase Commitments.—As discussed in the "Accounting Principles" section of this chapter, provision should be made for unrealized losses on purchase commitments. The auditor should review the record of purchase commitments, paying particular attention to commitments long outstanding; if the client does not maintain such a record, the auditor should examine open contracts and purchase orders for materials. Purchase commitments should be related to inventories and to expected sales. For example, if purchase commitments have been made at prices in excess of current market prices, but nevertheless a normal margin of profit seems assured from the sale of the finished article, no provision for loss will be necessary. On the other hand, if there are substantial purchase commitments and the inventory is excessive in quantity, or market or sales prices are declining, consideration should be given to possible loss on purchase commitments. Purchase commitments are of two kinds: (1) commitments with suppliers for materials to be used in the ordinary course of business, and (2) futures contracts for the purchase or sale of commodities under which delivery usually is not made and which may represent either a hedge or a speculation.

Inventory Certificate.—This certificate confirms statements made by the client as to the method of taking inventory, the ownership of the inventory, and the basis of its valuation, and avoids misunderstandings as to these matters between the auditor and the client. In addition, it reminds the client that the primary responsibility for inventories rests with him rather than with the auditor. The request for such a certificate is a customary procedure and in no way reflects upon the integrity of the client. In initial engagements it is desirable to obtain a similar certificate covering inventories at the beginning of the period. The status of purchase commitments may be covered in this certificate or in the liability certificate discussed in Chapter 16. The inventory certificate may take the following form, with variations appropriate to the circumstances:

INVENTORY CERTIFICATE

of auditor)

consolidated   _Oregon Oil Products_

..1 with your examination of the balance sheet of (name of
.1t (balance sheet date) I hereby certify that the inventory at
which the following is a summary, _12/31/64_

..il—before goods in—transit .... $ _138,852.97_

At lower of cost or market .... _74,917.70_

                                          _12/26/64_ $ ....

was taken under my direction, and that to the best of my knowledge and belief:

1. The quantities are correct and were determined by actual count, weight,
   or measurement as at (physical inventory date). (if a physical inventory was not taken at one time, substitute a statement as to the adequacy of the perpetual inventory system and statements as to the
   frequency and coverage of physical tests and the agreement of the
   quantities and amounts so determined with the perpetual inventory
   book record);

2. The entire inventory is the unencumbered property of the company,
   has not been pledged as collateral, and includes no items billed by the
   company up to and including the balance sheet date nor any items
   held on consignment; _except $63.00 on consignment_.

3. Each item or specified group of items of the inventory is priced at cost
   or market, whichever is lower, and not in excess of net realizable
   value; _at retail;_

4. The basis of pricing and method of computation is the same as was used
   at the end of the previous fiscal period. The general basis on which
   cost is determined is as follows (first-in, first-out; average; last-in,
   first-out; etc.);

5. No obsolete, slow-moving, damaged or unusable materials or merchandise are included in the inventory at prices in excess of net realizable
   value; _$74,917.70_

6. The amount stated above is a fair and proper valuation of the inventory
   for inclusion in the balance sheet at (balance sheet date).

                                          Very truly yours,

                                          (Name of company)

                                          (Name and title of person signing)

(Date signed)

Coordination of Examination with That of Related Accounts.—The
auditor's examination of inventories is closely related to his examination of cost of sales; a satisfactory determination of inventories, in
many cases, is of primary importance in a fair statement of income,

The review, analyses, and tests of cost of production and of its flow into cost of sales usually are largely accomplished when the auditor has completed his examination of inventories. He will usually trace charges to overhead for such items as depreciation and taxes to the related allowance or accrued liability accounts.

When quantities or units in opening and closing inventories can be reconciled with production and sales, it is sometimes possible to obtain a proof of the sales account by extension of quantities sold at selling prices.

Time of Examination.—Physical inventories are often taken at a date prior to that of the balance sheet. This permits the earlier issuance of financial statements and helps to relieve the year-end pressure on both the auditor and the client's accounting staff. The practice is desirable when there is reasonable assurance that interim transactions are properly recorded and are susceptible to a reasonable review. Thus, the bulk of the auditor's examination of inventories may take place prior to the balance sheet date.

STATEMENT PRESENTATION

Introduction.—Inventories, to the extent current, are carried in current assets, usually following accounts receivable. Since determination of inventories requires the exercise of judgment, and since the differences between various methods of valuing inventories may be great, it is important that the basis of valuation be adequately described.

Disclosure of Components.—It may or may not be significant to disclose the amounts of raw materials, supplies, work in process, and finished stock. If the relative investment in the different categories is normal, no useful purpose may be served by a breakdown. On the other hand, if one category is abnormally large it may be important to disclose its amount, as when the quantity of finished stock might indicate an unhealthy sales situation. It is frequently the practice to use such a caption as "Inventories of raw materials, supplies, work in process, and finished stock" if all such components are represented and no segregation is deemed necessary.

When progress payments under long-term contracts have been deducted from inventories, the amount deducted is frequently disclosed, thus indicating the gross amount of the physical assets on hand.

When materials included in the inventory are to be used, to an indeterminate extent, for either construction or maintenance or for a product which may either be sold or leased, it is appropriate to disclose this fact.

Disclosure of Basis of Valuation.—It is desirable that a brief description of the basis of inventory valuation be given in the balance sheet, together with further disclosure of any unusual aspects. Accounting Research Bulletin No. 43, Chapter 3, Section A, states that, where practicable, indication of the method of determining cost (e.g., average cost, first-in—first-out, last-in—first-out, etc.), should also be given.

Allowances and Reserves.—When inventories are reduced to a generally accepted basis by means of allowances, deduction of the allowances may or may not be disclosed, depending upon their significance. Disclosure may be appropriate of an allowance under the base stock method, or of a substantial allowance based on estimate or judgment rather than on exact calculation, such as an allowance for reduction of a relatively large contract in process to estimated net realizable value.

A provision for replacement of basic Lifo inventories, set up when such inventories have been used and are expected to be replaced, is usually included among the current liabilities. After the inventory has been replaced, the provision must preferably be treated as a deduction from inventories, provided such treatment does not jeopardize the use of the Lifo method for income tax purposes.

When provision is made for purposes other than valuation on a generally accepted basis, such as a reserve for future decline in inventory prices, it should not be deducted from inventories, but should be shown as appropriated earned surplus.

Disclosure of Liens and Encumbrances.—Borrowing accompanied by pledge or other encumbrance of the inventory should be stated as a liability and the amount of inventory pledged should be revealed. Examples of such borrowings are bank loans and advances by factors, by finance companies, or by customers. Retention of protective title by lenders should be disclosed. Ordinarily, borrowings should not be shown as a deduction from inventories. The treatment as a deduction from inventories of partial payments received on inventories under contracts with the United States Government is acceptable.

Disclosure of Adjustments in the Statement of Income.—The reduction of inventories and commitments to market may result in a charge to income so large that the reader of the income statement receives a distorted impression of the results of operations unless disclosure is made; the preferable method of disclosure is a segregation of these charges from cost of sales. On the other hand, inventory charge-offs are normally recurring in some businesses; when their segregation may convey the erroneous impression that these losses are nonrecurring it may be better not to disclose them.

Lack of Consistency or Comparability.—Consistency in inventory methods is of great importance, particularly to the determination of income. Disclosure should be made, preferably in a note to financial statements, of any material change in principle or in the application of a principle during the accounting period which materially affects the comparability of the financial statements with those of the previous period. Disclosure should include the dollar effect upon net income when practicable. This effect is usually indicated by stating that, under the method formerly followed, the net income would have been increased or decreased by a stated amount. It is also appropriate to disclose a change which will have a material effect upon future statements although its effect upon the current statements is not material. See Chapter 6 as to the statement which should be included in the opinion.

CHAPTER 12

PROPERTY, PLANT, AND EQUIPMENT

ACCOUNTING PRINCIPLES

General Principles.

BASIS OF INCLUSION.—Investment in property, plant, and equipment comprises a substantial portion of the total assets of many companies. It includes all tangible assets with a service life in excess of one year that are used in the conduct of the business and, in the ordinary course of operations, are not to be sold. Such assets generally fall into three categories :

1. Property ordinarily subject to neither depreciation nor depletion, such as land ;
2. Property subject to depreciation, such as buildings, machinery and equipment, and large tools ; and
3. Property subject to depletion, such as mines, oil wells, and timber.

The propriety of the recorded amounts for property, plant, and equipment of a going concern depends not only on accounting for the initial acquisition, but also on the policy adopted for subsequent additions, replacements, retirements, and repairs.

BASIS OF STATING PROPERTY, PLANT, AND EQUIPMENT.—As a general rule, property, plant, and equipment should be recorded at cost, less an allowance either for depreciation or depletion depending upon the nature of the asset. While cost is the accepted basis, other bases are used in practice and, under certain conditions, may be justified.

An appraisal of property, plant, and equipment may show a valuation which differs substantially from the amounts at which recorded. Such valuation may represent economic usefulness, replacement cost less depreciation, or probable sales price. It is proper to adjust to appraisal amounts, whether greater or less than book amounts, when the amounts of other asset and liability accounts are also subject to adjustment in a reorganization or quasi-reorganization. It may be proper to adjust the carrying amount of property, plant, and equipment to correct past errors in recording depreciation, additions, or retirements, and an appraisal may be helpful in establishing, or as a check on, the computed amount of such adjustments. It is not good practice to reflect upward adjustments based on an appraisal that mainly reflects change in price levels (see below), unless the adjustments are in connection with a reorganization or quasi-reorganization involving appropriate restatement of all the assets. The SEC has consistently viewed upward restatements of only property, plant, and equipment as not being in accordance with present-day accepted accounting principles. This view would also prohibit the recording of purchased plant at appraised or other amount higher than cost, even though the cost may be claimed to represent a bargain price.

The treatment of surplus accounts when property, plant, and equipment is properly recorded at appraised amounts is discussed in Chapter 19, and the recording of these items when there has been a pooling of interests rather than a purchase is treated in Chapter 21.

In recent years, considerable thought has been devoted by accountants, businessmen, bankers, economists, labor leaders, and others to the subject of depreciation and high costs. During periods of greatly increased price levels, management is faced with the problem of replacing plant facilities at costs much greater than those of the original facilities. Working capital provided as the result of depreciation charges based on lower-cost property may not be adequate for its replacement, necessitating additional financing for the higher cost. Many have suggested that the problem be met by periodically recording current appraised amounts for all properties, with comparable increased depreciation charges against current income. In Accounting Research Bulletin No. 43, Chapter 9, Section A, the Committee on Accounting Procedure reaffirmed its opinion to the effect that:

It would not increase the usefulness of reported corporate income figures if some companies charged depreciation on appraised values while others adhered to cost. The committee believes, therefore, that consideration of radical changes in accepted accounting procedure should not be undertaken, at least until a stable price level would make it practicable for business as a whole to make the change at the same time.

The committee disapproves immediate write-downs of plant cost by charges against current income in amounts believed to represent excessive or abnormal costs occasioned by current price levels. However, the committee calls attention to the fact that plants expected to have less than normal useful life can properly be depreciated on a systematic basis related to economic usefulness.

Components of Cost.

INCLUDIBLE COMPONENTS.—The cost of property, plant, and equipment includes all expenditures necessary to make property usable by the concern on whose balance sheet it is reflected. Cost of acquisition or construction includes not only invoice or contract price, but also the cost of other items of materials, supplies, labor, and services consumed or employed in the construction and installation of the plant, preliminary engineering studies and surveys, and expenditures necessary to establish title.

Certain regulatory commissions, such as the Federal Power Commission, prescribe uniform systems of accounts providing detailed classifications of property, plant, and equipment. Cost is prescribed as a basis for charges to these accounts, but, as discussed elsewhere in this chapter, cost as defined by such regulatory bodies is original cost, that is, cost to the person first devoting the property to public service. For enterprises other than certain public utilities, cost means cost of acquisition to the present owners.

Cash Discounts.—Cash discounts deducted from payments for property, plant, and equipment usually are considered as reductions of costs and not income, and the net amount paid is recorded as the cost of assets acquired. Although this treatment is generally accepted as good practice, many companies consider the total amount of cash discounts as insignificant and accordingly record discounts on purchases as income. This latter procedure is acceptable when amounts involved are not material.

Interest During Construction.—The principle of including as a cost of construction interest paid during the construction period on money borrowed for construction purposes is not frequently applied by companies other than public utilities.

It is general practice for public utilities to capitalize as interest during construction the net cost of borrowed funds and a reasonable rate on the utility's own funds used for construction. Such procedure is prescribed in the uniform system of accounts adopted by the Federal Power Commission, which system is typical of those promulgated by state public utilities commissions. In practice, there are wide variations in the application of this principle. Some utilities, as a matter of conservatism, do not capitalize any interest during construction. Others capitalize interest only on important projects, or on projects involving certain minimum expenditures, generally varying from $1,000 to $500,000. Some capitalize interest on borrowed capital only. Others capitalize interest on both borrowed capital and equity capital using as the equity capital rate the theoretical cost of money used. When a new company builds its first plant, if interest were not capitalized, a deficit would be incurred prior to the beginning of operations.

There is general agreement that interest should be capitalized only on those projects under construction for more than a month, and that the period of capitalization ends when the property is placed in service even though costs are not transferred from the construction in progress account to the plant accounts until a later date. It is generally considered undesirable to use a capitalization rate higher than that currently expended on borrowed capital used to finance construction, since the use of a higher rate results in the capitalization of theoretical profits or earning power.

When income bonds are outstanding during construction periods and it is believed that the interest will be paid for those periods, it is proper to accrue and capitalize the interest, even though its payment depends on income being sufficient to pay the interest and on the authorization of the payments by the directors.

Overhead When Concern Erects Buildings or Manufactures Its Own Equipment.—The determination of the amount of overhead to be capitalized when a company constructs its own buildings or manufactures its own equipment presents some problems. The recognized ceiling is that the overhead added should not increase the cost to an amount greater than that at which the property could be acquired through arm's-length transactions in the open market. Generally, only overhead directly attributable to the project should be added to the asset cost. In the event that a concern erects its own plant or makes its own equipment for less than it would cost if purchased from outsiders, good accounting practice precludes capitalizing an amount equivalent to the assumed saving. The benefit of the saving, if any, will be realized through lower depreciation charges.

Most large companies have departments which handle improvements and new construction as well as maintenance and repairs. Supervisory and indirect expenses of these departments are usually considered as overhead and distributed prorata to maintenance and construction jobs. Only overhead costs of these departments should be included in this overhead; ordinarily, general expenses of the company or overhead costs of operating departments would be excluded. Some services may be performed for maintenance departments by other service departments, such as those for purchasing or accounting; however, the costs of these services are usually negligible.

Additions to Property, Plant, and Equipment.

LAND AND LAND RIGHTS.—*Includible Costs.*—These asset accounts should reflect the purchase cost of land owned in fee and of rights, interests, and privileges held in land owned by others. They should include all costs directly attributable to the acquisition of the property and to conditioning it for use.

Commissions to agents and costs of examining, insuring, and registering title, including attorneys' fees and any other expenditures for establishing clear title, as well as expenditures for draining and filling, for installing buried bulkheads, and for clearing and grading land, are capitalizable items. Costs of removing, relocating, or reconstructing property of others in order to acquire possession, in addition to expenditures for improvements such as streets, sidewalks, and sewer lines, whether constructed directly by the owner or by public authorities who levy special assessments to defray the costs, should also be capitalized. When assessments for betterments are paid in instalments, the entire amount of the assessment should be recorded and the unpaid portion shown as a liability. Interest, if any, on deferred payments should be treated as an expense. Assessments for transitory services, such as lighting, sprinkling, and cleaning streets, snow removal, and protection of trees, when the benefit is temporary, should be charged to expense.

During the course of clearing land to make it useful for the purpose acquired, salable timber may be recovered. Since the clearing costs are capital items, amounts realized from the sale of the timber should be credited to the land account. When land acquired is held for a considerable period of time before being cleared, and there has been a substantial increment in the market value of the timber, only the estimated realizable value at the time of acquisition should be credited to the land account and the balance of the sales price should be recorded as other income.

Allocation of Cost of Demolished Buildings.—When land and buildings are purchased with the intention of demolishing the buildings, the original cost, plus cost of demolition of the buildings less salvage, represents the cost of the land. When the decision to demolish is made subsequent to purchase, the cost of demolition less salvage plus the cost allocated to the buildings at time of purchase, less accumulated depreciation to the date of demolition, may represent a realized loss or an additional cost of land, according to circumstances. When the demolition follows the discovery of unexpected defects in useful value, the entire cost of removal of the buildings, less salvage, and the original cost, less accumulated depreciation to the date of demolition, should be charged against income.

Accounting for Land Held for Development and Sale.—1. *Carrying charges on undeveloped property.*—When unimproved property is held for development or sale, taxes and other carrying charges may or may not be added to the cost.

When undeveloped property is carried as an investment and its development is deferred as a part of a well-defined plan and not because development would be unprofitable, reasonable carrying charges may be capitalized. When there is a possibility that undeveloped property may be disposed of at a loss, discretion should be used in capitalizing such expenditures. Capitalization of carrying charges should not be continued to a point beyond a reasonable valuation of the property. On the other hand, while it may be expedient or conservative to charge off such expenditures, it may not be good accounting practice to do so, since it may unduly reduce profits arising from current operations and understate the cost of the asset.

2. *Other costs incurred during development period.*—Most expenditures incurred up to the time when property for development is ready to be marketed should be treated as additional cost of the property. Such items would include the cost of grading and paving of streets and the cost of water and sewer installations. Related administrative and preliminary selling expenses, such as advertising, publicity, printing, and the preparation of maps, should be charged off or segregated as deferred expenses.

When development is completed and the property is to be sold by lots, the total cost should be allocated to the salable lots, on a basis such as expected selling prices or area, so that there may be a measure of gain or loss on each parcel sold.

BUILDINGS.—*Includible Costs.*—A building is a relatively permanent structure designed to house or safeguard property or persons, and its total cost should include not only the cost of the shell, but also expenditures for service equipment and fixtures made a permanent part of the structure. In addition to direct costs of construction, it is permissible to capitalize such items as permits, architects' and engineers' fees, interest on borrowed money, legal fees, and overhead directly applicable to construction.

Recorded costs of buildings should include, among other items, expenditures for exposed bulkheads and piling, coal bins and bunkers, boilers and furnaces, permanently attached floor covering, retaining walls, vaults, screens, storm doors and windows, partitions, railings and platforms, and the initial cost of painting.

The building account usually reflects costs of service equipment, such as fire protection, heating, refrigerating, plumbing, and electrical wiring systems, as well as the cost of lighting fixtures, elevators, and other improvements. Some companies, however, prefer to record such items in separate asset accounts so that varying rates of depreciation may be applied to the respective items rather than using a composite rate for buildings as a whole.

MACHINERY AND EQUIPMENT.—*Includible Costs.*—Expenditures for the purchase or manufacture of machinery and equipment should be capitalized together with all costs of installation. The latter would include transportation expenses borne by the purchaser, labor charges, cost of materials and supplies consumed, and other expenditures incurred in unloading and placing the equipment in readiness for operation. Costs of tests during an experimental period are proper capital items; proceeds from sale of energy generated by an electric utility during a period in which a new generator is tested should be credited to the asset account.

Costs of large tools, such as lathes, looms, and motors, are usually included under this classification. Costs of small tools, such as hammers, saws, and shovels, which may be lost or stolen or which have a relatively small value, should be excluded from fixed assets and accounted for as later described.

Development Expenditures.—Many industrial concerns maintain machine shops for the construction of part or all of the equipment used in the business. If substantial development expenditures are incurred in constructing new models of machinery, the cost of the first machines produced would exceed the cost of those manufactured subsequently. A reasonable amount of these development expenses may be deferred and allocated to the cost of additional machines constructed. Excess costs arising from errors in construction should not be included in the cost of construction. Generally, expenditures incurred after such machines have been placed in operation, such as expenditures for tests, correction, and improvement in installation, should be considered as expenses and not as additions to cost of the equipment.

Purchases on Deferred Payments.—When machinery is purchased on a partial payment or instalment plan, only the cash purchase price should be recorded in the machinery account. The gross purchase price should be credited to the vendor, and the excess of that price over the cash price, representing the charge for deferred payments, should be accounted for as interest expense, either at once or, if the amount warrants deferment, over the period of the instalment payments.

Purchases Under Royalty Agreements.—Machines are sometimes purchased under an agreement which also provides that royalties are to be paid on units of production. Such royalty payments are not costs of acquisition and they should be charged to operating expenses. When machines are installed under contracts whereby so-called royalties or rentals may be applied against the purchase price, and the intent is to purchase the machines, the accounting should be the same as that for machines acquired on a deferred payment basis.

TRANSPORTATION EQUIPMENT.—Costs of airplanes, automobiles, motor trucks, trailers, and similar equipment, and costs of garage equipment, such as battery-charging machines, repair shop equipment, and portable gasoline and oil pumps, should be capitalized. The initial cost of accessories should also be capitalized; however, subsequent replacements should be charged to expense. To facilitate allocation of depreciation to expense accounts, it is preferable to classify transportation equipment in the plant accounts according to function, such as production, sales, or administrative.

FURNITURE, FIXTURES, AND OFFICE EQUIPMENT.—This classification of fixed assets includes such items as desks, chairs, and desk equipment, partitions, shelves, bookcases, floor covering, safes, and tables. It is good accounting practice to establish a policy as to the minimum price of units of property within this group which are to be capitalized. In the absence of such a policy, the accounts may become cluttered with innumerable minor items of small value. The cost of accounting for such minor items over their service lives may easily exceed the original purchase price.

Furniture, fixtures, and office equipment should be classified on a functional basis to facilitate allocation of related depreciation charges.

SMALL TOOLS.—Since many hand and other portable tools are worn out, lost, or stolen, it is often impracticable to treat them as property, plant, and equipment to be written off through depreciation charges. Some companies take physical inventories of tools periodically and adjust the accounts accordingly. Others treat small tools as supplies inventory and charge them to expense when they are put into use, considering only new tools which have not been placed in service as an asset.

RETURNABLE CONTAINERS.—Returnable containers include steel drums, barrels, kegs, boxes, cartons, bottles, syphons, and other types of containers, which are necessary in many businesses for the shipment of products and which the customer is expected to return. To provide an incentive for their return, a charge is usually made, frequently in an amount in excess of the cost of the container. When certain bottled goods are sold for cash, the purchaser's deposit is refunded when the container is returned. In other instances, the customer's account is credited when the container is returned or, if the container has been lost or destroyed, the account is settled by a cash payment.

Sizable containers of substantial construction such as steel drums and reels for heavy wire or cable have service lives in excess of one year and usually are classified as depreciable fixed assets. Returnable containers are frequently carried in two accounts, one for containers on hand, and the other for containers held by customers.

Smaller, more fragile, and less valuable containers, such as carboys, generally have service lives of less than one year and are carried as supply inventories; accounting for these items is discussed in Chapter 11.

IMPROVEMENTS AND BETTERMENTS.—When an expenditure not only replaces a fixed asset but increases the rate of output, lowers operating cost or extends useful life, some part of it should be capitalized. The amount which should be added to the plant account frequently is difficult to measure. If the original cost of the asset retired can be determined, the problem may be solved by adopting the preferred accounting procedure of charging the cost of the improvement to the plant account and crediting that account with the original cost of the asset retired.

Costs of alterations that do not create improvements from which future operations may benefit, but merely modernize buildings or equipment, should not be capitalized. If the allowance for depreciation contains, as it should, provision for obsolescence, all or part of such costs may be charged against the accumulated allowance for depreciation.

COSTS OF REHABILITATIONS.—Rehabilitation implies something more than ordinary repairs. It implies a complete overhauling and reconditioning, which may not result in expanded capacity of a facility, but which will materially extend its useful life and assure its continued productivity. Under these circumstances, because it may be difficult or impossible to identify the cost of items removed, a charge to the allowance for depreciation of a part of the total cost of rehabilitation may be acceptable rather than removal from plant accounts of the original cost of items displaced.

When partly worn-out or run-down plants are purchased with the intention of rehabilitating them so that they can be operated efficiently, it may be assumed that the purchase price takes into consideration the poor condition of the plant. Under these circumstances, the entire cost of repairs and renewals required to bring the plant to a satisfactory operating condition, including applicable overhead expense, should be capitalized.

PROPERTY ACQUIRED FOR CONSIDERATION OTHER THAN CASH.— *Property Acquired in Trade.*—When property is acquired in exchange for other property, it is sound practice to record the acquired property at the carrying amount of the property disposed of, provided that such amount is reasonable and based on accepted accounting principles. Any cash required to equalize the exchange should be added to or deducted from the amount capitalized. If the asset disposed of is overstated or understated on the books by reason of inadequate or excessive allowances for depreciation, the recorded amount of the new asset should be adjusted accordingly. If the acquired property has been appraised recently or has a readily obtainable market value, this value may be a guide to the valuation to be recorded and to any profit or loss resulting from the exchange.

Property Acquired in Exchange for Company's Stock or Bonds.— As a general rule, cost of property so acquired should be determined either by the fair market value of the consideration given or by the fair market value of the property acquired, whichever is the more clearly evident. When neither is readily determinable, the situation requires careful consideration.

When bonds alone are issued, it may be presumed that the principal amount of the bonds represents the purchase price; however, the principal amount of the bonds alone may not be an adequate measure of value because of other conditions. For example, if 2 per cent bonds are issued at a time when similar corporations are issuing 5 per cent bonds, the presumption that the bonds are worth their principal amount is unreasonable, and an attempt should be made to establish fair value. The difference between the principal amount of the bonds and the fair value of the property presumably represents bond discount, which is discussed in Chapter 15.

When stock alone is issued, the par or stated value of the stock usually cannot be relied upon as a reasonable basis for recording the cost of the property acquired. If the fair value of stock is not readily determinable, some appraisal of the property must be made, either by the management or by outside parties, taking into consideration all pertinent factors.

Property Acquired as a Contribution or Donation.—Contributed or donated property should be appraised when received and recorded in the accounts at the appraised amount.

Property Acquired as Part of a Package.—When a going concern is purchased for a lump sum, it is sound accounting practice to allocate the sum of the amount paid and the liabilities assumed to the various categories of assets acquired. After the amounts allocable to current assets and to liabilities have been determined, the remainder, if any, may be considered to relate to fixed assets and, possibly, to intangible assets acquired. Fixed assets should be appraised, and, if the value so determined is less than the amount assignable to such assets, the difference may be considered to represent cost of intangibles. If the appraisal amount exceeds the balance assignable to the fixed assets, the excess should be deducted from the appraisal amounts, usually on a prorata basis.

PROPERTY ACQUIRED UNDER LONG-TERM LEASE ARRANGEMENTS.—Financing of property additions, usually land and buildings, through buy-build-sell-lease transactions has become rather common in recent years. Although details vary, a typical example is where the owner of land builds to his own specifications, sells the improved property, and simultaneously leases it from the new owner for a period of years; the lessee assumes all expenses and obligations of ownership except payment of any mortgage indebtedness on the property. Such an arrangement may, in substance, be equivalent to an instalment purchase of the property, especially when the lease permits purchase of the property for a nominal amount after a specified period, or when rentals are higher than market for similar properties so that the excess may be considered partial payments under a de facto purchase plan. Accounting Research Bulletin No. 43, Chapter 14, discusses this problem, and concludes:

> Since the lessee in such cases does not have legal title to the property and does not necessarily assume any direct mortgage obligation, it has been argued that any balance sheet which included the property among the assets and any related indebtedness among the liabilities would be incorrect. However, the committee is of the opinion that the facts relating to all such leases should be carefully considered and that, where it is clearly evident that the transaction involved is in substance a purchase, the "leased" property should be included among the assets of the lessee with suitable accounting for the corresponding liabilities and for the related charges in the income statement.

Retirements and Disposals of Property, Plant, and Equipment.— When detailed records of property, plant, and equipment are maintained and depreciation is computed on a unit life basis, the accepted accounting treatment of retirements is well defined. At the time a unit of property is retired from service, the cost should be credited to the appropriate plant account, the related accumulated depreciation should be charged to the allowance for depreciation account, and the profit or loss, adjusted for salvage value and cost of removal and disposition, should be reflected in the income account. However, Accounting Research Bulletin No. 43, Chapter 8, states that "material charges or credits resulting from unusual sales of assets not acquired for resale and not of the type in which the company generally deals" may be excluded from the determination of net income for the year, "and they should be excluded when their inclusion would impair the significance of net income so that misleading inferences might be drawn therefrom."

When a company computes depreciation on a composite rate basis, as described in Chapter 13, the accepted accounting treatment for plant units retired in the normal course of business is that cost is credited to the appropriate property account and such cost, plus the cost of removal and less salvage value, is charged to the allowance for depreciation. No profit or loss is recognized in the accounts, since the composite rate contemplates retirements of items in the group both before and after the expiration of the estimated average life. However, when retirements are abnormal or unusual, profits or losses should be recorded in the accounts, since composite rates do not provide for such retirements. Examples of this last type of retirement include the disposal of all items of a certain class of plant because of an obsolescence not considered in arriving at the composite rate and the retirement of facilities for the production of a discontinued major line of product.

Mines.—Practices peculiar to mining determine the accounting for exploration (work performed to determine if a mineralized area has commercial probabilities), development (work performed to prepare a mineralized area for commercial production), and plant and equipment acquired for production.

Prior to beginning commercial operations, costs of exploratory and development work, less proceeds of sales of production, are capitalized. Generally, when the major portion of the mineral production is obtained from workings other than those opened for the purpose of development, or when the principal activity of the mine becomes the production of developed ore as opposed to the development of additional ores for mining, it is considered that a mine has entered the producing stage. From that point on, the cost of development work is usually charged to expense because of the practical difficulty of segregating development costs from operating costs.

As extraction proceeds, shafts may become deeper and working faces recede, with the result that more track, cars, and other equipment will be necessary to produce the same quantities as were produced at the beginning of operations. If expenditures for such equipment do not increase the production of the mine or decrease the cost of production, they are usually charged to expense.

Oil and Gas Wells.

LEASES.—Frequently, oil companies enter into lease agreements with the owners of the land, and wells are drilled by independent contractors. These leases usually provide for payment of a bonus to the lessor upon execution and for the payment annually of a stated amount per acre as rental, with stipulations as to development of the property by the oil company. Rental ceases when production begins; thereafter, the lessor receives a royalty, or share of the production, usually one-eighth in commercial leases and one-sixth in Indian Agency (Government) leases. Thus, in a commercial lease, seven-eighths of the production accrues to the oil company.

An undeveloped lease sometimes is carried at the sum of the bonus referred to, expenses incurred in obtaining the lease, and the cost of geological and geophysical work performed. Such cost is amortized over the life of the lease or, if production is obtained before the expiration of the lease, amortization is discontinued at the date of production and depletion is recorded on the remaining net investment. Rentals are charged to expense as they accrue. An alternative method is to capitalize the bonus, rentals, and other costs and expenses, carrying the lease at the aggregate of these amounts until relinquishment or development of production. Under this plan, if the lease is relinquished, the cost is written off; in the event of production, the investment is subject to depletion.

USEFUL LIFE.—The original or flush production of a well is no criterion of the later flow, and no one can foretell accurately the commercially useful life of a well. However, based on experience and knowledge of oil and gas formations, geologists and petroleum engineers can estimate the amount of oil or gas, or both, recoverable from a well. These estimates are used generally as the bases for computing depletion and depreciation sustained as a result of production.

DEVELOPMENT EXPENDITURES.—Costs of drilling and equipping wells are usually capitalized. Sometimes the so-called intangible costs, such as labor and other items which have no salvage value, are charged to expense and other costs capitalized. After development is completed and production begins, the recorded costs of the investment in property should be amortized on the basis of the estimated units recoverable.

Changes in the policy of capitalizing development expenditures may produce widely varying results. Assume, for example, that a company expended in two accounting periods identical amounts on its development program, but that in the first period it capitalized all of the costs, whereas in the second period it charged intangible costs to expense. In comparison with the first period the expenses recorded in the second period have been increased by the amount of the intangible costs less the amount of depletion applicable thereto had such costs been capitalized. Such a change in policy and its effect on net income should be clearly explained.

Costs Prescribed for Public Utility Companies.—The uniform systems of accounts prescribed for public utilities regulated by the Federal Power Commission, Federal Communications Commission, and state utility commissions require that, when plant comprising an operating unit or system is acquired by purchase, merger, consolidation, liquidation, or otherwise, the original cost (cost to the person first devoting it to public service) shall be charged to plant in service accounts and the related accumulated depreciation and amortization shall be credited to appropriate allowance accounts. Amounts paid by utilities in arm's-length transactions in excess of the net recorded original cost of plant so acquired are recorded in plant acquisition adjustment accounts and disposed of as directed by the regulatory commissions. Usually the commissions require that such excess amounts be amortized by periodic charges to income over a period of years. Since such charges represent the write-off of actual cost of property, and are therefore comparable to depreciation, they usually should be classified as operating expenses. Under certain circumstances, however, commissions have required utilities to record the write-off as income deductions.

While the balances in plant acquisition adjustment accounts are usually debits, occasionally such balances are credits. Disposition of credit adjustments is subject to the same restriction as that of debit adjustments.

Before original cost requirements became effective, many utilities recorded revaluation write-ups in their plant accounts. These amounts in excess of original cost arose principally from reproduction cost studies and from acquisitions, frequently from affiliated interests, through the issuance of securities. The uniform systems of accounts required that utilities record such write-ups in plant adjustments accounts. In most instances, the commissions required that these excesses be disposed of by direct charges to surplus. Since the advent of original cost requirements, transactions which might give rise to such write-ups are closely scrutinized and controlled by the commissions with the objective of eliminating them.

Appraisals.

PURPOSES.—Appraisals may be made to determine values for many purposes, such as for consideration of adequacy of insurance coverage, or for segregation of various plant assets acquired in a lump-sum purchase. They may also be made to determine fair values in contemplation of the sale or purchase of a business, to determine fair values for tax purposes or to determine the adequacy of procedures in recording retirements of plant and depreciation.

STANDARDS OF THE SECURITIES AND EXCHANGE COMMISSION.—The Securities and Exchange Commission has issued stop-orders when, on investigation, it found that so-called appraised values expressed in balance sheets did not meet certain standards. The Commission insists that an appraisal must be more than an arbitrary determination and must be based on scientific methods; that the appraiser must be in fact independent; and that there must be a fair and accurate application of the methods purported to be followed. Even though valuations are in the final analysis expressions of judgment, the Commission does not consider that this warrants departure from these standards. The Commission holds that a balance sheet containing an untrue statement through overvaluation of an asset is not acceptable even if a footnote discloses the overvaluation. The Commission has not criticized downward restatements of plant costs, but has been disinclined to accept upward restatements.

UPWARD RESTATEMENT OF PLANT COSTS.—In the decade following 1929, there was little inclination to record plant or intangible assets at appraised values, probably because appraisals at reproduction cost would have been lower than cost less depreciation. With the rise in prices during and after World War II, the subject of reproduction cost again received considerable attention; however, as stated earlier in this chapter, the Committee on Accounting Procedure does not endorse the practice of recording current appraised values.

DOWNWARD RESTATEMENT OF PLANT COSTS.—Downward adjustments of recorded amounts for property are usually made to eliminate appreciation previously set up, to reduce plant accounts on the basis of an appraisal, or to write down the property balances to an arbitrary amount such as $1.

A write-down of book amounts that reverses previously recorded appreciation of fixed assets may represent a change in accounting policy or imply that management feels such appreciation should not have been recorded in the first place. Whether it is proper to go further and reduce book amounts of fixed assets to amounts below their depreciated cost depends on many considerations. The goal may be merely to record sound values, based on present reproduction cost. In appraisals consideration may also be given to such factors as future useful value, anticipated future earnings, idle plant facilities, possibility of obsolescence before full utilization of the complete plant, and relation of total productive capacity of an industry to anticipated demand for its product. Occasionally a company offers for sale a portion of its land, buildings, and equipment that is no longer needed in the business. If such property has an estimated sales value appreciably less than its depreciated cost, it should be written down to the estimated sales value.

Nothing can be said in favor of writing down plant accounts to an arbitrary amount. By writing a useful plant down to $1, future profits will be overstated and future losses understated by the amount of the depreciation thereby anticipated. It is altogether misleading both to stockholders and to prospective investors, for it suggests ultraconservatism on the part of the management, when it may conceal gross extravagance.

INTERNAL CONTROL

Internal Accounting Control.—The policy governing accounting for additions to, and deductions from, property, plant, and equipment accounts should be well defined, and responsibility for its administration definitely fixed. In establishing such a policy, the following procedures are essential to provide adequate accounting controls over transactions affecting the fixed asset accounts:

1. Adoption of a written statement of policy and instructions with respect to the accounting for additions to plant as opposed to maintenance and repairs;
2. Preparation of a budget of construction expenditures preferably for the accounting year, and approval of this budget by the board of directors or its executive committee;
3. Adoption of the practice of requiring advance approval by designated responsible persons of expenditures for projects specifically described in the construction budget and of all disposals of plant;
4. Installation of procedures, preferably described in a manual, for initiating requests for plant additions and disposals, indicating the forms to be used and the principles of accounting to be followed;
5. Maintenance of adequate property records;
6. Development of reports of changes in property accounts for review by designated responsible persons; and
7. When practicable, occasional physical inventories of plant items for comparison with the book records.

PROPERTY, PLANT, AND EQUIPMENT RECORDS.—Property, plant, and equipment controlling accounts should be supported by detailed records in which plant assets are appropriately classified. The most satisfactory control is exercised when the subsidiary accounts are, in turn, supported by an individual record on cards or sheets for each item of property, plant, and equipment in each classification, setting forth pertinent information. These records should include data with respect to all items in use, including fully depreciated assets as well as plant facilities owned by others. In addition to the dollar amount, the record for each plant item should include information such as the date purchased or constructed, voucher or work order numbers, an adequate description including the vendor's serial number, unit number assigned, and location in the plant. The detailed records should be balanced periodically, at least annually, with the general ledger controlling accounts.

Additions to Property, Plant, and Equipment Accounts.—Requests for authorization to construct, purchase, or install plant facilities are usually initiated by the plant engineer, plant superintendent, department heads, or other supervisory employees. Requisition forms used should set forth information such as the reason for the expenditure, estimated cost, budget item number, description, and proposed disposition of plant to be replaced, if any, and accounts to be charged or credited. They should be submitted for approval to the person to whom appropriate authority has been delegated.

Approved requests are usually known as appropriations and are numbered to facilitate their identification and control. Costs of acquisition and installation should be accumulated on work orders under these appropriation numbers. All appropriations should be controlled through a construction work in progress account in the general ledger and the detailed work order records should be balanced periodically with this controlling account.

After an installation has been completed, a statement of the appropriation should be prepared showing a comparison of actual costs with the cost estimate in the original requisition, and substantial differences should be satisfactorily explained. The appropriation should then be transferred from construction work in progress to the appropriate property, plant, and equipment accounts.

When a company constructs, purchases, and installs substantial property additions by using its own employees, costs of labor, material, supplies, and construction overhead should be accumulated and charged to construction work in progress under the appropriation or work order provided. The accounting for these costs should be subject to the same controls as those exercised over operating expenditures recorded through payrolls, vouchers, and other media. The accumulation of these costs should be watched carefully throughout the construction period to avoid, if possible, exceeding the original cost estimate. Timely information may permit appropriate corrective action during the construction period.

Reductions in Property, Plant, and Equipment Accounts.—Control of retirements of property, plant, and equipment should be similar to that of additions. Requests for authorization to retire, sell, transfer, dismantle, or abandon property may be submitted to the person authorized to approve additions or to other designated persons. Such requests should set forth the reason for the proposed transaction, a description and the recorded cost of the item to be retired, estimated salvage, estimated cost of removal, and accounts to be charged or credited. After approval, retirement work order numbers should be assigned for convenience in accumulating costs of the retirement; preferably cost accumulations should be controlled through a retirement work in progress account in the general ledger; and procedures in all ways should be similar to those relating to additions.

PHYSICAL INVENTORIES AND RECORD COMPARISONS.—When records are kept of individual plant items, physical inventories of those items susceptible of actual count should be taken occasionally and compared with detailed accounting and engineering records. If feasible, physical inventories should also be taken of plant items used by the company, but owned by others, and of items owned by the company and leased to others. Accounting records of units of property not susceptible of physical inventory should be compared with available engineering records.

Internal Check.—The inventory preferably should be taken by persons not responsible for either the custody or accounting functions and who are reasonably familiar with these assets. Differences developed through these processes should be reported promptly to the persons charged with the responsibility for approving adjustments.

AUDITING PROCEDURES

Objectives.—The auditor's fundamental objective in the examination of property, plant, and equipment accounts is to determine the basis at which such assets are stated in the accounts and whether such basis is in accordance with generally accepted accounting principles consistently applied in past as well as current periods.

The auditor's responsibility for property, plant, and equipment differs somewhat from that for current assets. If his report is unqualified, he should have arrived at an opinion as to the existence, basis of statement, and realizability on a going concern basis of the amount at which current assets are stated. The auditor is not responsible for substantiating the existence of property, plant, and equipment by physical tests and inspections. However, in addition to evidence obtained from the examination of accounting and other records, most auditors consider it desirable to make an inspection tour of the property as a whole, not only to acquire assurance that there is a plant in existence, but also to acquire a background for his examination of the records.

The auditor has no responsibility as to the realizability of the amounts at which property, plant, and equipment used and useful in the business are recorded; he should attempt, however, to determine that such assets as a whole are fairly stated in the accounts. If he is advised of or discovers a material amount of surplus equipment held primarily for sale, he should insist that it be segregated in the accounts and recorded in an amount not in excess of that estimated as realizable. When the auditor finds that title does not rest in the company, he should determine the nature and extent of the company's interest.

General Auditing Procedures.

EXAMINATION OF OPENING BALANCES.—When financial statements are being examined for the first time, the auditor must decide to what extent it is necessary to examine plant accounts prior to the beginning of the year or years under examination. If financial statements for prior years have been examined and reported upon by independent public accountants of good repute, his examination may be quite limited. Otherwise, he should review available plant records and may prepare or obtain analyses reflecting annual changes in prior years. His review should disclose the accounting procedures and principles employed by the company in recording additions and retirements and the consistency with which they have been applied since the inception of the existing plant accounts. Further, he may wish to examine evidential matter in support of substantial additions and reductions and, in particular, he should investigate unusual items in an effort to learn of any revaluations or other important adjustments. Charges for property paid for by issuance of common stock or bonds, especially when mixed aggregates of property were acquired, should be investigated to determine the basis on which these acquisitions were recorded, and to determine the basis for any allocations resulting from lump-sum purchases. The examination of the property accounts should be coordinated with historical analyses of long-term debt, capital stock, and surplus accounts, as discussed in Chapter 4.

EXAMINATION OF CURRENT TRANSACTIONS.—In determining the extent of audit procedures in examining current transactions, the auditor should consider the importance of plant additions and retirements in relation to other items in the balance sheet. For example, the investment of a public utility company in plant, and the additions and retirements during a period are usually substantial, and, further, such investment is an important factor in determining the rate base. Accordingly, considerable attention is usually given to the examination of plant accounts of such companies. In other types of business, investment in fixed assets may be relatively unimportant and there may be little movement during a period; here, the auditor is justified in reducing procedures to a minimum.

The auditor's procedures in examining property, plant, and equipment accounts for the period to be reported upon may be modified by the apparent effectiveness of the system of internal accounting control over recorded transactions. Control of additions to plant by a system of appropriations, supported by work orders which accumulate charges to the various projects, facilitates the differentiation between plant and expense charges for similar types of expenditure. When charges are made directly to classified accounts, the auditor may experience difficulty in judging the propriety of the classification, since the purpose of the expenditure is not as clearly evident as when a work order system is used.

The discussion which follows indicates procedures which might be appropriate when the fixed asset accounts are of considerable importance; when they are not, the examination will be more limited in scope.

Application of Auditing Procedures.

UNDER A WORK ORDER SYSTEM.—When a work order system is used for plant additions and retirements, the work orders are usually identified by number, and charges and credits thereto controlled through construction work in progress accounts in the general ledger. Preferably, separate controlling accounts should be maintained for additions and for retirements to facilitate proper balance sheet classification.

If the system of internal accounting control of property additions and retirements seems adequate, the auditor may confine his examination of work orders to a review of accounting procedures to satisfy himself that the system is operating properly. In this respect, as to additions, he may:

1. Determine that the aggregate credits to the construction work in progress account for a selected period are reconcilable with charges representing additions to plant accounts;

2. Select a representative number of completed and uncompleted work orders and determine that they have been properly authorized, examine vouchers and other evidential data in support of selected charges, test the appropriateness of accounting classifications, and examine completion reports and related engineering data;

3. Test the mathematical accuracy of charges accumulated on the work orders, the accounting for completed work orders transferred from construction work in progress to plant in service accounts

and the validity of the balance of the construction work in progress account at the end of an accounting period;

4. Make a test comparison of expenditures authorized or estimated with the actual costs charged to completed work orders as finally determined, obtain explanations of substantial variances, and, if the variances cannot be explained satisfactorily, investigate further the accuracy of the accounting for expenditures; and

5. Satisfy himself that the balances of uncompleted work orders at the end of the accounting period under examination represent costs applicable to uncompleted work and that charges to work orders applicable to abandoned projects, if any, have been eliminated from the construction work in progress account.

Under similar circumstances, with respect to plant retirements, the auditor may:

1. Determine that the aggregate charges to the retirement work in progress account for a selected period, representing costs of plant disposed of, are reconcilable with credits to the related property accounts;

2. Select a representative number of completed and uncompleted retirement work orders and determine that they have been properly authorized, examine journal vouchers in support of credits to plant accounts for costs of plant disposed of, determine that such costs represent all elements including installation costs and overhead, examine vouchers and other evidential data in support of charges for cost of removal and credits for salvage recoveries either through returns to stock or sales;

3. Test the mathematical accuracy of charges and credits accumulated on the retirement work orders, the accounting for completed retirement work orders in accordance with the depreciation policy adopted by the company, and the validity of the balance of the retirement work in progress account at the end of the accounting period; and

4. Satisfy himself that the charges and credits remaining in the progress account at the end of the accounting period apply only to retirement work orders for disposals or salvage transactions which have not been physically completed.

To satisfy himself that physical retirements have been recognized in the accounts, the auditor may supplement his procedural reviews by inspecting records indicating sales of scrap, by making inquiries of the engineering staff, construction superintendent, or production head, and by exploring other available sources of information.

Retirements from property accounts which appear on the books at appraised amounts should be made on the basis of such amounts.

When, in view of the company's system of internal accounting control, the auditor believes that procedural reviews, such as those described above, would not afford sufficient evidential matter, he may decide to extend his audit tests. Such extension usually would involve the examination of additional vouchers and other evidential data in support of changes in the plant accounts, other than those reflected on the work orders tested.

In Absence of a Work Order System.—When a work order system is not in use, the auditor should adopt procedures appropriate to the situation.

When plant additions consist of units acquired from outside vendors, invoices may be examined. The auditor should also determine whether these purchases, or at least purchases of the principal items, have been properly authorized.

Insignificant small items should not be capitalized. Additions to plant accounts for a given period should be grouped, and the client can usually furnish a description of the principal additions and improvements which have been undertaken or completed during the period.

Even though capital expenditures are not controlled through work orders, materials used are usually kept in a storeroom and become charges to plant accounts when issued on storeroom requisitions.

After the lapse of time, it may be impossible to determine by inspection of supporting vendors' invoices or storeroom requisitions what account should have been debited. Nevertheless, the auditor may compare a number of the documents supporting charges to property accounts with the related ledger entries, not only to ascertain that the entries have been correctly posted with respect to both account and amount, but also that, insofar as he can determine, they relate to items properly applicable to the accounts to which they have been charged.

In any examination of original data in support of accounts other than property, plant, and equipment, such as maintenance and repairs, the auditor should note the policy in accounting for these expenses and watch for items that should have been charged to property accounts rather than to expense.

If construction work to be capitalized is based on contracts, the auditor may examine the contracts and compare charges to property accounts with amounts called for by the agreements. After contracts have been signed, changes in the specifications are frequently authorized. The auditor should determine that extras have been properly approved and appear to be justifiable additions to the cost of construction.

Frequently an architect's or engineer's certificate relating to cost as well as to performance is required before final payment is made to the contractor. The auditor may examine such a certificate, but he should not place too much reliance on it, although it may be useful when the contract calls for a lump-sum payment and detailed costs are not available for the auditor's inspection.

If a contract for construction work by an outside contractor is a cost reimbursement type contract, or if the final price to be paid under the contract is in any way dependent upon the amount of costs incurred by the contractor, the owner or the architect should check the contractor's costs as the work progresses. This is usually done by having a representative of the owner or the architect, or both, at the job site at all times to review and approve payroll lists, reports of materials received from outside vendors or from the contractor's warehouse, equipment rental reports, vendors' invoices, and other cost supporting data. As a part of his regular examination, the auditor should determine whether the company has any such construction contracts in progress or about to be started, and whether it makes current examinations of the contractor's costs.

The auditor may review whatever collateral evidence of ownership and amount of property, plant, and equipment additions is available. Deeds, tax receipts, insurance policies, purchase contracts, all may be confirmatory of book entries or point to errors or omissions in accounting for property and equipment.

REAL ESTATE.—Ownership of real estate may be indicated by the absence of expenditures for rent, by unchallenged use and occupancy of the premises, or by the receipt of rental income. Expenditures for such items as taxes, building repairs, and interest on mortgages payable should indicate to the auditor that the company probably is the owner of an equity. Inspection of deeds, purchase contracts, settlement papers, insurance policies, minutes, and correspondence may further substantiate ownership. While such evidence is not always conclusive, the auditor is justified in accepting it as prima facie evidence of the ownership of real estate.

The auditor is not expected to pass upon legal questions of title. If he finds indications that there may be a question as to title to real estate carried in the accounts, the most practicable procedure is to secure from the company's attorney, or from a title company, a letter or certificate stating such information as may be applicable in the circumstances, as, for example,

1. Whether title to the real estate as it appears, or is described on the books, is in the name of the individual, firm or corporation under examination;

2. Whether the real estate is free from encumbrances, such as the following:
   (a) Mortgages,
   (b) Judgments,
   (c) Taxes or other municipal liens,
   (d) Possibility of reverter, because of failure to fulfill conditions in the contract of sale, such as, for example, that a plant will be erected within a stated time or that a specified number of men will be employed.

If possible, the cost of building sites should be segregated in the accounts from the cost of buildings and other improvements. If improved real estate is purchased, the auditor should review the data on which the apportionment of the cost of the property between land and improvements was based. Frequently tax assessment valuations, amounts of insurance coverage, and current appraisals are used for this purpose.

BUILDINGS.—When substantial amounts are expended on new or old buildings, vouchers and related supporting data should be examined or tested by the auditor. The construction as a whole should be checked with authorizations of the board of directors or responsible executives, and with bids or estimates submitted before the work was begun.

MACHINERY, TOOLS, FIXTURES, AND OTHER EQUIPMENT.—Purchases of machinery, large tools, fixtures, and other equipment should be analyzed to determine whether they represent actual additions to plant or renewals of existing facilities. Vendors' invoices should be examined in support of large items and in support of other items selected at random. Tests should be made to determine the propriety of installation costs, freight, labor, and other charges to the equipment accounts.

When machinery is purchased on a deferred payment plan, the auditor should examine the contracts and determine whether the total cost was charged to the asset account at the time of acquisition, and that provision is made for depreciation on the full cost. The status of instalment payments should be investigated, since if any instalments are overdue at the time the balance sheet is prepared, or if instalments have not been paid promptly, the equity may have been lost through right of repossession by the manufacturer.

If machinery is leased rather than purchased, there is no basis for including in the plant accounts any amount for leased machinery, since the lessee has no equity in the title. The auditor should examine lease agreements to determine the lessee's status. Frequently, memorandum records of leased equipment are maintained; these should be reviewed by the auditor in connection with his examination of the lease agreements.

Detailed records are often maintained in the form of a loose-leaf ledger or card file showing the particulars of the cost of machinery and equipment. The record should show how and when items were acquired, as well as such information as the cost of acquisition and installation, the annual allowance for depreciation, and the location in the factory. If the auditor determines that this record is reliable and is in agreement with the control account, it may be helpful to him in his tests of the changes in the accounts during the period under examination. In the absence of a formal detailed property record, an informal record may be kept for insurance purposes and should be examined for whatever information it may reveal.

TRANSPORTATION EQUIPMENT.—In his examination of the transportation equipment accounts, the auditor should employ basically the same techniques used in connection with his tests of changes in the machinery and equipment accounts.

The auditor should determine the number of vehicles in use to see whether those sold, exchanged, or scrapped have been properly accounted for. Although all vehicles depreciate rapidly, and the useful life of automotive equipment is usually short, the nature of these assets is such that repairs may prolong their lives.

The file of ownership certificates issued to owners in most states and containing information such as the kind, motor number, and registered owner of the vehicles may be useful to the auditor in his examination. Similar information may be found in automobile insurance policies.

PATTERNS, DRAWINGS, AND LASTS.—Patterns, drawings, and lasts frequently involve large expenditures, and recorded amounts are sometimes difficult to substantiate. If they are used for stock or regular production, their value depends on their life and on the probability of continued use. If acquired or made for special jobs, their residual value is small, and their cost should be charged to the special jobs. The auditor should review these items and seek substantial proof to support any material valuation.

Demands of the public change, and patterns must be made to suit the changing taste. When demand ceases, patterns become worthless and should be written off. In some lines of business, change in demand can be anticipated considerably in advance. The auditor should inquire about prospective changes and determine whether adequate allowance for obsolescence is being made for patterns capitalized on the books.

RETURNABLE CONTAINERS.—When the company requires deposits, the examination of the returnable containers account should include inspection of at least a part of the quantities on hand and computation of the quantities held by customers at the balance sheet date. Memorandum records should be available which show the number of containers held by customers or, if the deposit liability account has been kept accurately, the number can be determined by dividing the amount of the deposit liability by the deposit per container. After sufficient experience has developed on which to base an estimate, the percentage of containers which will never be returned should be estimated and entries made periodically to remove the cost of these containers from the property account and the deposits from the liability account, taking profit or loss to the income account.

When containers are furnished free with an obligation to return them, it must be assumed that customers treat the obligation lightly and that, in addition to the usual losses and breakages, a considerable portion will not be returned. If feasible, an attempt should be made at some convenient time to inventory containers on hand and those in the hands of customers that are believed to be recoverable. A comparison of such an inventory with the book inventory may provide a sound basis for determination of an expense rate or for estimating an allowance for depreciation.

When containers, such as kegs, crates, and syphons, are used without a deposit requirement, the customer being obligated to return them, the most common and probably the most satisfactory method of accounting for them is to note the quantities in the sales book and to post them in columns provided on both debit and credit sides of the customers' ledger. A test should be made of the records of returnable containers in the hands of customers.

MINES.—In the examination of mine accounts, the auditor should follow procedures previously suggested for examination of real estate, insofar as title and encumbrances are concerned.

In examining the amount at which mining property is carried, the auditor may not have much to guide him. As operations proceed, value of the mine property decreases, unless development and exploration work discloses new values. Improvements in extraction or reduction methods, in transportation, or in market prices may give value to ores previously considered worthless. An analysis of original cost, taking into consideration engineers' estimates of total contents, is a valuable check on the allowance for depletion. Engineers' records may not be submitted to the auditor, but he should be aware that no well-managed mining company attempts operation on a large scale unless fortified by scientific calculations of skilled engineers.

Appraisals.—When amounts reported as the result of appraisals are recorded, the auditor should secure a copy of the appraiser's report, inquire as to the basis on which the appraisal was made, and examine the resulting adjustments to determine whether they properly reflect the appraisal amounts.

The auditor should not accept appraised values without question, even when the appraisal is made by a reputable firm of appraisers. This does not imply that the auditor should criticize the appraiser's report as if he were a qualified appraiser, but rather that the auditor should read the appraiser's report to determine the basis on which the appraisal was made.

In some highly specialized industries, professional appraisers may not be considered as well qualified to determine the proper value of special machinery, dies, patterns, and molds peculiar to the industry, as are those intimately connected with their operation. When appraisals have been made by engineers or officers of the company, the auditor should inquire as to the qualifications of the appraisers and as to the methods used by them.

An entire plant may be acquired in exchange for common stock of the acquiring company. In the absence of an appraisal, the problem of valuation is a difficult one unless there is a readily determinable fair value for the common stock. Rather than assign the task to independent appraisers or company engineers, the board of directors may undertake to value the property and fix the value of the assets acquired at an amount sufficient to offset the par or stated value of the stock issued therefor. Since the directors may not be expert and certainly are not independent, the auditor should review available information and consider whether he should, in his report, take exception to the values established.

If, as a result of an appraisal, property, plant, and equipment accounts are revised downward, the auditor should investigate the basis for the revisions and review the entries recording the adjustments as comprehensively as if the adjustment had been upward.

Coordination of Examination with That of Related Accounts.— During the course of his examination the auditor should have in mind the relation to other accounts of the information and documentary evidence he is examining in support of property accounts. For example, examination of original documents supporting the acquisition of equipment may indicate that liens of various kinds exist, that the equipment was purchased on an instalment basis, or that a balance is due at some later date. The auditor should determine the nature of such liens, their present status, and that the accounts correctly reflect the liens themselves as well as unpaid instalments or balances still payable.

The accumulation of data for yearly additions and retirements in previous periods will expedite the review of accounts for repairs and allowances for depreciation. Data on additions and retirements should be accumulated in a form that will facilitate comparison with authorizations in directors' minutes or elsewhere.

Examination of plant accounts may indicate whether expenditures for maintenance and repairs have been capitalized; examination of expense accounts may indicate whether expenditures for plant assets have been charged to maintenance and repairs.

Time of Examination.—In the auditor's first examination, substantially all of his investigation of property, plant, and equipment acquired in prior periods may be made well in advance of the balance sheet date. He can not only analyze the general ledger accounts, but also summarize available records which may indicate the principles or procedures on which the accounts have been established. Additions and retirements can be summarized by years. Collateral and historical data can be reviewed. Major additions and acquisitions can be investigated, and all the assembled information studied to formulate an opinion on the reasonableness of the book amounts.

In subsequent annual examinations, the auditor can expedite the review of property, plant, and equipment accounts by a preliminary audit of transactions recorded for, possibly, the first ten months of the period. After the close of the year, he may examine transactions of the remaining two months.

STATEMENT PRESENTATION

General.—No one designation of property, plant, and equipment on the balance sheet has been accepted to the exclusion of others. "Property, plant, and equipment," "fixed assets," "land, buildings, machinery, and equipment," "general property," "properties," "plant, equipment, and real estate," and numerous other captions will be found in published financial statements. In condensed balance sheets, only one amount may appear to show the aggregate amount of the items to which the caption applies.

Preferably, nondepreciable property, such as land, should be segregated from depreciable property, such as buildings and machinery. Real estate not used in the business should be stated separately. Excess land, buildings, and equipment being offered for sale, if material in amount, should be stated separately from property in use, at amounts not in excess of estimated realizable value. Construction work in progress, if significant in amount, may be stated separately, or, if included with completed projects, may be indicated parenthetically.

If a company is in the business of buying and selling real estate, properties held for sale constitute inventory and should not be included under property, plant, and equipment. It is the practice of some such companies to reflect in their statements only their equity in property held for sale, when purchased subject to a mortgage or other liens. When liability under a mortgage is assumed by the purchaser, the proper treatment is to show the mortgage as a liability and the property at its gross amount.

Accumulated allowances for depreciation or depletion should be shown on the balance sheet either as deductions from the group of assets to which they relate, or as a deduction from the total of depreciable or depletable assets. Sometimes plant assets are shown after deducting the related allowances for depreciation or depletion; allowances should then be indicated parenthetically or in a footnote.

Ordinarily allowances for depreciation and depletion should not be shown on the liability side of the balance sheet. However, the uniform systems of accounts prescribed by many state regulatory commissions for use by certain public utilities provide for showing such reserves on the liability side of the balance sheet. Some utilities so reflect the reserves in their reports to the commissions and in their published reports to stockholders. The uniform system of accounts adopted by the Federal Power Commission contains similar provisions; however, that Commission's annual report forms require the reserves to be shown as deductions from the related assets. Similarly, Regulation S-X which prescribes the form and content of financial statements required to be filed with the Securities and Exchange Commission states in Rule 3.11 that "valuation and qualifying reserves shall be shown separately in the financial statements as deductions from the specific assets to which they apply."

Gross cost of facilities purchased under an instalment plan should be shown among the assets, with an indication of any material lien. Unpaid instalments should be shown among the liabilities. It is not good practice to state only the client's equity in instalment purchases, even though title to the property remains in the vendor until completion of the purchase contract.

Property Stated on Cost Basis.—It has long been an accepted principle of balance sheet presentation that, unless there is a notation to the contrary, the reader may assume that property, plant, and equipment is carried at cost less allowance for depreciation. Cost means cost in cash or its equivalent. Preferably, the words "at cost" are appended to the principal plant caption to avoid any possibility of misunderstanding.

When plant assets are carried at cost less accrued depreciation, there is no need for reporting replacement values. Some lawyers and corporation officials, however, have been apprehensive about stating plant assets at cost less depreciation allowance at a time when current replacement cost may be materially above or below the net book figure, for fear that, in the absence of explanation, such presentation might be construed by the courts as false or misleading. The question may be regarded as significant, for example, when an appraisal at reproduction cost of property covered by mortgage bonds offered for sale in a period of declining prices may be less than the actual amount paid for the property. There is no objection to appending a note to the balance sheet avowing that the amount carried for plant and property does not purport to represent reproduction cost or present value, or to stating any facts deemed to bear on the value of the property.

Property Stated on Bases Other Than Cost.

APPRAISAL AMOUNTS.—When plant assets are carried at appraised amounts, not cost, the balance sheet should clearly so indicate. It is good practice to indicate in the descriptive matter the fact that the appraisal was made by independent appraisers and the date and basis of the appraisal. The appraiser should be informed of the language proposed to be used and his approval or suggested modifications sought.

If the appraisal was made by the board of directors, by company engineers, or by other employees who may not be considered independent, that fact should be indicated clearly. As stated elsewhere, if study of available data indicates that amounts recorded are not reasonable, the auditor should suitably qualify his report.

RESTATEMENTS.—When property, plant, and equipment accounts are restated pursuant to orders of regulatory bodies or to plans of reorganization or corporate readjustments, the nature and amount of the restatement should be indicated clearly.

Restatements of plant accounts may be made in connection with a quasi-reorganization. The Securities and Exchange Commission states in Accounting Series Releases Nos. 15 and 16, dated March 16, 1940, that when a quasi-reorganization has been effected with the approval of the stockholders the transactions incident thereto should be disclosed in financial statements filed with the Commission by registered companies for the year involved and for at least three years subsequent to the date the new bases were established and, further, if such approval has not been obtained, the disclosure should be made in all statements thereafter filed with the Commission.

Idle Plant, Reserve, and Stand-By Equipment.—Plant assets on the balance sheet may include property in use and property held with reasonable expectation of its being used in the business. It is not customary to segregate or indicate the existence of temporarily idle plant, reserve, or stand-by equipment. Property abandoned but not physically retired and facilities still owned but no longer adapted for use in the business, if material in amount, should be removed from plant accounts and recorded separately at estimated realizable amount, appropriately explained.

When a material portion of plant and equipment has been idle for a protracted period with no apparent likelihood of resuming operations, the amount should be set forth separately with an appropriate caption. Such idle plant facilities involve a continuing expense, and creditors, stockholders, and others interested should be apprised of the fact that property, plant, and equipment exceeds apparent reasonable needs.

Fully Depreciated Items.—As the allowance for depreciation is at best an estimate, facilities may be operating after full depreciation has been provided on the books. One of the following treatments of fully depreciated plant may be adopted:

1. The amount of fully depreciated items may be included in the gross amount of property, plant, and equipment, and the related allowance for depreciation may be included in the accumulated allowances for depreciation.

2. The amount of fully depreciated items may be removed from the respective property, plant, and equipment and the related accumulated depreciation accounts, and shown separately in the balance sheet.

3. The amount of fully depreciated items may be written off against the related allowance for depreciation, so that no amount appears in the balance sheet.

If the facilities are being used, either the first or second method is preferable. If the first method is selected, it would be appropriate to disclose the amounts involved either parenthetically or in a footnote to the statements.

CHAPTER 13

DEPRECIATION AND DEPLETION

ACCOUNTING PRINCIPLES

Introduction.—This chapter deals principally with the methods of computing provisions for depreciation and depletion in accordance with generally accepted accounting principles. Such methods do not necessarily coincide with methods acceptable for federal income tax purposes. When depreciation and depletion provisions computed for financial statement purposes differ materially from allowable deductions for income tax purposes, it may be desirable to apply the principle of tax allocation discussed in Chapter 22.

Plant facilities which have been certified, in whole or in part, by the federal government as necessary for defense purposes, generally known as "emergency facilities," are allowed rapid amortization for income tax purposes, which may or may not agree with depreciation based on expected useful life. Problems arising from the amortization of emergency facilities are also discussed in Chapter 22.

Depreciation.

INTRODUCTION.—The subject of depreciation is one which has engaged the attention of accountants and engineers for many years. The necessity for an allowance for depreciation of tangible fixed assets is generally accepted, but the difference between the accountant's concept of depreciation accounting and the engineer's concept of observed physical depreciation is not generally clear in the lay mind. Accordingly, nonprofessional readers of financial statements often fail to comprehend the significance of the provisions and allowances for depreciation reflected in financial statements. Depreciation as used in accounting is not the same as physical depreciation.

Physical depreciation of property, plant, and equipment is generally understood to be the loss in useful life or efficiency caused by wear and tear from operation and by deterioration resulting from chemical reactions from air, water, gas, or other elements. In varying degrees it takes place whether plant and equipment is operated or is idle, whether it is well cared for or neglected, whether it is built from materials of good quality or constructed from scrap. Usually no direct relationship exists between physical evidence of depreciation and book allowances reasonably and carefully determined by the application of generally accepted principles of depreciation accounting.

The Committee on Terminology of The American Institute of Certified Public Accountants, in Terminology Bulletin No. 1, defines depreciation accounting as follows:

Depreciation accounting is a system of accounting which aims to distribute the cost or other basic value of tangible capital assets, less salvage (if any), over the estimated useful life of the unit (which may be a group of assets) in a systematic and rational manner. It is a process of allocation, not of valuation. *Depreciation for the year* is the portion of the total charge under such a system that is allocated to the year. Although the allocation may properly take into account occurrences during the year, it is not intended to be a measurement of the effect of all such occurrences.

CONSISTENCY IN APPLICATION.—The accounting recognition of depreciation and the reasonableness of depreciation allowances necessarily are based upon an estimate of useful life. Useful life may be less than physical life because of such factors as obsolescence and inadequacy. The estimate of useful life should be based on experience and intelligent consideration of existing circumstances and future possibilities.

When a sound depreciation policy has been decided upon, it should be applied consistently until fundamental conditions change to such a degree that its application no longer produces reasonable results. If accounting provisions for depreciation are not consistently computed, comparisons of statements of income for the affected periods may be either useless, misleading, or both.

The maintenance of a consistent policy does not necessarily imply or require that the rates of depreciation must be inflexible. Circumstances may arise which make it desirable to accelerate or decelerate provisions for depreciation. For example, when production is abnormally heavy, physical depreciation may be greater than was expected when the rates were established because there is less opportunity to repair and maintain machinery properly or because the machinery may suffer from operation by several persons in a multiple-shift operation. When cessation of demand is foreseen or radical new inventions threaten the ability of old machines to compete, an effort should be made to absorb the undepreciated cost of equipment during its remaining useful life. Conversely, as time passes, actual experience may indicate that the original estimates of useful lives were too conservative, and that the useful lives may be considerably longer than originally anticipated. When such conditions arise, studies should be made to determine whether the useful life has been shortened or lengthened and, if it has, to what extent this should be reflected in revised rates for the existing facilities and for future acquisitions of similar facilities.

BASIS OF DEPRECIATION ACCOUNTING.—It has long been recognized by business management, public accountants, and certain regulatory bodies that the proper basis for computation of depreciation is cost. Unrecorded increases or decreases in market value of the property and the fact that cost of replacement may be greater or less than the amount at which stated in the accounts should have no bearing on the amount to be recovered through depreciation charges to operations.

Chapter 12 contains a discussion of the subject of depreciation and high costs and the position taken by the Committee on Accounting Procedure on that subject. It also discusses the circumstances, such as reorganization or quasi-reorganization, when fixed assets may be written up or down justifiably to appraised amounts.

The Committee on Accounting Procedure has expressed its opinion in Accounting Research Bulletin No. 43, Chapter 9, Section B, to the effect that:

When appreciation has been entered in the books income should be charged with depreciation computed on the written-up amounts. A company should not at the same time claim larger property valuations in its statement of assets and provide for the amortization of only smaller amounts in its statement of income. When a company has made representations as to an increased valuation of plant, depreciation accounting and periodic income determination thereafter should be based on such higher amounts.

ACCOUNTS USED FOR APPLICATION OF DEPRECIATION METHODS.—Two broad types of accounts are in general use for applying depreciation rates; namely, the unit and the composite or group account. Under the unit account method, the useful life of each item is considered individually in determining a proper rate for depreciation. When an item is retired before the end of its estimated useful life, the resulting profit or loss is reflected in the income account for the period during which the transaction takes place.

The composite or group account method is predicated on the theory that the group of items to which it is applied has a reasonably determinable average useful life and that the period by which the actual useful life of certain items falls short of the general average will be compensated for by useful lives of other items extending beyond the average. It is assumed, for example, in a group of assets with an average useful life of ten years that items retired at the end of seven years will be offset by the continuance of other items, equivalent in dollars, for thirteen years of service. If composite accounts are used, it is desirable that the assets be segregated into as many classified or functional groups as are appropriate under the circumstances. This segregation will facilitate the initial determination of reasonable rates and provide a basis for subsequent periodic reconsideration of the reasonableness of the rates selected. The composite rate should be redetermined whenever substantial changes occur in the "mix" of the account, i.e., in the relation of long- or short-lived items weighted in dollars.

In the composite account method, upon normal retirement the cost of property retired is credited to the account and such cost, plus cost of removal, less salvage value, is charged to the accumulated allowance for depreciation. As a result, the remaining undepreciated balance of cost of retirements made before the average life is spread over periods beyond the average.

When assets in a group account are retired because of casualty or "extraordinary obsolescence," any resulting loss should be reflected in the income account. The allowance for depreciation should be charged only with an amount equal to estimated depreciation, including normal obsolescence, accrued to the time of such retirement, and the undepreciated balance of the cost, less salvage, should be charged to income.

DEPRECIATION RATES.—A reasonable rate of depreciation is based on the prospective useful life of the property from date of acquisition.

In estimating useful life, the conditions under which the property is used, normal obsolescence, probable salvage value, and the policy of maintenance, repairs, and replacements should be considered. Depreciation rates should be reviewed periodically and adjusted if changes in operating conditions warrant.

Useful Life.—The useful life of depreciable assets is based on their period of usefulness to the company and not their inherent life. For example, a machine tool may be useful to an automobile manufacturer for a foreseeable period of some fifteen years. The finer tolerances required in this industry may render the machine unusable after that period. However, it may give satisfactory performance in other industries for many more years. The automobile manufacturer should use a rate based on a fifteen-year life and an allowance for estimated net salvage recovery at the expiration of use.

Where group accounts are maintained for hundreds or thousands of different types of equipment, it is obvious that many variations will be encountered between the original estimates for each component and the actual life experience. One advantage of the group method stems from the probability of offset in deviations from estimate; while some assets in the group will last longer, others will be retired sooner than expected. Thus, changes in estimates need not be handled on a unit basis.

If the enterprise is one which deals with depletable assets, consideration must be given to the possibility that available coal, metal, oil, gas, or timber of commercial value may be exhausted before the expiration of the physical life of other assets and, as a result, shorten the anticipated useful service life of equipment used in production of wasting assets. It is not unusual to find that, when a mine closes down, equipment on hand is worthless because dismantling and removing it from the mine would cost more than would be realized from its sale. When these factors have been taken into consideration, the period over which the entire cost of depreciable assets will be written off may not represent the estimated physical service life of the assets, but rather the period of usefulness to the company while used for the purpose for which they were acquired.

Salvage.—Salvage, as used in depreciation computations, is the amount recovered by proceeds of sales, scrap value, fair value of reused or usable parts, or components of retired assets, etc., less dismantling costs and other costs of realizing such recovery. The probable salvage recovery at the end of the customary period of usefulness, based on current price levels, should be estimated at the time of acquisition. If single-item accounts are maintained, past recoveries on similar assets may provide the basis for an estimate.

For group accounts, the determination of a salvage recovery ratio is made by determining the aggregate proceeds from sale, scrapping, or value of reused parts for a representative period of years; this total is compared with the gross cost of assets retired during the period for all causes.

Allowance for Obsolescence.—No manufacturer can depend on keeping his plant operating profitably and successfully merely by replacing existing equipment with similar equipment. He must be prepared to replace machinery with improved equipment as it becomes available and when such replacement would provide related operating benefits and economies. It is inevitable that such improvements will be made over a period of time. Accordingly, normal obsolescence which is inherent in existing property, as opposed to so-called extraordinary obsolescence, should be recognized in determining depreciation rates. It is not contemplated that extraordinary obsolescence, such as that which might result from legislation, regulation, or entirely unexpected and radical developments, be considered in determining depreciation rates.

Normal obsolescence occurs when equipment becomes inadequate. Over a period of years most successful concerns increase the volume of production or service, necessitating the discarding of equipment of small capacity before it is worn out in favor of equipment of greater capacity which can be operated more economically.

Relation of Repairs and Replacements to Depreciation.—The useful life of equipment will vary considerably depending on the degree of preventive maintenance and timing of repairs. Therefore, when considering the reasonableness of charges to operations for depreciation, due regard should be given to expenditures for current upkeep or maintenance.

The policy of a company may be to classify as maintenance expenses the cost of major parts of machines that are continuously wearing out and breaking. Practically all moving parts of some machines are renewable, and it is not unusual to find that eventually the machine has been substantially rebuilt. The machine may be relatively efficient until immediately before it is scrapped; however, under the accounting concept, depreciation accumulates during the entire period of useful life of the machine. Under the unit account method, if neither obsolescence nor inadequacy is evident toward the end of the originally estimated life, and it appears that the machine can be maintained in efficient operating condition for some additional time beyond the original estimate, it would be proper to decrease the depreciation rate. Similar adjustment may be proper under the group account method.

Depreciation rates on identical equipment owned by different companies may vary because of different maintenance policies, even though the elements of obsolescence and of wear and tear not covered by maintenance and renewals are similar. Maintenance policies may vary physically as to the degree of efficiency at which equipment is maintained, and as to the accounting treatment of maintenance whether as an expense or as a replacement charged to the accumulated allowance for depreciation.

Physical depreciation of certain assets is so rapid that conventional depreciation methods may not be appropriate. Small tools, dies, jigs, and molds are examples of items which are consumed so rapidly that periodic inventorying would be required for allocation of expenditures to operating expenses. Charging the cost of replacements of such items to maintenance in lieu of depreciating them is usually a satisfactory alternative.

METHODS OF COMPUTING DEPRECIATION.—There are numerous methods which may be used in computing depreciation charges. All acceptable methods are based on estimated useful life. The methods adopted may vary within a single business as to the different classes of property. The generally accepted methods most frequently used at the present time are:

1. Straight-line,
2. Declining-balance,
3. Sum-of-the-years-digits, and
4. Unit-of-production and hours-of-service.

Other methods used in the past, infrequently encountered today, and generally not accepted by accountants, include the appraisal method and the gross operating revenue method. The appraisal method contemplates frequent appraisals of property and the determination of the charge for depreciation as the difference between the appraised values of the property at the beginning and end of the period. Basically, this method generally ignores expected or normal obsolescence and assumes that the allowance for depreciation is limited to the amount indicated by observed physical depreciation. Accordingly, the portion of any loss attributable to normal obsolescence upon retirement of equipment falls in the period in which the disposal is made. This practice violates the basic concept of depreciation accounting because it does not fairly allocate the cost of depreciable property to income over its useful life.

The gross operating revenue method of charging income with amounts based on percentages of revenue fails to recognize whether or not the amounts so accumulated will be sufficient to absorb the cost of property over its service life. The percentage is not usually increased if gross revenues do not come up to expectations. As a result, depreciation due to deterioration and obsolescence, which continues in periods of declining revenues, is not absorbed in costs of those periods. It is obvious that this method may result in extreme fluctuations in the provision for depreciation from period to period.

Straight-Line Method.—Many manufacturing companies compute depreciation charges by the straight-line method under which depreciation is provided in equal annual amounts over the estimated useful life.

It has been contended that the unit-of-production or hours-of-service method distributes cost more reasonably than does the straight-line method; however, if such unit methods are used and volume falls substantially below normal, it may be necessary to increase the depreciation charged to income in the period to a reasonable minimum. When production or hours of service materially affect the life of the asset, it may be preferable to use such a basis, but when depreciation is not materially affected by hours of service, or when exhaustion of useful life cannot be related reasonably to products produced, the straight-line method is preferable.

Declining-Balance Method.—The Committee on Accounting Procedure has stated in Accounting Research Bulletin No. 44, October, 1954, that "The declining-balance method is one of those which meets the requirements of being 'systematic and rational.' " Similar endorsement was expressed for other methods, including sum-of-the-years-digits, which produce substantially similar results.

Under the declining-balance method, depreciation is assumed to be greatest in the first year and smaller in each succeeding year during the useful life of the asset or group of assets. A rate is determined, based on a formula, that, when applied to the diminishing balance of cost periodically determined, will reduce the initial cost to estimated salvage value by the end of the useful life. The estimated salvage is not deducted from the cost in computing the annual depreciation. Proponents of this method claim that the allowance for depreciation should be relatively higher during the early years of the useful life of a depreciable fixed asset, when repairs and maintenance are usually lower, and that in later years, when repairs and maintenance are higher, the allowance for depreciation should be lower. Furthermore, in some industries there is great exposure to risks of competition, new processes and products, and

rapid changes in consumer preference, which require higher depreciation during such early years.

When using the declining-balance method, it is necessary to apply
a rate greater than would be required to depreciate the asset over the
same number of years by the straight-line method. Otherwise, a sufficient allowance would not be provided over the useful life of the
asset. For example, if a fixed percentage of 10 per cent were applied
to the original cost on a declining-balance basis to an item costing
$1,000.00 with a useful life of ten years and an anticipated salvage
value of $100.00, an undepreciated balance of cost of $348.68 would
remain at the end of the tenth year, instead of $100.00 under the
straight-line method. On the other hand, application of a 20 per cent
rate under the declining-balance method will result in an undepreciated
balance at the end of the tenth year of $107.38. Theoretically, a rate
slightly more than double the straight-line rate is needed to provide
for the residual balance of 10 per cent of the asset cost at the end of its
useful life. As a practical matter, double the straight-line rate is used
generally because it is the maximum permitted by the Internal Revenue
Code of 1954. Using double the straight-line rate, there always remains at the end of the estimated useful life of a single item a residual
of cost, so that no allowance for salvage value is made in the computation.

Sum-of-the-Years-Digits Method.—This method is similar in effect
to the declining-balance method in that it provides a greater proportion
of depreciation during the earlier years as compared with the later years
of useful life. It differs from the declining-balance method in that it
accumulates 100 per cent of the amount being depreciated by the end
of the estimated life. Therefore, the cost should be reduced by the
estimated salvage before applying this method.

The application of the sum-of-the-years-digits method to a unit
account is as follows: The rate of depreciation is successively lower
for each year. It is determined from a fraction in which the numerator
for each year represents the remaining estimated life of the asset in
such year and the denominator is an amount which is obtained by
adding the years of estimated life numbered successively from one
through the last year of expected life. For example, assuming a property item has an estimated useful life of ten years, the sum of the years
from 1 to 10 is 55 and the respective annual depreciation rates are 10/55
for the first year, 9/55 for the second year, and so on to the tenth year
when the rate would be 1/55. Using the half-year averaging convention, the respective annual depreciation rates are 5.0/55 for the year of

acquisition, 9.5/55 for the following year, then 8.5/55, and so on to the tenth year after year of acquisition when the rate would be 0.5/55.

The method illustrated above is not applicable to group accounts because (1) without reduction of cost for retirements, the items in the group would be fully depreciated at the end of the average life, even though some items remain in service for an additional period, and (2) if the cost and allowance for depreciation are reduced for subsequent retirements, a balance will remain at the end of the average life, but the method provides no way for depreciating it. Therefore, the Treasury Department's Regulations prescribe a "remaining life plan," under which the computed depreciation for group accounts results in a charge to income for each of the years of the total useful life of the asset group. This plan is acceptable for general accounting purposes.

Comparisons of Results of the Above Methods.—There is shown below a comparison of annual and cumulative depreciation for a single item under straight-line, declining-balance, and sum-of-the-years-digits methods, assuming an asset cost of $100, a 10-year useful life, and salvage value of $10 at the end of the useful life and assuming a full year's depreciation in the first year.

| | Straight-Line Method | | Declining-Balance Method | | Sum-of-the-Years-Digits Method | |
| | Rate—10% | | Rate—20% | | | |
Year	Annual	Accumulated	Annual	Accumulated	Annual	Accumulated
1st	$9.00	$ 9.00	$20.00	$20.00	$16.36	$16.36
2d	9.00	18.00	16.00	36.00	14.73	31.09
3d	9.00	27.00	12.80	48.80	13.09	44.18
4th	9.00	36.00	10.24	59.04	11.45	55.63
5th	9.00	45.00	8.19	67.23	9.82	65.45
6th	9.00	54.00	6.55	73.78	8.18	73.63
7th	9.00	63.00	5.24	79.02	6.55	80.18
8th	9.00	72.00	4.20	83.22	4.91	85.09
9th	9.00	81.00	3.36	86.58	3.27	88.36
10th	9.00	90.00	2.68	89.26	1.64	90.00

Unit-of-Production and Hours-of-Service Methods.—Under the unit-of-production method, depreciation is provided for in the ratio that the number of units of production during a period bears to the estimated total number of units which a plant or a part thereof may be expected to produce during normal useful life, and is appropriate if the life span thereof can be calculated within reasonable limits in units of production. This method is considered appropriate in such cases as blast furnaces and coke plants, and in the extractive industries.

Generally there are not many classes of plant and equipment with useful lives that can be reasonably estimated in terms of production units; accordingly, the difficulties involved in computing depreciation under this method usually preclude its use.

The hours-of-service method which attempts to relate loss of useful life to hours of actual use of property is subject to the same limitations as the unit-of-production method.

Other Methods.—A number of variations and refinements of methods of computing depreciation have been devised to meet varying conditions. Some of these variations have been designated by special terms such as the declining-rates method and the multiple straight-line rates method. These methods are not often found in practice.

Depreciation on Additions During the Year.—Some companies begin depreciation in the month after acquisition; various other conventions have been adopted. One frequently used is based on the assumption that all additions are acquired on July 1 of each year and sustain one-half year's depreciation. Where a disproportionately large addition is made toward the beginning or end of the year, it may be subject to separate computation so as not to distort income.

Another convention in some use is to begin depreciation with the first of the year following the year of acquisition.

LAND.—From the accountant's viewpoint, land is not subject to depreciation. It is not subject to physical wear and tear, and its economic obsolescence, if any, is not determinable. An exception might be that arable land may depreciate through use when not currently restored through proper agricultural practices.

CONSTRUCTION WORK IN PROGRESS.—Many concerns clear all charges for new equipment and construction through a work-in-progress account and transfer accumulated costs to the appropriate asset accounts upon completion of installation or construction. Depreciation should not be computed on uncompleted construction since depreciation for accounting purposes is assumed to begin only after the unit of property under construction is available for operating use.

PURCHASED PLANT.—Acquired properties are ordinarily recorded at cost. Since a portion of the useful life of such property has expired, careful consideration should be given to the estimate of its remaining useful life and classification of depreciable assets. Under the "accounting" prescribed for utility companies, property is generally required to be stated at its original cost to the person first devoting it to public service, and the difference between this original cost and the cost to the purchaser is included in a separate account to be disposed of according to commission regulations.

IMPROVEMENTS TO LEASED PROPERTY.—Department stores, hotels, theaters, and office buildings often are erected on land which is leased for a definite term of years, and tenants may make extensive improvements to leased buildings. The general rule to be followed by lessees is to amortize the cost of improvements to leased property over the life of the lease or to depreciate them over the useful life of the improvement, whichever is shorter.

For depreciation purposes the life of a lease is its original term, without regard to options to renew unless and until such options are actually, or obviously will be, exercised. Substantial expenditures made toward the close of the lease period may indicate that renewal is likely. When the lessee elects to exercise the option, any unamortized portion of improvements should be distributed over the period between the date the option is exercised and the extended expiration date of the lease, or over the remaining useful life of the improvements, whichever is the shorter.

When a lease requires the restoration of the premises to their original condition, reasonable wear and tear excepted, the estimated expenses of such restoration should be spread over the lease term.

REPLACEMENT ACCOUNTING AND RETIREMENT RESERVE ACCOUNTING.—These accounting methods were at one time used extensively. Railroads are required to follow replacement accounting as to track components. With this exception, such methods are today virtually nonexistent and are not generally considered acceptable substitutes for depreciation accounting.

Depletion.

INTRODUCTION.—Depletion represents the absorption of investment in natural resources through amortization of its cost by charges to operations over the period during which the quantities or units of such resources are extracted or exhausted.

An allowance for depreciation is identified with the amortization of cost of productive facilities, but an allowance for depletion is identified with the amortization of cost of natural resources. Enterprises exploiting depletable assets generally employ both depreciable and depletable assets.

When plant and equipment remain idle, depreciation not only continues, but may be accelerated. Cessation of operations does not ordinarily affect the units of natural resources since they remain to be extracted in the future. Obsolescence rarely affects natural resources.

OMISSION OF ALLOWANCE FOR DEPLETION.—Some companies engaged in nonferrous metal mining omit depletion allowances from their financial statements. In support of the practice they contend that it is impossible to obtain information sufficiently accurate for use as a basis upon which to calculate depletion, and, therefore, any allowance would be arbitrary and possibly misleading. They further contend that an allowance for depletion is of no importance because investors in such enterprises expect the managements to extract and sell the depletable assets as efficiently and economically as possible and to distribute to the investors the amounts realized from such extraction. The corporation laws of some states permit extractive industries to determine income available for dividends without providing allowances for depletion.

Available information about future productivity varies greatly in different mines. Many large mines were developed extensively prior to the beginning of extraction operations, because development was necessary for assurance of sufficient quantities of minerals to justify investment in costly installations of mining equipment, power plants, railroad lines, and other facilities. In smaller properties, however, frequently no more than a few years' supply of mineral was developed in advance of extraction. It may be unjustifiably expensive in some types of mines to develop the data necessary to estimate with reasonable accuracy the total units available. Probable and possible mineral contents may be indicated, but frequently definite assurance of additional commercial mineral is sought only as extraction progresses.

After preliminary development ceases and commercial operations begin, extraction and development proceed together. Some companies contend that, when later development indicates that the quantity of assured mineral equals approximately the quantity in sight at the beginning of commercial operations, the necessity for depletion charges is eliminated by charging the cost of such development to operations.

Companies which provide for depletion support their position as follows:

1. While it is recognized generally that it is often impossible to make accurate provision for depletion, nevertheless the determination of a provision based on the best available current information is preferable to the absence of any provision in the accounts.

2. There can be little criticism of determination of depletion provisions on the basis of the best available information, even if the rates require frequent adjustment.

3. While it is probably true that investors in closely held wasting-asset companies are not greatly concerned about deduction of depletion provisions in arriving at distributable income, the ordinary in-

vestor not closely associated with management may be confused and misled by financial statements giving no recognition to depletion.

Most companies in extractive industries, other than nonferrous metals, recognize depletion provisions in arriving at net income.

The authors believe that in all extractive industries allowances should be made for depletion of the book amounts of natural resources through charges to income.

BASIS OF DEPLETION.—Ordinarily the basis for depletion is cost. When the assets have been reappraised, the revaluation amounts should form the basis for depletion.

METHODS OF COMPUTING DEPLETION.—*Production Method.*—This method, based on production or output, is most widely used in computing depletion for accounting purposes. The depletion rate may be determined in relation to mineral reserves actually assured, that is, blocked out or in sight, or in relation not only to such assured reserves but also to probable and possible reserves. Under the former procedure, the unit rate applied to extractions during the year is determined by dividing the unamortized cost of the asset at the beginning of the year by the units of mineral in sight at the end of the year plus the units extracted during the year. If, as extraction proceeds, development continues to be successful, this method will result in higher depletion charges in the earlier years of the mine life than in later years. When probable or possible minerals are included in the depletion computations, the depletion rate may remain unchanged for a number of years or until conditions indicate the necessity for a change. If estimates of probable or possible minerals prove to have been optimistic, depletion allowances will have been inadequate. Depletion provisions should not be based on probable or possible minerals unless competent geological or other evidence has indicated a high degree of probability.

Percentage Method.—Under the percentage depletion provisions of the Internal Revenue Code and Regulations, applicable to all minerals, depletion is computed on the basis of a fixed percentage of gross income from the property (5 to 27½ per cent, depending on the nature of the product extracted), limited to 50 per cent of net income from the property, computed without depletion allowance. This method is not generally accepted for general accounting purposes.

DEVELOPMENT COSTS.—Until commercial operations begin, development costs are ordinarily not charged against income but are included in the mine property account, or recorded in a separate account. If depletion is recognized in the accounts, deferred development costs are usually amortized simultaneously with mineral costs.

In determining when a mine has passed from a development to a producing status, it is usually considered that the producing stage is reached when the major portion of mineral production is obtained from workings other than those opened for the purpose of development, or when the principal activity of the mine becomes the production of developed mineral rather than the development of additional minerals for mining.

The Internal Revenue Code provides that a taxpayer may elect either to deduct expenditures made in the development of a mine or other natural deposit (other than an oil or gas well), whether incurred before or after the production stage is reached, in the year they are incurred, or to defer the expenditures and deduct them ratably as the ore or mineral is sold.

MINING PROPERTIES.—If the quantity of minerals contained in a property could be definitely determined upon its acquisition, an exact ratable portion of the property cost could be allocated to each unit extracted and sold. Under such circumstances, the accumulated allowance for depletion at any date would represent the portion of the original property cost applicable to units extracted. Because of the difficulties in estimating the mineral contents of a property, the depletion charge can only be based on an estimate of the approximate unit cost of these assets. Ordinarily an exact unit rate of depletion is not determinable at the inception of a mining venture; however, a reasonable and consistent basis can usually be found for the computation of a depletion rate.

Theoretically, a mining property has been partly depleted whenever any mineral has been extracted. In practice, however, depletion may be recognized first at any one of a number of different points between the extraction and the sale of the mineral product. For example, in metal mines, depletion is variously computed upon tons of ore mined, tons of ore milled, tons of concentrate produced, or units of metal sold.

Depletion may be computed on the unit of metal, such as the pound of copper or ounce of gold, or upon the mining unit such as the ton of ore. Since the unit of sale is usually not a ton of ore but rather a pound or ounce of metal contained therein and since the percentage of metal contained in ores in different sections of a mine may vary widely, depletion rates applied to units of metal would seem to produce more equitable results. Obviously, since value is inherent only in the metal, the prices at which metal mining properties are bought and sold depend not upon tons of ore but rather upon quantities of metal. Accordingly, if depletion is determined on the basis of tons of ore, the charge will be the same for a ton of high-grade ore as for a ton of low-grade ore and will be distorted.

OIL AND GAS RESOURCES.—No one can predict accurately the commercially useful life of an oil well. The probable reserves of oil or gas are usually estimated by geologists.

When production is obtained, depletion of development costs and depreciation of equipment costs should be computed at rates per unit of production applied to such costs. These rates should be determined by dividing the costs to be depleted or depreciated by the units of probable reserves estimated by geologists.

TIMBER AND TIMBERLANDS.—Cutting of timber depletes timberlands just as the extraction of mineral deposits depletes a mine. There should be written off each year that proportion of the cost of the timber as the quantity of timber cut during the year bears to the quantity standing at the time of its purchase. Allowance for the value, if any, of the cut-over lands should be made in determining the amount of the charge for depletion.

Since it is easier to determine accurately the quantity of timber standing on a tract of land than it is to determine the contents of a mine, it follows that depletion (stumpage) charges for timber can be arrived at more accurately than can depletion charges in mining operations.

The accounting recognition of accretion in value of timberlands resulting from natural growth has been given considerable attention by accountants and others. It has been pointed out that many industries dependent on wood have found it desirable to operate timberlands on a continuing basis. While there may be merit to recognizing accretion in the accounts, it is seldom done in practice. When sums are spent in clearing and reseeding cut-over lands to insure second growth, such expenditures may be capitalized and depleted when the new timber is cut.

INTERNAL CONTROL

In General.—All companies should clearly define policies governing accounting for purchase, construction, retirement, and replacement of property, plant, and equipment, and for maintenance and repairs. These policies necessarily affect depreciation and depletion accounting policies. Therefore, internal control of depreciation and depletion accounting is closely related to internal control of property and maintenance accounts. When subsidiary depreciation and depletion records are maintained, the amounts shown therein for the current provision and the accumulated allowance should be balanced periodically with general ledger control accounts. In addition, transactions recorded in the accounts for allowances for depreciation and depletion should be reconciled with transactions recorded in other accounts. Thus, debits recorded in allowance accounts should be reconciled with credits to property, plant, and equipment accounts; and credits recorded in allowance accounts should be matched with charges to appropriate expense or cost accounts.

At the end of the accounting period it is customary to prepare summaries of transactions recorded in allowance accounts. Ordinarily, these summaries are prepared in comparative form, which adds materially to their usefulness.

AUDITING PROCEDURES

Objectives.—The auditor's objective in examining provisions and allowances for depreciation and depletion is to satisfy himself that the current and accumulated provisions or allowances appear to have been made in accordance with generally accepted accounting principles consistently applied. When provisions or allowances appear to be inappropriate or unreasonable, or if the principles of depreciation or depletion accounting have not been consistently followed, the auditor should see that an appropriate explanatory footnote is included in the financial statements or state the facts clearly in his report; further, he should take exception if the principles or practices followed do not result in a fair and consistent presentation of financial position and earnings.

Examination of Opening Balances.—When the financial statements are being examined for the first time, the auditor must determine the extent of his examination of depreciation and depletion provisions for years prior to the beginning of the period under examination. Unless the financial statements for prior years have been examined and reported upon by independent public accountants of good repute, he should attempt to obtain summary analyses of annual changes in the allowance accounts from the date of organization to the beginning of the period under audit. Investigations and analyses previously made in connection with registration statements or reports filed with the Securities and Exchange Commission or in determining invested capital for excess profits tax purposes are helpful and may facilitate the investigation of changes during earlier periods.

Examination of Accounts.—Comparisons of depreciation policies with those of other companies in similar types of business, comparison of rates in use with those advocated by various authorities or commissions, and inspection of physical plant may indicate to the auditor possible weaknesses in depreciation policy, but the information thus developed is not necessarily controlling. The useful life of depreciable assets used under certain conditions may be quite different from the useful life of similar equipment used under different conditions and policies by some other company. In general the auditor should satisfy himself that depreciation policies are in reasonable conformity with the actual experience of the company and are based upon intelligent consideration of present conditions and future probabilities.

To a great extent the auditor's examinations of property, plant, and equipment accounts and of depreciation and depletion allowance accounts are interdependent. Ordinarily, the charges made against allowance accounts will be substantiated by the auditor's examination of property, plant, and equipment accounts. Credits to allowance accounts should be substantiated on the basis of depreciation or depletion policies defined by the company under audit.

The auditor should review the allowance accounts and satisfy himself that the entries are in accordance with accepted accounting principles. The mathematical accuracy of the transactions recorded during the period should be tested, and the auditor should assure himself that authorized depreciation and depletion policies are being consistently followed. He should note any changes in the depreciation or depletion policy and arrive at an opinion on their propriety. The auditor should also satisfy himself that additions to allowance accounts representing provisions for depreciation or depletion are properly reflected as charges in the income statement.

OBSOLESCENCE.—The extensive construction of emergency facilities during the period beginning with World War II, the intensive competition in many industries since the war, the marked increase in automation, and the greater emphasis on development of new processes and products have accelerated the rate of obsolescence of plant facilities. The auditor should review with management the property, plant, and equipment accounts which may have been and are expected to be so affected; adjustment of the estimated remaining useful life may be advisable.

PROPERTY COMPLETELY DEPRECIATED.—When property has been completely depreciated on the books and still is in use, the annual depreciation may have been computed at too high a rate or replacements that should have been charged to asset accounts may have been treated as current expenses. If the amount involved is substantial, the auditor may, with propriety, recommend adjustment of the accounts to reflect more nearly cost less depreciation that should have been accrued.

EXCESSIVE DEPRECIATION.—Sometimes there may be a tendency toward excessive depreciation allowances for machinery whose important parts can be and are renewed from time to time. If depreciation has been provided at a rate which contemplates charging renewals to the accumulated allowance for depreciation, but the cost of these renewals has been charged to maintenance expense, the accumulated allowance for depreciation usually is overstated after a few years. The auditor should review the accounting and, if necessary, suggest appropriate adjustments.

DEPRECIATION DEDUCTED FOR TAX PURPOSES.—Provisions for depreciation recorded in the accounts may differ materially from amounts deducted for income tax purposes. When the differences are substantial, the auditor should investigate and obtain appropriate explanations. While amounts allowed for income tax purposes are not controlling, due consideration should be given to the reasons for material differences. See Chapter 22.

DEPLETION.—When depletion is recognized in the accounts, the auditor should determine that the method of computation is reasonable. If a mining enterprise consistently computes depletion on the basis of the best information available, its procedures may be considered reasonable. There can be no serious objection to changes in depletion rates resulting from bona fide revisions in estimates of recoverable mineral; such revisions may be made annually or less frequently.

The auditor should, if possible, receive a written statement from a geologist, mining engineer, or other responsible and informed person stating the depletion basis and giving his opinion that the current depletion rate is reasonable. Mining men are usually reluctant to commit themselves to an estimate of ore. Consequently, when the depletion allowance is based not only on developed ore, but also on estimates of probable and possible ore, the auditor may have difficulty in securing responsible written opinion concerning the depletion rate. A request for such an opinion is reasonable and when not complied with the auditor is on notice that the depletion rate may be inadequate or excessive. If the auditor cannot secure responsible written corroboration or other satisfactory evidence in support of the depletion rate, or if depletion is not provided in the accounts, he should consider the need for an appropriate exception in his report.

In well-managed timber operations, the quantity of standing timber will have been estimated and verified (cruised) and, with this as a starting point, the depletion to be charged is computed. Obviously, any attempt to determine depletion based only on an examination of money values is extremely hazardous. The records should show quantities of timber as well as dollar amounts. If they do not, they should be regarded as insufficient.

Coordination of Examination with That of Related Accounts.—As previously indicated, the examination of accounts for allowances for depreciation and depletion is closely related to that of property, plant, and equipment accounts. Additions to allowance accounts are based on amounts in depreciable or depletable plant accounts and charges to allowance accounts usually accompany credits to plant asset accounts.

In the examination of credits to allowance accounts, depreciation included in costs or expenses is substantiated, and charges to allowance accounts may be an element in determining profit or loss on disposal of plant assets.

Time of Examination.—Much of the examination of transactions recorded in allowance accounts can be made advantageously prior to the balance sheet date. The auditor may review procedures and methods, evaluate the effectiveness of internal control and, if the accounts are being examined for the first time, summarize and review transactions recorded in the accounts prior to the beginning of the period under examination.

In the event that the number of transactions recorded in the allowance accounts during the period under audit is substantial, the auditor may proceed effectively with his examination to, say, one or two months before the balance sheet date. If he follows this timing, only a minimum amount of work will be required after the balance sheet date to complete his examination of these accounts.

STATEMENT PRESENTATION

General Rule for Balance Sheet.—As a general rule, allowances for depreciation should be deducted from the costs of related assets, or the total of the allowances may be shown as a deduction from the total of depreciable assets. When depletion is recognized in the accounts, the amounts for assets subject to depletion may be shown after deduction of these allowances, or the allowances may appear as deductions from the related assets.

Certain public utilities offer an exception to this general rule when they show the allowance for depreciation on the liability side of the balance sheet in accordance with systems of accounts prescribed by regulatory authorities; reporting requirements of the Securities and Exchange Commission and the Federal Power Commission, described on page 264 of Chapter 12, prohibit this practice in financial statements filed with these Commissions.

Representation to Reader of Balance Sheet.—The distinction between allowances for depreciation and depletion and valuation reserves should be emphasized. There are many factors which must be considered in arriving at an amount which fairly represents the worth of assets to owners or possible purchasers. It is not intended for the reader of a balance sheet to believe that the amount shown as cost of depreciable or depletable assets, less the respective allowances, represents a realizable amount in the event of the sale of these assets. When the balance sheet shows the gross amount of property, plant, and equipment, the related allowance for depreciation or depletion, and the remaining balance, it purports to convey only the following information:

1. The cost, unless otherwise indicated, of depreciable or depletable assets at the balance sheet date;
2. The portion of the cost of such assets which has been absorbed by charges to operations in periods preceding the balance sheet date; and
3. The remaining portion of the cost of such assets to be absorbed by charges to operations in future periods.

Allowances for depreciation and depletion are not valuation reserves inasmuch as they do not attempt to indicate economic worth. They are not to be construed as liabilities. They do not constitute allocated surplus, for the amounts measure charges to income in recognition of the expiration of a portion of the useful life of depreciable property or a reduction in the number of depletable units.

A periodic provision for depreciation by a charge to income and a corresponding credit to allowance for depreciation does not guarantee the existence of any fund from which future replacements of property, plant, and equipment may be financed. Usually cash retained by a profit-making enterprise as the result of depreciation charges to income will be invested in inventories, marketable securities, or some other asset. It follows that the mere existence of an allowance for depreciation, accumulated by periodic charges to income, is not to be interpreted as indicating the availability of funds to replace plant assets. Consideration should be given by management to the source from which such replacements are to be financed.

Depreciation and Depletion in the Income Statement.—The desirability of disclosing the amount of depreciation included in the statement of income is discussed in Chapter 7.

When depletion is recognized in the accounts, the accepted method is to compute it on the basis of extraction, charge it to production costs, and thus include an appropriate amount as a component of inventory costs.

Depletion based on units extracted is sometimes charged to income rather than to costs of production and consequently is not included in inventory amounts. This procedure results in charging income with depletion on quantities which differ from quantities sold. When depletion is charged on the basis of units sold rather than units extracted, the portion of property costs applicable to inventories remains in plant assets.

CHAPTER 14

LONG-TERM INVESTMENTS, INTANGIBLE AND CONTINGENT ASSETS

Introduction.—Long-term investments may be mortgage notes, investment real estate, mineral interests, joint ventures, securities of, or long-term advances to, affiliates or related organizations, or cash surrender value of life insurance. Marketable securities, considered in Chapter 9, are often held as long-term investments by investment trusts, insurance companies, banks, and institutions, but their ready marketability distinguishes them from the investments considered in this chapter.

The accounting and auditing principles and procedures applicable to real estate and mineral interests held as long-term investments are substantially the same as those pertaining to similar assets used in the conduct of the business. Such assets and related allowances for depreciation and depletion are discussed in Chapters 12 and 13.

Intangible assets have been broadly classified by the Committee on Accounting Procedure of the American Institute of Certified Public

Accountants in its Accounting Research Bulletin No. 43, Chapter 5, as follows:

(a) Those having a term of existence limited by law, regulation, or agreement, or by their nature (such as patents, copyrights, leases, licenses, franchises for a fixed term, and goodwill as to which there is evidence of limited duration);

(b) Those having no such limited term of existence and as to which there is, at the time of acquisition, no indication of limited life (such as goodwill generally, going value, trade names, secret processes, subscription lists, perpetual franchises, and organization costs).

The excess of a parent company's investment in the stock of a subsidiary over its equity in the fair value of net assets of the subsidiary at the date of acquisition is sometimes shown as an intangible asset in consolidated financial statements of the parent and the subsidiary. This asset may represent intangibles of limited existence or of indefinite duration (see Chapter 21).

Contingent assets are those whose value is contingent upon the fulfillment of conditions regarded as uncertain. Most business concerns have claims which are in dispute, but which are considered collectible at least in part, such as those for overpaid taxes, patent infringements, or unfulfilled contracts. While these are not usually included among the assets in the balance sheet, they must be considered and, if significant, suitable disclosure, usually by footnote, should be made in the financial statements.

ACCOUNTING PRINCIPLES

Mortgage Notes and Mortgages.—Mortgage notes and mortgages should be recorded at cost or, if equity is impaired by decline in value of the mortgaged property, at cost less allowance for such decline.

Occasionally premiums are paid by insurance companies and other investors for the acquisition of mortgages. Such premiums are in effect an adjustment of the indicated interest rate and should be amortized by periodic charges against income received on the mortgages. If mortgages are acquired at a discount, the discount should be amortized only if it is clear that the discount represents an adjustment of interest rate; if the discount represents doubt as to the ultimate realization of the obligation, it should not be amortized.

Investments in Subsidiaries.—Investments in subsidiaries for the purpose of control are ordinarily recorded at cost. Changes in the market price of such securities should not affect the amounts at which they are carried. Investments in subsidiaries may be carried at amounts adjusted periodically to reflect underlying net assets of the subsidiaries, but this practice, while having some logical basis, has generally fallen into disuse, and is not recommended. It is not the function of the accounts and statements of the parent to show profits and losses of affiliated enterprises as a whole. The practice of adjusting investment accounts to reflect underlying net assets of subsidiaries is less objectionable when the subsidiaries are primarily domestic operating divisions of the parent.

If investments in subsidiaries are carried at cost, book amounts must be reduced by dividends paid from other than earnings since acquisition. When subsidiaries have sustained substantial losses since acquisition and it appears highly unlikely that such losses will be overcome by subsequent income, it is desirable to write down the investment on the parent company's books, even though such losses are offset by undistributed profits of other subsidiaries.

Consolidated financial statements are considered in detail in Chapter 21.

Bonds, Notes, Long-Term Advances, and Mortgages of Subsidiaries.—Bonds, notes, long-term advances, and mortgages of subsidiaries should be recorded at cost unless circumstances, such as default of interest or principal, indicate the desirability of a write-down.

Joint Ventures.—Occasionally several companies will finance a project on a joint basis. Their interests may be represented by capital stock, some form of interest-bearing obligation, or advances. Usually the interests and obligations of the parties are contained in a written agreement. The accounting principles relating to such investments follow those of the form of security received by the investor.

Cash Surrender Value of Life Insurance.—Cash surrender value of life insurance should be stated at amounts determined from tables in insurance policies and confirmed by insurance companies. Such amounts should include accrued dividends from mutual insurance companies and additional cash surrender value acquired by application of dividends left on deposit with the insurer.

Intangible Assets.—Accounting for intangible assets is considered in Accounting Research Bulletin No. 43, Chapter 5, which makes the following recommendations: Intangible assets should be recorded at cost; cost of noncash acquisitions may be determined either as the fair value of the consideration given or as the fair value of the property acquired, whichever is the more clearly evident.

The cost of intangibles of limited existence should be amortized by systematic charges to income over the period benefited. The cost of an intangible of indefinite duration may be amortized by charges to income if the company decides the intangible may not continue to have value during the entire life of the enterprise; the cost should be amortized in like manner when it becomes reasonably evident that the term of existence of the intangible has become limited; and any unamortized balance of cost should be written off when it becomes reasonably evident that the intangible has become worthless. The write-off of an intangible because of worthlessness should be by charge to income except that, where the amount of the write-off is so large that its effect on income may give rise to misleading inferences, the charge should be to earned surplus.

In discussing a limitation on write-off of intangibles, Accounting Research Bulletin No. 43 has this to say:

> Lump-sum write-offs of intangibles should not be made to earned surplus immediately after acquisition, nor should intangibles be charged against capital surplus. If not amortized systematically, intangibles should be carried at cost until an event has taken place which indicates a loss or a limitation on the useful life of the intangibles.

The principal objection to the previous rather common practice of lump-sum write-offs of intangibles to earned surplus was that partial or complete loss of value of such intangibles was never reflected as a charge in the income statement. The authors believe that the position taken in Bulletin No. 43 with respect to voluntary amortization is open to serious objection in that intangibles may be written off against income over a period when their value and earning power are as high or higher than at date of acquisition, with the result that net income may be understated by the amount of intangible amortization in years when there is no diminution in value of intangible assets.

PATENTS.—Cost of patents may include expenditures for government fees, attorneys' fees and expenses, and expenditures for experimentation and development. The cost of developing a patent may be capitalized or charged off as current expense. Frequently it is difficult to determine which course to pursue. It may be obvious, after a period, that the experiments under way are not yielding satisfactory results; then the cost is clearly an expense. More often the result is doubtful, and then it is permissible to elect whether to capitalize or charge off the costs. If a patent application is denied, accumulated costs should be charged to expense. Legal and other expenses of patent application or interference suits may be deferred until a settlement has been made. If a patent applicant is successful in an interference proceeding in the Patent Office, the expenses of the proceeding should be considered as patent application cost.

Expenditures for unsuccessfully defending or prosecuting patent infringement suits should be charged to expense when incurred. If such defense or prosecution is successful, costs may be capitalized to the extent of the evident increase in the value of the patent. When costs of defending a suit have been currently expensed over a relatively long period, successful outcome would not usually justify retroactive adjustment.

It is usually necessary to determine a fair value for a patent which has been acquired in exchange for capital stock. If at the time there is a free and active market for the shares, the capital stock, priced at market, may be considered the fair value of the patent. When the market for the shares is not active, other evidence must be sought to support a valuation. Valuation may be determined by the amount of a bona fide cash offer to purchase the patent by a financially responsible person, by capitalization of royalties obtained from the patent, or by capitalization of other earnings attributable to it.

Expenditures for additional patents, including improvements in basic patents, may be capitalized and amortized over the useful life of the new patents. Patents should not be written up, even though the value appears to be much in excess of cost. If several patents are acquired for a lump sum and it is impossible to assign a separate cost to each patent, computation of annual amortization should be based on the group as a unit using an average life which gives consideration to the expiration dates of the principal patents.

In this country patents are granted for a term of seventeen years. The cost may be distributed prorata over this period or over the period between the date of application and the date of expiration unless it appears that the patent will have a shorter period of commercial value; then the cost should be distributed over the period of expected benefit. The cost of patents of no commercial value should be written off immediately.

The period of time which will elapse between the date of application and the date of granting cannot be known until the patent is granted. The argument is often advanced that there is no necessity for writing off any portion of the patent until the patent has been granted. In practice, however, spreading the cost over the entire period between date of application and date of expiration or earlier date of expected loss of value of a patent is sounder procedure, even though estimates may have to be used for the earlier years.

Some companies amortize patent costs over a twenty-year period beginning at the application date on the theory that on the average three years elapse between date of application and date of issue of letters patent. If the three-year period can be substantiated by the client's experience, there is no objection to this procedure; but when the patent is granted, it is good practice to spread the remaining cost over seventeen years; if the application is rejected, the remaining cost should be charged off.

Patents should be reviewed periodically and when value has disappeared, because of obsolescence or for some other reason, any remaining unamortized balance of cost should be written off.

Patent development costs are frequently charged to expense as they are incurred, particularly by businesses with research departments continually experimenting with new developments. The cost of a patent which has been developed usually bears no relation to what it earns or should earn and is often nominal in amount.

TRADE-MARKS, BRANDS, AND TRADE NAMES.—Trade-marks, brands, and trade names should be recorded at cost which includes attorneys' fees, registration fees, and other expenditures definitely identifiable with their acquisition. The determination of what portion of advertising cost may be considered a cost of developing trade-marks and trade names, and consequently a capital expenditure, is usually so difficult that all such items should be treated as current expenses. Some companies have capitalized their advertising expenditures only to find upon cessation or reduction of their advertising that the drawing power of a trade-mark or trade name has to be constantly nourished. What they had been capitalizing was, in fact, maintenance.

Under federal statute, trade-marks and trade names may be registered for a period of twenty years and may be renewed indefinitely for additional like periods. They may be registered also under the laws of most states and in some states there is no time limit on the effectiveness of the registration. However, there is a significant distinction between patents and copyrights, and trade-marks and trade names. The right to a patent or copyright arises from registration under the statute; the right to a trade-mark or trade name is a common-law right based on its usage. It is customary, therefore, to consider trade-marks or trade names as being of value only so long as they are used. Usually they are carried at cost less recorded amortization. The basis of amortization, if any, is a matter of judgment.

COPYRIGHTS.—Cost of copyrights may include expenditures for government fees, and attorneys' fees and expenses. Many of the considerations which apply to patents apply also to copyrights. The term of a copyright is twenty-eight years and in certain circumstances it may be extended for another twenty-eight years. Most copyrights diminish in value irregularly and amortization usually should be based on periodic revaluations of each copyright rather than on statutory life.

ROYALTY AND LICENSE CONTRACTS AND FRANCHISES.—Royalty and license contracts granted under patents and copyrights are not usually given financial recognition in the accounts of the person to whom the rights are granted. Fees of attorneys drafting the contracts may be capitalized, but in practice minor amounts are charged to expense. When royalty and license agreements have been assigned for a consideration, the cost of obtaining the assignment may be capitalized.

Royalty and license contracts capitalized should be amortized over the life of the agreement or over the expected period of utility, whichever is shorter.

Fair value assigned to franchises acquired in exchange for capital stock may be tested by methods described for reviewing the fair value of patents similarly acquired. Franchises should be amortized over the period of their duration, or charged off when they have demonstrably become worthless.

GOODWILL.—Goodwill on a balance sheet usually represents the value attached to a business at some prior date over and above the value attributed to the other stated assets. It is almost exclusively related to the ability of an organization to produce a higher than normal rate of return on the amount of the tangible assets of the enterprise.

A losing business usually does not possess salable goodwill unless there are obvious signs of mismanagement. The basic element of salable goodwill is the probability that the public will continue to buy products or services from the successors of those who have built up a profitable business. When the earnings, the confidence, and other factors of the past cannot be transferred, goodwill has little value.

The purchaser of goodwill is more interested in the future than in the past. Past earnings are of interest as indicating what has been done, but in the mind of the purchaser they are important only as an indication of possible future earnings. Unprofitable companies have been sold on a basis of gross earnings, the buyers expecting to reduce expenses sufficiently to turn operating losses into net profits. However, goodwill attaches to a business only when it is believed to possess possibilities of continuing to be or becoming profitable.

Lists of subscribers to newspapers and magazines or of customers of dairies, bakeries, and laundries have business value although the enterprises themselves may not be profitable. This value is based on the estimated cost of securing customers.

Only purchased goodwill is recognized in the accounts, and it should be recorded at cost. While the value of goodwill varies with earnings, it is not customary to record such variations currently, although if it appears that a material and permanent decline in value has occurred, or can be foreseen within a reasonable period, write-down or amortization of the book amount is proper.

Many new businesses require several years to become firmly established. Net operating losses in these first few years have sometimes been capitalized as goodwill on the theory that operating expenses in excess of income were in reality development expenditures essential to the establishment of a steady patronage and the good name of the concern. In general, this practice should be condemned. If specific expenditures can be identified with building future business and prestige, it is permissible to treat them, to that extent, as deferred charges. To capitalize net losses arbitrarily as goodwill, even during the initial stages of an enterprise, usually is misleading.

Occasionally it is necessary to determine the value of goodwill. When a business is sold, both the seller and the buyer may want to determine a reasonable value for goodwill. When a business established prior to March 1, 1913, is sold, it has often been necessary to determine the value of the business at that date to arrive at the taxable profit on the sale, and this value may include goodwill.

As has been indicated, the value of goodwill is predicated on earning power, and the courts, in the absence of other evidence, have frequently resorted to a formula under which, after allowing for a fair return on tangible assets employed in the business, any excess of average annual earnings over a representative period of years (at least five) is capitalized at a reasonable rate of return. While, in a number of tax cases, the assumed rates of return frequently have been 8 per cent on net tangible assets and 15 per cent on intangibles (particularly in cases involving established commercial or mercantile enterprises), figures have been used ranging from 6 to over 11 per cent on tangibles and from 8 to over 33 per cent on intangibles depending largely upon the degree of stability or risk, of the particular business.

When a company acquires the stock of a subsidiary at a price in excess of capital stock and surplus as recorded on the subsidiary's books, this excess may represent goodwill to be stated separately in consolidation, or it may represent a valuation of net tangible assets in excess of their book amount. This is discussed at some length in Chapter 21.

Since goodwill may be considered the cost of expected earnings in excess of a fair return on net tangible assets, some contend that it should be amortized by charges to income over the period in which excess earnings are expected. This contention appears justified in those instances where the company does not endeavor to preserve the value of its goodwill or where it may be foreseen that the circumstances which have caused the excess earnings, such as unusually low costs, will be of limited existence. Successful enterprises, however, tend to maintain their relative superiority despite temporary reversals; and, in general, it is not practical to measure in the accounts diminution, if any, which may occur in future earnings. If goodwill is amortized, the basis necessarily will be somewhat arbitrary. Most accountants believe that no objection should be made to continuing to reflect it at cost, but there are also those who believe otherwise. Reasonable discretionary amortization, even when there is no evidence of loss of value, is generally considered permissible. The position of the Committee on Accounting Procedure of the American Institute of Certified Public Accountants is set forth in the following excerpt from Accounting Research Bulletin No. 43, Chapter 5:

> When a corporation decides that a(n) . . . . intangible may not continue to have value during the entire life of the enterprise it may amortize the cost of such intangible by systematic charges against income despite the fact that there are no present indications of limited existence or loss of value . . . . and despite the fact that expenditures are being made to maintain its value. Such amortization is within the discretion of the company and is not to be regarded as obligatory. The plan of amortization should be reasonable; it should be based on all the surrounding circumstances, including the basic nature of the intangible and the expenditures currently being made for development, experimentation, and sales promotion. Where the intangible is an important income-producing factor and is currently being maintained by advertising or otherwise, the period of amortization should be reasonably long. The procedure should be formally approved and the reason for amortization, the rate used, and the shareholders' or directors' approval thereof should be disclosed in the financial statements.

Tax Refund Claims.—Tax refund claims, usually with a contra allowance account, should be booked so that they will not be overlooked during the interval between the filing of the claims and their subsequent allowance or rejection and to call attention to the running of the statute of limitations and the necessity for instituting suit if the limitation date is imminent.

Present practice in reflecting tax refund claims varies greatly among companies, particularly as to determination of the proper time to recognize such claims in the financial statements. Generally, refund claims arising through application of net operating loss carry-backs, replacement of basic Lifo inventories, and similar circumstances when the applicable Internal Revenue Code sections are relatively noncontroversial, may be reflected in the accounts even though no approval has been granted. Tax refund claims based on more controversial code sections are in the nature of contingent assets and until agreed upon by final reviewing authorities of the Internal Revenue Service probably should not be recognized in the financial statements. Suitable disclosure in the footnotes should be made when the claims are significant in amount and ultimate collection appears probable.

INTERNAL CONTROL

Internal Accounting Control—Long-Term Investments.

AUTHORIZATION FOR TRANSACTIONS.—Authority for purchase, custody, sale, and modification or exchange of long-term investments should be clearly defined and should be exercised by officials designated by the directors or trustees. It is good procedure to require that changes in investments be authorized or approved in the minutes of meetings of directors or trustees.

RECORDS AND PROCEDURES.—A detailed record of investments should be maintained. It should include a description sufficient to distinguish each investment and should show, where applicable, identifying or certificate numbers, principal amounts, maturity, interest or dividend rate, cost, basis of amortization of premium, and a description of collateral held. A detailed record of income receivable or accrued also should be maintained, either as part of the foregoing record or separately, and a check should be made periodically to determine that all income has been recorded. The detailed records should be balanced periodically with general ledger control accounts.

For mortgage loans it is desirable that a record of documents received and their location be maintained. This record may be in the form of a check-off listing. In addition, tickler files are generally necessary to insure that copies of such documents as insurance policies and paid tax bills are submitted by the mortgagor at appropriate times.

The accuracy of the detailed records of long-term investments should be verified at least annually by confirmation with the debtor or issuer and by inspection of physical evidences of such investments or, if held by outside custodians, by confirmation. When investments are numerous and the records and procedures are well organized, it may be satisfactory to substantiate these records on a test basis.

At regular intervals, long-term investments should be appraised or priced at current market quotations, and the comparison of such amounts with book amounts should be reviewed by responsible officials.

INVESTMENTS DEEMED WORTHLESS.—Investments which are deemed to have little, if any, recoverable value and which have been written down or written off, should be under accounting control and reviewed periodically until it is finally determined that no recovery is possible.

Internal Accounting Control—Intangible and Contingent Assets.— The suggestions for internal accounting control of long-term investments made in the preceding paragraphs are generally applicable to intangible assets as well.

A detailed record of each contingent asset should be maintained, and the status of these assets should be reviewed periodically by responsible officials. It is good practice to maintain accounting control of contingent assets through the use of offsetting asset and allowance accounts in the general ledger.

Internal Check—Long-Term Investments.

ASSIGNMENT OF DUTIES.—The custodian of the investment documents, the detailed records bookkeeper, the general ledger bookkeeper, and the cashier should be independent of each other. Persons independent of all of the above should be assigned the functions of obtaining confirmations from debtors or issuers periodically, inspecting physical evidences of investments on hand and confirming those held by outside custodians, reconciling the total of detailed records with the general ledger control, and comparing investments at market prices with related book amounts. Independent persons should also be assigned the responsibility for approving modifications of investments, for authorizing the receipt, delivery, and write-off of worthless investments, and for endorsing investments to make them negotiable.

CUSTODY.—When investments are kept in a safe deposit box or vault under the control of the company, it is desirable that access thereto require the presence of at least two designated officers or responsible employees. Officers or employees so designated should not participate in cash functions nor in the maintenance of accounting records including the detailed records of investments.

Investments should be registered in the name of the company or an accredited nominee. However, if circumstances make it necessary or expedient to register investments in the name of an individual, appropriate assignments should be obtained promptly to protect the company's interest.

Internal Check—Intangible and Contingent Assets.—Intangible and contingent assets, because of their inherent characteristics, require little internal check beyond assigning to persons independent of each other the responsibilities of authorizing transactions, recording authorized transactions, and reviewing the entries made.

AUDITING PROCEDURES

Objectives.—The auditing procedures for long-term investments are similar to those for marketable securities. The auditor should satisfy himself that they are the property of the company and that they are stated at amounts determined in accordance with generally accepted accounting principles. Such amounts for cash surrender value of life insurance are those computed as realizable; for other long-term investments they are usually cost or cost adjusted to reflect any decline in value believed to be permanent.

The auditor's consideration of intangible assets is usually influenced by conservatism. The absence from a balance sheet of any indication of the existence of intangibles, even though they may exist, has little significance; the amount at which included usually has no relation to their current value.

The auditor should not neglect these assets merely because they are intangible. In his examination he should determine that both the gross amount and the provision for amortization, if any, are stated in accordance with generally accepted accounting principles.

Mortgage Notes and Mortgages.—The auditor should examine both mortgage notes (bonds) and the mortgages supporting them. He should determine whether the client is designated as payee and mortgagee, or whether the note and mortgage have been assigned to him and whether the mortgage and any assignment have been recorded. Laws concerning mortgages differ in various jurisdictions and, while an auditor is not expected to pass on the legal sufficiency of a mortgage, he should be familiar with procedures, forms, and recording requirements customary in the jurisdiction in which he practices.

The amount at which a mortgage is booked should be substantiated as not in excess of cost or cost adjusted to reflect any decline in value believed to be permanent. The auditor should make inquiry as to whether taxes or other assessments are in arrears and whether the mortgagee's interest in the property is protected by insurance. The mortgagee will frequently hold policies covering losses from fire or windstorm, executed in his favor or assigned to him, as well as an attorney's opinion or guaranty of title. If an apparently trustworthy appraisal, of recent date and identified with the mortgaged property, is available, the amount should be compared with the unpaid balance of the loan.

The auditor may find it desirable to inquire about the financial responsibility of the maker and any endorsers of the notes for which the mortgage is collateral. The mortgagee should keep informed as to the general condition of all properties on which he holds mortgages and as to circumstances affecting their values. This information may be requested by the auditor if payments against principal, interest, or taxes on the mortgaged properties are in arrears or if the amounts of the loans are out of proportion to the amounts of recent appraisals. If loss on a mortgage seems to be in prospect, the auditor should inquire whether the mortgagee is taking proper steps to protect his interests.

Amounts due on mortgages at the balance sheet date, if significant, should be confirmed by direct correspondence with the mortgagor. Partial payments reducing the original amount may be endorsed on the note, but this procedure is not always followed and the auditor's reliance should be placed on direct confirmation of the balance due. When the number of mortgages on hand is large, and internal accounting control and internal check is good, confirmation procedures may be on a test basis. The auditor may examine papers and correspondence usually accompanying mortgages, and the records of the original purchases and collections of principal and income relating to some of the mortgages not subjected to confirmation procedures. On occasion, canceled or fictitious mortgages have been submitted to the auditor for examination. Although he cannot accept responsibility for discovering forgeries, a review of the documents as indicated above may disclose obvious irregularities.

Investments in Subsidiaries and Affiliates.—Stocks, bonds, notes, long-term advances, and mortgages of subsidiaries and affiliates should be substantiated by examination of evidences of ownership or by direct correspondence with custodians of these evidences. These investments are usually held over a long period, and it is customary for the auditor to record, in his permanent working papers, certificate and bond numbers and other pertinent facts about them. Reference to this record when the evidences of ownership are being examined may reveal transactions otherwise unknown to the auditor.

Cash Surrender Value of Life Insurance.—The amount at which cash surrender value of life insurance is recorded may be substantiated approximately by computation from tables in the policies, and should be confirmed by direct correspondence with the insurance companies. The computation usually involves discounting the cash surrender value shown for the end of the current policy year back to the statement date, the discount being figured at the policy loan interest rate prescribed by the policy. In addition to the cash surrender value, the auditor should request confirmation of the beneficiary, assignments, dates to which premiums have been paid, accumulated dividends, loans made against the policies, interest prepaid or due on these loans, and any reservations of rights. If the insured has the right to borrow money on the policies or to change the beneficiary, the concern paying the premium may have no equity in the cash surrender value.

In most forms of life insurance other than term or group insurance, a substantial portion of each annual premium payment is immediately reflected in increased cash surrender value. That portion of the premium not added to cash surrender value may be included in prepaid insurance, and written off to expense over a suitable period. Where this practice is followed, the auditor should determine that amounts reported as prepaid insurance do not duplicate amounts included as cash surrender value.

Intangible Assets.—The auditor should analyze the patent account to determine whether it contains entries that relate to other intangibles. Whether or not they are combined in one item on the balance sheet, different kinds of intangibles should be carried in separate accounts on the books.

The auditor should examine patent papers and assignments, documentary evidence of trade-marks, brands, trade names, copyrights, royalty and license agreements, and franchises. Frequently the status or existence of such intangibles can be confirmed by direct correspondence with the client's attorneys.

Book amounts of these intangibles should be substantiated as being in accordance with generally accepted accounting principles. The auditor should investigate compliance with accounting provisions of royalty and license agreements, and franchises. An opinion from the client's counsel may be desirable, particularly if there are restrictions which are legal rather than accounting.

The goodwill account should be analyzed to determine the nature of the transactions that gave rise to its recognition and the basis of the amount at which it is recorded. The auditor should determine that both capitalization and amortization of goodwill, if any, are authorized, by examining minutes of meetings of stockholders and directors, partnership agreements, and other written evidence.

Common stock may have been issued as a bonus to subscribers to preferred or common stock, and the amount at which the bonus stock was credited to capital was offset by a charge to goodwill. Such a transaction, if proper at all, usually has nothing to do with goodwill, and the amount so charged to goodwill should be written off over a reasonable period. The auditor should satisfy himself that the goodwill account contains no such item.

Tax Refund Claims.—The auditor should examine supporting details of tax refund claims, investigate the basis of the claims, inquire as to the status of negotiation with the taxing authority, and consider the probability of collection by his client. His opinion as to whether the claim should be reflected in the financial statements and the appropriateness of the method of disclosure will necessarily depend upon the attending circumstances, including the company's past experience in tax examinations, the known attitudes of the taxing authority, and the likelihood of offsets or additional assessments.

Interest receivable from the government on tax refund claims is usually not taken up in the accounts until the claim has been finally allowed by the taxing authority. The auditor should check the computation of any interest so accrued.

Contingent Assets.—The auditor may establish the amounts of contingent assets or the existence of contingent assets of undetermined amount by inquiry and by examination of supporting written evidence.

Coordination of Examination with That of Related Accounts.—In his examination of long-term investments, intangible, and contingent assets, the auditor may have accumulated information substantiating in whole or in part the following accounts:

Dividends receivable from subsidiaries and from mutual life insurance companies

Interest income and interest receivable

Gain or loss on sales of long-term investments

Life insurance expense

Amortization or write-off of intangible assets.

Time of Examination.—Many of the auditing procedures in substantiating long-term investments, intangible, and contingent assets may be performed prior to the date as of which the examination is made. Acquisitions of these items up to an interim date may be substantiated during the year and subsequent changes substantiated later. Evidences of ownership of mortgage notes, mortgages, investment real estate, mineral interests, and investments in subsidiaries and affiliates may be examined prior to the year end, and may be controlled under seal until the year end. Minutes of meetings of stockholders and directors may be examined at an interim date and later brought up to the year end.

STATEMENT PRESENTATION

Mortgage Notes and Mortgages.—Investments in mortgage notes and mortgages are usually stated at cost less amortization of premiums paid, if any. If a decline in the market value of the mortgaged property has made it necessary to provide an allowance against the related mortgage, the asset should be shown on the balance sheet either gross less the allowance, or net, preferably with the amount of the allowance indicated in the caption heading.

Investments in Subsidiaries and Affiliates.—Investments in stocks, bonds, notes, long-term advances, and mortgages of subsidiaries and of affiliates and related organizations, when these investments are made for purposes of control, affiliation, or other continuing business advantage, should be classified on the balance sheet as noncurrent. Amounts at market quotations, if available, may be indicated, but it is not general practice to state them. Such market quotations are less important than those for marketable securities, because there is usually no present intention of disposing of the investments. It is customary to state the basis on which the investments are carried and to indicate the equity in underlying net assets of subsidiaries. Any subordination of notes receivable from subsidiaries or affiliates to notes payable by them to banks should be disclosed.

Cash Surrender Value of Life Insurance.—While cash surrender value of life insurance is sometimes classified as a current asset when the funds to be received on the death of the insured are unrestricted as to use by the beneficiary, classification of this asset as noncurrent is customary and is recommended in Accounting Research Bulletin No. 43, Chapter 3. The usual function of this asset is distinctly noncurrent; its purpose ordinarily is not to provide working capital until the death of the insured.

Intangible Assets.—Intangible assets of limited existence and those of indefinite duration should be shown separately on the balance sheet, if practical. They are usually the last item on the balance sheet, although they may be included with fixed assets, particularly in statements of public utilities. The important elements of intangibles of public utilities are often rights of way and franchises which are closely related to plant assets. In consolidated statements of public utilities the excess of amounts paid by the owning company over the underlying book amount of investment in subsidiaries is also classified with plant accounts. This excess is usually shown as a separate item in one amount because of the impracticality of allocation to tangible and intangible assets.

The basis of the valuation of intangible assets should be indicated; cost is assumed to be the basis unless another basis is stated. The fact and basis of amortization of intangible assets, if any, should be clearly indicated.

Tax Refund Claims.—Claims which appear sufficiently certain of collection to warrant their inclusion among the assets on the balance sheet are classified as current or noncurrent, depending upon when their collection reasonably may be expected.

Contingent Assets.—There is rarely any necessity for mentioning contingent assets, but if material in amount and there seems reasonable likelihood of their realization, failure to disclose them may result in concealing important information.

Significant contingent assets may be disclosed in a footnote; or they may be shown in the assets, indented, and not included in the aggregate assets; or in the assets with a contra provision deducted from the assets or included in the liabilities. Disclosure of contingent assets in a footnote is preferred since it implies less certainty regarding probable realization.

Tax Refund Claims.—Claims which appear sufficiently certain of collection to warrant their inclusion among the assets on the balance sheet are classified as current or noncurrent, depending upon when their collection reasonably may be expected.

Contingent Assets.—There is rarely any necessity for mentioning contingent assets, but if material in amount and there seems reasonable likelihood of their realization, failure to disclose them may result in concealing important information.

Significant contingent assets may be disclosed in a footnote; or they may be shown in the assets, indented, and not included in the aggregate assets; or in the assets with a contra provision deducted from the assets; or included in the liabilities. Disclosure of contingent assets in a footnote is preferred since it implies—due caution regarding probable realization.

CHAPTER 15

PREPAID EXPENSES AND DEFERRED CHARGES

Introduction.—Although the terms "prepaid expenses" and "deferred charges" are often used interchangeably, a distinction between them may be necessary since prepaid expenses are often classified as current assets and deferred charges as noncurrent, as discussed in the section of this chapter on statement presentation. Both types represent portions of expenditures or accruals made prior to the balance sheet date that are proper charges to income of subsequent periods. Prepaid expenses are generally considered to represent the balance of amounts paid for services not yet received from the payee, such as insurance premiums for which the insurance company still must provide coverage. Deferred charges on the other hand usually represent the balance of amounts paid for goods or services which have been received and for which the payee has no further obligation. Thus, the prorata amount of rent paid applicable to the unexpired portion of a lease is a prepaid expense, while the cost of experimental work that may reasonably be expected to produce income in the future is a deferred charge.

ACCOUNTING PRINCIPLES

The discussion which follows generally applies to a going business when it is expected that future income will be sufficient to absorb prepaid expenses and deferred charges relating to such income. If it is expected that there will be no future income or that such income will be insufficient to absorb prepaid expenses and deferred charges, general rules do not apply, and the facts and circumstances should be considered in determining what part, if any, of prepaid expenses and deferred charges should be carried forward in the balance sheet for allocation to subsequent periods.

Allocation of Prepaid Expenses and Deferred Charges to Periods Benefited.—One of the major objectives of accounting is the proper determination of net income through the process of matching applicable costs and expenses against revenues. In line with this objective, where practicable, costs and expenses which are charges against revenues of more than one period should be apportioned to the periods involved. Accordingly, prepaid expenses representing advance payments for services should be apportioned to those periods during which the services will be performed. On the other hand, since deferred charges relate to services with respect to which the payee has no further obligation, they may or may not be properly allocable to several periods. If future periods are expected to be benefited, the period of allocation may extend up to the date when benefit may reasonably be expected to cease.

The basis for allocating prepaid expenses and deferred charges varies with their nature. When they have a time limit, they should be apportioned equitably over their effective life. Each accounting period will usually bear its proportionate share of such expenses as rent, interest, and insurance. When prepaid or deferred items relate to production or to sales, they generally should be apportioned on the basis of units of production or sale. When the benefits to be derived cannot be related to specific periods or to production or sales, it is not usual to defer any part of such costs or expenses, even though future periods may benefit to some extent; accepted accounting practice requires that if such items are deferred they should be written off as rapidly as may be reasonable in the circumstances, usually in equal though arbitrarily computed instalments.

An exception to the principle of allocating costs and expenses to periods deriving benefits is recognized in accounting for commissions and taxes paid on premiums received by fire insurance companies. Fire insurance companies treat commissions and taxes paid as expenses of the period in which they are incurred and take premiums into income over the period of the policy. In view of the possibility of loss of many times the amount of such commissions and taxes, fire insurance companies believe there is little merit in attempting to carry forward, as assets, such costs and expenses.

Deferment of preliminary survey and investigation expenses may be proper under certain conditions, but when doubt exists as to the benefits accruing to subsequent periods, such expenses should be written off as incurred.

Production start-up costs are sometimes set up as deferred charges and written off over subsequent periods. This treatment may present more fairly the position of the company at a balance sheet date and results of its operations for the period then ended than would the charge-off of such expenses as they are incurred. To charge these expenses to operations in the year incurred may be misleading if income from them may reasonably be expected to be derived in subsequent years.

Annually recurring expenditures, not material in amount, may be charged to income when the expense is incurred even though the subsequent period is definitely benefited. This practice is not objectionable if it is consistently followed from year to year; for example, advertising bills for copy which is to appear in January publications may be paid and charged to expense in December.

The principle of deferment does not extend to deferring losses that should be charged off. For example, extraordinary costs of repairs and renewals arising from uninsured damage from accidents or storms should be charged off when incurred.

Prepaid Insurance.—Mutual insurance companies require advance payment of a premium that includes an amount in the nature of a deposit. Since profits from operations in a mutual company are returnable to policyholders in the form of dividends, the amount returnable to the insured at the expiration of a policy will probably include dividends as well as the amount of the deposit. These amounts may be returned in cash, but customarily they are deducted from gross premiums billed for the succeeding policy period. In practice, identification of the amount of the deposit is seldom possible. However, the amount of the return premium, representing deposit and dividend, usually can be estimated with reasonable accuracy and, if material, should be segregated from gross premiums and only the remainder considered in computing prepaid insurance.

Prepaid Taxes.—If the period assigned for absorption of property tax expense extends beyond the date on which the liability for an entire year is recognized, the unamortized portion is included among prepaid expenses. The question of the period to which property tax expense should be allocated is discussed in Chapter 22.

Inventory of Supplies.—Unused supplies, other than operating supplies, are in the nature of deferred charges. The cost of supplies such as letterheads and printed forms is often charged to expense when the supplies are purchased, but some companies prefer to charge expense as the supplies are used, and then the cost of the portion unused at a balance sheet date becomes a deferred charge. Either method is acceptable if it is followed consistently from period to period.

Prepaid Commissions.—Many companies allow their salesmen drawing accounts to be applied against earned commissions. When an excess over commissions earned is charged off at the end of the year, the drawing account may be in effect a minimum salary. Sometimes these excesses are carried forward as prepaid commission, to be offset by commissions earned in the subsequent period. This practice is permissible if experience has shown that commissions earned in subsequent periods customarily have been sufficient to offset such excesses. If a salesman leaves the employ of a company, a balance in his drawing account in excess of earned commissions is rarely collectible. After adjustment for additional commissions on orders presently unfilled which later, it is expected, will be credited to his account, the balance should be charged off as expense of the period in which the salesman leaves.

Advances to Employees for Expenses.—Advances to employees for expenses are ordinarily not charged to operations until their use is reported; prior to such reports they are considered prepaid expenses and are distinguished from loans to employees which are accounts receivable.

Cost of Annuities Based on Past Service.—In establishing pension plans requiring payments to outside agencies such as insurance companies and trustees, costs may be incurred which are based on past service of employees. Past service costs may be paid in a lump sum at the inception of the plan, or in instalments over a period. Such payments may be written off over an actuarially determined period, or arbitrarily over a shorter period. Any unamortized balance is a deferred charge to future operations. The Treasury Department permits those who qualify to deduct past service pension costs, in certain circumstances, over a ten-year period. Many companies have elected to follow this practice in their accounting; this practice is considered acceptable.

The principles set forth above are generally applicable as well to self-administered and informal plans. Further discussion of accounting for pension plans is given in Chapter 20.

Unamortized Debt Discount and Expense.—Bonds are sold at a discount because the rate of interest specified in the indenture is less than the rate that the issuing company must pay for the use of money. This discount, together with the expense of issue, is customarily charged to unamortized debt discount and expense and written off over the period from the date of issue to the date of maturity of the bonds. The sum of the interest paid and the amortization of debt discount, by periods, represents the effective rate of interest on the outstanding bonds.

Discount that would ordinarily be amortized during a period of construction may be capitalized; after construction is completed, periodic amortization is chargeable to expense.

Some large real estate operators have capitalized the entire discount on a bond or mortgage, the proceeds of which are used in the construction of buildings that they plan to sell or lease. They contend that the cost of obtaining funds for construction purposes is as much a part of the cost of the building as expenditures for more tangible items, since the building could not be erected without the financing. They claim that the cost of obtaining funds has value throughout the life of the building and accordingly should be amortized. There is a degree of reason in this point of view, but it has not been approved by the accounting profession. The authors believe that capitalization of bond discount should be limited to that portion applicable to the period of construction and that apportionment to the construction period should be based on the life of the bond issue, not on the life of the building.

When bonds are exchanged for property rather than sold for cash, the cost of the property may be considered to be the face amount of the bonds exchanged unless there is evidence that the fair value of the bonds is less. For example, if bonds given in exchange for property are immediately sold by the recipient at less than the face amount, an amount equal to the discount suffered by the seller of the bonds ordinarily should not be included by the issuer in the cost of the property, but should be segregated as bond discount. The sale price of the bonds by the recipient may usually be considered their fair value.

Under current generally accepted accounting principles, bond discount and expense should be written off over the life of the issue by periodic charges against income. In the past, debt discount and expense was often charged off to earned surplus at the date of issue, or at a later date; this procedure is no longer acceptable.

Various methods are used in disposing of the unamortized balance of bond discount and expense of single-maturity bonds and serial bonds; and of the unamortized discount, expense of issue, and redemption premium of bonds refunded.

The straight-line method is most frequently used in computing the amortization of debt discount and expense of single-maturity bonds. This method distributes discount and expense ratably over the life of the issue. The compound interest method has been used in the past, but is not now frequently employed.

The bonds-outstanding method may be used in disposing of the unamortized balance of bond discount and expense of serial bonds. Under this method, the total discount and expense is allocated to each interest period during the life of the issue in the ratio which the amount of the bonds outstanding in the interest period bears to the aggregate of the bonds outstanding in the several interest periods over the life of the issue. The amount of discount and expense allocated to each interest period is then charged off in that period. The Treasury Department's method of determining allowable deductions for discount on serial bonds produces the same charge for bond discount. However, the Treasury method requires that expenses incident to the issue of bonds maturing serially be treated differently than bond discount. Total expenses are allocated prorata to each series of bonds, and the allocated expense is amortized over the life of the bonds in the series.

Three methods for the disposition of unamortized discount, issue cost, and redemption premium on bonds refunded (hereinafter referred to as unamortized discount) have been considered in Accounting Research Bulletin No. 43, Chapter 15. They are:

1. A direct write-off to income or earned surplus in the year of refunding;
2. Amortization over the remainder of the original life of the issue retired; and
3. Amortization over the life of the new issue.

In the past, each of these methods has had support in court decisions, in determinations by regulatory agencies, and in accounting literature. In recent years method (1) has been considered acceptable; method (2) has been the preferred method, conforming more closely than any other to current accounting principles; and method (3) has been considered unacceptable unless the life of the new issue is less than the remaining life of the old issue.

A compromise between the first two methods is sometimes effected by spreading the unamortized discount over a period that is shorter than the unexpired term of the refunded issue. Accelerated amortization is acceptable provided that the charge is made against income and the charge in any year is not so large that income in that year is distorted.

If bonds are retired before maturity and the debt is not refunded, the balance of unamortized discount and expense should be written off, usually against income. If the amount is so material that its inclusion in income charges would impair the significance of net income, the amount, less the related reduction in income taxes, should be charged to earned surplus.

Experimental, Research, and Development Expenses.—Experimental, research, and development work is undertaken with the expectation that future benefits will result, and, if results were always as originally planned, there would be no question that the total costs should be spread over the periods benefited. The only problem is to estimate at the outset the period of amortization. In practice much experimental and development work fails to produce the results anticipated; when it becomes apparent that this work is unsuccessful, the cost should be charged off to expense at once.

Because of the uncertainty of the duration of benefits, and, in many cases, because of the uncertainty that benefits will be realized, the accounting treatment of experimental and development expenditures is optional. They may be capitalized during the progress of the work and the accumulated balance amortized over a definite even though arbitrary period, over a definite output of product, or written off immediately.

When experimental and development expenditures are characteristic of the business, the practical treatment is to charge them to expense currently. Chemical companies, for example, find continuous experimental work necessary to develop new products and to improve processes for manufacturing existing products. The most practical treatment is to charge these expenditures to expense currently, for it is usually difficult to determine in advance the benefit that may result therefrom in future periods.

In some industries, experimental and development expenditures may be infrequent and, when incurred, they are often related to a definite project. While such costs may well be charged to expense currently, it is not improper to accumulate them as deferred charges until the results of the work are determined. If the objectives are attained, the deferred charges may be amortized over an arbitrary, but usually relatively short, period. Such deferred charges should be written off rapidly and once the period has been fixed, charges should be made on a systematic basis. If the work is not successful, the unamortized balance should be charged off at once.

Consistency of treatment of these expenditures is essential to maintain the comparability of the income statement of one period with those of other periods.

Organization and Reorganization Expenses.—Expenditures incident to the original incorporation of a business such as those for government fees, stamp taxes, and attorneys' fees are capital items. However, it is customary to charge them against earnings over a short period after the business begins to earn profits. Such expenditures do not produce future profits or savings comparable to the benefits which may be derived from development expenditures. Many accountants approve the amortization of these expenses over a period of years, but abuse of the practice leads the authors to advocate charging them off as they are incurred.

There is some divergence of opinion among accountants whether promotion fees and expenses, as distinguished from corporate organization expenses, should be permanently capitalized, treated as a deferred charge, or written off. The authors believe that the best practice is to write off these charges as they are incurred. Certainly they should not be concealed in overvalued property accounts; that practice has been frequently condemned by the Securities and Exchange Commission, and rightly so.

Expenditures incurred in a reorganization or recapitalization of a corporation are usually charged against capital surplus resulting from the reorganization.

A distinction should be made between expenditures incident to incorporation or to the creation, rehabilitation, or modification of the capital structure of a business and other expenditures, perhaps equally necessary to its initial development, but from which future operations will benefit. For example, the cost of installing an accounting system is sometimes included as a part of organization expense. Expenditures of this kind preferably should be charged to expense currently but may be treated as deferred charges to be written off against future operations.

INTERNAL CONTROL

Internal Accounting Control.—Capitalization, amortization, and write-offs of prepaid expenses and deferred charges should be properly authorized. The distribution of routine prepaid expenses and deferred charges may be authorized by an officer or employee to whom such authority has been delegated. The accounting treatment of debt discount, expense and premium, experimental and development expense, organization and reorganization expense, and other unusual items should be authorized by someone at the executive level.

At established intervals a responsible employee should review items classified as prepaid expenses or deferred charges to determine that they are proper charges to future accounting periods.

Insurance coverage should be reviewed periodically by a responsible person who is familiar with insurance practices and insurable values. If this review is customarily made by an officer or employee who is not well qualified as to insurance matters, it may be worth while to arrange for a periodic review of the adequacy of the insurance coverage by an independent insurance specialist.

Use of appropriate subsidiary records, controlled by general ledger accounts, for prepaid expenses and deferred charges facilitates internal accounting control. Appropriate records may include, among others, an insurance register, tax register (or due date file), supplies inventory records, and experimental and development project cost sheets. The subsidiary records should be balanced periodically with general ledger control accounts.

Major supplies inventories merit the same internal accounting control as other inventories. See Chapter 11.

Internal Check.—Prepaid expenses and deferred charges are not generally types of assets that may be misappropriated. Expenditures that become prepaid expenses and deferred charges should be subject to the internal check procedures outlined for purchases in Chapter 20, accounts payable in Chapter 16, and cash disbursements in Chapter 8.

It is preferable that subsidiary records be maintained by an employee other than the one who posts the general ledger control accounts, so that one record will act as a check on the other.

Internal check of major supplies inventories should follow the procedures discussed in Chapter 11.

AUDITING PROCEDURES

Objectives.—The over-all objective of examining prepaid expenses and deferred charges is to determine that they are properly allocable to future periods in accordance with generally accepted accounting principles and that the amounts reasonably represent the cost of benefits which will be reflected in future operations. The extent of the examination of prepaid expenses and deferred charges should be based on appraisal of the effectiveness of internal accounting control and the significance of the amounts involved.

Subsidiary Records.—Under a well-organized accounting system, the auditor will find subsidiary records showing details of the computations of prepaid expenses and of the balances of deferred charges, supported by proper authorizations and by other related documents and data. If adequate subsidiary records are not maintained, the auditor should substantiate balances in prepaid and deferred accounts by reference to whatever documentary evidence is available.

Prepaid Insurance.—An insurance register, or schedule of prepaid insurance, should show for each item:

Policy number
Insuring company
Coverage (type and amount)
Co-insurance
Date of policy
Expiration date
Prepaid amount at beginning of period
Premium paid during period under review
Charged to expense in the period
Prepaid amount at end of period.

If an insurance register is not maintained, a schedule of prepaid insurance should be prepared, preferably by the client's staff. The auditor should check or test-check the data shown in the register or schedules. Insurance policies and vouchers supporting premiums should be examined on a test basis, noting, in addition to the items tabulated above, the beneficiary, special assessment clauses, and any evidence of liens on the insured property. If the insurance policies are not available for inspection, the auditor should determine why. Since lenders often hold insurance policies as collateral for loans, the absence of policies may indicate the existence of liens on the property. The auditor should request that the client obtain the policies for his examination. If there is evidence that insurance is in effect for which the client has not been billed, appropriate liability, expense, and prepaid amounts should be recorded.

Computations of amounts prepaid at the end of the period may be checked approximately. If the company is a going concern, the basis of computation is customarily prorata, not the short cancellation rate. Prepaid liability and compensation insurance, when premiums are based on payrolls, may be checked by a review of payrolls since the effective date of the policies to determine that charges to expense for this insurance coverage appear proper. Premiums due may exceed the advance payment so that at the end of the period there may be a liability rather than a prepayment.

Total prepaid insurance per the register or schedule should be compared with the general ledger controlling account.

The auditor is not an expert in determining insurable values, but he may render helpful service to his clients by comparing the amount of coverage with the insurable value (if available) and book amount of the property insured. If overinsured, a useless expense is incurred; if underinsured, an unjustifiable risk may be assumed.

Fidelity bond coverage should be reviewed to determine whether requirements of by-laws or company policy, if any, have been met and whether the amount of coverage seems adequate. If the amount of fidelity bond coverage appears to be inadequate, the auditor should urge a reappraisal of the requirements.

Prepaid Taxes.—The auditor should determine that the amount set up as prepaid taxes is actually an expense applicable to future periods. Reference should be made to tax bills and tax laws of the jurisdiction to which the client is subject, since taxes are imposed under the authority of the several states and their subdivisions by statutes that vary widely in their provisions. Significant variances in prepaid taxes at the beginning and end of the period should be investigated.

Inventory of Supplies.—Inventories of supplies, if substantial in amount, should be subjected to the same auditing procedures as those for inventories in Chapter 11.

Test counts of physical inventories may be recorded and compared with perpetual and book records. If no physical counts or tests have been made, supply accounts should be reviewed and balances at the close of the period should be compared with those at the beginning. Significant differences should be investigated. Obsolete items should not be included in inventory amounts.

Prepaid Commissions.—The propriety of amounts of prepaid commissions should be investigated. In connection with this investigation, the auditor may examine contracts with salesmen or obtain from the management an authoritative statement of the terms of employment. Commission records or other evidence of commissions earned may be reviewed; entries in the salesmen's accounts may be traced from commission records and from cash records. If there are many salesmen, the examination may be limited to the accounts of only a few of them or to the entries for only a limited period. Transactions of the last month of the period and the first month following the end of the period may be reviewed to determine that commissions have been allocated to the proper period. Confirmation of prepaid commission accounts may be requested from the salesmen. If there is a subsidiary ledger for prepaid commission accounts, the balance of the controlling account should be compared with the trial balance of the subsidiary ledger and any differences investigated.

Advances to Employees for Expenses.—Advances to salesmen and other employees for expenses may be tested by an examination of cash disbursements, expense reports, and cash receipts. If employees are advanced amounts as working funds on an imprest basis, the auditor may examine reimbursements in the month following the end of the period to determine whether expenditures of material amount prior to the end of the period had not been reimbursed. Advances may be confirmed by correspondence with the employees. The controlling account should be compared with the subsidiary ledger and any difference investigated.

Cost of Annuities Based on Past Service.—Deferred costs of annuities based on past service should be substantiated by reference to pension plans, reports of actuaries, contracts with insurance companies or trustees, or other available documentary evidence. The auditor should determine whether amortization has been properly authorized and computed on the authorized basis.

Unamortized Debt Discount and Expense.—The auditor should determine that accounting for unamortized discount, redemption premium, and expense on bonds retired or refunded is in accordance with the accounting principles previously set forth. He should check the computation of amounts charged to expense or capitalized by charges to construction during the period. He should determine that when part of an issue of bonds is retired, the related discount and expense is written off, leaving as the unamortized balance the amount relating to the unretired bonds. He should also determine that capitalizations, amortizations and write-offs of debt discount and expense have been properly authorized, usually by the board of directors or other executive body.

Experimental, Research, and Development Expenses.—The auditor should determine that experimental, research, and development expenses set up to be distributed over subsequent periods fairly reflect these expenses and that the basis of amortization is reasonable. He should check the computation of amounts periodically amortized and satisfy himself that the policy of amortization has been properly authorized and consistently followed from period to period. The status of projects on which expenses are deferred should be reviewed to determine the propriety of the deferment.

Organization and Reorganization Expenses.—The auditor should examine the certificate of incorporation, minutes of stockholders' and directors' meetings, agreements with underwriters and stock salesmen, and correspondence with attorneys to determine that amounts deferred as organization and reorganization expense fairly reflect such expense. He should determine that the accounting treatment of these expenses is defensible, that the basis of amortization is reasonable, that computations of amortized amounts are substantially correct, and that the amortization policy has been authoritatively established and consistently followed.

Suspense Debits.—Deferred charges may include suspense debits representing expenditures for which the final distribution has not been determined at the balance sheet date. They may be charged ultimately to plant accounts, to other assets, or to expense. This classification of accounts is authorized by certain regulatory bodies and is found more frequently in public utility companies than in industrial companies. In general, this classification should be discouraged and the client urged to determine the distribution of these amounts before the end of the period.

When suspense debits are encountered, the auditor should review the components to determine whether the amounts are fairly stated and represent assets rather than expenses which should be charged off. He should satisfy himself that distribution is in fact not determinable at the balance sheet date.

Other Prepaid Expenses and Deferred Charges.—Examples of other items included in prepaid expenses and deferred charges are interest, rent, and royalties. The auditor should satisfy himself as to the propriety of the classification and of the period over which the expense is to be distributed. The expenses should be substantiated by reference to related documents, and computations of the amounts of amortization should be checked or tested.

Coordination of Examination with That of Related Accounts.—Concurrent examination of prepaid expense and deferred charge accounts and related items included in the balance sheet or statement of income may often be made.

Time of Examination.—Most of the auditor's work in substantiating prepaid expense and deferred charges may be done before the end of the period. If the client maintains an insurance register, prepaid insurance may be examined at an earlier month end and entries between the date of the examination and the end of the period reviewed later. Physical inventories of supplies may be taken at an interim date and subsequent entries reviewed. Activities resulting in debt discount and expense, experimental and development expense, and organization and reorganization expense are often completed before the end of the period, and the resulting expenses may be examined as soon as all or most of them have been recorded. Amounts of amortization can be computed only when the total for the year is known, but this computation can frequently be made before the end of the period.

Other examinations, such as those of prepaid taxes, prepaid commissions, advances to employees, and suspense debits are usually made shortly after the end of the period, although some preliminary analyses may be made at an earlier date.

STATEMENT PRESENTATION

Current or Noncurrent.—The following basis for determining the classification of prepaid expense as current or noncurrent is set forth in Accounting Research Bulletin No. 43, Chapter 3, Section A:

For accounting purposes, the term *current assets* is used to designate cash and other assets or resources commonly identified as those which are reasonably expected to be realized in cash or sold or consumed during the normal operating cycle of the business. Thus the term comprehends in general such resources as . . . . prepaid expenses such as insurance, interest, rents, taxes, unused royalties, current paid advertising service not yet received, and operating supplies. Prepaid expenses are not current assets in the sense that they will be converted into cash but in the sense that, if not paid in advance, they would require the use of current assets during the operating cycle.

The ordinary operations of a business involve a circulation of capital within the current asset group. Cash is expended for materials, finished parts, operating supplies, labor, and other factory services, and such expenditures are accumulated as inventory cost. Inventory costs, upon sale of the products to which such costs attach, are converted into trade receivables and ultimately into cash again. The average time intervening between the acquisition of materials or services entering this process and the final cash realization constitutes an *operating cycle*. A one-year time period is to be used as a basis for the segregation of current assets in cases where there are several operating cycles occurring within a year. However, where the period of the operating cycle is more than twelve months, as in, for instance, the tobacco, distillery, and lumber businesses, the longer period should be used. Where a particular business has no clearly defined operating cycle, the one-year rule should govern.

This concept of the nature of current assets contemplates the exclusion from that classification of such resources as . . . . long-term prepayments which are fairly chargeable to the operations of several years, or deferred charges such as unamortized debt discount and expense, bonus payments under a long-term lease, costs of rearrangement of factory layout or removal to a new location, and certain types of research and development costs.

In practice, if a material portion of prepaid expense will be absorbed within the operating cycle, the total may be classified as current. If the noncurrent amount is so large that its inclusion in current assets impairs the significance of working capital, an appropriate amount should be shown as noncurrent.

Credit Balances in Prepaid Commission Accounts.—Credit balances in prepaid commission accounts, if significant in amount, should be shown as current liabilities.

Unamortized Debt Discount and Expense.—Unamortized debt discount and expense is customarily shown as a deferred charge, usually stated separately. Disclosure of the method of amortization is not mandatory except in statements filed with the Securities and Exchange Commission.

Organization and Reorganization Expenses.—Organization and reorganization expenses when deferred are usually shown separately on the balance sheet, toward the end of the list of noncurrent assets. Some regulatory bodies prescribe the inclusion of these expenses among fixed assets. If the balances are being amortized, it is desirable to describe the method of amortization.

Suspense Debits.—Items included in suspense debits pending final disposition by regulatory bodies, if significant in amount, should be disclosed and adequately described.

CHAPTER 16

CURRENT LIABILITIES

Introduction.—In Chapter 7 a definition is given of the term "liability" as used in accounting. The principal balance sheet classifications of liabilities are current and noncurrent (long-term). Certain types of liabilities, such as short-term notes to banks and accounts payable to trade creditors are usually current; others, such as bonds and mortgage notes, are usually noncurrent; certain accruals or deferred credits may be either current or noncurrent depending on circumstances. This chapter will be devoted to a discussion of current liabilities; long-term debt and other long-term liabilities are considered in Chapters 17 and 18; tax liabilities are discussed in Chapter 22.

ACCOUNTING PRINCIPLES

Definition.—Accounting Research Bulletin No. 43, Chapter 3, Section A, states:

The term *current liabilities* is used principally to designate obligations whose liquidation is reasonably expected to require the use of existing resources properly classifiable as current assets, or the creation of other current liabilities. As a balance-sheet category, the classification is intended to include obligations for items which have entered into the operating cycle, such as payables incurred in the acquisition of materials and supplies to be used in the production of goods or in providing services to be offered for sale; collections received in advance of the delivery of goods or performance of services; and debts which arise from operations directly related to the operating cycle, such as accruals for wages, salaries, commissions, rentals, royalties, and income and other taxes. Other liabilities whose regular and ordinary liquidation is expected to occur within a relatively short period of time, usually twelve months, are also intended for inclusion, such as short-term debts arising from the acquisition of capital assets, serial maturities of long-term obligations, amounts required to be expended within one year under sinking fund provisions, and agency obligations arising from the collection or acceptance of cash or other assets for the account of third persons.

The term "operating cycle" is discussed in Chapter 7. A one-year period is generally considered to be the basis for segregation of current liabilities from long-term or noncurrent liabilities. An exception to the one-year rule is made when the operating cycle is longer than one year.

Notes Payable and Other Evidences of Indebtedness.—Short-term indebtedness may be represented by notes payable to banks, suppliers, customers, subsidiaries, or affiliates, usually incurred to finance receivables or inventories; these liabilities present no problem of classification as current.

Loans on insurance policies on lives of officers are usually current liabilities, but, if definite assurance can be obtained that the loan will be liquidated only from proceeds of the policy upon maturity or cancellation, the loan may be classified as noncurrent or may be deducted from the cash surrender value of the policy included with noncurrent assets.

Trade acceptances are frequently used for financing domestic purchases for short periods and may be issued on individual invoices or monthly statements. Trade acceptances have stated maturities, may be discounted by the vendor who draws them, and are presented for payment through the holder's bank. Ordinarily they do not represent a lien on goods purchased.

Commercial letters of credit are extensively used in financing imports. A letter of credit is a guaranty by the bank issuing the credit that drafts drawn by a seller in compliance with stipulated terms will be honored when presented for payment. Drafts drawn by a seller against a letter of credit may be sight drafts or time drafts. Sight drafts require payment on presentation. Time drafts are customarily discounted by the seller of the merchandise at his own bank which forwards the drafts for acceptance and payment at maturity to the bank that issued the letter of credit. Sight drafts are paid and time drafts accepted by the bank against shipping documents. If the merchandise is shipped by the seller against a time draft which in due course is accepted by the drawee bank, the merchandise when received is generally released by the accepting bank to the purchaser against trust receipts.

Serial bond maturities, sinking fund payments, and payments under note agreement provisions, due within one year, should be classified as current liabilities. Occasionally supplemental agreements provide for earlier maturities of long-term debts under certain conditions; under these agreements all or part of the debt may require classification as current. Maturities of certain types of obligations may depend on various factors so that the amount due currently must be estimated; examples are equipment trust certificates to be liquidated out of rents or revenues received, obligations whose maturities are measured by depletion of natural resources, and advances by customers to be liquidated by delivery of products. If indebtedness payable at the option of the debtor is being liquidated at regular intervals as a matter of policy, payments scheduled within the next twelve-month period should be classified as current.

Certain exceptions to the classification of maturing long-term debt with current liabilities are discussed in Chapter 17. Exception in the classification of sinking fund instalments due within one year is referred to later in this chapter.

Accounts Payable.—The term "accounts payable" includes those debts and obligations that are not evidenced by notes, bonds, acceptances, or other specific promises to pay. They usually represent open accounts arising from completed transactions, principally with trade creditors.

In Chapter 11 considerations of title in recording invoices for inventory items are discussed, and the conclusions reached are generally applicable in recording other invoices. Generally, liability for payment is recorded when goods or services are received, or when an invoice indicates that shipment has been made, whichever is earlier. If material has been ordered and the goods have not been received nor has title passed to the purchaser at the balance sheet date, the transaction is a commitment which need not be recorded as a liability.

Agency obligations arise when cash or other assets are collected or accepted for the benefit of third parties. Social security taxes on salaries and wages and the statutory withholding for income taxes must be deducted from the employees' compensation by the employer; taxes on dividends paid to foreign stockholders must be withheld by the corporation paying the dividend; taxes on rents, royalties, or other forms of income paid to nonresident aliens, foreign partnerships, or foreign corporations must be withheld by the payers of such income; in certain localities local taxes on wages or on retail sales must be collected by the payer or the vendor; and union dues, hospitalization and group insurance premiums, amounts due on contributory pension contracts, and other items may be withheld from wages paid to employees. Rent collection agencies collect rentals from tenants for the benefit of the landlords.

Obligations arising from transactions of this nature are current liabilities when the cash or other assets collected become part of current assets. If, however, the assets received are segregated as restricted deposits and classified as noncurrent, the related liability should also be shown as noncurrent.

Current Liabilities Related to Government Contracts.—Business organizations which have substantial sales to U. S. Government departments or agencies are subject, under certain conditions and limitations, to renegotiation of sales prices when it has been determined that profits realized were excessive. Such excessive profits, when determined through renegotiation proceedings, must be refunded to the U. S. Government; the refund is reduced by the applicable federal income tax paid. Renegotiation proceedings may extend over relatively long periods, but often an estimate can be made of the probable refund, if any, based on experience of the company or of companies in the same or similar line of business. When the refund can be reasonably estimated, the liability is usually reflected as current at the gross amount reduced by applicable federal and state income taxes.

Certain government contracts contain price redetermination provisions whereby contract prices are set at provisional amounts and are then subject to review and retroactive adjustment based on experience in supplying a portion of the goods or services contracted for. If it appears that downward retroactive adjustments of prices for goods or services delivered prior to the balance sheet date are reasonably assured, provision for such adjustments, estimated, if necessary, should be included in current liabilities. When the related account receivable has not been collected, such adjustments may be made appropriately through direct reduction of the receivable or through an allowance deducted from the receivable in the balance sheet.

When it appears that fixed-price government contracts uncompleted at the balance sheet date will result in a loss, provision should be made for such loss. This provision may be included in current liabilities or applied as a reduction of inventory, depending on the circumstances.

Accrued Expenses.—Accrued expenses are those for which a liability has been incurred on or before a given date, payable at some future time, such as accruals of wages, salaries, commissions, rentals, royalties, and taxes, usually due to specific persons, and computable with reasonable accuracy. Other accrued expenses, such as costs in connection with product guaranties, must be estimated, and persons to whom payments will be made may not be identified.

ACCRUED VACATION PAY.—An agreement for vacation pay usually specifies the period of vacation and the period upon which it is based; for example, two weeks' paid vacation may be granted to each employee continuously employed for the period May 1 to April 30. The agreement may be either written or oral. The estimated cost of paid vacations to be taken after April 30 should be accrued by charges to expense during the year then ended and the ratable portion included in current liabilities at the balance sheet date. It is not usual to accrue vacation costs for office employees and others not covered by wage agreements; but, when a company has committed itself to grant vacations in the succeeding year to such employees, a ratable portion of vacation pay may be accrued. Legal opinion may be required to determine the existence of a liability for vacation pay.

Deferred Credits.—Unearned revenues, such as collections on or billings for ticket sales, magazine or other periodical subscriptions in advance, advances on uncompleted contracts, and unearned interest or rentals, are frequently described as deferred credits or deferred income. Current liabilities should include the portion of these deferred credits equal to the estimated cost of realizing such revenues in the following period. The remaining portion of unearned revenues, representing profit, may be excluded from current liabilities and designated as deferred income.

The authors believe that the above treatment is sound, but Bulletin No. 43, quoted on page 324, indicates a preference for the inclusion of collections received in advance in current liabilities. General practice, as reported in "Accounting Trends and Techniques," indicates that the position taken in Bulletin No. 43 may not have received general acceptance. For example, magazine and other subscription revenue received in advance is usually excluded from current liabilities. Subscription income of magazine and newspaper publishers generally contributes but a small portion of total revenue compared to advertising revenue, which normally is not received in advance. Subscription income of publishers of services, such as income tax, legal, financial, and credit information, is relatively large, but expenditures required to make the data currently available may have been made and charged off in the past. Deferred income of shipping companies on uncompleted voyages is not usually classified as a current liability, and contra deferred expenses on uncompleted voyages are excluded from current assets.

Advance Payments for Merchandise.—When part of the sales price has been collected in advance, such amounts should be reflected as liabilities until sales have been fully consummated.

Customers' advance payments received by department stores usually relate to so-called "lay-away" or "will-call" sales, under which the selected merchandise is set aside for delivery upon completion of payments. These arrangements frequently call for regular payments over a period of time, and they are akin to instalment selling except that the goods are not delivered until paid for in full. Advance payments are common also when special orders are received for goods not regularly in stock, and balances due on these orders become collectible upon delivery of the goods. Advance payments are usually required when customers have not established credit standing. When part of the sales price has been collected in advance, some department stores record the transaction as a sale in the full amount of the sales price, booking the difference between that amount and the advance as an account receivable. This is done when the balances are customarily collected in due course, and the merchandise has been segregated for delivery or provision has been made for the cost of goods not on hand at the time the order is received.

Security Deposits.—A utility company may require deposits to secure payments of bills and may pay interest on these deposits. Under regulations of some state utility commissions, companies are required to pay interest periodically, either in cash or by credits to billings. Otherwise, interest is not usually paid until the deposit is returned or credited to the depositor's account, possibly many years later. Many receipts are lost or destroyed, and return of the deposit may never be requested. Under uniform systems of accounts prescribed by public utility regulatory bodies, these deposits are reflected as current liabilities.

Interest, if payable, should be accrued until sufficient time has elapsed after discontinuation of service to indicate that return of the deposit is unlikely. Under the laws in some states, unclaimed deposits are turned over to the state after the lapse of a statutory period.

Landlords occasionally require a deposit from the tenant to be applied as payment of rent for a final period of the lease. Since the landlord's obligation involves a long-term deferment of delivery of the service, the deposit need not be classified by the landlord as a current liability until a year before expiration of the lease.

Product Guaranties.—Many articles are sold under guaranty of material, workmanship, or serviceability for varying periods based on time or usage. These guaranties may provide for free repair or replacement and may require the seller to disburse substantial sums in labor, material, and transportation charges to fulfill his obligations. When the cost of making good the guaranty may be large and the guaranty period covers several years, it is good accounting practice to accrue currently, by charge to income, an estimate of the amount which will be required to make good the guaranty on current sales. It is usually feasible to base such estimate on past experience and knowledge of the characteristics of current products. It is not usual to accrue such costs for volume sales of small cost items when the claims are not numerous and are likely to be made in a relatively short period following the date of sale.

Returnable Containers.—Deposits are required in certain industries to cover the cost of containers in which product is shipped; these deposits are to be refunded when the containers are returned. The cost or other valuation of the containers is included either in inventory or in fixed assets. These deposits usually are recorded through charges to accounts receivable and offsetting credits to a container liability account, although they may arise through cash receipts. If charges to accounts receivable are customarily settled by credits for the return of containers, the container liability account may be offset against accounts receivable; therefore, it is desirable to segregate in the accounts the liability for containers arising from cash receipts. If customers habitually pay container charges, the container liability account should not be offset against accounts receivable and segregation is not necessary.

The experience in some businesses (for example, manufacturers of large-sized wire and cable) is that customers often do not return the reels promptly. It is proper to estimate the portion of the total liability for returnable reels which will not be refunded for more than one year for classification as a long-term liability.

Beverage companies frequently reflect their container deposit liability as noncurrent. This treatment is permissible provided the containers are not included in current assets.

Customers often do not return containers. The deposit liability account should therefore be adjusted periodically so that the balance reflects estimated refunds that may be expected to be paid for returned containers. The estimate may be based on past experience, or the company may assume that containers held for a specified period will not be returned. The cost of containers not expected to be returned should be eliminated from the asset account and the difference between the deposit and cost charged or credited to the income account. Deposits not yet refunded on containers which have been returned may be shown either as accounts payable or in the container deposit liability account.

Basis of Recording.—Current liabilities based on completed transactions are fixed and definite in amount, and present no problems as to the basis of recording. Such items as accrued wages, rentals, salesmen's commissions, royalties, and traveling expenses can be computed with reasonable certainty when the period covered or other basis of the service to be rendered is known. Accrued liabilities for such items as taxes or costs of product guaranties may be susceptible of less certain computation, but past experience will generally furnish a sufficiently reliable guide.

Accounts payable are usually recorded at amounts due after trade discounts but before cash discounts have been deducted. Trade discounts ordinarily should not appear on the books of account since they are direct deductions from list prices.

Practice with respect to cash discounts is not uniform. Some companies which take advantage of all cash discounts deduct the discount from the amount of the invoice and record the net amount in accounts payable. Others reflect the amounts of invoices in accounts payable before application of cash discounts, and record discounts only as they are realized by payment of the invoices. Either practice is acceptable if followed consistently.

INTERNAL CONTROL

Internal Accounting Control.

NOTES AND ACCEPTANCES PAYABLE.—The system of internal accounting control should provide for the authorization, preparation, and subsequent payment, renewal, and recording of notes and acceptances payable.

Borrowings on notes executed in the corporate name of the company and renewals of these notes are usually authorized by the board of directors or other management group. Minutes of the board meeting should set forth the names of the banks or others from whom funds may be borrowed, the officers empowered to negotiate the loans, limits in amounts such officers are permitted to borrow, interest rates and terms, and collateral, if any, which may be pledged.

The books of account should clearly indicate details of notes issued. If borrowings are frequent, a note register or other subsidiary notes payable record should be maintained and the aggregate amount of notes outstanding, as shown by this record, should be reconciled periodically with the general ledger control account. The note register will usually include the following information for each note: principal amount, name of payee, date of issue, interest rate, due dates for principal and interest, payments made on account of principal and interest, and collateral pledged.

ACCOUNTS PAYABLE.—An adequate system of internal control for accounts payable should provide effective procedures for checking invoices before entry and payment, as discussed in Chapter 20. Other desirable procedures include balancing the aggregate of unpaid vouchers as indicated by the voucher register or other record with the general ledger control account at regular intervals, comparing vendors' statements with recorded liabilities, payment of invoices before the discount dates, and approval of adjustments of recorded accounts payable.

Debit memoranda for returned merchandise should be under numerical control, issued promptly upon receipt of proper authorization, recorded promptly when issued, and approved by a responsible person. If these procedures are not followed, overpayments to vendors or an overstatement of accounts payable may result.

ACCRUED LIABILITIES.—Internal accounting control over accrued liabilities, such as wages, commissions, rentals, royalties, and taxes, is exercised mainly through control of related expenses. It is good procedure to maintain detailed records of accrued liabilities and reconcile them periodically to the general ledger control accounts. Reviews of account balances and charges and credits to the accounts should be made periodically by responsible employees. Charges to accrued accounts for disbursement of cash should be subjected to regular routines for vouchers; charges arising from sources other than cash disbursements should be approved by responsible employees.

DEFERRED CREDITS.—Procedures for internal accounting control of deferred credits are similar to those required for accrued liabilities.

Internal Check.

NOTES AND ACCEPTANCES PAYABLE.—When borrowings on notes are not formally authorized by the board of directors, the signatures of two officers should be required to validate the borrowing instrument, and such officers should be independent of each other. These requirements should deter an officer or employee from borrowing funds in the corporate name and diverting such funds to his own use.

The employee who records entries in the note register should be independent of cash functions, and the periodic reconciliations of the register with the general ledger control account should be checked by persons independent of those who maintain the two records. Unissued notes should be in the custody of employees independent of cash, general ledger, and note register functions, and persons with such independence should account for the sequence of numbered notes, issued and unissued.

When a note has been paid, it should be returned to an employee other than the one who maintains the note register, examined for endorsements, effectively canceled, and retained in the files of the company.

ACCOUNTS PAYABLE.—A detailed listing of processed invoices, including vendors' names, should be maintained in a purchase journal, voucher register, or cash disbursement book by persons independent of purchasing, receiving, cash disbursement, and general ledger posting functions. Consecutive numbers should be assigned these invoices and all numbers should be accounted for. The reconciliation of unpaid items on the listing with the general ledger control account should be made by an employee independent of cash disbursement and invoice processing functions. Employees independent of invoice processing functions should reconcile vendors' statements with reported liabilities and approve any adjustment of these liabilities.

Employees who are assigned the responsibility of numbering and approving debit memoranda should be independent of purchasing, receiving, and invoice processing functions.

Some companies have established procedures whereby internal auditors or other independent employees make tests of recorded vendors to determine that such vendors actually exist and are not fictitious corporations established by dishonest employees.

ACCRUED LIABILITIES.—Employees maintaining detailed records of accrued liabilities should be independent of cash, voucher, and general ledger functions. Still other independent persons should be responsible for approving unusual charges and credits to the accounts and reviewing periodically entries and balances in the accounts. The reconciliation of the detailed records with the general ledger controls should be prepared or at least checked periodically by persons independent of general ledger functions and the maintenance of detailed records of accrued liabilities.

DEFERRED CREDITS.—Procedures for effective internal check of deferred credits are similar to those for accrued liabilities.

AUDITING PROCEDURES

Objectives.—An important objective of the examination of current assets such as accounts receivable or inventories is to establish a proper basis for stating their amounts in the balance sheet. As indicated previously in this chapter, the basis of recording current liabilities is not usually a problem, although there may be exceptions when, for example, income tax liabilities are unsettled because of complex tax controversies with the Internal Revenue Service. The auditor's main problem in the examination of current liabilities is to satisfy himself that all material liabilities subject to current payment, liquidation, or settlement are included in reasonably accurate amounts in the balance sheet. The possibility of deliberate omission of current liabilities from the balance sheet is greater when the current position is weak, when the business is unprofitable, when note or bond agreements contain restrictive clauses based on working capital, or when an examination is undertaken on behalf of creditors or receivers.

Notes Payable.—A list of outstanding notes payable should be prepared, preferably by the client's employees. The list should indicate payees, amounts of the notes, dates drawn, due dates, interest rates, endorsers, details of collateral hypothecated, if any, and the amount of the interest accrued or prepaid at the balance sheet date. The auditor should compare data on this list with the notes payable record and reconcile the total with the general ledger control account. If loans are customarily authorized by the board of directors, the list should be checked to authorizations or approvals appearing in minutes of directors' meetings; notes outstanding at dates during the period may be similarly checked.

Notes paid during the period under audit, properly canceled by the payee or a bank, constitute vouchers. If they are not so canceled, they should be marked to prevent their subsequent misuse. If notes are issued from a book with stubs, or if specially numbered forms are used, tests may be made to ascertain whether all stubs or numbers are accounted for. Careful consideration of notes issued during the period and an examination of notes paid and canceled between the date of the balance sheet and the date of examination will assist the auditor in determining whether all notes outstanding are reflected in the balance sheet.

It is customary for the auditor to obtain from holders of notes payable written confirmation of the amount payable and of any assets pledged as collateral. Notes held by banks can usually be confirmed simultaneously with the bank balances. Each bank with which the company may be doing business should be asked for a statement of direct and indirect obligations of the client. The form of request for confirmation illustrated in Chapter 8 usually will be found suitable.

In examinations of financial statements of stockbrokers, confirmations of loans payable are usually requested separately from those of bank balances. The following form has proved satisfactory for separate confirmation of collateral loans:

(Date)

(Name of creditor)
  (Address)

Dear Sirs:

Please confirm direct to our auditors, (name and address of auditors), the correctness of the following statement of your loans to us and the collateral held by you as at the close of business (date).

In replying to our auditors please inform them if we were otherwise liable to you as at that date, either directly or contingently.

A return envelope is enclosed for your convenience.

Very truly yours,

(Signature of client)

Date of Loan	Due Date	Amount ....
Collateral		

The above statement is correct.

(Signature of creditor)

When notes payable to bearer have been sold through note brokers, the request for confirmation of notes sold should be addressed to the brokers through whom the notes were sold. One form for this purpose follows:

(Date)

(Name of note brokers)
  (Address)

Dear Sirs:

Our auditors, (name and address of auditors), are engaged in an examination of our financial statements. They ask that you confirm to them the amount of notes sold through you and outstanding as at the close of business (date).

Please send the desired information direct to our auditors and, at the same time, inform them if, as at that date, we were otherwise liable to you either directly or contingently.

A return envelope is enclosed for your convenience.

Very truly yours,

(Signature of client)

Deliberate omission of notes payable from the books or financial statements is sometimes difficult to detect, because the owners or those authorized to negotiate loans for them may issue notes and possibly dispose of the proceeds without making a record in the accounts. If the lender is one to whom inquiries would not normally be addressed, the existence of these obligations may be concealed for some time. These notes may pass into the hands of innocent holders, who, under the law of negotiable instruments, are holders in due course; in any event, the company issuing the notes may be liable. Unusual items of cash receipts, interest, discount, bonuses paid, or unusual entries in personal accounts of partners or officers may furnish a clue to discovery of unrecorded notes payable.

Audit procedures for acceptances payable should be similar to those described for notes payable. In requesting confirmation from banks of acceptances outstanding, the auditor should also inquire about related collateral.

Consideration should be given to a possible liability for acceptances not recorded in the books. It is possible for a company to purchase goods, arrange for a bank's acceptance of the vendor's draft, receive and place the goods in stock, and yet make no record of the liability until the acceptance becomes due.

A test comparison of order and receiving records with purchase invoices should disclose discrepancies arising from carelessness. Comparison of creditors' statements with corresponding ledger accounts may not disclose acceptances because an acceptance usually covers specific invoices and after the receipt of an acceptance the creditor probably will not include the invoices covered by it in his statements, even though they are in fact still unpaid. Banks make a charge for services in accepting drafts, and payments of these charges should be test-checked with recorded acceptances.

Accounts Payable.—The auditor should test footings of the trial balance of accounts payable and compare the total with the general ledger control account. Comparisons should be made of some details of the schedule of accounts payable with amounts reflected by the ledger or the voucher record. The auditor should determine whether balances represent only specific and recent items; if they do not, he should inquire into the reason for delay in discharging the liabilities.

When accounts are past due, the auditor should consider the possibility that notes may have been given in settlement without recording the change in status of the accounts. Because of the difference in the legal status of negotiable notes and open accounts, if it is found that unrecorded notes have been given to settle open accounts, the books should be adjusted to reflect the facts.

Statements received by the client from creditors are useful in substantiating the amounts recorded as accounts payable. The auditor may request the client to obtain statements at the balance sheet date from selected vendors shown by the records to be creditors, as well as from companies with whom the client regularly does business, even though no obligation is reflected in the accounts at that date. Although many business houses do not regularly issue statements, they will usually furnish a memorandum of the amount due at any stated time.

If the accounts payable appear to be irregular in any respect, or if the auditor has reason to believe that the client may be attempting to conceal or otherwise understate accounts payable, he may request statements or written confirmation of balances direct from all creditors with whom the client normally does business. Even though none of the accounts appears to be irregular, the auditor may well request direct confirmation of balances from certain creditors at each examination for the purpose of testing the records because of the nature and size of the transactions, or because large purchases have been made from suppliers unknown to him. Under unusual circumstances it may be desirable to compare names of vendors appearing on the list of accounts payable with information appearing in credit publications to determine the existence of the named vendors.

The auditor should compare entries in the receiving records, immediately before and after the balance sheet date, with the purchase journal or voucher record to determine whether the liability for materials received just before the close of the fiscal period is properly recorded, and to see that purchases are not recorded in the current period for materials not included in inventory.

When the auditor's examination is not completed until some time after the balance sheet date, the voucher record and, if appropriate, the cash disbursement record, of the subsequent period should be examined to determine whether any invoices entered therein are applicable to the audit period. It should be remembered that the date of an invoice may not represent the date of shipment; invoices are sometimes dated forward.

Totals of expenses and of various sections of the expense accounts for the last month of the current period may be compared with corresponding totals for the previous period. Abnormal differences should be investigated, as they may lead to the discovery of unrecorded liabilities.

Some companies do not record invoices for materials until the materials have been received and checked for quality and quantity. At the end of an accounting period, therefore, a liability may be unrecorded both for material in transit and for material received but not checked. Although this practice may not seriously misstate income, both inventory and accounts payable may be understated by a significant amount.

If the auditor's examination reveals evidence that goods have been received on consignment, the records should be examined to determine whether consigned goods have been sold without a record in the accounts. Amounts currently due consignors for goods sold may be classified as trade creditor accounts in the balance sheet. It is often desirable to obtain direct from the consignor a letter or statement of unsold consigned goods and the amount due at the balance sheet date for goods previously sold.

The auditor should determine that allowances for retroactive discounts based on volume of business, as indicated in agreements with suppliers, have been recorded.

Debit balances in the voucher register or accounts payable ledgers, if significant in amount, should be investigated and given the same consideration as to collectibility as is given to accounts receivable. Investigation of the debit items may indicate that they are payments of unrecorded invoices, in which event appropriate adjustment should be made by recording the liability. Investigation may also show that such items are deductible upon payment of invoices already recorded, in which event they are properly treated as deductions from accounts payable.

Amounts Withheld from Employees or Others.—The auditor should determine whether there is an obligation to make such withholdings and to make remittances to others, and, if there is, he should assure himself that the amount of the liability is fairly stated in the books of account. A review of copies of reports or tax returns accompanying payments after the balance sheet date may indicate unrecorded liabilities at that date. It may be necessary to estimate or calculate amounts withheld and to compare the estimate with the aggregate of funds collected for the several purposes.

Withholding procedures should be reviewed to determine whether they seem adequate, and tests should be made to assure that they are functioning properly.

Advances on Government Contracts.—When advances on fixed-price government contracts are based on inventory in which title is vested in the government by virtue of such advances, care must be taken to assure that computations of inventory, computations of percentage advances based thereon, and computations of application of advances against billings for completed products are fairly stated. Significant overstatement or understatement of accounts receivable and inventory could result from undetected errors in such computations and offset applications.

Deposits.—The auditor should make appropriate tests which will indicate whether the total of the detail deposit records agrees with the control account. Deposits of material amounts should be confirmed by correspondence with depositors.

Dividends Declared but Unpaid.—The auditor should see that the liability for dividends declared but unpaid is supported by the shares outstanding as shown by the capital stock records and by the rate of dividend declarations of the board of directors.

Unclaimed Dividends.—Frequently stockholders cannot be reached and dividend checks may be returned by the post office. The liability for unclaimed dividends may remain undischarged for some time, and the auditor may examine evidence on a test basis to support charges to this account. Experience has shown that dormant items of this character are a temptation to dishonest employees.

It is appropriate for the auditor to suggest that a definite policy be adopted for the disposal of such items at regular intervals, usually not longer than one year after an established waiting period has elapsed. If such a policy has been adopted, the auditor should make suitable tests and inquiries to determine that it is being followed.

Many of the larger corporations, particularly those which have numerous stockholders or bondholders, turn over to fiscal agents the details of dividend or bond interest payments. Under these arrangements, the corporations usually consider their dividend or interest obligations discharged when they deposit the amount of the aggregate required payments with the fiscal agent. In these circumstances, the auditor is not concerned with unpaid dividend checks or uncashed bond coupons which have become obligations of the agent. He should, however, investigate the handling of unclaimed dividends no longer an obligation either of the agent or of the corporation because of the statute of limitations.

Damages and Other Unliquidated Claims.—It is customary to insure against liability for damages claimed by employees or the public, but insurance policies do not cover unlimited liabilities and not all companies carry adequate insurance. Furthermore, unusual claims for damages may arise from alleged breach of contract, failure to deliver goods, existence of foreign substances in the company's product, and other causes. The auditor should inquire about possible liabilities of this general character and request a letter from the client's attorneys indicating and commenting upon any pending claims or suits. Such a request is illustrated on page 376.

Claims may have arisen which have not been referred to counsel. For example, salesmen may claim commissions in excess of those paid or accrued, or employees who have been dismissed may claim salaries or other compensation for uncompleted terms of service. Such claims are often handled as purely administrative matters and may not be referred to counsel unless substantial in amount. If the auditor learns of a possible material liability for such claims, he should request the opinion of client's counsel with respect to the probable liability.

Advances from Officers, Employees, and Others.—Loans from officers, employees, and others are occasionally made, especially in small concerns, with the accounts as the only evidence of the indebtedness. The auditor should confirm such liabilities by correspondence, and circumstances surrounding these obligations should be investigated. An apparent advance may be a partial payment on subscriptions to capital stock or on the purchase of real estate or other assets of the corporation.

Judgments.—Occasionally a company disputes a claim, resorts to litigation, and has a judgment entered against it. If the case is appealed, execution of the judgment may be stayed if a bond is given pending final decision. These judgments are seldom entered on the books. Many businessmen consider a record in the books an admission of liability, and they will not permit a claim which they propose to fight to be shown as a liability.

The existence of judgments may be detected in several ways. An inspection of lawyers' bills may furnish a clue. If a company is able to pay but does not do so on principle, the auditor may have no difficulty in learning the facts. If a company obviously is in serious financial difficulties, the auditor may suspect that judgments have been obtained. In any event, he should request a written statement from the company's counsel as to any judgments of which the latter has knowledge, and under unusual circumstances he may even request an independent report based on a search of public records.

Unclaimed Wages.—Unclaimed payroll currency or checks should be deposited in the bank with a corresponding credit to a liability account.

The auditor should examine or test recorded transactions in the unclaimed wages account and satisfy himself that charges represent authorized payments or transfers.

If unclaimed wages remain a liability indefinitely, the auditor should suggest that a policy be adopted whereby unclaimed wages outstanding for a specified time will be transferred to income periodically or otherwise disposed of, depending upon applicable state law. If such a policy has been adopted, the auditor should determine that it is being followed.

Accrued Liabilities.—Accrued expenses, such as compensation to employees, rents, taxes, interest, and similar items, should be recorded as at the balance sheet date and charged to the appropriate expense accounts. When the accounts provide for accruals currently, it is probable that material accrued liabilities will have been recorded as a matter of routine. Nevertheless, the auditor should consider the possibility of accrued expenses for which provision has not been made; he should compare the details of amounts of such accruals at the end of the period with those at the end of the previous period. The likelihood of accrued interest may be suggested by notes or bonds payable, by accounts payable past due, or by accounts with finance companies. Evidence of extensive use of equipment and a relatively small investment in equipment may indicate royalty or rental expense, part of which may be accrued. Nearly all businesses have a liability for accrued wages, some for accrued bonuses to officers and employees, and many for accrued commissions to salesmen. In companies which have been engaged in labor controversies, reference to union agreements or other inquiry may disclose substantial amounts of unpaid retroactive wages. Frequently the initial deposit on compensation insurance is inadequate, and at the date of the balance sheet an additional liability may exist. Provisions of retirement pension plans, profit-sharing trusts, management contracts, and labor union agreements should be referred to by the auditor to discover accrued liabilities not recorded in the books.

When the auditor checks an accrual computation of one of the client's employees, he should not insist upon an adjustment of the books or the financial statements if his independent calculation produces a result only slightly at variance with that of the employee. Substantial differences should of course be investigated and errors corrected.

SALARIES AND WAGES.—The substantiation of accrued salaries and wages offers few difficulties. Most companies can furnish an exact computation of the accrual at the end of an accounting period. This computation may be tested by the auditor through a review of the method used. In the absence of an exact computation, the approximate amount of the accrual may have been estimated by the client by proration of the payrolls for the overlapping period. The arithmetical correctness of such an estimate may be easily checked.

OTHER EMPLOYEE BENEFITS.—Review of labor union contracts may disclose that the company has a liability for vacation pay, contributions to employees' welfare funds, or other so-called fringe benefits. When vacation periods are based upon length of service, a detailed computation of the accrued liability should be prepared by the client. The auditor should review the method in use and make sufficient test checks of the computation to satisfy himself that the amount provided is substantially correct. The approximate amount of the accrual should be estimated by the auditor on an over-all basis, whether or not a detailed computation is available for testing.

It is possible that a published statement of company policy, relied upon by employees, may create liabilities for rights which accrue to them even without formal labor contracts. Opinion of counsel may sometimes be necessary to determine if there is a legal liability at the balance sheet date. Contracts and policies of this nature do not always clearly indicate whether the employees' rights accrue ratably over a period or come into existence in their entirety at a specific date.

BONUSES TO OFFICERS AND EMPLOYEES.—The auditor should determine that the liability for authorized bonuses to officers and employees is computed in accordance with the authorization. Provisions for bonuses payable in a corporation's capital shares are not current liabilities unless the company must acquire the shares in the market.

Amounts due officers and employees under profit-sharing plans become a liability in the period during which the profits are earned. If the exact amount of the liability cannot be definitely fixed until a later date, it may be estimated at the balance sheet date. If amounts are payable over several years, the noncurrent portion should be segregated.

TRAVEL EXPENSE AND COMMISSIONS.—The auditor may obtain a list of employees with expense accounts and make appropriate tests to determine whether all expenses have been reported and recorded in the books during the period in which they were incurred. He may test related post-balance sheet date entries to determine whether any of them were applicable to the prior period.

Provision should be made for all commissions payable on sales billed to customers. Since commissions are frequently not payable to salesmen until the customers have remitted, accrued commissions are sometimes omitted from the books. However, as they must be paid from the proceeds of sales on which the full profit has already been taken into the accounts, they should be recorded as liabilities at the time the receivable and sale are recorded.

ROYALTIES.—In determining the amount of royalties payable at any given date, the auditor should examine royalty and licensing contracts and extract important provisions for his permanent files. Many such contracts provide that a minimum royalty must be paid whether or not any liability for royalties accrues on a unit basis. Oil and gas producing companies frequently enter into leases which require periodic payments even when no oil or gas has been produced. Such payments are usually termed "lease rentals."

Coal leases often call for minimum annual payments regardless of the fact that the leasing company may not have extracted any coal. Publishing companies enter into agreements with authors which provide for a sliding scale of royalties dependent upon the number of copies sold.

The auditor should attempt to determine from the royalty contract whether the payments are actually royalties, or whether, in fact, they represent payments for the purchase of a patent or other property covered by the agreement. If the contract is in reality a purchase agreement, the asset and liability should be set up at the date of the contract, and depreciation or amortization of the asset charged to expense. The so-called royalty payments should not be charged to expense if these payments represent a reduction in the purchase liability.

If provisions of the royalty contract are not clear, the auditor should request a legal interpretation of ambiguous provisions.

Royalties Based on Sales.—If royalty payments are based upon sales, computations may be checked against recorded sales. Selective tests of statements of royalties due may be made to substantiate recorded amounts.

Royalties Based on Production.—In some instances royalty payments are not based on sales but on the quantity or value of goods produced. Then the auditor should review documents on file supporting amounts accrued and make suitable tests of underlying data. If accounting records are not kept in sufficient detail to give the essential data, it may be necessary to analyze production records to obtain the required information.

Confirmations.—When the data on which a royalty is based is solely in the possession of lessors or vendors, it is desirable to secure from them statements of liability under royalty agreements. A request for confirmation may bring to light serious differences in interpretation of contract provisions.

INTEREST PAYABLE.—Many liabilities bear interest. Occasionally accounts payable bear interest and the auditor should explore that possibility. Loan accounts of partners and corporate officers usually bear interest; judgments, overdue taxes, and other liens often bear interest at high rates. If bond interest is in default and the indenture provides that interest shall accrue thereon, provision should be made for this interest.

The computation of accrued interest at the balance sheet date normally may be checked with little or no difficulty.

INCOME AND OTHER TAXES.—Chapter 22 includes a discussion of auditing procedures which may be followed in determining whether the liabilities for federal, state, and local taxes are fairly stated.

PRODUCT GUARANTIES.—The auditor should review the terms of the guaranty under which product is sold and the accounting policy followed in making provision for probable costs. The estimated liability may be included in current liabilities, in long-term liabilities, or apportioned between them on a reasonable basis, as circumstances indicate. The amount may be shown net of the related tax effect (see Chapter 22).

If the sales volume is large, substantiation of the adequacy of the warranty service provision even by a test examination may involve considerable study of statistical data. Facts ordinarily pertinent to such a determination include (1) the percentage of total units sold which may require service, (2) the average annual cost of service, and (3) the warranty period. From such data a reasonable estimate of the required service cost can ordinarily be computed. Subsequent expenditures for this service should be charged against the liability provision.

Certain products are built according to specifications with the understanding that the manufacturer is required to bear the expense of correcting any variation from specifications or latent defects disclosed by tests. If experience shows that such adjustments may be expected, provision for the obligation should be made by a charge against income and the liability retained in the accounts until the products have been finally accepted by the customer.

Deferred Credits.—The auditor should examine records and computations supporting the balances of deferred credits or deferred income accounts. His examination of subscription revenues should include the steps necessary to support unearned revenues at both the beginning and end of the period.

Advance sales of tickets for theatrical or sports events should be substantiated by reference to inventory of unsold tickets, certifications from printers of the number of tickets printed, reports from agencies of tickets disposed of and on hand, approved complimentary ticket lists and, if feasible, subsequent confirmatory records, such as certificates of incineration, reports to taxing authorities for admission taxes, and attendance reports. It may be advisable to attend the event, observe procedures, and possibly test-check turnstile counts by a count of ticket stubs deposited at selected turnstiles.

Rent and interest received in advance can usually be tested as part of the examinations of rental and interest income.

Unrealized profit on major sales of property or other assets may be substantiated in connection with the examination of related receivables or other assets resulting from the sale. The tax related to the realization of such deferred profits may require special attention from the auditor to assure the propriety of income tax rates applied. If the capital gains rate is ruled to be inapplicable, the additional tax involved may be very substantial. Agreements may have been reached with the United States Treasury Department controlling both the applicable tax rate and basis of reporting.

Attention should be given to the tax reporting basis of advance collections or other deferred income to assure that the treatment of significant differences in the bases of tax and financial reporting will not distort income. See Chapter 22.

In examining deferred credits or deferred income, the auditor should pay particular attention to charges other than transfers to current operations against these balances and authorizations therefor. He should also satisfy himself that the policy in disposing of these deferred balances is followed consistently.

TRADING STAMPS AND PROFIT-SHARING COUPONS.—Trading stamps, profit-sharing coupons, and the like issued to customers when merchandise is sold create obligations for redemption. The auditor should review the client's prior experience in the redemption of these obligations, estimate the percentage that may ultimately be redeemed, and so approximate the amount of the liability on outstanding coupons.

Some accountants refer to these liabilities as contingent, but in the authors' opinion such obligations should be recorded and classified as current liabilities. Usually the amount of the liability cannot be determined exactly; however, since experience has demonstrated that a substantial part of these premiums will be redeemed at a later date, reported income will be overstated unless the estimated liability is booked, rather than disclosed as a contingency.

Subordinated Debts.—The chief purpose of subordination of obligations is to protect other creditors. The auditor should analyze the general provisions of subordination agreements to determine their effect on the balance sheet; if there is any doubt, and if questions of recording and disclosure arise, legal opinion should be obtained.

Provisions of Bond Indentures and Note and Preferred Stock Agreements.—Violation of the provisions of such indentures and agreements may constitute default which, under certain conditions, may transform long-term liabilities into current liabilities. Provisions most frequently encountered include covenants for the maintenance of minimum working capital, for sinking funds, for the disposition of proceeds of mortgaged property sold, and for restrictions on dividends or other distributions to stockholders. The auditor should read the indentures and agreements and determine whether any of these covenants appear to have been violated. See Chapter 17 for further discussion of this subject.

Undisclosed Liabilities.—One of the auditor's most difficult tasks is determination of liabilities to which no direct reference appears in the accounts. Clues to such obligations may be discovered in unexpected places, and the auditor should be constantly alert for indications of their existence. In the preceding discussion some suggestions are made for determining unrecorded accrued expenses; not all undisclosed liabilities are accruals.

Responses to requests for confirmation of bank loans may list as collateral securities or other assets which do not appear on the records. These may have been borrowed from affiliated companies or from others. Liabilities in respect to borrowed securities or other property should be confirmed with lenders and reflected either in the body of the balance sheet or by footnote.

The assignment of fire insurance policies on merchandise or materials is likely to indicate the hypothecation of inventories, with a corresponding liability, possibly unrecorded.

Distributors of nationally advertised branded merchandise sometimes enter into agreements with agents and franchised dealers to supply advertising and demonstration materials. These contracts should be examined by the auditor and any undisclosed liability determined.

Manufacturers of machinery and equipment often sell their products at a price which includes cost of installation. The auditor should determine that adequate provision has been made for the cost of completing the installation of equipment sold, the profit on which has been recorded in the period under examination.

The cancellation of purchase commitments frequently involves a penalty. Particularly in a period of declining prices, the auditor should consider the possibility of liabilities by reason of such cancellations. Correspondence with creditors may be necessary to establish a liability for the cancellation of purchase commitments.

In the audit of a contractor's accounts, interrogation of executives and employees may disclose that important portions of jobs supposedly finished may require additional work at the contractor's expense. Matters of this kind are not always ascertainable from the accounts, but the information must be sought, since it may be essential to sound financial statements.

If a client is self-insured, the auditor should satisfy himself as to pending claims.

Liability Certificate.—Many auditors request from their clients written assurances that, to the best of their knowledge and belief, all liabilities have been entered in the books or disclosed to the auditors. This procedure is advisable since it provides written evidence that the auditor made proper inquiry from company officials about liabilities not otherwise determinable from the records. The information should be obtained and the letter dated as near as possible to the date of completion of the field work.

The liability certificate should be signed by a chief executive, and usually should also be signed by the officer responsible for accounting. In rare instances, an officer or chief executive may refuse to sign a liability certificate. If the auditor desires to express an opinion in the face of such refusal, he should satisfy himself that the refusal is not based on serious reservations or intentional misrepresentation.

The following specimen certificate may be modified to meet special requirements. If, in any business, there is a type of liability not common to business in general, it is advisable to refer specifically to this liability in the certificate. It should be understood that a liability certificate complements the auditor's examination and is not a substitute for audit procedures; it serves as a reminder of liabilities which the client may have overlooked.

LIABILITY CERTIFICATE

(Name and address of auditors)

Dear Sirs:

consolidated

In connection with your examination of the balance sheet of (*name of company*) as of (*balance sheet date*), I hereby certify that, as of that date, to the best of my knowledge and belief:

1. All liabilities have been taken up on the books of account, including the liability for all purchases to which title had passed prior to the stated date.

2. No asset of the company was pledged or is now pledged as security for any liability except as follows: *Chattel mortgages on equipment*

3. Unused balances of letters of credit outstanding, against which no drafts had been drawn, were as follows:

4. There were no contingent liabilities except as follows:

    (I understand the term "contingent liabilities" to include among other things:

    Notes, drafts, and acceptances receivable which have been discounted or sold with recourse; endorsements, warranties, sureties, or guaranties; pending suits, proceedings, hearings, or negotiations possibly involving retroactive adjustments; unsettled judgments or claims; taxes in dispute.)

5. There were no purchase commitments in excess of normal requirements or at prices in excess of the prevailing market prices, nor agreements to repurchase items previously sold, except as follows:

6. There were:

    (a) No commitments for purchase or sale of securities or to repurchase the company's stock or any other securities; nor any options given by the company, including options on company's capital stock; nor any bonus or profit-sharing arrangements, except as follows:

    (b) No other commitments, contracts, or leases, which, in my judgment, might adversely affect the company, except as follows:

7. There were no defaults in principal, interest, sinking fund, or redemption provisions with respect to any issue of securities or credit agreements, or any breach of covenant of a related indenture or agreement, except as follows:

8. Contractual obligations for plant construction and purchase of real property, equipment, and patent or other rights amounted to approximately $ 0

9. Except as are reflected in the balance sheet, there were no agreements under which any of the liabilities of the company had been subordinated to any other of its liabilities nor were any receivables owned by the company subordinate to any other liabilities of the debtor companies.

[handwritten: the on State of Minnesota]

10. ~~Federal~~ income tax returns have *[handwritten: not]* been examined and reported upon by the Internal Revenue Service, through (*date*); returns of years since (*date*) are still open; the provision for unpaid federal income taxes reflected in the balance sheet is adequate to cover any additional assessments resulting from examinations already made or from those to be made by the Service.

11. There have been no material changes since (*balance sheet date*) in respect of any of the above Items 4 to 10, inclusive, except as follows:

[handwritten: (a) Tornado damage to store in Fridley of which minimum portion of loss not expected to exceed $2300.]

Very truly yours,

....
(Name)

....
(Title)

....
(Date signed)

....
(Name of company)

Coordination of Examination with That of Related Accounts.— Whenever possible the examination of accounts classified as current liabilities should be coordinated with the examination of related accounts. Schedules of notes payable, acceptances payable, and other loans outstanding during any part of the year should be prepared to show interest paid and accrued on these loans, from which interest expense for the period may be determined readily.

Analyses of accrued accounts should be prepared so that amounts credited to these accounts may be traced to the related expense accounts. These analyses may be particularly important when the auditor also prepares income and franchise tax returns. Information required for tax returns should be accumulated during the regular audit; this facilitates preparation of returns at a later date without the necessity for additional analyses of the accounts.

The examination of deferred credits classified as current liabilities will often be feasible in conjunction with the examination of related subscription, transportation, admissions, rental, interest, or other revenue and income accounts.

Time of Examination.—Because of the rapidly changing nature of current liabilities, much of the auditor's examination of these accounts cannot be made until after the accounts have been closed as of the balance sheet date.

However, some work can be performed at an interim date to expedite completion of the final examination. The applicable features of the system of internal control can be reviewed; notes payable and other loan accounts can be analyzed for nine or ten months, their authorization reviewed, and paid notes examined.

Accounts for taxes and other amounts withheld can be analyzed prior to the year end to see that funds are being paid to the proper authorities, and that the accounts are cleared at regular intervals. Certain accrued accounts can be analyzed at an interim date, and consideration can be given to classification of the balances when finally determined as current or noncurrent.

After the close of the period, analyses and other schedules should be completed and brought into agreement or reconciled with the closing balances shown in the accounts.

STATEMENT PRESENTATION

Current liabilities ordinarily appear as the first group of items on the liability side of the balance sheet. Frequently, subgroupings of current liabilities are listed in the order in which they will become due. However, it is accepted practice to state notes payable as the first item of current liabilities, even though other current liabilities may be liquidated before the notes are due.

The section on accounting principles in this chapter has discussed in some detail the classification of certain liabilities such as deferred income, security deposits, and returnable containers as current or noncurrent.

Notes and Acceptances Payable.—For some purposes it is desirable that loans from banks, notes sold through note brokers, demand loans, notes to trade creditors, and notes to officers and others be clearly distinguished from each other, because the sources of credit may throw considerable light on financial policies of the business.

It is important that liabilities against which assets have been pledged be shown separately and that the amount of any assets pledged be indicated and related to the liability. When pledged merchandise has been released under a trust receipt, it is not always feasible to identify this merchandise after it has been started through processing procedures. Part of the merchandise may be in raw materials, part in process, and part in finished goods. This problem may be met by including a note to the balance sheet indicating the amount of merchandise that has been released under trust receipts.

Indebtedness to finance companies should be separately stated, with an indication of the amount and type of assets pledged against it.

It is desirable to distinguish between notes payable to trade creditors or trade acceptances payable, and bankers' acceptances payable. The

proper description of acceptances payable is important; if merchandise is pledged as security this should be indicated, since the assets so pledged are not available for other creditors. Following are two captions either of which ordinarily will adequately describe a company's direct liability under bankers' acceptances:

1. Acceptances under letters of credit against merchandise received under trust receipts, or
2. Bankers' acceptances against merchandise received under trust receipts.

Some creditors and creditors' organizations have urged that unused amounts of commercial letters of credit be disclosed on balance sheets of companies to which banks have issued letters of credit. The authors believe that such disclosure would rarely be essential to a proper understanding of financial position, but there is no objection to disclosing such information in a footnote along the following lines:

Note: Unused balances of commercial letters of credit at December 31, 19— were $............

In the authors' opinion, the interest rate on short-term notes and acceptances payable, even though higher than the legal or prevailing rate, need not be shown on the balance sheet unless this information is required by the person to whom the balance sheet is to be submitted. It may be of interest to creditors, but it is of more interest to competitors; and the possibility of unfavorable effect outweighs the desirability of disclosure. In setting a rate there may be mitigating circumstances or compensating factors which cannot be satisfactorily explained on a balance sheet.

Accounts Payable.—The term "accounts payable" may be used as a general caption under which may be listed separately items such as trade indebtedness, advances from officers, dealers' deposits, payroll withholdings of federal and state taxes, government bond purchases, and union dues.

When the term is not qualified, the reader is justified in assuming that it represents largely amounts due trade creditors as a result of ordinary business transactions. Current debit balances that are not direct offsets to accounts payable, if material, should be segregated and reflected in the balance sheet as current assets.

Accounts payable other than to trade creditors may be grouped in a separate total including such items as customers' credit balances, advance payments and deposits, advances by officers and employees, dividends and royalties payable, taxes collected on behalf of taxing authorities, and claims or awards. Any significant item should be stated separately.

Accounts payable to affiliated companies should be stated separately.

Receivable and payable balances with the same persons are not generally offset against each other if separate settlement of these balances is expected.

Current Liabilities Related to Government Contracts.—In connection with basic accounting problems common to cost-plus-fixed-fee (CPFF) contracts, Accounting Research Bulletin No. 43, Chapter 11, Section A, states in part:

An advance on a CPFF contract usually is made for the purpose of providing a revolving fund and is not ordinarily applied as a partial payment until the contract is completed or nears completion. It therefore appears to be preferable to offset advances on CPFF contracts against receivables in connection with the contracts only when it is expected that the advances will be applied in payment of those particular charges. In any case, amounts offset should be clearly disclosed.

Contracts terminated by the government often contain provisions whereby the contractor may recover allowable costs incurred to date of termination and, possibly, a related portion of estimated profit. Advances and partial payments made by the government on terminated contracts are usually deducted separately from amounts of termination claims. Loans under which such claims have been pledged as collateral should be shown as current liabilities, whether or not guaranteed by the government.

There may be one or more subcontracts for portions of the work which the contractor arranged with other companies. The liability of the corporation to subcontractors will finally be determined by their approved claims and usually will be included in the same amount in the contractor's termination claim.

It is permissible to treat subcontractors' claims either as current liabilities (at actual or estimated amounts) or as contingent liabilities, with appropriate disclosure. If the latter treatment is adopted, the receivable for the contractor's termination claim will not include subcontractors' claims. The subject of balance sheet treatment for subcontractors' claims on terminated government contracts is dealt with in Accounting Research Bulletin No. 43, Chapter 11, Section C, which states that the committee expresses no preference for either of the alternatives and considers either to be acceptable.

Advance payments on government contracts are frequently made on the basis of a percentage (running up to 90 per cent) of inventory accumulated for performance of the contract. Title to such inventory may vest in the government, and the company has a claim against the government for its equity in the inventory. Percentage advances or progress payments may be treated as deductions from inventory. Disclosure should be made that title to the remainder of the inventory is held by the government.

Accrued Liabilities.—Obligations of a continuing character, not due at the balance sheet date, and often likely to be larger in amount at their maturity, are generally set out separately from those based on completed transactions. In a detailed statement the various types of accrued liabilities may be shown separately because they reflect different phases of the business, but it is not improper to combine them in one amount if they are not abnormal in character or amount. The kinds of accruals represented may be indicated in the title.

It is preferable to state separately the estimated liability for federal income taxes. United States Treasury Tax Anticipation Certificates of Indebtedness and other government securities, if the intent is to use them to liquidate the tax liability, may be deducted from the liability for these taxes. This presentation may be considered acceptable under the stated conditions, but inclusion of such securities in current assets is preferable.

Accounting Research Bulletin No. 43, Chapter 3, Section B, states that the application of United States Government securities other than those which, by their terms, may be surrendered in payment of taxes as a deduction from the liability for federal taxes on income is a deviation from the general rule against offsets, but is not so significant a deviation as to call for an exception in an accountant's report. The bulletin further states that extension or application of this exception to cash or other assets or against amounts owing to the federal government other than income tax obligations is not to be regarded as acceptable practice. This seems to be a roundabout way of saying that the deviation with respect to government securities is acceptable practice.

No one has ever explained to the authors' satisfaction why it is acceptable for United States securities, which may be converted into cash but which may not be used for payment of federal taxes on income, to be applied as an offset against liability for such taxes, but it is not acceptable that the same amount of cash be similarly offset. When such offsetting started, auditors failed to take exception to offsetting United States securities other than those acceptable in payment of income taxes and, as a result, find themselves in what the authors believe is an indefensible position.

Sinking Fund Requirements Due Within One Year.—Some accountants believe it is sufficient to indicate in a note to the financial statements or parenthetically in the description of the issue the amount of sinking fund instalments due within one year for the retirement of bonds. In the authors' opinion, provision for these instalments, if material, should be included with current liabilities, unless the company has set aside and segregated from current assets sufficient funds or securities to care for them. Sinking fund instalments for the retirement of stock are somewhat similar, although some accountants believe that legal capital should not be reduced on the basis of a prospective payment for the account of stockholders. Any instalment in default should be indicated in a note to the balance sheet.

Subordinated Debts.—Full disclosure of any subordination should be made in the balance sheet. Subordinated items should not be included in accounts payable, even though explained in a note; they should be stated separately, as current or long-term liabilities, depending upon the circumstances. If the subordination is temporary, the time limitation should be clearly indicated lest creditors assume a continuation of the subordination after it has ceased to exist.

Sinking Fund Requirements Due Within One Year.—Some accountants believe it is sufficient to indicate in a note to the financial statements or parenthetically in the description of the issue the amount of sinking fund instalments due within one year for the retirement of bonds. In the auditor's opinion, provision for these instalments, if material, should be included with current liabilities, unless the company has set aside and segregated from current assets sufficient funds or securities to care for them. Sinking fund instalments for the retirement of stock are somewhat similar, although some accountants believe that legal capital should not be reduced on the basis of a prospective payment for the account of stockholders. Any instalment in default should be indicated in a note to the balance sheet.

Subordinated Debts.—Full disclosure of any subordination should be made in the balance sheet. Subordinated items should not be included in amounts payable when they are subjoined in a note; they should be shown separately, either as current or non-current liabilities, depending upon the character of the subordination when necessary, the note should so clearly indicate its restrictions that creditors do not assume a continuation of the subordination after it has ceased to exist.

CHAPTER 17

LONG-TERM DEBT

Introduction.—The section of the balance sheet between current liabilities and capital generally includes such items as long-term debt, other long-term liabilities, and minority interest in common stock and surplus of subsidiaries. Long-term debt is discussed in this chapter, other long-term liabilities in Chapter 18, and minority interest is covered in Chapter 21, Consolidated Statements.

Certain types of credit balances may represent either long-term liabilities or capital, depending on circumstances. Such items are usually included with liabilities, properly described, until circumstances change. Examples of such credit balances are:

(a) Debts to stockholders or partners which may be specifically subordinated to claims of other creditors, or assessments paid by stockholders and carried on the corporation's books as loans payable, which may prove to be capital.

(b) Deferred credits representing advance collections for services to be provided in a period starting more than one year from the date of the balance sheet. The total includes not only unearned income (eventually to be added to income) but a liability for the cost of the service. A discussion of these items is included in Chapter 16.

355

(c) Estimates of amounts of long-term liabilities such as product guaranties, litigation in progress, and tax controversies. It is prudent to overestimate rather than underestimate such amounts, and therefore some portion of the estimate eventually may be transferred to income or surplus.

ACCOUNTING PRINCIPLES

Long-Term Debt.—Long-term debt is frequently negotiated to finance the acquisition of assets of relatively long life, whereas short-term borrowings more often finance short-term working capital needs. The long-term lender often has a lien on specific properties, but he also looks to the earning power of the debtor company for security.

Common examples of long-term debt are bonds, mortgage notes, long-term notes or debentures, receivers' certificates, deferred purchase money obligations, and long-term loans from affiliated companies.

Most bonds and some long-term notes and debentures are issued subject to terms set forth in a trust indenture or note agreement. In addition to recitals setting forth the terms of the issue and a description of the pledged property, the instrument includes various covenants for protection of lenders.

Treasury Bonds.—Bonds purchased or otherwise acquired by the issuing company and not retired are called treasury bonds. If they are purchased with the intention of resale, it is proper to record them at purchase cost. Any profit or loss is not taken up in the income account until the resale or retirement.

There is a distinction between treasury stock and treasury bonds which warrants different treatment of the excess of par, stated value, or face amount over the purchase cost when there is no intention to resell. When bonds are bought in at less than their face amount and are not to be resold, the outstanding debt should be reduced by their face amount and the profit should be credited direct to income. Unamortized discount or premium on bonds purchased should also be charged or credited to income.

If the bonds were originally issued or assumed as part of the purchase price of property, purchase at a substantial discount or partial forgiveness of debt by arrangement with the mortgagee within a relatively short period of time may indicate that the original issue price was overstated. In these circumstances, the credit arising from the purchase or from forgiveness of debt should be credited to the property account.

Bonds of Subsidiary Company Purchased by Parent.—Bonds of a subsidiary company purchased by a parent for investment rather than retirement should be carried in the parent company's accounts as an investment at cost. Similar transactions between members of an affiliated group also should be so recorded. In a consolidated statement the parent and its subsidiaries are regarded as a single unit and the treatment is the same as when a corporation acquires its own bonds.

Premium on Bonds Sold.—When bonds are sold at a premium, the amount received in excess of the face amount represents in effect a reduction of the future interest cost. It should be carried as a deferred credit and distributed over the years to which it applies. For instance, a corporation may sell its 5 per cent ten-year bonds at 105, indicating that credit is rated on a basis of about $4\frac{1}{2}$ per cent; that is, if a $4\frac{1}{2}$ per cent bond had been issued, the corporation would have realized about face amount. The excess received at the time of sale should not immediately be credited to income or to surplus, but should be carried as a noncurrent deferred credit and so reflected in the balance sheet until extinguished by amortization. Conversely, when bonds are sold at a discount, the amount of the discount is considered as additional interest cost and is treated as a deferred charge and amortized over the life of the bonds as discussed in Chapter 15.

Separate premium and discount accounts should be maintained in the general or subsidiary ledger for each class or series of bonds issued or assumed by the corporation. Ordinarily, unamortized premium and unamortized discount on bonds are not offset.

Bond Premium Payable at Maturity.—When bonds are to be redeemed at maturity at a premium, good accounting practice requires that the amount of the premium be accumulated by annual charges to expense. This is in the nature of an adjustment of interest expense and creates a deferred credit to offset the premium to be paid.

INTERNAL CONTROL

In general, internal accounting control and internal check relating to issues of long-term debt are similar to those described in Chapter 16 for notes and acceptances payable.

Internal Accounting Control.—The borrowing of funds and the execution of indentures, bonds, notes, mortgages, and the like should be authorized by the board of directors or the stockholders or both. Copies or digests of borrowing instruments should be supplied to the accounting department, and their terms should be compared with authorizations.

When an independent registrar and transfer agent are not employed, it should be required procedure that unsigned and unissued bonds and long-term notes be prenumbered by the printer and held in the custody of a responsible officer of the company, and that all surrendered certificates be effectively canceled and filed. The company should also record in a bond ledger details of bonds issued, canceled, and outstanding, and all numbers should be accounted for. In the absence of an independent interest-paying agent, control should be exercised over the payment of coupons. All paid coupons should be canceled and preserved after cancellation. Proper control should be maintained, equivalent in scope to that used in safeguarding regular cash funds, over the preparation, signing, and mailing of checks for interest on bonds and notes, and over the accounting for outstanding interest checks.

When registrars, transfer agents, and independent paying agents are employed, periodic reports of charges and outstanding balances should be required; information in these reports should be reconciled to company records.

Internal Check.—The custodian of unsigned and unissued bonds should be independent of cash functions, general ledger functions, and maintenance of detailed note or bond records; the person who reconciles the detail record with the control account should have similar independence, as should the person who accounts, by number, for unissued and issued bonds or notes.

Most large corporations and some smaller ones employ an independent registrar and transfer agent who perform the functions listed above. Employment of independent interest or coupon paying agents should provide satisfactory internal check of those payments.

AUDITING PROCEDURES

Objectives.—Long-term debt is usually substantial in amount, and plant or other assets of the company are frequently pledged as security therefor. The auditor should consider whether all long-term obligations are fairly stated, reasonably described, and properly classified in the balance sheet. He should determine whether stocks, bonds, accounts receivable, or other assets have been pledged as collateral for long-term notes or loans payable.

Bonds.—So many different classes of bonds have been devised that no attempt will be made to classify them except in a general way. Formerly, if not otherwise designated, bonds were presumed to have real property pledged against them; now many bonds are issued under terms of indentures which may include restrictive provisions, and real property is not pledged against them.

Corporations which issue bonds should have available a signed copy of the indenture stating the terms under which they are issued. The auditor should read the indenture, abstract important provisions relating to amounts authorized to be issued, interest rate (or rates, since changes are sometimes made), due date or dates (frequently provision is made for instalment payments of principal), property pledged, sinking fund, maintenance fund, working capital and dividend restrictions, basis of issuance of additional securities, and other important provisions.

When bonds are issued under an indenture which provides for a trustee as registrar of the outstanding bonds, the auditor should obtain confirmation in writing direct from the trustee of the amount of bonds issued and outstanding at the balance sheet date.

All bonds which have been certified by the trustee and delivered to the corporation should be accounted for. If they have been sold for cash or issued for property, the auditor should determine that the proceeds have been properly recorded in the accounts. The auditor should count authorized but unissued bonds on hand.

When an independent trustee has not been appointed, the auditor should determine that the aggregate of bonds outstanding as shown by the company's detail bond record is in agreement with the general ledger control account. Canceled bonds, treasury bonds, and unissued bonds should be inspected or otherwise accounted for.

The auditor should determine whether interest accrued on bonds in the hands of the public has been recorded in the accounts and whether the amount due has been paid. Often the payment of coupons is effected through an independent paying agent, with which the debtor corporation deposits the total interest due on each payment date. The terms of the indenture usually determine whether the liability for interest is legally discharged on deposit of the necessary funds with the independent paying agent; regardless of legal responsibility, it is customary to treat the obligation on the books of the debtor corporation as discharged when deposit is made if the paying agent is financially responsible. The auditor usually should confirm by correspondence with the paying agent the date to which interest has been paid.

Some corporations retain control of the payment of coupons by making their payments through an agent who does not assume liability for ultimate payment and who may or may not be independent of the debtor corporation. The function of such a paying agent is similar to that of a commercial bank which handles a separate payroll account. Accounts should be kept for deposits in the hands of the paying agent and for the equivalent liability for matured coupons not presented for payment. The auditor will usually confirm the amount on deposit, analyze the unpaid coupon liability account, and examine sufficient supporting evidence, including the detail record of paid coupons, to satisfy himself as to the fairness of the remaining liability.

The auditor's investigation should disclose lack of compliance with the various requirements of the bond indenture which are pertinent to his examination. Examples of these requirements are those for sinking fund payments and the disposition of sinking fund balances; maintenance of certain ratios, such as the relation of net current assets to the amount of bonds outstanding; restrictions on payment of dividends; insurance requirements; and disposition of proceeds of sale of collateral or properties subject to the lien of the indenture.

Mortgage Notes.—Mortgages usually are recorded in governmental registries since otherwise they are invalid as a lien on the property mortgaged as against innocent third parties. Substantiation of the existence of these obligations can be made by inspecting the public records. The search may also reveal the existence of other unsatisfied obligations, liens, or judgments not recorded on the books. Auditors should not be expected to make such a search since it is in the nature of legal service. The auditor may request a report from a local attorney or title company based on a search of pertinent records. If the auditor considers that special search by legal counsel is not necessary in the circumstances, he should substantiate the amount, the due date, the interest rate, date to which interest has been paid, and the property pledged by examining the indenture and obtaining confirmation by correspondence direct from the mortgagee.

Long-Term Leases.—The use of long-term leases as a method of financing has become widespread. There are many variations in lease provisions. Some leases contain an option for acquisition of the property by the lessee and others require that the lessee purchase the property at the expiration of the lease. In buy-build-sell-and-lease transactions, the purchaser of land builds to his own specifications, sells the improved property, and simultaneously leases the property for a period of years.

In Accounting Research Bulletin No. 43, Chapter 14, the committee expresses an opinion (in respect to lease arrangements which, in substance, are no more than instalment purchase arrangements) that:

. . . . the facts relating to all such leases should be carefully considered and that, where it is clearly evident that the transaction involved is in substance a purchase, the "leased" property should be included among the assets of the lessee with suitable accounting for the corresponding liabilities and for the related charges in the income statement.

The auditor should note the existence of leases during the course of his work and make appropriate inquiry and investigation to determine the substance of long-term leases, in the sense that the word "substance" is used in the committee pronouncement.

Disclosure of significant guaranties, obligations, and annual rentals under long-term leases is required by Bulletin No. 43 as well as by Regulation S-X of the Securities and Exchange Commission.

Short-Term Notes.—Short-term notes are generally used for temporary financing. Obligations coming within this category usually mature in from one to five years and except for the shorter maturity differ very little from some types of bonds. They are normally issued under a trust agreement and may or may not be supported by a mortgage or collateral. The audit procedure is similar to that described for long-term debt.

Convertible Debenture Notes.—Although these unsecured notes are frequently issued with twenty-year or longer maturity, increasing market value of capital shares into which they are convertible at stated conversion prices may lead to extensive exercise of conversion options or to redemption calls for entire issues long before their maturity. When options have been exercised or notes called for redemption, the auditor should review the transactions to determine that they were in accordance with provisions of the indenture, and he should examine the canceled notes converted or redeemed. If these transactions were numerous, the examination may be on a test basis supplemented by review of the adequacy of internal accounting control and internal check.

Purchase Money Obligations.—These liabilities represent obligations given as part of the purchase price of property and frequently are payable in instalments over a period of years. If they are given for the purchase of real estate, they may be secured by first or junior mortgages; if for personal property, by chattel mortgages. Procedures set forth in this chapter with respect to mortgages apply to their examination.

Coordination of Examination with That of Related Accounts.—The auditor's examination of long-term liabilities usually is correlated with his examination of certain other accounts. As part of the examination of long-term debt, the auditor should determine that the proper amount of interest has been paid, accrued, and charged to expense. If there is an unclaimed interest account, he should examine transactions recorded therein with particular reference to authorizations for the charges to this account. The auditor also should review the accounting principles followed and test the accuracy of balances in the unamortized debt discount and expense, and the unamortized premium on bond accounts as at the balance sheet date and of their amortization as shown in the income account.

Time of Examination.—The examination of long-term liabilities and related accounts cannot be completed until after the books have been closed for the period under review. However, preliminary analyses and review of these accounts can be made prior to the closing.

STATEMENT PRESENTATION

Classification.—Long-term liabilities, with few exceptions, are classified separately on the balance sheet. They are often subdivided into two groups, the first of which includes long-term debt, such as bonds and notes issued under an indenture or other formal agreement, and the second, other long-term liabilities, such as deferred credits, customers' deposits, product guaranties, and estimated liabilities for tax or other disputed claims, which are discussed in Chapter 18.

If part of the liability matures or otherwise becomes payable within one year after the balance sheet date (or the current operating cycle, if longer), accountants classify that portion as a current liability. For example, the portion of a serial issue of bonds, or the total of any issue currently due and not to be refunded, ordinarily would be included with current liabilities. If refunding arrangements have been concluded with respect to a maturing issue, or if such arrangements are in process and reasonably certain of being successfully concluded, the maturing issue may be properly treated as long-term rather than current debt and the circumstances described in a note to the balance sheet. If funds have been provided to retire the maturing obligation and are segregated as noncurrent assets, the maturing liability should remain in the long-term debt category.

It is permissible to classify long-term debt as a single item following current liabilities on the balance sheet, disclosing the maturing current portion in the caption, provided that total current liabilities are described as "exclusive of $.......... long-term debt shown below."

If an entire convertible debenture note issue has been called for redemption and conditions at the time of the call and experience in similar circumstances indicate unlikelihood that cash funds will be required to satisfy the obligation, the appropriate amounts, including premiums, may be included in the capital section of the balance sheet with an appropriate explanatory note. This note should indicate the reasons for such treatment and amounts and description of capital shares expected to be issued.

As an alternative presentation, the entire convertible issue may be shown as a long-term liability with appropriate disclosure in a footnote of pertinent facts, but in these circumstances no part of the issue should be classified as a current liability, despite stated maturity within one year from the balance sheet date.

It is not considered good practice to deduct long-term debt from assets pledged against them. There may be exceptions to this rule. For example, when a company, engaged in buying, selling, and operating real estate, purchases property subject to a mortgage, the liability for which it does not assume, it may show the investment at gross purchase price (plus any additions at cost) and deduct therefrom the amount of the mortgage not assumed rather than showing the mortgage as a liability.

Disclosures.—In addition to the title of the long-term debt, its description should include the amount registered, issued, outstanding, and in treasury, the rate of interest, due dates, and call price, if any; this may be shown on the balance sheet or in a footnote.

Often real estate or personal property is pledged with an issue of bonds; sometimes a bond is a first lien on certain assets and a second lien on others. As a rule, balance sheets do not describe in detail the real estate pledged under a mortgage, but personal property, such as securities, so pledged should be identified.

Convertibility of bonds into capital stock should be indicated, usually in the description of the bond. Subordination of long-term debt by agreement with the lenders should be disclosed.

If there has been a default in principal, interest, sinking fund, redemption, or other requirements of the indenture, appropriate disclosure of the facts and amounts should be made in a notation to the balance sheet and reference thereto may be desirable in the auditor's report.

Disclosure of other indenture provisions, such as requirements for maintenance of working capital and restrictions on payment of dividends, is discussed in Chapter 7.

Treasury Bonds.—Treasury bonds held for resale may be shown separately as an investment, at cost. Reacquired bonds, not held for resale, should preferably be treated as a reduction, at par, of bonds outstanding on the liability side of the balance sheet; it is the usual practice to show only the net amount of bonds outstanding. If bonds were acquired to be held in a sinking fund, they may be listed with sinking fund assets at cost with an indication of the principal amount.

CHAPTER 18

OTHER LONG-TERM LIABILITIES

Introduction.—Other long-term liabilities discussed in this chapter include all noncurrent liabilities except those arising from borrowings under bond, note, or other agreements, which are discussed in Chapter 17. Such noncurrent liabilities should be presented in the balance sheet between current liabilities and capital and comprise three types of items: (1) the noncurrent portion of liabilities which may be found also in the current liability section of the balance sheet, such as deferred credits and liabilities for security deposits, return of containers, estimated additional taxes, renegotiation refund, and cost of product guaranty, all of which are discussed in Chapter 16; (2) estimates of admitted or probable liabilities of indeterminate amount, not payable within the operating cycle, in the past often designated as "reserves," discussed below; and (3) contingent liabilities, which implies that the transformation to a real liability in the future is a possibility but not a probability. Contingent liabilities are most frequently shown on the balance sheet in footnotes; since they are seldom of a short-term or current nature, they are also discussed in this chapter.

ACCOUNTING PRINCIPLES

Use of the Term "Reserve."—The Committee on Terminology of The American Institute of Certified Public Accountants issued (1953) a "Review and Résumé" (Bulletin No. 1) in which the use of the term "reserve" is discussed in some detail. It concludes that the use of the term should be limited

. . . . to indicate that an undivided or unidentified portion of the net assets, in a stated amount, is being held or retained for a special purpose, as in the case of a reserve (a) for betterments or plant extensions, or (b) for excess cost of replacement of property, or (c) for possible future inventory losses, or (d) for general contingencies.

The authors agree with the committee's recommendation that the term "reserve" should be limited to the sense described above, and that such reserves should be classified in the capital section of the balance sheet. Such reserves are therefore discussed in Chapter 19.
    The committee also points out that the term has been used

. . . . to indicate an estimate of (a) an admitted liability of uncertain amount, as in the case of a reserve for damages, (b) the probable amount of a disputed claim, as in the case of a reserve for additional taxes, or (c) a liability or loss which is not certain to occur but is so likely to do so as to require recognition, as in the case of a reserve for self-insurance.

The committee concludes that "the items in this area which have been described as reserves are therefore better designated in some such way as *estimated liabilities* or *liabilities of estimated amount.*" The American Institute's publication "Accounting Trends and Techniques" indicates that the committee's recommendation is finding increasing acceptance.

Liabilities of Estimated Amount.—This class of liability comprises those not precisely determinable in amount, although susceptible to reasonable estimate and for which some degree of liability is conceded. There may be no question of the fact of liability under an adopted pension plan, but the amount of liability depends on actuarial estimates, themselves based upon variable factors. Counsel may concede liability under suits for damages, patent infringement and the like, but amounts ultimately paid may depend on the findings of a judge or jury. A liability for warranty of product is based upon conditions of sale, but the amount may be estimated, usually based on experience. Liability under a self-insurance plan for workmen's compensation claims may be established or reasonably estimated.

Other long-term liabilities frequently appearing are those for repairs and renewals, deferred compensation plans, and employees' welfare or benefit plans.

Provisions for these liabilities are ordinarily charged to income. The amounts of these liabilities usually are estimates at the time the provision is made, and accumulated balances of provisions at any balance sheet date seldom are identical with subsequently determined liabilities at the same date. Necessary adjustments are ordinarily made in the income statement in the year in which determined; the treatment of adjustments of material amounts is discussed in Chapter 7.

FIRE LOSSES.—Most companies carry fire insurance so that all or a substantial part of a loss is recovered when a fire occurs; in effect the cost of the loss, or the cost of protection against loss, is spread over income of many years by means of allocating fire insurance premiums. Some companies elect to assume the risk of absorbing losses from fire without the protection of fire insurance policies.

In the latter case, some companies attempt to provide for fire losses by charging income with not more than the annual cost of comparable fire insurance premiums. Others do not attempt to provide for fire losses which may never occur; while losses may occur, they do not believe the amount of losses can be predicted. Still others have segregated portions of surplus, described as reserves for fire losses.

The authors believe that while all of these methods are subject to question in theory, they have been so sanctioned by practice that the auditor should not take exception to them. There are, however, some aspects to which he should give attention:

1. When provision for estimated liability for fire losses is made by periodic charge to income, the accumulated balance should not exceed a reasonable total at a balance sheet date.

2. When no provision has been made by charge to income, fire losses, when suffered, must be charged to income unless they are so material as to impair the significance of net income.

3. When portions of surplus have been segregated as a reserve for fire losses, actual fire losses may not be charged to such reserve.

REPAIRS AND RENEWALS.—In some plants the necessity for repairs and renewals is constant, and the aggregate maintenance cost is about the same from year to year. In other plants major repairs and renewals are required less frequently, and maintenance expense fluctuates from year to year. For example, refractory and steel companies may reline their furnaces and gas utilities may paint their storage tanks every four or five years. Under these circumstances, it is accepted practice in some industries to establish a liability account by setting aside a fixed annual amount based on the average cost over a period of years. Actual expenditures for repairs and renewals are then charged against such liability account.

If expenditures exceed the liability previously provided, the provision is proved inadequate, and the basis should be re-examined. It is not proper to carry forward to future periods debit balances representing such excess of expenditures over provisions made.

DEFERRED COMPENSATION.—Many companies have adopted compensation plans for officers and key personnel, usually based on profits and charged to expense year by year, but payable in instalments over future periods, often for as long as five years. The principal reasons for deferring the payments are to provide tax savings for the recipients and to retain the services of the officers and key employees. There are many varieties of such plans since they are generally tailored to fit the needs of the particular company. Such a plan gives rise to a deferred liability for the excess of the amount set aside over the amount due within one year. See Chapter 7 for a discussion of problems in connection with the determination of amounts available under deferred compensation plans and Chapter 22 for a discussion of the tax considerations arising from them.

LIABILITY UNDER PENSION PLANS.—Accounting for costs of pension plans is discussed in Accounting Research Bulletin No. 47. Chapter 20, in addition to dealing with the problem of allocating pension costs, discusses disclosure on the balance sheet of liabilities under pension plan arrangements. Differences of opinion exist whether the full liability, estimated on an actuarial basis for all employees under the plan at the balance sheet date, must be shown, or whether, such full accrual being unnecessary or unwise, no such liability need be shown. The committee concluded, in view of these differences in opinion, that

. . . . as a minimum, the accounts and financial statements should reflect accruals which equal the present worth, actuarially calculated, of pension commitments to employees to the extent that pension rights have vested in the employees, reduced, in the case of the balance sheet, by any accumulated trusteed funds or annuity contracts purchased.

This opinion is not intended to apply to informal arrangements subject to change or discontinuance at the employer's will; under such arrangements, the pay-as-you-go method of accounting for pension costs is appropriate, although the accrual method is equally appropriate if costs can be estimated with reasonable accuracy.

LEASES.—Provisions of leases may call for substantial penalties if renewal options are not exercised. If it appears clear that penalties will be incurred for nonrenewal of a lease, the actual liability should be accrued. Similarly, estimated costs of reconditioning or restoring property at termination of a lease are often definite liabilities which should be accrued.

Disclosure of pertinent provisions of lease agreements which are material is required by good accounting practice and Regulation S-X (Rule 3.18) of the Securities and Exchange Commission.

Accounting Research Bulletin No. 43, Chapter 14, states the opinion of the committee regarding such long-term leases that:

(a) disclosure should be made in financial statements or in notes thereto of:

(1) the amounts of annual rentals to be paid under such leases with some indication of the periods for which they are payable and

(2) any other important obligation assumed or guarantee made in connection therewith.

Contingent Liabilities.—The term "contingent liability" should be used in the accounting sense to designate a possible liability of presently determinable or indeterminable amount which arises from past circumstances or actions, which may or may not become a legal obligation in the future, and which, if paid, gives rise to a loss or expense or an asset of doubtful value. The uncertainty as to whether there will be any legal obligation differentiates a contingent liability from an actual liability.

In accounting practice, the term has been used to describe items of expenses or losses representing admitted or probable liabilities which can be computed with reasonable accuracy; in the authors' opinion, the term should not be so used. These items are those described above as liabilities of estimated amount and should be reflected in the accounts.

Losses which may arise from possible future events are sometimes wrongly referred to as contingent liabilities. For example, the possibility that property may be damaged by tornadoes in certain sections of the country does not create a contingent liability and requires no recognition in financial statements. Commitments to purchase inventory, fixed assets, and securities are sometimes referred to erroneously as contingent liabilities.

DISCLOSURE OF EXISTENCE.—If amounts involved are or may become material, the existence of contingent liabilities should be recognized and appropriately disclosed in the balance sheet. The fact that a precise amount cannot be established is no justification for failure to indicate the existence of a material contingent liability.

CONTINGENT LIABILITIES OF INDETERMINABLE AMOUNT.—By definition, contingent liabilities are those which are possible, but not probable or admitted. The following may describe either actual or contingent liabilities, depending on the degree of certainty of liability:

> Matters in litigation, such as alleged patent, copyright, and trade-mark infringements, or breach of contract;
>
> Possible claims by employees for back compensation under laws, the interpretation of which is uncertain;
>
> Proposed additional taxes for prior periods, which the company believes are unwarranted;
>
> Possible liability for refunds arising from renegotiation, which the company believes unjustified;
>
> Claims which counsel believes may be adequately defended, and with respect to which the amount of liability, if any, will be fixed by judge or jury subsequent to the balance sheet date;
>
> Guaranties of a new product.

Liability under product guaranties may be uncertain when a new product is introduced and experience gives no indication of the likelihood of claims. The company should determine whether amounts claimed under various types of litigation or government regulation represent actual or contingent liabilities.

Many companies carry fire and casualty insurance with mutual insurance companies; in addition to making deposits greater than a normal year's premium, the insured is contingently liable for assessment in the event abnormal losses are experienced by the insurance company. In view of the infrequency with which such assessments have been made in the past, and because any material increase in losses is usually reflected in higher premiums or lower dividends in subsequent years, it is not usual practice to recognize such a contingency on the balance sheet.

CONTINGENT LIABILITIES OF DETERMINABLE AMOUNT.—This classification includes items the amounts of which are usually determinable and which may become actual liabilities if a primary obligor defaults in payment. Included in this group are liabilities arising from the following transactions:

> Sale, pledge, or assignment of accounts receivable or instalment obligations when the transfer attaches a liability to the seller, pledgor, or assignor in the event of noncollection;

Discount, sale, or transfer of notes receivable, trade acceptances, bank acceptances arising under commercial letters of credit, or domestic and foreign drafts;

Endorsement of notes;

Accommodation endorsement of commercial paper;

Guaranty of payment of interest or principal on bonds of another person;

Sale of real estate subject to a mortgage when the vendor's liability continues under a bond.

In most of the above examples the amount of the contingent liability is the possible maximum loss, not necessarily the actual loss, which may be suffered. When accounts receivable are sold with recourse, for example, it is not likely that all will prove to be uncollectible by the assignee.

Most of the above contingent liabilities may give rise to contingent assets; i.e., if default necessitates payment by endorsers or guarantors, a right of action against the primary obligor ensues. The fact that contingent assets may arise on default does not relieve the company of the necessity of disclosure of these contingent liabilities, because the necessity of payment by the secondary obligor is generally prima facie indication of the doubtful value of a claim against the primary obligor. In exceptional circumstances, contingent liabilities may be fully offset by contingent assets which would be acquired if the liabilities should become actual.

ACCOUNTS RECEIVABLE SOLD.—Ordinarily an account receivable may be assigned legally without notifying the debtor of the assignment. In some states, however, an assignment of an account receivable is valid only if some act, such as the filing of public notice, is performed.

When accounts receivable are sold, they are usually guaranteed and, if the debtor fails to make payment, the vendor is obligated to make good the default by assigning other accounts receivable or returning cash. Less frequently, accounts receivable are sold outright without guaranty, and the vendor has no continuing or contingent liability.

Accounts receivable may be guaranteed for a consideration, a condition found in the relationship between textile mills and their factors. Provision for the estimated probable loss should be reflected in financial statements of the factor or guarantor. The amount of loss which is possible, but not probable, should be indicated in the balance sheet as a contingent liability.

DRAFTS SOLD.—When drafts against foreign shipments are sold to banks at the time of shipment and the cash received is credited to customers' accounts, the books of account will not disclose the amount of contingent liability on these drafts, but such information may be available in a subsidiary record.

The terms on which business is conducted with foreign countries may range from 30 days' sight to 90 days' sight and 120 days' dating. Therefore, a large portion of drafts drawn against foreign shipments and sold to banks in the last few months prior to the close of the period may be outstanding at the balance sheet date; contingent liability for these unpaid drafts should be recognized.

ACCEPTANCES.—An acceptance is a draft or bill of exchange across the face of which the drawee or acceptor has written the word "Accepted" and his signature. Usually the date of the acceptance is also indicated. When the acceptor is not a bank, the name of the bank or the place at which the acceptance is payable is also inserted.

An accepted draft may be immediately discounted by the drawer at his bank or sold in the open market. The drawer may be held liable as an endorser if the acceptance is not paid at maturity, and consequently a contingent liability exists with respect to the drawer until the acceptance is paid by the acceptor.

ENDORSEMENTS.—In addition to the contingent liability for notes discounted for the benefit of the endorser, there may be a liability based on endorsements for the benefit of others. These are known as accommodation endorsements. From a practical point of view it may be assumed that every endorsement, whether by an individual, firm, or corporation, may become an ultimate liability of the endorser. Promissory notes are usually negotiable instruments, and, so that they may circulate freely, an innocent purchaser who acquires such a note for value, without notice of any defect, may sue the maker and all endorsers. Knowledge on the part of the purchaser that an endorsement is an accommodation endorsement does not relieve the accommodation endorser of liability.

Assumptions that the maker will pay, or that the notes will not find their way into the hands of outsiders, have been disproved so often that accommodation endorsements must be considered contingent liabilities.

GUARANTIES.—Almost all the remarks under "Endorsements" apply with equal force to guaranties. However, the liability of an endorser is as set forth in the law of negotiable instruments, but the liability of a guarantor or surety depends upon conditions set forth in the contract of guaranty. With this exception, there is a similar likelihood that ultimate payment may be required.

GUARANTIES OF SUBSIDIARIES' OBLIGATIONS.—Good accounting practice requires full disclosure of contingent liabilities arising from endorsements and guaranties of subsidiaries' obligations and commitments running beyond the date of the balance sheet. Holding companies may guarantee the fulfillment of contracts made by subsidiaries, such as those for merchandise to be delivered at future dates. Full disclosure of these contingent liabilities should be made in the parent company's balance sheet. Such a guaranty would not usually affect the consolidated financial position of the company and subsidiaries, since the primary obligation is a liability of the consolidated group.

Holding companies sometimes guarantee specified dividends or interest on securities of subsidiaries in the hands of the public. If arrears of dividends so guaranteed have not been paid by the holding company, the liability and the fact of guaranty of future dividends should be disclosed in the balance sheet of the holding company.

INTERNAL CONTROL

Other Long-Term Liabilities.—Internal accounting control over recognition in the accounts of other long-term liabilities discussed in this chapter includes proper authorization, preparation and review of journal entries creating or adjusting the liability, and periodic review of the reasonableness of the balances. Charges to those accounts should be controlled by the procedures applied at the source, usually cash disbursements, payrolls, or issues of material. Internal check requires independent review of journal entries affecting these liabilities and of current balances. Appropriate internal check procedures relating to sources of charges to such liability accounts have been mentioned in the internal control sections of other chapters.

Contingent Liabilities.—Contingent liabilities, because of their nature, are subject to little or no internal accounting control or internal check. Effective liaison between the accounting and legal departments, however, contributes to control over such matters. When the contingent liability is such that the maximum amount can be established, such as liability for accounts receivable sold or notes discounted, the amount may be controlled through procedures established for control of the related notes or accounts receivable.

AUDITING PROCEDURES

Other Long-Term Liabilities.

OBJECTIVES.—The auditor's objectives are to determine that other long-term liabilities have been set forth in the financial statements in accordance with generally accepted accounting principles consistently followed, and that computations, under plans or bases followed, have been correctly made.

LIABILITY FOR WORKMEN'S COMPENSATION AND EMPLOYEES' PENSIONS.—Some companies have established provisions for workmen's compensation claims. Under these self-insurance plans, savings may be effected, representing the profit that would normally accrue to an insurance company and the amount by which a company can reduce its loss and expense ratios below the averages for the industry through safety engineering and education. Some companies administer their employees' pension plans, saving the profit that would normally accrue to an insurance company.

The auditor should determine that annual provisions for workmen's compensation and employees' pensions are based on actual payrolls, that they are in authorized amounts, and that under the plans followed the computations are correct. He may compare these annual premiums with commercial premiums, but often annual provisions will be less than commercial premiums inasmuch as one of the purposes of self insurance is to reduce expense.

Charges to these accounts should be reviewed to determine that they are proper.

The auditor should form an opinion whether balances in these accounts seem adequate for possible claims or losses resulting from known events up to, or even beyond, the balance sheet date. In this he will be guided by the client's experience, the experience of other companies in similar activities, and inquiry from company personnel and legal counsel. If the company maintains a claims department, he may wish to review available reports of claims pending, claims settled, and company estimates of costs of final settlement.

GENERAL.—The auditor should examine credits to other long-term liability accounts to determine that they are made in amounts as authorized and result in apparently adequate provision for the liabilities they are intended to cover. He should determine whether charges to these liability accounts are proper.

TIME OF EXAMINATION.—The auditor will find it desirable at the time of his interim examination to review other long-term liability accounts. Analyses of these accounts up to an interim date may reveal adjustments that should be made prior to closing the books. After the end of the period these analyses should be brought up to date and the balances in the accounts reviewed in the light of circumstances at the year end.

Contingent Liabilities.

AUDITOR'S RESPONSIBILITY.—Experienced auditors know that contingent liabilities seldom appear as such on books of account and that their existence is often difficult to establish. It may be impossible to determine their existence if a deliberate attempt is made to conceal them. Nevertheless, the auditor must make every reasonable effort to uncover and report upon material contingent liabilities of every description. He should not be expected to determine the probability that a contingent liability may become an actual liability.

The following are some general procedures which are usually followed.

INSPECTION OF MINUTE BOOKS.—If the auditor is to submit his opinion on financial statements, he should insist on inspection of the minutes of meetings of stockholders, board of directors, and executive and other committees of the board for the period under examination and up to the date of his report. These minutes may reveal contracts, possible or pending litigation, and other matters indicating contingent liabilities to be investigated and possibly recognized in the financial statements.

INSPECTION OF CONTRACTS.—The auditor may examine contracts and agreements to which his client is a party if he believes they would disclose any material contingent liabilities that should be reported in the financial statements.

INQUIRY AND DISCUSSION WITH OFFICERS AND EMPLOYEES.—The auditor should review with management the possibility of contingent liabilities. Frequently this review will bring to light the existence of such liabilities not determinable from the accounts. A statement of management as to contingent liabilities is included in the liability certificate discussed in Chapter 16.

INFORMATION FROM BANKERS AND ATTORNEYS.—Contingent liabilities may be revealed by the banks' replies to confirmation requests suggested in Chapter 8; these include a request for a statement of the client's liabilities as acceptor, endorser, or guarantor of notes, drafts, and acceptances.

The auditor should receive information from the client's attorneys about the status of suits and pending litigation; this may reveal possible liabilities of substantial amount. The client's records should be scanned for the names of attorneys who have been engaged or to whom retainers or fees have been paid, and usually information should be requested from all of them. For the protection of the auditor, written replies should be requested. A suggested request form follows.

(Name of legal counsel)
(Address)

Dear Sirs:

In connection with their (usual) examination of our financial statements as at (balance sheet date), our auditors, (name and address), have requested information regarding pending or contemplated litigation in which we are involved or represented in any way. They particularly desire information as to estimated minimum and maximum amounts of our contingent assets or our contingent liabilities, direct or indirect, from issues unresolved, from contracts and agreements involving disputes, or from outstanding judgments.

We shall appreciate your courtesy in promptly supplying the requested information direct to our auditors. Brief summaries of the current status of cases in litigation, amounts at issue, and causes of action will be appropriate, supplemented by such additional information as you feel will assist them in arriving at an opinion concerning our financial position. Please inform them also as to amounts due you or accrued and unbilled for services and costs advanced as at (balance sheet date).

A return envelope is enclosed for your reply.

Very truly yours,

(Name of client)

ACCOUNTS RECEIVABLE DISCOUNTED.—Accounts receivable may have been discounted with discount companies and the transaction not recorded in the books. The auditor may find a clue to this if the books indicate transactions with discount companies such as receipts of cash or payments of interest. Indications of dealings with discount companies should be investigated to determine whether a contingent liability exists.

COMMITMENTS OF SUBSIDIARIES.—The auditor should inquire about commitments of subsidiaries guaranteed by the parent company. These may not appear in the parent company records but may represent a contingent liability that should be recognized.

BONDS OF OTHER CORPORATIONS.—A corporation may guarantee the payment of the principal of bonds of another corporation and perhaps interest and sinking fund payments as well. When the guarantor is a parent company and the bonds guaranteed are those of an affiliate or subsidiary, the existence of the guaranty should not be difficult to detect. When there is no apparent relationship between the guarantor and the obligor corporation, and the guarantor has not been called upon to make payments under the guaranty, the auditor must rely for his information upon review of corporate minutes and inquiries from officials of the corporation. Past transactions may indicate the existence of a guaranty, as when properties subject to a bond issue have been transferred to another corporation, and the transferor has guaranteed new substitute bonds issued by the transferee.

PROFIT LIMITATIONS ON GOVERNMENT CONTRACTS.—Profits on certain government contracts are subject to limitations imposed by the Vinson Act, as amended, which applies to contracts for the construction of naval vessels and navy and army aircraft, or by Renegotiation Acts, which apply to contracts (including subcontracts and purchase orders) of many types. Since one of the tests of renegotiability is end use of the product or service, and since purchase orders or subcontracts may not indicate end use, the auditor should make investigation and inquiries appropriate in the circumstances, to determine whether any material amount of contingent liability arising from possible renegotiation proceedings exists. The auditor may investigate the status of the client under other acts and consider whether any contingent or actual liability should be recognized in the financial statements.

TIME OF EXAMINATION.—The examination of contingent liabilities will usually be made in conjunction with that of related assets and liabilities. Certain examinations may be continued up to the date of completion of field work and, sometimes, even up to the date of the report; events up to these dates may be of importance in determining that all material contingent liabilities have been recognized.

SUBSEQUENT EVENTS.—Statement on Auditing Procedure No. 25, issued in October, 1954, relating to the auditor's responsibility in connection with the disclosure of events occurring or becoming known subsequent to the date of statements concerning which he is expressing an opinion, sets forth the general rule that such financial statements should be adjusted to recognize liabilities determined subsequent to the balance sheet date and prior to the time his report is submitted.

Thus, liabilities properly considered contingent on the balance sheet date, if determined to be actual during the auditor's examination, should be treated as though such later determination had been known at the balance sheet date, and the financial statements should be appropriately adjusted.

STATEMENT PRESENTATION

Other Long-Term Liabilities.—Items included under this caption are those which are not expected to be paid or payable until after the next succeeding operating cycle, or, at a minimum, one year. If definite in amount, or experience or legal opinion provides a basis for a reasonable estimate of the amount of a liability, the amount should be stated in the balance sheet. When the existence of a liability is admitted or probable, but the circumstances do not permit a reasonable estimate of its amount, a disclosure of the facts may be made in a note to the balance sheet. Although this form of disclosure is similar to that for contingent liabilities, care should be taken to indicate that the liability is probable or actual, since the uncertainty exists only as to amount and not as to the obligation itself. If the amount may be material, the auditor should consider whether qualification of his opinion is necessary.

Most, if not all, items referred to earlier in this chapter as other long-term liabilities may be or become, in whole or in part, current liabilities. A damage suit may be settled, and the payment become due in one sum or in a series of payments, sometimes over a period of years; it is often possible to estimate the portion of product guaranty liability to be liquidated currently. The current portion of otherwise long-term liabilities should usually be so classified in the balance sheet.

While it is desirable to describe other major long-term liabilities so as clearly to indicate their nature, occasionally such disclosure would be clearly to the disadvantage of the company. A company may believe it has a liability under a suit, damage claim, or tax dispute, but it may be reluctant to disclose on its balance sheet its estimate of the amount it may have to pay. The authors believe it permissible under such circumstances to include these liabilities under a general caption such as "Other" or "Miscellaneous"; it is not accepted practice to include them under the caption "Reserve for Contingencies."

Contingent Liabilities.—The characteristics of contingent liabilities are such that it is usually not possible to show them in dollars in the conventional manner with direct liabilities on the balance sheet. For example, while the amount of notes receivable can be stated in dollars, the contingent liability for notes sold has not become actual at the date of the balance sheet; the liability for damages, if any, for breach of contract may not be determinable until awarded by a jury and approved by the court. The existence of contingent liabilities is most frequently disclosed in an explanatory note, which may be placed on the liability side of the balance sheet immediately preceding the capital section or as a footnote. The position of the notation on the balance sheet is not important, but a clear statement of significant information is.

Whether a contingent liability is material is sometimes a troublesome question. The potential amount involved may be large, but the possibility of the contingent liability's becoming actual may seem to be very remote. By custom, the contingent liability for receivables discounted is usually disclosed even if not material in amount, because readers of the balance sheet may be interested in how the company obtains working capital.

Disclosure of contingent liabilities does not require disclosure of information that might be detrimental to a company or its stockholders. In opposing disclosure of lawsuits or other claims, the liability for which the company denies, it is sometimes argued that a balance sheet stating the existence and amount of these claims might be offered in evidence by opposing attorneys as admission of liability. The auditor should, of course, give full consideration to the position of his client, but usually it is possible to explain a contingent liability and at the same time avoid harmful admissions. A statement may suffice that the amount of a contingent liability is indeterminable at the balance sheet date but may be substantial and that counsel considers the possibility of its becoming a determined liability of material amount to be remote.

Notes and Acceptances Discounted.—After the date of discounting notes or acceptances but before maturity, the amount of the contingent liability of the endorser, usually expressed as the principal amount of the notes or acceptances discounted, should be disclosed. It is not sufficient to state that notes or acceptances have been discounted without stating the amount.

CHAPTER 19

CAPITAL AND DIVIDENDS

Introduction.—"Capital" is the term used by accountants to describe the owners' equity in a business. It is represented by the excess of total assets over total liabilities (hence, "net assets") and may be described as the property or cash paid in as investment of the owners together with increments or decrements arising during the course of business. The terms used to describe the different types of capital should indicate the sources from which they are derived.

The terms "capital" or "net assets" are preferred by accountants to "net worth," which was widely used some years ago. Net worth has the disadvantage of suggesting present realizable value. Since the assets shown in a balance sheet prepared in the usual manner are generally a mixture of known values (cash), estimates of current or going concern values (receivables and inventories), and historical costs (fixed assets and intangible assets), the proprietary equity or excess of assets over liabilities, as reflected by the accounts, rarely approximates present worth of the business.

ACCOUNTING PRINCIPLES

Capital of a Business Corporation.—A corporation differs from a sole proprietorship and a partnership in that a corporation is a legal entity separate from its stockholders, whereas a business owned and operated by a sole proprietor or a partnership has no legal standing apart from that of its owners. However, it is convenient for accounting purposes to endow a business with an identity independent of its owners, although it is primarily in incorporated businesses that this distinction is recognized legally. The capital section of the balance sheet of a business owned by an individual or a partnership reflects the equity of the proprietor or partners in the assets of the business; the capital section of the balance sheet of a corporation reflects the equity of the stockholders of the corporation in its assets. The caption "Stockholders' Equity" is appearing more frequently in published reports of corporations.

TERMINOLOGY.—In recent years, corporations have presented the capital sections of their balance sheets in terms more meaningful to the various classes of stockholders and considered more clearly representative of the nature and sources of the elements constituting stockholders' equity. The use of the term "surplus" on the balance sheet without a descriptive adjective has practically ceased. The proper distinction to be made is not between capital and surplus, but between the origins of capital such as (a) capital derived from contribution or proprietary investment of stockholders (ordinarily further divided, when the circumstances exist, into "capital stock" and "capital surplus," the latter category representing capital contributions in excess of the amounts assigned to capital stock) and (b) capital derived or accumulated by the retention of earnings, most frequently called "retained earnings" or "earned surplus." This chapter will discuss the classifications of capital in terms of three broad areas: capital stock, capital surplus, and earned surplus.

The American Institute's Committee on Terminology has recommended the use of terms other than capital surplus and earned surplus to help eliminate confusion over the origin of capital; although the authors agree with the committee's recommendation, they will continue to use the traditional terms until alternate terms are more firmly established by usage. The committee's recommendations are discussed in the Statement Presentation section of this chapter.

CAPITAL STOCK.—Capital stock represents that part of the amount of capital contributed by the stockholders which the corporation is expected to maintain intact (other than as reduced by losses or by appropriate legal action) for the protection of creditors. Such amount may be expressed as capital stock with par value, or as capital stock without par value, with or without stated or assigned value; it does not necessarily represent the full amount contributed by the stockholders.

Authorized stock is the maximum number of shares that may be sold or issued by a corporation under the terms of its charter, and that number usually may not be increased or decreased without the approval of the stockholders and appropriate charter amendment.

Issued stock may be reacquired by the corporation either through gift or by purchase. Reacquired shares, unless retired, remain issued stock and are referred to as "treasury stock." From an accounting standpoint, *outstanding stock* generally is considered to be stock issued and in the hands of stockholders and would not include shares reacquired by the issuing corporation; from a legal standpoint, treasury stock is considered *outstanding* until all necessary legal steps for formal retirement thereof have been accomplished.

Capital stock of a corporation is divided into shares, or certificates of ownership, and any owner thereof enjoys proportionately the same rights and privileges as other owners of the same class of stock. Corporations often divide their capital stock into various classes, the most usual being common stock and preferred stock, which may in turn be divided into separate classes enjoying different rights. Sometimes other classes such as debenture stock and founders' stock are authorized.

The rights, privileges, and responsibilities of stockholders are governed by the laws of the state under which the corporation is organized and by the charter and by-laws of the corporation.

Par Value Stock.—The par value of capital stock has no inherent relation to its actual worth, nor does it necessarily fix the price at which it will be sold. It is an arbitrary figure which should not be mistaken for real value. If capital stock is sold by the company on original issue at a price below par, it is not legally fully paid, and the stockholders may be liable to creditors for the difference between the price paid and the par value. This difference, in states which permit this practice, is known as "discount on capital stock."

No Par Stock.—Most states permit the issuance of stock without par value. Each certificate of no par stock merely states the number of shares which it represents. Some states require that the total number of shares authorized also be shown on the certificate.

No par stock may be recorded on the books of the corporation at a stated or assigned value, which may be equal to, or less than, the subscription price of the stock. Sometimes a portion of the price paid is credited to paid-in surplus and may be available for dividends. Payment of dividends from this source is discussed later in this chapter.

Another accepted method of accounting is to credit the capital stock account with the net proceeds of the sale of the no par stock, notwithstanding the fact that it may have been sold at different prices and at different times. Sometimes, the above procedure is confined to the sale of the original issue with subsequent issues then being credited at the same amount per share and the difference being charged or credited to paid-in surplus.

Both par and no par preferred stocks are sometimes stated at minimum liquidation prices; this treatment is explained under Statement Presentation in this chapter.

Expenses of Stock Issues.—Underwriting discounts, professional fees and related expenses are properly considered a reduction of the proceeds of a stock issue before determining the amount to be capitalized. These expenses include commissions to selling agents; attorneys', engineers', or accountants' fees; printing costs; SEC filing fees; and other expenses clearly and directly attributable to realization of proceeds of the shares issued. If the offering price is at least par value but expenses of issue bring the net proceeds below par or stated value, the stock should be shown at par and the difference charged first to any available paid-in surplus on issues no longer outstanding, and the balance against earned surplus.

Common Stock.—Common stock represents the residual ownership in the business. If there is no preferred or other special class of stock, common stock and capital stock of the corporation are synonymous. Common stockholders are not entitled to any distribution of earnings or assets until the respective prior claim of preferred stockholders as to each such type of distribution is satisfied.

Common stockholders, by virtue of their ownership in the business, have certain basic rights : usually, to vote and thus to participate in the selection of management; to share in the profits of the business by receiving dividends when and if declared by the directors; and, when the corporation is dissolved, to share in the distribution of assets in accordance with the terms of the charter. Depending on the laws of the state of incorporation or on the charter, common stockholders sometimes have a fourth right, called the "pre-emptive" right, which prevents dilution of the stockholders' equity without their consent; i.e., they may have first call to purchase additional common stock issued by the corporation in proportion to their holdings at the time of the new issue.

Preferred Stock.—Classes of stock that have been granted certain preferences or privileges ahead of the common stock are known as preferred stocks. They may be accorded preference as to dividends, in liquidation, in voting, or in other matters.

1. *Dividend preference.*—Holders of preferred stock generally are entitled to receive a fixed dividend (expressed either in dollars per share or as a percentage of the par value of the stock) before a distribution is made to common stockholders. The payment of this dividend is not automatic; it is dependent upon declaration by the directors.

The dividend preference may be either cumulative or noncumulative. If the dividend preference is cumulative and if a dividend on the preferred stock is not paid in any year, this dividend (and any other unpaid cumulative preferred dividends) must be declared and paid before the directors may properly declare a dividend payable to the common stockholders. There may be circumstances when these accumulated dividends are never paid, but, if they are not, distribution may not be made to the common stockholders. Therefore, unpaid cumulative dividends on preferred stock constitute a lien on undistributed profits which requires disclosure on the balance sheet. If dividend preference is noncumulative and the directors fail to declare a dividend in any particular year, preferred stockholders lose their right to that dividend and are entitled only to regular dividends in future years. There are also instances of what might be termed "cumulative when earned" preferred stock, which means that if the preferred dividend is earned in any year and the directors fail to declare the dividend, then no dividend on common stock may be paid until the directors pay the preferred stock dividend previously earned.

Stocks preferred as to dividends may also be classified as participating or nonparticipating. The participation of the preferred stock may be either partial or full. A fully participating preferred stock receives its fixed dividend for the year, the common stock receives a prescribed amount (usually an equivalent amount per share), and any further distribution made for the year is shared equally by common and preferred stock, share for share. A partially or limited participating preferred stock shares in the residual distributable amount after payment of the annual fixed dividend on preferred stock and after a specified dividend has been paid to common stock, such sharing being limited to a specified maximum amount per share. Any additional dividends paid during the remainder of the year are paid to common stock only.

A nonparticipating preferred stock is entitled to its fixed dividend only, not sharing with the common stock in any additional dividends paid. Unless the charter specifies otherwise, preferred stock is nonparticipating.

2. *Assets on liquidation.*—After claims of all creditors have been settled, preferred stockholders generally receive a fixed amount per share before distribution is made to common stockholders. This fixed amount is often slightly larger in voluntary than in involuntary liquidation. Preferred stockholders are usually entitled to receive accrued or unpaid dividends before assets are distributed to common stockholders.

Preferred stock may also be participating as to assets when the corporation is liquidated. For instance, the preferred initially may receive $100 per share upon dissolution and, after the common receives $100 per share, participate equally with the common in the distribution of remaining assets. The amount to which each is entitled is dependent upon the preferred stock agreement.

3. *Voting.*—Unless the charter provides otherwise, preferred shares have the same voting rights as common shares. However, the charter usually either deprives the preferred stock of voting power or limits it. Frequently preferred stock is entitled to vote only under certain conditions, such as when dividends have not been declared for a specified period, or when working capital, net assets, or earnings fall below a

specified minimum, or in the event of default in other provisions of the corporate charter. Preferred stock is usually given the right to vote on matters such as the issuance of additional preferred stock or other senior securities, the sale of corporate assets, or changes in the by-laws affecting rights of the preferred stockholders.

4. *Convertibility.*—A privilege sometimes granted to preferred shareholders is the right to convert preferred stock, usually into common stock at a specified ratio, at the option of the holder. This is done with the thought that the conversion privilege will make the preferred stock more attractive to prospective purchasers. Conversion generally must be effected within a specified period, and the conversion ratio may change with the passing of time.

5. *Redemption.*—Most preferred stocks are redeemable after a certain date at the option of the corporation, sometimes in whole and sometimes in part selected by lot. When the stock is called, the corporation usually is required to pay to the stockholder either the par value of the preferred plus a premium and accrued dividends or a stipulated redemption price and accrued dividends, depending upon whether the stock is a par value stock or a no par value stock.

6. *Premium and call expense on redeemed or converted issues.*— In general, premium and call expense on preferred stock redeemed should be charged to earned surplus. Under certain circumstances, however, premium and call expense, in whole or in part, may be charged to paid-in surplus. For example, if upon original issue a premium over the par or stated value was received and credited to paid-in surplus, premium and call expense on retirement may be charged to paid-in surplus to the extent of the prorata premium received on issue of such shares. Further, if paid-in surplus has been created by previous transactions in this issue (see "Treasury Stock"), or if paid-in surplus remains on other preferred issues redeemed in their entirety, such paid-in surplus may be used to absorb any remaining premium or call expense.

Frequently, preferred stock on which a call for redemption has been issued may be converted into common stock prior to the settlement or other specified date. It is often advantageous to the preferred stockholder to convert rather than receive cash because of the favorable market price of the common stock. The corporation may have called the preferred issue anticipating that most preferred stockholders will convert. In the event of conversion, the excess of the par or stated value of the preferred stock over the par or stated value of the common stock issued in exchange, less expenses, should be credited to paid-in surplus.

Other Classes of Stock.—There are various other types of stocks which are found rather infrequently in this country. Common stock may be divided into Class A, Class B, and sometimes Class C common. Often one or more of these classes of common stock have all the rights usually associated with preferred stock and are common stock in name only. Sometimes the classes vary only with respect to their voting privileges.

Debenture stock may be preferred stock under another name. When debenture bonds have no due date, they resemble preferred stock.

Founders' stock, rarely seen in the United States, is usually issued to founders, promoters, or organizers of a corporation; it frequently claims a larger proportion of declared dividends than the remainder of the common stock. For example, 5 per cent of the common stock, the so-called founders' shares, may be entitled to 15 or 20 per cent of the total dividend declared payable on the common. Voting rights may or may not be the same as those of other shares.

Treasury Stock.—Treasury stock is a corporation's own stock which has been issued and subsequently reacquired by purchase or by donation, but not retired. Generally it should not be considered as an asset of the company but as a reduction of capital. An exception to this rule may arise when treasury stock has been acquired for the specific purpose of resale to employees or others; then it may be so described and shown on the asset side of the balance sheet at cost. Reacquired stock remains treasury stock until it is either retired, resold, given as compensation to employees, distributed as a dividend, or exchanged for property. Treasury stock cannot be voted.

1. *Dividends on treasury stock.*—Ordinarily, cash dividends are not paid on treasury stock. When dividends are paid through a dividend paying agent, they may be paid on treasury stock, but upon receipt these dividends should be applied as a reduction of the amount of dividend distribution and not taken into dividend income.

When stock dividends are paid, some companies prefer to issue the stock dividend on treasury stock in order that the treasury shares may retain the same proportionate ownership. This practice is permitted by some states and not by others; it is not essential from an accounting viewpoint. When stock dividends are issued on treasury stock, the accounting treatment should be the same as that for shares held by the public, as described on page 405; the cost basis of the total treasury shares after the stock dividend remains the same as that before the dividend.

2. *Retirement of treasury stock.*—As a general rule, upon the retirement of treasury stock, the applicable par, stated, or assigned value is deducted from the appropriate capital stock account. Any excess of cost over the amount so deducted is charged first to any related paid-in surplus applicable to the retired shares on a prorata basis, then to any paid-in surplus from a class of stock no longer outstanding, and the remainder to earned surplus. Any excess of amount deducted from capital stock over the cost of the shares is credited to paid-in surplus. Treasury stock of no par or stated value which had been issued at varying prices per share is usually deducted from the related capital accounts at either the amount originally received for the shares reacquired or, more usually, at the average issue price of all stock of the class. As a practical matter, it is not always feasible to determine the amount originally received for the specific shares reacquired.

While the foregoing may be stated as the general rule, it is advisable to consult legal counsel when stock is retired so that book entries and financial statements may be prepared in conformity with counsel's interpretation of applicable state laws.

3. *Transactions in treasury stock.*—When treasury stock is resold rather than retired, the problem arises of disposition of the difference between the cost and the selling price of the shares.

Accounting Research Bulletin No. 43, Chapter 1, Section B, reads in part as follows:

> Apparently there is general agreement that the difference between the purchase price and the stated value of a corporation's common stock purchased and retired should be reflected in capital surplus. Your committee believes that while the net asset value of the shares of common stock outstanding in the hands of the public may be increased or decreased by such purchase and retirement, such transactions relate to the capital of the corporation and do not give rise to corporate profits or losses. Your committee can see no essential difference between (a) the purchase and retirement of a corporation's own common stock and the subsequent issue of common shares, and (b) the purchase and resale of its own common stock.

The Securities and Exchange Commission issued an opinion of the Chief Accountant (Accounting Series Release No. 6) which reiterated the same reasoning in similar language, and concluded, "There would seem to be no logical reason why surplus arising from the reacquisition of the company's capital stock and its subsequent resale should not also be treated as capital."

Loss on the sale of treasury stock may be charged to paid-in surplus arising from similar transactions; if no such surplus exists the loss should usually be charged to earned surplus. It would be improper to charge a loss on the sale of treasury stock to paid-in surplus arising from issue of shares outstanding, but it would be proper to charge such a loss to paid-in surplus arising from a class of stock previously retired through purchase or redemption.

When treasury shares or unissued shares are given in exchange for services or property other than cash, the issue price is usually deemed to be the fair market value of the shares, and the difference between such price and cost is charged or credited as indicated above. If no fair market value for the shares is determinable, the fair value of the property or services is used.

Stock Options.—Stock options represent rights given by a corporation, usually to a bondholder, stockholder, underwriter, officer, or employee, which permit the holder to purchase shares of the corporation's stock at a specified price, during a certain period, and in accordance with conditions set forth in the option. Options, or warrants as they are often called, may be attached to bonds or to preferred stocks to increase the marketability of the issue. The options may be detachable or nondetachable. If detachable, the purchaser of the bond or preferred stock may sell the warrant, exercise it, or permit it to expire. If nondetachable, he must either exercise it, sell it with the security to which it is attached, or let it lapse at the expiration date.

1. *Stock options as compensation.*—Stock options may be given to officers or employees of a corporation for various reasons, for example, as compensation for work previously performed or as an inducement or incentive to greater effort.

Employee stock purchase plans are frequently part of a corporation's program to secure equity capital or to obtain widespread ownership among employees; when they are, no element of compensation need be considered to be present if the purchase price is not lower than is reasonably required to interest employees generally or to secure the desired funds.

When a limited number of officers and key employees are granted options to purchase stock at fixed prices over extended periods, an element of compensation may be involved. Generally, such options are issued as inducements for continued employment and greater effort in managing the company in order that its success will be reflected in increased market valuation of the stock. The option agreement usually provides that during a specified period and upon the performance by the grantee of certain stipulated conditions, the grantee may, at his own election, exercise the option in accordance with its terms. If the option price is considerably below the market price of the stock at the date of the option agreement, there is usually no question but that the element of compensation exists, and its amount may readily be computed. When, however, the option price is at, near, or above the market price at the date of the option agreement, the company has parted with no material consideration and no accounting recognition of compensation is required, even though the privilege to purchase stock at a later date, when a market increment may have occurred, at no risk in the interim, may prove to be of considerable value to the grantee.

The problems involved in the accounting for any such compensation are twofold—first, measuring the value of the option right, and, second, determining the date as of which it should be valued.

In considering the measure of value of such option rights, Chapter 13, Section B, of Accounting Research Bulletin No. 43 states in part:

.... there is no such objective means for measuring the value of an option which is not transferable and is subject to such other restrictions as are usually present in options of the nature here under discussion. Although there is, from the standpoint of the grantee, a value inherent in a restricted future right to purchase shares at a price at or even above the fair value of shares at the grant date, the committee believes it is impracticable to measure any such value. .... On the other hand, it follows in the opinion of the committee that the value to the grantee and the related cost to the corporation of a restricted right to purchase shares at a price *below* the fair value of the shares at the grant date may for the purposes here under discussion be taken as the excess of the then fair value of the shares over the option price.

There has been disagreement in the past as to whether the option should be valued on the date of the agreement, on the date the option becomes exercisable, on the date the option becomes the property of the grantee, or on the date on which it is finally exercised. There is now general agreement with the bulletin on this point, which states in part:

.... it may be assumed that if the stock option were granted as a part of an employment contract, both parties had in mind a valuation of the option at the date of the contract; and accordingly, value at that date should be used as the amount to be accounted for as compensation. If the option were granted as a form of supplementary compensation otherwise than as an integral part of an employment contract, the grantor is nevertheless governed in determining the option price and the number of shares by conditions then existing. It follows that it is the value of the option at that time, rather than the grantee's ultimate gain or loss on the transaction, which for accounting purposes constitutes whatever compensation the grantor intends to pay. The committee therefore concludes that in most cases, including situations where the right to exercise is conditional upon continued employment, valuation should be made of the option as of the date of grant.

Usually, the circumstances and terms under which options are granted, including any conditions as to exercise of the options or disposal of the stock acquired, are the most significant evidence available as to the nature and purpose of a stock option plan. Many plans maintain a fixed price, determined at the date of grant, for all shares optioned, even though the options may be exercised only in instalments during the period covered by the grant. Some plans provide that option prices be based upon a specified number of points below average market quotations for the year preceding exercise, and require the company to purchase shares in the open market to make them available for the optionees. The element of compensation is more obvious in the latter plan.

When compensation is involved, its amount as determined at the date of grant should be charged to income in the period during which the services are rendered, and, when the period is not specifically set forth in the agreement, the apportionment should be reasonable in the light of the attendant circumstances. The offset to the income charge should be set up in an account similar to that covering subscriptions to capital stock; this account should be reduced by appropriate credits to the capital accounts as the options are exercised or lapsed.

The Internal Revenue Code provides for special tax treatment of restricted stock options, as defined. In general, if specified conditions are met, the grantee is taxed only on resale of the stock and then only for a long-term capital gain (provided he holds the stock for more than six months). When the option does not qualify as a restricted stock option, the Treasury Department takes the position that the date exercised is the proper date for determining the value of the option, and that compensation should be recognized at that date to the extent the fair value of the stock exceeds the amount paid. Corporations are entitled to income tax deductions for compensation so recognized.

CAPITAL SURPLUS.—The term "capital surplus" has been used to describe any type or amount of "capital" in excess of stated capital, other than earned surplus. But if surplus is merely one form of capital, the term "capital surplus" is redundant; when "surplus" is used to indicate capital derived from the conduct of the business, the term "capital surplus" is in conflict with the term "earned surplus." The confusion surrounding the use of the term "capital surplus" has resulted in many recommendations that its use be discontinued and that it be replaced by more specific terms which describe its source. Forms of capital which, by tradition, have been included in the capital surplus category are discussed in this section. Until suitable alternatives are firmly established by usage, the term "capital surplus" cannot be avoided entirely.

If used at all, the term "capital surplus" should be used only to describe varieties of paid-in surplus, but sometimes published balance sheets include in this caption amounts arising from revaluations or excess of book amount of net assets of a subsidiary over cost of investment therein.

Paid-in Surplus.—The term "paid-in surplus" usually means capital contributed by stockholders in excess of par or stated value of capital shares. It is sometimes referred to as "paid-in capital" or "premium on capital stock." The following conditions are characteristic of those wherein paid-in surplus may arise:

1. Sales of par value capital stock for consideration in excess of par, which excess is known as premium on capital stock.

2. Sales of no par stock in which part of the proceeds is designated as the stated value of capital stock and the remainder is allocated to paid-in surplus.

3. The reduction of the par or stated value of previously issued capital stock. This credit may be best described as "paid-in surplus arising from reduction in par (or stated) value of capital stock."

4. Conversion of securities with higher stated values than those into which converted.

5. Capitalization of earnings in the form of stock dividends to the extent of amounts in excess of par or stated value of the stock issued. See the discussion of stock dividends on page 405.

6. Sale of stock donated by stockholders or the donation of property to the corporation by stockholders (donated surplus).

7. Assessments, levied against stockholders, of amounts in excess of par or stated value.

Other forms of paid-in surplus arise from forfeited stock subscriptions, and from the sale or retirement of treasury stock. Frequently, amounts derived from the above sources are combined and shown as one amount of paid-in surplus.

Until a particular class of stock has been fully redeemed or retired, paid-in surplus arising from transactions in it is deemed to be allocated to the class and may not absorb charges from other classes (e.g., premiums and expenses of called issues—see discussion on page 387). After redemption or retirement, remaining paid-in surplus applicable to such stock may be used to absorb charges from other classes which may have exhausted their own paid-in surpluses. Paid-in surplus applicable to preferred stock which has been converted to common stock becomes a part of the common stock paid-in surplus. Actual segregation of paid-in surplus by classes of stock within the accounts is desirable; such segregation is seldom seen in published balance sheets other than those of regulated utilities.

Some accountants feel that any form of paid-in or capital surplus may be used to absorb premiums, discounts, and expenses of stock issuances and calls, thus distinguishing net capital contributions of stockholders from undistributed earnings. They argue that earned surplus should represent all the company's accumulated earnings not distributed, unaffected by capital transactions; to accomplish this, they are willing to permit reductions in contributed capital of one class of stock by charges applicable to another class. The authors believe it is more important to preserve the contributed capital of each class. Furthermore, the balance of earned surplus may not represent all undistributed earnings, as when earnings have been capitalized in the form of stock dividends. Redemptions of senior issues are usually motivated by the desire to make available more earned surplus for future distribution to common stockholders by eliminating preferred dividend requirements. Accordingly, earned surplus should bear charges for those premiums and call expenses which are not properly chargeable to paid-in surplus as stated in the foregoing section relating to such charges.

Donated Surplus.—When a corporation's own stock (issued fully paid and nonassessable) which has been reacquired by donation is subsequently disposed of, the proceeds of the sale become donated surplus.

Until sold or retired, donated treasury stock may be entered on the books at no value or at a nominal amount of $1, with an offsetting credit to donated surplus. The latter account should be adjusted as the shares are subsequently disposed of.

If capital stock is issued for the acquisition of property and it appears that, at about the same time and pursuant to a previous agreement or understanding, some portion of the stock so issued is to be donated to the corporation, consideration needs to be given to whether or not an adjustment of the purchase price of the asset is necessary. Usually it will be found that only the *net* shares issued should be considered as the purchase price of the asset. In such cases, donated shares, while nominally treasury stock, should be treated as unissued shares from an accounting standpoint, with no donated surplus being recognized as a result of their resale.

Donated surplus sometimes arises from a direct capital contribution in cash or property from a stockholder, or a parent company. When a public utility receives assistance from customers or municipalities in the construction of its facilities, the amounts are not usually shown as donated (contributed) surplus, but separately under some such caption as "contributions for extensions."

Stock Assessments.—Even when shares of stock are fully paid and nonassessable, corporations occasionally levy a prorata assessment on all shares outstanding. Such a levy might occur when the corporation is facing bankruptcy or is undergoing a reorganization. Since it results in an increase in the capital funds of the corporation, paid-in surplus should be credited with the amount received, adequately described.

Forfeited Stock Subscriptions.—When a subscriber to capital stock remits a portion of the subscription price and fails to pay the balance, the corporation must act in accordance with the laws of the state of incorporation. In some states, the subscriber, after a certain period has elapsed, forfeits his payment, and the corporation may resell the stock. If the stock is resold at an amount which, together with the amount forfeited, exceeds par or stated value, a form of paid-in surplus arises.

Retirement or Sale of Treasury Stock.—In most states the excess of par or stated value over cost of treasury stock retired or not reissuable should be credited to an account such as paid-in surplus. Net profits on the resale of treasury stock should be similarly classified, as discussed on page 389.

Revaluation Surplus.—Appreciation, frequently described as revaluation surplus, may be recognized when assets are restated on a basis higher than cost less accumulated depreciation.

If the higher amount based can be shown to result from excessive provisions for depreciation or charges of capital items to maintenance, the excess represents a prior year adjustment and may be carried to earned surplus and appropriately explained. If, however, the higher amount arises from increases in price levels, the excess should not be credited to earned surplus but to revaluation surplus. Such appraisals are discussed in Chapter 12.

In Chapter 13, the viewpoint of the Committee on Accounting Procedure (Bulletin No. 43, Chapter 9, Section B) was stated with respect to basing depreciation charges on higher appraisal amounts rather than on cost; the committee did not express an opinion as to the ultimate disposition, if any, that is to be made of appraisal surplus. It is the authors' opinion that appraisal surplus should be viewed as permanent capital and therefore not available for subsequent transfer to earned surplus as realized through depreciation or sale; also, that it may not be used for purposes appropriate for paid-in surplus, such as absorption of premiums on retired issues or transfers to capital under pooling arrangements. Such surplus would, however, be disposed of in connection with a quasi-reorganization.

Surplus Arising from Consolidation.—When, in the preparation of a consolidated balance sheet, a credit arises from the acquisition of a subsidiary at a cost below the book amount of its net assets at acquisition date, such credit may sometimes be shown in the capital surplus section. The principles applicable to revaluation surplus may be, and in many instances are, equally applicable to this credit. For a discussion of this credit, and the authors' views thereon, see Chapter 21.

Other Transactions Affecting Capital.—In accordance with generally accepted accounting principles, some items may be properly charged or credited to surplus other than earned surplus. Transactions in treasury stock and premiums and call expenses on redeemed issues have been previously discussed in this chapter. Examples of other transactions which may affect capital are discussed below.

1. *Dividends.*—Ordinarily, dividends are not charged to any surplus other than earned surplus. In unusual circumstances, when permitted by statute and authorized by the directors, certain dividends may be charged to capital surplus. The treatment of these dividends is discussed under Sources of Dividends on page 407.

2. *Organization expenses.*—Organization expenses of newly formed corporations are sometimes charged to paid-in surplus arising from the sale of stock at a premium, provided the directors authorize and the laws of the state of incorporation permit such a charge. The more usual method of disposing of organization expenses is to charge them to earnings over a short period, such as three to five years.

Expenditures and write-offs incident to reorganization, recapitalization, merger, or consolidation are charged either against paid-in surplus resulting therefrom or against earned surplus.

3. *Quasi-reorganizations.*—A quasi-reorganization may be defined as a procedure recognized in accounting by which the accounts of a corporation may be restated to the same extent they would be if a new corporation were created and acquired the business of the existing corporation; a new basis of accountability for assets, liabilities, and capital is established.

In 1934, on recommendation of the special committee on cooperation with stock exchanges, the American Institute of Certified Public Accountants formally adopted the following rule relating to surplus other than that arising from profits retained in the business:

Capital surplus, however created, should not be used to relieve the income account of the current or future years of charges which would otherwise fall to be made thereagainst. This rule might be subject to the exception that where, upon reorganization, a reorganized company would be relieved of charges which would require to be made against income if the existing corporation were continued, it might be regarded as permissible to accomplish the same result without reorganization provided the facts were as fully revealed to and the action as formally approved by the shareholders as in reorganization.

Formal consent of the shareholders is required for a quasi-reorganization. The effective date of the readjustment should be as near as practicable to the date consent is given; usually the close of the fiscal year is selected.

The adjustments should be made in such a manner that income of subsequent periods will be fairly stated and will be comparable to that of a new corporation commencing operations under business conditions existing at the time of the reorganization. Assets should be carried forward at fair and not unduly conservative amounts, determined with due regard for the accounting to be employed thereafter. Provision should be made for maximum probable losses or charges known to have arisen before the date of the reorganization; subsequent adjustments to these provisions should be carried to capital surplus.

When the amounts to be written off in a readjustment have been determined, they should be charged first against earned surplus to the full extent of such surplus; any balance may then be charged against capital surplus. Frequently, the capital surplus needed to absorb these charges is created by a reduction in par or stated value of capital stock, approved by the shareholders at the time consent to the quasi-reorganization is given.

It is implicit in a quasi-reorganization that there should be no remaining balance of earned surplus and that no deficit should exist in any surplus account. A new earned surplus account should be established and described as being accumulated from the effective date of the readjustment. This dating should be disclosed in financial statements until such time as the effective date is no longer deemed significant. It is not expected that quasi-reorganizations will be repeated at frequent intervals, if at all. The Securities and Exchange Commission has suggested (Accounting Series Release No. 15) that after restatement of surplus:

. . . . until such time as the results of operations of the company on the new basis are available for an appropriate period of years (at least three) any statement or showing of earned surplus should, in order to provide additional disclosure of the occurrence and the significance of the quasi-reorganization, indicate the total amount of the deficit and any charges that were made to the capital surplus in the course of the quasi-reorganization which would otherwise have been required to be made against income or earned surplus.

After the quasi-reorganization, material transactions relating to the prior period should not be reflected in the new earned surplus account. Dividends received from subsidiaries declared out of earnings prior to the adjustment represent capital adjustments and not credits to income. Earned surplus of subsidiaries at the date of quasi-reorganization should not be carried forward as consolidated earned surplus in the consolidated balance sheet.

The foregoing principles are in agreement with those set forth in Chapter 7, Section A, of Accounting Research Bulletin No. 43.

Plant accounts may be written down in a quasi-reorganization to more realistic amounts, with the result that depreciation charges in subsequent income statements are less than depreciation deducted for income tax purposes; such "tax benefit" is received by the reorganized company during the remaining life of the related plant.

Similarly, when a company undergoing quasi-reorganization has suffered losses in the immediately preceding years, such losses may be availed of by the reorganized company to reduce taxable income in the immediately succeeding years.

Many accountants believe that when realization of such tax benefits by the reorganized company seems likely, they should be recognized at the date of reorganization by setting them up as deferred charges with subsequent charge to income of the tax benefits applicable to each year; as an alternative, with respect to plant accounts the estimated tax benefits may be recognized in arriving at the amounts to which plant accounts are written down. Depreciation of amounts added to plant under this alternative method will eventually equal the total tax benefits, except that if the depreciation rates are changed, they may not offset, year by year, the tax benefits received. If at the time of reorganization, subsequent taxable income seems unlikely, and therefore the amount of "tax benefit" to be realized cannot reasonably be estimated, those accountants believe that recognition should be deferred until realization, when income should be charged and capital surplus credited with the amount applicable to the year of realization. Other accountants believe that tax benefits realized in any subsequent year should be reflected in income of that year.

In the authors' opinion, the preferable treatment is to exclude from income and earned surplus subsequent to reorganization any tax benefits arising from deductions or losses attributable to periods prior to reorganization.

EARNED SURPLUS.—Earned surplus has been defined by the Committee on Terminology (Bulletin No. 1, par. 34) as:

> The balance of net profits, income, gains and losses of a corporation from the date of incorporation (or from the latest date when a deficit was eliminated in a quasi-reorganization) after deducting distributions therefrom to shareholders and transfers therefrom to capital stock or capital surplus accounts.

The term "earned surplus" has been criticized because its meaning is so often misunderstood. Many accountants and others concerned with the preparation of financial statements have turned to expressions such as *earnings (or income, or profits) retained in the business.* The purpose of using this description is to avoid the concept of an available surplus or undivided profits from which stockholders may expect dividends. While it is legally possible to declare dividends to the full extent of earned surplus, and in some states, of capital surplus also, most corporations consider earned surplus as permanent capital to the extent that such undistributed earnings are used for expansion of the business; dividends are frequently limited to a portion of current earnings.

The authors in this edition have not attempted to abandon completely the use of the term "earned surplus," but they recognize the force of the arguments in favor of replacing it with a more precise term. The recommendations of the Committee on Terminology are discussed under Statement Presentation later in this chapter.

Unappropriated Earned Surplus.—When a portion of earned surplus has been appropriated or set aside for one or more designated special purposes, the balance of earned surplus is generally referred to as unappropriated earned surplus. Extraordinary charges and credits permitted to be made directly to unappropriated earned surplus rather than to income are discussed in Chapter 7.

Appropriated Earned Surplus (Surplus Reserves).—Portions of earned surplus (representing an undivided portion of the assets) may be set aside by management for general or specific purposes; such segregations are commonly referred to as surplus reserves. Examples of these reserves are sinking fund reserves, reserves for retirement of preferred stocks, for working capital, and for general contingencies. The only purposes served by surplus reserves are to conform with the provisions of agreements with respect to bonds, notes, preferred stocks, etc., and to give some indication to stockholders of the amount of possible losses in the future. The principles applicable to these reserves are summarized on the following page.

1. Appropriations of earned surplus do not represent liabilities. If the reserve is required to provide for an existing or reasonably estimable liability or loss, it should be classified as a liability and the provision therefor charged to income.

2. Costs or losses should not be charged to a surplus reserve, and no part of the reserve should be transferred to income or in any way used to affect the determination of net income in any year.

3. When such a reserve or any part of it is no longer required, it should be returned to earned surplus.

4. Such reserves should preferably be classified in the balance sheet as segregations of earned surplus.

Some of the more important types of surplus reserves are discussed below.

1. *Sinking fund reserves.*—Many issues of bonds, notes, and preferred stock contain provisions providing for their payment or retirement through operations of a sinking fund. For example, the annual provision for this purpose may be specified in amount, it may be a specified percentage of the outstanding issue, a stated percentage of net earnings, or it may be based on realizations of wasting assets.

Some agreements specifically state that sinking fund provisions are to be made "out of earnings (or profits)." Accordingly, an appropriation of earned surplus may be made in annual amounts equal to those specified as sinking fund payments. When the agreement provides that such payments are to be made out of earnings, counsel should be consulted for advice whether such appropriation is legally required under the agreement. The requirements of some agreements are ambiguous, but a correct understanding of the intention of the investors (as well as the intention of the corporation) is of great importance. The result of such appropriation is to indicate in the financial statements the aggregate total of assets accumulated out of earnings which have been, or shortly will be, devoted to reduction of debt or retirement of preferred stock.

While the setting up of this type of reserve is a convenient device for measuring the assets which have been, or shortly will be, devoted to retirement or acquisition of related securities, the procedure cannot be considered as a guaranty, of itself, that the requisite assets will be available in the form required when needed; hence, retirement or sinking fund reserves are sometimes (but not necessarily) accompanied by the segregation of cash or other assets to insure payment when the sinking fund instalment is due.

Even though the reserve account, because of periodic retirements, may exceed the principal amount of the issue remaining to be retired, it is not usually proper to transfer any part of the reserve to unappropriated earned surplus until the issue has been completely retired, unless the agreement so provides. On retirement of the entire issue, the balance in the reserve may be returned to earned surplus.

2. *Reserves for retirement of preferred stock.*—Under the terms of agreements to retire preferred stock, a portion of earned surplus may be appropriated annually to restrict dissipation of assets by means of dividends on common stock. The principles outlined above with respect to sinking fund reserves are equally applicable to reserves for retirement of preferred stock.

3. *Reserves for working capital.*—The segregation from earned surplus of a reasonable amount as a reserve for additional working capital may be temporary or permanent, at the discretion of the directors. The reserve is a voluntary and revocable segregation of earned surplus. It may be advisable to accumulate a substantial surplus, and the directors may believe that the temptation to declare dividends will be less if the earned surplus account is diminished and some other surplus account is created. Such segregation of surplus should have directors' approval.

4. *Reserves for fire and similar losses.*—Corporations which are self-insurers sometimes carry reserves for fire and similar losses. Such reserves are segregated surplus if they originated by charges to earned surplus.

5. *Reserves for future inventory declines.*—Even if inventories are fairly stated at the lower of cost or market, management may feel that prices may go lower, and may segregate a portion of earned surplus as a conservative measure. The account may be entitled "Reserve for Future Inventory Decline," or otherwise described. Such a reserve should not be used to absorb inventory losses and eventually should be returned to earned surplus; it should not be shown as a reduction of inventory.

6. *Reserves for excess replacement costs.*—When it can be foreseen that necessary plant replacement will require expenditures considerably in excess of original cost of plant to be replaced, a portion of earned surplus may be appropriated as a reserve for this purpose. Such reserve would indicate to stockholders the approximate amount of earnings which management feels should not be disbursed as dividends, but should be retained in the business until needed for the stated purpose.

7. *General purpose contingency reserves.*—Management may set up general purpose contingency reserves which are not required at the

time under generally accepted accounting principles and whose purposes are not specific. Such reserves are those created:

1. For general undetermined contingencies,
2. For a wide variety of indefinite possible future losses,
3. Without specific purpose reasonably related to operations of the current period, or
4. In amounts not determined on the basis of reasonable estimates of costs or losses.

No costs or losses should be charged to these reserves, and no part of them should be transferred to income or in any way used to affect the determination of net income in any year. They should be restored to earned surplus directly when no longer considered necessary. Chapter 6 of Accounting Research Bulletin No. 43 considers these reserves, and its recommendations have been summarized in this chapter.

8. *Secret reserves.*—Occasionally capital is understated either inadvertently or intentionally through the creation of secret reserves. This term implies the existence of proprietary equities concealed through the understatement or omission of assets, the overstatement of liabilities, or the inclusion of fictitious liabilities.

From an accounting standpoint, there is no justification for flagrant understatement of net assets in any circumstances. The principal argument used in support of secret reserves is that stockholders insistent upon dividends form the opinion that a surplus available for dividends, but not so distributed, is evidence of poor management. However, when profits of good years have been distributed in their entirety, they become bitterly critical when the inevitable poor year arrives and dividends must be passed. In the authors' opinion, there is no merit in the use of secret reserves in lieu of fair presentation of asset and liability amounts in accordance with generally accepted accounting principles. The authors believe that a stockholder capable of interpreting financial statements realizes that dividends are generally paid from current earnings and that to the extent indicated in the financial statements, earnings of the past have been reinvested in expanding the operations of the business. It is apparent that a stockholder who sells his stock without the knowledge that reported financial position and earnings have been understated is at a great disadvantage as compared with a prospective purchaser who happens to have that knowledge.

Surplus in Mergers, Consolidations, and Acquisitions of Subsidiaries.—When two or more unaffiliated corporations merge or consolidate, the action may be considered either a pooling of interests or a purchase of a subsidiary (or its assets) by the acquiring company. These alternatives exist whether or not one of the old corporations survives, a new corporation is formed, or a parent-subsidiary relationship emerges. The distinction between these alternatives and the applicable accounting principles is more fully discussed in Chapter 21.

If a pooling of interests is deemed to have taken place, the individual components of the capital sections of the balance sheets of the constituent companies are combined by classifications. Any excess of the combined stated capital stock amounts over the amounts required for the stated or par value of the stock of the new entity is transferred to paid-in surplus; any insufficiency is made up first from the combined paid-in surplus, to the extent available, and then from the combined earned surplus.

When consolidated financial statements are prepared subsequent to a purchase of a subsidiary, capital accounts of the subsidiary at the date of acquisition are eliminated against the investment. Only undistributed earnings of the subsidiary since acquisition are included in consolidated earned surplus. See Chapter 21.

When there is a merger of a subsidiary with a parent company, or a liquidation of a subsidiary into its parent, it is permissible to include in earned surplus of the parent company the subsidiary's undistributed surplus earned since the date of acquisition by the parent. Similarly, if two companies owned by the same parent are merged, say, by the issuance of additional stock of one company in exchange for the stock of the other, with the resulting subsidiary subsequently merged with the parent, the undistributed earned surplus of both subsidiaries since the dates of original acquisition may be taken over as such by the parent company.

When a corporation wishes to change its domicile to another state and for that purpose a corporation with the same corporate powers and capitalization is formed in that state to acquire the business of the first corporation, it is permissible for the new corporation to take over the earned surplus of its predecessor.

If the effective date specified in an agreement for corporate merger or for purchase of a business is prior to the actual date of passing of title to the properties, it may be practical to consider that the operations of the new (successor) enterprise began on the earlier date. Use of the earlier date is not objectionable if changes in surplus in the interim period are not significant.

Dividends.—A dividend has been defined as a prorata distribution to the stockholders of a corporation. Dividends may be classified as to the medium of payment (cash, property, or stock) or the source (earned surplus or paid-in capital). Usually the term "dividend" without qualification indicates a prorata distribution in cash, paid out of earned surplus to all stockholders of a given class.

The board of directors of a corporation decides when and in what amounts dividends shall be paid. It should take into consideration the financial position and earnings of the company, the general business outlook, and future plans of the company. Often it is advisable to have counsel pass on the legality of proposed dividend actions.

Dividends are declared by a formal vote of the board of directors indicating the amount (or percentage of par) per share to be paid, the payment date, and the record date; the declaration should be recorded in the minutes of the directors' meetings. Only those persons owning stock as of the record date are entitled to dividends declared.

When a dividend other than a stock dividend has been declared and public notice of it has been given to the stockholders, the dividend is a legal obligation and may not be rescinded without the consent of stockholders entitled to receive the dividend. Accordingly, earned surplus is charged with the appropriate amount at the time of declaration. Stock dividends may be rescinded without stockholders' consent at any time before issuance of the additional stock.

The treatment of dividends on treasury stock is discussed on page 388 under Treasury Stock.

MEDIUM OF PAYMENT.—Dividends may be paid in cash, in other assets, in capital stock of the distributing corporation, or in scrip. Payment of dividends in cash is by far the most usual, and the accounting for such dividends presents few problems.

Stock dividends are paid in capital stock of the corporation making the distribution. A dividend on one class of stock is usually paid in the same class of stock, but it is sometimes paid in stock of another class. Occasionally, dividends are declared payable in property, such as marketable securities of other corporations. Some distilling companies have paid dividends from finished stock inventory. Usually the difficulty of apportioning property, other than securities, among many stockholders owning various proportions of the outstanding stock discourages the payment of dividends in property.

When a corporation otherwise in a position to pay dividends lacks cash or other assets suitable for distribution, it may resort to the payment of dividends in dividend scrip. Dividend scrip is usually an issue of short-term interest-bearing notes payable to stockholders in cash at a future date.

Dividends Paid in Property Other Than Cash.—There are two alternatives as to the amount to be charged to surplus of the disbursing corporation upon payment of a dividend in property. One is that earned surplus be charged with the cost of the property to the disbursing corporation; the other, with the market value of the property at the date the dividend is declared, any difference between market value and cost being reflected as a charge or credit to income or earned surplus of the period. Generally, the first alternative is used, although problems arise under either treatment, and it is not always possible to determine a fair market value. Income tax considerations may have an important bearing on the accounting treatment selected.

If dividends are paid in property having a readily determinable market value appreciably in excess of the amount at which the property is carried on the books and these dividends are charged to surplus at book amount, the amount of this difference should be clearly indicated in the current financial statements. This is particularly important when there is more than one class of stock and the property is being distributed to a class other than common stock. Preferred stock with a fixed dividend rate should not profit by receiving dividends in property the value of which exceeds the fixed rate.

Stock Dividends and Stock Split-ups.—Although they appear to be similar, stock dividends and stock split-ups are fundamentally different and must receive different accounting treatment. Chapter 7, Section B, of Accounting Research Bulletin No. 43, defines a stock dividend as "an issuance by a corporation of its own common shares to its common shareholders without consideration and under conditions indicating that such action is prompted mainly by a desire to give the recipient shareholders some ostensibly separate evidence of a part of their respective interests in accumulated corporate earnings without distribution of cash or other property which the board of directors deems necessary or desirable to retain in the business." This bulletin defines a split-up as "an issuance by a corporation of its own common shares to its common shareholders without consideration and under conditions indicating that such action is prompted mainly by a desire to increase the number of outstanding shares for the purpose of effecting a reduction in their unit market price and, thereby, of obtaining wider distribution and improved marketability of the shares."

A stock dividend purports to distribute earnings of a corporation in a form other than cash; actually neither earnings nor assets are distributed. The percentage distribution is usually small and the issuance of the additional shares required to pay the stock dividend results in little or no decrease in the per share market price of the shares. The committee's recommendation is quoted on the following page.

The committee therefore believes that where these circumstances exist the corporation should in the public interest account for the transaction by transferring from earned surplus to the category of permanent capitalization (represented by the capital stock and capital surplus accounts) an amount equal to the fair value of the additional shares issued. Unless this is done, the amount of earnings which the shareholder may believe to have been distributed to him will be left, except to the extent otherwise dictated by legal requirements, in earned surplus subject to possible further similar stock issuances or cash distributions.

In the authors' opinion, the date of declaration of a stock dividend is the most logical point at which to determine fair value of the shares issued. While the ex-dividend date and the date of payment have been used, these dates are less defensible. It should also be stated that the section of the bulletin quoted above is not necessarily applicable to closely held corporations where all the stockholders may be presumed to be aware of the implications of a stock dividend payment.

With respect to stock splits, Bulletin No. 43 states:

Where this (reduction in the unit price of shares) is clearly the intent, no transfer from earned surplus to capital surplus or capital stock account is called for, other than to the extent occasioned by legal requirements. It is believed, however, that few cases will arise where the aforementioned purpose can be accomplished through an issuance of shares which is less than, say, 20% or 25% of the previously outstanding shares.

Stock split-ups are often more conveniently effected in the form of a stock dividend, as, for example, a 100 per cent stock dividend (two-for-one split). In such split-ups, if the use of the word "dividend" cannot be avoided, the transaction should be described as a "split-up effected in the form of a dividend."

Any amount required to be transferred to capital stock from paid-in or earned surplus is confined to the par or stated value of the additional shares issued. When the par or stated value is, by formal action, reduced in proportion to the share split, or when no par stock is after the share split at the aggregate contributed capital amount, no change in the dollar amount of stated capital is required.

Dividends Payable in Cash or Stock at Option of Stockholder.— After a stock dividend (as previously defined), the percentage of the total shares held by each receiving shareholder in the class of shares being paid remains the same as before the distribution. A dividend payable in stock or cash at the option of the stockholder may not be a true stock dividend for it may not be a prorata distribution of shares; the proportions will be changed if cash is taken by some shareholders. However, a corporation which gives the stockholder the choice of a cash dividend or a stock dividend usually makes the offer in such terms that the choice of stock is more attractive to the recipient.

When significant amounts of cash are paid in any such distribution, the amount of earned surplus to be capitalized for the entire distribution should be at a rate per share not less than that of the optional cash dividend.

SOURCES OF DIVIDENDS.—From a common-sense business standpoint, dividends should be paid to stockholders only from accumulated earnings. Dividends have been charged to paid-in surplus or to a surplus other than earned surplus without a clear indication of the source of the dividend and without violating state regulations. That this can be done reflects no great credit to lawmakers, since the incongruity of contributing to the capital of a corporation and then receiving part of it back in the guise of ordinary dividends should be sufficiently evident to encourage making the practice legally impossible. Apart from the legality of such dividends, however, directors may be violating their trust if they declare dividends out of capital without making it clear to the stockholders that the dividends are not distributions of earned income. Some states have legislation which provides that shareholders shall be notified when dividends are paid out of capital.

Investment companies often declare two types of dividends—one representing a distribution of investment income, the other a distribution of gains from sales of investment securities. Such dividends are frequently declared by companies considered under the Internal Revenue Code as regulated investment companies, whose income from these sources is substantially tax free to the company if properly distributed currently in the form of dividends.

Availability of Surplus of Subsidiaries for Distribution by Parent Company.—Companies often purchase subsidiaries which have substantial surplus accounts. Surplus earned by a subsidiary prior to acquisition should be excluded from consolidated earned surplus and dividends paid to the parent company out of surplus accumulated by the subsidiary prior to its acquisition should not be treated as income but should be credited to the investment account on the parent company's books.

With respect to earnings subsequent to acquisition, there may be limitations on the payment of dividends by subsidiaries to the parent company. Provisions of bond indentures and stock agreements of the subsidiary companies may restrict the payment of dividends to the parent from the earned surpluses of these companies. In such instances, any material effect upon the availability of consolidated earned surplus for dividends should be disclosed.

Liquidating Dividends.—Dividends paid with the express intent of reducing the capital of the corporation, and with a view toward partial or complete dissolution, are known as liquidating dividends or distributions of capital. Accounting for such dividends should follow the intent expressed in resolutions of the directors or stockholders.

Dividends Paid from Amounts Specifically Included in the Price of the Stock.—When specific amounts equal to accrued dividends per share are included in the prices at which shares of capital stock are sold by the issuer, with the intention that these amounts are to be returned to the stockholders as part of the first dividends to be distributed to them, such amounts should be shown as a liability and not included in the proceeds of the sale of the stock. This usually occurs when a corporation issues preferred stock at a price plus accrued dividends, and the first dividend is paid for a period beginning prior to the date of issuance of the stock. Also, certain types of investment trusts are required by their certificates of incorporation to segregate a portion of receipts from the sale of capital stock equal to the per share amount of undistributed realized or unrealized net income. This procedure is designed to maintain, for the benefit of the existing stockholders, the per share amount of distributable income which might otherwise be reduced upon the issuance of new shares.

There appears to be no reasonable or practical basis for objection to these practices, even though the amounts received equivalent to accrued dividends technically might be considered premiums.

Dividends of Extractive Industry Corporations Paid Out of Capital. —The statutes of some states permit the determination of distributable income without a deduction for depletion by companies engaged in the metal, timber, oil, and other extractive industries. Consequently, in those states, the entire realization from capital invested in these assets may legally be paid out in dividends. If this dividend policy is followed, it is desirable that financial statements disclose the amount of capital distributed as dividends in the current year as well as the accumulation of these distributions to date. Tax regulations require that when depletion is omitted and dividends are paid from capital, due notice must be given to stockholders. However, some companies omit depletion allowances in financial statements and in paying dividends make no attempt to distinguish between distributions of earnings and distributions of capital; the authors do not approve either of these procedures. Arguments for and against the omission of depletion in the determination of distributable income are found in Chapter 13. Regardless of what is legally permitted by state laws and under court decisions, the auditor should uphold the principle that paid-in capital should not be impaired by the repayment to stockholders of any of their contributed capital in the guise of ordinary dividends.

CONSTRUCTIVE DIVIDENDS.—Constructive dividends are distributions to stockholders in the ratio of their shareholdings without formal action of the board of directors in declaring and paying a dividend. The constructive dividend has received attention mainly because of income tax determinations. In a closely held corporation, if salaries or bonuses are paid to officers who comprise practically all of the stockholders of the company and if such salaries or bonuses are not based upon the value of their services but bear some relation to their stockholdings, the Treasury Department may consider all or part of such payments as distributions of profits for tax purposes and not as business expenses.

Capital of Businesses Other Than Corporations.—Business organizations other than corporations range from individual proprietorships to organizations tantamount to corporations. The more common types are individual proprietorships, business partnerships, limited partnerships, partnerships with transferable shares, and Massachusetts voluntary trusts with transferable shares. The last type mentioned so closely resembles a corporation that it is taxed like one.

As in a corporation, the types of capital and rights of participants depend upon the laws of the state in which the business is formed and the articles of copartnership or association.

Capital of Nonbusiness Enterprises.—Nonbusiness enterprises include such organizations as churches, fraternal orders, educational institutions, hospitals, and clubs. They may adopt one of several forms of legal organization, but usually there are no stockholders. In general, they are not subject to income taxes.

The capital of these enterprises represents mainly donations, which may be in the form of cash contributions, legacies, or endowments. The trustees may be permitted to use earnings from the funds and the funds themselves at their discretion, but often donors place restrictions upon both income and principal.

The accounting for capital in these enterprises may not follow generally accepted accounting principles in all respects. Legal restrictions placed upon the discretion of the trustees may require accounting treatment differing from that found in business enterprises. For example, profits or losses on the sale of stocks or bonds may be considered as changes in capital rather than credits or charges to income.

FUND ACCOUNTING.—Frequently, the operations of nonprofit organizations are sufficiently complex to require an accounting for several funds as separate entities; for example, such funds as general funds, endowment funds, restricted funds, and plant funds. When presented on the balance sheet, assets equal to the amount of each fund are separately stated. Transfers between funds, when legally permissible and properly authorized, should be recorded to recognize these entities.

INTERNAL CONTROL

Internal Accounting Control.

CAPITAL STOCK.—The extent of a corporation's internal accounting control over its capital stock will vary depending on whether an independent transfer agent and a registrar are employed. Corporations with stock listed on an exchange are required, in accordance with listing agreements, to maintain a transfer office or agency and, in addition, a registrar other than the transfer agent. When stocks are not listed but are widely held and transfers are numerous, independent agents are also frequently employed.

A transfer agent is responsible for maintaining stockholders' records, approving transfer instruments, and issuing new stock certificates. A registrar controls the issues of stock and registers stock as issued.

The use of these agents facilitates the recording of transfers, relieves the corporation of keeping detailed records and the responsibility for their accuracy, minimizes the possibility of fraud or error, and reduces the possibility of incurring penalties in connection with stock transfers because of inadequate knowledge or facilities. Stock certificates should be delivered to these agents only on specific authorizations of a designated official of the company. The only other control necessary is the comparison of the periodic reports of the agents with the general ledger.

More exacting controls are required when such agents are not employed; among the more important procedures are the following:

1. Blank stock certificates and stubs should be prenumbered and issued in numerical sequence.
2. The officers authorized to sign stock certificates should be designated by the board of directors.

3. Adequate records should be maintained for each class of stock, including stock ledgers, transfer journals, window tickets, registers of certificates received, ledger and stock control records, stock transfer records, and registers of authorized signatures. Subsidiary records should be balanced periodically with controlling accounts.

SURPLUS AND SURPLUS RESERVES.—Unusual entries in the surplus and surplus reserve accounts should be approved by the board of directors.

Periodically, analyses of surplus and surplus reserve accounts summarizing all changes in these accounts should be reviewed by a company official, preferably the comptroller or chief accountant.

DIVIDENDS.—Many large companies employ a dividend-paying agent to handle the payment of dividends to stockholders. When such an agent is employed, the requirements of internal accounting control procedures within the company are appreciably reduced.

Dividends should be properly declared and recorded in the minutes of the board of directors; notification to the agent should be signed by a designated company officer; and a check transferring to the agent the amount of the total dividend on the outstanding stock should be signed by the treasurer, and possibly countersigned by another responsible official. The notification should include all pertinent information as to the payment and record dates, and the authorized recipients. Dividend checks should be imprinted with the name of the corporation, signed by the paying agent, and mailed to reach the stockholders on the date dividends are declared payable.

When a company acts as its own dividend-disbursing agent, the need for internal control is greater. The dividend should be properly declared as previously noted. A separate bank account should be maintained for dividends; controls over disbursements from the dividend account should include those relating to bank accounts in general, discussed in Chapter 8.

It is important that total dividends paid do not exceed the amount determined by multiplying the number of shares of outstanding stock (not including treasury stock) by the dividend rate. This may be accomplished by transferring the total dividend to the special dividend account and checking the total of the individual dividend checks to the amount transferred before sending them out. Checks should be compared individually with the stockholders' ledger.

After a short period, unclaimed dividends may be transferred to a separate account so that the dividend payable account will reflect only current dividends payable. Unclaimed dividends should not be left on the books indefinitely, but, if the laws of the state permit and counsel so advises, they should be returned to surplus after an appropriate period has elapsed.

Internal Check.

CAPITAL STOCK.—For proper internal check each of the following functions should be performed by employees who have no cash functions and who are independent of each other:

1. Custodianship of blank certificates and maintenance of stock certificate books. These should be stored in a suitable safe or vault.
2. Signing and countersigning certificates. Preferably, two signatures should be required. Signing in advance should be prohibited.
3. Maintenance of stockholders' ledger.
4. Accounting for sequence of certificate numbers. Unused certificate books should be examined periodically for possible unauthorized extractions. This control should be maintained when stock certificates are accessible to personnel of the corporation, even when the issuance is under the control of a registrar.
5. Reconciliation of stock certificate books (or agents' reports) with stockholders' ledger and general ledger.

When certificates are surrendered for transfer or exchange, they should be returned to someone other than the person maintaining the detailed records. Such certificates should be examined for proper endorsement and should be effectively canceled and reattached to their original stubs. Persons signing the replacement certificates should be instructed to examine the related canceled certificates. Lost certificates should be replaced only after approval of the board of directors and receipt of an affidavit of loss accompanied by an indemnity bond.

Treasury stock should be registered in the company's name, physically segregated from unissued certificates, and under the control of a responsible official divorced from all stock certificate functions.

DIVIDENDS.—For proper internal check, each of the following functions should be performed by employees who are independent of each other:

1. Preparation and recording of checks.
2. Signing and mailing of checks. This person should also prove the mathematical accuracy of the total disbursement, that is, see that the aggregate amount paid does not exceed the dividend rate times the number of shares outstanding.
3. Preparation of bank reconciliations of the special dividend account.
4. Control of and authorization for disposition of unclaimed dividend checks.

AUDITING PROCEDURES

Capital Stock.—In an initial examination, the auditor should review the corporation's charter or certificate of incorporation and the by-laws and all pertinent amendments; the extent of review of prior years' minutes of meetings of the board of directors and stockholders and other documents and of capital stock accounts will depend upon circumstances and whether the financial statements have previously been examined by independent certified public accountants of good repute. In subsequent examinations, only changes within the period under examination need be reviewed.

When capital stock has been sold to the public, it is also advisable to review agreements with underwriters and others, and the prospectus filed with the SEC. These sources may disclose certain requirements, such as those for maintenance of minimum working capital or minimum earned surplus.

The auditor should include in his permanent file of working papers information as to the kinds of stock authorized, the number of shares of each class authorized, par or stated values, provisions concerning dividend rates, redemption values, priority rights to dividends and in liquidation, cumulative or noncumulative rights to dividends, participation or conversion privileges, and other pertinent data.

If there is an independent transfer agent, the number of shares outstanding at the balance sheet date should be confirmed with him. If there is a registrar, a similar confirmation should be obtained from him.

Some accountants advocate correspondence with the Secretary of State of the state in which the client is incorporated, to obtain direct confirmation of the number of shares and classes of capital stock authorized. This procedure is advisable on a new engagement; it is often followed in others when there are indications that minute books and other corporate records do not contain a complete record of changes in originally authorized capital stock.

The number of shares and amounts of unpaid subscriptions should be substantiated by reference to subscriptions on file or other supporting documents. If stock has been sold on the instalment plan, the auditor should determine whether collections have been received in accordance with the terms of the sale. Special terms granted to any stockholder should be approved by the board of directors. Confirmation of unpaid balances is often desirable.

The auditor should compare the number of shares outstanding and subscribed for (as evidenced by his examination of stock certificate stubs, stockholders' records, subscription records, and confirmations) with ledger accounts and with the certificate of incorporation and its amendments, to determine whether the number of shares of each class of stock issued and subscribed for is properly reflected in the books of account and is within the amount authorized. In his examination of stock certificate books, the auditor should be alert for evidence which may indicate the issuance of certificates without proper approval and record on the stock certificate stubs. He should note that all surrendered certificates have been effectively canceled and reattached to their respective stubs; the sequence of numbers and unused certificates should be accounted for. Many of these procedures may be performed on a test basis when the volume of activity is large and adequate controls are present.

Proceeds from the sale of capital stock shown by the records to have been issued should be traced to the accounts. If stock has been issued for property or assets other than cash, the minutes of the corporation should specify the authorized basis of the exchange.

The auditor cannot assume responsibility for determining that the stock issued is legally fully paid, but he should familiarize himself generally with provisions of the laws of the state in which the company is incorporated relating to the legal consideration for an issue of capital stock. Reference to requirements in issues of no par stock and the repurchase of the client's own stock are especially important. In many states, promissory notes or future services are not acceptable as payment or part payment for any issue of capital shares. If the auditor has any doubt as to the legality of the consideration for stock issued, he should ask the client to obtain opinion of counsel on the point. The balance sheet treatment of stock determined by counsel to be in fact not legally fully paid requires careful consideration.

When large corporations maintain their own transfer departments, the auditor may, as a part of his review of internal accounting control, make a surprise examination of this department. This examination may include a count of all securities on hand, checking of all transactions for a selected period, and examination of correspondence files.

OPTIONS AND WARRANTS.—The auditor should determine that transactions in options and warrants have been properly recorded, and that any exercise thereof has been in compliance with the terms of their issue.

TREASURY STOCK.—Certificates for shares reacquired and in the treasury should be examined and compared with entries in the treasury stock account. Treasury stock certificates should be in the name of the company, endorsed to the company, or accompanied by a properly executed power of attorney. If treasury stock is not in the possession of the corporation, confirmation should be requested from the custodian. Transactions in treasury stock should be examined for propriety of accounting treatment.

The legal steps in retiring shares held in the treasury may vary considerably with state laws, company charters, or by-laws. The auditor may wish to inquire from legal counsel whether proper steps have been taken and their effect on authorized and issuable stock.

FEDERAL STAMP TAXES ON ORIGINAL ISSUES OF CAPITAL STOCK. —The federal government and some states impose a stamp tax on original issues of stock, and the auditor should assure himself that the tax has been paid by noting that the proper stamps have been affixed to the certificate stubs. If the stock records are in charge of independent agents, reference may be made to cash records for assurance that original issue taxes have been paid.

RECORDS ON FILE IN PUBLIC OFFICES.—In most states it is possible to determine from public records the powers and purposes of a corporation, the kinds and amount of capital stock or obligations authorized for issue, the rights of the holders of the various kinds of securities, provisions for sinking funds, and redemption and conversion features of each issue. Records of the corporation should contain most of this information, but, if they do not, examination by counsel of official public records may be deemed necessary. As a general rule auditors are justified in relying on information of this type obtainable from the corporate records.

TREATMENT OF UNEXCHANGED CAPITAL STOCK IN RECAPITALIZATIONS.—When a corporation is recapitalized, new shares of a different par value or with different provisions are often exchanged for shares previously outstanding. After the final date for making the exchange or the expiration of the period during which the old shares may be traded on a security exchange, some of the old shares still may be outstanding. The auditor should examine the recapitalization plan and available data to determine that exchanges were made in accordance with the terms of the plan and that accounting was proper. He should satisfy himself as to the number of shares unexchanged after the final exchange date and see that proper reference is made to them in the financial statements.

Capital Surplus and Earned Surplus.—On an initial examination the auditor should analyze the surplus accounts from the beginning in order that he may determine whether all entries were in accordance with generally accepted accounting principles then prevailing. When examinations have been made previously by other independent certified public accountants of good repute, he may limit his procedures to a review of analyses made by previous auditors. The basis for the origin of such surplus accounts as Revaluation, or Donated Surplus, their authorizations, and amounts set up for consideration other than cash should be reviewed. Entries in these accounts should also be reviewed for consistency of treatment from year to year. The analyses of paid-in surplus and capital surplus should segregate balances by classes of stock outstanding. These analyses of surplus accounts should be retained in the auditor's permanent file of working papers so that current year changes may be readily reviewed for consistency in treatment.

In connection with the initial analyses of surplus accounts, the auditor may find it desirable to make a parallel analysis of accumulated earnings and profits as determined under Treasury Department regulations. Such an analysis provides information about the company's federal income tax experience which may be helpful currently in estimating the tax status of dividends. It should be retained in the permanent file of working papers and brought up to date each year.

All surplus reserves should be analyzed or reviewed. The creation of new reserves and changes in existing reserves should be checked to authorizations in the minutes of the board of directors' meetings. Entries in surplus reserve accounts should be checked for conformity with generally accepted accounting principles.

Minutes of the meetings of directors and stockholders should be examined for authorizations of transactions that have been or should be recorded in the surplus and surplus reserve accounts. For example, when capital surplus has been created or increased by reducing the par or stated value of outstanding capital stock, such action may require the approval of the stockholders and directors.

When subscribers to capital stock have not paid their subscriptions in full and part payments have been credited to paid-in surplus, the auditor should satisfy himself, usually by inquiry of counsel, that the corporation has a legal right to retain the amounts paid in.

Inquiry should be made concerning restrictions upon the surplus accounts; related indentures, loan agreements, stock provisions, etc., should be carefully reviewed in this connection. Computations of currently restricted amounts should be checked.

Dividends.—The auditor's procedures in the examination of dividend accounts should be designed to assure him that all declarations are authorized by the board of directors, that authorized amounts are paid on the designated dates to recorded stockholders, and that all distributions, cash or otherwise, are reflected in the accounts in accordance with generally accepted accounting principles. The auditor should be familiar with the type of problems which may arise with the declaration, recording, and payment of dividends and realize when advice of counsel should be obtained. One of the auditor's responsibilities is to arrive at an opinion whether the intentions of the board, as indicated in the resolutions authorizing the dividends, are properly reflected in the financial statements.

The minutes of meetings of the board of directors should contain formal declarations of dividends. In the absence of a formal declaration, distributions to stockholders should be examined, and, if the evidence indicates a dividend in fact, the auditor should recommend that the distribution be ratified at the next meeting of the board.

When the total amount to be paid as dividends is transferred to a disbursing agent, the auditor should substantiate the computation of the total and the transfer of funds. If the dividends are paid by the corporation, rather than by a disbursing agent, the auditor should determine that the aggregate of the amounts paid is correct; that is, that for each dividend the number of shares outstanding multiplied by the dividend rate specified in the minutes of the board meeting equals the total amount paid. If internal accounting control is not good, he may, in addition, check or test amounts paid to individual stockholders, by multiplying the shares owned of record by the dividend rate.

If the funds have been placed in a special bank account, the auditor may reconcile the account and determine that it is being used for no other payments. Sometimes a minimum balance is carried in such an account and this is usually grouped with general cash accounts. Cash procedures outlined in Chapter 8 are generally applicable to dividend disbursements.

The unclaimed dividend account including the accounting treatment of dividends unclaimed after expiration of the legal holding period, should be reviewed.

The auditor should familiarize himself with any of the corporation's agreements which may contain provisions relating to dividend policies. When a company legally pays dividends and charges them to paid-in surplus, and there exists a balance of earned surplus, the auditor should point out to the directors the objections to this practice and insist upon full disclosure in the financial statements.

When stock dividends are paid, the auditor should determine whether the accounting treatment has been proper and whether the statements disclose the amount of surplus capitalized, its source, and the number of shares issued.

The auditor should review preferred stock agreements. While he is entitled to a lay opinion as to whether the provisions have been complied with, questions of interpretation should be referred to counsel.

Holders of noncumulative preferred stocks ordinarily have no claim to dividends in a year when the amount of the dividends has not been earned, except possibly when dividends earned in a prior year have been improperly withheld. Dividends paid on common stocks may have encroached upon the rights of holders of noncumulative preferred stocks. If the auditor discovers such a situation, he should remind his client of the terms of the preferred stock issue and suggest that counsel be consulted about a possible liability to holders of noncumulative preferred stock.

When the price of stock sold has included accrued dividends, the auditor should satisfy himself that the accrued dividends have been correctly computed and that the accounting treatment has been proper.

When a dividend on common stock is payable in preferred shares, the auditor should determine, usually by inquiry of counsel, that the corporation has complied with requirements for the consent of holders of senior shares and with the various formalities for the issuance of new or additional preferred shares. He should determine as well that the capitalization of earned surplus is in accordance with generally accepted accounting principles.

If a dividend has been paid on preferred stock in common stock, the auditor should satisfy himself, usually by inquiry of counsel, that statutory requirements and provisions of the preferred stock agreement have been complied with and that the proper amount of earned surplus has been capitalized. When such a dividend is paid, due consideration to the relative interests of the different classes of stockholders requires that little discretion be allowed directors in determining the amount of earned surplus to be capitalized, especially when the preferred stock upon which the dividend is paid is cumulative or participating.

The auditor should determine whether proper procedures have been followed not only in accounting for regular distributions, but also in accounting for stock split-ups, dividends payable in scrip, and dividends payable in assets other than cash. In the distribution of a stock dividend or in a stock split-up, it is important to note whether the capital stock authorization is exceeded, and that consideration has been given to shares reserved for stock options or conversions of other issues.

Individual Proprietor's Capital.—In an individual proprietorship there will seldom be formal documents for capital paid in. The excess of assets over liabilities at any given date represents the proprietor's capital. Changes in capital between one audit date and another should be analyzed and substantiated. It is desirable to summarize the changes in capital between balance sheet dates in order that those interested may readily determine the results of operations as distinguished from capital contributions and withdrawals.

Partnership Capital.—As part of his examination of partnership financial statements, the auditor should read the partnership agreement. Ordinarily these agreements not only show the basis on which profits and losses shall be shared but also contain provisions for fixed amounts of capital to be maintained by the various partners, loans by partners in certain circumstances, interest on partners' capital and loans, limitations on withdrawals, and similar matters. The auditor should analyze and substantiate changes in partnership capital between statement dates, and report any failure to carry out provisions of the partnership agreement.

Some partnerships conduct business without written partnership agreements. In these circumstances the auditor should inquire whether the partners understand the bases on which the accounts are kept, particularly with respect to distributions of profits or losses and interest on partners' capital. It is good practice to ask that each partner sign the financial statements on which the partners' accounts appear or, as an alternative procedure, ask the partners to confirm the balances in their accounts.

If partners' withdrawals are made in currency, partners should approve their accounts as they appear in the ledger. The practice of permitting drawings of small amounts at frequent intervals without evidence of receipt is an invitation to dishonesty on the part of the cashier. Auditors should criticize this practice and suggest to partners that withdrawals be by check only and that personal bills be paid through personal bank accounts.

Capital of Nonbusiness Organizations.—For nonbusiness organizations the auditor should consider procedures similar to those previously discussed, where appropriate. The terms of donations or bequests are frequently of considerable importance and should be reviewed to determine that restrictions are being observed.

The auditor should review changes in capital between balance sheet dates and make such tests as appear advisable to assure himself that items whose disposition is specified in articles of organization or incorporation, stipulations in bequests, or resolutions by the trustees, directors, or members as embodied in the organization's minutes, have been disposed of in accordance with the specific provisions.

Time of Examination.—The auditor's examination of capital stock and surplus accounts cannot be completed until the close of the fiscal period under review. However, when these accounts are active, the auditor may make preliminary analyses and review the accounts prior to the end of the year, bringing his examination up to date after the close of the period.

STATEMENT PRESENTATION

Capital of Business Corporations.—It is important that capital be so stated that each stockholder and prospective investor may have a clear picture of the capital structure of the company.

TERMINOLOGY AND FORMAT.—The confusion resulting from the use of traditional accounting terms in the presentation of the capital section of a corporation has been discussed in the first part of this chapter. The elimination of this confusion requires the adoption of better terminology and a clearer format for this section of the balance sheet.

The Committee on Terminology (Accounting Terminology Bulletin No. 1) has recommended that:

(1) The use of the term *surplus* (whether standing alone or in such combination as *capital surplus, paid-in surplus, earned surplus, appraisal surplus,* etc.) be discontinued.

(2) The contributed portion of proprietary capital be shown as:

(a) Capital contributed for, or assigned to, shares, to the extent of the par or stated value of each class of shares presently outstanding.

(b) (i) Capital contributed for, or assigned to, shares in excess of such par or stated value (whether as a result of original issue of shares at amounts in excess of their then par or stated value, or of a reduction in par or stated value of shares after issuance, or of transactions by the corporation in its own shares); and

(ii) Capital received other than for shares, whether from shareholders or from others.

(3) The term *earned surplus* be replaced by terms which will indicate source, such as *retained income, retained earnings, accumulated earnings,* or *earnings retained for use in the business.* In the case of a deficit, the amount should be shown as a deduction from contributed capital with appropriate description.

(4) In connection with 2(b) and 3 there should, so far as practicable, be an indication of the extent to which the amounts have been appropriated or are restricted as to withdrawal. Retained income appropriated to some specific purpose nevertheless remains part of retained income, and any so-called "reserves" which are clearly appropriations or segregations of retained income, such as those for

general contingencies, possible future inventory losses, sinking fund, etc., should be included as part of the stockholders' equity.

(5) Where there has been a quasi-reorganization, retained income should be "dated" for a reasonable time thereafter; and where the amount of retained income has been reduced as a result of a stock dividend or a transfer by resolution of the board of directors from unrestricted to restricted capital, the presentation should, until the fact loses significance, indicate that the amount shown as retained income is the remainder after such transfers.

(6) Any appreciation included in the stockholders' equity other than as a result of a quasi-reorganization should be designated by such terms as *excess of appraised or fair value of fixed assets over cost* or *appreciation of fixed assets.*

In the same bulletin the committee concluded that the use of the term "reserve" should be restricted to the designation of surplus reserves and that other terms such as *less estimated losses in collection, less accrued depreciation,* and *estimated liabilities* be used for other types of items sometimes called reserves. However, it would appear that the use of an expression such as "retained earnings appropriated for contingencies" rather than "reserve" would be more consistent with the recommendation that the expression "earned surplus" be avoided.

It should be noted that the recommendations of the terminology bulletins are considered as desirable objectives by the American Institute but they are not issued as formal pronouncements by the Committee on Accounting Procedure. Many corporations have adopted terminology similar to that recommended. This chapter has previously discussed the elements of capital in these broad areas: capital stock, capital surplus, and earned surplus. The authors believe that the reader is capable of making the required substitution of terms when confronted with the task of statement presentation. Basically, the format should be as follows:

CAPITAL (OR STOCKHOLDERS' EQUITY)

Contributed or paid-in capital:			
Capital stock (at par or stated values)	$xxxx		
Capital paid in or contributed in excess of par or stated values, including amounts assigned to shares issued as stock dividends	xxxx	$xxxx	
Appreciation of fixed assets (revaluation or appraisal surplus)		xxxx	
Retained earnings:			
Appropriated for (indicate purposes)	xxxx		
Unappropriated, less amounts (indicate dollars) capitalized in the form of stock dividends	xxxx	xxxx	$xxxx

Any presentation which adds capital surplus to earned surplus, to indicate a total surplus, is undesirable, particularly when capital surplus includes paid-in capital. While such inclusion is in accord with the legal concept of surplus in many states, this concept should not influence the accounting presentation. When capital surplus arises from different sources, it should be classified accordingly.

An alternative presentation would be to show as capital stock the full amount contributed by stockholders with a parenthetical notation of the amount of legal capital.

CAPITAL STOCK.—If there is more than one issue of stock, the several classes should be stated in the order of the priority of their rights in liquidation, which is usually the same as the order of priority in participation in earnings. Under this standard, preferred stock is usually stated first. The description of each issue of stock should include its legal title; whether it is par or no par value stock and the par value per share or, if no par value, the stated or assigned value per share, if any; the number of shares authorized; the number and aggregate dollar amount of shares issued and outstanding; and, if preferred stock, the nature of the preference, the dividend rate, whether cumulative or non-cumulative and, in circumstances discussed below, the redemption and liquidation amounts. The amount assigned to capital stock, regardless of class, may include amounts paid in excess of par or stated value. If shares of any class of stock are reserved for issue on conversion of other classes of stocks or of bonds, the number of shares so reserved should be indicated in the description of the issue reserved or in a note to the balance sheet.

No par value stock is variously stated on balance sheets. If no stated value per share has been assigned, the aggregate net proceeds from each class issued are usually indicated. State laws may require that a minimum value be ascribed to no par value shares. However, this is only a minimum value; if the corporation has designated a higher value, the higher amount should be included in the balance sheet.

Many stock agreements contain restrictive and preference provisions. The balance sheet should describe adequately the various classes of stock so that owners of junior securities may ascertain the existence of prior liens in dividend distributions, redemptions, and liquidation. Frequently, these disclosures are provided in footnotes.

Redemption or Liquidating Prices Above Par or Stated Values.— When redemption or liquidating prices of preference stocks are above their par or stated values, the facts should be clearly set forth in order that holders of junior shares may realize the extent to which surplus will be reduced if senior issues are retired or the company is liquidated. It is good practice to indicate in dollars the aggregate excess of involuntary liquidation price of preference stock over par or stated value.

The Securities and Exchange Commission's Regulation S-X, Rule 3.19, requires that, if "the excess involved is material there shall be shown (i) the difference between the aggregate preference on involuntary liquidation and the aggregate par or stated value; (ii) a statement that this difference, plus any arrears in dividends, exceeds the sum of the par or stated value of the junior capital shares and the surplus, if such is the case; and (iii) a statement as to the existence, or absence, of any restrictions upon surplus growing out of the fact that upon involuntary liquidation the preference of the preferred shares exceeds its par or stated value." As administrative policy the Commission has also required, when the excess involved is significant, an opinion of counsel as to whether there are any restrictions upon surplus by reason of these differences and also as to any remedies available to stockholders before or after the payment of any dividend that reduces surplus to an amount less than that by which the aggregate preference of such stock on involuntary liquidation exceeds its aggregate par or stated value.

Many companies show no par preferred stock on the balance sheet at the amount of preference in liquidation, rather than at a lower amount paid in, or at a lower legal stated value. The difference should have been charged either to paid-in surplus or to earned surplus, as permitted by the accounting principles described earlier in this chapter. One alleged advantage of stating no par preferred stock at the amount of preference in liquidation is that it simplifies the evaluation of common stock since all other capital, except that which may be applicable to unpaid cumulative dividends on preferred stock, is then identified with the common stock. Another advantage claimed is that it obviates the possibility of surplus being reduced by dividend declarations below the amount required to preserve the liquidation value of the preferred stock. If the client wishes to state no par preferred stock on the balance sheet at the amount of preference in liquidation and this is permitted by the statutes of the state in which the company is incorporated, the auditor can offer no objection providing the basis is adequately disclosed.

Some preferred issues require periodic redemption of amounts based on excess earnings determined in accordance with a prescribed formula or based upon other terms of the charter. Amounts equal to the redemption amount of preferred stock which must be so redeemed within the next fiscal year should preferably be deducted from the capital section and shown among the current liabilities.

Subscriptions to Capital Stock.—When subscriptions to capital stock have been taken, and the stock is to be issued only when the subscription price has been fully paid by the subscriber, the liability to issue such stock should be separately stated in the capital section of the balance sheet. The capital section of the balance sheet should indicate the aggregate amount to be received for the stock to be issued and the number of shares to be issued.

When a subscriber has the right to cancel his subscription and to have refunded the amounts paid in, it is preferable to state the subscriptions at the amounts paid in, described as common (preferred) stock instalments, and disclose the number of shares subscribed, aggregate subscription price, and other pertinent provisions of the plan.

Discount on Capital Stock.—Discount on capital stock other than preference shares generally should be deducted from the capital stock to which it relates; it may be deducted from the total of capital stock and surplus. If part of a class of stock is sold at a discount and the balance at a premium, discount and premium may be offset.

When the discount applies to preference shares, it is good practice to show it as a deduction from paid-in surplus arising from other sales of the same issue (or from issues no longer outstanding) or from earned surplus. There is no logical basis for writing off the discount periodically by charges to income.

Unexchanged Stock in Recapitalization.—No hard and fast rule can be laid down for the presentation in the balance sheet of the unexchanged capital stock after the date of recapitalization. Usually the new capital stock should be shown as though all the old shares had been exchanged, with an explanatory statement either in the body of the balance sheet or as a footnote indicating the number of old shares still outstanding which for balance sheet purposes are assumed to have been exchanged and the basis upon which the exchange will be made upon receipt of the old certificates. Disclosure should be made of any dissents entered by stockholders who disapprove the merger or consolidation plans and who have applied to the courts for an appraisal of stock values, as provided by state statutes. The capitalization should not reflect the exchange of the shares held by dissenting stockholders.

Subordinated Indebtedness Treated as Capital.—Corporations sometimes issue long-term debentures with provisions subordinating them to other corporate obligations, including general creditors. These are frequently issued to stockholders who may be willing to accept a subordinate position. In some instances, the interest on the debentures is payable only if earned and is noncumulative. If only common stock is outstanding, these debentures, on liquidation of the company, have substantially the standing of preferred stock.

Debentures of this type are sometimes classified with capital rather than as liabilities. Ordinarily there should be no objection to such presentation if full disclosure is made. On a balance sheet illustrative of this treatment, the capital section is headed "Capital and subordinated debentures" and the debentures, listed first, are described as:

Twenty-year 6% Debentures, due August 1, 19—, redeemable in whole or in part at the option of the corporation on 90 days' written notice at par and accrued interest but subordinate, in the event of liquidation, in every respect to claims of creditors.

Stock Warrants and Options.—Terms of stock warrants and options granted should be adequately disclosed on the balance sheet, so that stockholders may know to what extent potential purchasers have options on stock which otherwise would be available for sale or issue. When option rights have been issued to officers and employees as compensation for services but have not been satisfied as yet by the issuance of shares, an amount equivalent to such compensation, to the extent it can be measured, should be shown in the capital section of the balance sheet in a manner similar to that for proceeds from subscriptions for capital stock. As the options are exercised, this amount will be relieved by transfer of appropriate amounts to a capital stock account and, possibly, to a paid-in surplus account, adequately described.

As to disclosure in financial statements with respect to stock option plans, Accounting Research Bulletin No. 43, Chapter 13, Section B, states:

In connection with financial statements, disclosure should be made as to the status of the option or plan at the end of the period of report, including the number of shares under option, the option price, and the number of shares as to which options were exercisable. As to options exercised during the period, disclosure should be made of the number of shares involved and the option price thereof.

Regulation S-X of the Securities and Exchange Commission requires the following disclosures in connection with stock options:

Rule 3.20 (d) *Capital Stock Optioned to Officers and Employees.*

(1) A brief description of the terms of each option arrangement shall be given, including (i) the title and amount of securities subject to option; (ii) the year or years during which the options were granted; and (iii) the year or years during which the optionees became, or will become, entitled to exercise the options.

(2) State (a) the number of shares under option at the balance sheet date, and the option price and the fair value thereof, per share and in total, at the dates the options were granted; (b) the number of shares with respect to which options became exercisable during the period, and the option price and the fair value thereof, per share and

in total, at the dates the options became exercisable; and (c) the number of shares with respect to which options were exercised during the period, and the option price and the fair value thereof, per share and in total, at the dates the options were exercised. The required information may be summarized as appropriate with respect to each of these categories.

(3) State the basis of accounting for such option arrangements and the amount of charges, if any, reflected in income with respect thereto.

(Note: Period, as used in the above context, denotes the period or periods for which income statements are furnished.)

The New York Stock Exchange revised its requirements for listing in September, 1956, with respect to the information required to be disclosed in annual reports to stockholders relating to the operation of a stock option plan, as follows:

The Corporation will disclose in its annual report to shareholders, for the year covered by the report, (1) the number of shares of its stock issuable under outstanding options at the beginning of the year; separate totals of changes in the number of shares of its stock under option resulting from issuance, exercise, expiration or cancellation of options; and the number of shares issuable under outstanding options at the close of the year, (2) the number of unoptioned shares available at the beginning and at the close of the year for the granting of options under an option plan, and (3) any changes in the exercise price of outstanding options, through cancellation and reissuance or otherwise, except price changes resulting from the normal operation of anti-dilution provisions of the options.

Treasury Stock.—The balance sheet should indicate the number of shares of stock held in the treasury and describe the issue. Treasury stock is usually deducted from total capital, at cost; but if it has been acquired for the specific purpose of resale to employees or others, it is permissible to show it separately on the asset side of the balance sheet, at cost, provided the reason for the treatment is disclosed in the balance sheet or in a note thereto.

The laws of many states provide that treasury stock may be purchased only when the purchase does not impair legal capital; in some states surplus available for payment of dividends or other purposes is restricted in the amount of the cost of treasury stock. Such restriction should be disclosed in a note to the financial statements.

When treasury stock is legally retired and canceled, the number of authorized shares is usually reduced accordingly. Retirement without cancellation does not reduce the authorization in some states, unless surplus has been reduced by the cost of treasury stock.

Formerly it was not uncommon to show treasury stock "as if" it were retired; the par or stated amount of treasury stock was deducted from capital stock, and the appropriate surplus accounts were adjusted for the difference between cost and par or stated value. In most states, this procedure reflected the situation as it would have been if the legal steps necessary for retirement of treasury stock had actually been taken. Serious objections to this method are that it implies a future retirement which may not take place, and does not indicate the possible effect on surplus of the restrictions arising from acquisition of treasury stock; therefore, it is not now considered the best practice.

Legal considerations have substantial weight in determining the proper display of treasury stock in the financial statements. The auditor should have some familiarity with the state laws concerning the accounting for and presentation of treasury stock and consult with legal counsel when necessary.

Some corporations have sold substantial blocks of stock prior to the close of the fiscal year under an agreement to repurchase the stock at the same price shortly after the beginning of the new period. This procedure may be simply a form of window dressing or the agreement may be so worded to protect the purchaser from loss on resale of the stock. In any event, commitments to repurchase a company's stock or to protect the purchaser from the effects of a falling market should be disclosed on the balance sheet.

SURPLUS.—Problems inherent in the presentation of the various classes of capital and surplus have been discussed previously in this chapter.

Corporations with long and complex financial histories may find it difficult to segregate surplus by sources and therefore may indicate surplus in one amount. If surplus is indicated in one amount, it is desirable to disclose in a note to the financial statements the reasons therefor and any known circumstances of its origin. Usually, however, it is possible to distinguish between undistributed profits (earned surplus) and surplus arising from other sources.

Regulation S-X, Rule 5.02, of the Securities and Exchange Commission, for statements filed with it under the Acts it administers, provides for commercial and industrial companies:

Surplus.—(a) Separate captions shall be shown for (1) paid-in surplus; (2) surplus arising from revaluation of assets; (3) other capital surplus; and (4) earned surplus (i) appropriated and (ii) unappropriated.

(b) If undistributed earnings of subsidiaries are included, state the amount thereof parenthetically or otherwise. However, in a consolidated statement the preceding sentence shall have reference only to the undistributed earnings of subsidiaries not consolidated in such statement.

(c) Subsequent to the effective date of a quasi-reorganization any description of earned surplus shall indicate the point of time from which the new earned surplus dates and for a period of at least three years shall indicate the total amount of the deficit eliminated.

(d) An analysis of each surplus account setting forth the information prescribed in Rule 11.02 shall be given for each period for which a profit and loss statement is filed, as a continuation of the related profit and loss statement or in the form of a separate statement of surplus, and shall be referred to here.

CAPITAL SURPLUS.—The various forms of capital surplus have been discussed previously in this chapter. It is desirable that each of them be separately stated in the balance sheet. When no one form of paid-in surplus is particularly significant, it is permissible to combine such amounts as shown in the model format previously illustrated. However, so-called capital surplus arising from sources other than contribution or paid in, such as from an appreciation or appraisal, or from excess of book amount of subsidiary company net assets over cost of investment therein, should be separately stated if material in amount.

EARNED SURPLUS.—Restrictions on earned surplus should be indicated in a footnote or in a parenthetical notation. Restrictions imposed by bond indentures, state laws, or charter provisions are examples of those which should be disclosed. Frequently bond indentures include restrictions not only on the payment of dividends but also on the use of assets for the purchase of capital stock. The amount of earned surplus free of these restrictions may be indicated, or the amount restricted may be given. When provisions of these agreements are not presently operative, but are likely to result in a material restriction in the immediate future, a disclosure of the future applicability of the provisions is desirable.

Restrictions upon the payment of dividends or stock purchases may be based upon the availability of earnings accumulated subsequent to a specified date, upon the corporation's ability to observe certain working capital requirements, or upon other considerations. When agreements impose more than one type of limitation, or when several issues are outstanding containing different provisions, disclosure may be made on the basis of the most restrictive covenants likely to be effective in the immediate future. When alternative restrictions are nearly equally restrictive, reference should be made not only to the covenant currently operative but also to other types of restrictions imposed by the indenture. A note similar to the following would be appropriate:

The Company's loan indenture restricts the payments of dividends (other than stock dividends) and payments for reacquisition of capital stock to the lesser of (1) the amount of earnings accumulated since December 31, 19___, which at December 31, 19___ amounted to $3,000,000 or (2) an amount which will not reduce working capital to less than $10,000,000; at December 31, 19___, working capital, as defined in the indenture, amounted to $14,000,000.

The subject of quasi-reorganizations with a resulting dating of earned surplus has been discussed on page 396. Accounting Research Bulletin No. 46 states that:

> The committee believes that the dating of earned surplus following a quasi-reorganization would rarely, if ever, be of significance after a period of ten years. It also believes that there may be exceptional circumstances in which the discontinuance of the dating of earned surplus could be justified at the conclusion of a period less than ten years.

There is some indication that the Securities and Exchange Commission shares the views expressed in this bulletin but the Commission reserves the right to consider a period of time other than ten years as appropriate for continuing dating of such surplus.

Earned Surplus Appropriations.—Terms of bond indentures, preferred stock agreements, or other contractual obligations often make mandatory the segregation from surplus of amounts otherwise available for dividends. Occasionally, amounts are voluntarily segregated from free surplus by action of a corporation's board of directors. Whether the segregation is voluntary or involuntary, it results in appropriated or allocated surplus; as previously outlined in this chapter, the mere allocation of surplus does not alter its essential character. It remains surplus subject to such restrictions as may be imposed by the conditions which dictated its segregation. If the auditor's examination discloses that there has been or should have been an allocation of surplus, before he submits his opinion on the balance sheet he should determine that the allocation has been properly authorized and make sure that the appropriation is adequately described in the balance sheet. Adequate description ordinarily includes recitation of the purpose of the appropriation.

It is permissible to characterize the appropriation as a reserve, but the term "reserve" does not, by itself, constitute an adequate description since it does not indicate the purpose of the appropriation. The inclusion of the term "reserve" in the description should serve notice on readers of the balance sheet that the amount to which it applies is appropriated surplus, but the frequent misuse of the word makes it inadvisable to presume that its implications will be clear to readers of the statement. There may be many surplus reserves and generally they immediately precede unappropriated earned surplus on the balance sheet.

SURPLUS STATEMENTS.—Balance sheets may contain analyses of each class of surplus showing a summary of the changes during the year. If the changes are too numerous to be clearly explained on the face of the balance sheet, the details may be presented as a continuation of the statement of income (if unappropriated earned surplus) or in a supplemental statement of surplus.

Surplus statements should contain full explanations of changes in all classes of capital surplus and earned surplus, including surplus reserves. In the interest of statement simplification, minor changes in surpluses other than unappropriated earned surplus are frequently disclosed in footnotes.

Occasionally, an auditor is requested to submit an opinion upon the balance sheet alone. While it is desirable to furnish income and surplus statements with balance sheets, it is permissible for the auditor to express an opinion upon the balance sheet alone. It is not essential that an analysis of surplus be given in such instances. The authors' views on this point have been presented in Chapter 7.

DIVIDENDS.—Dividends paid or declared are usually shown in the analysis of surplus, whether it be in the surplus section of the balance sheet, a continuation of the income statement, or a separate surplus statement. It is customary to indicate the total dividend for each class of stock, the medium of payment if other than cash, and if the dividends were paid in whole or in part out of surplus other than earned to so indicate. Ordinarily, the amount or rate per share is indicated; Regulation S-X (Rule 11.02) of the Securities and Exchange Commission requires that per share amounts be given and that the medium of payment be expressly stated.

Since there are many variations in the requirements of corporate agreements and state legislation, a company may legally declare dividends out of a source other than earnings which, because of the absence of accompanying explanatory comment, may be misinterpreted by uninformed stockholders as distributions of earnings. The auditor should suggest adequate disclosure of the circumstances and source of such dividends; if such disclosure is not made, he should state an exception in his report.

When a liquidating dividend has been declared and all the legal steps taken requisite to the reduction of the stock, but the payments to stockholders have not been made, the balance sheet should show the outstanding stock at its reduced amount and the liquidating dividend as a current liability, adequately described.

When dividends are paid in property, the value of which may be a matter of opinion or may have been determined arbitrarily, it is good procedure to indicate in the financial statements the basis used by the board of directors in determining the dollar value of the property distributed.

Dividends declared but unpaid at the balance sheet date are deducted from surplus and included among the current liabilities. Stock dividends declared but unissued at the balance sheet date are not shown among the liabilities; the amount to be capitalized may be shown as a separate classification in the capital section with an indication of the number of shares to be issued. When the shares are issued shortly after the balance sheet date and the statements are released some time thereafter, the balance sheet may give effect to the issuance of the shares, with appropriate explanation. It is permissible, however, not to reflect any change in the balance sheet as a result of the declaration, other than to disclose by footnote the nature of the declaration and the amount of surplus to be capitalized.

The balance sheet may reflect stock split-ups accomplished shortly after the balance sheet date, provided adequate explanations are given.

Dividends in Arrears.—When unpaid dividends on preferred stock have accumulated, the amount unpaid, or the date since which unpaid dividends have accumulated, should be disclosed in the balance sheet. The Securities and Exchange Commission Regulation S-X, Rule 3.19, requires that "arrears in cumulative dividends per share and in total for each class of shares shall be stated." This information may be indicated in a parenthetical note in the description of the preferred stock or in a note to the balance sheet.

Capital of Business Partnerships.—In a partnership, the balance sheet may show a summary of the changes in each partner's capital since the date of the previous statement or a summary of the changes in the combined capital; changes within the period in the capital of each partner, including contributions, withdrawals, share of current profits or losses, interest credits or charges, and salary allowances should be shown in detail in a supplementary statement.

Capital of Nonbusiness Organizations.—Capital of nonbusiness organizations is frequently stated on the balance sheet under headings sufficiently descriptive to indicate general restrictions of their use. Such capital may be stated as current funds, plant funds, or endowment funds, or in other classifications as indicated by restrictions on the accounts. Capital changes during the period should be disclosed, either on the balance sheet or in a separate summary. The balance at the beginning of the period, changes during the period, the sources of additions, the nature of distributions, and the allocation of the balance at the date of the financial statements should all be shown.

CHAPTER 20

REVENUE, COSTS, AND EXPENSES

433

Introduction.—In Chapter 7, it is emphasized that the statement of income is historical and not prophetic, although it should reveal as far as possible the earning power of the enterprise; informative classification, description, and annotation of both the balance sheet and the statement of income are helpful in attaining this objective.

Historically, the income statement has been and to some extent still is influenced by accounting principles followed in preparation of the balance sheet. Principles of valuation applied to current assets, policies adopted in the capitalization and depreciation of plant, and methods of recognizing liabilities, all have their effect on the income statement and thus on surplus. In recent years emphasis has been placed on accounting principles that produce the fairest determination of income, with consequent effect on the balance sheet, thus recognizing the reversal of the former relative importance attributed to these statements.

Accounting Terminology Bulletin No. 2, March, 1955, discusses the use of the terms "revenue," "income," "profit," and "earnings." The Committee on Terminology recommends that the word "revenue" be used to include net sales, net gains on sale of assets other than stock in trade, interest and dividends earned, and other increases in the owner's equity except those arising from capital contributions and capital adjustments. Frequently the term "gross income" is used as the equivalent of "revenue," but the committee recommends that this usage be avoided.

The words "income" and "profit" may be misleading unless preceded by a qualifying adjective, except when used as the title of a statement showing the results of operation, as in "income statement." Otherwise, qualifying adjectives such as "gross" or "net" should be used. "Gross profit," or preferably "gross profit on sales" or "gross margin," describes the excess of operating revenue over cost of goods sold. The term "net income" or "earnings" refers to the results of operations after deducting from revenues all related costs and expenses and all other charges and losses assigned to the period, excluding dividends or comparable withdrawals.

ACCOUNTING PRINCIPLES

General.—In general, net income for any period should reflect all items of profit and loss recognized during the period, including corrections of estimates of prior years' income, except extraordinary items when their inclusion would materially impair the significance of net income (see Chapter 7 and Accounting Research Bulletin No. 43, Chapter 8).

The doctrine of conservatism when applied to the income statement requires that income be recognized only after realization in cash or its substantial equivalent and that provision be made not only for incurred but also for probable costs, expenses, and losses which may be related to the period ended on the balance sheet date. Sound judgment is required in the application of this doctrine, since it is susceptible of abuse. Conservatism in the deferment or capitalization of expenditures requires that borderline items be charged off currently.

Revenue—Sales of Products.—Sales represent the revenue received or receivable from the transfer of inventories to customers in the ordinary course of business and usually involve physical delivery and passage of title. Revenue from sales of services and of allied commodities may be included under this caption; occasional sales of property other than inventories ordinarily should not be included with sales, and the related profit or loss should be accounted for as other income or other charges.

RETURNS, ALLOWANCES, AND DISCOUNTS.—Returns represent cancellations of previous sales and usually involve return of merchandise. Allowances comprise credits to customers to adjust for errors in pricing, shipments of the wrong merchandise, defects in quality, shortages in shipments, and the like. Selling prices are frequently quoted gross, and discounts allowed generally fall into three classifications: quantity discounts, which vary as the name implies with the quantities purchased; trade discounts, which depend upon the classification of the customer as manufacturer, wholesaler, or retailer; and cash discounts, which are allowed for prompt payment, usually at the rate of 2 per cent or less. The absorption of freight charges or taxes by a seller is often considered to be an allowance or a discount. Accounts for sales are customarily maintained to show separately the gross selling price and the various reductions for returns, allowances, and discounts; cash discounts are sometimes accounted for as other deductions rather than as a reduction of sales.

Provision should be made in the accounts, at least at the year end, for material amounts of returns, allowances, and discounts which can reasonably be expected to result from past sales; even though the amount of credits to be allowed may be disputed, a provision can usually be determined with reasonable accuracy in the light of past experience.

CASH SALES.—When merchandise is sold for cash, questions as to timing the accounting recognition of income are minimized; however, cash received in advance of the delivery of merchandise or services ordinarily should be credited to a liability or deferred income account and taken into income when the sale is consummated by the delivery of merchandise or performance of services. See page 328 for discussion of department store accounting for "will call" and "lay away" sales.

CONSIGNMENT SALES.—Shipments of merchandise on consignment or any similar basis should not be recorded as sales until the merchandise has been sold by the consignee, at which time commission expense is also recorded by the consignor.

C.O.D. SALES.—While title to shipments under collect-on-delivery terms remains with the seller until the merchandise has been delivered to the purchaser and paid for by him, such shipments may be recognized as sales either when shipped or after collection from the purchaser. If a sale is recorded when the merchandise is shipped, the collectibility of the related receivable must be considered. Department stores and other retail organizations usually account for C.O.D. shipments as sales since this method facilitates merchandise control under a perpetual inventory system.

INSTALMENT SALES.—Automobiles and large household appliances have been sold on the instalment basis for some years; more recently the practice has been extended to include practically all consumer goods. Instalment financing may range from plans whereby the seller carries the instalment paper himself to plans under which a bank or finance company takes over the receivables without recourse, relieving the seller of further financial risk. Instalment sales commonly involve retention of protective title under a conditional sale, chattel mortgage, or some similar arrangement depending on the laws of the state in which the merchandise is sold. Additional charges to the purchaser may include interest, service fees, and insurance.

Instalment sales should generally be accounted for on the same basis as other sales. While the collection risk on instalment sales is usually greater than that on other sales, this risk may be met by appropriate allowances, and it does not justify reporting revenue in a later period. Under the instalment method, which is rarely used, sales and gross profit on sales are reported as collections are made. The Treasury Department permits use of the instalment method for tax purposes under certain circumstances, and its use may substantially defer payment of income taxes, even though the books are kept on the conventional accrual basis. The portion of revenue representing charges for financing and servicing is properly deferred and taken up as income over the period of collection and servicing, respectively. Chapter 22 discusses the problem of tax allocation in these circumstances.

Long-Term Contracts.—Accounting Research Bulletin No. 45 discusses long-term contracts. When completion of construction or other types of contracts requires a long period of time, income may be recognized under the percentage-of-completion method or under the completed-contract method. Under the former, as work progresses, sales and gross profits are reported in instalments based on estimates of costs incurred or work completed. Since considerations other than those acceptable as a basis for the recognition of income frequently enter into the determination of the timing and the amounts of interim billings on these contracts, progress billings are not usually an acceptable basis for reporting. Recognition of sales and income only when the contract is substantially completed, under the completed-contract method, may be preferable when lack of dependable estimates or inherent hazards cause forecasts to be unreliable.

Export Sales.—Sales to customers in foreign countries are usually recorded when shipments are made. Occasionally, when the customer has difficulty in obtaining United States dollars for payments, the seller may retain title to the merchandise under an arrangement, such as a sight draft with bill of lading attached, and account for such shipments as sales when collection is made.

Intracompany and Intercompany Sales.—Frequently transfers of semifinished and finished products from one department or plant to another are recorded as sales at current market prices. In some businesses there may be several distinct stages in the manufacturing process between raw materials and finished stock. Competing businesses may have one or more of these identical stages and what is a finished product for one company may be a raw material for another. For instance, one steel company may mine ore and manufacture pig iron whereas another may purchase pig iron as a raw material. Thus a primary purpose of accounting for transfers of products within a company as sales is to show the departmental results on an independent basis. These sales should be segregated in the accounts to facilitate their elimination in the income statement and the elimination of the unrealized profit from inventories.

Sales between affiliated companies are usually recorded at current market prices so that each company can produce financial statements on an independent basis; intercompany sales should be segregated in the accounts to facilitate their elimination and the elimination of intercompany profits from inventories in consolidated financial statements. See Chapter 21.

BY-PRODUCT SALES.—Some manufacturing processes yield a primary product and a by-product. If the by-product is relatively unimportant, proceeds from its sale are usually applied as a reduction of the manufacturing cost of the primary product. If the by-product is important, sales may be treated similarly to those of the primary product.

SALES OF SCRAP.—Almost every manufacturing process produces a certain amount of scrap material. The scrap is generally accumulated, sometimes sorted, and held for sale to a scrap dealer or to some other manufacturer. Proceeds from the disposition of scrap are usually applied as a reduction of manufacturing cost.

Revenue—Sales of Services.—Revenue from the sales of services is generally recorded as income in the period in which the service is rendered. Services may be sold by public utilities or by companies principally in the business of renting equipment or selling periodicals, technical services, or entertainment. Public utilities sell transportation by railroad, air, bus, truck, boat, or over a toll bridge, or furnish electric power, water, gas, steam, telephone, or telegraph service. Governmental regulatory bodies prescribe uniform systems of accounts for these utilities. Other enterprises that sell services usually record receipts as deferred income and record revenue only when the service is rendered or the commodity delivered. However, when receipts in advance are regular and recurring, such as those from ticket sales, it is generally considered permissible to record income at the time of receipt.

Other Income.—Other income includes income from sources outside the normal operations of the enterprise. Thus, dividends are usually classified as other income except when, as in an investment company, they are one of the principal sources of income.

CASH DISCOUNTS ON PURCHASES.—As stated previously, cash discounts on purchases are preferably considered a reduction of invoice price or cost of sales, although sometimes they are treated as other income.

DIVIDENDS.—Cash dividends, with the exceptions discussed below, constitute income and are usually recognized as such in the accounts on the ex-dividend or record date. Dividends are infrequently paid in property, and, when they are, they usually represent income in the amount of the property's fair market value.

Some of the recognized exceptions to the treatment of dividends as income are as follows:

1. Dividends paid from surplus of a subsidiary earned prior to acquisition of control by the parent are not income to the parent; after a reduction for applicable income taxes, they usually should be credited to the parent's investment in the subsidiary. This treatment may be extended to dividends from companies other than subsidiaries, particularly when a large dividend was clearly earned prior to acquisition of the investment.

2. Dividends on a company's stock held in its treasury are not income; they should be treated as a reduction of dividends paid.

3. Dividends in common stock of the paying company to its common stockholders should not be treated as income by the recipient.

4. Dividends in liquidation or from surplus other than earned surplus should rarely be treated as income.

Laws of the various states governing probate accounting and federal and state income tax laws may require accounting for dividends that varies from that indicated by generally accepted accounting principles.

INTEREST.—Interest received regularly from solvent debtors is usually accrued currently in the accounts. Interest should not be accrued when it is not being received regularly, or when there is some doubt as to its receipt. When investments include a substantial amount of bonds purchased at a premium, the premium is frequently amortized over the period to the earliest call date or maturity. Discount on bonds may be similarly amortized, but this practice is less frequent. Discount on speculative bonds should not be amortized when its eventual realization is uncertain.

RENTS.—Rents are received for the use of real or personal property, and ordinarily they should be recorded as income as they accrue. Rents received in advance should usually be deferred for inclusion in income in the appropriate accounting period. Rents are generally classified as other income except when, as in a real estate company, they are one of the principal sources of income.

ROYALTIES.—Royalties are usually based on agreements for the use by others of patents, copyrights, secret processes, and the like or for the extraction of natural resources. They should be taken into income in the period in which earned.

PROFITS ON SALES OF SECURITIES AND FIXED ASSETS.—When the entire holding of an issue of securities is sold, there is no problem of apportioning the total cost. However, if a holder of securities sells only a portion of his holding of an issue, the cost of the holding must be apportioned to determine the cost of the securities sold. In apportioning cost, the first-in first-out or average cost bases are preferable to specific identification since they offer less possibility of arbitrarily increasing or decreasing reported profits. For federal income tax purposes, if specific cost of securities sold cannot be identified, the first-in first-out method of costing sales should be used.

Accounting for profits on sales of fixed assets is largely affected by the related depreciation methods. If the composite life method is used, no profit or loss is recognized unless it involves the disposition of an entire group or a major unit. Profits on the sale of fixed assets should not be recorded until title has passed or until receipt of the sales price is certain.

Cost of Sales.—In general, cost of sales includes all direct and factory indirect costs of purchase and production of goods sold. The cost of sales of many manufacturing companies represents cost of production adjusted by opening and closing inventories; it usually includes such items as write-down of inventories to market, royalties paid for the right to manufacture and for use of patented equipment, amortization of preproduction and tooling costs, and services and other costs under product warranties, and is reduced by sales of relatively unimportant by-products and scrap.

Operating Expenses.—This designation is used for costs and expenses applicable to the production of revenue from sales of services. In a public utility they consist of direct production and distribution costs of the service or commodity furnished—such indirect costs as depreciation, maintenance and repairs, property, and other operating taxes; cost of service departments; income taxes; and those expenses classified in a manufacturing company as selling, general, and administrative.

Depreciation and Amortization; Maintenance and Repairs.—Chapter 13 is devoted to the various methods of recognizing in the accounts the depreciation or amortization of plant and property over its useful life as well as the methods of accounting for related expenses of maintenance and repairs. Chapter 12 discusses the capitalization of expenditures for property, plant, and equipment. Chapter 14 describes the methods of amortizing intangible assets and discusses the capitalization of related expenditures.

Experimental and Development Expenses.—Continued experimental and development expenses are characteristic of many industries, and they are necessary if products are to be improved or production costs reduced. Although these expenditures generally relate not to current but to future production, they are usually charged off as incurred. Deferment of these expenditures is permissible if (1) future periods, rather than the current period, will benefit from them and (2) continuing value at least equal to the amount deferred is reasonably assured. The considerations against deferment, which are usually more persuasive, are that future benefits may be intangible and impossible to measure, the length of the future period which may be benefited is usually impossible to determine, and the continuing value of the expenses may be uncertain. As more fully discussed in Chapter 22, with respect to experimental and research expenses, taxpayers may adopt either the current write-off or amortization basis for federal income tax purposes.

Selling, General, and Administrative Expenses.—This group of expenses represents costs of selling the product and administering the enterprise. Selling expenses include salesmen's salaries, commissions, and expenses, advertising, overhead of the sales department, entertainment of customers, and the like. General and administrative expenses include salaries and expenses of the general executives, of the general accounting and credit departments, such corporate expenses as transfer agents' fees and expenses of reports to stockholders, certain taxes, contributions, and legal and auditing fees. Other expenses not related to production and not outside the usual activities of the enterprise are usually included in this category.

Pension Plan Expense.—Widespread adoption of pension plans for employees, the frequent broadening of benefits payable, and variations in such plans have created a number of accounting problems involving the recognition of pension cost liabilities and the allocation of such costs.

Informal arrangements by which voluntary payments are made to retired employees, in amounts usually not fixed until about the retirement date and often related to the employee's financial need, are not considered pension plans. Under such informal arrangements, the pay-as-you-go method of accounting for pension costs generally is appropriate, but if costs can be estimated in advance with reasonable accuracy, the accrual method described below may be equally appropriate.

When a formal pension plan is adopted, it is reasonable to assume that it will continue indefinitely, even though its continuation is at the company's discretion and its terms are subject to modification. Present and future costs incurred by the adoption of a plan are costs of doing business, and they should be recognized in the accounts on an accrual basis, even though a strict legal interpretation of obligations under the plan might indicate otherwise. The accrual need not be governed by funding arrangements, whereby independent trustees or agencies undertake the payments to pensioners.

DETERMINATION OF PENSION COSTS.—A number of factors, such as the age at which an employee may elect to retire, employee turnover, length of life of employees, and future compensation levels, prevent the precise advance determination of the total cost of pensions. Actuarial computations will, however, permit reasonably accurate estimates; these should be reviewed periodically and, if necessary, revised.

A plan when first adopted usually recognizes services rendered prior to adoption of the plan as well as services to be rendered in the future. Actuarial estimates of pension costs allow for these past service and future service periods in accordance with terms of the plan. Computations of cost may be made for each employee, for categories (by age, length of service, or rate of pay), or they may be based on the average expected service life of all covered employees.

METHODS OF PROVIDING FOR PENSION COSTS.—Opinions differ considerably as to the proper accrual and allocation of pension costs; circumstances will govern the selection of one of the methods discussed below. Principles of tax allocation described in Chapter 22 may be applied to insure proper treatment of applicable income taxes.

As a minimum, accruals should equal the present worth, actuarially calculated, of pension rights which have vested in employees, reduced by accumulated trusteed funds or annuity contracts purchased.

The preferred method requires full accrual and allocation of all past service costs together with current pension costs, regardless of funding arrangements, in order to effect a reasonable matching of costs and revenues. However, past service costs may be funded in instalments over a period of years or may be recognized only when funding payments are made.

ALLOCATION OF PENSION COSTS.—When pension costs are recognized under any of the above methods, they are charged to expense during the period of active service of covered employees on a systematic basis that will not distort operating results in any one year. Since pension plans are adopted in expectation of current and future benefits to the company, past service costs should be charged to operations of the current and future periods benefited, not to earned surplus.

Generally, past service costs are charged to income over a reasonable period of time, although opinions differ considerably on what constitutes a reasonable period. Past service costs have often been charged off over a ten-to-twelve-year period (approximately the period allowable for federal income tax purposes) ; they have also been charged off over longer periods of twenty or thirty years.

The Committee on Accounting Procedure of the American Institute of Certified Public Accountants has dealt with pension accounting problems in two research bulletins: Accounting Research Bulletin No. 43, Chapter 13, Section A, and Accounting Research Bulletin No. 47, issued in September, 1956. The foregoing principles are substantially in agreement with the committee's statements, but in Accounting Research Bulletin No. 47, the committee states its belief that

. . . . in the case of an *existing plan* under which inadequate charges or no charges for past services have been made thus far and the company has decided to conform its accounting to the preferred procedure expressed in this bulletin (full accrual), it may be appropriate to charge to earned surplus the amount that should have been accumulated by charges to income since inception of the plan.

The authors disagree with this portion of the opinion of the committee and feel that the cost of past services should always be allocated to current and future periods, since they believe that the benefits of the pension plan as a whole, including past service costs, will accrue to the company in the future; these benefits include better employee morale and the attraction and retention of desirable personnel.

Since costs of pension plans are generally material, footnotes to the financial statements are usually required in the year in which a plan is adopted, in the year in which an existing plan is amended materially, in the year in which a change in accounting for pension costs materially affects the results of operation, or when reasonable provision has not been made for past or current service costs material in amount.

Other Deductions.—Other deductions represent charges to income not related to normal operations, or financial charges for the cost of borrowed money.

CASH DISCOUNTS ON SALES.—Some companies still classify cash discounts on sales as other deductions on the theory that they represent a financial expense, but these discounts are more frequently deducted from sales.

INTEREST, DEBT DISCOUNT, AND EXPENSE.—The determination of interest is usually a matter of simple arithmetic. Occasionally, interest on obligations may be contingent (e.g., on earnings), and it should be accrued in accordance with the terms of the obligation. The amount of interest will vary slightly with different methods of computation used by banks, brokers, the United States Treasury, and others.

Long-term obligations are frequently sold at prices above or below face amount, giving rise to a premium or discount. This premium or discount should be amortized over the life of the debt by periodic credits or charges to income. Expenses of issue, such as legal fees, expenses of registration and underwriting, and brokers' fees should be similarly treated.

Unamortized debt discount, expense, and redemption premium on an issue which is being refunded may be charged off in the year of refunding or amortized over the remainder of the original life of the old issue, but it should not be amortized over the life of the new issue unless the new issue has a shorter life than the old. Accounting for unamortized discount, expense, and redemption premium on bonds refunded is discussed in Chapter 15, and the related reduction in income taxes is considered in Chapter 22.

LOSSES ON SALES OF SECURITIES AND FIXED ASSETS.—Considerations similar to those previously expressed with reference to profits on sales of securities and fixed assets apply to losses on these sales. However, the doctrine of conservatism dictates that probable losses be recognized, whereas probable profits are not. For instance, it may be desirable to recognize a loss even though the final steps in a sale have not been completed or to provide, in advance of an expected disposal, a valuation allowance charged to other deductions.

Consistency.—In Chapter 6 it is stated that the selection of one accounting principle rather than another, or the selection of one method of application of an accounting principle rather than another, may have little effect on income over a long period, but that it may have a material effect within a single period. Consistency and comparability in statements of income are important largely because of the conclusions that the reader may draw from the statements. It is well known that market prices of stocks are based, to some extent, on a capitalization of earnings and that they are also strongly influenced by the trend in earnings. Any increase or decrease in earnings may be reflected in changes in stock prices; consequently, it is important to the investor that the increase or decrease represent actual changes in earnings rather than the result of changes in accounting principles or methods of their application. While consistency is desirable, changes in principle and in methods of application may be made, and, in fact, the average enterprise is continually making minor changes and may occasionally make a major change. It is important that the reader of the income statement not be misled or confused by undisclosed changes or by frequent major changes.

Interim Statements of Income.—The auditor frequently is faced with the problem of arriving at an opinion whether statements of income covering a period less than a full fiscal year are fairly presented. Some clients publish income figures quarterly or semiannually, and wish them to be accompanied by the auditor's opinion. Others request their independent auditor to review these figures before publication, and he will wish to call attention to inaccurate or misleading representations in these statements. Registration statements filed with the SEC often include statements of income for the period following the close of the latest fiscal year; these may or may not be accompanied by an independent auditor's opinion, but if they are not, the underwriters usually ask that the auditor review the interim statements and report on this review in letter form. This subject is discussed in Chapter 25.

It is not uncommon, of course, to prepare quarterly or other interim financial statements in the course of routine monthly closings and to publish them subject to year-end adjustments. When care is used in monthly closings, year-end adjustments are usually not significant, and interim statements of earnings would not be materially affected by them.

However, the application of the general principle that costs and expenses should be reasonably matched against revenue may require special consideration in the preparation of interim statements of income. Methods of allocating revenue under various conditions have been discussed earlier in this chapter. Allocation of various costs and expenses have also been discussed in the chapters relating to balance sheet items. Generally, allocation of such items as rents and taxes may be made on a time basis; variable factory overhead expenses on the basis of production; and advertising costs on a sales or budget basis. The allocation methods must always be considered by the auditor in examining or reviewing interim financial statements; he should form an opinion on the propriety of the methods used. An allocation method may be appropriate when applied to the year as a whole but inappropriate when applied to an interim period. A few situations of this kind are discussed below.

INCOME TAXES.—A seasonal business may consistently show losses for the first six months of the year and profits in the second six months sufficient to produce taxable income for the full year. If no adjustment is made for income taxes in the first six months, the tax provision for the second six months will be understated since it receives the benefit of the first six months' loss. If taxable income for the year seems reasonably assured, the first six months' loss should be reduced by the amount of the tax reduction determined by application of the tax rate to the loss; this treatment is comparable to that of a full year's carry-forward or carry-back tax loss.

OTHER COSTS AND EXPENSES.—When variable factory overhead expenses and selling and general expenses, such as advertising, are allocated within the fiscal year on the basis of estimated sales, production, or other forecasted amounts, the auditor should review any deferred charge or credit remaining after the allocation. He should compare the forecasted basis with that experienced to the interim date and consider whether the resulting deferred amounts are reasonable in the circumstances. If allocations have not been made, but their omission has resulted in distorted interim statements, the auditor should suggest proper adjustment.

INVENTORIES.—Inventory valuations often present problems in the preparation of interim statements, especially when cost records are not complete; special tests may have to be developed to assure the auditor that inventory valuations are fairly stated. When inventories are priced on the Lifo basis, the valuation of inventories at an interim date may be difficult, since complete information about price levels and increase or decrease in inventory quantities over the Lifo base is usually available only at the year end.

LOSSES.—Losses of one kind or another may be realized early in the fiscal year, but they may be spread equally over the twelve months of the year to avoid distortion of earnings for internal reporting purposes. While the earnings for the full year may be properly stated on this basis, published interim earnings should reflect the full amount of the realized loss.

INTERNAL CONTROL

Internal Accounting Control.

SALES OF PRODUCTS.—When the size and kind of business permit, the cycle of operations in initiating and consummating sales should include the following steps: (1) receipt and acceptance of the customer's order; (2) preparation of an order form and, in some cases, a contract; (3) confirmation of the order; (4) preparation of other supporting documents, including sales invoice, shipping order or advice, material requisition, and packing slips—possibly in one operation through the use of multiforms; (5) preparation of a production or purchase order if items requested are not in stock; (6) withdrawal of merchandise from stores; (7) shipment; (8) recording of the transaction and transmittal of invoice to customer; and (9) receipt of payment. The steps that may not pertain to all sales are the preparation of the contract and initiation of a production or purchase order. The remaining steps should usually be followed consistently, and controls should be established to insure promptness and accuracy in observing them.

Orders received from customers should be reviewed by the sales or order department to determine that the material is available and that the terms are acceptable, and by the credit department to appraise the financial status of the customer, evaluate the risk involved, and set any desirable limitations of credit. The approvals of these departments should be indicated on the customers' orders.

Since purchase orders received from customers vary in form, a standard sales order form should be prepared by the sales or order department, in a number of copies sufficient for distribution to those concerned. The original may be retained in the sales or order department, or a detailed listing may be made, showing customers' names and quantities ordered, and information about shipments and billings.

Invoices, stock requisitions, shipping advices, and packing slips should be prepared in sufficient copies—simultaneously, if possible—from information available on approved customers' orders. Two copies of the stock requisition usually go to the storekeeper, one to be retained in support of the issuance of the material and the other to be forwarded to the billing department for comparison with shipping documents. The shipping department should retain the original shipping advice and send one copy to the billing department on which has been indicated data about the shipment, such as date shipped, items, route, carrier, and freight charges to be added to the billing. As an alternative to the last two steps, when the storekeeper does not retain a copy of the requisition he may forward the copy to the shipping department where the shipping data are added, and the copy is then sent to the billing department. The billing department may then complete the invoice to conform with the shipping data, mail the original invoice to the customer, and send one copy to the accounting department for recording in the accounts.

Numerical control should be maintained over sales orders, shipping orders, and invoices, and they should be adequately cross-referenced. Unfilled orders and unmatched shipping advices should be reviewed periodically. Invoices should be checked for accuracy of quantities billed, prices used, extensions, footings, and terms before they are sent to the accounting department. A detailed listing of invoices (usually in the form of a sales register) should be prepared, and provision should be made for the inclusion of all types of sales. Total sales for the period should be reconciled with receipts from cash sales and charges to accounts receivable.

CASH SALES.—Cash sales may be controlled by the use of serially numbered tickets or slips; cash registers are widely used in effecting this control.

RETURNS, ALLOWANCES, AND DISCOUNTS.—A receiving report should be prepared for all returned merchandise, and copies should be sent to the sales and accounting departments indicating the reason for the return and its physical disposition. Credit memoranda for returns should be under numerical control, based on receiving reports, issued promptly, and approved by a responsible employee. Rebates and special allowances, including freight, should be reviewed and approved by an authorized employee. Trade discounts should be checked to standard terms at the time the invoice is prepared.

SUMMARIES AND ANALYSES.—The classification of sales is an important feature of internal accounting control; they may be classified by type of product, by type of customer, by areas, or by salesmen. Each of these classifications may be used as a cross-check; for example, when one type of customer receives a trade discount, it may be feasible to prove the over-all accuracy of trade discounts allowed in this classification by computing the percentage of total discount to gross sales.

SALES OF SERVICES.—Revenue from services rendered by public utilities involves a type of control different from that in a manufacturing or merchandising concern. Such revenue is subject to metering, or may be controlled through the sale of tickets or tokens. To a greater extent than in commercial enterprises, revenue of public utilities is broken down into functional groups according to the type of service, classification, and location of customers, and a careful review of revenue accounts is an important feature of internal accounting control. Charges to customers are standardized in that they are based on rates approved by regulatory bodies. The following outline lists some of the important controls that are applicable to revenue subject to metering:

1. All applications for service should be subject to review and approval before acceptance by the service and credit departments.

2. Procedures should be designed to insure the forwarding of all meter readings to the billing department.

3. Periodic bills should be checked for accuracy of consumption, rates, and extensions before they are mailed to consumers.

4. Meter history cards should be maintained and periodically checked to customers' ledger and route sheets to see that a customer is being billed for each meter in service, that meter constants (or multipliers) are correct, and that other pertinent data are in agreement.

5. Service cutoffs should be approved by a credit manager or other responsible official.

When transportation tickets are sold by an agent, he may be charged with the face amount of the tickets delivered to him and account for that amount in either unsold tickets or cash.

OTHER INCOME.—The items which comprise other income may be regularly recurring and subject to controls similar to other revenue, or they may be sporadic. Budgeting of miscellaneous income and comparison of budgeted income with actual income usually provide effective internal accounting control.

Cash Discounts on Purchases.—One method of accounting control that insures the reporting of cash discounts lost is to record accounts payable gross and provide accounts for discounts available and for discounts lost. Discounts available are charged to the former account when invoices are recorded; this account is relieved (1) by a charge to accounts payable on payment of the invoices when discounts are taken or (2) by a charge to the discounts lost account when discounts are not taken. Another method is to record accounts payable net and to charge discounts not taken to a discount lost account. Usually, however, audits of invoices when vouchered and of vouchers when paid will be sufficient to assure that maximum discounts are being taken.

Rents.—Real estate, equipment, or other assets for the use of which rental is received should be controlled through the maintenance of adequate records of their location, terms of rental, and rent due. Income indicated by these records as due should be checked periodically to recorded receipts, and any differences should be followed up promptly. The records should also include a summary of expenses so that proper control of net income may be maintained.

Royalties.—A record should be maintained of the important terms of royalty agreements; this is frequently kept by the legal department. Reports of licensees should be reviewed and checked with terms of agreements.

Interest and Dividends.—The employment of an independent custodian of investments, such as a bank or trust company, is in itself an important control in that the custodian usually has procedures to insure the receipt of all income due its custody accounts. However, whether or not such a custodian is employed, income from investments should be substantiated by computation of interest at established rates and by reference to published investment services that report dividends paid. Interest from sources other than investments, such as from instalment receivables, is usually subject to verification by computation.

Miscellaneous.—Many companies receive revenue from activities such as cafeterias or clubs conducted for employees. While these types of revenue usually do not result in net income and the activities are frequently conducted at a loss as a matter of policy, gross revenue may be substantial. There is often a tendency toward laxity in maintaining adequate records and controls of these types of revenue. These activities should receive the same attention as those of other departments, and they should be similarly controlled.

PURCHASES.—The purchasing department should be headed by a responsible official well versed in purchasing techniques, who should approve all purchase orders issued and any subsequent changes. All purchases should be supported by a properly approved requisition. A standard purchase order form properly approved and containing all pertinent information should be prepared with a sufficient number of copies for distribution perhaps as indicated below. These should be under numerical control and listed in detail; the list should show vendors' names, quantities, and prices. The listing may be in the form of a purchase order register or a file of copies of purchase orders. While the distribution of copies will vary, a common distribution is as follows: (1) original and one copy to the vendor, the copy to be returned as an acknowledgment of the order; (2) one copy to stores; (3) one copy to the person initiating the request, if other than the storekeeper; (4) one copy to the receiving department, so that it may have a description and specifications of the material ordered in advance of its receipt to facilitate quality determination; (5) one copy to the accounting department against which the receiving report and vendor's invoice may be checked for quantities and terms as part of the voucher audit procedure; and (6) one or two copies to be retained in the purchasing department.

Adequate records should be maintained of the status of unfilled orders to facilitate prompt follow-up. When applicable, all orders should be supported by complete data on bids received and the basis for the selection of a particular vendor; these data should be reviewed periodically, particularly when contracts are large. Procedures and controls relating to the receiving function were discussed in Chapter 11.

Procedures should be established for a check of invoices and supporting documents by the accounting department before payment is made. Invoices should be listed on receipt and maintained under numerical control, and all unprocessed invoices should be reviewed periodically. Invoices should be checked to purchase orders and the evidence of receipt of materials or services to determine the propriety of prices, terms, transportation charges, and other conditions agreed upon at the time the order was approved. All mathematical computations should be proved. The invoices or vouchers should indicate by initials or rubber stamp that all the foregoing checking has been done. Accounting distribution should be indicated by the accounting department and reviewed by an authorized employee. Invoices sent to the treasurer for payment should be approved by the head of the accounting department or a capable designee; the approval should be based on careful review of all pertinent documents and should not be perfunctory.

The shipping clerk should keep a separate record of purchases returned to vendors, and this record should be checked periodically to see that proper credits are received and reflected in the accounts.

Chapter 16 contains a further discussion of the internal accounting control of invoices (or vouchers) after they have been approved for payment. Chapter 8 discusses the control of cash disbursements.

PAYROLLS.—An employment record should be kept for each employee showing his rate of pay along with other data; additions or other changes should be made in this record only on proper written authorization. In large organizations this record is usually maintained by the personnel department. From time to time, payroll records should be compared with employment records as to name, dates of beginning and terminating employment, and rate of pay. If possible, time clocks or other mechanical devices should be used in conjunction with time or piecework records, and these records should be checked periodically to production schedules and payroll distribution records. Procedures should be instituted for checking clerical operations in preparing payrolls.

If employees are paid by check, many of the controls for check disbursements discussed in Chapter 8 are applicable; among them are the use of prenumbered checks and control of used, unused, voided, and old outstanding checks.

Control should be maintained over unclaimed wages by listing all checks and pay envelopes not distributed, which should be turned over to the accounting department promptly; receipts for subsequent distributions should be examined by the accounting department. After a designated period unclaimed wages should be returned to general cash and credited to a liability account for unclaimed wages.

COST OF SALES.—As stated in Chapter 11, good internal accounting control presupposes an adequate cost system for determination of the cost of goods manufactured.

Charges to cost of sales should be related to physical shipments. Entries in the cost of sales account usually originate in the cost section of the accounting department, and quantities and costs may be checked or test-checked internally to records of units shipped and to inventory prices. Entries reflecting the difference between production cost and inventory cost and inventory adjustments should also originate in the cost section; they are subject to the controls outlined in Chapter 11.

JOURNAL ENTRIES.—While many costs and expenses are charged directly to income when the expenditure is made, frequently expenditures are charged initially to asset accounts, and charges to income are subsequently recorded through the medium of journal entries. These journal entries reflect the sale of inventories, absorption of prepaid expenses such as insurance and taxes, the usage of expense inventories, traveling and other expenses paid from funds advanced to employees, depreciation and amortization of plant and other assets, bad debt provisions and write-offs, and expenses arising from accruals of taxes, insurance, and other current liabilities. It is important that journal entries originate with responsible employees and that they be properly reviewed and approved. Mechanical control of journal entries includes standard journal entry numbers for recurring transactions, under numerical control to assure their recognition each month.

BUDGETARY CONTROL.—A budgetary system has been generally recognized for many years, even in small companies, as an effective device in attaining efficient operation. Circumstances may be such that a comprehensive budget plan is not economically feasible, and certain procedures may be limited. Therefore, the following discussion relates to the more general features of a budget plan.

Budgetary control requires (1) the selection of a budget supervisor, responsible for the compilation, administration, and reporting of the budget; (2) the establishment of budget figures or standards (these normally originate with departmental supervisors and are transmitted to the budget supervisor or budget committee for review and appraisal before inclusion in the budget); (3) the use of a chart of accounts arranged to facilitate comparisons of actual and budgeted income and expenses; (4) periodic reports to management on forms that contain explanations of variations between budgeted and actual results and other appropriate comments; and (5) the effective use of the budget by management.

The period for which a budget is prepared will vary, particularly when a business is seasonal. The sales budget should recognize production factors, such as available labor and the capacity to produce. Since all phases of the budget program are directly related to sales, the budget must be sufficiently flexible to permit prompt adjustment when sales trends differ from those originally anticipated.

The various budgets normally prepared in arriving at an over-all budget are those for revenue, production, purchasing, inventory, labor, factory expenses, selling and administrative expenses, and capital expenditures. In addition, special financial budgets of receipts and disbursements of funds and forecasted profit and loss statements are frequently prepared.

Budgetary control formalizes the company's proposed plan of operations, fixes responsibilities, and may localize certain weaknesses in operations that, when brought to the attention of management, may be corrected with considerable financial saving. For example, comparison of budgeted sales figures with actual may suggest changes in the production program or, conversely, when production costs of certain items far exceed the estimates, changes in the sales policy.

A budget assumes the existence of suitable expense classifications so that expenses subject to direct control by shop foremen or department supervisors can be clearly segregated. When monthly reports show actual performance in comparison with the budget, controllable expenses should be shown separate from noncontrollable expenses such as rent, depreciation, taxes, and insurance.

Internal Check.

REVENUE.—Employees of the sales, shipping, billing, and cash receipts departments should be independent of each other, but their functions should be coordinated to produce a smooth flow of operations.

Sales orders should be approved for propriety and credit by someone other than the salesman or the person who prepares the order. The latter should not be responsible for accounting for the sequence of order numbers. Sales to employees, as well as incidental sales of scrap and equipment, should be handled in the same manner as sales to customers.

Invoices should be checked for authorization and evidence of shipment by an employee whose duties involve neither authorization nor shipment. The accuracy of sales classifications should be checked periodically by employees independent of those preparing the original analyses.

Collections should be received and placed under accounting control by an employee who does not participate in authorizing sales, making shipments, or maintaining customers' ledgers. For example, meter readers should not act as collectors; in addition, it is desirable to rotate their routes periodically. Similarly, the employee responsible for the collection of rentals should not have access to the controlling records. The employee checking interest and dividend income should not have access to securities nor participate in accounting for them.

When merchandise is sold for cash, a routine should be established to insure that merchandise is released only against appropriate sales tickets. Frequently it is possible to separate the function of receiving cash from that of delivering merchandise or services. If tickets or tokens are sold by an employee who also receives cash from other sources, registers may serve as an additional control.

PURCHASES.—The employees of the purchasing, receiving, accounts payable, and cash disbursements departments should be independent of each other. Purchase orders should be approved by supervisory employees other than the employee who makes purchases or the employee who prepares the purchase order. Purchase requisitions should not be initiated by the purchasing department. Purchases for employees or unusual purchases should be subject to the same routine as other purchases.

PAYROLLS.—The method of preparing the payroll should be so devised that the various steps involved are divided among a number of employees and each step is independently checked. Internal check of payroll preparation is strengthened by rotation of employees' duties from time to time so that any irregularity may not go long undetected. A cardinal principle is that no person involved in payroll preparation, custodianship of cash funds, or the maintenance of accounting records should sign and distribute payroll checks or participate in the disbursement of payroll funds. Individual employment records should be maintained by someone independent of those who authorize changes, prepare the payroll, or distribute wages.

Payrolls should be audited periodically by someone independent of payroll functions, such as an internal auditor, and the examination should include, in addition to tests of the accuracy and propriety of the recordings, review of conformity with government labor legislation, accounting for liabilities incurred in connection with payroll deductions, and reconciliation of payrolls with salaries and wages included in the various social security and withholding tax returns.

TRAVEL AND ENTERTAINMENT.—Internal check over these expenditures depends largely upon the extent of the detail evidence the employee is required to furnish in support of his report of expenditures. Generally, the more exacting the requirements for supporting data, the better the internal check. Sometimes standard allowances for meals, hotels, and miscellaneous expenses are a satisfactory means of check and serve to reduce the necessity for detailed examination.

Vouchers for reimbursement of expenses of all officers and employees should be approved prior to payment. The board of directors sometimes approves reimbursement of expenses of the principal executive officer. Advances should be confirmed periodically by management or the internal auditor.

OTHER EXPENDITURES.—The propriety of the accounting distribution of other expenditures, particularly those for maintenance, repairs, and capital improvements, should be reviewed by someone independent of operations. The use of a postage meter is useful in preventing minor defalcations in postage expense.

AUDITING PROCEDURES

Objectives.—The usual purpose of the auditor's examination of the statements of income and surplus, made in accordance with generally accepted auditing standards, is to form an opinion whether such statements present fairly the results of operations for the period in conformity with generally accepted accounting principles consistently applied. Reference should be made to Chapters 3 and 5 for the relation of the system of internal accounting control to the scope of the auditor's examination, the responsibilities he assumes, and those he does not assume, particularly for the detection of defalcations and similar irregularities. Techniques of reviewing and testing, when skillfully applied, usually may be relied upon to furnish a basis for the auditor's opinion. In his examination, the auditor assumes less responsibility for the proper classification of items in the income statement than for items in the balance sheet.

Basic Procedures.—The auditor's examination of the statement of income usually comprises an examination of related balance sheet accounts, a review and test of the systems of internal accounting control and internal check, and review, analyses, and perhaps additional tests of the operating accounts.

EXAMINATION OF RELATED BALANCE SHEET ACCOUNTS.—Proper statement of the balance sheet accounts at the beginning and end of the period in accordance with generally accepted accounting principles consistently followed insures that the reconciling amount of net income is necessarily properly stated in accordance with such principles, except for possible errors in classification between income and surplus. If the system of internal accounting control is not good, review and tests of income and expense accounts may lead to corrections of balance sheet accounts; for example, when fixed asset additions are erroneously charged to expense.

In the sections on auditing procedures in the various balance sheet chapters, it was stressed that the examination of many balance sheet accounts would also, with little or no additional effort, tend to establish the integrity of related accounts in the statement of income. Some of the more important relationships are again discussed below.

Examination of accounts receivable and inventories should indicate that a proper cutoff of revenue was observed, and confirmation of receivables tends to establish the validity of sales. Examination of the balance sheet amount of allowances for sales returns, sales allowances, and discounts tends to assure that revenue is not overstated.

Examination of accounts payable and accrued liabilities should give assurance that all determinable costs and expenses have been initially recorded; examination of inventories establishes in large part the propriety of cost of sales; examination of prepaid expenses and deferred charges tends to assure that charges to current income are proper; examination of plant accounts and allowances for depreciation supports charges for depreciation and gives assurance that maintenance expenses have not been improperly capitalized; and examination of estimated liabilities for taxes and other expenses supports charges for these items in the statement of income.

Closely related to the above auditing procedures, which more or less accomplish the objectives of both the balance sheet and the income examination, are those undertaken concurrently for purposes of convenience, such as the substantiation of interest and dividends from investments when the investment accounts are examined.

REVIEW AND TEST OF INTERNAL ACCOUNTING CONTROL AND INTERNAL CHECK.—The auditor's opinion of the nature and apparent effectiveness of the company's systems of internal accounting control and internal check is especially important in the selection, scope, and timing of audit procedures in his examination of revenues, costs, and expenses. As discussed in Chapter 3, the auditor's responsibility for income statement classification and for detection of defalcations and other similar irregularities is limited. In Chapter 5, the investigation of internal accounting control and internal check and their relation to the audit program are discussed.

REVIEW, ANALYSES, AND TESTS OF OPERATING ACCOUNTS.—The auditor will find it helpful to review the client's detailed internal reports and compare individual operating accounts with those of prior periods. Review of reports comparing actual and budgeted income and expenses may also be helpful.

The auditor may prepare, or ask his client to prepare, analyses of those accounts for which he requires further breakdown. Preparation of these analyses by the client usually results in substantial savings of the auditor's time. If the client knows he is to prepare them, he will usually see to it that the accounts are maintained in sufficient detail to facilitate analysis. Analyses prepared by the client may be reviewed, checked, or test-checked by the auditor as the circumstances indicate.

When additional tests of the operating accounts are to be made, there are two general methods for testing underlying transactions : certain accounts may be analyzed and substantial portions of the supporting original documents examined; or original documents, journal entries, postings, and footings in a selected period may be checked or tested irrespective of the accounts involved.

Frequently an operating account can be substantiated approximately by an over-all computation; any substantial variation between the result of the computation and the recorded amount should be investigated.

Revenue.

SALES OF PRODUCTS.—The auditor's examination of the details of sales and related returns, allowances, and discounts does not usually cover an extended period or a large percentage of the transactions. He places his chief reliance on the evaluation of internal accounting control, the examination of receivables and inventories, and the over-all review of the revenue accounts.

The auditor may prepare, or procure from his client, monthly analyses of sales, broken down by principal products or other logical classifications, showing gross sales, returns, allowances, discounts, and, preferably, cost of sales and gross profit. These analyses may be compared with comparable figures of other months or of the previous year. The auditor can then investigate unusual trends in sales or unexplained variances in profit margins.

After the auditor understands the order, billing and shipping procedures, and related controls, he may undertake a limited detailed examination of sales, selecting either a period for all sales accounts or certain accounts for more extended periods. Since the chief value of such an examination is in determining whether good procedures and controls are in force, it is more important to examine fewer original documents with greater care than to cover a large number of transactions at the sacrifice of thoroughness. The examination may include some or all of the following auditing procedures for the period chosen :

1. Trace totals of the sales recapitulation to the sales and receivable controlling accounts.
2. Foot or test-foot the sales recapitulation.
3. Compare or make test comparisons of amounts on invoices with entries in the sales recapitulation and the individual customers' accounts receivable.

4. Account for the numerical sequence of all or part of the invoices.

5. Compare or make test comparisons of quantities on invoices with advices from the shipping department, transportation receipts, and customers' orders.

6. Check or test-check prices on invoices with sales orders or price lists; test computations on invoices.

The auditor should assure himself of the propriety of the cutoff of sales at the end of the accounting period. If shipping advices are numbered in the order in which shipments are made, the auditor may examine invoices recorded a few days before and after the end of the period to determine that transactions of the period include all invoices recorded by the shipping department as shipped before the close of the period, but not shipments after that date. If shipping advices are not so numbered, the date of shipment on the shipping advice or on the transportation receipt may be used as a check. The examination of inventories and the confirmation of receivables at the end of the period offer additional assurance of a proper cutoff.

An effective over-all test of sales is the correlation of units produced, adjusted by opening and closing inventories, with units sold. This correlation is not always possible; it is usually practicable when the products are few and prices uniform. It may be useful even though the correlation is only approximate.

Returns, Allowances, and Discounts.—The analyses of sales previously mentioned, prepared by the auditor or the client, should include analyses of returns, allowances, and discounts. The auditor may compare the ratio of these to total sales from month to month or from period to period and obtain reasonable explanations of unusual fluctuations in the ratios.

The auditor's examination of returns, allowances, and discounts may include some or all of the following procedures for the period chosen:

1. Obtain a recapitulation of the credits issued or refer to the credit register if one is maintained; test footings and postings to accounts receivable, returns, allowances, and discounts controlling accounts in the general ledger.

2. Test-check the numerical sequence of credit memoranda; compare credit memoranda with the recapitulation or credit register.

3. Test-check credits recorded in the register or recapitulation to customers' accounts and compare them with original invoices to customers.

4. Test a representative number of credit memoranda for authorization and, when possible, inspect evidences of receipt of returned merchandise.

5. Determine that merchandise returned by customers for credit is charged to the proper inventory account with a corresponding credit to cost of sales and that these charges and credits are correlated with corresponding entries in returns and allowances and accounts receivable.

6. Check credits appearing in selected customers' accounts receivable to approved credit memoranda.

Credits issued after the end of the accounting period may be tested to determine their effect on sales for the period under review and the advisability of providing an allowance for them at the year end. If returns are excessive, shipments unauthorized by customers may have been made prior to the end of the period to inflate sales and increase reported profits. Review of the supporting evidence for these credits may indicate that merchandise was returned prior to the year end and included in inventory without reversing the sale. Excessive returns may also indicate defects in the product, suggesting possible revision of inventory pricing and the necessity for a provision at the year end for costs of correcting the defects.

The client's trade and quantity discount policies should be reviewed and the terms of any special agreements noted. In addition to the investigation of unusual fluctuations a test may be made of the discounts allowed to a representative number of customers or for a selected period. Provision should be made for substantial trade or quantity discounts which are expected to be allowed to customers after the year end on sales made during the year. It is good practice, but not obligatory, to provide for cash discounts.

Cash Sales.—When the volume of cash sales is large, the importance of the auditor's examination of related internal accounting control and internal check procedures should be emphasized. Weaknesses in the control of cash sales may have serious consequences. The circumstances of cash sales vary so greatly that it is hardly possible to include here a list of all detailed outlines of procedure which might be followed in examining or testing cash sales. It is often possible to make over-all checks of cash sales, even if sales are also made on credit.

Consignment Sales.—Consignment sales are, in fact, not sales, but inventories held by the consignee for the account of the consignor. The inclusion of shipments on consignment in regular sales will ordinarily be revealed in the confirmation of receivables. Auditing procedures for inventories on consignment are discussed in Chapter 11.

C.O.D. Sales.—Aside from a review of procedures and controls for handling C.O.D. sales, the auditing procedures involved are similar to those applied to other sales. In conjunction with his examination of inventories and receivables the auditor may investigate the final disposition of C.O.D. shipments in transit at the balance sheet date and consider the necessity for a provision for returns if these shipments were recorded as sales.

Instalment Sales.—Audit procedures in the examination of instalment sales may include confirmation of part of the receivables; examination of supporting documents, such as conditional bills of sale and serial notes; and tests of footings and summaries of these sales.

OPERATING REVENUES OF UTILITY COMPANIES.—A typical utility company serves a large number of small customers and a smaller number of large customers, and bills its customers monthly or bimonthly for the service rendered. Internal accounting control is usually good and often includes extensive internal auditing. Therefore, the auditor customarily confines his examination to a small portion of the revenue and relies to a great extent on internal accounting control, analyses and over-all tests. One or more billing centers may be selected for a test examination, including the confirmation of accounts receivable, chiefly for the purpose of determining that established procedures are being followed. Over-all review of operating revenue will usually include tests of summarization and investigation of major fluctuations. Variations in revenue are usually watched carefully by management, and a study of reports on these variations may be helpful to the auditor.

RENTAL REVENUE OF REAL ESTATE COMPANIES.—The auditor should prepare or obtain from his client a summary of rental properties and of rents receivable from each property; this summary may also indicate the rent due during the period. The auditor should make test examinations of related leases or, if rentals are not under lease, review informal rent agreements with someone in authority, preferably one whose functions do not include the receiving of rents. Floor plans of buildings may be checked to see that all space is accounted for, vacancies may be checked by a visit to the premises, and rentals received may be tested by confirmations from tenants. The auditor will usually be able to determine whether substantially all rents due have been received or are receivable and whether they are subject to satisfactory accounting control.

When leasing of properties and collections of rentals are handled by a reputable agent, the scope of the auditor's examination may be reduced if the agent's reports are comprehensive and are reviewed by a responsible person in the client's organization. If the authenticity of the reports seems doubtful, the transactions may be confirmed directly with the agent.

Frequently a lease requires a deposit by the lessee as a guaranty of performance. If such deposits are specified in the lease, the propriety of their treatment in the accounts should be substantiated.

REVENUE FROM DUES AND SUBSCRIPTIONS.—The auditor may check dues received by an association or club against a list of members which may be published and which usually has been approved by the board of trustees or some responsible official. The computation of income classified as earned and as deferred may be tested.

Auditing procedures for revenue from subscriptions are similar to those for revenue from dues. The auditor should also review the systems of internal accounting control and internal check; these should be designed to provide maximum control of receipts.

Other Income.—Auditing procedures which may be applied to some of the more usual types of other income are discussed below.

CASH DISCOUNTS ON PURCHASES.—The auditor should determine whether payment procedures take full advantage of all cash discounts. If the information is available, he may review the ratio of discounts earned to purchases and compare this ratio with that of the preceding year. If no account is maintained for discounts lost, he may note in his examination of vouchers and report to the client any substantial cash discounts which appear to have been lost.

DIVIDENDS AND INTEREST.—Dividends and interest from investments are ordinarily examined in conjunction with the examination of the related assets. Analyses of investment accounts should include information necessary for tests of investment income. Dividends may be checked by reference to independent reporting services, and particular attention should be paid to stocks purchased or sold around the record date. Interest on investments may be tested by computation. Interest from other sources should be subjected to appropriate tests.

RENTS.—Many companies receive rental income from miscellaneous properties leased to others. Auditing procedures for this income are similar to those discussed above under Rental Revenue of Real Estate Companies.

ROYALTIES.—Royalty agreements should be examined and pertinent data on rates, reports required, effective dates, and methods of settlement abstracted for the auditor's permanent file. The terms of royalty agreements usually call for periodic reports from the licensee, and income received or accrued should be based on these reports. If the licensee's reporting date and the date at which the financial statements are being examined do not coincide, it may be necessary to ignore royalties accrued from the date of the latest report. Reports received from the licensee during the fiscal period should be reviewed and the computation of royalties due checked against terms of the agreement.

PROFIT OR LOSS ON THE SALE OF FIXED ASSETS OR SECURITIES.— The auditor should test-check profits or losses on sales of fixed assets or securities in conjunction with his examination of fixed asset and investment accounts. He should satisfy himself that they are properly computed.

Costs and Expenses.—The auditor's examination of costs and expenses is usually not detailed, and his chief reliance is on examination of related balance sheet accounts, review and test of the system of internal accounting control and internal check, and an over-all review of the accounts.

The auditor should familiarize himself with procedures and controls for purchases, payrolls, and other expenditures and with the method of originating journal entries for cost of sales and other expenses.

He should obtain analyses of costs and expenses, classified in groups appropriate to the business being examined and, preferably, comparing current monthly costs and expenses with those of the previous year.

Based on his review of internal accounting control and the above-mentioned analyses, the auditor should decide whether he will make a further examination of vouchers and underlying data.

VOUCHERS.—An examination of vouchers such as is outlined below is made principally to determine the effectiveness of the system of internal accounting control and the extent to which prescribed procedures are being followed.

Most companies maintain a voucher register for recording purchases and other liabilities to be discharged by cash payments. The register will usually serve as the starting point for the examination of vouchers; the examination may include some or all of the following steps for a selected period:

1. Test postings from the voucher register to the general ledger.
2. Test footings of the voucher register.
3. Compare selected vouchers with entries in the voucher register.
4. Compare information on such vouchers with information on supporting data, such as invoices, receiving reports, and purchase orders.

5. Check selected invoices for evidence of audit prior to payment.
6. Test the mathematical accuracy of such invoices.
7. Review the accounting distribution of such invoices.
8. Examine selected receiving reports for signatures of authorized recipients.
9. Examine the related purchase orders, noting their propriety and prices, quantities, and discounts.
10. Compare selected voucher register entries with entries in the cash disbursements record and with paid checks.

Vouchers occasionally cannot be located. Unless the number of missing vouchers or the amounts involved are comparatively large, or explanations obtained from officers or employees of the client are unsatisfactory, the auditor should not regard the failure of the client to submit every voucher as serious. Experience indicates that in normal business operations vouchers may be temporarily mislaid or misfiled, and that when an employee enters an irregular or wholly fictitious payment he is usually careful to support it with an authentic-looking voucher. However, the auditor should satisfy himself that material items for which vouchers cannot be located are properly supported by correspondence or other documents in the files.

Occasionally, adequate vouchers are not available to support charges to expense accounts, and the auditor may be told that the disbursement represents confidential bonuses or commissions, legal expense, dues, contributions, or other expenditures, details of which are not appropriate for inclusion in the regular files. When an adequate voucher is not available, the auditor should obtain approval of the expenditure from an employee at least as high in authority as the employee who would have authorized the payment originally had a formal voucher been prepared. He should assure himself that disbursements of material amount are made with the knowledge and approval of high company authority. The auditor may wish to request approval by the board of directors of significant expenditures not properly supported.

The auditor's procedures in determining that all invoices have been recorded at the end of the accounting period are outlined in Chapter 16.

Invoices for goods or services purchased should be in the name of the client and not in the name of its officers or employees, except in those cases where, as a matter of policy, employees are given the advantage of the company's purchasing facilities to obtain better prices.

PAYROLLS.—One or more payrolls in the period under examination may be selected for examination, depending on the number of persons employed and the degree and apparent effectiveness of internal accounting control and internal check. The primary purpose of this examination is to determine that the company is following prescribed procedures. Suggested procedures to be followed in a payroll examination are as follows:

1. On a test basis compare the names appearing on payrolls with personnel records or other satisfactory evidence of employment.
2. For employees paid on an hourly or piecework basis, test-check payroll hours or production by reference to time clock cards, production tickets, or other supporting data.
3. Test-check rates of pay by reference to approved schedules of hourly or piecework rates, or to approved salary schedules.
4. Test computations of gross pay and net pay.
5. On a test basis substantiate deductions by computation or by reference to proper authorizations.
6. Test payroll extensions and footings.
7. Compare the net amount of the payroll tested with the disbursement voucher and trace the accounting distribution indicated on the voucher to the accounts.
8. When considered desirable, attend and control a pay-off and observe the controls in payroll disbursement procedures.

JOURNAL ENTRIES.—Journal entries are often the source of charges to income for costs and expenses. The auditor's examination of journal entries may be accomplished through examination of vouchers and analyses of various accounts, or through a review of journal entries for a selected period. The auditor may wish to review special or nonstandard entries that may reflect unusual transactions.

COST OF SALES.—In his examination of inventories, as outlined in Chapter 11, the auditor may have obtained or prepared inventory analyses which show cost of production, charges and credits to inventories, and production costs not chargeable to inventories, such as unabsorbed overhead and inventory write-downs. If these analyses are available, they should be compared with cost of sales appearing in the income statement. The auditor may have reviewed monthly fluctuations in gross profit in connection with the analysis of sales referred to in this chapter, and he may have compared gross profit with that of the previous year; such a review preferably should be made of gross profit before recognition of such items as unabsorbed overhead and cost variations. Factory overhead is usually substantial in amount and includes a number of different kinds of expenditures. An analysis of it is often desirable. The auditor should not underestimate the importance of factory overhead because it loses its identity in a cost system.

The foregoing discussion of inventories and cost of sales assumes that an adequate cost system is in operation; if there is not a satisfactory cost system, audit procedures should be adapted to the circumstances.

The auditor's examination of cost of sales for a selected period may include the following procedures:

1. Determine whether the accounting system is such that the sale of inventories should produce charges to cost of sales; tests may be limited when physical shipment should automatically produce a cost of sales entry.
2. Test-check the application of cost to shipments.
3. Test other charges to cost of sales, such as unabsorbed overhead and inventory write-downs.

The correlation of units produced with units sold previously described as a procedure in the examination of sales may be amplified to substantiate cost of sales as well by extending the units sold at cost. This procedure is possible only in certain circumstances, but its possibilities should not be overlooked.

The auditor may review the cost of sales account for the period and determine the propriety of entries unusual in amount or in source.

OTHER COSTS AND EXPENSES.—The test or examination of other costs and expenses, including certain items often included in factory overhead, may follow the scope indicated for vouchers or for payrolls, or it may be necessary to conduct the examination along different lines. Any such test or examination should be designed to determine whether expenditures are properly authorized, made only on evidence of receipt of goods or services, subjected to adequate internal examination, and properly recorded in the accounts.

The auditor may obtain or prepare analyses of other costs and expenses. These should be reviewed and unusual fluctuations from the previous month or the previous year should be investigated.

In most well-ordered businesses, expense accounts will be maintained in sufficient detail to facilitate such a review, and the auditor's examination of individual items will be restricted to tests to establish generally the propriety of the account classifications and to the examination of material individual vouchers. Since the auditor's examination of expense accounts may vary considerably, depending on circumstances, it is not practicable to summarize the procedures in detail. In the following paragraphs some appropriate procedures for the examination of certain costs and expenses are discussed.

Freight.—The auditor is not expected to be an expert on freight rates. However, if he is not satisfied that freight bills are being satisfactorily reviewed by reasonably well-informed personnel, he should suggest that a study be made to improve procedures. When reviewing freight expense, the auditor should determine whether transportation charges are correlated with receipts and shipments. He may wish to determine that freight charges on incoming shipments are not being paid twice; i.e., that freight is not also being charged by the vendor when materials are shipped f.o.b. shipping point. On outgoing shipments, customers should be charged freight if the terms are f.o.b. factory and the client prepays the freight.

Depreciation and Amortization; Maintenance and Repairs.—Examination of provisions for depreciation and amortization of fixed and intangible assets is discussed in Chapters 13 and 14; charges to income should be reconciled with amounts credited either to the related allowance accounts or directly to the asset accounts. The auditor may review and test charges to maintenance and repair accounts or work orders to determine whether they include items that should have been capitalized. His examination of additions to fixed assets should enable him to determine whether items that should have been charged to maintenance and repairs have been capitalized.

Insurance.—Insurance expense may represent the absorption of amounts originally charged to prepaid insurance or charges directly to expense as they are accrued or paid. The former may be examined in conjunction with the examination of prepaid accounts; the latter, in conjunction with the examination of accrued accounts or vouchers. Sometimes insurance expense can be reconciled with actual payments during the period adjusted by opening and closing balances in prepaid and accrued accounts.

Rents and Royalties.—Rent and royalty expense can usually be substantiated by reference to lease and license agreements. Provision should be made for royalties on completed production which may not be payable until after the end of the period.

Salesmen's Commissions.—The auditor may make a test of salesmen's contracts and determine whether their provisions are properly reflected in the expense accounts. He should note whether commissions are payable when goods are shipped or when accounts are collected, on gross or net sales, or after reduction for returned sales. His tests should enable him to determine whether commissions earned during the period have been properly accrued.

Compensation of Officers.—Compensation of officers, whether in the form of salary, bonus, or a share of profits, should be checked to authorizations of the board of directors or the executive committee. If any part of the compensation is based on a computation, such as a percentage of profits, the auditor should check the calculation.

Donations.—If donations are material, this account may be analyzed and substantial items vouched. Large donations should be checked to authorizations in the minutes of the board of directors if they have been authorized by that group.

Legal.—This account is usually analyzed and major items vouched, since it may give the auditor clues to unrecorded and contingent liabilities.

Miscellaneous.—Since the account "Miscellaneous Expense" may contain items properly chargeable to other accounts, it is usually reviewed or analyzed by the auditor.

Taxes.—The auditor's examination of tax expense may be made in conjunction with his analyses of prepaid and accrued taxes.

Tax returns or tax bills are customarily examined in support of major items, and computations of tax accruals are checked by reference to data such as taxable income and taxable salaries and wages. Since the public accountant is usually skilled in income tax matters, he should be able to arrive at an opinion on this tax expense. The final determination of taxes depends on government administration of the tax law as well as on the law itself, and exact determinations are usually not possible at the time of audit; however, it is usually possible to make reasonable estimates of this expense. A more complete discussion appears in Chapter 22.

Other Deductions.—In addition to cash discounts on sales discussed above, other deductions usually consist of items that are subject to satisfactory control, or items that can be examined in detail or in total, such as interest on funded debt, debt discount and expense, and losses on sales of fixed assets and securities.

Time of Examination.—If possible, examination of the statement of income should be largely completed before the end of the fiscal year. Review of internal accounting control and internal check, and partial analyses and test examinations of operating accounts, as a practical matter, are better performed prior to the end of the year.

STATEMENT PRESENTATION

General.—In Chapter 7, where the general form of the income statement was discussed, it was indicated that the usual and conventional presentation discloses the following as a minimum; revenue from sales of products and services; cost of sales or operating expenses; selling, general, and administrative expenses; other income; other deductions; income taxes; and net income. It is also brought out in Chapter 7 that, while it is customary to indicate profit figures at the various stages, such as gross profit on sales, frequently the single-step income statement is used, placing all items of income in one group and all costs and expenses in another group and subtracting the latter from the former to arrive at net income. Income statements comparing current and preceding periods are strongly recommended by most accountants and analysts.

Although the purpose of the statement of income is to reveal to the reader in summary form the results of operations, disclosure of certain details of operating accounts and certain features of the accounting principles followed may be considered desirable. It is not possible to lay down specific rules for disclosure, but, in general, consideration should be given to disclosure of facts that may materially affect a reader's interpretation of the income statement. Information that would be harmful to the company if disclosed and whose omission will not mislead the investor should not be disclosed, but it is sometimes difficult to determine whether failure to disclose such matters results from management's desire to suppress information that should be revealed or from its hesitancy to divulge information that is legitimately confidential. Disclosure should not necessarily be limited to what is ordinarily revealed by conventional financial statements, but should be considered in the light of what an intelligent investor would consider important.

CHAPTER 21

CONSOLIDATED FINANCIAL STATEMENTS

Introduction.—Many corporations carry on some of their operations through subsidiaries. Subsidiary corporations may be formed, or a company may be acquired and its business continued under its previous corporate structure, because of legal or tax considerations, or because of operating or financial advantages. When a corporation controls other corporations through stock ownership, the question arises as how best to display its financial position and results of operations. Financial statements of a parent company alone are inadequate to disclose essential information if a substantial portion of the group's operations is conducted by subsidiary companies or if a substantial amount of assets is owned by these subsidiaries. On the other hand, statements of the parent, plus separate statements of the subsidiary companies, may comprise so voluminous a mass of data and the relations of the companies may be so complex that intelligent summarization is necessary for an understandable presentation of the financial picture. Consolidation of financial statements of a group of companies has been found to be the most useful method of summarizing the over-all financial information and has become a usual practice in stating the financial position and results of operations of a company and its subsidiaries.

When business interests wish to combine their operations, such combinations may be effected through many different means, depending on legal, tax, accounting, and various kinds of business considerations. The legal means by which these combinations are effected vary considerably according to the requirements of state law, and there are legal differences between mergers, consolidations, exchanges of shares, and purchases which may, although they often do not, affect the accounting treatment.

When unaffiliated businesses combine in one form or another, the accountant must determine whether the combination is in effect the purchase of one by the other or whether they are pooling their interests to continue operations as one enterprise. If a purchase has taken place, a new accountability arises, dependent largely upon the purchase price; if a pooling has taken place, the old accounting bases continue. These distinctions and the applicable accounting principles are discussed later in this chapter.

Except to the extent that the accounting for purchases and poolings of interest differs, the accounting principles for consolidated financial statements given in this chapter are applicable to all business combinations.

ACCOUNTING PRINCIPLES

General.—Consolidated financial statements look through the form of corporate organization and present the financial position and results of operations of a group of companies as if they were those of a single enterprise operating through divisions or branches rather than through subsidiary companies.

In accounting terminology, "subsidiary" means a company, the majority of whose voting capital stock is owned or controlled by another company, usually referred to as the parent company. An "affiliate" is one of a group of related companies all of which are under common ownership or control. Sometimes "associated" is used to designate companies which are closely connected through operating or other contractual arrangements, but where voting control is absent.

A consolidated balance sheet is one which sets forth the combined assets and liabilities of a parent company and some or all of its subsidiary companies as if the enterprise were a single entity. Items reflecting relationships within the group, such as intercompany receivables and payables and the parent's investments in consolidated subsidiaries, are eliminated.

Similarly, a consolidated statement of income presents the combined results of operations of a parent company and its consolidated subsidiaries after elimination of sales, costs, expenses, profits, and losses arising from transactions between consolidated companies.

Pooling of Interests.—The majority of consolidated financial statements represent business combinations arising from the acquisition of a majority interest in one or more subsidiaries' capital stock. In recent years a number of business combinations have been effected through an arrangement known as a pooling of interests, which for accounting purposes is described by Accounting Research Bulletin No. 48 as:

. . . a business combination of two or more corporations in which the holders of substantially all of the ownership interests in the constituent corporations become the owners of a single corporation which owns the assets and businesses of the constituent corporations, either directly or through one or more subsidiaries, and in which certain other factors discussed below are present.

The bulletin further states that the single surviving corporation may be one of the constituent corporations or it may be a new corporation; while the net assets of all the constituent corporations will in a large number of cases be held by a single corporation, the continuance in existence of one or more of the constituent corporations in a subsidiary relationship to another of the constituents does not necessarily prevent the combination from being a pooling of interests if:

. . . . no significant minority interest remains outstanding, and if there are important tax, legal, or economic reasons for maintaining the subsidiary relationship, such as the preservation of tax advantages, the preservation of franchise or other rights, the preservation of the position of outstanding debt securities, or the difficulty or costliness of transferring contracts, leases or licenses.

From the accounting standpoint, the importance of distinguishing between a purchase and a pooling of interests lies in the different accounting treatment applied to them. When a combination is deemed to be a purchase, the capital stock or assets acquired should be recorded at cost; when a pooling has taken place, different accounting is appropriate, as discussed below.

POOLING OF INTERESTS VS. PURCHASE OF SUBSIDIARIES.—For accounting purposes, the distinction between a *purchase* and a *pooling of interests* is to be found in the attendant circumstances rather than in the designation of the transaction according to its legal form (such as a merger, an exchange of shares, a consolidation, or an issue of stock for assets and businesses), or in the number of corporations which survive or emerge, or in legal or tax considerations (such as the availability of surplus for dividends).

The basic consideration which differentiates a pooling of interests from a purchase is whether continuity of ownership in the constituent corporations exists, or whether new ownership of one of the constituents is introduced. Ownership, as used in Accounting Research Bulletin No. 48, refers basically to common stock, although in some cases the term may include other classes of stock having senior or preferential rights as well as classes whose rights may be restricted in certain respects.

The bulletin further states:

5. In determining the extent to which a new ownership or a continuity of old ownership exists in a particular business combination, consideration should be given to attendant circumstances. When the shares of stock that are received by the several owners of one of the predecessor corporations are not substantially in proportion to their respective interests in such predecessor, a new ownership or purchase of the predecessor is presumed to result. Similarly, if relative voting rights, as between the constituents, are materially altered through the issuance of senior equity or debt securities having limited or no voting rights, a purchase may be indicated. Likewise, a plan or firm intention and understanding to retire a substantial part of the capital stock issued to the owners of one or more of the constituent corporations, or substantial changes in ownership occurring shortly before or planned to occur shortly after the combination, tends to indicate that the combination is a purchase. However, where a constituent corporation has had two or more classes of stock outstanding prior to the origin of the plan of combination, the redemption, retirement, or conversion of a class or classes of stock having senior or preferential rights as to assets and dividends need not prevent the combination from being considered to be a pooling of interests.

6. Other attendant circumstances should also be taken into consideration in determining whether a purchase or a pooling of interests is involved. Since the assumption underlying the pooling-of-interests concept is one of continuity of all of the constituents in one business enterprise, abandonment or sale of a large part of the business of one or more of the constituents militates against considering the combination as a pooling of interests. Similarly, the continuity of management or the power to control management is involved. Thus, if the management of one of the constituents is eliminated or its influence upon the over-all management of the enterprise is very small, a purchase may be indicated. Relative size of the constituents may not necessarily be determinative, especially where the smaller corporation contributes desired management personnel; however, where one of the constituent corporations is clearly dominant (for example, where the stockholders of one of the constituent corporations obtain 90% to 95% or more of the voting interest in the

combined enterprise), there is a presumption that the transaction is a purchase rather than a pooling of interests.

7. No one of the factors discussed in paragraphs 5 and 6 would necessarily be determinative and any one factor might have varying degrees of significance in different cases. However, their presence or absence would be cumulative in effect. Since the conclusions to be drawn from consideration of these different relevant circumstances may be in conflict or partially so, determination as to whether a particular combination is a purchase or a pooling of interests should be made in the light of all such attendant circumstances.

ACCOUNTING FOR ASSETS AND CAPITAL.—Contrary to the rules for statement of assets when there has been a purchase, a new basis of accountability does *not* arise when a combination is deemed to be a pooling of interests. The carrying amounts of the assets of the constituent corporations should be carried forward, assuming that they are stated in conformity with generally accepted accounting principles, with the understanding that it is permissible to adjust them when deemed necessary to place them on a uniform basis.

The combined earned surpluses and deficits, if any, of the constituent corporations should be carried forward, except to the extent otherwise required by law or appropriate corporate action. While adjustments of assets or of surplus which would be in conformity with generally accepted principles in the absence of a combination are ordinarily equally appropriate if effected in connection with a pooling of interests, the pooling-of-interests concept implies a combining of surpluses and deficits of the constituent corporations, and it would be inappropriate and misleading in connection with a pooling to eliminate the deficit of one constituent against its capital surplus and to carry forward the earned surplus of another constituent. Even though one or more of the constituent companies continues in existence as a subsidiary, if the requirements of a pooling of interests have been met, the new enterprise is nevertheless regarded as a continuation of all the constituent corporations; the rule applicable to purchased subsidiaries that earned surplus created prior to acquisition does not form part of consolidated earned surplus does not apply. However, if *prior to* the pooling of interests one of the constituent companies had acquired a subsidiary by purchase, the parent's share of the subsidiary's earned surplus prior to acquisition through purchase should not be included in earned surplus of the pooled corporations.

If a single corporation survives in a pooling of interests, the stated capital of such corporation may be either more or less than the total of the stated capital of the constituent corporations. If more, the excess may be deducted first from the total of any other contributed capital (usually paid-in surplus) and then from the total of any earned surplus of the constituent corporations. If less, the difference should appear in the balance sheet of the surviving corporation as other contributed capital (paid-in surplus), analogous to that created by a reduction in stated capital where no combination is involved.

STATEMENT OF INCOME.—When a pooling of interests has taken place, the statement of income of the combined corporations for the calendar (or fiscal) year in which pooling took place should ordinarily include the combined results of operations of the constituent interests for the entire year. If combined statements are not furnished for the portion of the calendar (or fiscal) year prior to the date of pooling of interests, statements for the constituent corporations should be furnished separately for such period.

When statements of income for years prior to that in which pooling of interests was effected are presented for comparative purposes, the results of operations may be stated on a combined basis, or shown separately where, under the circumstances of the case, that presentation is more useful and informative.

TAX ASPECTS OF BUSINESS COMBINATIONS.—In its discussion of poolings of interests as contrasted with purchases, the committee on Accounting Procedure points out that the distinction will be found in the attendant circumstances and not, among other things, in the tax considerations. The attendant circumstances to which the committee refers have already been discussed. The auditor in the course of his review of combinations of the type discussed should be aware that there are instances where the rules laid down to guide accounting treatment will differ from the required tax treatment.

To illustrate, under the Internal Revenue Code, in order for certain combinations to qualify as tax-free reorganizations with a carryover of basis, the rules are precise as to the requirement that the acquiring corporation issue solely voting stock in exchange for at least 80 per cent of the voting stock and at least 80 per cent of the total number of shares of all other classes of stock. The failure to meet such test would result in a taxable transaction, essentially equivalent to a purchase. The bulletin is not nearly so exact in its requirements, and the failure to meet the Treasury test would not necessarily bar the combination from being treated as a pooling of interests for accounting purposes.

Similarly, the relative size of the corporations being combined and the degree of continuity in management have no bearing whatever on whether a combination is a tax-free reorganization or a taxable transaction.

In view of the variance in the rules applied, the auditor should be cognizant of the tax aspects of combinations for tax liability purposes.

Consolidated Statements—General.—Consolidated financial statements do not always furnish all the information that may be desired by shareholders, creditors, and financial analysts, since the parent and each subsidiary are individual entities under law. Separate statements for the parent company may be required by creditors if a loan to the parent is involved, although if all the subsidiaries are in effect operating divisions, a separate statement of the parent's income is not of great significance. If the parent company's earned surplus is small, and substantial amounts of retained earnings of the subsidiaries have been invested in fixed assets or retained to provide working capital, the position of the parent by itself should be of particular interest to its shareholders, who look only to the parent company for dividends. When a parent company is a registrant in filings with the Securities and Exchange Commission, its separate financial statements must be furnished in addition to consolidated statements, except under conditions specified by the rules of the Commission as stated in Chapter 25. Minority stockholders of a subsidiary cannot obtain information as to the position of the subsidiary from consolidated statements; they are interested in the statements of that subsidiary alone. Bankers and other lenders frequently wish to see individual statements of subsidiaries in addition to the parent company and consolidated statements, since the status of bondholders and other creditors and the assets against which their claims rank may be shown clearly only by such individual statements.

The purposes of presenting both the consolidated and the individual company positions and results of operations may be accomplished by an analytical statement in which columns are provided for each company and for the consolidation. Such analytical statements are generally known as consolidating statements. At times subsidiaries with common characteristics, as, for example, those operating domestically and those in foreign countries, those organized for manufacturing and those for distribution, are grouped in such presentations.

It is often feasible to disclose supplementary information necessary to the proper understanding of consolidated financial statements in footnotes, rather than in the more cumbersome analytical statement in columnar form described above. For example, if material, it is usual to indicate in a footnote amounts of net assets and of net current assets of foreign subsidiaries included in consolidated net assets, especially if such assets may not be available to the parent in the usual course of business. The amount contributed by foreign subsidiaries to consolidated net income, if material, is usually similarly reported. The composition of consolidated surplus, working capital, or other data, between parent and subsidiary companies, if significant, may also be disclosed in a foot-note. The auditor should exercise his best judgment in devising and recommending methods of presentation that will give the reader information necessary for a proper understanding of the consolidated financial statements.

Basis of Inclusion or Exclusion of Subsidiaries in Consolidation.— When the parent company owns 100 per cent of the voting stocks of its subsidiaries, and they are in effect its operating divisions, con-solidated financial statements usually provide the best means of pre-senting fairly the position and results of operation of the group. Parent companies often own less than 100 per cent of the voting stocks, and in such circumstances policies in consolidating subsidiaries vary consider-ably. Usually more than 50 per cent ownership of voting stock is neces-sary for legal control; but even though the parent has legal control, the relationships between the companies or the character of their operations may be such that consolidation does not produce the fairest presentation.

Often the type of business of a subsidiary differs from that of the group as a whole, so that consolidation of its financial statements with those of the other companies would lead to unnecessary complexity. Under these circumstances a fairer presentation may result from includ-ing in the consolidated balance sheet the investment of the parent in the subsidiary and presenting separate financial statements for the subsidi-ary. Such a situation is found when an industrial company controls a bank, an insurance company, a utility, or any other company whose operations would not normally be activities of an industrial company. There is less reason to consolidate subsidiaries that do little intercom-pany business with the group as a whole or are independently managed, than subsidiaries closely integrated with major operations of the group. On the other hand, there is at present a trend to greater diversification within business organizations which may make managements less in-clined to exclude subsidiaries because of dissimilar operations. Bond or stock indentures of subsidiaries may place such restrictions on cur-rent assets or surplus that it may be desirable not to consolidate these subsidiaries. A consolidated statement including these subsidiaries would be misleading unless these restrictions were adequately disclosed. A subsidiary about to be disposed of or one over which control is being exercised only temporarily frequently is excluded from consolidated statements. Insolvent, bankrupt, or inactive subsidiaries are sometimes not included. It is often advisable to omit from consolidation foreign subsidiaries that may be subject to uncertain economic, financial, or political conditions. (See the discussion later in this chapter and in Accounting Research Bulletin No. 43, Chapter 12.)

Another reason for possible exclusion of certain subsidiaries from the consolidation is that their fiscal years do not coincide with the period for which consolidated statements are prepared. However, when fiscal years of foreign or other subsidiaries forming a minor part of the whole enterprise close one to three months in advance of the fiscal year of the consolidated group, it is usually feasible to include them in the consolidation. In such instances, intercompany accounts with such subsidiaries on the books of other companies in the consolidation must be reviewed for the interim period to determine adjustments that may be necessary to avoid duplication or omission of assets or liabilities in consolidated statements arising from the difference in closing dates.

When a subsidiary has been omitted from consolidation for these or other reasons, the auditor should consider whether the consolidated financial statements nevertheless fairly present financial position and results of operations. If they do not, the auditor should suggest that the data concerning the omitted subsidiary be presented in a footnote or otherwise; if necessary, they should be included as information in the auditor's report.

The policy as to inclusion or exclusion of subsidiaries in the consolidation is often disclosed in the financial statements, and disclosure is required in statements filed with the Securities and Exchange Commission.

Technique of Preparation of Consolidated Statements.—The mechanics of preparation of consolidated financial statements are explained in books dealing with accounting procedure. Usually statements are prepared in columnar form by companies, with additional columns for combined group totals, for elimination of intercompany accounts and transactions, and for final consolidated amounts. Preparation of elimination entries and the disposition of differences between intercompany amounts shown on parent and subsidiary books involve many questions of accounting principle which are dealt with in succeeding paragraphs of this chapter.

Consolidated Balance Sheet.

ACCOUNTING FOR PURCHASED SUBSIDIARY.—Accounting Research Bulletin No. 48 states that:

When a combination is deemed to be a purchase, the assets acquired should be recorded on the books of the acquiring corporation at cost, measured in money, or, in the event other consideration is given, at the fair value of such other consideration, or at the fair value of the property acquired, whichever is more clearly evident. This is in accordance with the procedure applicable to accounting for purchases of assets.

When a corporation acquires the majority interest in a subsidiary's capital stock by purchase, it has in effect purchased a proportionate interest in underlying net assets of the subsidiary. The mechanics of giving effect to the rule stated above are to eliminate the cost of the parent company's investment in the purchased subsidiary against the acquired portion of the latter's capital stock and surplus at the acquisition date. The difference, if any, between the book amount of the acquired proportion of underlying net assets at date of acquisition and the cost to the parent company requires adjustment in the preparation of the consolidated balance sheet, as discussed in succeeding paragraphs.

Excess of Cost of Investment in Purchased Subsidiary over Book Amount of Its Net Assets.—The Committee on Accounting Procedure in Accounting Research Bulletin No. 43, Chapter 5, has stated that:

. . . . there is a presumption that the parent company, in effect, placed a valuation greater than their carrying amount on some of the assets of the subsidiary in arriving at the price it was willing to pay for its investment therein. The parent corporation may have (a) paid amounts in excess of carrying amounts for specific assets of the subsidiary or (b) paid for the general goodwill of the subsidiary. In these cases, if practicable, there should be an allocation, as between tangible and intangible property, of the cost of the mixed aggregate of property or of the excess of a parent's investment over its share of the amount at which the subsidiary carried its net assets on its books at the date of acquisition. Any amount allocated to intangibles should be further allocated to determine, if practicable, a separate cost for each type. . . . .

When the cost of the investment in a subsidiary is in excess of the book amount of its net assets, officials of the parent company should analyze the motives underlying the purchase and, if appropriate, by means of independent appraisal determine for which class of assets the excess was paid. It may be found that the excess was paid for inventory, fixed assets, a favorable long-term lease held by the subsidiary, or for intangible assets (such as trade names, patents, patent rights, or goodwill) not on the books of the subsidiary, or for a combination of assets. The auditor should examine corroborative evidence such as reports of company personnel or independent appraisers and correspondence to satisfy himself that the allocation of the excess cost is reasonable.

If the excess is properly allocable to specific assets, it should not be written off immediately. There would be no more reason for doing so than there would be for writing off a portion of the cost of any other asset when there has been no loss in usefulness or other evidence of decline in value. If the excess represents a type of intangible, such as goodwill, having no limited term of existence and as to which there is, at the time of acquisition, no indication of limited life, its disposition should follow the principles discussed in Chapter 14.

Excess of Book Amount of Net Assets of Purchased Subsidiary over Cost of Investment to Parent Company.—If the book amount of net assets of a subsidiary at date of acquisition is greater than the price paid for the stock, the transaction should be analyzed to determine the nature of this excess. It may be that certain assets of the subsidiary are overstated on its books, and the difference represents an amount to be deducted from tangible or intangible assets in consolidating the accounts. Under other circumstances the difference might appropriately be carried to a liability account in the consolidated balance sheet to provide for estimated shrinkage, estimated losses, or costs of rehabilitation of assets of the acquired subsidiary. In exceptional cases, the excess has been treated as surplus arising from a transaction clearly recognized to be a "bargain purchase," when, for example, all assets of the subsidiary are current and realizable at book amount.

Occasionally, no effort is made to reduce assets by the amount by which the net book amount exceeds the purchase price and, in consolidation, the excess is then described by wording such as "excess of book amount of net assets over cost of subsidiary company stock." This treatment has precedent as its only support. The authors fail to see how a surplus can arise from a purchase. When a company's net assets are purchased, the consideration paid, not the book amounts used by the seller, is the proper cost basis. The authors see no distinction between a purchase of net assets and a purchase of capital stock and hope that the occasional practice of using a basis for the net assets acquired that is in excess of the price paid will soon be discontinued.

Subconsolidations.—When the stock of a company owning one or more subsidiaries is acquired, the amount to be adjusted in consolidation should be computed first by consolidating the balance sheet of the purchased company with those of its subsidiaries to determine consolidated net assets of this group, and then by comparing the amount of such consolidated net assets with the amount paid by the purchasing company. Differences between cost and equity in underlying net assets should be disposed of in both the subconsolidation and the top consolidation in accordance with principles previously discussed.

Acquisitions at Various Dates.—If control of a subsidiary is established over a period of time by the acquisition of blocks of shares at various dates, the determination of the equity in underlying net assets at dates of acquisition presents certain problems. If the stock has been acquired in numerous small lots over a relatively short period, the practice is to group the purchases, and compute amounts to be eliminated on the basis of the balance sheets of the subsidiary at dates near the focal dates of such groupings. There have been instances of a company holding a minority interest, say 25 per cent, in another company for some time and later acquiring an additional 50 per cent of the outstanding stock. The question arises whether the parent is then entitled to reflect in consolidated earned surplus the earned surplus of the subsidiary applicable to the original 25 per cent during the period prior to acquisition of control.

The authors believe that, as a general rule, all acquisitions of a subsidiary's stock through the date when a controlling interest has been accumulated should be considered as a unit and their aggregate cost compared with the equity in underlying net assets of the subsidiary at the date control was obtained. In principle, for each subsequent purchase of stock an elimination should be made against the proportionate share of the subsidiary's net assets at the date of each acquisition. Exceptions to these general rules may depend on the length of the period over which acquisitions were made, on dividends paid, or on considerations of materiality.

If there are subholding companies in the consolidated group with minority interests, transfers of stocks of subsidiaries between subholding companies may also affect the aggregate difference between cost of subsidiaries' stocks to subholding companies and equities in underlying net assets at acquisition because of the change in relationship of interests.

See Surplus in Mergers, Consolidations, and Acquisitions of Subsidiaries in Chapter 19.

Addition to Investment Through Subscription to Capital Stock of Subsidiaries.—When additional capital stock is issued for cash by a subsidiary to majority and minority interests in ratable proportion, no change occurs in the percentage of minority interest or in the difference between the parent company's investment and related net assets of the subsidiary. If the majority interest subscribes to more or less than its ratable proportion, the computation of the difference will be affected because of the change in the percentage of ownership of the underlying net assets.

Subsequent Changes in Net Assets at Acquisition.—Determination of the amounts of assets and liabilities of a company at the date of acquisition of its capital stock by another company involves the same problems encountered in the preparation of a statement of financial position at any date. Passage of time is frequently necessary to determine facts upon which financial position at acquisition date is properly stated. Allowances or provisions for deferred maintenance, for bad debt losses, or for contingent liabilities may be established as at the acquisition date, but such estimates are subject to adjustment when actual liabilities or losses are later determined. Such adjustments relate to the previously determined amounts of assets and liabilities of the subsidiary at date of acquisition, and consequently will be reflected in consolidated financial statements as adjustments of accounts in which the difference, if any, between cost of capital stock and the underlying book amount of net assets is reflected. Any such adjustment of net assets should be definitely related to the position at the acquisition date, and it is customary to adhere rather strictly to the rule of materiality. Unless adjustments are material, they may be reflected in income, and the various accounts at date of acquisition should not be held open for an indefinite period awaiting possible adjustment.

ELIMINATION OF OTHER INTERCOMPANY HOLDINGS OF SECURITIES.—Unless they are held in a special fund or under other restrictions, bonds and notes of affiliated companies owned within the consolidation should ordinarily be eliminated from the assets and liabilities of the consolidated balance sheet so that only those owing to the public are shown as liabilities. Elimination will ordinarily involve adjustment of unamortized debt discount or premium balances relating to the intercompany securities and of consolidated income or earned surplus.

Capital stock of the parent company held by subsidiaries should be reflected in the consolidated balance sheet as treasury stock, and any dividends thereon received by the subsidiaries and charged by the parent against earned surplus should be eliminated.

INTERCOMPANY RECEIVABLES AND PAYABLES.—Intercompany accounts within a consolidated group which may be found in the regular accounts receivable and accounts payable records, in addition to accounts between companies carried separately in the general ledger, should be eliminated in the consolidated balance sheet. Intercompany accounts may give clues to intercompany income, costs, and expenses which require elimination in the preparation of the consolidated income statement. If intercompany accounts are not in balance, they should be reconciled so that adjustment for items in transit may be made, either in the accounts themselves or in the process of consolidating them.

ADVANCES TO SUBSIDIARY COMPANIES OPERATING AT A LOSS.— Parent companies frequently must make cash or other advances to subsidiaries operating at a loss if the subsidiary is to remain in business. The parent company may carry these advances as assets; but, to the extent that such advances appear uncollectible, an allowance for the probable loss should be provided for in the parent company balance sheet. On consolidation, the advance is eliminated against the liability on the subsidiary's balance sheet; the allowance for the probable loss is restored to consolidated earned surplus since the losses of the subsidiary are charged against consolidated earned surplus.

INVENTORIES SOLD WITHIN THE GROUP.—Any material intercompany profits in inventories arising from purchases from affiliated companies at prices in excess of costs to the selling companies should be eliminated from inventory amounts in the consolidated balance sheet. This treatment is based on the well-established principle that, treating the group as a whole, a profit is not realized until the products have been sold outside the group. If intercompany transfers in the ordinary course of business involve additional costs such as freight, there is no objection to allowing such costs to remain as part of consolidated inventory cost. Frequently intercompany profits in inventories are eliminated by setting up an allowance for these profits on the books of the parent company. Indeed, it is good practice to provide an allowance for intercompany profits not realized by ultimate sale when nonconsolidated statements of the parent company are presented.

Some questions about eliminations arise when there is a minority interest in a subsidiary. The minority interest is entitled to its share of profits earned by the subsidiary company regardless of the company's affiliations. Should only the portion of intercompany profit in consolidated inventories applicable to the majority interest be eliminated, or should the entire intercompany profit in inventories be eliminated? While there may be theoretical arguments for following the first method, the authors consider it better practice to exclude all intercompany profit from inventories so that the consolidated balance sheet will consistently reflect the principle of not taking up profits until goods have been sold outside the consolidated group.

When intercompany profit is completely eliminated and there is a minority interest in the constituent selling company, the authors believe that the portion of the elimination applicable to the minority interest should be deducted from that interest in the consolidated balance sheet. The minority interest in surplus is thus stated at the amount of the minority's equity in net assets reflected in the consolidated balance sheet. This method is consistent with the theory that consolidated statements present the position of the group from the point of view of the controlling interest. Others contend that the entire elimination should be borne by the parent and deducted from consolidated surplus, rather than applied in part against the minority interest in surplus.

This method states the minority interest in surplus at the amount of the minority's equity in net assets shown on the financial statements of the subsidiary; in the authors' opinion, however, the minority should look to the subsidiary's balance sheet for this information.

When inventories include items which were sold by one company to another company of a consolidated group before the parent company acquired control of the selling company's stock, no intercompany profits should be eliminated. Profits realized by a subsidiary prior to the date of effective control are represented in the net assets of the company which were purchased by the parent company.

If companies within the consolidated group file separate federal income tax returns, unrealized intercompany profit in consolidated inventories may have resulted in substantial current income tax payments or accrual of tax liabilities by the affiliate that sold the items at a profit. Under such circumstances, an amount equal to the income tax on the unrealized intercompany profits should be credited to consolidated income tax expense and added to the amount of consolidated inventories.

Occasionally, items are purchased from affiliated companies at current market prices which are lower than actual cost to the selling companies. Such losses in inventory would not usually be restored in consolidation, since they represent in effect write-downs to market. Items may also be purchased from affiliated companies at arbitrary prices which are lower than either actual cost to the selling companies or current market prices. Restoration of such losses in consolidation should be made in such amounts as will not increase the consolidated valuation for these items above the lower of cost or market.

FIXED ASSETS SOLD WITHIN THE GROUP.—When fixed assets are sold at a profit by one company to another company of a consolidated group, the profit should generally be eliminated so that the fixed assets of the group may be stated at cost to the consolidation. In theory, losses on fixed assets sold by one affiliated company to another should be restored in consolidation, because such intercompany transactions usually do not establish a proper basis for lower valuation; in practice, however, such losses are not usually restored unless either the amount of the loss or the required consolidating adjustment of annual depreciation is material.

Consolidated Statement of Income.

INCLUSION OF EARNINGS OF PURCHASED SUBSIDIARY.—The consolidated statement of income should include the net operating results of purchased subsidiaries only from the dates of acquisition. For the year during which an acquisition is effected, the income statement of the acquired subsidiary is usually included only from date of acquisition to the close of such year. To preserve comparison of total business activity of the year of acquisition with subsequent years, some accountants feel that it is desirable to include in that year the full year's income statement of the acquired subsidiary and to deduct, as a single item, the net income for the period prior to the date of acquisition. In the author's opinion, this latter method is acceptable under certain circumstances.

ELIMINATION OF INTERCOMPANY ITEMS IN THE STATEMENT OF INCOME.—Intercompany items should be eliminated from the various account classifications of the consolidated income statement so that results of operations may reflect only transactions with the public. Intercompany sales and costs of sales should be eliminated from consolidated sales and cost of sales, and any material intercompany profit in inventories at the beginning and end of the year should be eliminated in the computation of consolidated cost of sales. Other intercompany items to be eliminated include interest charged by a consolidated company on loans to another consolidated company, dividends on stocks of subsidiaries held by the parent, administration service charges, rentals, and commissions.

UNIFORMITY OF ACCOUNT CLASSIFICATION AND FISCAL PERIOD.— Care should be taken to see that the classification and summarization of accounts within a consolidated group are comparable.

Income statements of consolidated subsidiaries preferably should be for the same fiscal period as that of the holding company. This is not always possible. If the fiscal periods of the subsidiaries cannot be made uniform, the auditor must use his best judgment in recommending necessary adjustments. As previously mentioned, accounts of foreign subsidiaries are frequently closed one to three months earlier than those of the parent company so that audited foreign statements may be available for review and consolidation when the parent's accounts are closed. Satisfactory consolidated statements can usually be prepared when minor subsidiaries close their books not more than two or three months in advance of the fiscal year of the consolidation. The Securities and Exchange Commission allows the accounts of a subsidiary to be consolidated under these circumstances, if the difference in dates is not more than 93 days and certain explanations are given.

The accounts of a subsidiary, if available, or, in any event, the parent's account with the subsidiary for the interim period should be reviewed by the auditor to see whether there have been any transactions that might have a material effect on the consolidated statements and for which adjustment should be made.

DEDUCTION OF EARNINGS OF SUBSIDIARIES APPLICABLE TO MI-NORITY INTERESTS.—The consolidated income statement should show separately the deductions for dividends paid or accumulated on preferred stocks held by minority interests. The portion of subsidiary company earnings applicable to minority holdings of common shares should be deducted in the consolidated income statement before arriving at the consolidated net income applicable to stock of the parent company. However, if the capital of a subsidiary in which there is a minority interest has been wiped out by deficits and it is operating at a loss, the entire loss should be charged to consolidated net income, since minority holders cannot ordinarily be expected to provide funds to take care of their share of the deficits.

A consolidated income statement sometimes shows first the income of subsidiary companies, after intercompany eliminations, coming down to the amount of net income from subsidiaries applicable to parent company holdings, after which the parent company's income is added and its fixed charges deducted. This form is especially appropriate when the parent is primarily a holding company and not an operating company, and it has been used principally by utility systems. It has the advantage of clearly segregating interest and dividend payments of the subsidiaries to the public from the parent company's fixed charges.

DEDUCTION OF CUMULATIVE PREFERRED DIVIDENDS ON SUBSIDIARY SHARES.—If a subsidiary that has cumulative preferred shares outstanding in the hands of the public does not pay or provide for preferred dividend requirements, provision should be made for accrued dividends payable to outsiders by a charge against consolidated income, and the liability for these dividends should be reflected in the consolidated balance sheet. This charge in the consolidated income statement is required not because of any obligation on the part of the parent company to pay these preferred dividends, but because they represent a claim ahead of the common stock owned by the parent company and therefore a diminution of its equity in such common stock.

DEPRECIATION, DEPLETION, OR AMORTIZATION OF CONSOLIDATED ASSETS.—The provision for depreciation for a consolidated group of companies, as for a single company, must be based on a plan for extinguishing the cost of the depreciable assets over their estimated useful lives. While each company of the group may have provided allowances for depreciation based on its cost or book amounts, the parent company may have paid more or less than the book amount of the subsidiary's stock, which excess or deficiency may be assignable to depreciable assets. The aggregate of the depreciation allowances made by the individual companies may require adjustment in consolidation in order to reflect allowances properly based on cost to the consolidation. A similar adjustment of depletion may be required in consolidation if it is determined that the excess or deficiency is assignable to properties subject to depletion.

If it is determined that an excess cost is properly assignable to intangible assets, amortization of this excess should follow the rules discussed in Chapter 14.

Consolidation and Translation of Financial Statements of Foreign Subsidiaries and Branches.—In consolidating financial statements of foreign subsidiaries or combining those of branches with statements of the parent and domestic subsidiaries, accounts kept in foreign currencies must be translated into United States dollars. This presented few problems when exchange rates established in a free market were relatively stable, and goods and funds flowed between countries without restriction. Under present conditions, however, rates of exchange in many countries are not established in a free market, and official rates may be far from meaningful. In addition, rates in effect may vary considerably depending on the type of transaction for which funds are to be used. Some countries have severely restricted the movement of funds out of their jurisdiction. Under these circumstances, the consolidation of foreign subsidiaries frequently is not the best way of presenting the position of the parent and its subsidiaries.

Nevertheless, circumstances with respect to certain countries are such that it still may be appropriate to consolidate the financial statements of the parent company with those of foreign subsidiaries located within those countries, provided adequate disclosure is made of the significance of foreign operations and assets. There are some generally accepted accounting principles which normally apply to the translation of foreign currencies into United States dollars when consolidation is appropriate, and these are equally applicable to a branch or a subsidiary. Accounting Research Bulletin No. 43, Chapter 12, states:

. . . . a sound procedure for United States companies to follow is to show earnings from foreign operations in their own accounts only to the extent that funds have been received in the United States or unrestricted funds are available for transmission thereto. Appropriate provision should be made also for known losses.

Any foreign earnings reported beyond the amounts received in the United States should be carefully considered in the light of all the facts. The amounts should be disclosed if they are significant, and they should be reserved against to the extent that their realization in dollars appears to be doubtful.

When only remitted foreign earnings have been included in income, the authors believe that it is inappropriate to present a balance sheet consolidating foreign assets and liabilities and including unremitted foreign earnings in the equity section. While such presentation is seen occasionally, the authors have been unable to find any justification for it other than a limited degree of precedent.

RATES APPROPRIATE FOR TRANSLATION OF FOREIGN CURRENCIES. —The bases for translating assets, liabilities, and income of foreign subsidiaries or branches stated in foreign currencies into United States dollars may vary under different circumstances. The rules given below are generally applicable to most situations. Current assets and current liabilities, except for accounts kept on a United States dollar basis by the subsidiary or branch, are usually translated at rates in effect at the balance sheet date. When both official and free rates are in effect, the rate most appropriate to the circumstances must be selected. In general, the rates at which funds in payment of dividends or on open account are received by the parent, or the rates at which the parent buys foreign currency for transmission to its affiliate, should be considered in deciding on the rate to be used. Fixed assets in foreign countries should be translated into United States dollars at rates prevailing when these assets were acquired or constructed, unless the properties were paid for by the parent in United States dollars. Deferred assets and long-term investments are similarly translated.

As a general rule, long-term liabilities are translated at rates in effect when the liabilities were created or, if the liabilities existed when a subsidiary was acquired, they are translated at rates in effect at the date of acquisition. Capital stock at date of acquisition is translated at rates in effect at that date. The amount of long-term debt payable in United States dollars does not require translation.

With certain exceptions, items in the statement of income are translated at average rates of exchange in effect during the period. If the earnings have been largely distributed to the parent as dividends, the rates at which such dividends were remitted may be proper for use in translating the income statement. Items such as depreciation, depletion, and amortization of intangibles or of deferred charges are translated at rates in effect at dates of acquisition of the related assets.

In recent years, foreign currencies have occasionally been devalued, recognizing a substantial and presumably permanent decline in the exchange rate. Under such circumstances, the procedures described above governing the translation of items such as fixed assets, inventories, long-term liabilities, and capital stock may not be applicable. Accounting Research Bulletin No. 43, Chapter 12, discusses the problems which may arise in the event of devaluation of foreign currencies and suggests acceptable procedures for translation.

DISPOSITION OF PROFIT OR LOSS ON TRANSLATION OF FOREIGN CURRENCIES.—When the parent company receives remittances from its foreign subsidiary or branch in settlement of open account or as dividends on its investment in subsidiary capital stock, it may realize a profit or loss measured by the difference between the rate of exchange at which funds advanced or earned were translated and the rate in effect when the cash transfer was made. Such profits or losses are usually reflected in the parent company's income when realized.

Unrealized profits or losses on translation of foreign currencies result from the translation of the accounts of a foreign subsidiary or branch to United States dollars. Since different rates are usually used in translating the various balance sheet and income accounts, a debit or credit is required to restore the balance of foreign accounts included in the consolidated statements. The policy usually followed is to charge unrealized loss to consolidated income, but to credit unrealized profit to a suspense account. An exception may be made if the credit arises from a recovery of the exchange rate from a level to which net assets were previously written down by a charge to income; such profit may properly be credited to income.

Investments in foreign subsidiaries are subject to the rules for long-term investments discussed in Chapter 14.

STATEMENT PRESENTATION

Headings.—When few companies are included in consolidated financial statements, they may be named in the heading; this is not feasible when many are included in the consolidation, but the companies consolidated are sometimes listed in the company's report to stockholders. When all subsidiaries are included, the heading is usually "X Company and Subsidiaries." If all are not included, the heading may be "X Company and Subsidiaries Consolidated" or, if appropriate, "X Company and Domestic Subsidiaries." Certain data frequently disclosed in consolidated financial statements are discussed below.

Pooling of Interests.—When there has been a pooling of interests, all relevant facts should be adequately disclosed in the financial statements for the year of combination as well as in any comparative statement of operations for a series of years which include the year of combination.

Minority Interests.—The accepted method of presenting the consolidated balance sheet is to include all the assets and liabilities of the group (except eliminated intercompany items) whether or not there are minority holders of subsidiary company shares. Minority interests are represented on the credit side of the consolidated balance sheet by the amounts of their proportionate shares in the subsidiaries' net assets (capital and surplus) included in the consolidated statement. The minority interest in subsidiary company preferred shares should usually be stated separately from that in common shares, and Regulation S-X requires that the minority interest in subsidiaries' surplus be segregated in consolidated balance sheets filed with the Securities and Exchange Commission. The amounts of such interests of outside stockholders are generally placed between liabilities and capital in the consolidated balance sheet.

Preferred Stock of Subsidiaries.—Amounts applicable to subsidiary company preferred stock of an industrial company not held by the parent company should be stated separately in the section of the consolidated balance sheet in which minority interests in subsidiary common stock and surplus appear, rather than grouped with the parent company's capitalization. Public utility balance sheets, however, usually classify such preferred stock in the same section as the parent company capital stock.

Preferred stock of a subsidiary held by the public is generally shown in the consolidated balance sheet at its par or stated amount as reflected in the books of the subsidiary plus any share in the subsidiary company's surplus to which it may be entitled. When the call or involuntary liquidation price of the subsidiary's preferred stock is in excess of that at which the stock is stated on the subsidiary's balance sheet, these prices should be indicated in the consolidated statements. If material, the excess of aggregate involuntary liquidation price over aggregate par or stated value should also be indicated. If the subsidiary has a deficit, no part thereof may generally be attributed to the preferred stock; it should be applied as a reduction of the equity of the common stock up to the amount of the common stock. If the equity in a subsidiary company's common stock has been wiped out through losses, the total equity in and possibly control of a subsidiary is vested in its outstanding preferred stock held by the public. However, the parent company may also have a substantial creditor position with respect to such subsidiary, and consolidation may nevertheless be appropriate.

The equity of the preferred stock in surplus of a subsidiary is determined in accordance with provisions of the indenture or articles of incorporation. In general, a noncumulative nonparticipating preferred stock may have no claim on surplus until a dividend is declared or until its redemption or liquidation. Accordingly, no part of the subsidiary surplus would be allocated to this type of stock in consolidation.

Cumulative preferred stock of a subsidiary company has an equitable claim on that company's surplus to be reflected in consolidated financial statements to the extent of accrued and accumulated unpaid dividends. The amount of unpaid cumulative dividends is usually added to the aggregate interest of outside preferred shareholders and, when the subsidiary's common stock is fully owned by the parent company, the accumulating diminution of the parent's equity is reflected by current charges against consolidated income as the arrears of preferred dividends accrue. If there is outstanding a minority common stock interest in the same subsidiary, a proportionate share of arrears of preferred dividends is chargeable thereagainst until the minority interest is extinguished.

When a subsidiary has a cumulative participating preferred issue, its surplus should be allocated first to preferred stock to the extent of unpaid cumulative dividends, next to common stock in the amount of the maximum dividend that could be paid thereon before the preferred shares begin to participate, and the remainder to preferred and common stocks according to the stated basis of participation in the balance.

There should be allocated to noncumulative participating preferred stock the amount of surplus to which it is entitled, despite the fact that unpaid dividends on such stock do not accumulate.

The guiding principle should be to allocate to participating preferred stock held by the public any portion of subsidiary surplus that clearly can be distributed only to such stock, either currently or in liquidation. A contingency distribution to participating preferred stock, which cannot be expressed in definite amount at the balance sheet date, should be disclosed in a note in both the consolidated balance sheet and the consolidated income statement.

Unconsolidated Subsidiaries.—It has been stated that there may be good reasons for excluding from the consolidation a subsidiary of which a majority of the voting stock is owned by the parent company. When a controlled subsidiary is excluded from the consolidation, certain questions arise as to presentation of the parent's investment in such subsidiary.

Investments in and Earnings of Unconsolidated Subsidiaries.—Capital stocks and obligations of unconsolidated subsidiaries owned by the parent or its subsidiaries ordinarily are carried in the consolidated balance sheet at cost. Chapter 14 includes a discussion of accounting principles and statement presentation of these long-term investments. Net assets of unconsolidated subsidiaries are usually indicated in a footnote to the consolidated balance sheet or in supplemental financial statements of such subsidiaries, particularly when the subsidiaries are foreign, or the parent's investment is a significant portion of its total assets, or the total assets or gross revenues of the unconsolidated subsidiaries are significant in relation to the consolidated assets or revenues; this information is required for consolidated balance sheets filed with the Securities and Exchange Commission. It is accepted practice to indicate, usually by footnote, the difference between dividends received by the parent company and the related earnings of the unconsolidated subsidiaries during the period; this information is also required by Regulation S-X.

CHANGES IN SUBSIDIARIES CONSOLIDATED.—If subsidiaries included in consolidated statements are not the same from one accounting period to the next with consequent effect on their comparability, this fact should be disclosed in a note to the financial statements. Any change in policy as to inclusion or exclusion of subsidiaries in the consolidated statement and its effect on comparability of financial statements should also be disclosed (see Chapter 6).

GUARANTIES OF UNCONSOLIDATED SUBSIDIARIES' OBLIGATIONS.— Holding companies may guarantee dividends or interest on capital stock or obligations of subsidiaries in the hands of the public, or they may guarantee leases or other contractual obligations of a subsidiary. These agreements represent continuing commitments or contingent liabilities of the holding company and should be disclosed if material. Arrearages of dividends or interest should be included in liabilities in the consolidated balance sheet.

Mortgage of Consolidated Subsidiary Not Guaranteed by Parent Company.—A question sometimes arises as to balance sheet presentation when a mortgage on real estate of a consolidated subsidiary is not guaranteed by the parent company. The description of the liability may include the statement that it has not been guaranteed by the parent company.

Hypothecation of Capital Stock of a Subsidiary.—When capital stock of a subsidiary is pledged as collateral to bond or note issues of the parent, the description of the liability for these bonds or notes in the consolidated balance sheet should indicate that a subsidiary's stock is so pledged, since the pledge of stock is equivalent to a pledge of assets of the subsidiary.

Availability of Surplus for Distribution.—The surplus of a subsidiary at the date of purchase of its capital stock becomes acquisition surplus to be eliminated in the consolidated balance sheet. If consolidated surplus is made up largely of surplus of subsidiaries earned since acquisition, it still may not be available for payment of dividends to the parent company. Bond indentures and preferred stock provisions of the subsidiaries may restrict their dividend payments. If restrictions require notation on balance sheets of the subsidiaries, this notation should be repeated on the consolidated balance sheet which includes these subsidiaries, provided that amounts so restricted on a consolidated basis are material in relation to consolidated surplus. Other limitations on the availability of consolidated surplus for distribution should be indicated in the consolidated financial statements.

Foreign Assets and Operations.—Financial statements consolidating significant foreign subsidiaries or branches should disclose briefly the nature and extent of assets and liabilities in foreign countries, the countries involved, and currency restrictions that may have been imposed. Also, if a significant portion of consolidated net income is derived from foreign sources, the amount of such income is usually either disclosed or indicated in the form of a percentage of total net income. Some companies with widespread foreign holdings and operations present condensed combined statements of foreign holdings and operations in addition to consolidated statements. Material unconsolidated foreign holdings and operations should also be adequately disclosed.

If unremitted earnings from foreign operations are not to be included in consolidated income, the amount of foreign earnings remitted may be added as a separate item in the consolidated income statement; or, if it is desired to show total activity, foreign operations may be consolidated, and the amount of foreign earnings not remitted deducted as a separate item.

CHAPTER 22

TAXES

Introduction.—Taxes have become one of the most significant items in financial statements. The auditor is constantly being confronted with situations requiring an awareness of the many tax considerations involved in business activities. His training and experience should equip him with an understanding of (1) the various types of taxes to which a business is subject, (2) the statutory methods for the determination of taxes payable, (3) the alternatives available for minimizing taxes, (4) the proper accounting for tax expense, and (5) the auditing procedures available to assure himself that liabilities for taxes are fairly stated in the balance sheet.

The number and variety of federal, state, and local taxes make it impractical in a book of this kind to do more than indicate a few of the more important matters that should be considered by the auditor; the complexities of tax legislation are such that for many years books have been devoted to federal income taxes alone. Accordingly, the discussions in this chapter are largely directed toward the last two areas mentioned above; namely, the accounting for tax expense and the auditing procedures available for determining that tax liabilities are fairly stated in the balance sheet.

ACCOUNTING PRINCIPLES

Tax Accounting Methods.—The Internal Revenue Code requires that taxable income shall be computed in accordance with the method of accounting regularly employed by the taxpayer in keeping his books. If the method in use does not clearly reflect income, the Treasury is empowered to recompute income under any method that clearly reflects income.

The most commonly used methods of accounting for tax purposes are the cash receipts and disbursements method, the accrual method, and certain hybrid methods which combine features of each. Variations of these methods include the instalment sales method and accounting for long-term contracts under either the percentage of completion or the completed contract basis. Whichever method is used, the Treasury requires that it be applied consistently. Consistency in application will frequently outweigh minor deviations from accepted methods.

If the method used of determining income for accounting purposes were generally the same as the method used for determining taxable income, accounting for the resulting tax expense would be relatively simple. For example, if income for tax purposes is the same as income for accounting purposes, the federal income tax determined to be payable would be a proper charge in the income statement. For many reasons, however, there are differences between the methods required or permitted for determining taxable income and the methods followed in reporting income under generally accepted accounting principles. When these differences are material, an allocation of the taxes payable may be necessary to determine the tax expense properly chargeable to the income shown in the statements.

Other differences between taxable income and book income may arise from the optional applications of federal income tax laws and regulations, involving, for example, depreciation and depletion methods, development and intangible drilling costs, and property tax accruals.

Allocation of Federal Income Taxes.—The problem of allocating federal income taxes to income of specified periods arises whenever the difference between income for federal tax purposes and that determined under generally accepted accounting principles is material, creating a significant difference between taxes computed on taxable income and taxes that would result from application of tax rates to book income.

The high current income tax rate for corporations accentuates the effect on net income of such differences. These differences may arise because the Treasury Department does not permit accrual of certain provisions for unrealized losses and expenses arising from current operations, or deferment of certain types of revenue received in advance; or they may arise from carrying to surplus extraordinary credits or charges that are includible in the determination of taxable income. Some businesses prefer to use methods of determining taxable income which differ substantially from those used in determining accounting income because of tax deferment advantages. There are many other examples, some of which are illustrated later in this chapter.

The subject of allocation of income taxes was dealt with by the Committee on Accounting Procedure in Accounting Research Bulletin No. 43, Chapter 10, Section B, and also in Chapter 9, Section C. The committee concluded that income taxes, like other expenses, are apportionable and should be apportioned between income and other accounts when transactions resulting in material increase or decrease in income taxes are not reflected in the income statement. This conclusion does not apply to transactions that involve normal and recurring differences between book and taxable income.

Application of this conclusion of the committee results in:

1. The elimination from income and the allocation to surplus of the tax related to credits or charges to surplus:

   (a) When an item that is credited to surplus results in a material increase in income taxes, surplus, not income, should be charged with the amount of the tax increase.

   (b) When an item that is charged to surplus results in a material decrease in income taxes, surplus, not income, should be credited with the amount of the tax decrease.

   For example, when substantial gains or losses on dispositions of property are reflected in earned surplus, the applicable increase or decrease in income tax payable should also be reflected in earned surplus.

2. The elimination from income of the tax effect of credits or charges not recognized therein:

   (a) When a material credit item is recognized as taxable income but is deferred in the balance sheet, the tax charge applicable thereto should not be recognized in the income statement. The liability for federal taxes applicable to such taxable income should be recognized with a corresponding charge to the related deferred credit account or to a deferred charge account. In subsequent periods, when the item is recognized in the income statement, income should be charged for the taxes previously determined as applicable thereto, and the account previously charged should be credited. This treatment would be used, for example, when rent received in advance is taxed in the year of receipt rather than in the years to which it is applicable.

(b) When a material debit item is deductible for tax purposes but is deferred in the balance sheet, the tax benefit should not be recognized in the income statement but should be credited to the related deferred charge account or to a deferred credit account with a corresponding addition to income tax expense charged to income. In subsequent periods, when the item is recognized in the income statement, the deferred charge or credit account previously credited should be charged for the taxes previously determined as applicable thereto and income tax expense correspondingly reduced. This treatment would be used, for example, when refunding premium and expenses on bonds are amortized over the life of the old issue but are deductible in full for income taxes in the year of refunding.

3. The recognition in income of the tax effect of credits or charges thereto that are not currently recognized for tax purposes:

(a) When a material credit item is recognized in the income statement but is taxable in a later period, the tax effect should be recognized in the period in which the item is included in income. For example, if income from instalment sales or from long-term contracts is accrued currently for accounting purposes, the estimated income taxes thereon should be accrued simultaneously, even though the income may not be taxable until collected or the contract completed in a subsequent period.

(b) When a material debit item is charged to income but is not deductible for tax purposes until a future period (for example, the accrual of certain types of estimated liabilities), the future tax reduction should be recognized in the period in which the item is charged to income by reducing income tax expense with a corresponding charge either to the estimated liability account or to a deferred charge account. In subsequent periods, when charges to the estimated liability are deductible for tax purposes, the income tax expense should be increased and the account previously charged should be credited.

The tax effect described in the foregoing paragraphs is usually the difference between the tax payable with and without including the item in the amount of taxable income. When the tax effect is applicable to future periods, it may be necessary to use an estimated rate expected to be in effect over such periods. The capital gains tax rate should be used on transactions taxable at that rate.

DEPRECIATION AND AMORTIZATION.—Depreciation accounting has been and probably will continue to be influenced by tax legislation and by decisions of federal taxing authorities. In general, the principles set forth in the Treasury's regulations on depreciation agree with generally accepted accounting principles. However, while the principles are the same, opinions of taxpayers and the Treasury frequently differ on the proper rates of depreciation to be used in computing the allowance for depreciation. This is understandable since the businessman must be prudent in providing for losses, while the Treasury usually seeks to allow the minimum amount.

Depreciation and amortization methods and rates used for tax purposes need not, and sometimes should not, be adopted for accounting purposes. Financial statements prepared by management to present financial position and results of operations should reflect existing conditions as fairly as possible, and they should not be distorted by the application of tax methods and rulings that are not appropriate in the circumstances.

ACCELERATED DEPRECIATION.—Under the Internal Revenue Code, the taxpayer generally has the right to select the straight-line method of computing depreciation for all property in service, the declining-balance method or the sum-of-the-years-digits method for certain additions subsequent to 1953, or any method that has been used consistently over the years and has been acceptable to the Internal Revenue Service. For each method there are technical requirements as to bases, rates, and methods of computation which, in themselves, are more significant from a tax than from an accounting viewpoint.

The so-called accelerated methods, namely, declining-balance and sum-of-the-years-digits, discussed in Chapter 13, have long been considered acceptable for accounting purposes since they meet the requirements of being systematic and rational. Many businesses desire to obtain the earlier tax deductions available under the accelerated methods, and will use them in determining taxable income. Some will use these methods on the books to avoid the necessity of keeping two sets of records; others may wish to record depreciation on the books on a straight-line basis. In Accounting Research Bulletin No. 44, October, 1954, the Committee on Accounting Procedure stated:

In those cases where the expected productivity or revenue-earning power of the asset is relatively greater during the earlier years of its life, or where maintenance charges tend to increase during the later years, the declining-balance method may well provide the most satisfactory allocation of cost. The conclusions of this bulletin also apply to other methods, including the "sum-of-the-years-digits" method, which produce substantially similar results.

When a change to the declining-balance method is made for general accounting purposes, and depreciation is a significant factor in the determination of net income, the change in method, including the effect thereof, should be disclosed in the year in which the change is made.

There may be situations in which the declining-balance method is adopted for tax purposes but other appropriate methods are followed for financial accounting purposes. In such cases it may be that accounting recognition should be given to deferred income taxes. However, the committee is of the opinion that, in the ordinary situation, deferred income taxes need not be recognized in the accounts unless it is reasonably certain that the reduction in taxes during the earlier years of use of the declining-balance method for tax purposes is merely a deferment of income taxes until a relatively few years later, and then only if the amounts are clearly material.

Although concluding that such deferred income tax credits need not be recognized in the ordinary situation, the committee also stated that there might be situations where accounting recognition should be given thereto. Many accountants feel that accounting for public utilities qualifies as such a situation; they believe that the relatively stable earnings of these companies may be particularly sensitive to the tax effect of differences between book and taxable income and that the percentage considered material as to the tax effect of such differences should not be as large as that for other business organizations. Many regulatory commissions have recognized this and require the deferment of income taxes whenever accounting and tax depreciation methods or bases differ. Some commissions permit a deferred tax credit to be shown in a restricted surplus account instead of a deferred credit account.

ACCELERATED AMORTIZATION.—The Internal Revenue Code provides that when a company obtains from the government a certificate of necessity to construct or purchase a so-called emergency facility, all or part of the cost, as stipulated in the certificate, may be amortized for income tax purposes over a period of 60 months. This amortization, if claimed, is in lieu of any depreciation deduction that might otherwise be allowable, and any portion not certified is subject to ordinary depreciation, if depreciable. If it is reasonable to expect that the useful life of the facility will, for all practical purposes, generally coincide with the effective period used for tax purposes, the tax allowance for depreciation and amortization may be considered a proper cost of operations during that period. However, if it is believed that the useful life of the portion of the property certified will be more or less than the five-year period, management should carefully consider all related factors in determining its accounting depreciation policy for this facility. On this problem, the Committee on Accounting Procedure stated in Accounting Research Bulletin No. 43, Chapter 9, Section C, that:

Sound financial accounting procedures do not necessarily coincide with the rules as to what shall be included in "gross income," or allowed as a deduction therefrom, in arriving at taxable net income. It is well recognized that such rules should not be followed for financial accounting purposes if they do not conform to generally accepted accounting principles. However, where the results obtained from following income-tax procedures do not materially differ from those obtained where generally accepted accounting principles are followed, there are practical advantages in keeping the accounts in agreement with the income-tax returns.

Where management appropriately decides to record depreciation of the certified portion of the cost of the emergency facility in an amount that is materially less than the amortization deducted for income tax purposes, and the income tax payable annually during the amortization period is significantly less than it would be if based on the income reflected in the financial statements, the reduction in income tax otherwise payable should be deferred. On this point the committee stated:

. . . . during the amortization period, where this difference is material, a charge should be made in the income statement to recognize the income tax to be paid in the future on the amount by which amortization for income-tax purposes exceeds the depreciation that would be allowable if certificates of necessity had not been issued. The amount of the charge should be equal to the estimated amount by which the income tax expected to be payable after the amortization period exceeds what would be so expected if amortization had not been claimed for income-tax purposes in the amortization period. The estimated amount should be based upon normal and surtax rates in effect during the period covered by the income statement with such changes therein as can be reasonably anticipated at the time the estimate is made.

In accounting for this deferment of income taxes, the committee believes it desirable to treat the charge as being for additional income taxes. The related credit in such cases would properly be made to an account for deferred income taxes. Under this method, during the life of the facility following the amortization period the annual charges for income taxes will be reduced by charging to the account for deferred income taxes that part of the income tax in excess of what would have been payable had the amortization deduction not been claimed for income-tax purposes in the amortization period. By this procedure the net income will more nearly reflect the results of a proper matching of costs and revenues.

The committee also pointed out that some accountants similarly recognize the necessity for giving effect to the amount of deferred income taxes but prefer to do this by charging the income account with an equivalent amount for additional amortization or depreciation and crediting the related allowance account. This procedure may be considered acceptable since it results in the same amount of net income as the procedure described above, which the committee recommends and prefers.

INCOME TAX ON APPRECIATION OF FIXED ASSETS.—The rule has previously been stated that when fixed assets are written up to appraised amounts, depreciation based on the written-up amounts should be charged to income. For federal income tax purposes, however, depreciation may be based only on cost. Fixed assets on which depreciation is not fully deductible are less valuable to a company than are identical fixed assets on which depreciation is fully deductible. If recorded in the accounts, an excess of appraisal amount over cost should be reduced, either directly or by means of an allowance, by the estimated reduction in income taxes that would result in future periods if depreciation on such excess were deductible for federal income tax purposes.

PERCENTAGE DEPLETION.—The basic concept of depletion is discussed in Chapter 13. When percentage depletion exceeds cost depletion, the amount allowable as a deduction for federal income tax purposes is computed on the basis of a fixed percentage of gross income from the property, limited to a fixed percentage of net income from the property. Percentage depletion is allowed even though the accumulated allowances exceed the cost basis of the property.

Percentage depletion has the effect of a continuing reduction of the income tax rate and bears no relation to depletion computed in accordance with generally accepted accounting principles. Accordingly, the reduction in income tax resulting from a percentage depletion allowance greater than that charged to accounting income is not subject to tax allocation rules.

EXPLORATION, DEVELOPMENT, AND INTANGIBLE DRILLING COSTS. —Expenditures paid or incurred during a taxable year for the purpose of ascertaining the existence, location, extent, or quality of a deposit of ore or other mineral, if paid or incurred prior to the disclosure of the existence of ores or minerals in commercially marketable quantities, are properly classed as exploration costs. For accounting purposes these costs are generally deferred and recovered ratably over the period in which the ore or mineral is sold. Under the Internal Revenue Code, the expenses may be deferred and cost recovered in the same manner, or they may be deducted up to $100,000 in any one taxable year. This option to deduct is limited to any four years, not necessarily consecutive, that the company may select. Exploration expenditures in excess of $100,000 per year, or incurred in years other than the four years for which an election to deduct or defer them is allowed, are added to the cost basis of the property and recoverable only through its depletion.

For federal income tax purposes, current expenditures deducted within the above limitations and the amortization of any deferred exploration expenditures are not considered to be depletion and are allowable in addition thereto, but any deduction so taken must be used in arriving at net income from the property for the purpose of determining maximum allowable depletion.

Mine development costs for federal income tax purposes (see discussion in Chapter 12) may be treated in the same manner as exploration expenses except that there is no limit on the number of years for which the deduction may be taken nor on the amount which may be deducted in any one year.

The Internal Revenue Code provides that a taxpayer may elect either to deduct intangible drilling and development costs of oil and gas wells as they are paid or incurred, or to capitalize them, recovering them ratably over the period the units are produced. The election once made is binding for all years thereafter.

In contrast with mineral exploration and development expenditures discussed above, the amortization of capitalized oil and gas development costs is deemed to be depletion. Therefore, percentage depletion, when claimed, is in lieu of amortization of such costs. Usually a taxpayer who expects to employ percentage depletion elects to deduct these costs rather than to capitalize them.

When intangible oil and gas drilling and development expenses are capitalized on the books but deducted for tax purposes, and when the same treatment is followed for some or all mine development and exploration expenses, the related tax benefits may be deferred in the accounts. Many companies do not defer these tax benefits because such costs usually recur annually in approximately the same amounts and the resulting tax deduction approximates the book amortization of previously capitalized costs.

TIMBER AND TIMBERLANDS.—Under a special provision of the Code, a company owning timber or a contract right to cut timber for a period of at least six months prior to the beginning of a taxable year may elect to treat the cutting of such timber as a sale at fair market price on the first day of the taxable year in which the timber is cut. The gain on the imputed sale is taxed at capital gain rates. The fair market value used in computing the gain or loss is considered thereafter as the basis of such timber for tax purposes. For accounting purposes the cut timber is carried at its depletable cost plus cutting costs and other expenses. Although proper, it is not general practice to defer such portion of the tax paid at capital gain rates, referred to above, as may relate to timber or products therefrom contained in the year-end inventory.

INSTALMENT SALES.—When taxpayers selling personal property on the instalment plan report taxable income on the instalment plan but report such transactions to stockholders on the accrual basis, an estimated liability should be accrued for the tax applicable to the income accrued but not received. Additions to the liability are made by charges to income in years when income tax payable is less than the tax computed on the accrual basis; income is credited and the liability reduced in years when tax payable is greater than the tax computed on the accrual basis.

EXPERIMENTAL AND RESEARCH EXPENSE.—Experimental and research expenditures may be charged off currently or, under certain circumstances, deferred for accounting purposes. If a proper election is made, the Internal Revenue Code permits the deduction of these expenditures currently. Under the Code, an election may also be made to defer these expenditures and amortize them over a period of not less than 60 months, provided they do not have a definitely determinable life. Amortization must begin with the month in which benefits from the expenditure are first realized. If material expenditures of this nature are deducted as expenses for tax purposes but capitalized or deferred on the books, allocation of the tax effect should be considered.

DEFERRED COMPENSATION PLANS.—Deferred compensation plans have become popular as a means of providing additional incentive to executives subject to extremely high individual tax rates. Such an arrangement usually is in the form of a contractual promise by the employer to pay certain amounts at designated future dates. To avoid early income recognition to the executive under the doctrine of constructive receipt, the contracts customarily include certain conditions which, if not complied with, remove the employer's obligation for future payments. These contingent requirements include continued employment for a specified period, availability for advisory services, and agreement not to compete after retirement. The plans may vary considerably in the payment terms and the period of deferment. Payments may be made in cash, in stock, or partly in cash and partly in stock.

Ordinarily, accruals for deferred compensation are not deductible for income tax purposes until the year of payment. While many companies that have adopted deferred compensation plans do not follow tax-effect accounting in respect thereto, recognition of the tax effect is desirable when the company is a profit-maker and may reasonably expect continued success. In the latter instance, the liability for deferred compensation payable in cash may be set up in an amount that recognizes the estimated future tax benefit. When stock is to be issued in payment, the tax benefit will need to be shown as a deferred charge. If by reason of increase or decrease in the market value of the stock between the contract date and the date of issue, a larger or smaller deduction is obtained than anticipated, there will be a difference between the estimated and the actual tax benefit. Opinions vary as to how such difference should be accounted for. Some believe credit adjustments should go to paid-in surplus, but debit adjustments should go to income, or if sufficiently material, to earned surplus; others believe the adjustment, if other than nominal, should go to paid-in surplus; in the opinion of still others, the adjustment should go to income unless sufficiently material to impair the significance of net income, when the adjustment should go directly to earned surplus. It is generally agreed that differences between the estimated and actual tax benefit occasioned by a change in tax rates should go to income.

Usually, the amounts of deferred compensation and deferred tax benefit should not recognize interim fluctuations in the market value of the capital stock that is to be used to pay deferred compensation.

ALLOCATION OF CONSOLIDATED PROVISION FOR FEDERAL INCOME TAXES.—*Consolidated Returns.*—The Internal Revenue Code of 1954 permits a parent company and subsidiaries that are at least 80 per cent owned to file federal income tax returns on a consolidated basis. The combined normal tax and surtax rate on consolidated taxable income is presently 54 per cent; the separate return rate is 52 per cent. The 2 per cent increase in rate does not apply to that portion of consolidated taxable income attributable to Western Hemisphere Trade Corporations or regulated public utilities as defined in the Code. Consolidated tax returns may be advantageous under certain conditions despite the 2 per cent penalty; for example, when one of the companies has a net loss, or when a subsidiary has paid large dividends to the parent company. The filing of consolidated returns creates the problem of allocation of the total tax liability to the individual companies. For the purpose of determining accumulated earnings and profits of individual members of a consolidated group, the 1954 Code permits a number of methods for allocating the consolidated tax. The following are most commonly used:

1. On the basis of the ratio which that portion of the consolidated taxable income attributable to each member of the group having taxable income bears to the consolidated taxable income (source of income method).

2. On the basis of the percentage of total tax which the tax of such member, if computed on a separate return, would bear to the total

amount of the taxes for all members of the group if so computed
(separate return tax method).

The source of income and the separate return tax methods described
above are sanctioned for accounting purposes by the Securities and
Exchange Commission under the Holding Company Act; provided,
however, that:

> (i) the tax allocated to each subsidiary company shall not exceed the
> amount of tax of such company based upon a separate return com-
> puted as if such company had always filed its tax return on a separate
> return basis; and

> (ii) any excess of tax which would be allocated to a company but for (i)
> above shall be apportioned among the other members of the group,
> including the holding company, in direct proportion to the reduction
> in tax resulting to such members as measured by the difference
> between their tax on a separate return basis and their allocated
> portion of the consolidated tax.

Other methods of apportionment of consolidated tax to the companies
included in the consolidated return may be appropriate in certain
situations. For example, special treatment may be in order when a
substantial consolidated net operating loss carry-forward is availed
of by a newly acquired member of the consolidated group. However,
it is usually not good practice to assign to each subsidiary a portion
of the consolidated tax equal to the tax of the subsidiary on an individual return basis and to charge or credit the difference to the parent
company.

If individual company financial statements are prepared and the
difference between the consolidated tax allocated to the company and
the tax computed on an individual return basis is material, the amount
of the difference should be disclosed in a note to the statements.

Separate Returns.—In the preparation of consolidated financial
statements good accounting practice requires the elimination of intercompany profits in inventories. When separate tax returns are filed
by the constituent companies, the income tax is levied on profits computed before this elimination; the tax expense related to the unrealized
profit may be deferred to the subsequent period or periods when the
profits are realized by the consolidated group. See also page 483.

When taxable income of a subsidiary is reduced by application of
net operating losses incurred prior to acquisition, the proper disposition
of the resulting tax reduction may present a problem. Tax recovery
may have seemed so assured at the date of acquisition that the amount
thereof was included in the assets of the subsidiary at that date; then
no problem arises when the reduction is realized. In other instances,

while the tax recovery seemed likely, treatment of the recovery in the consolidated financial statements may have been delayed until the recovery is assured.

In the authors' opinion, the preferable treatment is to exclude from consolidated income and earned surplus subsequent to acquisition of the subsidiary any tax benefits arising from losses attributable to periods prior to acquisition of the subsidiary. If the amount involved was not treated as an asset of the subsidiary at the time of acquisition, this exclusion may involve adjustment of whichever account was debited or credited with the difference between cost to the parent company and the amount of net assets shown in the balance sheet of the subsidiary at date of acquisition.

However, if, at the time of acquisition of the subsidiary company, it seemed unlikely that any such subsequent tax benefit would be realized, the authors believe that the tax benefits, when realized, may be reflected in income or earned surplus in the year of realization.

Income Taxes on Undistributed Earnings of Subsidiaries.—Earnings of foreign and domestic subsidiaries become available for distribution to parent company stockholders only when they are paid to the parent company in the form of dividends or when the subsidiary is liquidated. The dividends so paid are factors in the determination of federal income taxes (and possibly state taxes) payable by the parent company, except domestic dividends eliminated when consolidated returns are filed. The question arises whether provision should be made currently for federal income taxes on undistributed earnings of subsidiaries included in the consolidated income statements and accumulated in consolidated earned surplus. These taxes will be assessed only when dividends are declared and paid by the subsidiaries, and, since the assessment may be long deferred, it is usually impossible to predict what portion, if any, of these dividends will be subject to tax or what rates will be in effect at that time. Under the Code the parent company generally is allowed an 85 per cent deduction for domestic dividends received, as a result of which the parent company may pay no tax or only a small effective tax on these dividends. Foreign dividends may be subject to foreign dividend taxes withheld at the source; however, the parent company is entitled to a credit for such taxes and, in certain circumstances, to a foreign tax credit for other foreign taxes paid by the subsidiary, so that the net tax, if any, on undistributed earnings of foreign subsidiaries usually cannot be predicted.

For these reasons, although permissible, it is not generally customary to provide for possible taxes to be paid in the future on undistributed earnings of subsidiaries, although a notation may be made to the effect that such undistributed earnings may be subject to federal income tax, when and if they are distributed to the parent company, at rates in effect at the time of distribution, and the approximate amount of the tax, computed at current rates, may be indicated.

However, when material dividend remittances subject to high tax rates seem likely to be made in amounts disproportionate to current earnings of the subsidiary, provision should be made for the tax payable on such estimated future remittances.

Claims for Refund.—Since their realization is often uncertain, claims for refund of federal taxes generally should not be included in the accounts prior to approval by the taxing authorities.

Claims for refund based on carry-back provisions of the Internal Revenue Code, however, have as definite a basis as has the computation of income taxes for the year. Therefore, amounts claimed as refunds of taxes paid in prior years as a result of the carry-back of an operating loss should be recorded as a receivable (see Chapter 10) and included in the income statement of the year in which the loss occurs.

When losses have been carried forward to a year of profit, the resulting reduction in federal income tax should be reflected in the year in which the carry-forward loss is availed of. This subject is discussed in Accounting Research Bulletin No. 43, Chapter 10, Section B.

Property Taxes.—Real and personal property taxes are based on the assessed valuation of property as of a given date, and the total tax usually becomes a lien on the property at a subsequent specified date known as the lien date. While these taxes are collected to provide for expenses of government for a certain period, they are not levied to cover ownership over a period of time. In this respect they differ from taxes on income, which generally accrue as income is earned.

The problem of determining the period to which property taxes should be allocated in the statement of income has been met in various ways. Accounting Research Bulletin No. 43, Chapter 10, Section A, indicates that in practice they have been charged against income of various periods, as follows:

Year in which paid (cash basis),
Year ending on assessment (or lien) date,
Year beginning on assessment (or lien) date,
Calendar or fiscal year of taxpayer prior to assessment (or lien) date,
Calendar or fiscal year of taxpayer including assessment (or lien) date,
Calendar or fiscal year of taxpayer prior to payment date,

Fiscal year of governing body levying the tax,

Year appearing on tax bill.

The bulletin states that:

Consistency of application from year to year is the important consideration and selection of any of the periods mentioned is a matter for individual judgment.

The authors believe that the most desirable basis of accounting for property taxes is generally proration over the fiscal year of the governing body levying the tax.

The 1954 Internal Revenue Code in an attempt to reduce variations between tax accounting and generally accepted accounting principles permits accrual-basis taxpayers, if they so elect in the first year in which the taxpayer incurs real property taxes, to prorate real property taxes over the period to which they relate. If this election is not made, the tax is deductible on some fixed date of accrual. A variety of dates for accrual have been approved by the Treasury and the courts in specific cases. These include the assessment date, the lien date, and the date personal liability attaches.

On the sale of real estate, the Code requires that the real property tax be apportioned between the seller and purchaser on the basis of the time the property was held by each party during the year covered by the tax. Proration is required whether or not the seller and purchaser actually apportion the tax and whether they are on the cash or the accrual basis.

Since the property tax becomes a lien on and after the assessment or lien date, it is customarily booked as payable on receipt of the tax bill. When the accounts of the company reflect payment or full liability for these taxes, either estimated or actual, and the period assigned for absorption of the tax expense for accounting purposes extends beyond the date on which the liability was recognized, the unamortized tax expense at a balance sheet date is shown as prepaid taxes.

INTERNAL CONTROL

Many large enterprises maintain a tax department that prepares or supervises the preparation of all tax returns, maintains the required analyses and information, and approves all tax payments. The scope of operations of a tax department and the amount of outside advice and assistance which it may require will vary with the tax and accounting complexities of the company and the ability of its personnel. The present high tax rates make it obvious that good control must be exercised over what may be the largest single expense of the business.

Because of the differences between income for tax purposes and income as determined under generally accepted accounting principles, an extensive set of supplementary records may be desirable to facilitate the preparation of tax returns and to identify clearly allowable costs and other deductions.

AUDITING PROCEDURES

Objectives.—The various types of taxes for which most companies are liable include, but are not necessarily limited to, the following:

Federal income taxes,

State income and franchise taxes,

Real estate and personal property taxes,

Excise taxes, including sales and use, manufacturers' excise, and gross receipts taxes,

Social security, unemployment, and disability taxes,

Employees' income tax withheld from wages.

The purpose of the auditor's examination of tax accounts is to form an opinion whether the client's computation of the provision for taxes is a reasonable allocation of this expense to income of the period under examination and whether the amounts deferred to future periods, or included among liabilities at the balance sheet date, are fairly stated. Determination of the estimated liability for federal and state income taxes is often difficult and complex, but the auditor should have sufficient knowledge of the major taxing statutes to make this determination. While excess profits taxes are not imposed currently, the auditor should have a working familiarity with them since the years to which excess profits taxes applied may not be closed. The discussion which follows is directed primarily to federal income taxes; however, the methods suggested may be adapted to the auditor's examination of state income taxes.

Federal Income Taxes.

CURRENT YEAR.—The auditor's examination of the provision for federal income tax for the current year will ordinarily include, but not necessarily be limited to, the following:

1. Review the reconciliation of net income per books with taxable income to be reported in the current year's tax returns, as computed by the client. Compare with prior year's reconciliation. Determine whether the taxable income computation gives effect to adjustments resulting from Treasury examinations of prior years which may affect the current year.

2. Summarize beginning and end-of-the-year balances of estimated liabilities and provisions not deductible for tax purposes, and trace net changes for the year to the reconciliation of book and taxable income.

3. Review changes in earned and capital surplus accounts for the year to determine whether any such changes should be reflected in the determination of taxable income for the current year.

4. Review operating losses, if any, for each of the five preceding years together with statutory adjustments, if any, required to convert them to a net operating loss deduction. Review capital losses for the same period. Determine to what extent such losses may be applied to the current year.

5. Review client's computation of federal income tax for the current year.

The Internal Revenue Code does not tax all corporations alike. Personal holding companies, insurance companies, and regulated investment companies are treated differently from ordinary trading or manufacturing companies; foreign corporations and Western Hemisphere Trade Corporations are taxed differently from ordinary domestic corporations. Certain charitable corporations and others, such as farmers' co-operatives, are exempt in whole or in part from income taxes. The auditor reviewing the income tax liability of a company falling within special classifications should consider whether the company has complied with the applicable requirements of the Internal Revenue Code and the regulations.

REMINDER LIST.—In addition to procedures outlined above, some auditors make use of a reminder list which is designed to insure consideration of some of the more common factors affecting the computation of federal and state income tax liabilities. It is impractical to list all possible matters for consideration, and the auditor's review should not be restricted to the items listed; nevertheless, a prepared standard list is a useful aid in the review of the adequacy of corporation federal income tax accruals. The following are examples of a few of the subjects, together with condensed explanations of their significance, which might be covered in such a list:

Consolidated Returns:
    (a) If a consolidated return was filed for the preceding year, the practice may have to be continued.
    (b) If a consolidated return was not filed for the preceding year, consideration should be given to any advantages that might result from filing consolidated returns.

Charitable Contributions.—There are limitations on the amounts that may be deducted; excess contributions may, however, be carried over to the next two succeeding years.

Dividends Received Deduction.—Tax deductions for dividends received from domestic corporations are allowed, subject to certain limitations.

Foreign Taxes.—The aggregate foreign income taxes paid or accrued may be either deducted from gross income or claimed as a credit against the tax.

Provisions for Contested Liabilities.—Accruals for contested liabilities are not deductible until liability is actually determined and fixed.

Unpaid Expenses and Interest.—Accruals for interest or expenses to be paid to cash-basis stockholders of closely held corporations are not deductible unless payment is made within 2½ months after the close of the year.

Property Used in Trade or Business.—Net gain on sale of depreciable or real property used in trade or business held over six months is subject to favorable capital gains rates. A net loss may be taken as an ordinary deduction.

Security Transactions.—Net gain on sale of securities or other capital assets, if held for more than six months, may be subject to favorable capital gains rates. Net losses are not deductible but may be carried forward. Taxable gains and losses are computed from the tax basis, which may be different from the book basis.

Personal Holding Company Surtax.—Corporations which are defined as personal holding companies are subject to additional surtax on undistributed net income.

Charges to Estimated Liability and Allowance Accounts.—Nondeductible provisions made in prior years give rise to deductions in the year of payment.

Tax Savings List.—Many times the independent certified public accountant's review of income tax liability in the annual examination of financial statements reveals opportunities for tax savings or tax postponements. Development of constructive suggestions may be aided by the use of a tax savings list which describes briefly many of the more common situations in which income taxes may be minimized or postponed, or lower statutory rates availed of. Many matters may be covered, but the following are illustrative of the type of material that might be included:

Utilization of Elective Features.—Lifo method for inventories, reserve method for bad debt deductions, accruals for vacation and holiday payments.

Changing Form or Timing of Transactions.—Adoption of completed contract basis for long-term contracts, making charitable contributions in the form of high-value, low-basis property, leasing in lieu of buying equipment.

Officers' and Employees' Benefits.—Various forms of stock option plans, pension, profit-sharing, stock bonus plans, deferred compensation contracts.

Transactions Involving Capital Assets.—Realization of ordinary income tax-free when net long-term capital gains exceed taxable income, offsetting realized capital gains by further sales of capital assets at a loss, avoidance of capital gains in loss years.

Acquisitions, Organizations, Reorganizations.—Allocations of purchase price to obtain maximum tax benefit, possible advantages of purchase of assets rather than stock, preservation of high basis in reorganizations, alternative methods of liquidating a corporation.

Foreign Operations.—Use of Western Hemisphere Trade Corporation or one of the foreign tax havens, timing of dividends from foreign corporations, taxing of income blocked by foreign exchange restrictions.

PRIOR YEARS.—As part of his examination, the auditor should be assured of the adequacy of the estimated liability for additional taxes and interest that may be assessed for years still open for assessment. For information upon which to base this opinion, the auditor should review copies of tax returns and the file of correspondence with the Treasury Department relating to those years that are still subject to adjustment. In an initial examination he should also review similar material for recent closed years. The possibility of an assessment of additional taxes may come to the auditor's attention as a result of his review of an agent's report challenging the treatment of certain items. Additional taxes are not always paid in the full amount of the proposed assessment, for the Treasury Department frequently cannot sustain its claims. Consequently, the auditor must consider whether the amount of proposed taxes, if material, should be included as a liability or disclosed in an explanatory footnote.

State and Local Taxes.—A corporation must consider the possible liability for taxes imposed by any state in which it does business. The fact that the company has sales representatives or maintains inventories in various states may be significant in determining whether it is subject to tax in those states. The auditor should summarize the various state tax liabilities accrued at the balance sheet date for current and prior years. If federal taxable income for prior years has been changed and such income is the starting point for computing state taxes, the revisions should be reported by the taxpayer to the state tax authorities in accordance with the applicable requirements, and the liability for additional state taxes should be recorded.

The auditor may not have knowledge of obscure or unusual taxes in distant or foreign localities in which he does not practice; however, to the extent that a tax liability may be material, the auditor should satisfy himself that adequate provision has been made.

Taxes Withheld.—Under various tax law enactments of federal, state, and local governments, companies must collect from employees and others taxes to be remitted to the proper taxing authorities. Neither federal nor state laws prescribe specific methods of accounting or record-keeping. The laws and regulations require that records be maintained so that government auditors may be able to determine the tax liability and compliance with the laws. Social security taxes payable by employees on salaries and wages and the statutory withholding for income taxes must be deducted by the employer from the employees' compensation; taxes on dividends paid to foreign stockholders must be withheld by the corporation paying the dividends; taxes on rents, royalties, or other charges paid to nonresident aliens, foreign partnerships, or foreign corporations must be withheld by the payers; in certain localities local taxes on wages or on retail sales must be collected by the taxpayer or the vendor. Amounts withheld represent liabilities to the various taxing authorities and are usually presented in the balance sheet as accounts payable other than to trade creditors.

Withholding procedures should be reviewed to determine their adequacy and tests should be made to determine that they are functioning properly.

The employer's share of social security and other payroll taxes should be accrued concurrently with the accrual of all regular payrolls. When a split-week payroll is accrued at a year end, the company may or may not accrue related payroll taxes, but the policy adopted should be consistently maintained.

STATEMENT PRESENTATION

General.—There are few fixed rules for the classification of taxes as expenses or deductions in the statement of income, except that the provision for federal taxes on income is almost invariably stated separately. It is also customary to show separately foreign taxes on income. Property taxes are usually included in cost of sales and state franchise taxes in general and administrative expenses. State income taxes are sometimes included with state franchise taxes and sometimes shown as a separate item with federal income taxes under a heading such as "Taxes on Income."

It is difficult to distinguish between state income taxes and state franchise taxes, since so-called franchise taxes may in fact be based on income and so-called income taxes may in fact be based on something other than income. The authors recommend classifying as income taxes only those state taxes that are officially called income taxes and are in fact based on income.

The authors also recommend the practice of showing provisions for income taxes in income statements in round amounts, thus emphasizing the fact that they are necessarily estimates, not exact computations.

Adjustments of Prior Years' Taxes.—A provision for possible additional assessments of taxes (generally federal income taxes) is usually included in each year's provision; if additional taxes are assessed for which no previous provision had been made, the amounts are usually charged to income of the year in which determined. If material in relation to the current year's provision, they may be stated separately; if so large as to distort net income for the year, they should be included in the statement of surplus.

Carry-Back and Carry-Forward Losses.—When (a) refunds of federal income taxes paid in a prior year are receivable as a result of the carry-back of losses to a prior year, or (b) a reduction of federal income tax of the current year results from losses carried forward from a prior year, Accounting Research Bulletin No. 43, Chapter 10, Section B, states:

> Either of two treatments is acceptable: (a) the amount of taxes estimated to be actually payable for such year may be shown in the income statement, with the amount of the tax reduction attributable to the amounts carried back (forward) indicated either in a footnote or parenthetically in the body of the income statement; or (b) the income statement may indicate the results of operations without inclusion of such reduction, which reduction should be shown as a final item before the amount of net income for the period.

The bulletin also states that if misleading inferences would be drawn from the inclusion in income of a reduction in federal income taxes because of carrying forward losses, the tax reduction should be credited to surplus.

Allocation of Income Taxes.

STATEMENT OF INCOME.—When income taxes or amounts in lieu thereof are charged or credited to income as a result of allocation under the principles discussed earlier in this chapter, the authors consider that such amounts, when material, should preferably be stated separately under the caption "Provision for Federal Income Tax," appropriately described. When material profits or losses are included in the statement of surplus after allocation of the related income tax, the allocation of such tax should be indicated in the statement of surplus.

BALANCE SHEET.—Whether or not tax allocations are necessary, the liability for federal income taxes shown among the liabilities should include the amount expected to be paid in the ensuing year. See the statement presentation section of Chapter 16 for a discussion of off-setting United States Government securities against the liability for federal taxes on income.

When tax-deductible items are not reflected as charges to income in the current year but will be charged to book income in future years, the temporary tax benefit derived should be shown as a deferred credit or deducted from the related asset or deferred charge. When items are included in taxable income in the current year but will be reflected in book income in future years, the amount of tax applicable thereto should be deferred and included among the assets or deducted from the related balance sheet liability. If the item is a book deduction in the current year, but the tax deduction will be taken in the future, the same principle applies, except when the transaction is such that no liability is created, then the expected tax benefit is necessarily included among deferred charges. Credit or debit amounts of taxes deferred under tax allocation principles should be included among current or noncurrent asset or liability captions, depending on the circumstances.

DEFERRED COMPENSATION PLANS.—When tax allocation principles are applied in accounting for liabilities under deferred compensation plans, the liability to be discharged by payment of cash or an equivalent may be reduced by the related tax effect. The amount of related tax effect may also be treated as a deferred charge and the gross liability for compensation shown. When the liability is to be met with the issue of capital stock, the gross liability should be included in the capital section of the balance sheet, with disclosure of the number of shares to be issued under the plan, and the related tax effect should be treated as a deferred charge.

CHAPTER 23

THE LONG-FORM REPORT

Introduction.—The auditor's short-form report is discussed in Chapter 6. The auditor frequently has occasion to present long-form reports containing more detail than that included in the short-form report. They may vary greatly in form and content depending on their purpose, and they may be given in addition to or in lieu of the short-form report. In addition to the basic financial statements, the long-form report customarily contains details supporting and comments on various items in the financial statements as well as comments on the scope of the examination.

When the auditor makes an examination of financial statements for the purpose of giving his opinion on them in a short-form report, he need not extend his examination merely because a long-form report is to be given in addition to the short-form report. The auditor should endeavor to distinguish clearly in his long-form report between qualifications and mere explanations, and he should avoid giving the impression that the report includes factual representations made by him; he should make clear that the report contains his opinion or reasons for lack of opinion on financial data consisting of management's representations.

Auditor's Responsibility for Financial Data in Long-Form Reports.
—Financial data in most long-form reports fall into the following
categories:

1. Basic financial statements, usually a balance sheet and statements of
   income and surplus, which present the financial position and the
   results of operations, and on which the auditor has stated, or is in
   a position to state, his opinion in a short-form report.

2. Supplementary financial statements and other details of the basic
   financial statements which, in the auditor's opinion, are not necessary for a fair presentation of financial position and results of
   operations.

3. Statistical data which the auditor usually has not examined.

4. Financial statements and related financial data for prior periods,
   submitted for comparative purposes, all, part, or none of which
   may have been examined by the auditor.

Statement on Auditing Procedure No. 23, issued in 1947, revised
in 1949, and incorporated in substance as the fourth reporting standard
in "Generally Accepted Auditing Standards" in 1954 is discussed in
Chapter 6. Because of its important relation to the long-form report,
this fourth reporting standard is quoted below:

The report shall either contain an expression of opinion regarding the financial statements, taken as a whole, or an assertion to the effect that an opinion
cannot be expressed. When an over-all opinion cannot be expressed, the
reasons therefor should be stated. In all cases where an auditor's name is associated with financial statements the report should contain a clear-cut indication
of the character of the auditor's examination, if any, and the degree of
responsibility he is taking.

The authors prefer that the basic financial statements (category 1
above) submitted with the short and long-form reports be identical,
and that the auditor's opinion on them be given either at the beginning
or at the conclusion of the long-form report. Some auditors incorporate
by reference a short-form report previously submitted; this treatment
is objectionable because the reader is not in a position to know whether
the short-form report contains explanations or qualifications.

The question arises as to the extent to which the auditor's opinion on
the fairness of the basic financial statements applies to other financial data
included in the long-form report, and as to the need for him to express
or disclaim an opinion on supporting or supplementary statements, or
on other financial data contained in the report. It is generally understood that the auditor's opinion on the fairness of presentation of financial statements is directed to the statements as a whole, and not to each

individual item or amount stated on them. The auditor's opinion on the basic financial statements is applicable to supporting or supplementary financial statements and other details (category 2 above) to the same extent that it is applicable to individual amounts in the basic statements; that is, to the extent of their relationship to the financial statements as a whole.

In the authors' opinion, the above-quoted reporting standard is not intended to require the independent auditor to report separately on supporting details of items shown on financial statements which might be included in the text or as supporting or supplementary statements in a long-form report, unless he has an exception to or reservation about certain portions of the data. His reservation may result from (1) facts brought to light in the course of his examination, (2) the fact that his examination did not include tests relating to the information contained in a supporting or supplementary statement or schedule, or (3) the fact that the information is presented in such a manner or context as to make likely misleading inferences.

When details of consolidating or combining statements by companies, divisions, departments, or products are given, the auditor may believe, as a result of his examination, that the statements present fairly the consolidated or combined financial position and results of operations, but one or more of the aforementioned considerations may preclude him from reaching the same conclusion about statements of individual subsidiaries, divisions, departments, or products. In this case he should make his position clear, usually in a paragraph early in the text.

When statistical or other data (category 3 above), usually taken from company records without examination by the auditor, are included in the long-form report, the auditor should state whether he has examined or tested such data. It is usually feasible to make such a statement at the point in the report at which the material is introduced.

When basic financial statements and related financial data for prior periods (category 4 above) are given for comparative purposes, the standards applicable to the preceding three categories should be applied, respectively, subject to the same considerations expressed in Chapter 6 on comparative statements in short-form reports.

The Committee on Auditing Procedure of the American Institute of Certified Public Accountants is considering a proposed statement on long-form reports which, if issued, should indicate the committee's opinion on the application of the fourth reporting standard to these reports.

The auditor may present long-form reports following limited examinations of the client's financial statements on which no opinion can be given or is expected. Some clients request their auditors to provide monthly or quarterly accounting services which might include the preparation of reports containing analyses and interpretive comments on periodic financial statements. These reports resemble long-form reports on the examination of annual financial statements, except that they should include in the opening paragraphs a statement of the auditor's inability to express an over-all opinion, together with his reasons.

Content of Long-Form Report on Examination of Financial Statements.—Even though a business organization has an accounting staff that prepares current reports of operations containing all financial information required by management, the client may request the auditor to submit a long-form report. A file of long-form reports prepared by the auditor provides a readily accessible record of significant financial data for the life of the enterprise, and these reports often prove of value many years after they have been written. Concerns without accounting staffs that regularly prepare summarized financial data often rely on the independent auditor to present annually, or at more frequent intervals, reports providing management with significant information in text and schedule form.

Most long-form reports on examinations of financial statements conform to the following broad outline:

> Text, including opinion, scope of examination, explanatory comments, comparisons, ratios, and statistical data;
> Basic financial statements;
> Supporting or supplementary statements and schedules.

TEXT.—Practices differ in selecting and arranging material to be included in the text of a long-form report. Material that might be included is discussed in the following paragraphs.

When both short-form and long-form reports are submitted, they usually bear the same date. This subject, together with that of addressing the report, is discussed further in Chapter 6.

COMMENTS ON SCOPE OF EXAMINATION AND OPINION.—When all required procedures have been followed and the opinion on the statements is unqualified, the language of the scope paragraph of the short-form report is an excellent condensed description of the scope of examination. Credit grantors frequently request additional information on the extent of auditing procedures. When auditing procedures are reported in greater detail, they may be stated in a separate section of the report where they will not detract from the clarity of the financial data presented, or it may be preferable to include these explanations under the discussion of balance sheet items or operating accounts to which they apply. When the auditor's opinion contains exceptions, he may discuss them in further detail under the appropriate captions of the text.

ORGANIZATION AND HISTORY.—When financial statements are being independently audited for the first time or a report is being made to new management, it may be desirable to present a summary of the organization and history of the company. The following subjects may appropriately be covered in this section of the report:

Date and state of incorporation.

Character of business.

Capital originally authorized and issued and subsequent changes therein.

Assets, cash or property, received on issuance of capital stock.

Description of predecessor companies if there has been a merger or consolidation.

Summary of earnings and dividends for a representative period (e.g. ten years) prior to first audit.

Description of major property additions in prior years.

Purpose of issues and description of long-term debt, such as bonds, debentures, and notes.

Description of subsidiary companies, if any, indicating degree of ownership, nature of business, and any other relevant data.

SUMMARY OF IMPORTANT CHANGES DURING THE YEAR.—Summarization of important changes during the year is usually desirable before beginning detailed comments. Financing operations may have refunded existing obligations or stock issues, or provided additional working capital. A description of the issues sold or retired, and the disposition of the proceeds for new plants, additional working capital, or research may be of interest. The company may have started to market new products, or to expand its markets for established lines. There may have been changes in sales or other policies that have a significant effect on operations. Inauguration of a pension or profit-sharing plan or developments in labor relations may be proper subjects for comment at this point.

COMMENTS ON RESULTS OF OPERATIONS.—A condensed comparative statement of income is often used as a starting point for comments on results of operations, as shown on the following page.

	Current Year	Pct. of Sales	Preceding Year	Pct. of Sales	Increases Decreases* in Net Income
Net sales	$230,000	100.0	$200,000	100.0	$30,000
Cost of sales	184,000	80.0	152,000	76.0	32,000*
Gross profit	$ 46,000	20.0	$ 48,000	24.0	$ 2,000*
Selling expenses	$ 14,000	6.1	$ 11,000	5.5	$ 3,000*
General and administrative expenses	14,000	6.1	10,000	5.0	4,000*
Total expenses	$ 28,000	12.2	$ 21,000	10.5	$ 7,000*
Income before federal taxes on income	$ 18,000	7.8	$ 27,000	13.5	$ 9,000*
Provision for federal taxes on income	5,400	2.3	8,500	4.2	3,100
Net income	$ 12,600	5.5	$ 18,500	9.3	$ 5,900*

The foregoing comparisons should prompt the auditor to inquire into the reasons for the variations. For example, he may inquire why the rate of gross profit showed a marked drop with increasing sales, and why selling expense per dollar of sales increased in spite of a substantial increase in sales since an increase in sales is ordinarily accompanied by lower selling expense per dollar of sales. He should want to know why general and administrative expenses increased 40 per cent when the volume of business increased only 15 per cent. The auditor should feel sure that he knows all the facts before commenting on variations in a comparative income statement.

Significant changes affecting the comparability of the results of operations of the current year with those of the preceding year should be described if they have not previously been included in the "Summary of Important Changes During the Year." The changes should be described in detail and amounts should be stated so that their effect is clearly evident. In addition, if the comparability of the operating results of the two years is sufficiently affected by inconsistency in the application of generally accepted accounting principles, details of the inconsistent treatment, with amounts involved, should be set forth at this point in the report. These details should support the exception to consistency taken in the opinion section of the report.

There are a number of possible variations of the form of condensed statements of income. The major items of revenue, costs, and expenses may be shown by products, geographical areas, companies, or other significant divisions. Sales units may be shown, and sales and costs may be stated in terms of dollars or thousands of dollars per unit.

COMMENTS ON BALANCE SHEET ITEMS.—In this section of the report it is appropriate to present the composition of principal items of assets and liabilities and an amplification of the description of bases on which they are stated. Additional comments on the scope of examination and findings of the examination may be included under the appropriate balance sheet captions. Data illustrative of material which may be included are mentioned in the paragraphs immediately following.

In discussing the various balance sheet items, the logical starting point for comment is usually the condensed balance sheets at the end of the current year and the preceding year. These may be presented in comparative form as follows:

	December 31		Increases Decreases*
	Current Year	Preceding Year	
Current assets:			
Cash	$ 83,000	$ 30,000	$53,000
Notes and accounts receivable, less allowance	160,000	169,000	9,000*
Inventories	220,000	180,000	40,000
	$463,000	$379,000	$84,000
Current liabilities:			
Notes payable	$ 30,000	$ 18,000	$12,000
Accounts payable	18,000	3,000	15,000
Accrued expenses	36,000	4,000	32,000
	$ 84,000	$ 25,000	$59,000
Working capital	$379,000	$354,000	$25,000
Other assets:			
Land	30,000	30,000	——
Buildings	68,000	65,000	3,000
Machinery and equipment	112,000	97,000	15,000
Allowance for depreciation	47,000**	46,000**	1,000*
Deferred charges	8,000	4,000	4,000
Total	$550,000	$504,000	$46,000
Represented by:			
Capital stock	$530,000	$500,000	$30,000
Earned surplus	20,000	4,000	16,000
	$550,000	$504,000	$46,000
Ratio of current assets to current liabilities	5½ to 1	15 to 1	

** Deductions.

Source and Disposition of Working Capital.—The condensed balance sheets show an increase of $25,000 in working capital. This increase may be explained by presenting a statement of the source and disposition of working capital.

Working capital is derived from earnings during the period, sales of fixed assets, increase of capital through issue of securities, or from other sources. Purchases of additional fixed assets, retirements of bonds or preferred stock, and payments of dividends are examples of transactions that decrease working capital.

In preparing a statement of source and disposition of working capital, consideration should be given to increases or decreases disclosed
by the comparative balance sheets that result from book entries that do
not affect working capital, e.g., provision for depreciation or amortization of noncurrent assets. Although depreciation and amortization provisions affect profits, they must be added back to net income in determining additions to working capital.

In the following illustration of a statement of source and disposition of working capital, which is not intended to be all-inclusive, it
should be noted that:

Capital stock in the amount of $30,000 was sold at par;

Net income was $36,000;

A cash dividend of $20,000 was paid;

Provision for depreciation in the amount of $7,000 was added to the
depreciation allowance account; and

Machinery and equipment which cost $12,000, and for which deprecia-
tion of $6,000 had been previously provided, was sold for $4,000,
showing a loss of $2,000.

STATEMENT OF SOURCE AND DISPOSITION OF WORKING CAPITAL
for the year ended December 31, _____

Source of working capital:		
From operations:		
Net income for the year		$36,000
Add, Deductions made in determining net income which did not affect working capital:		
Provision for depreciation	$ 7,000	
Loss on sale of fixed assets	2,000	9,000
Total from operations		45,000
Proceeds from issue of additional capital stock		30,000
Proceeds from sale of fixed assets		4,000
Total derived from above sources		$79,000
Disposition of working capital:		
Dividend paid		$20,000
Additions to fixed assets:		
Buildings	3,000	
Machinery and equipment	27,000	30,000
Increase in noncurrent deferred charges		4,000
Total disposition of working capital		$54,000
Net increase in working capital		$25,000

A statement of this type, sometimes called "Statement of Source and
Application of Funds," discloses changes in financial position not always apparent from a comparison of balance sheets. The form of statement may be varied to emphasize significant information. For ex-

ample, it may be desirable to prepare a statement of the source and disposition of cash funds. Certain changes in net current assets, such as the additional borrowing on notes payable in the illustration above, may be brought into the statement as a source of funds. Or, if an issue of bonds is the most important source of funds during the period, the statement may start with the proceeds of the bond issue. The statement may be one of the most useful in the long-form report, since many businessmen understand it more readily than the more conventional financial statements on which it is based.

Cash.—An unwarranted number of vouchers or unauthorized employee advances and loans in working cash funds might call for comment in the report. Unusually large balances on deposit with small banks or small balances that might be consolidated to avoid service charges may well be mentioned.

Accounts Receivable.—Readers of a report are usually interested in the status of the accounts receivable from customers and the auditor's opinion of the adequacy of allowances for losses on collection. If the company is a borrower on short-term credit, the lender may wish to see an analysis of accounts receivable by age, preferably compared with a similar analysis for the preceding year. If some accounts are past due, an indication of the amounts collected since the balance sheet date may be of interest. Because of special problems that may arise in the collection of accounts of foreign customers, it is well to segregate foreign accounts receivable. The average period of collection may be computed and compared with the company's credit terms. Unusual credit terms involving large amounts of receivables and exceptionally large percentages of sales to individual customers may be proper subjects for comment. Credit insurance coverage, if any, should be indicated. A summary analysis of the allowance for doubtful accounts for the year, showing opening balance, additions, deductions, and the ending balance, may be included. The extent of requests for confirmation of accounts receivable balances and replies received in response to these requests may be indicated. Large advances to and receivables from officers and employees may be listed in detail.

Inventories.—As a result of his examination of inventories, the auditor should have a comprehensive knowledge of the client's methods of inventory control, inventory-taking, and pricing and should be able to comment on these methods and suggest improvements if any are needed. A summary schedule of inventories by classification or location may be of interest; a statement of obsolete or slow-moving material and provisions for estimated loss might be informative.

The report may also describe in some detail the basis on which the inventory is stated and the method of computing cost or market. If cost is determined by the Lifo method, the year the method was adopted is usually of interest.

Plant Assets.—Supplemental information about plant and property, depreciation and amortization allowances, and the policy in accounting for repairs may be of interest. If assets are carried at amounts other than cost, the basis should be described. A summary by plant classification indicating beginning balances, changes during the period, and closing balances of plant asset and related accumulated allowance accounts together with depreciation and amortization rates is often of interest. Significant changes in depreciation rates and policies in accounting for fixed assets may be discussed.

Deferred Charges.—The long-form report usually includes a more detailed list of these items than is customarily shown on the face of the balance sheet. The basis of the amount at which intangibles are carried in the accounts and the policy as to amortization thereof may well be given; amounts amortized during the year may be stated.

Notes Payable.—Details of notes payable to banks and other creditors may be tabulated. Significant provisions of loan agreements are usually set forth in notes to the financial statements.

Accounts Payable.—It may be desirable to summarize trade accounts payable by age, that is, by the months in which they were billed, especially if it appears that substantial amounts are not being paid in accordance with the usual trade terms. A tabulation of significant amounts of miscellaneous accounts payable, such as advances, deposits, and taxes withheld from salaries and wages, may be set forth in the report. If payables include amounts due officers, stockholders, or affiliated interests, a listing of the individual amounts is in order. A summary of the changes during the period in such accounts or other unusual accounts payable may be of interest to the reader.

Accrued Accounts.—A summary of the accounts under this caption in the balance sheet is usually of interest to the report reader. When profit-sharing or bonus plans are in effect, a brief description of the terms of the plan, a calculation of the amount of extra compensation accrued during the period, and the current and noncurrent portions of the liability may be included in the report. If these plans require approval by stockholders, the date of the latest approval should be indicated.

A summary of the accrual provided for federal taxes on income and renegotiation is usually of interest. It may well be accompanied by an indication of the latest year examined by representatives of governmental authorities and the disposition of any adjustments proposed.

Comments on accrued royalties, if significant in amount, may include a recital of the important terms of license agreements, a summary analysis of the accrued royalty account, and a statement of the computation of important royalties accrued during the period under review. Reports of special examinations of royalties accrued may be referred to under this caption.

Accrued salaries, wages and commissions, taxes other than federal income taxes, and interest ordinarily do not merit extended comment unless circumstances are unusual.

Long-Term Liabilities.—Most bonds and some long-term notes and debentures are issued subject to terms set forth in a trust indenture. The auditor's report may recite significant accounting provisions in the indenture and refer to any violations of the provisions that his examination may have disclosed. Pertinent information about such matters as interest rates, maturities, and sinking fund requirements may be given.

Capital Stock.—Changes in the capital structure during the year may be outlined here if they were not discussed in the "Summary of Important Changes During the Year" at the beginning of the report. Operations of sinking funds for retirement of preferred stock during the period may be described. If the company has a stock option plan, the long-form report may include a description of the terms and conditions of the plan, a statement of options granted, exercised, and expired during the period, and information about options outstanding at the end of the period. Such detailed comments on options amplify information included in the notes to the financial statements.

Surplus.—If the statements of surplus included in the financial statements are condensed, any amplification that may be desirable should be included here. If adjustments affecting both capital stock and surplus were made as a result of a reorganization, the effect of the adjustments may be indicated, possibly in a tabulation. The financial statements should refer to any restrictions on surplus resulting from loan agreements or indentures and should state the amount of surplus either restricted or free from the restrictions at the balance sheet date.

Contingent Liabilities and Commitments.—Although reference to significant contingent liabilities and commitments is required in the notes to financial statements, it is customary to comment upon these matters in some detail in the text of the long-form report. When adverse claims and suits are pending, reference should be made to their current status, the amount of the liability estimated by counsel, and the provision, if any, that has been made for them in the financial statements.

Unusual commitments to purchase raw materials, significant expenditures that will be required to complete plant additions authorized at the balance sheet date, and contractual obligations under long-term lease or lease-back arrangements may be discussed.

Pension plans are generally of interest to the reader of the report. These plans may be described briefly to indicate whether they are contributory or noncontributory, the eligibility requirements, the number of employees covered by the plan, the provisions for benefits, and the actuarial status of the plan with particular emphasis on unfunded past service costs and the plan, if any, for funding them. The total cost of the plans for the current year and for the preceding year may be stated. If appropriate, a description of the contributory feature of the plan should be included.

COMMENTS ON AUDITING PROCEDURES.—It is appropriate to include comments on auditing procedures in the textual material discussed above, or to include such comments in a separate section. Auditing procedures followed in confirming accounts receivables and observing physical inventories are usually described in comments under the related captions. A detailed recital of all auditing procedures included in the examination is not likely to be of interest to the reader.

COMMENTS ON INTERNAL ACCOUNTING CONTROL AND INTERNAL CHECK.—Evaluation of (1) accounting controls designed to assure an accurate and suitable recording and summarization of authorized financial transactions and (2) controls directed primarily to the safeguarding of assets against defalcations or other similar irregularities is an integral and important part of the auditor's examination. The importance of these controls and the auditor's methods of investigating and test-checking their operation are discussed in Chapter 5.

The auditor will wish to assist his client by reporting promptly to him constructive suggestions for improvements in existing internal accounting control or internal check resulting from observations during the course of his examination. Matters to be reported may be discussed informally with the client, and, if of major importance, they should be put in writing, possibly in the long-form report or, more usually, in a supplemental report or letter.

If the auditor reports on internal accounting control and internal check following an examination of financial statements, he should clearly indicate that the weaknesses discussed are only those that came to light in the course of an examination for the purpose of forming an opinion on the financial statements.

The system of internal control reflects practical choices based on materiality and relative risk. After reviewing the system the auditor may report that he believes that the internal control is "good and appropriate to the needs of the business"; he should, however, make it clear that such a review can never be sufficiently comprehensive to preclude the existence of some undetected weakness.

COMPARISONS, RATIOS, AND STATISTICAL DATA.—To make reports interesting and informative, the auditor may include statistical and comparative information on earnings and operations of the current year with previous years that he may or may not have examined. If such information is furnished, the report should clearly indicate whether the data were examined or whether they were taken from the client's records without audit; this point is discussed earlier in this chapter.

The significance of financial data may be more readily comprehended when they are converted to ratios. Probably the working capital ratio is the one most widely used; it expresses the relationship of current assets to current liabilities. Following are other ratios and figures that may be included to advantage in a long-form report:

Ratio to net assets of:
  Net income for the year
  Fixed assets
Turnover of inventories
Turnover of accounts receivable
Ratios of:
  Cash to current liabilities
  Profits before interest to interest on long-term debt
  Net income to preferred dividend requirements
Percentage to net sales of:
  Cost of sales
  Expenses
  Net income
Net income per share of common stock outstanding
Net assets per share of common stock outstanding

There are wide variations in methods of financing working capital, property additions, and other financial needs of different types of business. The auditor may review the policies of the business on which he is reporting, and develop ratios that will indicate the effect of these policies on financial position.

Financial ratios are most useful when compared with standards such as the company's ratios for preceding periods. These comparisons facilitate a study of trends. The ratios may assume even greater value when compared with those of other companies operating under similar conditions. Data from which ratios of comparable companies may be computed may often be obtained from statistics published by financial and credit agencies, government publications, or trade association bulletins. Sometimes ratios developed from published financial data of a recognized leader in the industry provide interesting and informative comparisons.

Financial ratios and other statistics developed from the financial statements, together with comparisons with those of prior periods and those for the industry, may be effectively presented in the long-form report in the following tabular form:

TABLE OF SIGNIFICANT FINANCIAL RATIOS

Description of Ratios	1957	1956	1955
Balance Sheet Ratios			
LIQUIDITY			
Cash to current liabilities	.19	.28	.36
Industry ratios (see note)		.24	.32
Current assets to current liabilities	1.96	2.53	2.72
Industry ratios		2.62	2.54
ACCOUNTS RECEIVABLE			
Average collection period of accounts receivable in days	24	24	28
Industry experience		32	31
INVENTORIES			
Cost of sales to inventory	2.43	3.38	3.60
Industry ratios		5.40	5.50
Inventory to working capital	1.49	1.12	.98
Industry ratios		.75	.76

Note: Industry ratios are median ratios of companies contained in the X industry published by the X Trade Association. The companies included in the study—50 in 1956 and 48 in 1955—had net assets ranging from $1,000,000 to $1,500,000. Industry data for 1957 are not available at this time.

Data for the industry should be selected with care, in order that data used are comparable with those of the company. It is always prudent to review the selection of industry statistics with company officials to assure reasonable comparability.

Presentations of financial ratios and other statistics in the long-form report should be limited to factual disclosure. It may be unwise to attempt to interpret the ratios presented.

In industries with a single unit of production, such as tons, pounds, barrels, or gallons, the sales accounts are usually kept in quantities as well as in amounts so that it may be possible to state income and expenses per unit of production or sales as well as in total dollars. Records of quantities and amounts, not only of sales, but also of materials consumed may make possible a comparison of the quantity of materials used with the quantity of finished product manufactured.

SUPPORTING OR SUPPLEMENTARY STATEMENTS AND SCHEDULES.— Additional data are often presented in long-form reports as supporting or supplementary statements and schedules. The details in which the data are presented may vary greatly, and the auditor must exercise his judgment in selecting those that may be appropriate and of interest to the reader.

It is customary to present a statement of cost of sales in some detail. Occasionally it will be helpful to furnish additional details in a supporting schedule. For example, the various elements of cost included in indirect labor and the major items of material cost might be included in supplementary schedules. It is customary to furnish detailed statements of selling expenses, administrative expenses, and general expenses; some items in these statements may also be supported by additional details in accompanying schedules.

A summary of plant and equipment and the related allowances for depreciation is a schedule frequently presented in support of the balance sheet; this schedule was described previously. Another balance sheet schedule frequently submitted is a schedule of investments owned together with the income received from each investment during the year. When a business carries insurance on the lives of its officers, long-form reports often include a schedule setting forth appropriate details of the insurance in force, the type of policy, annual premiums, and the cash surrender value at the close of the year under review.

Information on the types of insurance in force may be summarized in tabular form in a supplementary schedule. The amount of fire insurance by locations may be compared with the book amounts of the assets covered, but if this is done, it should be made clear that the book amounts may not represent insurable values. Co-insurance provisions of the policies should be indicated. The amount and limits of coverage under use and occupancy insurance, steam boiler, theft, and public liability policies, and blanket or position fidelity bonds may also be indicated.

Special Long-Form Reports.—The problems of reporting on examinations of nonprofit organizations, companies keeping their accounts on a cash basis or modified cash basis, and other types of business following special accounting practices are discussed in Chapter 6. When long-form reports on such examinations are presented, the principles discussed in this chapter for the preparation of reports on profit-making organizations are equally applicable.

Long-form reports may also be issued on examinations made for limited purposes. Reports on these examinations do not normally include complete financial statements because of the limited character of the examination. Included in this group are reports on the examination of specific accounts (such as rentals, royalties, profit-sharing bonuses, and the like) and reports on special investigations and surveys (such as those dealing with defalcations, systems and methods, contemplated purchases, and tax matters). If a limited opinion (that is, one restricted to certain phases of the accounts) can be expressed by the auditor, the areas of limitation must be clearly defined. Descriptions of the contents of some reports falling in this group are set forth in the following paragraphs.

SPECIFIC ACCOUNTS.—The auditor may occasionally be asked to make examinations of specific accounts, such as cash and securities. He should make clear to the client the limitations of such an examination, but there is no reason why he should not accept such an engagement. The auditor may be asked to examine all accounts at a specific location, such as a branch or factory. Examinations of consigned stocks of merchandise, or of lessees' accounts when the rental is based on a percentage of sales or net income are not uncommon. The auditor may be called upon to determine whether the terms of royalty or licensing agreements have been observed. These agreements frequently include a provision that the periodic reports of the licensee or lessee are to be examined by an independent public accountant.

DEFALCATIONS.—The primary responsibility for the prevention and detection of defalcations and similar irregularities rests with management, but irregularities may be discovered by the public accountant during the course of his examination. When irregularities become apparent, a number of questions arise: What is the extent of the money damage? Who are involved in the irregularities? What methods were used to conceal the shortage? Can the amount of the shortage be established to the satisfaction of the bonding company? Does it exceed the amount covered by the bond? Can the accumulation of the loss be identified by dates, especially if there are periods not covered by bond, or covered by different bonding companies? Is there possibility of recovery from sources other than the bonding company? Is the amount likely to be of such serious proportions that creditors, stockholders, or other interested parties should be notified promptly?

Often the management feels that the advice and expert knowledge of the independent certified public accountant should be availed of to assist in obtaining prompt and reliable answers to these questions. The examination made will depend on many considerations, such as the records available, the extent to which the existing system of internal check might have permitted extension of the known irregularity, the position of the defaulter in the organization, and other matters. The auditor should consult and cooperate with legal counsel and with representatives of the bonding companies so that the client's interest may be best served. His report should be designed to answer the questions previously raised and to provide other information helpful to interested parties.

PROPOSED BUSINESS ACQUISITIONS.—An examination made on behalf of a prospective purchaser usually covers a number of years, and some of the information desired is more general than that ordinarily obtained in the course of the usual audit. Much of this information is of continuing interest, and if the business is acquired the data should be retained in the auditor's permanent file. The following indicates information that may be obtained:

1. History of the business. Data on the origin of the concern; its incorporation; location and subsequent growth; formation, acquisition, and purpose of subsidiaries; and corporate powers reflected in articles of incorporation and by-laws.

2. Products. Description of principal and secondary products and by-products; source of demand for products—consuming public or other manufacturers; and characteristics of demand—fluctuating, seasonal, or relatively constant.

3. Production methods and processes. Relative importance of raw materials, fixed investment, and labor in the manufacturing process; principal raw materials, source of supply, kind of market; kind of labor, skill, sex, union affiliations, and apparent availability; and relative magnitude and kind of machinery used in the manufacturing process.

4. Methods of sale and distribution. Number and characteristics of consumers; whether sales are made through salesmen, branch offices, dealers, or jobbers; type of advertising employed; and relative importance of selling and distribution expenses.

5. Status of company in the industry. Comparison of production with that of competing companies in the same industry and with total for the industry; basis of competition with competitors—quality, price, and service; whether concern has strategic advantage over competitors in location (nearness to raw materials or to markets), or in labor costs; and dependence on tariff protection, patents, secret processes, and formulae.

6. Management and control. Distribution of stock ownership; identity of management with stock ownership; form of organization and organization chart; interrelationship and control of the various departments—sales, production, engineering, financial, and re-

search; personal data on executives—age, experience before and after affiliation with concern, salaries and bonuses; extent to which management relies on monthly or other periodic reports as a guide to management policies; extent to which reports are prepared but not used by those for whom intended; and extent of coordination of departmental activities.

7. Other data. Inventories may raise questions of obsolescence, overstocking, or unbalance. Purchase commitments and unfilled orders may assume even more than their usual significance. If any substantial portion of the company's operations is conducted in leased premises, terms of leases—which may be advantageous or disadvantageous to the lessee—should be determined. Schedules of sales in detail for as many as ten years, classified on as many bases as statistical records will permit; comparative statements of costs and expenses, with ratios to net sales; analyses of surplus showing rates and amounts of dividends for a period of years; and other details suitable to the circumstances may be included.

Long-Form Report on Financial Statements When No Examination Is Made.—The preparation of financial statements from books of account without examination is well within the scope of the certified public accountant's services, but such work should be differentiated from auditing.

Financial statements issued in a cover of an accounting firm, without a report or statement of the scope of the examination, may create the impression that the statements have the endorsement of the auditor, though that may not be the client's intention in showing them to third parties. Unexamined financial statements for which the auditor takes no responsibility should preferably be submitted on plain paper without the auditor's watermark or letterhead and, if bound, should preferably be in plain covers without the auditor's name. If the auditor's name appears on the paper or cover, the words "without audit" should be prominently displayed under the description of the financial statements on the cover and the headings of the statements in the report should also include such wording as "without examination" or "unaudited." The report should clearly state that the statements have been prepared without audit from data submitted by management.

Mechanical Preparation of Report.—All reports, whether short or long-form, should be typed in the auditor's office in the number of copies required for distribution, with at least one copy for the auditor's permanent file.

The mechanics of report preparation are usually concentrated in a special department of the auditor's office. The work is frequently divided into three categories: typing, proofreading and verification of arithmetic, and review for correctness of grammar and cross-references. This department should be so organized and staffed that it may be entrusted fully with the accuracy of these details, leaving the principal free to review reports for matters of accounting policy, adequacy of disclosure, form of presentation, style, and suitability.

The typing of audit reports is a specialized task which can be accomplished satisfactorily and economically only by typists of considerable training and experience in this field. Acquaintance with various reproducing equipment and other mechanical aids is important.

Reports should be proofread and reviewed by experienced persons with some knowledge of accounting. It should be an invariable rule that a report does not leave the auditor's office until it has been carefully read and checked by the report department. The accountant in charge should review a typed copy of the report before it is released.

Reports on examinations of independent public accountants, whether the covering opinion is qualified or unqualified, should be bound in durable covers bearing the auditor's name and typed on good quality paper.

Date of Report.—Dating of long-form reports is discussed on page 69.

Discussion of Draft of Report.—Usually, a conference with the client is desirable before a long-form report is finally issued so that the auditor may be assured that the report fulfills the client's requirements. Close cooperation between the auditor and the client's officers promotes efficient conduct of an examination.

divided into three categories: typing, proofreading, and checking of authors beyond services for references of original and cross-references. This department should be so organized and staffed that it may be entrusted chiefly with the accuracy of these details, leaving the principal free to review reports for matters of accounting policy, adequacy of disclosure, form of presentation, style, and suitability.

The typing of audit reports is a specialized task which can be accomplished satisfactorily and economically only by typists of considerable training and experience in this field. Acquaintance with various report-placing equipment and other mechanical aids is important.

Reports should be proofread and reviewed by experienced persons with some knowledge of accounting. It should be an invariable rule that a report does not leave the auditor's office until it has been carefully read and checked by the report department. The accountant in charge should review a typed copy of the report before it is released.

Record...

Date of Report.—Dating of long-form reports is discussed on page 66.

Discussion of Draft of Report.—Usually a conference with the client is desirable before a long-form report is finally issued so that the matter may be verified that the report reflects the set of circumstances. There...

CHAPTER 24

MANAGEMENT SERVICES

THE PUBLIC ACCOUNTANT AND
MANAGEMENT SERVICES

Introduction.—Businessmen expect their independent public accountants to provide many types of special services related to the general management of their businesses. This is particularly true in areas where accounting and statistical reports may be used by management as tools to assist in planning and controlling operations and increasing profits. They expect the accountants to be able to suggest procedures that are essential to good control.

Public accountants are expected to be expert in such matters as organization plans, methods and procedures for accounting and record-keeping, and the characteristics of various types of clerical labor-saving devices. They must be informed of the latest technological changes in office machines and methods for rapid communication and processing of data and realize the possibilities for making use of electronic computers and modern devices for automatic data processing.

Some companies have within their own organizations employees with all types of specialized technical abilities. Others prefer to call on outside specialists as needs for their services arise. Under either policy, the public accountant should be prepared to assist the client in obtaining the specialized management services he requires.

In companies that employ within their own organizations experts in accounting methods and data processing, the public accountant may serve as consultant to a study committee reporting directly to top management, charged with the review, research, and development of data processing methods. Study committees are frequently formed to include the controller, the cost accountant, the head of the systems and procedures division, and, from time to time, other department heads who may be interested directly in the problems under review. Sometimes it may be advisable to include a representative of the president to give the committee authority to cross departmental lines and to implement its recommendations. These committees are particularly useful for the extensive preliminary studies that must be made before installation of electronic computers. The public accountant may be called upon to analyze operations and assemble data for these committees.

Other companies may not include within their own organizations personnel qualified to determine the best methods, or those with the necessary qualifications may be overburdened with other duties. Under these circumstances, clients often turn to their public accountants for assistance. The public accountant should be qualified and ready to perform for these companies the same types of services provided by competent controllers or systems and procedures men.

Because of the intense competition characteristic of present business conditions and the rapid improvements being made in data processing methods, the time is ripe for a general overhaul of accounting and clerical operations and routines. Every business, regardless of size, should employ the most efficient methods and procedures appropriate to conditions prevailing in the enterprise. Modern methods are available for the elimination of duplicated clerical operations on original data; depending on circumstances, they may make use of electronic devices, common language tapes, tabulating equipment, standard office machines, or simple devices such as carbon paper or pegboards.

Qualifications for Management Services.—The public accountant specializing in management services should have a background of general accounting and business experience. He should have a natural interest in solving problems and constructive planning, and ability in converting ideas into reality. He should inform himself of control reports, systems, methods and procedures in use by well-operated companies, and the great variety of mechanical devices and equipment available for saving clerical labor. He should have imagination, be capable of original thinking, have perseverance in the face of difficulties, and, having arrived at a solution to a problem, he should be able to convince others of the soundness of his solution. He should be able to get along with people of widely varying personal characteristics and to deal impressively with management.

The procedures followed by public accountants in the examination of financial statements provide them with an unusual opportunity to become familiar with many kinds of managerial problems. The problems often have elements of similarity or are susceptible of solution by the application of common principles. Experience in public accounting develops powers of observation and critical analysis, and an objective point of view. It is, therefore, to be expected that public accountants should have these qualifications that are so essential in providing management services.

One rule is of fundamental importance: No public accountant should hold himself out as expert in any specialized field of service unless he has qualified himself as an expert in that field.

Approach to Management Services.—It is particularly important to the public accountant providing management services that he obtain and maintain the interest and cooperation of the top echelon of management. Before any work is undertaken, top management must understand and believe in the objectives of the study to be made. In no other way can there be assurance that when solutions have been found to the problems being studied, the necessary executive action will be taken to carry out recommendations made. Moreover, the problems, point of view, and working characteristics of top management should be understood by the public accountant, so that details of the plan to be developed may be fashioned to serve the needs of those who carry managerial responsibilities.

Any plan to improve or expedite information will require a change in work routines. It is human nature to resist change; any good idea must be sold to individuals before it can be put into effect. It is necessary, therefore, to enlist the cooperation of those who make the executive decisions, first in accepting the objectives of the study and later in effecting the changes necessary to make the plan work.

Competent personnel should be available to operate the revised plan, procedure, or system. It is futile and damaging to the reputation of the independent public accountant to design a system, deliver it to a client, and depart without assurance that it will operate to the client's satisfaction. Company personnel to operate a revised plan should be selected early in the development of the program of study, and they should participate in all phases of the program. Employees should receive full credit for their ideas; the public accountant will have the best assurance that the plan will operate successfully if employees feel that they have contributed to it and that their contribution is recognized.

The principal objective of revisions in methods or procedures is to enable management to increase the net income of the business. The public accountant should weigh total costs of obtaining information against total costs of not having it, taking into account long-term benefits that may accrue.

Every enterprise has problems which are related to those of the industry or activity of which it is a part. It is essential that the public accountant view the enterprise in true perspective and understand whether the basic problems lie within or outside the particular enterprise.

Independence in Management Services.—The public accountant can provide management services without losing his independence. His proper function is to bring to the attention of the client ideas, facts, recommendations, and assistance pertaining to the problems under consideration, in a staff capacity without active participation in management decisions. This requires a fine sense of professional responsibility; if the facts disclosed by investigation and research clearly indicate a course of action, the public accountant should not hesitate to express his recommendations. If equally acceptable alternative courses are available, they should be clearly described with full explanations of their advantages and disadvantages.

The independent public accountant in his professional capacity as a management advisor is expected to be free from any bias or prejudice that may influence the thinking of the client's personnel. His advice and suggestions have added weight since they are free of considerations that might militate against the objectivity of client's employees.

The authors believe that it is definitely in the public interest for independent public accountants to offer both auditing and management services to the same client. The public accountant providing management services will usually bring to his engagement a considerable knowledge of the client's affairs and internal management problems, obtained in connection with his auditing services. He will already be known to the client's employees. He can usually assist in obtaining improvements in methods and procedures with less disruption of the existing organization than can other outside consultants. His recognized objective point of view and his knowledge of total company operations may permit him to cross departmental lines with less friction than could company employees.

Responsibilities of the Public Accountant.—The public accountant who is observant in his auditing engagements will usually have little difficulty in discerning opportunities to assist his client in eliminating waste and unnecessary expense. He may be certain that his client will welcome any suggestions that will increase net income.

The public accountant should consider it one of his responsibilities to offer management services to his clients. Clients who engage public accountants for expert services in auditing and taxation are entitled to expect expert services in any area related to accounting, record-keeping, finance, and statistics.

Management services will sometimes disclose problems unrelated to accounting, record-keeping, finance, and statistics, and the public accountant should recognize that these problems should be solved by engineers or members of other professions. Public accountants should cooperate with the other professions. When services in other professions are offered by the independent public accountant, it is the opinion of the authors that the practitioner or partner of a firm of public accountants responsible for the performance of the management services engagement should himself be technically competent to pass judgment as an expert on the quality of the other professional services offered.

Scope of Management Services.—The scope of management services to be offered should be determined by the public accountant on the basis of his qualifications for providing services in the various areas. The authors prefer to confine the scope of management services to areas related to accounting, record-keeping, and financial and statistical matters and to recommend to clients the employment of specialists in other unrelated areas.

The scope of business operations is so vast that it offers many opportunities for specialization. The public accountant, since he is a specialist in accounting and its many adaptations, can provide a great variety of services to management. Some public accountants may become expert in accounting problems of various types of industry, or in some specialized field of accounting, such as federal income taxes, reporting under SEC regulations, or other fields common to many industries. Others may become expert in the many types of services to management that are enumerated in this chapter. The types of management services which are discussed below are intended to be illustrative rather than complete.

TYPES OF SERVICE

Organization.—Top management should delegate responsibilities and permit junior executives to make decisions. Those to whom these responsibilities have been delegated should be held responsible and rewarded according to their performance. Delegations of responsibility should be accompanied by clear lines of authority, and the organization plan must be understood and accepted by all persons affected.

An organization chart is important and, in itself, may point out to management weaknesses in organization that may be improved. The chart may, however, portray only a theoretical organization. No matter how good an organization may look on a chart, intensive study may be required to determine whether it functions effectively and according to plan.

REVIEW OF ORGANIZATION PLAN.—In any comprehensive study of a business enterprise the public accountant engaged in management services will necessarily examine the framework of the organization. He will observe the extent to which employees at various levels of authority and responsibility understand and actually perform the duties expected of them. He will determine whether the assignments of duties are clear, whether the organization is operating smoothly, and whether the delegations of authority and responsibility are clearly defined.

No enterprise is static, and its organization plan should be adjusted as the business grows. Authorities and responsibilities are sometimes reassigned or divided without adequate consideration of earlier delegations. Persons in positions of responsibility may not always be competent, and the public accountant may recommend that duties be reassigned to those who can perform them adequately.

The organization plan should serve the major objectives of the business and yet be adapted to the capabilities of available personnel, assuming that these capabilities are adequate for performance of required duties. The organization plan will influence the determination of departmental groups, the design of systems and procedures, the chart of accounts, and the form of the reports to be submitted to various levels of management.

RESPONSIBILITY ACCOUNTING.—The middle and lower levels of management often hold the key to effective operations. The principle of responsibility accounting is applicable even at the lowest management level. While usually this is the foreman level, frequently group leaders subordinate to the foreman should be included in the review of the organization plan.

ORGANIZATION CHARTS AND MANUALS.—An organization chart based on duties actually performed will call to the attention of management the points where lines of authority need clarification. If the chart is properly designed, it will set forth levels of authority so that weaknesses will become apparent.

Actual duties and responsibilities frequently are not accurately reflected in published organization charts. Periodic comparisons by management services specialists of actual duties and responsibilities with those published may lead to a revision of the organization chart or a reassignment of duties and responsibilities.

When assignments of authority and responsibility are described in writing, questions of definition invariably arise. A manual defining the organization plan in some detail is usually helpful in perfecting a smoothly operating organization.

Internal Management Reports.—The major purpose of internal accounting is to provide management with the data essential for the decisions which will produce the maximum profit for the enterprise. Internal management reports, whether prepared for the top or lower levels of management, should be prepared to accomplish that purpose. Reports should be produced promptly and at proper intervals to be of the greatest service and at minimum expense consistent with the major purpose.

The accounts should be so classified that reports based on them disclose results of operations by areas of responsibility. Reports should compare the current period with the previous period or with the same period in the prior year, so that trends from one accounting period to another may be determined. They should show operating efficiencies by comparison of actual with predetermined standards of performance; review of deviations from such standards offers an effective means of controlling operations.

Reports may be recurring, such as monthly statements of net income or periodic analyses of inventories, or they may be single-purpose reports, such as those designed to assist management in deciding whether to buy or produce components of the end product. Reports are often prepared on a recurring basis when single-purpose reports would be equally effective and save both the clerical labor of preparation and the reading time of executives.

The form and content of reports are important. Reports should be designed to meet the requirements of the management levels for which they are intended, making use of appropriate summarizations, graphic presentations, or other techniques. Reports designed for top management should highlight deviations from planned performance; those issued to shop foremen should use shop terminology rather than technical accounting language.

PLANNING.—The most successful managements make full use of internal accounting and statistical reports, not only for controlling costs and expenses, but for planning future operations based on analyses of their markets, distribution costs by products, cost-price-volume relationships, production costs by material, labor, and overhead components and by fixed and variable expenses, and other factors which influence profits. Several types of reports are required to enable management to establish a forward plan and modify it in the light of changing circumstances. Some of the principal reports are considered below.

Budget Reports.—Budgets presenting a plan for a specified period are particularly helpful to management. To be effective, budget data must be reported in sufficient detail to permit comparison of actual and estimated costs in each area of responsibility. Budget reports should be designed so that changes in volume, facilities, production methods, product mix, and other elements affecting revenues and costs may be reflected readily therein.

Several reports are required in a well-designed budgetary system. Various estimates aid in the preparation of production and purchasing schedules; among them is an estimate of sales by products, in dollars and quantities, based on an appraisal of future market conditions and the company's share of the market. Schedules of plant capacity by production centers may be prepared and related to proposed production schedules to aid in determining whether proposed production exceeds normal capacity. If normal capacity is to be exceeded, reports may be prepared comparing marginal costs of producing in excess of normal capacity, or of purchasing components, with costs resulting from plant expansion. These reports together with reports of prior years' operations modified to reflect changes in volume, labor rates, performance, or other conditions should be furnished to those responsible for preparation of the budget.

Unless reports required to produce the budget are completely integrated, effort will be wasted and the reliability of the budget will suffer. Budgets or partial budgets may be produced by various short-cut methods; their reliability is no greater than that of the approximations permitted in the underlying data.

Forecasts.—Comparisons of long-range forecasts of income and financial position with actual statements of income and the balance sheet enable management to appraise the progress in obtaining results anticipated by the forecast. Forecasts of capital expenditures and cash position guide management in arranging for financing or in deciding to curtail or expand operations, to reschedule production, or otherwise to revise its plans.

Some well-managed companies have developed their budget reports and forecasts to the extent that they produce each month a running forecast for several months, comparing last month's forecast for the current month with this month's actual results. This type of report gives management excellent control of its production schedules. It also provides top management with a means of interrogating junior executives in the event that actual results differ from estimates they previously submitted.

Special Reports.—Many companies find it desirable to formalize their long-term planning by preparing forecasts for five- to ten-year periods. This is particularly valuable in planning plant improvements and expansion. Important considerations in this area of forward planning are the cost already invested in plant facilities and whether the company will be able to continue or can afford to abandon its present investment in favor of modern or labor-saving facilities. This type of report requires the collaboration o. engineers and accountants and must give effect to all of the factors that bear on the economic justification of the proposals.

Financial Statements.—The form and content of internal financial statements are important to management since they are the basis for day-to-day decisions. Too frequently these statements are conventional in form, rather than designed to meet the particular needs of those receiving them. The needs and individual preferences of those receiving reports should be surveyed; reports should be designed to give the executive information which he can and will use. After such a survey has been made, the wishes of all interested persons should be correlated and financial statements designed to provide essential data to meet their requirements. Financial and operating statistics to be used in conjunction with the financial statements or as separate reports are considered below.

Financial and Operating Statistics.—In most businesses, certain relationships within the financial and operating data are recognized as normal and offer management a means of evaluating performance. Statistical information, such as accounts receivable turnover, inventory turnover, gross profit ratios by products, return on investment, units of production per machine-hour, and ratios of manufacturing overhead to direct labor by departments may assist management in controlling operations.

Comparison of the ratios suggested above with statistical data published for the industry or with other published data may further assist management in making sound decisions. In the analysis of financial data by ratios, it is important to present comparisons with earlier periods so that the trend of changes may be observed.

Sales Analyses.—Automatic devices, particularly tabulating equipment and electronic computers, have now made it possible to obtain analyses of sales in great detail as a by-product of records prepared for general accounting purposes. Analyses of sales by type and sizes of product, by salesmen, by commission rates, by geographical areas, by credit terms or other classifications may now be readily obtained from records so voluminous that analyses by manual methods were previously out of the question. Manual methods of sales analyses have also been improved by various sorting devices so that analyses may be obtained even when less voluminous records do not warrant the use of automatic equipment. The information obtained from such analyses has formed the basis for many suggestions for improving distribution methods and decreasing distribution costs. The analyses also provide basic data necessary for budget estimates and forecasts.

Market Analysis.—Analysis of a company's market for its products is a specialized branch of statistical research requiring review of economic data, investigation of general business conditions, familiarity with the company's products, and knowledge of the public's acceptance of the products of both the company and its competitors. Sales analysis is a first step in market analysis. All public accountants are not equipped by experience and training for market research, but statistical and data-handling areas are within their competency.

Return on Investment.—The ratio of net income to capital is frequently helpful in comparing the operating effectiveness of different companies, the operating results of divisions within one enterprise, and the performance of individuals within specific areas of responsibility.

To apply return on investment ratios properly as a management tool, the accounting system and procedures must be established to reflect clearly operations of each plant and division to which the measurement is to be applied. This requires accounting for all transactions between plants and divisions at fair prices and the allocation of common expenses on an equitable basis. It also requires an allocation of capital investment to each plant and division. When fixed assets are acquired at various price levels, capital may be adjusted to reflect present values so that the return on investment ratios may be prepared on a comparable basis.

The return on investment technique has been widely adopted by large companies as a concept of management control, and it has been used with profitable results.

COST REPORTS.—Many cost reports are prepared but never read. It is wasteful to assemble cost data each time an operation is repeated when variations in costs are negligible; an occasional cost study would serve management better. Cost reports should be streamlined to serve a particular need or purpose. When properly designed, they are an indispensable tool for controlling and reducing costs, for budgeting and forecasting, and frequently for serving as a guide in establishing prices.

When cost reports are based on standards carefully prepared, they provide the means of reporting variances from standards and thus permit management to control operations by reviewing these variances. To be effective, the cause of the variances as well as their nature should be determined. Properly prepared variance reports can point out areas of weakness where corrective action may be profitable. Frequently, the form and content of these reports may be improved by reporting separately variances requiring corrective action from those that have been anticipated, such as purchase price variances.

INTERNAL AUDIT REPORTS.—The independent public accountant can often be of assistance in organizing an internal auditing department. He can assist in outlining the scope of the work and in designing programs to use effectively the time and efforts of the internal auditing staff. Advice can be given as to the form of internal audit reports so that emphasis will be placed on major deviations from authorized procedures and on matters that require corrective action or policy decisions by management.

Systems and Procedures.—An important area of management services is the design and installation of accounting and control systems and related procedures necessary for assembling data for internal financial and statistical reports. For many years, public accountants have assisted in the installation of systems of accounts. The use of internal accounting as a management tool to control operations has been developed tremendously during the past twenty years, so that today there are many opportunities for specialization in this field. Public accountants should be prepared to consult with their clients on these matters and, if the occasion requires, to supervise or undertake system installations.

CHARTS OF ACCOUNTS.—When budgetary or cost control programs are adopted, existing charts of accounts are usually inadequate and require redesigning, possibly to segregate costs and expenses by departments or cost centers. When companies retain their identity as divisions in mergers, the preparation of consolidated financial statements dictates the adoption of a uniform chart of accounts insofar as the operations of the various divisions permit. Differences in accounting principles and policies should be resolved and the records and reports of the merged organizations brought into conformity.

When an industry has expanded or branched into multiplant operations, the listing of account names and numbers may no longer adequately indicate the proper use of the accounts, and it may be desirable to prepare descriptions of the accounts that will enable employees to code documents properly.

ACCOUNTING AND PROCEDURE MANUALS.—Uniform recording and reporting usually cannot be obtained by organizations with branch or multiplant operations without accounting and procedure manuals. Similarly, the processing of documents may vary in departments unless a uniform processing procedure has been established.

Assistance of a public accountant in preparing these manuals and other operating manuals may be desirable since his approach is impartial and he is not faced with problems of personal relationships that may confront a company employee.

GENERAL ACCOUNTING RECORDS.—When systems and procedures are designed and installed by persons without accounting training, cost determinations tend to be made without reconciliation with financial transactions recorded in the general books of account. It is an accepted principle of system installation that all data used should be coordinated and reconciled with actual financial transactions recorded in the general accounts of the enterprise. The accounting methods of utilizing controlling accounts and requiring that subsidiary records of details be balanced frequently within controlling accounts, and the practice of analyzing variances from standards by reference to actual amounts recorded in the general books of account, go far to ensure the reliability of financial and statistical data reported to management. The general accounting records must be designed to control cost details, to record verified data, and to provide a smooth flow of information from the field of operations into the final reports.

It is important in any installation of general accounting records to make certain that adequate internal control is provided. Methods of proving figures by balancing, or matching or comparing the results of selected clerical operations, should ensure that original data are correctly summarized through the records into financial or other reports. Internal checks should be provided which, together with physical protection, will safeguard the assets of the enterprise.

REVIEWS OF GENERAL PROCEDURES.—It has been stated that an accounting system begins to deteriorate the day it is installed. Few businesses remain static; they expand or contract, produce new products and drop old ones, add new departments and consolidate or discontinue others, or change managements or management's viewpoint. Accounting procedures, accordingly, cannot be expected to remain static. New ideas make old procedures obsolete; new office equipment opens opportunities for improved data processing. Unless general accounting and statistical procedures are reviewed and revised periodically, they are likely to become inadequate.

It is rare indeed to find an accounting organization in which some suggestions for the improvement of internal control cannot be made. One employee often performs duties involving cash and at the same time performs duties that give him access to accounts receivable or accounts payable or other duties incompatible with safeguarding assets. Proofs of accuracy of accounting records are sometimes omitted when they could easily be obtained, or perhaps verifications are duplicated by employees in several departments.

A review of purchasing procedures may disclose records that are duplicated elsewhere, or that could be maintained more effectively by departments other than the purchasing department. The review may reveal that procedures designed for purchases of large quantities are being applied unnecessarily in purchases of insignificant amounts and that processing costs are therefore high in relation to the value of the merchandise purchased.

In many companies billing and related accounting are time-consuming clerical operations; if procedures are obsolete or inadequate, the ineffective use of personnel may create substantial waste. For example, many companies whose customers are principally industrial, paying on the basis of invoices rather than statements, expend wasted effort in continuing to send monthly statements to all customers. In many instances substantial clerical expense may be saved by eliminating accounts receivable ledgers and the posting operations required to maintain them.

The trend toward bigger and better employee benefits, incentive or profit-sharing plans, and more detailed distribution of payroll costs has complicated the already complex job of payroll accounting. Many companies have turned to machine accounting for payroll, even though not mechanized elsewhere, because of the complexities of computing problems. Companies acquiring electronic data processing equipment frequently apply it first to payroll because payroll accounting offers the biggest headache. Since mechanization of payroll accounting frequently proves to be uneconomic, the advantages of a proposed machine installation should be compared with those of modern manual methods.

A review of procedures of the credit department will sometimes disclose that records maintained virtually duplicate accounts receivable records. This situation may have developed because of lack of cooperation between the credit and the accounts receivable departments or, possibly, from a well-intended effort to strengthen internal control. A procedure should be designed that will provide the credit department with necessary information without the duplication of records.

PROPERTY ACCOUNTING.—The immediate benefits of complete property records sometimes appear to management to be nebulous when contrasted with the cost of establishing and maintaining such records. Management may not be convinced that such records are necessary until a calamity happens, such as an unrecoverable fire loss or a substantial tax deficiency. However, with the ever-mounting investment of industry in mechanical devices to replace manual labor and the consequent increasing proportion of total manufacturing cost represented by fixed charges, the matter of adequate records for property, plant, and equipment becomes more and more important.

During their earlier years, many older companies kept inadequate records of costs of additions and retirements, or they may have used unacceptable methods of capitalizing assets constructed by their own employees. Sometimes a physical inventory of assets on a reconstructed cost basis may be recommended as a starting point for adequate records.

Property accounting records are frequently inaccurate because of absence of control over retirements by sale, abandonment, or rebuilding. Procedures should be established that will make certain that movements of plant assets are reported and that retirements are properly recorded in the accounts.

The basis of plant assets for federal income tax purposes is often different from the cost basis required for the corporate books of account. It may be necessary to provide procedures to record current retirements and allowances for depreciation and bring forward asset and reserve balances on both bases.

Expenditures for physical properties are frequently controlled by procedures requiring formal requests indicating estimated costs, and, possibly, approval by the executive committee or board of directors. As the work progresses, costs are accumulated on plant orders. Completed and estimated costs are compared, and additional approval is required for material overexpenditures.

COST ACCOUNTING SYSTEMS.—Cost information should be presented in a form that will assist management in making decisions that will increase net income, i.e., that will increase revenue or decrease costs and expenses. In companies manufacturing many products, the determination of costs by products will usually be an important objective.

Product Costs.—There are many methods for determining product costs. Some managements assign only direct costs to products. Other managements allocate all expenses to products according to some allocation method considered rational under the circumstances. Most of these methods of allocation serve useful purposes if they are thoroughly understood by those who use the cost information.

In some industries management does not have complete control over product mix, as in the packing and refining industries. When the unit cost of joint products is determined by allocating common costs in proportion to selling prices, true costing has been abandoned. Nevertheless, the study of process costs in these industries is a valuable management tool for cost control and cost and expense reduction.

Selection of Cost Centers.—Considerable time and research are often required to select cost centers that will properly disclose changes in costs resulting from changes in volume, product mix, or other cost factors. Areas of supervision may not correspond with desirable segregations of cost factors; frequently, two logical cost centers may be using joint facilities.

Cost centers should be selected so that unit or average costs derived from them may serve some useful purpose consistent with the expense of maintaining them. To attain this objective, operations in a center or department should be similar, or they should produce a product in whose cost management is interested. Mixtures of high- and low-cost machines or of mechanical production and bench work are to be avoided, and labor rates should not be so diverse or subject to such fluctuations that the usefulness of average labor costs derived from the center is destroyed.

Production Reporting Methods.—Accurate counting of physical units and statistical reporting of production are essential to the success of any cost system. Sometimes production personnel may require production reports of a different type or in a different form than that useful to cost accounting personnel. They may set up their own records, frequently duplicating information accumulated in other departments. Production reporting procedures and records should be integrated to avoid wasteful duplication.

Reports of Material Consumption.—In some businesses the material cost of the product may be very high and the labor cost low; in others the reverse is true. Few businesses can ignore losses due to scrap or spoiled or reworked material. Special reports may be needed to control these losses.

Careful consideration should be given the question whether materials consumed should be reported in physical quantities or in dollars or both. The reports should be integrated with requirements of the several departments of the business, such as cost accounting, production control, inventory control, purchasing, and general accounting.

Time Reporting and Payroll Distribution.—In many companies time-reporting procedures have not been changed for years. Even though many of its other accounting operations may have been mechanized, there is often resistance to changing timekeeping procedures. Comparison of costs of obsolete timekeeping methods with estimated costs of proposed procedures will frequently alert management to the need for change. Payroll is often distributed by inefficient and expensive methods. Forms can usually be designed to simplify this operation by manual methods, or, if the volume is sufficient, mechanical equipment is available to distribute the payroll expeditiously and economically. Often time-reporting and payroll distribution procedures may be combined.

Overhead Rate Determination.—There are several acceptable bases for determination of overhead rates. The basis selected must be thoroughly understood by those who are to use the costs, particularly if job costs are to be used for price estimating. For example, overhead based on full machine capacity rather than on normal capacity may be satisfactory when pricing small jobs that will absorb some of the fixed charges. Such a pricing policy should be used only by persons who recognize its limitations and who would not apply it to decrease prices on large orders that supply the volume on which normal capacity and over-all profits have been estimated.

Before determining overhead rates, normal capacity of production must be determined on a basis selected by management, e.g., on current sales forecasts, long-term sales forecasts, full physical capacity, or some other basis. Such determination is not difficult if the necessary data have been accumulated, but it becomes complex if there is no system for accumulating such data.

Fixed and Variable Expenses.—Decisions whether an individual classification of expense is fixed or variable are not easy to make. For example, on a one-shift operation, supervision may be fixed, but it may become variable if a two-shift operation becomes necessary. Indirect expenses usually increase in steps as volume increases. It becomes necessary to designate many semivariable expenses as either fixed or variable. In making such designations, the over-all situation must be balanced to minimize the effect of errors introduced by arbitrary decisions. Even expenses which appear ordinarily to be entirely fixed and uncontrollable may prove to be otherwise in periods of depression or low-volume operation when physical assets may be sold or abandoned and key employees discharged.

Nevertheless, classification of expenses as fixed and variable has proved helpful. It has encouraged the preparation of flexible budgets so that expenses may be estimated at various assumed levels of production, and it has permitted the study of break-even points. Managements often do not realize how high their break-even points have become.

Reviews of Operating Standards.—The reliability of any cost accounting system depends in large part on underlying nonfinancial operating standards, such as the producing speeds of machines, bases for distribution of power, heat or light to departments, estimated time required to complete units of work, proportions of chemicals or other materials in a mix, or a wide variety of physical factors significant in a particular business. Operating standards used in an established cost accounting system are frequently obsolete or incorrectly applied; they should be reviewed and brought up to date periodically. Public accountants are competent to review operating standards on the basis of discussions with engineers and operating personnel.

Distribution Costs.—Not only are distribution costs, including selling costs, material in amount, but they are important in a competitive market. They should be given the same measure of attention and the same analysis and close supervision that management commonly gives to production costs. In the past, cost accounting systems have been less frequently used in this area than in the determination of production costs. Most of the management services described in this chapter, including organization, reports, budgeting, cost reduction plans, and electronic data processing apply to selling and distribution activities as well as to manufacturing and production. They are equally applicable to businesses organized for distribution—retail, wholesale, department, chain, and specialty stores, and transportation—and to manufacturing enterprises.

Cost Control.—Many cost systems have been installed for the sole objective of obtaining actual costs of units of products, processes, or jobs. They may be used even more importantly as a means of controlling and reducing costs and expenses. With this objective in mind, standards are usually established, variances from standard are analyzed, and corrective actions instituted to bring actual costs into agreement with planned costs.

Cost Reduction Plans.—During recent years many companies have experienced a marked increase in sales without a corresponding increase in profit, and they have been forced to turn their attention to cost reduction programs in order to retain a competitive position in their industry, or even to remain in business.

A most effective method of controlling costs is the use of standards, based partially on experience and historical cost records and, more importantly, on an estimate of costs that should be incurred with the best practices and planning that can be employed. Standards based on historical cost records tend to perpetuate past errors and inefficiencies. To be useful for cost reduction, standards should be engineered, which means that they should reflect all of the know-how of operating personnel and the best advice available for efficient operation.

Reports should be obtained currently of scrap materials, spoiled work and rework, and corrective action taken when variances indicate that actual losses are excessive. Reports of productivity, by employee, machine, or department, and of absenteeism, excessive set-up time, machine failures, excessive repairs and maintenance, time lost waiting for materials, and similar information obtained by analyses of variances will indicate actions to be taken to reduce direct labor or overhead expenses.

The use of a cost system for cost control and cost reduction raises many questions not present when a system is designed only to determine product costs. The program should be integrated with other operating and accounting activities, such as production reporting, inventory and material control, budgetary reporting, and the general books of account.

Incentive Plans.—Many types of incentive or profit-sharing plans have proved useful under the particular circumstances in which they were applied. Some companies have effected substantial savings in costs and expenses by awarding prizes to employees for their suggestions. Employees are often in a position to observe opportunities for conserving materials or supplies, or to suggest improved methods of operation that save labor or overhead expenses. Recognition of these suggestions has proved profitable to the company and to the employees. Some have been of only temporary benefit; others have been successful for long periods.

INVENTORY CONTROL.—It is important to the successful operation of any business that the capital tied up in inventories be kept at a minimum consistent with operating requirements. An interruption of production or the loss of sales because of failure to receive materials or supplies at the right time can be extremely expensive. An inventory should be a live asset; the turnover of each item should be known and related to the requirements for its use in terms of minimum and maximum quantities determined with reference to the demands for it and the time requirements for reordering and delivery.

Problems of inventory control are common to most businesses. In many balance sheets, inventories are the largest current asset and often, particularly work in process, the most difficult asset to control and value. Inventory records serve many purposes in many departments.

Inventory records are frequently duplicated in whole or in part in several departments. The production control staff, requiring accurate data on material flow, economic production quantities, and timing, may keep complete quantity records of raw materials on hand, ordered, and assigned to production orders, and of production in process and finished goods inventory balances. Purchasing, requiring information on probable future purchases, may keep records of quantity usage and balances. Cost accounting, requiring costing data, may keep records of purchases and monthly usage in both quantities and dollars. The sales order department, requiring information on material on hand, may keep quantity records of finished goods and of production in process. General accounting, being charged with the responsibility for providing control for protection of the asset and with obtaining statistical data on turnover and obsolescence, may maintain complete records in both quantities and dollars.

Inventory records and data processing procedures should be designed to provide information required by the several departments, as well as to control inventories. A knowledge of the many techniques for maintaining inventory records as well as the utilization of the data by the departments is vital in designing an integrated inventory control system.

PRODUCTION CONTROL.—The scheduling of operations to avoid waste in set-up time and provide a smooth flow of the movement of materials and efficient application of labor is essential in manufacturing operations. In mass production industries, such as automobile manufacturing, the control of the movement of materials has virtually eliminated the stocking of many materials; suppliers deliver materials directly to production and assembly operations in accordance with daily requirements.

The design of a production control system should be integrated with the requirements for inventory control, production records, purchasing, and cost accounting to eliminate duplication of records and clerical effort.

QUALITY CONTROL.—The use of statistical sampling techniques for control of quality has in many instances resulted in a substantial reduction in inspection costs without significant deterioration of quality. The management services specialist should be familiar with these techniques on which may be based a quality control system with a rejection formula satisfactory to the client.

COST ESTIMATING FOR PRICING.—Frequently selling prices are set entirely by competition, but in many instances management can encourage sales of high-profit products and discourage sales of low-profit items. Sometimes the prices of different products are interrelated; for example, when a total line of items must be sold in order to sell the profitable items, the pricing method must be related to the probable volume of the entire line to produce maximum total revenue.

In some companies, prices are established by bidding based on estimated costs. Often, such costs can be accumulated by operations on which standards have been set, and the aggregate of such costs, when adjusted for anticipated variances from standard, provides a sound basis for setting the price. Cost estimates are frequently based on historical costs for similar jobs; the resulting pricing may sometimes produce substantial losses, or the order may be lost because of excess profits included in the bid.

Work Simplification.—Not only should an accounting system provide adequate and timely data, but it should provide this data as efficiently as feasible and at minimum expense.

Frequently, when enterprises have merged or grown rapidly without opportunity for adequate revision of clerical operations, reports once initiated are still produced although no longer required, forms once considered necessary are still used although they are obsolete, or clerical operations may be unnecessarily duplicated in several departments. These conditions may also exist in old, well-established, and profitable organizations that have continued to operate year after year without considering the usefulness of forms and reports or the efficiency of procedures. A periodic study on a company-wide basis with a view to eliminating unnecessary clerical operations and reports will be worth while in almost every company.

PROCEDURE ANALYSIS—PAPER-WORK SURVEY.—A flow chart of the movements of all copies of forms and reports will frequently reveal to a trained analyst areas of duplication and of unnecessary collection and reporting of data. His survey will include gathering samples of all forms and reports in use and discussing with the client's employees the actual use of each copy.

In a typical organization, such a survey may reveal that many reports serve little or no purpose, that copies of detailed reports are routed to individuals who require only summary information or only small segments of the detail, and that the same information appears in several reports. It may also disclose that substantially the same information is being recorded on several forms, that different forms are used for recording the same type of transactions, that copies of forms are prepared for and filed in departments requiring limited data that could be obtained from copies prepared for other departments, and that some data recorded on forms are not used at all. Review of processing procedures may reveal that the same data are verified in more than one department, and that forms are routed to departments which can obtain the required data from other sources. Relating the forms with processing procedures may reveal that forms are not designed to be prepared readily from original documents or to make subsequent processing as easy as possible.

FORMS CONTROL.—Although a paper-work survey and redesign of forms will serve to bring forms up to date, unless a forms control program is continuous, deterioration of forms and reports will begin as soon as there is any change in the organization.

Many companies have established a forms control department and require clearance of new forms and of reordered old forms through this department. Each new form is reviewed for its usefulness and for duplication of other forms, and each reordered form is reviewed for improvement in format, for possible combination with other forms, and for continued usefulness.

RECORD MAINTENANCE.—Storing the vast amount of paper created is a serious problem. Although reduction of the volume of paper created gives some degree of relief, the filing of necessary documents is still an expensive activity.

Record Retention Program.—Most records and documents, or all but one copy of documents, can be destroyed shortly after they have been prepared. However, the cost of sorting out records that should be retained for longer periods or in perpetuity is frequently so great that it is cheaper to maintain the files in storage than it is to purge them.

Companies with properly organized record retention programs have no problems of wasteful storage; worthless copies of documents never reach the files. Duplicate copies of forms and reports are destroyed as soon as they have served their purpose. Destruction dates are set for all records, and filing is arranged in accordance with the destruction dates.

The design of a record retention program requires extensive survey of the probable and possible uses of documents subsequent to filing. Filing methods must be designed to give ready access to data by departments that have destroyed their copies of the form. Destruction dates should be determined, based on the cost of filing as contrasted with possible costs or losses resulting from not having the information available and on legal requirements.

Filing Systems.—In connection with a record retention program, or as a separate engagement, the management services specialist may be called upon to review the filing system. He should be familiar with filing methods and equipment. He should know the advantages and disadvantages of filing by terminal digits or by other than straight alphabetical or numerical order. He should be able to suggest types of filing equipment best suited for the particular situation. He should know the applicability and limitations of microfilming and be able to evaluate the use of this equipment as compared with placing old records in an outside record center.

EXPEDITING CLOSINGS.—The importance of early reporting of operating results is recognized by most managements. To meet the demands of early closings considerable overtime is frequently required at the end of each accounting period. The reason for late closing or excessive overtime by the accounting staff can usually be traced to improper programming of the work load throughout the accounting period and improper emphasis on certain accounting details.

Simplification of the work of the accounting department, with substantial reduction in time consumed in closing at the end of interim accounting periods, has been achieved by a new approach to the recording of data. This recognizes that reports may be issued before data are fully recorded in the books of account and that careful estimates may provide management with just as satisfactory a basis for making operating decisions as fully recorded data.

This approach may be illustrated by a few examples. Computations of allowances for depreciation may be based on balances at the end of the prior month unadjusted for changes during the month; the computation may be made at any time before the end of the month. Taxes, insurance, and other prepaid expense allocations may be based on balances at the end of the prior month. The voucher register may be closed shortly after the end of the month and outstanding liabilities recorded on the basis of open purchase orders for material and services received. Unposted sales at the end of the month may be entered in total and details posted and accounts receivable balanced during the following month.

Clerical Efficiency.—Any evaluation of clerical efficiency should take into consideration the relative total expense of alternative methods. Although manual operations may appear to require less immediate cash outlay, costs of delayed reports and the unavailability of certain analyses and other information must also be considered. If new equipment is proposed, rentals or interest on capital invested, space costs, and other machine costs should be considered in addition to direct labor costs.

CLERICAL WORK STANDARDS.—The success of programs designed to increase efficiency of production workers by measuring their performance against predetermined work standards has suggested the possibility of using similar methods to increase efficiency of clerical workers. Such programs have met with considerable resistance from the office worker when traditional techniques, such as time and motion studies, have been attempted.

Most clerical work measurement programs that have been successful use other approaches to establish standards. When tasks are routine and consist of only a few operations (such as posting accounts receivable ledgers), synthetic standards may be effective. Such standards may be constructed, motion by motion (such as moving hand to ledger tray) or operation by operation (such as hand-posting of eight digits). The use of motion picture cameras to record the operations will usually be less offensive to the clerical employee than other methods. Another method of establishing clerical work standards that has been successful and causes little or no employee resistance is work sampling using statistical techniques. This might, for example, consist of observations of clerical workers as busy or idle, taken at regular time intervals during the working periods.

OFFICE MECHANIZATION.—Manual methods formerly adequate have proved to be inadequate for the requirements of many companies after substantial expansion of their operations. These companies have sometimes hurried into commitments for equipment that was not the best available for the operations to be performed or that was not economically justified.

Some companies rush into the purchase of equipment without considering the adaptability of the equipment for several purposes or the possible effect of changes in procedures. As a result, the usefulness of the machines selected may be restricted, or the selection may result in expense for redesigning forms and procedures that might have been avoided. Whenever office equipment is purchased, the design of forms and procedures should be integrated with other requirements of the accounting system, and maximum adaptability of the equipment should be sought.

The management services specialist should be interested in every type of labor-saving office appliance from check-writers, postage meters, letter-openers, and sorting racks to bookkeeping machines and electronic computers.

Equipment Utilization.—In mechanized offices, additional or improved machines are frequently requested. Before deciding to acquire additional equipment, the percentage of capacity at which present machines are operated should be considered. Proper scheduling of work or a revision of methods may eliminate the need for additional equipment.

Statistical sampling techniques by which machines are observed at random intervals are useful in determining the time a machine is operating, thus isolating machine usages that require detailed study before a decision is reached to buy new equipment.

INTEGRATED DATA PROCESSING.—The term "integrated data processing" is widely misunderstood. It is frequently thought to be linked primarily with electronic data processing. Although integrated data processing is essential to an electronic data processing system, most integrated data processing systems make use of manual methods or office machines.

Companies that are not large enough to require electronic data processing equipment are turning to integrated data processing methods to increase clerical efficiency. They must do this to stay in competition with larger firms using electronic equipment. In medium-sized companies, many of the systems are correlated with punched-card methods. In smaller companies, manual methods or simple office machine methods are used.

Manual Methods.—The pegboard is an important tool in manual methods of integrated data processing. Complete accounting and financial reporting systems have been built around its use. In other applications, the pegboard is used for limited operations, such as the preparation of payroll or sales analyses. One application of pegboard methods is to assemble subsidiary reports on a board, extend total amounts and prepare a photocopy of the board for a summarized report.

A simple system of integrated data processing may use only a typewriter, printed forms, and carbon paper. For example, a typist may prepare simultaneously an acknowledgment of an order, invoices covering the order, packing slip, bills of lading, labels, and office copies used as (1) sales register, (2) sales distribution media, (3) sales commission register, and (4) unit accounts receivable ledger. Simultaneously with the writing or typing, other forms produce unit documents which may be sorted by account distribution.

Duplicating Equipment.—Many integrated data processing systems are designed around duplicating equipment. By the use of variable masters or other techniques, data originally typed on the master can be modified or supplemented to produce forms or reports for other purposes. This method is often used for sales order–work order–billing routines.

Common Language Machines.—Probably the greatest impetus to the development of integrated data processing has been the attachment of punched-paper tape equipment to office machines. Machines producing or operating from common-language punched-paper tape now include typewriters, adding machines, tag readers, accounting machines, and cash registers. In many instances, effective use of this equipment requires that the tape be converted to punched cards for further processing. In simpler applications, the tape-reading facilities of machines, such as typewriters, may make the application economically sound without conversion to punched cards.

Many companies having sales offices, warehouses, or manufacturing plants at widely separated locations transmit telegraphically accounting and statistical data on automatic sending and receiving machines using common-language tape or wire recording. By expediting reports, these devices have made possible improvements in management control of operations.

ELECTRONIC DATA PROCESSING.—The development of electronic data processing equipment has brought about a revolutionary change in all problems related to the recording and reporting of financial, accounting, and statistical data. The speeds with which this equipment can process coded information are so great that the effects on record-keeping and auditing methods cannot be foreseen at present. In designing a system of flow of data to and from an electronic computer, existing methods and procedures must be reappraised. It is not enough to program existing procedures on electronic devices; it may be possible to eliminate some procedures and to obtain more detailed and useful information than before. The nature of the duties performed by many clerical employees may change from posting and bringing down balances to the preparation of source information.

The design and installation of an electronic data processing system requires specialists understanding the operations of the equipment and experienced in the installation of accounting and other record-keeping systems. Without this combination, the potentials of the equipment cannot be realized.

Justification of Acquisition.—Electronic data processing equipment is at present not only expensive but subject to rapid obsolescence because of the continuing experimental and development work in this field. Few companies have the necessary volume of transactions to justify installation of the largest of the electronic computers. Many companies, however, can use the small and medium-sized computers to advantage.

A study period of two years is frequently required to determine the justification for this equipment and to plan rearrangements of source data, output data, and reports. Extensive study may disclose that procedures can be revised to accomplish substantial economies without the acquisition of electronic equipment.

Installation of System.—The public accountant should participate with his clients in the installation of electronic equipment. It is possible with this equipment to eliminate many intermediary records, such as registers, journals, and historical ledgers, and to produce financial statement balances directly from original documents. Many original documents as we now know them may disappear, and the equipment may be activated directly by the transactions as they occur. Nevertheless, all the detailed data required to permit management to control operations must be provided. It will always be necessary to analyze portions of the data and reconcile them with completed financial statements.

The records produced on electronic equipment will require auditing by governmental agencies as well as by public accountants. In addition to satisfying himself about the built-in programs, the auditor will require satisfaction about program modifications or data that may be introduced into the equipment manually through the console. Participation by the public accountant in the system installation will give him knowledge of the built-in program that will help him in subsequent audits. It will also give him an opportunity to make certain that reliable internal and external controls, with adequate proofs, balances, and storage, are provided, and that the fundamental requirements for audit are given proper consideration.

In many instances, the client will train its own personnel in programming and operating the electronic data processing equipment during the period of the survey for justification of acquisition and thus develop a staff capable of doing most, if not all, the programming. In other instances, the client may call upon the public accountant to make a complete installation, including programming. To accept such an engagement, the accountant must have a trained staff of experts competent for this type of work.

Special Problems of Financial Management.—Many types of management services lie in areas outside regularly recurring financial reporting or the operation of accounting systems. Clients frequently turn to their independent public accountants for consultation and advice when they are expanding by purchase or merger or contracting by sale or other disposition. Problems may arise in connection with refinancing or recapitalization or in determining the profitability of alternative courses of action. Other services may be requested in solving accounting and financial problems of compliance with statutory requirements and with provisions of contracts and agreements. Still others relate to personnel, their procurement, training, and compensation.

PROBLEMS OF EXPANSION OR CONTRACTION.—A few of the types of service that the public accountant can provide in connection with problems of expansion or contraction are discussed below.

Plant Locations.—A proposal to expand by adding facilities at another location, or to move plant facilities, raises many questions that should be answered before a company has an informed basis for a decision. Accessibility to raw materials, processors, and markets should be weighed. Transportation facilities and rates should be studied. The availability of labor and the possible effect of a new industry on the labor market should be determined. State and local taxes should be investigated.

Accounting Aspects of Appraisals and Valuations.—When the accounting basis of plant and equipment changes because of transfer to another company or for other reasons, problems arise in recording the new valuations. Even when detailed appraisals are available, descriptions of property in the appraisal frequently bear little or no relation to descriptions of properties in the plant and equipment records. The property components listed in the appraisal may be entirely different from classifications in the records. In some instances, valuations may have been established by negotiation with little or no detail available.

The process of reconciling descriptions with book amounts and establishing a new property ledger is one that requires painstaking identification of property units in the appraisal and in the records and the determination of amounts for the details of assets that were appraised as a group. In the absence of a detailed appraisal, the task may be primarily one of allocation of a total amount on an equitable basis acceptable to management and for accounting and tax reporting.

Profitability of New Ventures and New Products.—When a company embarks on a new venture or the manufacture of a new product, a study should be made of the anticipated profitability of the venture or product.

In the study of a new venture, a company may have no experience on which to estimate costs, and general averages or other data must be assembled. In the study of a new product, management can usually provide reasonably accurate estimated direct costs. However, the effect on manufacturing overhead, distribution costs, and administrative expense should be studied at various sales levels of both new and old products to determine the probable effect on the company's total profit.

Financing Acquisitions.—Expansion by purchase of new plants or facilities requires capital and unless this has been accumulated in advance by the retention of earnings, negotiations must be entered into with banks, insurance companies, investment houses, or other capital sources. Several alternative plans are usually developed that must be analyzed not only for financial aspects but also for their effect on the future welfare of the company. Pro forma financial statements and forecasts may be of great assistance in clarifying what may otherwise be vague and confusing. The public accountant often participates in negotiation conferences as an advisor to his client.

Recapitalization Problems.—After some years of operation, companies often outgrow their original capital structures. They usually seek advice on the relative advantages and disadvantages of various alternatives, such as short-term or long-term borrowings and offerings of preferred or common stocks. Accounting questions may arise on the capitalization of retained earnings or the future burden of interest charges or alternative dividend policies. Frequently federal income tax, stamp tax, state franchise tax, and other tax questions are involved; sometimes registration statements are to be filed with the SEC; possibly negotiations are to be carried on with state "blue-sky" commissions; or conferences with officials of stock exchanges may become necessary.

In these circumstances, public accountants may be of assistance in preparing pro forma statements and forecasts and in participating with clients in their planning and negotiations.

Liquidation Problems.—When a company sells its assets and plans to distribute the proceeds to its stockholders, or gets into financial difficulties and operates under the supervision of a creditors' committee, or goes into bankruptcy, a new series of problems and questions is encountered. Many of these have income tax implications for both the corporation and its stockholders as individuals. Special procedures and records often should be instituted. Accounting systems and reports designed for a going concern may no longer be appropriate, and steps should be taken to revise them as expeditiously as possible.

COMPLIANCE WITH STATUTORY OR CONTRACTUAL REQUIREMENTS. —Public accountants may provide a number of types of services in accumulating data for use in meeting statutory requirements and provisions of contractual agreements. Some typical examples are discussed in the following paragraphs.

Insurance Claims.—Frequently, when fire, theft, defalcations, or other disasters cause losses, detailed costs of properties destroyed or stolen must be reconstructed as a basis for seeking reimbursement from insurance companies. When policies include coinsurance clauses, additional data on the total value of assets must be submitted.

Filing an insurance claim may be relatively simple for companies maintaining complete accounting and property records. When such records are not maintained, a search of detailed records and documents may be necessary, and, frequently, corollary information must be substituted for original documents.

Cost and Price Determinations and Redeterminations.—Many government contracts and subcontracts for materials or services contain price determination and redetermination clauses. Actual costs, including overhead, must be submitted to the governmental agency, but the government's definitions of overhead exclude certain classifications of expense not considered applicable and therefore differ, in most instances, from overhead in the records of industrial companies. An important problem in assembling costs for price determination or redetermination is usually the allocation of overhead to the product manufactured under the contract. Other problems frequently encountered are the determination of preproduction expenses, starting load, plant rearrangement costs, termination costs, and the charge for tools used commonly for both government and private production.

Determination of Contract Profits.—Frequently it becomes necessary to determine profits from work performed under a single order or contract. When materials are manufactured or services provided using facilities and personnel also used in the regular business or for other contracts, problems arise that are foreign to normal business activity. Even though a good cost accounting system is in effect meeting the ordinary requirements of the company, problems of allocating administrative and general expenses may still arise. If a standard cost system is in effect, variances applicable to material produced under the contract must be isolated. In the absence of a cost system, or if it is inadequate, many analyses and allocations must be made to determine profits under a single contract.

Renegotiation of Profits Under Government Contracts.—Companies with both renegotiable and nonrenegotiable business frequently request their public accountants to represent them in presenting their cases to the renegotiation boards. Every effort should be made to assemble all pertinent accounting and operating data so that the client may receive proper credit for use of his own funds rather than funds furnished by governmental agencies, for contributions of improvements to the product, for assistance to other contractors, and for other factors that may be considered by the renegotiation boards.

Determinations Under the Robinson-Patman Act.—To support its position under the Robinson-Patman Act, a company should have detailed and precise records of its total costs by products and of its bases for distribution of overhead. Frequently, in situations that give rise to action, elements of overhead expenses, in the opinion of the management, do not apply to the particular product and, in accordance with the Act, the product may be priced lower than if an over-all overhead allocation were made. To support this position, it is often necessary to reconstruct financial statements to show the effect on costs of other products if the questioned product had not been produced.

Events of Default.—Recoveries or assessments under default provisions of contracts often create problems of cost determination. Expenditures may be fully recoverable even though the work was not completed. One complication in the allocation of overhead rests in the fact that the amount of overhead properly allocable to a product in process may not be proportionate to that allocable to a finished product. For example, the purchasing department may have completed its work, whereas the inspection department may have had little or no work in connection with the contract.

Acting as Arbitrator.—In the examples of management services that have been discussed in this section, services in the determination of costs have been emphasized. Objective approach and the reliance of other parties on the impartiality of the conclusions are important factors in services in cost determinations. Because of these same attributes the public accountant is sometimes called upon to serve as arbitrator in questions on accounting matters.

The speed and relatively low cost of arbitration as against a court hearing have induced many persons to write arbitration clauses into contracts and partnership and other agreements. The public accountant should be familiar with the work of the American Arbitration Association, and his services in this field may be an important contribution to his community.

Interpreting Contract Formulae.—Contracts that have been written without consultation with the company's public accountant sometimes contain cost accounting or other formulae that are ambiguous, unworkable, or patently contrary to the understanding of the parties. Services may be provided in interpreting the formulae and in obtaining an understanding between the contractors of the agreed basis for computing costs, allocating overhead, or other computations of the formulae.

PERSONNEL.—Many special problems of management concern methods for properly compensating personnel. Many plans have been devised for supplementing basic wages and salaries of workers and management in proportion to their contribution to the company's profit. The management services specialist should be familiar with such plans if he is to provide services of the following types.

Executive Compensation.—Because of the present tax structure, many companies have difficulty holding their executives merely by increasing salaries. They must provide income that will be taxable at lower rates or provide some inducement in lieu of current income. Most successful plans are based either on enabling the executive to realize a capital gain or on deferring payment until after retirement when he will be in lower income tax brackets. The tax features of executive compensation plans must be equitable both to the company and to the individual.

Middle Management Incentives.—Middle management incentive plans have received too little notice. Although management has recognized that this group may be largely responsible for the success or failure of a company, few companies have been able to devise a formula for relating compensation to successful performance. There is, however, recognition that middle management incentives that are based on contributions to the company's profit may be an important factor in reducing costs.

One of the principal problems in devising formulae for supplemental compensation based on contributions to profits is the segregation of income and expense elements that do not result from the efforts of the person being compensated. For example, increased volume may increase departmental profits without any effort on the part of the supervisor in charge. The management services specialist, who has a comprehensive picture of operating conditions throughout the company, is in a position to segregate such factors as volume changes and to devise formulae that will prove beneficial to both the company and the middle management personnel.

Pension and Profit-Sharing Plans.—Pension plans have grown rapidly in popularity. Usually, both management and workers participate. Pension plans have an advantage to the employer over profit-sharing plans that disburse profits currently in that they reward those who stay with the company and thus tend to reduce turnover of personnel. Pertinent regulations of the Internal Revenue Service must be considered.

Fringe Benefits.—In some companies, fringe benefits have been granted as a result of negotiated agreements with labor unions; in others, they have been adopted in order to attract workers; and in still others, they have resulted from the employer's interest in the welfare of employees. Whatever the motivating cause for fringe benefits, the principal advantage to the employee rests in the fact that they represent tax-free income. Further expansion of such benefits may be expected.

Management sometimes grants a benefit and then discovers that the expense involved is substantially greater than estimated. Projected future costs should always be computed when additional fringe benefits are being considered.

Statistical Aspects of Union Negotiations.—During the course of negotiations with labor unions, it is frequently necessary to assemble considerable statistical data to determine profits that may be shared with employees in the form of increased wages. Such data may have many ramifications, such as amounts invested in equipment per worker, return on investment, history of reinvestment of profits in plant expansion, and pro forma statements reflecting wage increases. Frequently the need for additional data develops suddenly during the course of the negotiations.

Training Programs in Finance and Accounting.—Another type of assistance by the public accountant in the field of personnel is in training programs. A number of companies have adopted continuing programs for training financial and accounting personnel. A common approach to this training is the case study technique, frequently making use of material drawn from the company's experience.

As such training programs develop, the management services specialist may frequently be called upon to serve as an instructor in some phase of the program. He may also be asked to assist in the assembly and organization of data used in the case studies.

MATHEMATICAL ANALYSIS.—Complex military, scientific, and engineering problems were successfully solved by higher mathematics during World War II. Since then great interest has been shown in the application of these methods to general business problems, particularly to inventory control.

The management services specialist, who is trained in mathematics, should watch for business situations in which it is possible to identify significant causative elements or statistical patterns and to express their relationships in mathematical form such that an effort to obtain the best solution of a complex situation by mathematical methods may be practicable.

General.—It has been said that every audit engagement should produce, in addition to an informed opinion on the financial statements, suggestions useful to the client in the betterment of his enterprise. Aside from the assistance directly related to management services which may be provided the client as a separate engagement, suggestions arising from a firm's competence in this field constitute a valuable by-product to a regular audit engagement. In furtherance of the development of such helpful suggestions, a reminder list is useful during the course of the audit engagement. Such list is designed to aid in pointing up the areas which, on the basis of observations made during the audit, appear to offer opportunities for economies or other improvement. These areas and the related suggestions for improvement are then brought to the attention of the client so that he may consider appropriate action.

CHAPTER 25

PROCEDURE UNDER THE FEDERAL SECURITIES ACTS

The Securities and Exchange Commission.[1]

STATUTES ADMINISTERED BY SEC.—The Securities and Exchange Commission (SEC) is an agency of the United States Government. Its principal function is the administration of the following statutes:

Securities Act of 1933

Securities Exchange Act of 1934

Public Utility Holding Company Act of 1935

Trust Indenture Act of 1939

Investment Company Act of 1940

Investment Advisers Act of 1940

In this chapter consideration will be given only to the accountant's duties under the 1933 and 1934 Acts.

ORGANIZATION OF SEC.—The main office of the SEC is in Washington. It has regional offices in New York, Boston, Atlanta, Chicago, Fort Worth, Denver, San Francisco, and Seattle, and branch offices in Cleveland, Detroit, St. Paul, Salt Lake City, and Los Angeles.

[1] The material in this chapter is taken largely from *SEC Accounting Practice and Procedure* by Louis H. Rappaport, CPA, published by The Ronald Press Company (1956). The reader is referred to that book for a more comprehensive discussion of SEC accounting and auditing matters, including numerous formal and informal decisions, reports, opinions, interpretations, and rulings, which, because of space limitations, cannot be included in this volume.

The Commission consists of five members appointed by the President with the consent of the Senate. One member is designated by the President to serve as chairman. The Commission employs a staff of lawyers, accountants, engineers, analysts, and others. The staff is organized into the following divisions and offices which are directly responsible to the Commission:

Executive Director—Division of Administrative Management
Division of Corporation Finance
Division of Trading and Exchanges
Division of Corporate Regulation
Regional Offices
Office of General Counsel
Office of Chief Accountant
Office of Opinion Writing
Office of the Secretary
Office of Hearing Examiners
Executive Assistant to the Chairman

The public accountant who has clients subject to the 1933 and 1934 Acts is concerned primarily with the workings of the Division of Corporation Finance and the Office of Chief Accountant.

The Division of Corporation Finance has duties in connection with most of the statutes administered by the SEC. The Division's principal responsibility is to prevent fraudulent offerings of securities to the public and the dissemination of false or misleading information about securities. A director supervises the work of the Division, and he is assisted by a number of examining sections, the Office of General Counsel, and the Office of Chief Accountant. Each examining section is headed by a securities analyst and includes accountants, lawyers, and examiners. When necessary, the sections have recourse to engineers, geologists, statisticians, and other experts. The accounting work in the Division is coordinated by the Chief Accountant of the Division who consults with the Chief Accountant of the Commission regarding new or important accounting or auditing problems.

Questions of accounting involving the work of the Division of Corporation Finance should be taken up first with that division. If exception is taken to a decision or opinion of that division, the question may be referred to the Office of Chief Accountant and, if necessary, to the Commission.

The Chief Accountant is the principal adviser to the Commission on all matters relating to accounting and auditing and supervises the execution of SEC policy in these fields. He drafts rules and regulations governing the form and content of financial statements filed with the SEC. He answers questions received from registrants or their public accountants dealing with accounting and auditing. Some of his opinions are published by the SEC as "Accounting Series Releases."

Familiarity with SEC Requirements.—Accountants undertaking examinations of financial statements filed under the 1933 and 1934 Acts should be informed of the requirements of the Acts and of the rules and regulations thereunder.

From time to time the rules and regulations are amended and new ones issued. Notices of new and amending rules and regulations and other information are given in releases. The SEC from time to time also publishes opinions (in the form of releases) of its Chief Accountant on major accounting questions, administrative policy with respect to financial statements, and certain other matters of importance to accountants. Public accountants should familiarize themselves with these releases which are published as the Accounting Series. They may be obtained by writing to the Commission and asking to be put on the mailing list for them.

The accountant who participates in a registration engagement is charged not only with a knowledge of the Commission's formal requirements but also with its pronouncements on accounting matters. In 1938 the Commission issued, in Accounting Series Release No. 4, the following statement of its administrative policy with respect to financial statements:

In cases where financial statements filed with this Commission pursuant to its rules and regulations under the Securities Act of 1933 or the Securities Exchange Act of 1934 are prepared in accordance with accounting principles for which there is no substantial authoritative support, such financial statements will be presumed to be misleading or inaccurate despite disclosures contained in the certificate of the accountant or in footnotes to the statements provided the matters involved are material. In cases where there is a difference of opinion between the Commission and the registrant as to the proper principles of accounting to be followed, disclosure will be accepted in lieu of correction of the financial statements themselves only if the points involved are such that there is substantial authoritative support for the practices followed by the registrant and the position of the Commission has not previously been expressed in rules, regulations or other official releases of the Commission, including the published opinions of its Chief Accountant.

Under the 1933 Act the SEC is empowered under certain conditions to declare the registration statement effective at a date earlier than the usual twenty days after the date of filing. To issuers and underwriters desiring to have a registration statement become effective at the earliest possible date, it is important that the registration statement as originally filed be free from errors of omission or noncompliance. This is further reason why public accountants should be thoroughly familiar with requirements of Regulation S-X, the applicable form and instruction book, published opinions of the Chief Accountant, and decisions and reports of the Commission.

Regulation S-X.—This is the principal accounting regulation of the SEC in its administration of the Securities Act of 1933 and the Securities Exchange Act of 1934. Promulgated originally in 1940, the regulation has been amended several times since that date. No public accountant should attempt an examination of financial statements intended for filing under these acts without having at hand an up-to-date copy of the regulation together with a copy of the form proposed to be filed, including applicable instructions.

Regulation S-X relates generally to the form and content of financial statements and supporting schedules required in most of the registration statements and reports under both acts. The regulation does not specify the dates or periods of financial statements; these requirements appear in the instructions accompanying the applicable registration statement or report form. Regulation S-X also does not specify for whom statements are to be furnished; whether for the registrant, the registrant and its consolidated subsidiaries, the unconsolidated subsidiaries, and others; these requirements appear in the instructions of the applicable form. To illustrate, Form S-1 (applicable to the registration of securities under the 1933 Act) contains instructions as to what statements are to be filed, the dates of the balance sheets, and the periods to be covered by the income statements, but Regulation S-X governs the form and content of these balance sheets and income statements.

To a public accountant who has conscientiously attempted to comply with all the instructions, it may come as a surprise that the SEC, after an examination of the certified financial statements, suggests that additional information be furnished, usually in notes to the financial statements. In the performance of its duties under the statutes it administers, the SEC is vitally concerned with the principle of full disclosure. Regulation S-X could never contain detailed instructions applicable to all situations. It is important therefore to remember that the instructions in the regulation represent *minimum* requirements.

FORM AND CONTENT OF INCOME STATEMENT.—Requirements for the form and content of income statements of most commercial and industrial companies are governed by Rule 5.03 of Regulation S-X. One provision of that rule deserves attention. Rule 5.03(a) provides in effect that all items of profit and loss given recognition in the accounts during the period covered by the income statement shall be included in the income statement. The significance of this instruction becomes apparent when it is observed that Captions 17 and 18 which follow immediately after "Net income or loss" (Caption 16) in the SEC's form of income statement are as follows:

17. Special items.—State separately and describe each item of profit and loss given recognition in the accounts, included herein pursuant to rule 5.03(a), and not included in the determination of net income or loss (caption 16).

18. Net income or loss and special items.

If a company has a gain or loss which, pursuant to generally accepted principles of accounting, is entered in earned surplus, the gain or loss must be shown in a SEC filing in the income statement caption 17, special items, except in the case of public utilities and similarly regulated companies.

Accountants do not ordinarily favor reporting the same transaction in different ways. An accountant may hesitate to show an item in surplus in a report to stockholders, and the same item as a special item (Caption 17) in the income statement filed with SEC. This inconsistency is more apparent than real and should not disturb the accountant or his client. Special items following net income are equivalent to direct credits or charges to earned surplus. (Accounting Research Bulletin No. 43, p. 64.) Hence, when an item is entered in earned surplus in the report to stockholders and as a special item in a SEC filing, the difference is one of form—not substance.

When, in harmony with provisions of Regulation S-X, additions to or deductions from net income are displayed at the bottom of the income statement, the figure of net income should be clearly and unequivocally designated so as not to be confused with the final figure in the income statement. The caption of the final figure should be descriptive of what it represents, such as "net income and special items," "net income and flood loss," "net loss and special items," or "profit on sale of subsidiary, less net loss." Any representation of earnings for the year or of earnings per share should be based on the amount designated as net income.

Independence of Certifying Public Accountants.—In any engagement involving filing financial statements with the SEC, the independence of the certifying accountant should receive early and careful consideration. In recognition of its functions under the statutes which it administers, the SEC has emphasized in several of its decisions and regulations the importance of complete independence of public accountants who practice before the Commission. In Regulation S-X, for example, the Commission states as follows :

Rule 2.01. Qualifications of Accountants.

(a) The Commission will not recognize any person as a certified public accountant who is not duly registered and in good standing as such under the laws of the place of his residence or principal office. The Commission will not recognize any person as a public accountant who is not in good standing and entitled to practice as such under the laws of the place of his residence or principal office.

(b) The Commission will not recognize any certified public accountant or public accountant as independent who is not in fact independent. For example, an accountant will not be considered independent with respect to any person, or any affiliate thereof, in whom he has any financial interest, direct or indirect, or with whom he is, or was during the period of report, connected as a promoter, underwriter, voting trustee, director, officer, or employee.

(c) In determining whether an accountant is in fact independent with respect to a particular registrant, the Commission will give appropriate consideration to all relevant circumstances including evidence bearing on all relationships between the accountant and that registrant or any affiliate thereof, and will not confine itself to the relationships existing in connection with the filing of reports with the Commission.

The SEC is in a strong position to enforce its views on the qualifications of accountants who certify financial statements for filing with it. Under Rule II(e) of its "Rules of Practice" :

The Commission may disqualify, and deny, temporarily or permanently, the privilege of appearing or practicing before it in any way to any person who is found by the Commission after hearing in the matter

(1) Not to possess the requisite qualifications to represent others; or

(2) To be lacking in character or integrity or to have engaged in unethical or improper professional conduct.

For the purpose of the rule, "practicing before the Commission" includes the preparation of any statement or opinion by an accountant filed with the Commission with the accountant's consent.

In addition to Rule 2.01 of Regulation S-X, the SEC in a long series of formal and informal rulings in cases and inquiries arising under the acts administered by it, has discussed a number of proscribed relationships between accountants and their clients which give rise to a presumption of lack of independence on the part of the accountant. In a few cases, in fact, the accountant's lack of independence resulted in disciplinary proceedings under Rule II(e) of the "Rules of Practice," and subsequent suspension from the privilege of practicing before the Commission. A few of these cases are discussed below.

When the accountant deliberately falsifies the facts, the SEC has said that there is a convincing demonstration of his lack of independence.

Any financial interest of the accountant in his client or its affiliates will ordinarily disqualify the accountant from certifying financial statements for filing with the Commission. A partner in an accounting firm owned 2 per cent of the preferred stock of a registrant at the time his firm made the audit of the accounts of the registrant. Despite the fact that the shares were sold subsequent to completion of the audit, the SEC ruled that the accounting firm of which the partner was a member was not independent for the purpose of filing with the Commission. A partner in another accounting firm which certified financial statements of a registrant owned 11,000 shares of the registrant's stock. In an apparent effort to avoid disqualification, an amended financial statement was filed which was prepared by an employee of the accountant and certified jointly by the employee and the accounting firm. The employee received from the registrant a cash payment for his services and had no other interest in the registrant. The Commission held that the purpose and intent of its rules relating to accountants' independence would be defeated and evaded if the accountant were to be disqualified by its provisions but his partner or employee were not, and concluded that the statements had not been certified by independent public accountants as required.

An accounting firm had rendered services to a registrant for which the registrant had not been able to pay. To guarantee payment of the account the registrant had pledged shares of its own stock and had given the accountants an option to purchase the pledged securities at the market price at the date the option was granted. The Commission ruled that the accountants were not independent for the purpose of certifying the registrant's financial statements.

If a partner in an accounting firm serves on the Board of Directors of a company but does not participate in any way in his firm's audit of the company's accounts, would the firm be disqualified for purposes of a SEC filing? The SEC has taken the position that the accounting firm in these circumstances could not be considered independent for the purpose of certifying the registrant's financial statements.

In a slight variation of the foregoing situation, a partner of the accounting firm was serving as a member of a registrant's Board of Directors. Another partner in the same accounting firm conducted the audit of the registrant and certified the financial statements in his own name, not in the firm name. The SEC held that the certifying accountant could not be considered independent.

In another case a partner in an accounting firm had served on the Board of Directors of a registrant but had resigned from that position prior to the close of the most recent fiscal year. This accountant had not participated in any way in the firm's audits of the registrant. The Commission ruled that the accounting firm could not be considered independent for the purpose of certifying financial statements of the registrant covering any period during which a partner of the firm was a director of the registrant.

The SEC has stressed the importance of separating the functions of record-keeping and independent auditing. In the Commission's view an accountant may not be considered independent when financial statements have been prepared from accounting records that he has kept.

In another case the accounting firm that certified the financial statements of a registrant had in the past drawn up the monthly journal records of the company from underlying documents that had been prepared by the registrant's staff. These journal records were posted to the appropriate accounts by the certifying accountants. At the end of the year the audit engagement was undertaken by personnel of the certifying accountant that had not participated in the original recording of accounting data. The Commission ruled that the accounting firm could not be considered independent for the purpose of certifying the financial statements of this registrant.

A variation of the above involved a small loan company that kept its accounting records on a cash basis. The primary records of the company consisted of daily cash reports that were prepared by the cashier and signed by the manager. The accountant who certified the financial statements of this company took no part in the preparation of these basic records. However, he did audit these cash reports each month and then entered the totals in a summary record which he in turn posted to the general ledger. The certifying accountant also made adjusting journal entries each month for insurance, taxes, depreciation, and similar items. The company was small and did not require the services of a full-time bookkeeper. The certifying accountant devoted about one day a month to the clerical or bookkeeping tasks described above. The Commission held that the accountant could not be considered independent for the purpose of certifying the financial statements of this registrant.

Keeping books even on a temporary basis may raise a question of the accountant's independence. In one case, members of a firm of certifying accountants set up a registrant's books and maintained them for about six months before the registrant engaged a bookkeeper. The

SEC ruled that the accounting firm could not be considered independent for the purpose of certifying the registrant's financial statements for the year in which the accountants kept the books.

Even when the accountant's work on the records is exceedingly limited, it may disqualify him for purposes of a SEC filing. An accountant certified financial statements which were filed with the Commission. Prior to certification, the accountant posted to the general ledger entries covering a month's transactions and prepared all the closing entries. The SEC ruled that the accountant could not be considered independent for the purpose of certifying financial statements filed by the registrant.

The Commission has also stated its opinion on the independence of public accountants who have indemnity agreements with registrants. The question arose in connection with financial statements filed with the Commission when the registrant had agreed to indemnify the certifying accountant from all losses and liabilities arising out of his certification to which the accountant might become subject under the 1933 Act or at common law, other than for willful misstatements or omissions. The Commission took the position that the existence of such an agreement removes or greatly weakens one of the major stimuli to objective and unbiased considerations of the problems encountered in an auditing engagement.

Space does not permit a listing of all the formal and informal rulings by the SEC involving independence of public accountants. Suffice it to say that when the accountant, or any partner, relative, or spouse of the accountant, has a financial interest in, or any managerial or other unusual relationship with, a client, or any affiliate of the client (parents as well as subsidiaries), or persons closely connected with the client, the accountant should consider carefully whether the interests or relationships are such that they are apt to raise a question of his independence for SEC purposes. If his independence is questioned, it is far better to have the question resolved early in the engagement than to learn the Commission's attitude after the registration statement has been filed, with the consequent loss of time and money involved in having an audit made by another accountant.

THE SECURITIES ACT OF 1933

Principal Provisions.—The Securities Act of 1933 provides for the registration of securities with the Commission before they may be sold to the public. Under the law the Commission has the authority to exempt from registration small offerings—that is, when the aggregate amount of the offering does not exceed $300,000. Also exempt from registration requirements are securities of governmental units and certain regulated companies, such as banks and common carriers. The law also exempts from the registration provisions transactions not involving a *public* offering.

The 1933 Act is a *disclosure* statute, the disclosure being provided by means of a registration statement and a prospectus. Under the law the function of the SEC is to see that all information pertinent to the company's business and its securities is available to the investor as a basis for deciding whether to purchase its securities. The merits of any security are not reviewable by the SEC. The SEC's chief interest is in seeing that the facts about the issuer of the security are truthfully told, and that no material information has been withheld. It is unlawful for anyone to represent that a registration statement is true and correct because it has been declared effective by the SEC. On the first page of every prospectus there must be a legend to the effect that the securities have not been approved or disapproved by the Commission nor has it passed upon the accuracy or adequacy of the prospectus.

If all the facts about a security are not truthfully told in a registration statement, or if important information is omitted, the Commission may require the registration statement to be appropriately amended.

The Act provides for the civil liability of the issuer of the securities, underwriters, and experts (including accountants) when representations have been materially false or inadequate. The law also imposes criminal penalties for fraudulent acts and practices in the sale of securities in interstate commerce whether or not they are registered with the SEC.

Registration Procedure.—The law provides that a registration statement shall become effective twenty days after it has been filed with the SEC, but empowers the Commission to declare the statement effective at an earlier date when valid reasons exist. As previously noted, this acceleration provision is of importance to accountants as well as to others participating in a registration engagement.

After the registration statement has been examined by the Commission's staff, the SEC usually issues a memorandum of comment (more commonly known as a "deficiency letter") suggesting changes in or additions to the material originally filed. The Commission's comments are often discussed informally by representatives of the issuer and the Commission's staff. If the registration statement is not appropriately corrected by amendment, the Commission may exercise its stop-order powers and refuse to allow the statement to become effective until it is amended.

Preliminary Considerations in Registration Engagements.

THE TIMETABLE.—Before detailed preparation of a registration statement is begun, a timetable is often prepared (usually by counsel) for the guidance of all concerned with the registration. Sometimes in great detail, sometimes in less detail, the timetable shows the steps that are to be taken in making the proposed offering, and the dates on which it is planned to complete each of the steps listed.

The independent public accountant who certifies the financial statements included in the registration document has an important part in accomplishing the proposed objective. A copy of the timetable is usually given to him; if it is not, he should always request it. The accountant should review the timetable, noting carefully those dates of immediate concern to him—such as that on which it is proposed to file the registration statement, that on which the SEC's deficiency letter is expected to be received, that on which it is planned to file the substantive amendment correcting the SEC's deficiencies and bringing the registration statement up to date because of changed conditions since the original filing date, that of the due diligence meeting, and that on which it is expected that the registration statement will become effective. All of these dates are important to the accountant in planning his work on the engagement.

READING THE REGISTRATION STATEMENT.—The accountant who participates in the preparation of a registration statement should make it a rule to read carefully the entire registration statement, not merely the financial data. There are several reasons for this.

First, the accountant is interested in determining that representations in the so-called "narrative" section do not conflict with representations in the financial section. If there are such conflicts, they must be resolved. For example, Item 12 in the Form S-1 registration statement calls for information about material pending legal proceedings to which the registrant or any of its subsidiaries is a party or of which any of their property is the subject. The auditor inquires about this in the course of his examination; obviously the response to Item 12 should confirm the results of the auditor's independent inquiry.

Second, there are usually few people, except the registrant's personnel, as familiar with the affairs of the registrant as the certifying accountant. For this reason the accountant almost invariably is in a position to make helpful and constructive suggestions for improving the narrative section of the registration. The information in that section is almost always prepared under the supervision of lawyers, and they welcome comments, suggestions, or criticisms which the accountant may make after reading the entire registration statement.

Third, there may be material in the narrative section of the registration statement which should be cross-referenced in the financial section, or vice versa. For example, the notes to financial statements must set forth some of the provisions of the company's pension plan if it has one, including a brief description of the plan together with a statement of annual cost and the unfunded cost of credits for service rendered prior to the adoption of the plan. Pensions are often described in the section of the prospectus dealing with employee relations. Rather than repeat all this information in the financial statements, it is desirable to make a cross-reference in the statement notes to the section of the prospectus that sets forth material otherwise required to be included in the financials. One of the general instructions of Form S-1 provides that cross-references of this kind shall be made to avoid duplication.

Fourth, the American Institute Committee on Auditing Procedure issued a bulletin[2] which deals with events subsequent to the date of financial statements. In one section of this bulletin the committee sets forth its views on special requirements for registration statements filed under the Securities Act of 1933. The committee stated that, in its opinion, a reasonable investigation would include the reading of the full text of the prospectus and review of pertinent portions of other sections of the registration statement.

READING THE UNDERWRITING AGREEMENT.—As soon as he can conveniently do so, the accountant who participates in the preparation of a registration statement should read the underwriting agreement. He should not wait until the underwriting agreement is signed; he should read it as soon as he can obtain a draft. At that time there is usually agreement in principle as to what is expected of all parties in the agreement.

There are a number of reasons why the accountant should read the draft of the underwriting agreement before it is final. In the first place, the underwriting agreement frequently contains provisions which affect the accountant in one way or another. For example, the agreement often provides that on or before the closing date (that is, the date on which the securities are delivered to the underwriters and paid for by them), the certifying accountant is to issue a letter or report in which he states that the financial statements, supporting schedules, and summary of earnings covered by his certificate comply in form with requirements of the Securities Act. Also, the accountant may be required to report on his review of unaudited financial statements

2 Statement on Auditing Procedure No. 25 (Oct., 1954).

included in the registration statement. Frequently the underwriting agreement also contains a provision to the effect that the accountant is to issue a letter concerning recent changes in the company's capital structure or adverse changes in its financial condition other than those disclosed in the registration statement or prospectus.

Second, underwriting agreements sometimes contain provisions requiring an accountant's opinion covering such matters as the amounts of additions to, and retirements of, fixed assets during the last five years. Where the matter in question is as simple as this, the accountant may be able to comply with this provision of the underwriting agreement without much, if any, additional work. If provisions of the agreement require considerable effort on the part of the accountant, the client may wish to consider the advisability of authorizing it. If the cost of the additional work is disproportionate to its value, the underwriter may be willing to waive this provision of the agreement.

Third, when the underwriting agreement provides that the accountant is to furnish letters about compliance, adverse changes, etc., it is advisable to clear with the interested parties in advance the form of such letters and opinions proposed to be issued in satisfaction of the underwriting provision. The objective is to agree in principle at an early date on the form of these letters. If, for some reason, the independent auditor finds it necessary to qualify the report called for by the underwriting agreement, that fact may have an important bearing on the underwriter's willingness to proceed with the offering, or it may put the underwriter on notice of an area that he should investigate further in his exercise of due diligence. At the closing there is no time to resolve differences between the accountant and the underwriter regarding the content of the accountant's report.

READING THE INDENTURE OR CHARTER PROVISIONS.—If the registration statement relates to a new issue of bonds, a new indenture is probably being drafted at the same time. This indenture will recite at length and in detail certain agreements (called "covenants") to which the borrowing company agrees as a condition to borrowing the money. Other statements may relate to a new issue of preferred stock, the terms of which may be governed by an amendment to the company's certificate of incorporation. Regardless of the form of the governing instrument—whether it be an indenture or an amendment to the certificate of incorporation—it is important that the certifying accountant read it in draft form before it becomes final.

Primarily it is important for the accountant to read the underlying instrument because the instrument is something that he will have to live with if he is to serve the company in the future. Indentures and charters frequently contain provisions relating to the payment of dividends on junior securities, such as preferred and common stocks. These dividends may be restricted to earnings accumulated subsequent to a stated date, or limited by such considerations as available working capital. Frequently the governing instrument may contain restrictions on a corporation's reacquisition of its own securities. An indenture may contain sinking-fund provisions that require payments into a fund for the repurchase or redemption of a corporation's own securities. The amount of the fund may be governed by the amount of net income available for that purpose as defined in the indenture.

Often an indenture provides that an independent accountant is to certify the amount of surplus available for dividends. An indenture may also provide that the accountant is to certify the amount to be paid into the sinking fund. It may require of the accountant certification in the future of his knowledge of defaults in indenture provisions. These provisions are not unusual, and, if they require an accountant's opinion, he should be informed of them in advance—preferably while the indenture or charter amendment is being drafted.

Experience has shown that the certifying accountant can be helpful in eliminating ambiguities in the indenture or other governing instrument. Because of his familiarity with the company, the industry, and the manner in which the financial statements are prepared from the accounts, he can frequently make suggestions that will be welcomed by all concerned.

BLUE-SKY REQUIREMENTS.—Most of the states have laws governing the sale of securities within those states. These laws are called "Blue-Sky" laws, and they vary considerably in different states.

When arranging an engagement under the Securities Act, it is desirable to inquire of counsel for the company and the underwriter about any additional work that may be required in blue-skying the securities. In some states the prospectus and registration statement filed with the federal authorities is not enough; additional information may be necessary. In Illinois, for example, certain classes of securities may require a certified balance sheet as of a date within sixty days of its filing.

New York's blue-sky law requires registration by dealers and the filing of dealers' statements under certain circumstances. The Attorney General of New York may grant exemptions, however, to seasoned corporations that comply with specified requirements for payments of interest and dividends in the past. The exemption is available for common stock "upon which dividends have been paid annually for a continuous immediately preceding period of six years at the rate of not less than 3 per cent of the book value of such common stock as shown by its balance sheet at the date of the close of the fiscal year in which such dividends were paid, *as certified by an independent certified public accountant.*"[3] (Emphasis added.)

Accountant's Liabilities Under the Act.—Under Section 11(a) of the Act:

> In case any part of the registration statement, when such part became effective, contained an untrue statement of a material fact or omitted to state a material fact required to be stated therein or necessary to make the statements therein not misleading, any person acquiring such security . . . . may . . . . sue . . . . every accountant . . . . who has with his consent been named as having . . . . certified any part of the registration statement . . . . with respect to the statement in such registration statement . . . . which purports to have been . . . . certified by him.

The section quoted above is significant to all persons connected with a registration engagement. To public accountants it is especially significant in that it appears that the registration statement speaks *as of its effective date.* As discussed later in this chapter, this means that the need for diligence on the part of the public accountant does not end with the completion of his work in the field.

As indicated above, the certifying accountant may be sued if he certifies false or inadequate financial statements in a registration statement. The law provides, however, that no person, other than the issuer, shall be liable who shall sustain the burden of proof that:

> . . . . as regards any part of the registration statement purporting to be made upon his authority as an expert . . . . he had, after reasonable investigation, reasonable ground to believe and did believe, at the time such part of the registration statement became effective, that the statements therein were true and that there was no omission to state a material fact required to be stated therein or necessary to make the statements therein not misleading. . . . . [Section 11(b)(3)(B) of the Act.]

The standard of reasonableness referred to above shall be that required of a prudent man in the management of his own property [Section 11(c) of the Act].

If the registration statement under the 1933 Act contains an untrue statement or material omission, any person acquiring the security may sue the certifying accountant regardless of the fact that he is not a client of the accountant. There need be no connection between the investor and the accountant; in other words, there need be no showing of privity.

Limitations of Actions to Recover.—Suit must be brought within *one year* after the discovery of the untrue statement or omission or

[3] New York Fraudulent Practices Act, Sec. 359-f(2).

after such discovery should have been made by exercise of reasonable diligence, and in any event within *three years* after the security was bona fide offered to the public (Section 13 of the Act).

No liability under the Securities Act applies to any act done or omitted in good faith in conformity with any rule or regulation of the Commission notwithstanding that such rule or regulation may thereafter be amended or rescinded or determined to be invalid (Section 19 of the Act).

Information Required in Registration Statement.—The law provides (Section 7) that a registration statement shall contain the information and shall be accompanied by the documents specified in Schedule A of the Act. The SEC is empowered, however, by rules and regulations, to waive any such information or document in respect of any class of issuers of securities if it finds the requirement inapplicable and adequate disclosure is otherwise made. Under this authority the SEC has devised numerous forms for registration of securities. The instructions accompanying each form make it clear in what situation it may be used. Any registration statement shall be deemed to be filed on the proper form unless objection to the form is made by the Commission prior to the effective date of the statement.

A registration statement usually consists of two parts: a prospectus containing the most significant information about the issuer of the security, and certain additional information which is not deemed to be of primary importance. Although this additional information may be omitted from the prospectus, it must be included in the registration document. The prospectus is also subject to disclosure provisions of the law, and a copy must be delivered to the buyer of the registered security.

Registration Statement Forms.—The principal registration forms currently in use are as follows:

Form S-1	General form for registration of securities of issuers for which no other form is authorized or prescribed
Form S-2	For securities of nonsuccessor commercial and industrial corporations having no subsidiaries and still in the development stage
Form S-3	For shares of mining corporations in the promotional state
Form S-4	For securities of closed-end management investment companies registered on Form N-8B-1
Form S-5	For securities of open-end management investment companies registered on Form N-8B-1

Form S-6	For securities of unit investment trusts registered on Form N-8B-2
Form S-8	For certain types of unincorporated employees' stock purchase and savings plans
Form S-9	For registration of nonconvertible fixed interest debt securities of issuers meeting the requirements of the form
Form S-10	For oil or gas interests or rights
Form S-11	For shares of exploratory mining corporations

Other forms for registration under the 1933 Act are not listed here since they do not require the inclusion of financial statements.

Notification Forms for Exempt Securities.—The 1933 Act contains provisions exempting certain securities, such as securities of the United States, any state of the United States, or any political subdivision of any state. In addition, the Commission has the authority, by rules and regulations, to add any class of securities to the list of exempted securities referred to above, provided the aggregate amount at which the securities are offered to the public is not more than $300,000. Under this authority the Commission promulgated Regulation A which provides a general exemption from registration requirements for certain securities, the aggregate offering price of which (together with other exempt offerings within a one-year period) is not over $300,000.

Regulation A requires an unseasoned company to use an offering circular, but seasoned companies do not need to use an offering circular except for issues over $50,000. The circular must inform the prospective investor of the nature of the enterprise and the essential facts concerning its securities and include financial data. The circulars are examined by the Commission to determine the adequacy of disclosure and whether there is any indication of the existence of fraud. This is important because, although securities may be exempt from the registration requirements of the Act, they are not exempt from the antifraud provisions of the Act.

Form 1-A is for use in notifying the Commission of an offering of securities to be made pursuant to Regulation A. The offering circular referred to in the preceding paragraph is filed with and is deemed a part of this notification.

Form S-1.—As will be apparent from the list on page 585, Form S-1 is a catch-all to be used where no other form is authorized or prescribed, and most business organizations use it in registering with the Commission.

A registration statement on Form S-1 consists of two parts: information required in the prospectus, and certain other information and documents which are not required in the prospectus. (As used here the term "prospectus" means a general prospectus, as distinguished from a prospectus in the form of a newspaper advertisement.)

The prospectus must contain among other things the following information: the name of the issuer, a description of the business and significant developments in the past five years, a description of the principal plants, mines, and other physical properties, a description of capital securities outstanding and being registered, names of underwriters and nature of the underwriting arrangements, names of directors and officers, the remuneration of certain persons, the provisions of material pension, retirement, bonus, and profit-sharing arrangements for the benefit of directors or officers, and the nature of claims or charges involved in legal proceedings. Also required in the prospectus are the summary of earnings and the financial statements specified in the Instructions as to Financial Statements.

The second part of the registration statement contains the exhibits, schedules supporting financial statements, and other data which may be omitted from the prospectus. Included in Part II are copies of the charter, by-laws, certain pension and deferred compensation plans, bonus or profit-sharing plans, stock option plans, indentures and contracts, an opinion of counsel on the legality of the securities being registered, a list of subsidiaries, certain historical financial information (see page 592), expenses of issue, and other information.

Financial Statements in Form S-1.—The instructions as to financial statements in Form S-1 specify the balance sheets and statements of income which are required to be filed as part of the registration statement. Regulation S-X governs the form and content of those statements, certification by accountants, and the required supporting schedules. In other words, the instructions for Form S-1 specify the dates and periods for which the statements are to be furnished, but they do not indicate, for example, how inventories are to be shown in the balance sheets; Regulation S-X specifies the information required for inventories, such as the basis of determining the amounts and segregation into major classifications.

The SEC's instructions as to financial statements to be filed as part of Form S-1 are set forth in the following pages.

FINANCIAL STATEMENTS OF THE REGISTRANT.—A balance sheet of the registrant (unconsolidated) is required to be filed as of a date within ninety days prior to the date of filing the registration statement. In lieu of this ninety-day statement, however, the balance sheet may be as of a date within six months prior to the filing date if *all* of the conditions listed on page 588 exist.

1. The registrant files annual and other reports (Form 10-K, for example) pursuant to Section 13 or 15(d) of the Securities Exchange Act of 1934;

2. The total assets of the registrant and its subsidiaries, as shown by the latest consolidated balance sheet filed, amount to $5,000,000 or more, exclusive of intangibles; and

3. No long-term debt of the registrant is in default as to principal, interest, or sinking-fund provisions.

The balance sheet required in the preceding paragraph need not be certified. If it is not certified, there must be filed *in addition* a certified balance sheet as of a date within one year prior to the filing date unless the fiscal year of the registrant has ended within ninety days prior to the date of filing, in which event the certified balance sheet may be as of the end of the preceding fiscal year.

The registrant must file an income statement (unconsolidated) for each of the three fiscal years preceding the date of the latest balance sheet filed, and for the period, if any, between the close of the latest of such fiscal years and the date of the latest balance sheet filed. Regulation S-X requires that an analysis of each surplus account shall be filed as a continuation of the related income statement or as a separate statement of surplus. The income and surplus statements must be certified up to the date of the latest certified balance sheet filed. If the income or earned surplus statements are included in their entirety in the summary of earnings (see page 595), the statements so included need not be otherwise included in the registration statement.

Notwithstanding what has been said in the preceding paragraphs, individual financial statements of the registrant may be omitted if (1) consolidated statements of the registrant and one or more of its subsidiaries are filed, (2) the conditions specified in *either* of the following paragraphs are met, and (3) the Commission is advised of the reasons for such omission:

(a) The registrant is primarily an operating company and all subsidiaries included in the consolidated financial statements filed are totally-held subsidiaries (as defined on page 591); *or*

(b) The registrant's total assets, exclusive of investments in and advances to the consolidated subsidiaries, constitute 85 per cent or more of the total assets shown by the consolidated balance sheets filed *and* the registrant's total gross revenues for the period for which its income statements would be filed, exclusive of interest and dividends received from the consolidated subsidiaries, constitute 85 per cent or more of the total gross revenues shown by the consolidated income statements filed.

CONSOLIDATED FINANCIAL STATEMENTS.—The registration statement must contain a consolidated balance sheet of the registrant and its subsidiaries as of the same date as each balance sheet of the registrant filed pursuant to the instructions set forth above. The consolidated balance sheet must be certified if the registrant's balance sheet as of the same date is certified. If the registrant's balance sheets are omitted as permitted by the instructions, the consolidated balance sheets filed must be as of the same dates as the balance sheets of the registrant which would otherwise be required; the consolidated balance sheet must be certified if the corresponding balance sheet of the registrant would be required to be certified.

The registration statement must include a consolidated income statement of the registrant and its subsidiaries for each of the three fiscal years preceding the date of the latest consolidated balance sheet filed, and for the period, if any, between the close of the latest of such fiscal years and the date of the latest consolidated balance sheet filed. Requirements of Regulation S-X indicated previously for surplus in financial statements of the registrant are the same for surplus in consolidated statements.

FINANCIAL STATEMENTS OF UNCONSOLIDATED SUBSIDIARIES AND 50 PER CENT OWNED COMPANIES.—Balance sheets and income and surplus statements that would be required if the subsidiary were itself a registrant must be filed for each majority-owned subsidiary not consolidated. Insofar as practicable, these statements must be for the same dates or periods as those of the registrant.

If it is impracticable to file a balance sheet of any unconsolidated subsidiary as of a date within ninety days prior to the date of filing, there may be filed in lieu thereof a certified balance sheet of the subsidiary as of the end of its latest annual or semiannual fiscal period preceding the date of filing the registration statement for which it is practicable to do so.

If the registrant owns directly or indirectly approximately 50 per cent of the voting securities of any company, and the remaining 50 per cent is owned directly or indirectly by another single interest, there must be filed for each such company the financial statements which would be required if it were a registrant. The statements filed for each such company must identify the other single interest.

Notwithstanding the instructions in the preceding paragraphs, there may be omitted from the registration statement all financial statements of any one or more unconsolidated subsidiaries or 50 per cent owned companies, if all such subsidiaries and 50 per cent owned companies for which statements are so omitted, considered in the aggregate as a single subsidiary, would not constitute a significant subsidiary.[4]

FINANCIAL STATEMENTS OF AFFILIATES WHOSE SECURITIES ARE PLEDGED AS COLLATERAL.—For each affiliate, securities of which constitute or are to constitute a substantial portion of the collateral securing any class of securities being registered, there must be filed the financial statements that would be required if the affiliate were a registrant. For the purpose of this instruction, securities of a company are deemed to constitute a substantial portion of collateral if the aggregate principal amount, par value, or book value as shown by the books of the registrant, or market value, whichever is the greatest, of such securities equals 20 per cent or more of the principal amount of the class secured thereby.

SPECIAL PROVISIONS.—*Reorganization of Registrant.*—If during the period for which its income statements are required, the registrant has emerged from a reorganization in which substantial changes occurred in its asset, liability, capital stock, surplus, or reserve accounts, a brief explanation of such changes must be set forth in a note or supporting schedule to the balance sheets filed.

If the registrant is about to emerge from such a reorganization, there shall be filed, in addition to the balance sheets of the registrant otherwise required, a balance sheet giving effect to the plan of reorganization. These balance sheets must be set forth to show, preferably in columnar form, (1) the balance sheet of the registrant prior to the reorganization, (2) the changes to be effected in the reorganization, and (3) the balance sheet of the registrant after giving effect to the plan of reorganization. By a footnote, or otherwise, a brief explanation of the changes must be given.

Succession to Other Businesses.—If during the period for which its income statements are required, the registrant has by merger, con-

---

[4] Regulation S-X defines the term "significant subsidiary" as follows:

The term "significant subsidiary" means a subsidiary meeting any one of the following conditions:

(a) The assets of the subsidiary, or the investments in and advances to the subsidiary by its parent and the parent's other subsidiaries, if any, exceed 15 per cent of the assets of the parent and its subsidiaries on a consolidated basis.

(b) The sales and operating revenues of the subsidiary exceed 15 per cent of the sales and operating revenues of its parent and the parent's subsidiaries on a consolidated basis.

(c) The subsidiary is the parent of one or more subsidiaries and together with such subsidiaries would, if considered in the aggregate, constitute a significant subsidiary.

solidation, or otherwise succeeded to one or more businesses, the additions, eliminations, and other changes effected in the succession must be appropriately set forth in a note or supporting schedule to the balance sheets filed. In addition, income and surplus statements for each constituent business, or combined statements if appropriate, must be filed for such period prior to the succession as may be necessary when added to the time, if any, for which income and surplus statements after the succession are filed to cover the equivalent of the three-year period.

If the registrant by merger, consolidation, or otherwise, is *about* to succeed to one or more businesses, financial statements must be filed for each of the constituent businesses, combined (pro forma) if appropriate, which would be required if they were registering securities under the 1933 Act. In addition, there must be filed a balance sheet (pro forma) of the registrant giving effect to the plan of succession. These balance sheets must be set forth to show, preferably in columnar form, (1) the balance sheets of the constituent businesses, (2) the changes to be effected in the succession, and (3) the balance sheet (pro forma) of the registrant after giving effect to the plan of succession. A brief explanation of the changes must be given by footnote or otherwise.

The two paragraphs immediately preceding do not apply to the registrant's succession to the business of any totally-held subsidiary[5] *or to any acquisition of a business by purchase.*

Acquisition of Other Businesses.—Financial statements must be filed for any business directly or indirectly acquired by the registrant *after* the date of the latest balance sheet filed pursuant to the instructions relating to financial statements of the registrant and the consolidation. Financial statements must also be filed for any business *to be* directly or indirectly acquired by the registrant. The financial statements to be filed for such business acquired or to be acquired are those that would be furnished if such business were a registrant.

The acquisition of securities is deemed to be the acquisition of a business if such securities, combined with securities already held, give control of the business. In addition, the acquisition of securities which will extend the registrant's control of a business is deemed to be the

[5] Regulation S-X defines the term "totally-held subsidiary" as follows:

The term "totally-held subsidiary" means a subsidiary (a) substantially all of whose outstanding securities are owned by its parent and/or the parent's other totally-held subsidiaries, and (b) which is not indebted to any person other than its parent and/or the parent's other totally-held subsidiaries in an amount which is material in relation to the particular subsidiary, excepting indebtedness incurred in the ordinary course of business which is not overdue and which matures within one year from the date of its creation, whether evidenced by securities or not.

acquisition of the business if any of the securities being registered are to be offered in exchange for the securities to be acquired.

Financial statements need not be filed, however, for any business acquired or to be acquired from a totally-held subsidiary. In addition, the statements of any one or more businesses may be omitted if such businesses, considered in the aggregate as a single subsidiary, would not constitute a significant subsidiary, provided, however, that the statements of any business may not be omitted where any of the securities being registered are to be offered in exchange for securities representing such business.

Filing of Other Financial Statements in Certain Cases.—The Commission may, upon the request of the registrant, and when consistent with the protection of investors, permit the omission of one or more of the required statements as set forth above, or the filing in substitution therefor of appropriate statements of comparable character. The Commission may also require the filing of other statements in addition to, or in substitution for, the statements required by these instructions when such statements are necessary or appropriate for an adequate presentation of the financial condition of any company whose financial statements are required or whose statements are otherwise necessary for the protection of investors.

HISTORICAL FINANCIAL INFORMATION.—The information required by the instructions set forth below must be submitted for each company or group of companies whose balance sheet is filed. The information is to cover the seven-year period preceding the three-year period for which income statements are filed. The information must be given for all the accounts specified below whether or not they are presently carried on the books of account. The information required by these instructions does not call for an audit, but only for a survey or review of the accounts specified. The information should not be detailed beyond a point material to an investor. What is more important, however, is that the information may be omitted for any company for which equivalent information for the period has previously been filed with the SEC pursuant to the 1933 Act or the 1934 Act.

Revaluation of Property.—If there were any material increases or decreases in investments, in property, plant, and equipment, or in intangible assets, resulting from revaluing such assets, a statement is required indicating (1) in what year or years such revaluations were made; (2) the amounts of such increases or decreases, and the accounts affected, including all related entries; and (3) if in connection with such revaluation any related adjustments were made in reserve accounts, the accounts and amounts with explanations. Information is not required of adjustments made in the ordinary course of business, but only of major revaluations made for the purpose of entering in the books current values, reproduction cost, or any values other than original cost. Information need not be furnished for any revaluation entry which was subsequently reversed or for the reversal of a revaluation entry recorded prior to the period if a statement is made disclosing the reversal.

Capital Shares.—If there were any material restatements of capital shares which resulted in transfers from capital share liability to surplus or reserve accounts, a statement must be made of the amount of each such restatement and all related entries. Information is not required for restatements resulting from the declaration of stock dividends.

If there was an original issue of capital shares, any part of the proceeds of which was credited to accounts other than capital share accounts, a statement must be made of the title of the class, the accounts, and the respective amounts credited thereto.

Debt Discount and Expense Written Off.—If any material amount of debt discount and expense on long-term debt still outstanding was written off earlier than as required under any periodic amortization plan, the following information must be given: (1) title of the securities, (2) date of the write-off, (3) amount written off, and (4) to what account charged.

Premium and Discount and Expense on Securities Retired.—If any material amount of long-term debt or preferred shares was retired, and if either the retirement was made at a premium or there remained, at the time of retirement, a material amount of unamortized discount and expense applicable to the securities retired, a statement must be made for each class giving: (1) title of the securities retired, (2) date of retirement, (3) amount of premium paid and of unamortized discount and expense, (4) the account charged, and (5) whether being amortized and, if so, the plan of amortization.

Other Changes in Surplus.—If there were any material increases or decreases in surplus, other than those resulting from transactions specified above, the closing of the income statement, or the declaration or payment of dividends, the following information must be furnished: (1) the year or years in which such increases or decreases were made, (2) the nature and amounts thereof, and (3) the accounts affected, including all material related entries. Information, however, need not be furnished for any revaluation entry which was subsequently reversed or for the reversal of a revaluation entry recorded prior to the period if a statement disclosing the reversal is made.

Predecessors.—Historical Financial Information shall be furnished, to the extent it is material, for any predecessor of the registrant from the beginning of the period to the date of succession, not only for the entries made respectively in the books of the predecessor or the successor, but also for the changes effected in the transfer of the assets from the predecessor. However, no information need be furnished for any one or more predecessors which, considered in the aggregate, would not constitute a significant predecessor.

Omission of Certain Information.—No information need be furnished for any subsidiary, whether consolidated or unconsolidated, for the period prior to the date on which it became a majority-owned subsidiary of the registrant or of a predecessor for which information is required above.

No information need be furnished for any one or more unconsolidated subsidiaries for which separate financial statements are filed if all subsidiaries for which the information is so omitted, considered in the aggregate as a single subsidiary, would not constitute a significant subsidiary.

Only the information specified under "Revaluation of Property" above need be given for any predecessor of any subsidiary thereof if immediately prior to the date of succession thereto by a person for which information is required, the predecessor or subsidiary was in insolvency proceedings.

SUPPORTING SCHEDULES.—A registration statement on Form S-1 must also include certain supplemental schedules. The form and content of these schedules are set forth in Regulation S-X.

FINANCIAL STATEMENTS INCLUDED IN PROSPECTUS.—A prospectus prepared for filing as part of a registration on Form S-1 must include all the financial statements required by the Instructions as to Financial Statements except as provided below:

1. All schedules to balance sheets and income statements may be omitted from the prospectus except Supplementary Profit and Loss Information (Schedule XVI), Investments in Securities of Affiliates—Banks (Schedule III-A for bank holding companies only), and Summary of Investments in Securities—Other than Securities of Affiliates (Schedule V for insurance companies other than life and title insurance companies). All Historical Financial Information may also be omitted from the prospectus.

2. If the income or earned surplus statements required are included in their entirety in the summary of earnings, they need not be otherwise included in the prospectus or elsewhere in the registration statement.

The prospectus of the ordinary industrial company will contain the prime financial statements, i.e., balance sheets, income and surplus statements, and earnings summaries, plus the information contained in Supplementary Profit and Loss Information, either in a separate schedule or in notes to the financial statements. All supporting schedules (except Supplementary Profit and Loss Information) and Historical Financial Information are included in Part II of the registration statement.

SUMMARY OF EARNINGS.—Item 6 of Form S-1 calls for the inclusion in the prospectus of a summary of earnings.

For Whom Furnished and Period Covered.—The summary presents in comparative columnar form the earnings history of the company or of the company and its subsidiaries consolidated, or both, as appropriate. The summary must be furnished for each of the last five fiscal years of the company, or for the life of the company and its immediate predecessors, if less, and for any period between the end of the latest of such fiscal years and the date of the latest balance sheet furnished, and for the corresponding period of the preceding fiscal year.

A registrant which is a company engaged primarily (1) in the generation, transmission, or distribution of electricity, the manufacture, mixing, transmission, or distribution of gas, the supplying or distribution of water, or in furnishing telephone or telegraph service or (2) in holding securities in such companies may, at its option, include a summary for a twelve-month period to the date of the latest balance sheet furnished, in lieu of both the summary for the interim period between the end of the last fiscal year and such balance sheet date and the summary for the corresponding period of the preceding fiscal year.

Although the summary must cover at least the last five fiscal years, the instructions provide that comparable data shall be included for any additional fiscal years necessary to keep the summary from being misleading. What this probably means is this: If the company's business during the required five-year minimum period was unduly influenced by extraordinary or nonrecurring conditions, such as war production, the summary should include a number of earlier years that are more nearly representative of the company's operations under normal conditions. Similarly, when a company's business is subject to extreme cyclical fluctuations, if the five-year period showed consistent profits and the preceding three years consistent losses, presumably the five-year period would not be representative and might be misleading.

Items of Information.—Subject to appropriate variation to conform to the nature of the business or the purpose of the offering, the following items of information must be included in the summary of earnings: net sales or operating revenues, cost of goods sold or operating expenses (or gross profit), interest charges, income taxes, net income, special items, and net income and special items. The summary must reflect the retroactive adjustment of any material items affecting the comparability of the results. (See page 606.)

Even though not specifically called for by the instructions, when charges for maintenance, repairs, and depreciation are significant— as in public utilities operations—the registrant may wish to set them out separately, either in the body of the earnings summary or in a footnote. The SEC's language in the preceding paragraph, "Subject to appropriate variation to conform to the nature of the business," may, in fact, require such presentation.

If the summary of earnings furnishes substantially all the information that would be contained in the formal income statement, the latter statement may be omitted.

If long-term debt or preferred stock is being registered, the instructions provide that there must be shown the annual interest requirements on such long-term debt or the annual dividend requirements on such preferred stock. To the extent that an issue represents refunding or refinancing, only the additional annual interest or dividend requirements shall be stated.

Necessary Information and Explanations.—In connection with the summary the instructions provide that "whenever necessary," information or explanations "of material significance to investors in appraising the results shown" shall be reflected; reference to such information or explanations set forth elsewhere in the prospectus is permitted.

In Accounting Series Release No. 62 (1947) the SEC states:

In order that investors may make proper use of the summary earnings table and to prevent the possibility of misleading inferences, certain explanatory data are usually necessary. If, for example, the reported earnings reflect the results of unusual conditions, or in certain years include significant nonrecurring items of income or expenses, an appropriate disclosure of such conditions or items is made either in the summary or in footnotes thereto.

In the same release the SEC pointed out that where the summary reflected operations of a predecessor, or where there had been violent or radical changes in the enterprise, appropriate disclosures or adjustments may be required; or the summary may, in fact, be entirely deleted, as follows:

Ordinarily, the summary earnings table will reflect the operations of the registrant, or of the registrant and its subsidiaries, during the period covered. However, under special circumstances, as where the registrant has succeeded to the business of one or more predecessors, it may be necessary for the summary to be specially constructed so as to reflect as far as possible for the period covered the earnings applicable to the enterprise now represented by the registrant. Where, for example, a predecessor operated as a partnership it is ordinarily necessary to indicate in an appropriate manner the adjustments required to place the partnership income on a corporate basis. In other unusual cases there may have been such violent and radical changes in the business of the registrant that a long summary of past earnings might be of very little or no value and might well be misleading. In several such cases, the registrant has been requested either to delete the summary entirely or to furnish only a brief statement of the over-all, aggregate results, without a breakdown as between the several years. In any case, where special and unusual circumstances exist, a decision as to the content of the summary and as to whether or not a summary should be furnished at all can only be reached after careful appraisal of the particular facts of each case.

If there has been a material wage increase in the latter part of the latest year covered by the summary of earnings, and the wage increase has not been compensated by a corresponding increase in the selling price of the company's product or a decrease in other costs, a disclosure should be made of the wage increase. Usually this can be done by reference to the narrative portion of the prospectus that discloses recent wage increases. The principle involved would be equally applicable to other cost increases not compensated by corresponding increases in selling price or rates, or by a decrease in other costs.

The preceding paragraph gives the requirements which, in the opinion of the authors, are applicable when there has been a recent material increase in costs. There remains to be considered the related question when there have been material reductions in selling prices or rates which are not compensated by corresponding reductions in costs or expenses. The principle enunciated in the preceding paragraph is also applicable here: if such reductions in selling prices or rates are material, are not reflected for approximately a year in the summary of earnings (or, as some suggest, for all of an interim period), and are not compensated by corresponding reductions in costs or expenses, they should be disclosed, either in a note to the summary or by reference to the narrative section of the prospectus that deals with the matter.

When a reference is made to material in another part of the prospectus, the auditor should make certain that the material incorporated by reference is such that it may be properly covered by his opinion.

Ratio of Earnings to Fixed Charges.—A registrant may, at its option, show in tabular form for each fiscal year or other period, the ratio of earnings (computed in accordance with generally accepted accounting principles after all operating and income deductions, except taxes based on income or profits and fixed charges) to fixed charges. The term "fixed charges" means:

1. Interest and amortization of debt discount and expenses and premium on all indebtedness;

2. An appropriate portion of rentals under long-term leases; and

3. In case consolidated figures are used, preferred stock dividend requirements of consolidated subsidiaries, excluding in all cases, items eliminated in consolidation.

Interest credits charged to construction by utilities should be added to gross income and not deducted from interest. If the ratio is shown, the pro forma ratio of earnings to fixed charges adjusted to give effect to the issuance of securities being registered and to any presently proposed issuance, retirement, or redemption of securities should be disclosed. Any registrant electing to show the ratio of earnings to fixed charges, in accordance with this instruction, must file as an exhibit a statement setting forth in reasonable detail the computations of such ratios. For the purpose of this exhibit and the pro forma ratio referred to above, an assumed maximum interest rate may be used on securities as to which the interest rate has not yet been fixed, which assumed rate should be shown.

Nothing in the instructions throws any light on the meaning of "an appropriate portion of rentals." Inquiries as to its meaning have been answered by reference to a publication dealing with this matter from which the following is quoted:

Capitalization of Fixed Charges.—As we pointed out in our earlier discussion of the composition of fixed charges, the latter are not confined solely to interest on funded debt. All or some part of annual rental obligations, interest and dividends guaranteed under lease or otherwise, and dividend requirements on subsidiary-company preferred stocks constitute fixed charges in computing over-all coverage. Similarly, for the purpose of comparing "funded debt" with tangible-asset values, net current assets, and stock equity at market, it is important to recognize that debt may be represented not only by bond issues but also by guaranteed stocks, by annual rental obligations, and effectively also by nonguaranteed preferred stocks of operating subsidiaries.

The principal amount of these obligations is usually stated quite clearly in the consolidated balance sheet of a public utility enterprise; but this may not be true in the case of a railroad company or an industrial or commercial concern, chiefly because its rental obligations are not likely to be reflected in its balance sheet. We suggest, therefore, that the "effective debt" of a railroad may be calculated by multiplying the "adjusted charges" by an appropriate figure, say 25. This is equivalent to capitalizing the adjusted charges at an assumed rate of 4%—in other words, to assuming that the true debt is that figure of which 4% will equal the adjusted charges.

A more difficult problem is presented by chain stores and other business enterprises which are obligated to pay rental for building space. To some extent these rentals are identical with fixed "overhead"—e.g., depreciation, taxes, general expense—which it has not been found feasible to add to bond interest for the purpose of figuring coverage. But to some extent they also partake of the nature of fixed charges. Our inquiries addressed to corporate officials and our study of available financial data for such enterprises lead us to the conclusion that one-third of such annual rentals should be regarded as fixed charges when computing earnings coverage for senior issues, and that this fraction of them should be capitalized at, say, 4% and the product added to bonds outstanding in order to obtain the "effective debt."[6]

The SEC apparently shares the sentiments quoted above which, in effect, do not consider depreciation and real estate taxes as constituting fixed charges. It considers only the portion of rents representing the interest factor on the cost or value of leased property as a fixed charge. The interest factor represents the owner's profit on his investment plus his interest charges, and this is the portion of the rent which is considered to be "an appropriate portion of rentals." This should not, however, be construed to mean that the SEC believes that the "appropriate portion of rentals" to be taken into account is necessarily always one-third of the rents paid.

Certification by Independent Public Accountants.—Earnings summaries in Form S-1 are not required by SEC to be certified by independent public accountants. In practice, however, underwriters usually require that the summary of earnings be certified at least for the period (usually three years) that the SEC requires certification of the income statements.

Accounting Series Release No. 62 (1947) provides, in substance, that if an accountant's name is used in connection with a summary—to the effect that he has reviewed or examined it—his certificate must be furnished. The release also provides that the accountant may not certify the summary of earnings unless the scope of his examination conformed to generally accepted auditing standards.

Unaudited Interim Periods.—In connection with any summary for an unaudited interim period or periods between the end of the last fiscal year and the balance sheet date, and any comparable unaudited prior periods, a statement should be made that all adjustments necessary to a fair statement of the results for such interim period or periods have been included. In practice the form of representation, as given on the following page, has been found to be acceptable.

[6] By permission from *Security Analysis,* 3d ed., by B. Graham and D. Dodd, p. 346. Copyright, 1951, McGraw-Hill Book Co., Inc., New York.

The summaries of earnings for the (periods) ended (date) and (date) have been prepared from the records of the Company without audit by independent public accountants, and, in the opinion of the Company, reflect all adjustments necessary to present fairly the results of operations for the periods.

In addition, there should be furnished, as supplemental information but not as a part of the registration statement, a letter from the registrant to the SEC describing in detail the nature and amount of any adjustments, other than normal recurring accruals, entering into the determination of the interim period results shown.

Earnings and Dividends Per Share of Common Stock.—If common stock is being registered, the summary must show the net income applicable to common stock. If cumulative preferred shares were outstanding during the period covered by the summary, cumulative dividends on such preferred shares, whether or not declared or paid, must be deducted from net income to compute net income applicable to common stock. If preferred dividends are payable quarterly and the earnings summary is submitted for, say, four months, there should be deducted from net income the preferred dividend requirements for four months even though in that period only one preferred dividend had been declared.

In addition, earnings and dividends declared per share of common stock for each period of the summary must also be included unless inappropriate.

Prospectuses Used More Than Nine Months After Effective Date. —After the registration statement becomes effective, the sale and distribution of securities is usually completed promptly. However, because of market or other conditions, the public offering date may be delayed or the public distribution may take considerable time. For example, an issue of preferred stock may have been registered with warrants attached entitling the holders to purchase common stock of the registrant at some future date; or debentures may have been registered, convertible into common stock at some future date on surrender of the debentures together with cash. In these and similar situations the issuer must furnish an up-to-date prospectus. The 1933 Act and the Commission's rules contain provisions for prospectuses used more than nine months after the effective date of the registration statement.

Section 10(a)(3) of the 1933 Act covers a prospectus used more than nine months after the effective date of the registration statement to which it relates. The section provides as follows:

. . . . when a prospectus is used more than nine months after the effective date of the registration statement, the information contained therein shall be as of a date not more than 16 months prior to such use so far as such information is known to the user of such prospectus or can be furnished by such user without unreasonable effort or expense.

Rule 427 under the 1933 Act provides as follows:

There may be omitted from any prospectus used more than 9 months after the effective date of the registration statement any information previously required to be contained in the prospectus insofar as later information covering the same subjects, including the latest available certified financial statement, as of a date not more than 16 months prior to the use of the prospectus is contained therein.

The following example illustrates how the above SEC rule works in practice.

Corporation A filed a registration statement which became effective March 15, 1957, in which were included financial statements as of December 31, 1956, and for the period then ended. Under Rule 427 these financial statements may be used in prospectuses without further supplement until April 30, 1958. After April 30, 1958, certified financial statements as of a date more recent than December 31, 1956, must be substituted; presumably by that date certified financial statements as of December 31, 1957, will be available and may be included in the prospectus.

Registration Statement Speaks as of Its Effective Date.—It was observed earlier in this chapter that the public accountant could be sued under the 1933 Act if the statements he certifies in the registration statement, *when it became effective,* contained a material misstatment or omission. The registration statement, when it becomes effective, must be true and there must be no material omissions. This imposes a duty on the independent accountant which does not end with the signing of his certificate and consent and the filing of the registration statement. After the filing and up to the effective date, the accountant must take reasonable steps to determine whether anything has happened in the interim that materially affects the statements he certifies. It is true that this is a responsibility which he shares with others, but it is not a good defense to say that his responsibility is only secondary, that the primary responsibility is the registrant's. Suppose, for example, that on the date of the statements and on the filing date an important lawsuit was pending and no provision had been or could be made for an adverse decision. Shortly after the filing date, a decision is handed down against the registrant. Under the law, unless this information is included in the registration statement, it might be construed as an omission of a material fact which would subject those participating in the registration to the liabilities provided in the statute.

In the *Shonts* case,[7] the court held the accountant not responsible for events occurring subsequent to the date of his certificate but prior to the effective date of the registration statement. This case is not a satisfactory one, raising as many questions as it answers. Until there is a better case, prudence requires the certifying accountant to keep in touch with the financial affairs of his client up to the effective date of the registration statement.

It seems to the authors that the accountant's job does not end with the filing of the registration statement; he may not relax his vigilance after the filing and sit back and wait for the SEC's memorandum of comments, and, finally, the effective date. On the other hand, the independent accountant as a practical matter cannot be expected to continue his audit until the effective date which may be weeks or even months after the certificate date. The authors have not interpreted the clause "at the time such part of the registration statement became effective" as requiring the accountant to continue his examination of the books and records to the effective date. The accountant should, however, keep in touch with the financial affairs of his client in some manner.

On this point the American Institute Committee on Auditing Procedure has said in Statement on Auditing Procedure No. 25 (Oct., 1954):

. . . . It is obvious that the accountant may encounter serious problems in keeping currently informed as to the happening of any extraordinary transactions or events bearing on the financial statements, and the procedures which may be involved would be unreasonably costly and impractical.

There are additional difficulties involved in keeping currently informed up to the time of the effective date by reason of the lack of recorded financial information during the period immediately preceding the effective date. Depending on the size of the company and the complexity of its operations this period of time may be substantial.

Suggestions for Review To Keep Currently Informed.—Before the registration statement is filed and from time to time thereafter before the effective date, the accountant should confer with responsible, informed officials of the registrant with a view to determining whether, since the date of his certificate, there have been any important developments in the affairs of the company which have a bearing on either the financial statements or his certificate. He should also review any statements of the company prepared for internal purposes. If develop-

---

[7] *Shonts v. Hirliman* (28 F. Supp. 478, S.D. Cal., 1939).

ments indicate that the certificate should be revised or that the financial statements should be changed, the auditor should require amendment of the registration statement before the effective date.

The primary purpose of this conference and the review of statements is to determine whether the over-all picture at the date of his certificate has changed materially because of recent developments in the company's business. Usually a conference at the company's main office should suffice for this purpose, and it should not be necessary to send staff accountants to every location visited in the audit. Matters discussed at such a conference will vary with each engagement, and the accountant will have to use his imagination and his knowledge of the company in making his inquiry.

The recommendations of the American Institute Committee on Auditing Procedure as to review in these circumstances follow:

The committee therefore is of the opinion that a "reasonable investigation" (a) as to point of time, should be construed as referring to a period ending sufficiently prior to the actual effective date as is consistent with the practical availability of financial information, etc., and (b) as to procedures, should comprise the following:

1. The reading of available minutes of meetings of stockholders, directors, and finance or executive committees, as applicable.

2. Reading of such available interim financial statements as are regularly prepared by the client.

3. The reading of the full text of the prospectus and review of pertinent portions of the rest of the registration statement.

4. Inquiry of one or more officers or key employees and of legal counsel, where appropriate, as to happenings which may be considered material in relation to the financial statements reported upon by the auditor and included in the registration statement. Such happenings, or the absence thereof, should be the subject of written representations.

5. Any other steps which the auditor deems necessary for a "reasonable investigation" under the particular circumstances.

It is obvious that the responsibility for the disclosure of post-balance-sheet events must, as a practical and reasonable matter, decrease following the close of the field work and that subsequent to that time the accountant must rely, for the most part, on inquiries of officers and key employees. In the case of an issuer with multiple offices and wide-spread operations, the officers and employees would be those at the home office level.

When a registrant has changed auditors, and the registration statement contains the reports of two or more auditors covering different periods, question may arise about the scope of current review required of the accountant who certifies the earlier periods. The Institute Committee's opinion is given on the next page.

The committee is of the opinion that when the independent accountant whose opinion is to be submitted in respect to statements for previous years furnishes such opinion he should have available the full text of the registration statement and prospectus in which his opinion will appear so that he can read or review . . . . anything included therein which apparently relates to his period. The committee is of the opinion that no duty rests upon the independent accountant for such earlier period to make any subsequent examination or review other than the suggested reference to the documents it is proposed to file or from such assurances as he may request from the registrant or its current accountants.

For a form of assurance as suggested in the foregoing quotation, see the recommended form of letter on page 612.

Unaudited Interim Financial Statements.—As stated earlier in this chapter, certain financial statements in a registration statement and prospectus are not required by law or SEC regulation to be certified by independent public accountants. However, directors or underwriters may request that the accountants review the interim statements, not for the purpose of certifying them but as a measure of assurance, short of an audit, about the method of preparation of the statements and the omission of obvious errors.

The review of these interim statements is of value not only to officers, directors, and underwriters but also to the accountant because:

1. He is interested in the transactions and developments during the interim period for whatever additional light they may shed on the statements he certifies. A tax audit in progress at the time of his last examination may have resulted in a substantial adjustment for which provision had not been made, or losses may have been sustained which were not adequately provided for in the certified statements.

2. He wishes to know whether there has been any change during the interim period in the application of accounting principles as compared with the practices followed in the certified statements.

3. The review is a means of bringing himself up to date on the affairs of his client (see page 602).

As a result of the review considered here, it is not to be expected that the independent accountant will be able to certify the interim statements; neither should he issue over his signature and for public information any letter or statement setting forth the scope of his review. It is true that the accountant is liable only for what he reports, but nevertheless the public is only too apt to see his name and not read what he says. To avoid any misunderstanding on the part of the public, it is better practice not to be identified in the eyes of the investing public with uncertified statements. On the other hand, management, directors, and underwriters understand the purpose and scope of the review, and there is no objection to an accountant's reporting privately to them.

Furthermore, the SEC has stated that an accountant may not express an opinion on an earnings summary of any period unless his examination of that period conformed to generally accepted auditing standards. Although the SEC's statement was directed to earnings summaries, it is undoubtedly applicable to all financial statements.

The statement of the SEC's Chief Accountant is, in part, as follows:

. . . . it is my opinion that it is generally improper and misleading for an accountant to permit his name to be used in connection with any period covered by a summary earnings table or to undertake to express his professional opinion as to the fairness of the representations made for such period in a summary earnings table unless he has made an examination for such period in accordance with generally accepted auditing standards applicable in the circumstances.[8]

LETTER COVERING REVIEW OF UNAUDITED FINANCIAL STATEMENTS.—A typical letter follows covering the accountant's review of unaudited interim financial statements and conformity of such statements with SEC requirements:

We previously submitted our reports dated _____ on our examination of the financial statements and supporting schedules of (name of company) and the consolidated financial statements and supporting schedules of that company and its subsidiaries as of (date) and for the years _____, _____, and _____, and the summary of earnings for the years _____ to _____, inclusive. The afore-mentioned statements, supporting schedules, and summary of earnings, together with said reports, are included in Registration Statement No. _____, filed by (name of company) with the Securities and Exchange Commission.

Pursuant to your request, we have reviewed and made a limited investigation, but not an audit, of the financial statements and supporting schedules of (name of company) and the consolidated financial statements and supporting schedules of that company and its subsidiaries as of (interim date) and for the (interim period) months then ended, and the summary of earnings for the (interim periods) ended (date) and (date), which statements, schedules, and summary are also included in the above-mentioned registration statement. Such statements, schedules, and summary were checked in detail by us with the face of the general accounts of the respective companies and were compared with similar data for prior periods. We also made inquiries of officers and other employees of the companies responsible for accounting matters about the consistency of accounting procedures and the existence and disclosure of any material contingent liabilities. Our review and investigation did not reveal to us any information which gives us reason to believe that the afore-mentioned

[8] Accounting Series Release No. 62 (1947).

financial statements and summary do not fairly present the position at (interim date) and results of operations for the (interim periods) ended (date) and (date) of (name of company) and of that company and its subsidiaries consolidated in conformity with generally accepted accounting principles applied on a basis consistent with that of the preceding fiscal year(s).

Insofar as we have determined from our limited review and investigation, the financial statements, supporting schedules, and summary referred to in the preceding paragraph appear to conform in all material respects with the pertinent requirements of the Securities Act of 1933 and the pertinent published rules, regulations, and instructions of the Securities and Exchange Commission.

It is understood that this letter is not to be reproduced, in whole or in part, or be referred to in the registration statement or in any amendment thereto or in the related prospectus, or in any literature used in connection with the offering of securities covered by the afore-mentioned registration statement, but such information may be furnished to members of the underwriting group.

Recasting of Previously Reported Statements.—Frequently, surplus adjustments are material in amount, and the public accountant may question the treatment to be accorded them when they affect the income of a period included in the registration statement. When such adjustments have a material effect upon income of prior years, the best practice is to restate those income accounts. Recasting may also be required of provisions made in prior years when costs or losses differ materially from the provisions for them, and for material adjustments of federal income taxes. Notwithstanding that this produces net income different from that previously reported, the guiding objective should be to make a fair presentation in the light of information obtained since the earlier statements were issued.

If a company wishes to make a thorough reallocation of prior year items—whether absorbed in surplus or in income—the accountant is hardly in a position to object. From the viewpoint of pure theory management's objective is certainly commendable. But from a practical viewpoint a line has to be drawn somewhere or the project is bound to bog down. It is doubtful whether any income statement can be so thoroughly refined that it contains no items relating to other years.

The desirability of recasting previously reported financial statements in the light of current knowledge has been suggested by the SEC. In Accounting Series Release No. 62 (1947), the Commission stated:

[Earnings summaries] usually embrace a suitable span of years and set forth in comparative form for each year appropriate information with respect to the major income and expense categories applicable to the business. Since such summaries are presented in the light of the circumstances existing at the date of registration it is often necessary and appropriate to recast the figures originally reported for earlier years to give effect to transactions or adjustments which were recorded in the more recent years but which are clearly applicable to the operations of the earlier years included in the summary.

Prior Representations by the Issuer.—Insofar as he can reasonably do so, the public accountant should determine whether representations in the registration statement are consistent with representations made elsewhere: for example, in annual reports to stockholders, in previous flotations, in Forms 10 or 10-K filed under the Securities Exchange Act, in listing applications and reports filed with stock exchanges, and in proxy statements.

If net income shown in a registration statement differs from net income for the same period previously reported by the company, the issuer should explain the difference in a note to the income statement.

Earnings for Part of a Year.—When income and expenses in an income statement submitted for an interim period may not be indicative of the rate of yearly earnings because of seasonal variations or for other reasons, a note so indicating should be included in the statement. A similar note should also be considered for the summary of earnings in the narrative section of the prospectus.

Whether True Statements Are Not Misleading.—The public accountant's examination should enable him to form an opinion not only whether individual items in the financial statements are fairly stated, but also whether the statements as a whole are true and not misleading. For example, a corporation, organized during World War II, had a phenomenal war production record and realized substantial profits with a very small capital investment. After the war the company was faced with serious problems in converting to peacetime production and in obtaining scarce materials because of the loss of wartime priorities. The owners of the company sold their stock to an underwriting group and began the preparation of a registration statement in anticipation of a public offering. The income statement required to be included in the registration statement covered the war period. In the circumstances, the auditors believed that the income statement could serve no useful purpose. They recommended, therefore, that the income statement be included in Part II of the registration statement and omitted from the prospectus. The advice of others prevailed, however, and the prospectus as initially filed included the income statement with appropriate disclosures. The Commission in due course issued a memorandum of comment recommending that in the circumstances of this particular registration all statements setting forth operating results should be omitted from the prospectus and filed as an exhibit. The registration statement and prospectus were amended accordingly.

SEC Requirements as to Certificates.—Most of the formal financial statements and supporting schedules included in a registration statement filed under the 1933 Act are required to be certified by independent public or independent certified public accountants. The Commission's requirements for certification are contained in Rule 2.02 of Regulation S-X which follows:

Rule 2.02.

(a) *Technical requirements.*—The accountant's certificate shall be dated, shall be signed manually, and shall identify without detailed enumeration the financial statements covered by the certificate.

(b) *Representations as to the audit.*—The accountant's certificate (i) shall state whether the audit was made in accordance with generally accepted auditing standards; and (ii) shall designate any auditing procedures generally recognized as normal, or deemed necessary by the accountant under the circumstances of the particular case, which have been omitted, and the reasons for their omission.

Nothing in this rule shall be construed to imply authority for the omission of any procedure which independent accountants would ordinarily employ in the course of an audit made for the purpose of expressing the opinions required by paragraph (c) of this rule.

(c) *Opinions to be expressed.*—The accountant's certificate shall state clearly: (i) the opinion of the accountant in respect of the financial statements covered by the certificate and the accounting principles and practices reflected therein; (ii) the opinion of the accountant as to any material changes in accounting principles or practices, or method of applying the accounting principles or practices, or adjustments of the accounts, required to be set forth by Rule 3.07; and (iii) the nature of, and the opinion of the accountant as to, any material differences between the accounting principles and practices reflected in the financial statements and those reflected in the accounts after the entry of adjustments for the period under review.

(d) *Exceptions.*—Any matters to which the accountant takes exception shall be clearly identified, the exception thereto specifically and clearly stated, and, to the extent practicable, the effect of each such exception on the related financial statements given.

Form of Certificate.—The standard short form of report or opinion (see Chapter 6) meets the Commission's requirements for certification. The certificate, however, is also required to cover the supporting schedules. A simple method of accomplishing this result is by adding the words "and the supporting schedules" (or similar identification) to the first paragraph, dealing with the scope of the examination, and to the last paragraph, which contains the opinion.

Underwriters sometimes object to this procedure on the grounds that the supporting schedules (except supplementary profit and loss information) are not contained in the prospectus, the document delivered to the investor, and reference to them in the accountant's certificate may imply that the schedules are essential to a showing of the position and results of operation. This objection may be overcome by phrasing the opinion paragraph as follows:

In our opinion, the accompanying financial statements (pages _____ to _____, inclusive) present fairly the financial position of _____ Company at (date), and the results of its operations for the years _____, _____, and _____, and the supporting schedules present fairly the information required to be set forth therein, all in conformity with generally accepted accounting principles applied on a consistent basis.

Bankers or their counsel may also object to this form of opinion for the reason that it contains a reference to schedules which are not contained in the prospectus. When they do, two separate certificates may be issued—one covering the statements in the prospectus, and another covering the supporting schedules. The latter certificate will not appear in the prospectus, but will accompany the schedules to which it relates, and may take the following form:

We have examined the balance sheet of _____ Company as of (date) and the related statements of income and surplus for the years 19__, 19__, and 19__, and the supporting schedules. Our examination was made in accordance with generally accepted auditing standards, and accordingly included such tests of the accounting records and such other auditing procedures as we considered necessary in the circumstances.

In our opinion, the supporting schedules (Exhibit _____, or pages _____ to _____, inclusive, of the registration statement) present fairly the information required to be set forth therein, in conformity with generally accepted accounting principles applied on a consistent basis.

Most prospectuses contain earnings summaries that have been reviewed by independent public accountants. Circumstances under which the accountant may properly express an opinion on earnings summaries, and the form of such opinions are set forth in its Accounting Series Release No. 62. As indicated in that release, if the statement is made that an accountant reviewed the summary, then his report or opinion must be furnished. Suggestions as to the form of the accountant's report on the earnings summary appear below.

CERTIFICATE FOR SUMMARY OF EARNINGS.—Because of the importance of earnings summaries, they should be presented in sufficient detail to permit expression of the independent public accountant's opinion that they fairly present results of operations. Usually little additional detail will be required, but certain supplementary information—

such as disclosure of dividends and other charges and credits to surplus, if material—should be included to enable the accountant to give an opinion that the earnings summaries fairly present results of operations.

Practice by the profession generally has not yet reached the point where an accountant can insist that his client furnish a tabulation of earnings conforming to the views expressed in the preceding paragraph. However, when he is named as having reviewed a summary of earnings, the public accountant should urge his client to present a tabulation that fairly presents results of operations rather than certain data.

The opinion covering the review of the summary may be furnished either as part of the accountant's certificate on financial statements for the three-year period, or in a separate report. In the first alternative, if the accountant has audited the entire period covered by the summary and the formal income statement, his opinion may take the following form:

We have made examinations of the balance sheet of X Company as of December 31, 19___, the related statement of income and earned surplus for the years 19___, 19___, and 19___, and the statement of income for the years 19___ to 19___, inclusive, which latter statement is included in this Prospectus under the heading, "Earnings." Our examinations were made in accordance with generally accepted auditing standards, and accordingly included such tests of the accounting records and such other auditing procedures as we considered necessary in the circumstances.

In our opinion, the financial statements (pages _____ to _____, inclusive) and the statement of income (page _____) present fairly the financial position of X Company at December 31, 19___, and the results of its operations for the years 19___ to 19___, inclusive, all in conformity with generally accepted accounting principles applied on a consistent basis.

The foregoing certificate, insofar as it relates to the summary of earnings, is appropriate only if the summary conforms to the recommendation above that changes in earned surplus be disclosed.

If the summary of earnings contains only selected data which do not present fairly the results of operations, the opinion may take the following form:

Certificate in the usual form relating to the years included in the income statement, followed by:

We had previously made yearly examinations, similar in scope to that indicated in the first paragraph above, of the financial statements which were reported by the Company for the years 19___ through 19___. We have reviewed the summary of earnings which appears under the caption "Earnings" in this prospectus and, in our opinion, it presents fairly the net income and other data shown therein for the years 19___ to 19___, inclusive, in conformity with generally accepted accounting principles applied on a consistent basis.

If the certificates covering the statements of any of the years were qualified and the need for the qualification still exists, the necessary qualifications should be included in the foregoing examples.

CERTIFICATE WHEN PART OF EXAMINATION IS MADE BY ANOTHER ACCOUNTANT.—Occasionally a public accountant reports on financial statements when part of the examination has been made by other public accountants. The accounts of an out-of-town branch, division, or subsidiary may be examined by auditors located near those offices. Sometimes the out-of-town auditor is engaged by the principal accountant, who reviews the work of the other accountant and pays his fee. Or the client may engage the out-of-town accountant and make his report available to the principal accountant as a basis for reporting on the over-all or consolidated financial statements. The variations in these arrangements are almost endless.

Rule 2.05 of Regulation S-X dealing with certification of financial statements by more than one accountant is as follows:

If, with respect to the certification of the financial statements of any person, the principal accountant relies on an examination made by another independent public accountant of certain of the accounts of such person or its subsidiaries, the certificate of such other accountant shall be filed (and the provisions of Rules 2.01 and 2.02 shall be applicable thereto); however, the certificate of such other accountant need not be filed (a) if no reference is made directly or indirectly to such other accountant's examination in the principal accountant's certificate, or (b) if, having referred to such other accountant's examination, the principal accountant states in his certificate that he assumes responsibility for such other accountant's examination in the same manner as if it had been made by him.

CERTIFICATE COVERING PORTION OF PERIOD UNDER REPORT.— When a client has changed auditors, the accountant who examines the balance sheet frequently has not examined the income and surplus statement for the entire three-year period. Inasmuch as the entire period must be certified by independent public accountants, the report of the accountant who examined the first year of the period may be similar to the following:

We have made an examination of the statements of income and surplus and supplementary profit and loss information of X Corporation for the year 19___. Our examination was made in accordance with generally accepted auditing standards, and accordingly included such tests of the accounting records and such other auditing procedures as we considered necessary in the circumstances.

In our opinion, the accompanying statements of income and surplus and supplementary profit and loss information present fairly the results of operations of X Corporation for the year 19___, in conformity with generally accepted accounting principles applied on a basis consistent with that of the preceding year.

Because of the passage of time since he was in touch with the company and its affairs, the accountant should take steps to assure himself that his certificate may properly be issued. If he examined years 1, 2, and 3 of a five-year period covered by a summary of earnings, he would be concerned with what happened in subsequent periods, for whatever light it might throw on years 1, 2, and 3. He would want to know that the accounting principles followed in the first three years were also followed in subsequent years; if not, the reason for the change and the effect thereof. If a surplus adjustment in a later year is retroactively applied to one of the first three years, the accountant should inquire into the nature of the transaction and the basis and method of its application. He should also review the entire registration statement and prospectus. The first accountant should also obtain a letter from the successor firm along the lines of the following :[9]

Dear Sirs:

This letter is furnished in connection with the opinion you are to give on the income and surplus statements of (name of company) for (year 3) and the summary of earnings for the (years 1, 2, and 3), which statements and summary are to be included by the company in its proposed registration statement to register under the Securities Act of 1933 an issue of (description of securities).

We have examined the balance sheet of (name of company) as of December 31 (year 5) and the statements of income and surplus for the (years 4 and 5); also the summary of earnings for such years, all as included in the aforementioned registration statement. In our opinion, there were no significant adjustments by (name of company) during the (years 4 and 5) which were applicable to operations for the (years 1, 2, and 3).

/s/ Successor Firm

OPINION AS TO DIFFERENCES BETWEEN BOOKS AND STATEMENTS. —Reference is made to Rule 2.02(c)(iii) of Regulation S-X appearing on page 608. This rule requires the accountant to state in his certificate the nature and his opinion of any material differences between the accounting principles and practices reflected in the financial statements and those reflected in the accounts. An example of a certificate showing compliance with this rule is the following:

Property, plant, and equipment in the accompanying financial statements differ from those in the accounting records of the Company. In the ac-

---

[9] The need for obtaining assurances along the lines indicated is suggested by Statement on Auditing Procedure No. 25 (Oct., 1954), p. 15. See the discussion beginning on page 603 of this book.

companying financial statements effect has been given to the elimination of appreciation of property, plant, and equipment. The inclusion in the financial statements of property, plant, and equipment at cost rather than on an appraisal basis, in our opinion, conforms to generally accepted accounting principles.

REPORT COVERING HISTORICAL FINANCIAL INFORMATION.—A registration statement on Form S-1 under the 1933 Act calls for information about certain asset revaluations and unusual adjustments of surplus during the seven-year period preceding the required three-year income statement. The information which must be reported under "Historical Financial Information" and the circumstances under which the information may be omitted are set forth beginning on page 592.

This information is not required to be certified, but, when practicable, the registrant or underwriters usually desire to have the response reviewed by independent accountants, not on the basis of an audit but on the basis of a survey of the accounts named. Below is a suggested form of opinion covering such review:

We have made a review, but not an audit, of the accounts maintained by (name of company) for the period from (date) through (date) corresponding to those named in Instructions as to Financial Statements on Form S-1 of the Securities and Exchange Commission covering matters to be reported under "Historical Financial Information" and, in our opinion, the information required to be reported under such heading is fairly presented above.

If the company's accounts were audited by the accountant during the period covered by the above report, the phrase "but not an audit" should be deleted.

Pro Forma Financial Statements.—Pro forma financial statements are often prepared and used in registration and proxy statements, although they are frequently of importance for other purposes as well.

Pro forma statements are of many kinds. Pro forma balance sheets may give effect to the receipt of funds from the proposed sale of new securities and the application of the proceeds toward payment of liabilities and purchase of new assets. They may set forth the financial position of two or more business enterprises whose merger is proposed. Pro forma income statements of merged companies which previously operated as separate enterprises may combine their operations for a period prior to merger to indicate operating results that might have been obtained had the companies merged earlier. When a company is no longer affiliated with others, pro forma statements may attempt to present the operating results that would have obtained had the company not received the benefits of consolidated tax returns. However, recognition of surplus charges and credits, adjustments of federal income taxes, and other similar retroactive adjustments to the years to which they apply does not change the essentially historical character of statements, and statements so adjusted should not be labeled "pro forma."

Pro forma statements often help the reader comprehend an otherwise confusing situation; sometimes they are essential to a proper understanding. Often these statements are more illuminating than the so-called "actual" statements on which they are based, and the public accountant must be alert to see that the prospective investor is furnished not only with all the financial information he needs but also that the information is presented in the most convenient and useful form. This latter consideration frequently dictates the use of pro forma statements, and in recent years prospectuses have placed increasing emphasis on these statements. There has been a tendency to abuse them, and this was the subject of extended discussion at a meeting in 1946 attended by representatives of several investment banking, legal, and accounting firms. It was the consensus of those present that it is not desirable to restate in an earnings summary covering several years, interest and other fixed charges on the basis of securities to be issued in the future. When such a computation is necessary to indicate the balance of earnings applicable to equity securities, it should be limited to the latest fiscal year, and, preferably, indicated in an explanatory note.

INSTITUTE PRONOUNCEMENTS.—In 1923 the membership of the American Institute of Certified Public Accountants adopted the following recommendations of a special committee on the subject of pro forma statements, which are still in effect:

I. The accountant may certify a statement of a company giving effect as at the date thereof to transactions entered into subsequently only under the following conditions, viz.:

(a) If the subsequent transactions are the subject of a definite (preferably written) contract or agreement between the company and bankers (or parties) who the accountant is satisfied are responsible and able to carry out their engagement;

(b) If the interval between the date of the statement and the date of the subsequent transactions is reasonably short—not to exceed, say, four months;

(c) If the accountant, after due inquiry, or, preferably after actual investigation, has no reason to suppose that other transactions or developments have in the interval materially affected adversely the position of the company; and

(d) If the character of the transaction to which effect is given is clearly disclosed, i.e., either at the heading of the statement or somewhere in the statement there shall be stated clearly the purpose for which the statement is issued.

II. The accountant should not *certify* a statement giving effect to transactions contemplated but not actually entered into at the date of the certificate, with the sole exception that he may give effect to the proposed application of the proceeds of new financing where the application is clearly disclosed on the face of the statement or in the certificate and the accountant is satisfied that the funds can and will be applied in the manner indicated. It is not necessary that the precise liability shown in the balance-sheet before adjustment should actually be paid out of the new money. It is sufficient, for instance where the balance-sheet before the financing shows bank loans, if the proceeds are to be applied to bank loans which are either identical with or have replaced the bank loans actually outstanding at the date of the balance-sheet. Ordinarily, however, the accountant should not apply the proceeds of financing to the payment of current trade accounts payable, at least not against a normal volume of such current accounts payable, because there must always be such accounts outstanding and the application of new moneys against the outstandings at the date of the balance-sheet results in showing a position which in fact could never be attained. The accountant may usually best satisfy himself that the funds will be applied as indicated by getting an assurance from the issuing house on the point.

III. In any description of a statement or in any certificate relating thereto it is desirable that the past tense should be used. It should also be made clear that the transactions embodied have been definitely covered by contract.

IV. When the accountant feels that he cannot certify to such a hypothetical statement, probably because of the length of the period which has elapsed since the accounts have been audited, he may be prepared to write a letter, not in certificate form, stating that at the request of the addressee a statement has been examined or prepared in which effect is given, in his opinion correctly, to proposed transactions (which must be clearly specified). Such letters should be given only in very special cases and with the greatest care.

SEC RULES.—The SEC has a rule under the 1933 Act regulating the use of certain kinds of pro forma statements; a similar rule was promulgated under the 1934 Act. The rule under the 1933 Act is as follows:

Rule 170. Prohibition of Use of Certain Financial Statements.

Financial statements which purport to give effect to the receipt and application of any part of the proceeds from the sale of securities for cash shall not be used unless such securities are to be offered through underwriters and the underwriting arrangements are such that the underwriters are or will be committed to take and pay for all of the securities, if any are taken, prior to or within a reasonable time after the commencement of the public offering, or if the securities are not so taken to refund to all subscribers the full amount of all subscription payments made for the securities. The caption of any such financial statement shall clearly set forth the assumptions upon which such statement is based. The caption shall be in type at least as large as that used generally in the body of the statement.

The SEC's rule permits the use of pro forma balance sheets giving effect to proposed financing when the underwriters agree to refund to subscribers all subscription payments in the event that all the securities are not taken by the underwriters. This rule permits the use of a pro forma balance sheet showing a financial position which may not, in fact, be attained. The reasoning behind the rule may be that, if the financial position is not attained because of the underwriters' decision not to take the securities, the investing public will not suffer because they will get back any payments they may have made on account of subscriptions.

If a public accountant is called on to assist in the preparation of a pro forma balance sheet of the type under consideration, he should first determine whether the underwriters' commitment is of the type that will permit the use of pro forma balance sheets under SEC Rule 170. Some underwriting agreements, for example, provide that the underwriter, acting as an agent, will use his best efforts to place the securities with investors, but the underwriter is not committed to buy any of the securities. When the underwriting agreement so provides, the SEC does not permit the use of pro forma balance sheets giving effect to the financing since the company may not be successful in disposing of all of the securities, and usually provision is not made for refunding investors' payments if all the securities are not sold.

At the time the pro forma balance sheet is prepared, the underwriting agreement is usually tentative—it does not become final, in fact, until shortly before the effective date of the registration statement when all its terms have been agreed upon. Usually, however, there is agreement in principle early in the engagement on the nature of the underwriting agreement. If the tentative agreement complies with SEC standards, the pro forma balance sheet may be prepared with the understanding that its use will depend on the final agreements between the company and the underwriters.

Although the accountant may have assisted in the preparation of pro forma financial statements, the certification of such statements by the accountant is subject to considerations discussed below.

CERTIFICATE OR LETTER COVERING PRO FORMA STATEMENTS.— If pro forma financial statements are intended for filing with the SEC, they should comply with the requirements of both the Commission (see page 615) and the American Institute of Certified Public Accountants (see page 614). Even though the statements comply with all these requirements, the public accountant should certify them publicly or privately only under certain conditions.

A pro forma *balance sheet* may be certified provided that:

(1) the underlying financial statements have been examined by the certifying accountant; and

(2) when the pro forma balance sheet gives effect to the sale of securities and application of the proceeds, the underwriters are firmly committed to take the issue.

If the underwriters are not firmly committed to purchase the securities, the accountant should not certify the pro forma balance sheet.

From the foregoing discussion, it will be observed that the SEC permits the use of pro forma balance sheets giving effect to financing in situations in which the accountant should not certify. The authors believe that the accountant may certify pro forma balance sheets only if the transactions given effect to have been consummated or there is definite assurance that they will be consummated.

A suggested form of certificate covering a pro forma balance sheet follows:

We have examined the accompanying pro forma balance sheet of X Corporation as of (date). This balance sheet is based upon the accompanying balance sheet of X Corporation as of (date) (which appears hereinafter with our certificate) and the pro forma adjustments identified in the headnote.

In our opinion, the accompanying pro forma balance sheet of X Corporation presents fairly, in conformity with generally accepted accounting principles, the financial position of the company as it would have appeared at (date) had the transactions set forth in the related pro forma adjusting entries been consummated at that date.

When the public accountant has not examined the underlying financial statements, he is in no position to certify the pro forma statements derived from them. He may, however, include in the letter covering his review (see page 605) a paragraph similar to the following:

We have also reviewed the pro forma balance sheet as at (date) which is also included in the above-mentioned Registration Statement. In our opinion, the adjustments set forth in the pro forma adjusting entries have been properly applied in the pro forma balance sheet.

The certification of pro forma income statements or earnings summaries presents a more difficult problem for the public accountant. Occasionally he may with justification object to having his name identified publicly with certain types of such statements or summaries. He should not refuse to certify pro forma income statements or earnings summaries that merely add the historical results of two or more businesses that have been combined into a single enterprise. This rule is not altered by the fact that intercompany transactions, if any, are eliminated in the pro forma statement. Other pro forma statements, however, should be considered on their merits, and the auditor should bear in mind that these statements are sometimes abused.

The Consent.—The 1933 Act provides that "if any accountant . . . . or any person whose profession gives authority to a statement made by him, is named as having prepared or certified any part of the registration statement, or is named as having prepared or certified a report . . . . for use in connection with the registration statement, the written consent of such person shall be filed with the registration statement." (Sec. 7 of the Act.) The consent must be dated and signed manually.

Below is a suggested form of consent that may be used by the certifying accountant with appropriate modifications:

We consent to the inclusion of the following reports in the registration statement to be used in registering, under the Securities Act of 1933, (title of issue) of the (name of company): (1) our report dated _____ accompanying the financial statements of (name of company) and of that company and its subsidiaries consolidated and the summary of earnings which are included in the prospectus; (2) our report dated _____ accompanying the supporting schedules listed in Item 31 of the registration statement; and (3) our report dated _____ accompanying the historical financial information listed in Item 31 of the registration statement.

(Name of certifying accountant)

(City)
(Date of signing)

If, as frequently happens, the accountant is named as having reviewed financial data in the registration statement, or if it is stated that any financial data are set forth upon the authority of the account-ant as an expert, the accountant must also consent in writing to such references (see page 619). This may be done by adding to the form suggested above the following additional paragraph: "We also consent to the references to our firm under the captions 'Earnings' and 'Experts' in the prospectus."

When financial data covered by the accountant's certificate are amended, his consent must be filed as part of the amendment. This may be accomplished by repeating in the amendment and re-signing and re-dating the consent that appeared in the original filing.

It has been the policy of the SEC to require consent of independent accountants to the use of their certificate in a bring-up prospectus (see page 600). A suggested form of consent to be used for this special purpose follows:

We consent to the inclusion of our report dated _____ accompanying the financial statements and summary of earnings of _____ _____ Company appearing in its prospectus dated _____ relating to its (title of issue), to be filed with the Securities and Exchange Com-mission under the provisions of the Securities Act of 1933.

This consent must also be dated and manually signed.

"Upon the Authority of an Expert."—The Securities Act of 1933 imposes possible liability for false or misleading statements, but provides that persons other than the issuer of the securities may not be liable for such misrepresentations in any part of the registration statement purporting to be made "upon the authority of an expert." Because of the protection afforded by this provision to officers, directors, and underwriters when statements are made upon the authority of an expert, lawyers for the company and the underwriters usually request a positive assertion in the prospectus and registration statement specifically bringing within the scope of this provision certified financial statements, summaries of earnings, supporting schedules, and other data.

Financial statements are primarily representations of the company; this has been recognized by the SEC. The language used in registration statements and prospectuses to identify financial representations should be equally clear in characterizing the accountant's responsibility for those representations. Accountants believe that, since the financial statements and earnings summaries are representations by the company, the expertizing declaration should be so phrased as to make it clear that the certificate or report of the accountants, rather than the financial statements or summaries, is the information given upon their authority as experts. Accountants therefore prefer that the reference to them in such declarations, when relating to financial statements and earnings summaries in the prospectus, be substantially in the following form:

The financial statements which appear on pages _____ to _____ of this prospectus and the summary of earnings which appears on page _____ have been examined by (name of accountants), independent public accountants, and are included in the prospectus in reliance upon the accompanying report of said firm which report is given upon their authority as experts.

Some lawyers insist that the expertizing declaration conform to the language in Section 11 of the Act. To meet this insistence, the final clause in the above paragraph may be revised as follows: ". . . . and are included in the prospectus in reliance upon the accompanying report of said firm and upon their authority as experts."

The language to be used should avoid such phrases as *have been prepared* by (name of accountants), independent certified public accountants," for they may attribute to the accountant greater responsibility for the financial statements than he intended to assume.

The Conformity (or Compliance) Letter.—As stated on page 581, the public accountant is sometimes required to report whether, in his opinion, the financial statements in a registration statement covered by his certificate comply with the Act and the Commission's rules and regulations thereunder. This opinion is usually given in the form of a letter—commonly called a "conformity" letter, or a "compliance" letter. A typical form of such a conformity letter follows:

(Name of client)
(Address)

We previously submitted our reports dated _____ on our examination of the financial statements and supporting schedules of (name of company) and the consolidated financial statements and supporting schedules of that company and its subsidiaries as of _____ and for the years _____, _____, and _____, and the summary of earnings for the years _____ to _____, inclusive. The afore-mentioned statements, supporting schedules and summary of earnings together with the said reports appear in Registration Statement No. _____ filed by (name of company) with the Securities and Exchange Commission.

In our opinion, the financial statements, supporting schedules, and summary of earnings covered by our reports conform in all material respects with the pertinent requirements of the Securities Act of 1933 and the pertinent published rules, regulations, and instructions of the Securities and Exchange Commission.

The conformity letter is ordinarily addressed to the client, but the accountant may furnish copies addressed to other interested parties, such as underwriters, if he is authorized to do so by his client.

On written authorization by the client, the accountant may address the conformity letter to third parties. A typical conformity letter addressed to underwriters would read as follows:

Messrs. (name of underwriters) as representatives of the several underwriters
    under the underwriting agreement of (name of company) dated (date).

Dear Sirs:

We have been requested by our client (name of company) to furnish to you our opinion, which follows, pertaining to Registration Statement No. _____ used in registering, under the Securities Act of 1933, (insert description of securities):

We previously submitted our reports dated _____ on our examination of the financial statements and supporting schedules of (name of company) and the consolidated financial statements and supporting schedules of that company and its subsidiaries as of _____ and for the years _____, _____, and _____, and the summary of earnings for the years _____ to _____, inclusive. The afore-mentioned statements, supporting schedules, and summary of earnings, together with said reports, appear in the registration statement.

In our opinion, the financial statements, supporting schedules, and summary of earnings covered by our reports conform in all material respects with the pertinent requirements of the Securities Act of 1933 and the pertinent published rules, regulations, and instructions of the Securities and Exchange Commission.

The date of the conformity letter is usually the effective date of the registration statement, or, when the letter is addressed to underwriters, the date of delivery of the securities (the closing date).

Letter Commenting on Adverse Changes and Capital Changes.— As has been previously indicated, the registration statement speaks as of its effective date. For that reason the underwriters are interested in knowing whether there have been any material adverse changes in the financial position of the company or any material changes in capitalization in the period between the date of the latest balance sheet filed and a date as near as practicable to the effective date. Occasionally the underwriting agreement provides that the accountants are to make a review, but not an audit, of subsequent transactions, which review will serve as the basis for a letter commenting on these changes.

The letter commenting on adverse changes and capital changes is not intended for the public and is frequently incorporated in the conformity (or compliance) letter or the letter covering the review of uncertified financial statements. The following paragraph has been found to be satisfactory in practice:

We have made a review and a limited investigation, but not an audit, of the financial statements of (name of company) for the period from (date) to (date), the date to which the general accounts of the company were recorded. We inspected minute books of the company for meetings of the Board of Directors through the meeting held on (date), meetings of the Executive Committee through (date), and the Finance Committee through (date). We made inquiries of officers and other employees of the company responsible for accounting matters about the nature of transactions subsequent to (date) through (date), and the existence of any material contingent liabilities. Our review and investigation did not reveal to us any information which gives us reason to believe that there have been any changes in the capital stock or funded debt of the company, or that there have been any material adverse changes in its financial position during the period from (date) through (date) other than as set forth in the prospectus.

The Due Diligence Meeting.—After the registration statement is filed but before it becomes effective, a meeting (called the "due diligence" or "information" meeting) is usually held under the auspices of the principal underwriters. Among those attending are representatives of the company whose securities are proposed to be offered, counsel for the company, the underwriters and their counsel, independent public accountants, engineers, and appraisers, if any. At this meeting the members of the underwriting group are afforded an opportunity to exercise due diligence before offering the securities to the public; they may ask questions about the company, its business, recent developments, and prospects. Questions are invited about any items in the registration document, including the financial statements. The accountant is frequently requested to answer questions about matters covered by his examination.

The accountant is almost invariably requested to attend the due diligence meeting. Some accountants consider this a burden, but, in the opinion of the authors, they should welcome the opportunity of attending. The questioning sometimes elicits answers from high-ranking officers of the corporation that frequently confirm information that the auditor has obtained in the course of his examination, particularly about recent developments in the corporation's affairs. The accountant will want to consider whether the information offered at the due diligence meeting is in conformity with financial data included in the registration statement.

THE SECURITIES EXCHANGE ACT OF 1934

Principal Provisions.—The Securities Exchange Act of 1934 provides for the registration of national securities exchanges, securities listed on such exchanges, and brokers and dealers trading in the over-the-counter securities markets. The law also prohibits market manipulation by means of wash sales, matched orders, any other deceptive device, or fraudulent practice. Under the law the Commission regulates the solicitation of proxies from holders of listed securities, such trading activities as short sales and stabilizing, the hypothecation of customers' securities, and the business of specialists and odd-lot dealers. Corporate insiders—that is, directors and officers of listed corporations and principal owners of its equity securities—are required to file statements of their holdings of the registered equity securities of their company and also to file monthly reports of changes in such holdings.

Accountant's Liabilities Under the Act.—Under Section 18 of the 1934 Act:

Any person who shall make or cause to be made any statement in any application, report, or document filed pursuant to this title or any rule or regulation thereunder or any undertaking contained in a registration statement as provided in subsection (d) of Section 15 of this title, which statement was at the time and in the light of the circumstances under which it was made false or misleading with respect to any material fact, shall be liable to any person (not knowing that such statement was false or misleading) who, in reliance upon such statement, shall have purchased or sold a security at a price which was affected by such statement, for damages caused by such reliance, unless the person sued shall prove that he acted in good faith and had no knowledge that such statement was false or misleading. . . . .

In its application to accountants certifying financial statements under the 1934 Act, it will be seen that liability is imposed for a misleading statement that results in a person buying or selling a security at a price affected by such statement. Since an income statement is misleading whether it overstates or understates net income, it follows that under this law an accountant may invite a lawsuit if he allows conservatism to influence his judgment to the extent that income is materially understated.

Limitations of Actions to Recover.—Suit must be brought within one year after the discovery of the facts constituting the cause of action and within three years after such cause of action accrued [Section 18(c) of the Act].

Registration of Securities Listed on Exchanges.—A corporation seeking to list its securities for trading on a national securities exchange must comply with two sets of requirements, those of the securities exchange and those of the SEC. To a large extent information—both financial and narrative—is duplicated, but this is unavoidable under existing regulations.

The Commission requires that a corporation must prepare an application for registration of its securities under the 1934 Act. This application is filed with the exchange and with the Commission. For most commercial and industrial companies, the application is prepared on Form 10, although other forms are prescribed for certain special types of securities.

Financial Statements Required by Form 10.—The SEC's instructions for financial statements to be filed as part of Form 10 are set forth in the following pages.

FINANCIAL STATEMENTS OF THE REGISTRANT.—A certified balance sheet of the registrant (unconsolidated) is required to be filed as of the close of its latest fiscal year unless such fiscal year has ended within 90 days prior to the date of filing the application on Form 10, in which case the balance sheet may be as of the close of the preceding fiscal year. (Note that this requirement is less stringent than a filing under the 1933 Act.) If the latest fiscal year of the registrant has ended within ninety days prior to the date of filing the Form 10 application and the required balance sheet is filed as of the end of the preceding fiscal year, there must be filed as an amendment to the application, within 120 days after the initial filing, a certified balance sheet of the registrant as of the end of the latest fiscal year.

The registrant must file a certified income statement (unconsolidated) for each of the three fiscal years preceding the date of the balance sheet specified in the preceding paragraph, and, by amendment, for the year preceding the afore-mentioned balance sheet that is required to be filed as an amendment within 120 days after the initial filing. Certified statements of surplus must be filed for the same periods as the statements of income, as a separate statement, or as a continuation of the income statement.

Notwithstanding the two preceding paragraphs, unconsolidated financial statements of the registrant may be omitted if (1) consolidated statements of the registrant and one or more of its subsidiaries are filed, *and* (2) the conditions specified in *either* of the following paragraphs are met:

(a) The registrant is primarily an operating company and all subsidiaries included in the consolidated financial statements filed are totally-held subsidiaries [as defined on page 591]; *or*

(b) The registrant's total assets, exclusive of investments in and advances to the consolidated subsidiaries, constitute 85 per cent or more of the total assets shown by the consolidated balance sheets filed and the registrant's total gross revenues for the period for which its income statements would be filed, exclusive of interest and dividends received from the consolidated subsidiaries, constitute 85 per cent or more of the total gross revenue shown by the consolidated income statements filed.

CONSOLIDATED FINANCIAL STATEMENTS.—The application on Form 10 must include a certified consolidated balance sheet of the registrant and its subsidiaries as of the close of the latest fiscal year of the registrant, unless such fiscal year has ended within 90 days prior to the date of filing the application, in which case this balance sheet may be as of the close of the preceding fiscal year. If the latest fiscal year of the registrant has ended within ninety days prior to the date of filing and the required balance sheet is filed as of the end of the preceding fiscal year, there must be filed as an amendment to the application, within 120 days after the initial filing, a certified consolidated balance sheet of the registrant and its subsidiaries as of the close of the latest fiscal year.

The application must also contain certified consolidated income and surplus statements of the registrant and its subsidiaries for each of the three fiscal years preceding the balance sheet mentioned in the first sentence of the preceding paragraph. If, pursuant to the instructions in the preceding paragraph, a more recent balance sheet must be filed as an amendment within the prescribed 120 days, certified consolidated income and surplus statements for the latest fiscal year must also be filed as an amendment.

FINANCIAL STATEMENTS OF UNCONSOLIDATED SUBSIDIARIES.— Balance sheets and statements of income and surplus that would be required if the subsidiary were itself a registrant must be filed for each majority-owned subsidiary not consolidated. Insofar as practicable these statements must be for the same dates or periods as those of the registrant. If the fiscal year of any unconsolidated subsidiary has ended within ninety days prior to the date of filing, or ends after the date of filing, the financial statements of the subsidiary may be filed as an amendment to the application within 120 days after the end of the subsidiary's fiscal year.

SPECIAL PROVISIONS.—*Banks and Insurance Companies.*—Notwithstanding the requirements in the instructions, financial statements filed for banks or insurance companies (other than title insurance companies) need not be certified.

Registrants Not in the Production Stage.—Notwithstanding the foregoing instructions, if the registrant falls within the terms of paragraphs (b) or (c) of Rule 5A.01 of Regulation S-X, the following statements, all of which must be certified, must be filed for the registrant and each of its significant subsidiaries, if any:

(a) The statements specified in

Rule 5A.02 (Statement of assets and unrecovered promotional, exploratory, and development costs),

Rule 5A.03 (Statement of liabilities),

Rule 5A.04 (Statement of capital shares),

Rule 5A.05 (Statement of other securities), and

Rule 5A.07 (Supporting schedules)

must be filed as of the end of the registrant's latest fiscal year unless such fiscal year has ended within 90 days prior to the date of filing the application with the exchange, in which case such statements may be as of the close of the preceding fiscal year.

(b) If the latest fiscal year of the registrant has ended within 90 days prior to the date of filing the application with the exchange and the statements required by paragraph (a) are filed as of the end of the preceding fiscal year, statements as of the end of the latest fiscal year must be filed as an amendment to the application within 120 days after the date of filing the application.

(c) The statement of cash receipts and disbursements specified in Rule 5A.06 must be filed for each of the three fiscal years preceding the date of the statements required by paragraph (a) above, and for the fiscal year immediately preceding the date of any statements filed pursuant to paragraph (b).

FINANCIAL STATEMENTS OF 50 PER CENT OWNED COMPANIES.

FINANCIAL STATEMENTS OF AFFILIATES WHOSE SECURITIES ARE PLEDGED AS COLLATERAL.

OTHER SPECIAL PROVISIONS.

Reorganization of Registrant.

Succession to Other Businesses.

Acquisition of Other Businesses.

FILING OF OTHER STATEMENTS IN CERTAIN CASES.

HISTORICAL FINANCIAL INFORMATION.

Provisions for the above are similar to those previously described in this chapter for registrations on Form S-1.

SUPPORTING SCHEDULES.—In addition to the financial statements indicated above, a Form 10 application must contain certain supplemental schedules. The form and content of these schedules are set forth in Regulation S-X.

CERTIFICATION BY INDEPENDENT PUBLIC ACCOUNTANTS.—The requirements for certification by independent public accountants are set forth beginning on page 608.

INCORPORATION BY REFERENCE.—The SEC's rule under the 1934 Act dealing with incorporation by reference is set forth on page 630. This rule makes it possible to avoid unnecessary filing with the SEC of information already on file with the SEC. In many cases financial statements filed for Form S-1 may be incorporated by reference in Form 10.

Annual Reports.—As a means of keeping up to date the application for registration under the 1934 Act, the SEC has prescribed the filing of annual reports. Of particular interest to public accountants are the annual reports which must be filed by:

1. Corporations which have securities listed for trading on exchanges.
2. Certain issuers which registered securities under the 1933 Act but which do not have securities listed for trading.
3. Certain exchange members, brokers, and dealers.

FORM 10-K.—The SEC has promulgated a series of "K" forms to be filed periodically by corporations having securities listed on securities exchanges. For corporations that registered on Form 10, the annual report form is 10-K. Most issuers of listed securities use Form 10-K.

Frequently in the past the only information available about companies not having securities listed on an exchange, but which registered under the 1933 Act, was that contained in the registration statement and prospectus filed under the 1933 Act. In other words, when an investor bought unlisted securities on the basis of information furnished him in a prospectus, he often had no access to later financial information about the company whose securities he had acquired. If a company registered under the 1933 Act was also listed and registered under the 1934 Act, it would be required to file annual reports (Form 10-K, for example) and other reports required of listed companies.

It seemed to many that investors in securities of a company registered under the 1933 Act should have access to the same financial information about that company that is available to investors in a listed company. On the other hand, companies should not be burdened with furnishing such financial information unless the original issue sold to the public is substantial, and they should not be required to furnish it when the issue outstanding becomes immaterial.

In 1936, legislation corrected this situation by means of an amendment, not to the 1933 Act but to the 1934 Act. Section 15(d) of the 1934 Act was amended to provide as follows:

Each registration statement hereafter filed pursuant to the Securities Act of 1933, as amended, shall contain an undertaking by the issuer of the issue of securities to which the registration statement relates to file with the Commission, in accordance with such rules and regulations as the Commission may prescribe as necessary or appropriate in the public interest or for the protection of investors, such supplementary and periodic information, documents, and reports as may be required pursuant to Section 13 of this title in respect of a security listed and registered on a national securities exchange. . . . .

The undertaking required by Section 15(d) quoted above, however, becomes operative only if the aggregate offering price of the issue plus the aggregate value of all other securities of the issuer of the same class outstanding, computed on the basis of such offering price, amount to $2,000,000 or more. The duty to file such information is automatically suspended when the aggregate value of all outstanding securities of the class to which the issue belongs is less than $1,000,000, computed on the basis of the offering price of the last issue of said class offered to the public.

FINANCIAL STATEMENTS REQUIRED BY FORM 10-K.—Form 10-K is the principal annual report form required to be filed by listed companies and by certain unlisted companies that registered under the 1933 Act. This report is required to be filed within 120 days after the close of the company's fiscal year. The SEC's instructions for financial statements to be filed as part of an annual report on Form 10-K are set forth in the following pages.

Financial Statements of the Registrant.—The annual report on Form 10-K must contain a certified balance sheet (unconsolidated) of the registrant as of the close of the fiscal year and certified statements of income and surplus for the fiscal year then ended.

Provisions for filing consolidated financial statements and omitting individual financial statements of the registrant are similar to those previously described for Form S-1, except that the 10-K statements will be only for one year.

Financial Statements of Unconsolidated Subsidiaries and 50 Per Cent Owned Companies.—A certified balance sheet as of the close of the subsidiary's most recent fiscal year and certified statements of income and surplus for such fiscal year must be filed for each majority-owned subsidiary of the registrant not consolidated. If the fiscal year of any unconsolidated subsidiary ends within 105 days before the date of filing the annual report, or after the date of filing, the statements of the subsidiary required above may be filed as an amendment to Form 10-K within 105 days after the end of the subsidiary's fiscal year.

Provisions for filing financial statements of 50 per cent owned companies and for omission of financial statements of unconsolidated subsidiaries and 50 per cent owned companies are similar to those previously described for Form S-1.

Financial Statements of Affiliates Whose Securities Are Pledged as Collateral.—Provisions for filing financial statements of affiliates whose securities are pledged as collateral are similar to those previously described for Form S-1, except that the 10-K statements will be only for one year.

Financial Statements of Banks and Insurance Companies.—Notwithstanding the foregoing requirements, financial statements filed for banks or insurance companies (other than title insurance companies) need not be certified.

Registrants Not in the Production Stage.—Notwithstanding the foregoing instructions, if the registrant falls within the terms of paragraph (b) or (c) of Rule 5A.01 of Regulation S-X, the following statements, all of which must be certified except as provided below, must be filed for the registrant and each of its significant subsidiaries, if any:

(a) The statements specified in

Rule 5A.02 (Statement of assets and unrecovered promotional, exploratory, and development costs),

Rule 5A.03 (Statement of liabilities),
Rule 5A.04 (Statement of capital shares),
Rule 5A.05 (Statement of other securities), and
Rule 5A.07 (Supporting schedules)

shall be filed as of the end of the fiscal year.

(b) The statement of cash receipts and disbursements specified in Rule 5A.06 shall be filed for the fiscal year.

The financial statements prescribed above need not be certified if all of the following conditions are met by the registrant and each of its significant subsidiaries, if any:

(1) Gross receipts from all sources for the fiscal year are not in excess of $5,000.

(2) The registrant has not purchased or sold any of its own stock, granted options therefor, or levied assessments upon outstanding stock.

(3) Expenditures for all purposes for the fiscal year are not in excess of $5,000.

(4) No material change in the business has occurred during the fiscal year, including any bankruptcy, reorganization, readjustment, or succession, or any material acquisition or disposition of plants, mines, mining equipment, mining right, or leases.

(5) No exchange upon which the shares are listed, or governmental authority having jurisdiction, requires the furnishing to it, or the publication of, certified financial statements.

Filing of Other Statements in Certain Cases.—Provision for filing other statements in certain cases are similar to those previously described for Form S-1.

Supporting Schedules.—In addition to the financial statements indicated above, an annual report on Form 10-K must include certain supplemental schedules. The form and content of these schedules are set forth in Regulation S-X.

Certification by Independent Public Accountants.—The requirements for certification by independent public accountants are set forth beginning on page 608. See also the discussion on page 574.

Incorporation by Reference.—The SEC's rule under the 1934 Act dealing with incorporation by reference is set forth on page 630. This rule makes it possible to avoid unnecessary filing with SEC of information already on file with SEC. The rule is also applicable to an annual report on Form 10-K and may be invoked whenever it is appropriate.

SUBSEQUENT TRANSACTIONS AND EVENTS IN FORM 10-K FILINGS.
—On page 601 it is indicated that in a filing under the Securities
Act of 1933 the truthfulness of the statements will be tested in the
light of the situation that existed on the effective date of the registra-
tion. What is the situation when a Form 10-K is filed under the
Securities Exchange Act of 1934?

Assume that a company having securities listed on a national securities exchange has a fiscal year ending December 31. It publishes an
annual report which it sends to stockholders early in the following
February. The financial statements in the published report are accompanied by the certificate of an independent public accountant dated late
in January. This company must also file a report on Form 10-K for
the same fiscal year and this report is not required to be filed before the
end of April. Ordinarily, the certificate of the independent public
accountant in the Form 10-K filing will bear the date of the certificate
in the published annual report to stockholders. Is there any obligation
on the part of the certifying accountant to review events and transactions between the date of his certificate in the published report to
stockholders and the date of filing the Form 10-K report? The view
of the profession generally is that there is no such obligation (Statement on Auditing Procedure No. 25, October, 1954). The applicable
portion of that statement is as follows:

> Frequently, a company's annual report on Form 10-K is prepared for filing
> after an interval has elapsed since issuance of a printed annual report to stock-
> holders. Sometimes the independent auditor finds it necessary to return to a
> client's office for additional work in connection with checking financial state-
> ments and schedules in the Form 10-K and sometimes such financial statements
> are prepared entirely or checked from information initially obtained during
> the regular audit. Inquiry indicates that most firms of independent account-
> ants date their opinion as of the same date as that on the opinion included
> in the printed annual report to stockholders. The committee approves this
> dating practice and recommends general observance. This is for the purpose
> of removing any implication that events of a later period may have been
> reviewed.
>
> It is the opinion of the committee that no duty rests upon the independent
> accountant to make a further investigation or inquiry as to events which may
> have occurred between the times of issuance of his opinion in the printed
> report to stockholders and the annual report on Form 10-K.

Incorporation by Reference.—Assume that a company files a registration on Form S-1 under the 1933 Act. At a later date it desires
to list its securities for trading and proceeds with the preparation of
an application for registration on Form 10 under the 1934 Act. Many
of the financial statements in Form S-1 are required to be included
in the application for registration on Form 10. The SEC permits the

registrant to incorporate the financial statements required in the filing under the 1934 Act by reference to the financial statements in the filing under the 1933 Act.

Rule X-12B-23 deals with incorporation by reference and provides in part as follows:

Any financial statement filed with the Commission pursuant to any Act administered by the Commission may be incorporated by reference in an application or report, filed with the Commission by the same or any other person, if it substantially conforms to the requirements of the form on which the application or report is filed. Any financial statement filed with an exchange pursuant to the Act may be incorporated by reference in any application or report filed with the exchange by the same or any other person, if it substantially conforms to the requirements of the form on which the application or report is filed. If any financial statement filed with the Commission is incorporated by reference in copies of an application or report filed with the Commission pursuant to Section 12 or 13 of the Act, copies of the financial statement may be filed with the exchange in lieu of the corresponding financial statement required by the form on which the application or report is filed.

Material incorporated by reference shall be clearly identified in the reference. An express statement that the specified matter is incorporated by reference shall be made at the particular place in the application or report where the information is required. Matter shall not be incorporated by reference in any case where such incorporation would render the statement incomplete, unclear or confusing.

In the example cited above, the financial statements in a Form S-1 filing were incorporated by reference in a Form 10 filing. A copy of Form S-1 was also required to be filed with the exchange.

An accountant's certificate appearing in a Form S-1 filing may also be incorporated by reference. If a certificate is incorporated by reference, the accountant must give his consent which may be in the following form:

We consent to the incorporation by reference in this application for registration of our report dated _____ appearing in the registration statement on Form S-1 (SEC File No. _____) of (name of company) filed with the Securities and Exchange Commission pursuant to the Securities Act of 1933.

The consent should be signed by the certifying accountant. While the foregoing consent is written for inclusion in an application for registration, the form may also be adapted for inclusion in other documents; for example, an annual report on Form 10-K.

The issuer may not incorporate an accountant's certificate without the accountant's written consent. This requirement effectively prevents the unauthorized use of an accountant's certificate without his knowledge.

Financial Statements Required by Form 8-K.—Issuers of listed securities are required to file a report on Form 8-K when certain designated events occur. This report must also be filed by issuers that registered under the 1933 Act if the undertaking referred to on page 627 is effective.

Item 2 of Form 8-K deals with an acquisition or disposition of a significant amount of assets otherwise than in the ordinary course of business. The financial statements specified below must be filed for any business whose acquisition by the registrant or any of its majority-owned subsidiaries is required to be described in answer to this item. For this purpose an acquisition or disposition is deemed to involve a significant amount of assets (a) if the net book value of such assets or the amount paid or received therefor upon such acquisition or disposition exceeded 15 per cent of the total assets of the registrant and its consolidated subsidiaries, or (b) if it involved the acquisition or disposition of a business whose gross revenues for its last fiscal year exceeded 15 per cent of the aggregate gross revenues of the registrant and its consolidated subsidaries for the registrant's last fiscal year.

A balance sheet of the business must be filed as of a date reasonably close to the date of acquisition. This balance sheet need not be certified, but if it is not certified, there shall also be filed a certified balance sheet as of the close of the preceding fiscal year. Income and surplus statements of the business must be filed for each of the last three full fiscal years and for the period, if any, between the close of the latest of such fiscal years and the date of the latest balance sheet filed. The income and surplus statements must be certified up to the date of the certified balance sheet. If the business was in insolvency proceedings immediately prior to its acquisition, the balance sheets referred to above need not be certified, but the income and surplus statements required must be certified to the close of the latest full fiscal year. Except as otherwise provided in the instructions, the principles applicable to a registrant and its subsidiaries in filing individual, consolidated, and group statements in an original application or annual report shall be applicable to the statements required to be filed.

Regulation S-X contains the requirements for certification and form and content of balance sheets and of income and surplus statements required in the preceding paragraph. No supporting schedules need be filed. The instructions for Form 8-K also contain provisions similar to those appearing in Form S-1 set forth on page 592 for filing other statements and for the omission of statements.

Financial Statements Required by Form 9-K.—Form 9-K is a semi-annual report that must be filed by certain issuers of listed securities and by certain issuers who registered securities under the 1933 Act. The report must be filed within forty-five days after the close of the first half of the fiscal year. The form of the report is as follows:

Profit and Loss and Earned Surplus Information

1. Gross sales less discounts, returns, and allowances
2. Operating revenues
3. Total of Captions 1 and 2
4. Extraordinary items
5. Net income or loss before taxes on income
6. Provision for taxes on income
7. Net income or loss
8. Special items
9. Earned surplus items
   Remarks:

The report must be filed only for the first half of the issuer's fiscal year. In the first report on this form filed by the registrant, the information must also be given for the corresponding six-month period of the preceding fiscal year.

COMPANIES FOR WHICH INFORMATION IS TO BE GIVEN.—The required information must be given for the registrant or, if the registrant files consolidated financial statements with its annual reports, it must be given for the registrant and its consolidated subsidiaries. If the information is given for the registrant and its consolidated subsidiaries, it need not be given separately for the registrant.

The required information must also be given separately for each unconsolidated subsidiary or group of such subsidiaries for which separate individual or group statements are required to be filed with the registrant's annual reports. It need not be furnished, however, for any such unconsolidated subsidiary which would not be required to file semiannual reports if it were a registrant.

PRESENTATION OF INFORMATION.—The form calls only for items of information specified; it is not necessary to furnish formal statements of income and earned surplus. There is no objection, however, to furnishing formal statements, or incorporating by reference published statements, provided copies of the statements are filed as an exhibit to the report on this form.

The information is not required to be certified by independent public accountants and may carry a notation to that effect and any other qualification considered necessary or appropriate.

If income is derived from both gross sales (Caption 1) and operating revenues (Caption 2), the two classes of income may be combined in one amount (Caption 3) if the lesser amount is not more than 10 per cent of the sum of the two captions.

If there is included in the total of gross sales and operating revenues (Caption 3) excise taxes in amount equal to 10 per cent or more of such total, the amount of such taxes must be stated separately.

There must be stated separately under extraordinary items (Caption 4) any material amounts of other income or income deductions of an unusual or nonrecurring nature included in the determination of net income or loss during the period covered by the report.

Any material amounts included in provision for taxes on income (Caption 6) which are applicable to periods other than the one covered by the report, or to items not included in the determination of net income, should be appropriately explained.

There must be stated separately and described under special items (Caption 8) each material item of profit and loss given recognition in the accounts and not included in the determination of net income or loss or reported under earned surplus items (Caption 9).

Under earned surplus items (Caption 9) the issuer is required to state separately any material additions other than net income, and any material deductions, including dividends, indicating clearly the transactions out of which the items arose. Items reported under special items (Caption 8) are not to be included in earned surplus items (Caption 9).

The issuer must furnish under Remarks any material information considered necessary or appropriate to make the information called for by this form not misleading, such as a statement that the information is not representative because of the seasonal nature of the business, or an explanation of an unusual increase or decrease in net sales or income.

DELAY IN FILING INFORMATION.—The information for foreign subsidiaries not consolidated may be omitted if it is impracticable to furnish it within the time specified for filing the report, provided it is indicated that such information has been omitted and the omitted information is furnished by amendment when available.

If the registrant has securities registered on a national securities exchange and publishes, pursuant to the regulations of such exchange, an earnings statement that it desires to incorporate by reference, the filing of a report on this form may be deferred until the earnings statement becomes available, provided the report is filed immediately thereafter.

If a delay in filing the report or in furnishing any of the required information becomes necessary under any other circumstances, a request must be made for an extension of time pursuant to the SEC rules.

SEASONAL INDUSTRIES.—For registrants having seasonal cycles or material variations in operating results from other causes, comparable figures for the same period of the preceding year, or figures for 12 months, as considered appropriate, may be given in addition to the required information.

Annual Reports of Certain Exchange Members, Brokers, and Dealers.—Rule X-17A-5 requires the filing in each calendar year of a report of his financial condition as of a date not more than 45 days prior to filing by:

1. Every exchange member who transacts a business in securities directly with nonmembers;
2. Every broker and dealer who transacts a business in securities through any such member;
3. Every registered over-the-counter broker or dealer.

For most brokers and dealers the report must be certified by an independent public accountant. At the date of this writing, the SEC is proposing to extend the certification requirements to all brokers and dealers.

FORM X-17A-5.—The annual report is designated Form X-17A-5 and consists mainly of a financial questionnaire. Regulation S-X does not apply to this report but the financial information is required to be certified by independent public accountants. While the form is of limited interest to most public accountants, there are two aspects which are of general interest: (1) a provision in the rule dealing with the accountant's certificate, and (2) minimum audit requirements set forth in the form.

The accountant's certificate must make certain representations about the audit. Among other things it is necessary to make a "reasonably comprehensive statement as to the scope of the audit made, including a statement as to whether the accountant reviewed the procedures followed for safeguarding the securities of customers . . . . ."

MINIMUM AUDIT REQUIREMENTS.—The minimum audit requirements prescribed in Form X-17A-5 are as follows:

The audit shall substantiate the stated assets and liabilities as of the date of the financial questionnaire and the scope and comprehensiveness thereof shall be such as would enable the independent public accountant to express an opinion as to the stated financial condition of the respondent as of that date. The scope of the audit shall include at least the following:

(1) Comparison of ledger accounts with the trial balances obtained from the general and private ledgers and proofs of the aggregates of subsidiary ledgers with their respective controlling accounts.

(2) Physical examination and comparison with the books and records of all securities, currencies, tax stamps, warehouse receipts, and such other assets on hand, in vault, or in box, or otherwise in physical possession.

(3) Verification of securities in transit or in transfer.

(4) Balancing of positions in all securities and spot and future commodities as shown by the books and records.

(5) Obtaining of written confirmations with respect to the following (see note):

(a) Bank balances (In addition to the reconcilement and confirmation of bank balances as of the date of the audit, the independent public accountant shall, at a later date, after giving ample time for clearance of outstanding checks and transfers of funds, obtain from depositaries canceled checks and statements of the bank accounts as of such date, and reconcile the balances shown thereon with the balances shown by the books of the respondent.);

(b) Open contractual positions and deposits of funds with clearing corporations or associations;

(c) Money borrowed and detail of collateral;

(d) Accounts, commodities, securities, and commitments carried for the respondent by others;

(e) Details of:
(i) securities borrowed
(ii) securities loaned
(iii) securities failed to deliver
(iv) securities failed to receive
(v) when issued contracts
(vi) delayed delivery and other similar open contracts
(vii) open commodity contracts with others

(f) Customers', partners', officers', directors', and respondent's accounts (Confirmation of these accounts may be in the form of a written acknowledgment of the accuracy of the statement of balances, security positions, and open contractual commitments, other than uncleared regular way purchases and sales, accompanying the first request for confirmation mailed by the independent public accountant.);

(g) Guarantees in cases where required to protect accounts guaranteed as of audit date;

(h) All other accounts which in the opinion of the independent public accountant should be confirmed.

(6) A written statement should be obtained from the proprietor, partner (if a partnership) or officer (if a corporation) as to the assets, liabilities, and accountabilities, contingent or otherwise, not recorded on the books of the respondent.

(7) The independent public accountant shall review the methods of internal accounting control of the respondent and its procedures for safeguarding securities.

Note to Item (5): Compliance with requirements for obtaining written confirmation with respect to the above accounts shall be deemed to have been made if requests for confirmation have been mailed by the independent public accountant in an envelope bearing his own return address and second requests are similarly mailed to those not replying to the first requests.

Regulation X-14—Proxy Statements.—Under the authority granted in Section 14 of the 1934 Act, the SEC has promulgated Regulation X-14 governing the solicitation of proxies in respect of securities listed and registered on a national securities exchange. Public accountants who serve listed companies should be familiar with those portions of the regulation which prescribe the filing of financial statements, especially since, as will be seen, the rules are somewhat flexible and leave room for exercise of judgment.

Regulation X-14 consists of certain rules and Schedule 14A. This schedule itemizes the information required in the proxy statement which must be furnished to the stockholder whose proxy is solicited. The information to be furnished depends in part upon the matters to be acted upon at the meeting to which the proxy relates.

FINANCIAL STATEMENTS.—Financial statements are required if action is to be taken with respect to:

The authorization or issuance of securities otherwise than for exchange (Item 12),

The modification or exchange of securities (Item 13), or

Certain mergers, consolidations, acquisitions of a going business or its assets, sale of a substantial part of the issuer's assets, or liquidation of the issuer (Item 14).

If any of the above items apply, there must be furnished for the issuer the same prime certified financial statements—i.e., balance sheets and income and surplus statements—and supplementary profit and loss schedule that would be required in an original application for registration under the 1934 Act, except as provided in the paragraph following. Usually registration would be effected on Form 10, and hence the prime statements and schedule in the proxy statement must be as of and for the period prescribed by Form 10. The requirements for financial statements in Form 10 are summarized on page 623. Financial statements must also be furnished for a business proposed to be acquired, but these need not be certified.

The Commission's rule provides that any and all otherwise required financial statements may be omitted when they are not material for the exercise of prudent judgment on the matter to be acted upon at the meeting if the reasons for such omission are stated. Such financial statements are usually deemed to be material when the authorization or issuance of a material amount of senior securities is proposed, but are not material for authorization or issuance of common stock, other than in exchange.

Proxy statements must be filed in preliminary form with the SEC, and definitive copies may not be sent to stockholders until at least ten days after such filing.

When the election of directors is one of the matters to be acted upon at the annual meeting and the proxy is solicited on behalf of the management of the issuer, Regulation X-14 requires that an annual report accompany or precede the proxy statement. The annual report must contain such financial statements for the last fiscal year as will, in the opinion of the management, adequately reflect the financial position and operations of the issuer. This annual report, including financial statements, may be in any form deemed suitable by the management. Special rules apply if proxies are being solicited in opposition to the management. By Commission rule, the annual report is not deemed to be proxy soliciting material or to be filed in a legal sense with the SEC or otherwise subject to the regulation or the 1934 Act except to the extent that the issuer specifically requests that it be treated as a part of such material or incorporates it in the proxy statement by reference.

APPENDIX

QUESTIONNAIRE FOR EVALUATION OF INTERNAL ACCOUNTING CONTROL AND INTERNAL CHECK

Introduction.—Chapter 5 of this book discusses internal control, the auditor's responsibility in relation thereto, and his methods of investigating and test-checking its operation.

A standard questionnaire prepared for the use of staff members on all engagements is a practical and useful device for investigating and recording the auditor's inquiries into a system of internal accounting control and internal check. Such a questionnaire, designed by persons fully conversant with problems of internal control, makes available a large fund of accumulated experience and furnishes a basis for evaluating the system under review.

An example of a questionnaire in actual use follows:

QUESTIONNAIRE

INSTRUCTIONS

Standards of field work approved and adopted by the American Institute of Certified Public Accountants in September, 1948, include the requirement that:

There is to be a proper study and evaluation of the existing internal control as a basis for reliance thereon and for the determination of the resultant extent of the tests to which auditing procedures are to be restricted.

Adherence to this standard is indicated principally in the answers and explanations in the completed questionnaire, in the formal audit program, and in the working papers. The evaluation of existing controls and determination of the extent of application of auditing procedures are based principally on data in the questionnaire and are made in oral consultations among partners and staff members.

The selection of auditing procedures and the extent of their application depend largely on the auditor's evaluation of the nature and apparent effectiveness of the client's internal accounting control. The attached questionnaire is designed to aid the auditor in making this evaluation by providing a means to elicit the required information about those accounting controls designed primarily to assure the accurate and suitable recording and summarization of authorized financial transactions (Internal Accounting Control). The auditor should report to clients suggestions for improvements in accounting control procedures following this evaluation.

The auditor should also report to clients suggestions for improvement in controls designed primarily for the safeguarding of assets against defalcations or other similar irregularities (Internal Check). Accordingly, certain questions are designed to elicit information for that purpose even though

a. The primary responsibility for safeguarding assets and preventing and detecting errors and fraud rests with management, and

b. The ordinary examination incident to issuing an opinion on financial statements is not designed and cannot be relied upon to disclose defalcations and other similar irregularities.

While apparent weaknesses in internal check probably will not lead to extensions of audit procedures to the same extent as might observed weaknesses in internal accounting control, the auditor's evaluation of the effectiveness of internal check may lead to reconsideration of the time of application of certain audit procedures for accounts receivable, cash, or inventories. For example, accounts receivable may be confirmed as at the balance sheet date rather than as at a date say one or two months prior thereto.

It should be understood that the review called for by this questionnaire is not a substitute for a systems examination and is not designed and cannot be relied upon to disclose all weaknesses in internal accounting control and internal check. Further, the questionnaire is not intended to imply that all procedures covered by the questions are necessary in all circumstances, nor is it intended to disclose all statistical, physical, or other controls that should be evaluated in determining the extent of application of auditing procedures and that may be considered in formulating suggestions to be made to clients.

This questionnaire should be prepared (1) for each new audit engagement and (2) at least once every three years for each recurring audit engagement. For each intervening year, the questionnaire should be reviewed to determine that the answers and other data are current in the light of changes in the client's procedures and personnel disclosed through inquiry, observation, and review of accounting manuals. Major changes should be recorded by revising the appropriate section or sections. After the original preparation of this questionnaire, the renewal requirements may be met on recurring audit engagements by preparing the several sections on a cycle basis provided all sections are prepared anew within each three-year period.

It is recognized that substantial portions of the questionnaire may not be applicable on specialized engagements such as the examination of bank, brokerage, investment trust, insurance, or institutional financial statements. Further, some organizations may be so small that the evaluation of internal accounting control and internal check may best be accomplished through methods other than the use of the questionnaire. However, the policies and principles set forth are applicable to all engagements. A list of sections omitted, showing the reasons for the omissions, should be filed with sections of the questionnaire that have been prepared. If use of the questionnaire is omitted entirely, a statement to that effect, together with the reasons therefor, should be filed in the permanent binder with the audit program for the engagement.

Most sections of the questionnaire are divided into two parts:

Part I—Internal Accounting Control—Questions that will bring responses indicating the existence or absence ("yes" or "no" answers) of accounting procedures or statistical, physical, or other controls designed to bring about *the accurate and suitable recording and summarization of authorized financial transactions* relating to the subject matter of the section.

Part II—Internal Check—Questions that will bring responses indicating the existence or absence ("yes" or "no" answers) of accounting procedures or statistical, physical, or other controls *which safeguard assets* against defalcations or other similar irregularities.

Many sections also include introductory questions, the answers to which are factual and establish the areas to be covered in Parts I and II.

Answer columns in which the "yes" and "no" answers may be checked should be provided on each questionnaire page.

Questions in Part I are designed to cover basic requirements of internal accounting control. All questions must be answered, unless the subject matter is not present or is insignificant; "not present" or "insignificant" should then be written in the answer column. Where there is a "no" answer, suitable explanations should be given on a sheet headed "Explanations" at the end of the section.

In general, answers to the questions in Part I are to be obtained and substantiated independently by the auditor through the application of auditing procedures, including the examination of documentary evidence. In the absence of documentary evidence, the auditor is to state in the questionnaire the basis for his answer.

Questions in Part II are designed to indicate procedures that are desirable to provide or enhance internal check. Explanations of "no" answers should include descriptions of alternative procedures which may be in use to provide the desired controls.

Answers to the questions in Part II may be obtained by the auditor through observation or by inquiry of persons who have full knowledge of procedures in use. Accordingly, provision should be made for separate columns to indicate the source of each answer: "A"—auditor, "C"—client.

Frequently, different procedures are followed at different locations in accounting for similar transactions, for various reasons. The question should then be answered on the basis of the principal procedures followed and, depending on the importance of the item, the alternative procedure may be explained on the sheet headed "Explanations," or a separate section may be prepared.

The staff member should sign and date the sections completed by him and indicate the names of company personnel consulted. The questionnaire may be separated into sections and parts, to facilitate preparation by different staff members at different locations, and, by placing Parts I and II in juxtaposition, to permit ready comparison of internal accounting controls with related internal check.

The senior in charge should consider with supervising company personnel the validity of the answers obtained, and should date and sign the questionnaire to indicate that he has discharged his responsibilities.

The supervisor of each engagement is responsible for reviewing the findings of the senior in charge and his proposals to restrict or extend auditing procedures in the current audit program. The supervisor should consult with the partner about those findings and proposals that involve major changes in the audit program.

The supervisor is also responsible for preparing or reviewing the proposed letter of suggestions to the client and for consulting with the partner about the letter. These letters are generally to be reviewed with clients before they are formally submitted.

GENERAL

PART I—INTERNAL ACCOUNTING CONTROL

1. Is a chart of accounts in use?

   A formal chart of accounts is a list of accounts, systematically arranged, indicating account names and numbers.

2. Is the chart of accounts supplemented by definitions of items to be recorded in the various accounts?

   The definitions of items to be included in the accounts promote consistency in recording and summarizing accounting transactions.

3. Is an accounting manual in use?

   Such a manual should prescribe procedures to be followed in recording and summarizing accounting transactions.

4. Is the assignment of accounting duties and responsibilities expressed in the form of an organization chart?

   Such a chart is a formal expression of assignments showing functional responsibilities; these assignments may also be expressed in the form of job descriptions.

5. Are all postings to general and subsidiary ledgers required to be supported by entries in books of original entry or journal entries?

6. Are ledger entries clearly referenced to indicate their source?

7. Are journal entries:
   - (a) Standardized for content and identification?
   - (b) Supported by readily identifiable data?
   - (c) Reviewed and approved by a responsible employee?

8. Are the original recording and summarizations of accounting transactions reviewed to assure adherence to:
   - (a) Chart of accounts?
   - (b) Accounting manual instructions?
   - (c) Assignments indicated by the organization chart?

   These reviews may be made by department heads, the chief accounting officer, or by other assigned personnel. When a formal chart of accounts, accounting manual, or organization chart is not in use, a file of instructions may contain equivalent data.

9. Are periodic reports to management compared with:
   - (a) Reports of prior periods?
   - (b) Budgets?

10. Is a specified employee or group of employees assigned the duty of accounting for and reporting on significant fluctuations disclosed by the comparisons referred to in Question 9?

> *This review may disclose errors in recording or summarizing transactions.*

11. Is a specified employee or group of employees assigned the duty of reviewing and revising:

    (a) Chart of accounts and related definitions?
    (b) Accounting manual?
    (c) Organization chart?

> *This review and revision may be made periodically under the direction of the chief accounting officer.*

PART II—INTERNAL CHECK

1. Are persons who control the recording and summarization of accounting transactions independent of those who:

    (a) Perform the operations of:
        (1) Selling?
        (2) Shipping?
        (3) Manufacturing?
        (4) Purchasing?
        (5) Receiving materials or merchandise?
        (6) Receiving cash?
        (7) Disbursing cash?
        (8) Extending credit?
        (9) Internal auditing?
    (b) Are custodians of:
        (1) Assets, such as:
            (a) Cash?
            (b) Petty cash?
            (c) Marketable securities?
            (d) Notes receivable?
            (e) Inventories?
            (f) Patents?
        (2) Unissued:
            (a) Checks?
            (b) Notes payable?
            (c) Bonds?
            (d) Stock certificates?

*Control of the recording and summarization of accounting
transactions includes the recording of transactions in books of
original entry, the summarization of recorded transactions, the
posting of transactions or summarizations to the general ledger,
and the preparation of periodic accounting reports.*

*The segregation of the functions of recording and summarizing
transactions from those of initiating transactions and of custody
of company property is fundamental to the safeguarding of
assets. More detailed questions about such segregation will
be found in each of the sections.*

2. Is the person who reviews and approves journal entries independent
   of:
   (a) Posting and balancing detail records?
   (b) Initiation of entries in books of original entry?

3. Do persons independent of those who record and summarize accounting transactions periodically:
   (a) Examine original data supporting recorded transactions?
   (b) Review recording and summarization of accounting transac-
       tions for adherence to prescribed policies?
   (c) Review the preparation of periodic reports to management and
       comparisons with trial balance accounts, reports of prior
       periods, and budgets?
   (d) Review reports on significant fluctuations disclosed by the com-
       parisons referred to in (c) above?

       *These examinations and reviews may be assigned to persons
       within the accounting department who are not responsible for
       initiating procedures and who are independent of the subject
       under examination. Frequently they are assigned to an internal
       auditor.*

4. Are the examinations and reviews referred to in Question 3 above:
   (a) Scheduled to cover all types of accounting transactions at regu-
       lar intervals?
   (b) Based on written audit programs?
   (c) Reported on in writing to persons independent of the subject
       of the examination?

5. Is the person who approves revisions of the chart of accounts and
   related definitions, the accounting manual, and the organization chart
   (Question 11, Part I) independent of:
   (a) Those who maintain the accounting records?
   (b) Those who report on adherence to prescribed policies?

. 6. Is access to accounting records limited at all times to persons whose duties require such access?

7. Are accounting department employees:
   (a) Rotated periodically when possible?
   (b) Required to take vacations at least annually?

Note:
Indicate in the space provided whether a fidelity bond is in effect. If it is, a complete description including the name of the carrier and type and amount of coverage should be filed in the working papers.

> *Although a fidelity bond does not provide a control for safeguarding assets, the above data are pertinent to the review of the existing system of internal check.*

CASH RECEIPTS

INTRODUCTION

Do receipts of currency, checks, and money orders include:
   (a) Receipts by mail?
   (b) Receipts over the counter or through collectors?
   (c) Receipts by outside salesmen or route men?

PART I—INTERNAL ACCOUNTING CONTROL

RECEIPTS BY MAIL:
   1. Is a detailed listing made showing names and amounts?

> *The detailed list may be in the form of entries in the cash book, the original or a copy of a written tabulation, adding machine tapes, deposit slips, copies of remittance advices, or groups of collection stubs.*
>
> *When the volume of mail collections and consequent posting of detail accounts is large, many companies use an adding machine tape as a control mechanism for amounts and prepare or use one of the following as a posting medium:*
>
> *(1) Remittance advices, which may be prepared on receipt of the payment or may represent a section of the original invoice torn off and sent with the payment by the customer.*
>
> *(2) Copy of the deposit slip, with details of source added.*
>
> *When one of these is used, the posting medium serves as the detailed listing of the names.*

Individual items of cash receipts should be totaled daily or periodically. These totals provide controls over bank deposits, entries in the cash book, and contra credits.

2. Are postdated checks and disputed items included in the list above?

> *If postdated checks and nondepositable items are included in the original listing, control is established over their subsequent disposition. If they are not so included, control may be otherwise established, by separate listing, physical segregation, or other means.*

3. (a) Is the total of the listing in the cash book compared with:
   (1) Deposit slip total?
   (2) Credits to accounts receivable control or other control accounts?
   (b) When a list other than that in the cash book is prepared, is the total of such list compared with the cash book total?

> *Assurance of the effectiveness of internal accounting control over total cash receipts is obtained by making the comparisons above. Correctness of detailed postings, especially to individual customers' accounts, would be assured by comparison of the detailed listing with detailed accounts receivable postings. In practice, this is seldom done. Frequently the accuracy of the accounts receivable posting medium is assured by simultaneous mechanical preparations of the detailed list and the posting medium. Detection of errors in posting from such lists usually depends on customers' complaints resulting from monthly statements or circularization.*

RECEIPTS OVER THE COUNTER OR THROUGH COLLECTORS:

4. If cash registers are used:
   (a) Do they prepare tapes?
   (b) Are the tapes retained?
   (c) Are the totals of the tapes reconciled with the cash collected at least once a day?
   (d) If the answer to (a) is "No," is the cash register cumulative total reconciled periodically with recorded receipts?

5. If counter sales slips, cashiers' receipts, or collectors' receipts are used:
   (a) Are retained copies prenumbered?
   (b) Are numbers accounted for?
   (c) Are totals of the slips or receipts reconciled periodically with the cash collected?

6. Are totals shown by the cash registers (tapes or readings), or totals of sales slips or receipts:
   (a) Summarized for recording each day?
   (b) Compared with:
      (1) Cash book totals?
      (2) Deposit slip totals?
      (3) Credits to contra control accounts?

RECEIPTS BY OUTSIDE SALESMEN OR ROUTE MEN:

7. Are salesmen charged for the merchandise furnished to them for sale?
   The charge may be made in dollars or in units of merchandise; it establishes control over subsequent transactions.

8. Are salesmen required to turn over cash and report transactions (sales and charges to customers) at regular fixed intervals?

9. Are cash receipts and charges to customers reconciled at least once a month with changes in inventories charged to salesmen?

10. Are items of merchandise held by the salesmen physically inventoried at the time reconciliations are made?

11. Are the aggregates of collection items (cash receipts and charge sales) compared with:
    (a) Cash book totals?
    (b) Deposit slip totals?
    (c) Debit(s) and credit(s) to accounts receivable control or other control accounts?

ALL RECEIPTS:

12. Are each day's receipts recorded promptly when received?

13. Are cash receipts at branch offices reported promptly to the main office?

14. Do the forms on which cash receipts are summarized provide for the inclusion of all known sources of cash receipts?
    When cash receipts information flows from many sources, such as a number of departments, cash registers, route books, vending machines and branch offices, practices should be followed which account for all collection points.

15. Are all bank accounts required to be authorized by the Board of Directors?

SEE CASH DISBURSEMENTS SECTION, PART I, FOR PROCEDURES COVERING TRANSFERS AND BANK RECONCILIATIONS.

PART II—INTERNAL CHECK

RECEIPTS BY MAIL:

1. Do the duties of the persons who prepare the detailed listing of receipts by mail exclude the functions of:

    (a) Preparing the bank deposit?

    (b) Posting customers' remittances to detailed accounts receivable?

    (c) Posting credits for cash received to general ledger accounts?

    (d) Entering amounts in the cash receipts book?

    To meet requirement (d) above, a prelisting of receipts may be prepared by independent persons in the incoming mail department, the treasurer's department, or the internal auditor's department.

    The independent listing of receipts indicated above minimizes the possibility of omissions from deposits and recorded receipts as well as concealment of these omissions by erroneous posting of credits. It is obviously important that no person having duties described above have access to the receipts before the listing is made.

2. Are cash receipts items withheld from deposit:

    (a) Reviewed by a responsible person independent of cash receipts or accounts receivable functions?

    (b) Released by a responsible independent person for return to payor, or for deposit?

3. Are cash receipts items, withheld from deposit but not listed or otherwise under accounting control, held by a responsible person independent of:

    (a) The person preparing the deposit?

    (b) Those responsible for posting detail accounts receivable or other contra accounts?

    In the absence of accounting control, responsible independent physical segregation may safeguard these items.

RECEIPTS OVER THE COUNTER OR THROUGH COLLECTORS:

4. Are the duties of the person(s) who receive such items independent of:

    (a) Other cash functions?

    (b) Custody of other negotiable assets?

    (c) Posting detailed accounts receivable?

    (d) Posting general ledger accounts?

The segregation of duties indicated above curtails the opportunity to conceal irregularities without collusion. When some of the above duties are assigned to one department, proper segregation of these duties within that department is important; satisfactory internal check may be provided by other control procedures, such as a check of these receipts and the accounting for them by someone other than the person receiving them.

RECEIPTS BY OUTSIDE SALESMEN OR ROUTE MEN:

5. Does someone independent of the salesmen or route men:
    (a) Check the merchandise at the time it is furnished to them?
    (b) Take or check the inventory which supports their reports?
    (c) Check the accounting for collection items?
    (d) Reconcile the reports with related book entries?

ALL RECEIPTS:

6. Are each day's receipts, exclusive of postdated items, deposited intact and promptly?

7. Are receipts by a branch office deposited locally subject only to main office withdrawal?

8. Are checks charged back by banks:
    (a) Received by a person independent of those:
        (1) Preparing the deposit?
        (2) Posting detailed accounts receivable?
    (b) Investigated by a responsible person independent of those responsible for receipt or entry of cash?

    These procedures aid in the discovery of lapping when misappropriations are covered by the use of worthless checks. Sometimes the company may redeem uncollectible items, i.e., purchase them for cash from the bank. Question 8(a) above applies also to the person making such redemptions.

9. Does a person independent of those preparing bank deposits, entering amounts in cash receipts book, posting customers' remittances, and posting credits for cash received to general ledger accounts:
    (a) Obtain directly from banks authenticated duplicate deposit slips for all deposits?
    (b) Compare authenticated deposit slips in detail with cash book entries?
    (c) Compare amounts on authenticated deposit slips in detail with the original listing and reconcile the totals?
    (d) Compare authenticated deposit slips with bank statement entries?

These procedures provide a control over checks and other items withheld from immediate deposit and disclose items not recorded in both the bank statements and the books.

When the bank compares deposit items with the deposit slip in detail, and this may be ascertained from the bank, the above procedures will tend to disclose lapping. When this comparison is not made by the bank, a person with the independence indicated above should compare the deposit items with the deposit slip before the deposit is made if lapping is to be curbed.

10. Have all banks been instructed:

    (a) Not to cash checks or money orders payable to the client?

    (b) Not to accept for deposit in special accounts (such as payroll or petty cash) checks of others payable to the client?

    While large banks may be reluctant to accept this instruction, many banks will accept it, and conversion of checks to cash then becomes more difficult.

11.   (a) Are totals of cash receipts compared with cash book and deposit slip totals, and with credits to accounts receivable control and other control accounts (Questions 3, 6, and 11, Part I) by persons independent of:

        (1) Cash receipts functions?

        (2) Accounts receivable functions?

        (3) Posting credits for cash received to the general ledger?

    (b) Are the totals of the listings verified?

    The footing of the cash column may be checked by the person making the independent bank reconciliation.

SEE CASH DISBURSEMENTS SECTION, PART II, FOR PROCEDURES COVERING TRANSFERS AND BANK RECONCILIATIONS.

CASH DISBURSEMENTS

INTRODUCTION

1. Are the following disbursements made by check:

    (a) All disbursements?

    (b) General disbursements of large amounts?

    (c) Payroll disbursements:

        (1) From imprest funds?

        (2) Other (describe)?

    (d) Disbursements for special purposes (describe)?

    (e) Petty disbursements:
        (1) From imprest funds?
        (2) Other (describe)?

2. Are the following disbursements made in currency:
    (a) General disbursements of large amounts?
    (b) Payroll disbursements:
        (1) From imprest funds?
        (2) Other (describe)?
    (c) Disbursements for special purposes (describe)?
    (d) Petty disbursements:
        (1) From imprest funds?
        (2) Other (describe)?

When payments such as those for payroll or petty expenses are made in currency, transfers from general funds to special funds for such purposes should be made by check.

When payroll or working fund disbursements, either by check or in currency, are made separately from general disbursements, it may be preferable to use a separate Cash Disbursements section of this questionnaire for each major payroll or working fund.

PART I—INTERNAL ACCOUNTING CONTROL

DISBURSEMENTS BY CHECK:

  1. Are checks signed, manually or in facsimile, only on the basis of approved vouchers?

Internal accounting control requires that cash be disbursed only in liquidation of liabilities recorded by approved vouchers which may include vendors' invoices or formalized requests for checks. The signing of checks in advance of presentation of the voucher defeats the purpose of the control.

  2. At the time of signing, does the signer:
    (a) Have written evidence that:
        (1) The payments are supported by approved vouchers?
        (2) The data on the checks have been compared with the vouchers?
    (b) Cancel the request for payment by appropriate means or deliver the vouchers for cancellation to a person who does not approve or prepare vouchers or checks?

The evidence may be the vouchers or initials or signatures on request for checks or on the checks themselves.

3. Are all checks prenumbered?

   Prenumbering of all checks provides a ready means of accounting for checks and of effecting periodic bank reconciliations.

4. When checks are prenumbered, is a record made of the disposition of all checks?

5. Are checks issued listed in detail?

   A tabulation or other record of checks issued should show in detail payees and amounts, to facilitate the posting of subsidiary records. The detailed list may be in the form of entries in the cash book, a written tabulation, adding machine tape, copies of checks or requests for checks to be issued.

6. Is the total of the listing compared with:
   (a) Cash book total (if listing is other than the cash book)?
   (b) Charges to accounts (vouchers) payable control or other control accounts?

   The above comparisons, often made as part of the posting procedure, enhance the effectiveness of internal accounting control over totals of cash disbursements.

7. Are transfers between bank accounts under accounting control?

   This control requires the use of a clearing account or other record and is necessary to assure that both sides of a transfer between banks are recorded in the same accounting period.

8. Are the following reconciled periodically:
   (a) Cash balances shown by bank statements and those recorded in the books?
   (b) Totals of debits and credits listed on bank statements and comparable book totals?
   (c) Detailed items listed on bank statements and cash items recorded on the books?

   These three procedures are frequently considered as one procedure, namely, a bank reconciliation. However, each procedure may be carried out independently, and each serves a separate purpose.

   Reconciliations of balances disclose any differences between net increases or decreases in recorded cash during the periods and net increases or decreases shown by the bank statements.

   Reconciliations of totals assure that there are no undisclosed items of receipts offset by items of disbursements recorded in the cash records but not in the bank statements, or vice versa.

Reconciliations of detailed items disclose the failure to recognize all items, including offsetting items, in both the books and the bank statements.

The above conclusions assume that transfers are under accounting control.

The need for applying all three procedures to effect satisfactory bank reconciliations varies with the extent of the accounting control over cash transactions. When control procedures tend to assure the deposit of all receipts and that all checks issued are recorded, the reconciliation of totals [Item (b) above] may not be required. When controls over total receipts and disbursements are satisfactory, it may be proper to rely on customers and creditors to report errors. Failure to effect reconciliation (a) above may necessitate reconciliations (b) and (c) to uncover the errors that impeded reconciliation (a). Under the block method of reconciling, reconciliations (b) and (c) will not be effected until differences appear.

9. Are such reconciliations (Question 8 above) made at least once during each accounting period?

   Usually the reconciliations are made as of the closing date of the accounting period to assure that all transactions applicable to the period are recorded. However, reconciliations of imprest, payroll, petty cash, and other fund bank accounts may be made at other times during the period.

DISBURSEMENTS IN CURRENCY:

These disbursements include expenditures from petty cash funds, travel advances, freight funds, special purpose advances, payroll funds, and from current receipts.

Many disbursements in currency are made from funds kept under the imprest system, which provides a convenient method for reviewing and accounting for them.

Some organizations, especially in the retail field, permit purchases to be made from currency included in cash receipts. Special procedures used to control these disbursements should be described by the auditor.

10. Are all expenditures supported by evidence indicating their purpose and amount?

    This support may consist of petty cash slips, invoices, payrolls, pay receipts, and reports on travel or special purpose expenditures.

11. Is there an established maximum amount for an individual expenditure?

> *Such a maximum tends to discourage the by-passing of regular procedures in procuring and paying for materials and services.*

12. Is the amount of the fund such as would ordinarily necessitate reimbursement at least once a month?

> *The need for reimbursement tends to assure reasonably current recording in the general books of disbursements from the fund.*

13. Is the fund counted periodically and reconciled with the general ledger control account?

14. Are requests for reimbursement of the fund accompanied by details of expenditures and supporting data?

15. Are amounts authorized but not disbursed:
    - (a) Reported promptly to a designated employee?
    - (b) Returned to general cash after a reasonable period?

> *These amounts might include undelivered pay envelopes and undisbursed travel or other special advances.*

PART II—INTERNAL CHECK

DISBURSEMENTS BY CHECK:

1. Are persons who prepare checks independent of persons who:
    - (a) Approve vouchers for payment?
    - (b) Subsequently compare data on checks with approved vouchers or other supporting data?

2. Are persons who sign checks manually or in facsimile independent of persons who:
    - (a) Prepare vouchers for approval?
    - (b) Approve vouchers for payment?
    - (c) Prepare checks?

> *This independence tends to assure the issue of checks only in payment of properly approved liabilities.*

3. When checks require two authorized signatures, must each signature:
    - (a) Mean that the signer has ascertained that payments are supported by approved vouchers?
    - (b) Be that of a responsible person independent of the other signer?

> *Requirement (a) assures that written evidence supports the disbursement.*
>
> *Requirement (b) serves to discourage fraudulent disbursements.*

Some countersignature procedures require that one of the signers, who is independent of the other signer, certify that the payments liquidate liabilities recorded by means of approved vouchers. If the second signer does not examine supporting vouchers, but signs in reliance on the first signature, such procedures may offer little, if any, protection beyond that afforded by the first signature.

4. When a mechanical check-signer is used:
   (a) Does the individual authorized to use the signature die have custody of the die when it is not in use?
   (b) Are procedures followed in using the die such that this individual knows that only authorized checks have been signed?

   Control over the mechanical check-signer may be exercised by the physical presence of the custodian when the die is in use, by control over checks issued to the operator, by a numbering device on the machine, or by a device for physically controlling signed checks such as a locked compartment.

5. Are amounts on checks protected against alteration by means of:
   (a) Protective paper?
   (b) A protective writing device, such as a check protector?
   (c) Inscribing amounts (if a writing device is used) prior to or simultaneously with the comparison of checks with approved vouchers?

   Use of the writing device at the earliest opportunity provides the most effective protection.

6. Are all checks drawn to the specific order of creditors and custodians?

   The practice of drawing checks to the order of specified payees limits the negotiability of these checks and provides a means for the acknowledgment of receipt by endorsement of the checks. Checks drawn to cash or bearer do not have these attributes.

7. Are signed checks retained in the custody of the signer until delivery (or mailing) and delivered (or mailed) by him or by a person directly under his control and independent of:
   (a) Voucher functions?
   (b) Payroll functions?
   (c) General ledger functions?
   (d) Cash receipts functions?
   (e) Petty cash or other cash fund functions?
   (f) Check preparation functions?

   The foregoing requirements tend to assure delivery or mailing of checks, unaltered, to specified payees.

8. Do persons independent of those who sign checks:

    (a) Have custody of unnumbered checks and insert check numbers?

    (b) Record and account for sequence of check numbers?

These procedures tend to disclose the disposition of all checks and to assure the entry in the cash disbursements records of all check numbers issued. Check numbers may be inserted by the printer or other independent person. The effectiveness of numerical control is enhanced when unnumbered checks are not available to the signer and numbers are independently inserted.

9.   (a) Is comparison of totals of the list of checks issued with cash book totals and charges to accounts (vouchers) payable or other control accounts (Question 6, Part I) made by persons independent of:

        (1) The person who prepared the list?

        (2) Check-signers?

        (3) Voucher functions (payroll functions for pay checks)?

    (b) Are the totals of the listings verified by such persons?

Totals of the list of payroll checks issued should be compared with (1) total of the related payroll, (2) related amount, if any, deposited in an imprest bank account, and (3) net total of payroll account classifications. Persons making the comparison should be independent of payroll functions.

The person making the independent bank reconciliation may check the footing of the list of checks issued (cash column of the disbursement record).

10. Are all transfers between banks as recorded in the books (Question 7, Part I) and transfers between banks as reflected in bank statements accounted for by persons independent of:

    (a) Check-signers?

    (b) Persons who prepare lists of checks issued?

This procedure is usually carried out by persons reconciling bank accounts and is required to guard against the deposit of a transfer check in one accounting period and the recording of the disbursement in a succeeding accounting period (kiting).

11. Are bank accounts reconciled by a person independent of:

    (a) Cash receipts functions?

    (b) Cash disbursements functions?

    (c) Voucher functions (payroll functions for payroll bank accounts)?

12. Does the reconciler:
    (a) Obtain bank statements direct from the bank or in an envelope sealed by the bank?
    (b) Maintain custody of the bank statement and other contents of the envelope until all reconciliation steps are completed?

13. Does the reconciler:
    (a) Determine the total of outstanding checks by detailed comparison of paid checks with the detailed list of checks issued for:
        (1) Dates?
        (2) Payees?
        (3) Amounts?
    (b) Examine paid checks for:
        (1) Signatures?
        (2) Endorsements?
    (c) Return inadequately endorsed checks to the bank for proper endorsement?

    This independent detailed comparison is necessary to disclose alterations in checks after listing, substitution of checks for checks listed, offsetting errors in the list of checks, unauthorized signatures, and improper endorsements. If the comparison called for has been made by a person other than the reconciler and independent of those who prepare the list of checks issued, the reconciler may derive the total of the amount of outstanding checks:

    (a) By identifying missing check numbers and supplying amounts from the detailed list of checks issued, or
    (b) By determining the excess of the amount of checks outstanding at the beginning of the reconciliation period plus the amount of checks issued during the period over the amount of paid checks returned by the bank during the period (block method).

14. Does the reconciler compare each item in the credit (deposit) column in the bank statement with amounts deposited as shown by the cash records?

    If such an independent comparison is made in connection with the cash receipts, the procedure need not be repeated for purposes of the reconciliation.

15. Does the reconciler:
    (a) Determine totals of bank credits and debits by footing either deposits or withdrawals shown by the bank statements and deriving the other total?

(b) Reconcile:
    (1) Book receipts and bank credits?
    (2) Book disbursements and bank debits?

These procedures are designed to disclose any offsetting items of receipts and disbursements recorded in the cash records but not in the bank statements or vice versa, provided the verifications called for by Question 9(b) above or Question 16 below have been made. If, in addition, Questions 13 and 14 above are answered in the affirmative, the application of these procedures assures the discovery of offsetting items within receipts, disbursements, deposits, or withdrawals.

16. Does the reconciler verify the footing of the detailed book record of cash receipts and disbursements?

For payrolls this record would be the check column of the payroll.

When the answers to Questions 13, 14 and 15 above are "yes" this question is inapplicable and should not be answered.

17. Does the reconciler substantiate all reconciling items by reference to supporting documents?

18. Does the reconciler account for the sequence of the numbers of all checks recorded as issued in the period up to and including the date of the reconciliation?

This procedure requires examination of the numbers on paid checks, examination of the numbers on voided checks if pre-numbered, and reference to the list of outstanding checks, and tends to assure the discovery of unauthorized checks issued. When the sequence of the check numbers of checks issued is required to be recorded and accounted for [Question 8(b), above], this procedure also serves as a check on the execution of that responsibility.

DISBURSEMENTS IN CURRENCY:

19. Is the primary responsibility for the fund vested in one person?

20. Are surprise counts of the fund made by an internal auditor or other independent person?

21. At such times, is the composition of the fund submitted to a responsible official for review?

22. Are checks for reimbursement made out to the order of the custodian?

This practice fixes responsibility and precludes subsequent denial of accountability.

23. Are data supporting disbursements:
 (a) Executed in a manner designed to make alterations difficult?
 (b) Receipted by the recipient of the funds?

24. Are the duties of the custodian divorced from:
 (a) Authorizing reimbursement of the fund?
 (b) Duties relating to other funds, including cash receipts?
 (c) Authorization of, or recording or posting, accounting distribution of disbursements?

25. Are authorized but undisbursed amounts returned to and held by persons having the independence indicated in Question 24 above?

26. Payroll funds:
 (a) Does an independent paying agency:
  (1)(a) Stuff pay envelopes?
   (b) If the answer is "no," is currency covering the payroll required to be:
    (i) Counted before the envelopes are filled?
    (ii) Denominated, so that it will be consumed exactly when all envelopes are filled?
  (2)(a) Distribute pay envelopes?
   (b) If the answer is "no":
    (i) Are paymasters independent of:
     (a) Payroll preparation?
     (b) Other cash functions?
    (ii) Are payoffs made on a surprise basis by persons independent of:
     (a) Custodian of the payroll fund?
     (b) Paymasters' functions?
     (c) Authorization of payroll?
     (d) Preparation of payroll?
 (b) Do persons independent of the custodianship of payroll funds, paymasters' functions, the authorization of payrolls, and the preparation of payrolls:
  (1) Check the receipts against the payroll for:
   (a) Dates?
   (b) Employees' names?
   (c) Amounts?
  (2) Account for names for which no receipts have been obtained?
  (3) Investigate the authenticity of each unclaimed envelope?

MARKETABLE SECURITIES AND LONG-TERM INVESTMENTS

INTRODUCTION

Do investments include:

(a) Securities of affiliated or subsidiary companies?
(b) Marketable securities?
(c) Mortgage loans?
(d) Cash surrender value of life insurance?

Although the accounting controls applicable to all classes of marketable securities and long-term investments are substantially similar, it may be desirable to prepare a separate copy of this section for each class of these assets held.

PART I—INTERNAL ACCOUNTING CONTROL

1. Are purchases and sales of investments authorized by a designated official?

2. Are detailed records of investments maintained showing:
   (a) Serial numbers?
   (b) Names in which registered?
   (c) Amounts?
   (d) Collateral held?

3. Is a reconciliation of the detailed records of investments with the general ledger control:
   (a) Prepared periodically?
   (b) Reviewed by a responsible employee?

4. Are confirmations obtained periodically from:
   (a) The issuers of investments as to amounts?
   (b) Independent custodians and lending institutions as to investments held for account?
   (c) Borrowers as to details of collateral pledged?

   Confirmation of actively traded securities is usually impractical. The issuer of negotiable instruments can usually confirm only that instruments with specified serial numbers are outstanding in the indicated amounts.

5. Is approval of a responsible official required for:
   (a) Modification in terms of investments?
   (b) Write-off of worthless investments?
   (c) Release of collateral?
   (d) Receipt and delivery of securities?

6. Are investments that have been written off:
   (a) Under accounting control?
   (b) Reviewed periodically by a responsible official?
7. Is a designated employee responsible for the custody of:
   (a) Investments?
   (b) Collateral?
8. Is the custodian of securities:
   (a) Informed of partial reductions in face amounts of securities?
   (b) Required to endorse reductions on the securities?
   (c) Required to keep a record of securities deposited or withdrawn?
9. Are investments periodically:
   (a) Inspected?
   (b) Compared to the detailed records?
10. Is collateral periodically:
    (a) Inspected?
    (b) Compared to the detailed records?
11. Are investments and related collateral appraised or valued at market quotations for comparison with related book value:
    (a) Periodically?
    (b) By or under the supervision of a responsible employee?

PART II—INTERNAL CHECK

1. Is the custodian of investments and related collateral independent of:
   (a) General ledger functions?
   (b) The maintenance of detailed records of investments and collateral?
   (c) Cash functions?
2. Are the employees who post the detailed investment records independent of:
   (a) General ledger functions?
   (b) Cash functions?
   (c) Voucher functions?
3. Are reconciliations of the detailed records with the control account prepared or checked periodically by a person independent of:
   (a) General ledger functions?

(b) The maintenance of detailed records of investments and collateral?

(c) Custodianship of investments and collateral?

4. Do persons independent of those responsible for custodianship of investments or collateral, posting of investment records, preparing the detailed listing used in support of the cash book entry and independent of those who negotiate investments, confirm investments by:

   (a) Checking confirmation requests to the detailed records?

   (b) Controlling confirmation requests until they are mailed?

   (c) Receiving reported differences direct?

   (d) Investigating reported differences?

5. Do persons with the independence indicated in Question 4 above:

   (a) Inspect investments?

   (b) Inspect collateral?

   (c) Compare items inspected with the detailed records?

   (d) Obtain confirmation of investments pledged or held by independent custodians?

   (e) Periodically prepare or check the comparison of investments at appraised value or at market quotations against related book values?

   (f) Periodically compare the custodian's record of securities deposited and withdrawn with accounting records of purchases and sales?

6. Do persons with the independence indicated in Question 4 above:

   (a) Approve changes in terms of investments?

   (b) Approve write-off of worthless investments?

   (c) Endorse securities when required to effect transfer?

   (d) Approve release of collateral?

   (e) Authorize the receipt and delivery of securities?

7. Have registered securities been transferred to the name of the client or its nominee?

8. Is the custodian of securities informed of partial reductions in face amounts of securities by persons independent of those maintaining detailed records of securities?

9. Is it necessary for more than one person to be present to obtain physical access to the investments?

10. Do transactions by the custodians require the authorization of more than one responsible official?

SALES, OPERATING REVENUE, AND ACCOUNTS RECEIVABLE

INTRODUCTION

Does internal accounting control of sales and operating revenue begin with:

(a) Sales orders?

(b) Sales invoices?

(c) Shipping or delivery advices or completion reports?

(d) Sales books?

(e) Sales reports?

(f) Cash registers, collection books, etc.?

(g) Deferred credit accounts?

(h) Other (describe)?

Internal accounting control of sales and operating revenue may begin with control of sales orders, with a record of sales invoices or with a listing of shipping or delivery advices, completion reports, sales books, sales reports, or cash register totals. The method of doing business and the volume of transactions will indicate the timing and kind of accounting controls applied. Questions in this section are designed to disclose such controls when they are present. When internal accounting control is not based on control of these documents, "no" answers do not necessarily indicate weaknesses.

PART I—INTERNAL ACCOUNTING CONTROL

SALES ORDERS:

1. Are sales orders, including any firm sales commitments, listed in detail, showing customers' names and quantities?

    Orders received from customers on their order forms or copies of orders written by client's personnel, including orders received over the counter for later delivery, and entries in an order book, provide a means of controlling both the disposition of orders and the recording of sales by the use of detailed listings to check against subsequent steps in completing transactions. The detailed list may be a written tabulation, tabulating machine cards, or copies of order forms.

2. Are such orders under numerical control?

3. Is the listing or are copies of sales orders compared in detail with:

    (a) Shipping advices or completion reports?

(b) Invoices or other documents originating charges to customers?

This comparison discloses whether the sales orders have been suitably executed.

4. Are unfilled sales orders or commitments reviewed periodically for:
   (a) Delivery period?
   (b) Terms of commitment related to current inventory and selling prices?

   When goods or services, for which commitments have been made in sales orders or sales contracts, are to be delivered or completed over long periods of time or are significant in amount, uncompleted or undelivered sales orders or contracts should be reviewed to determine whether there is a commitment to deliver goods or services at prices below current or estimated future costs or in excess of capacity to fill orders.

5. Are sales orders and changes therein subject to approval before acceptance:
   (a) By a responsible person in the sales or order department?
   (b) By the credit department?

   These procedures are necessary to assure that orders are accepted only on terms and conditions acceptable to the company and for products or services offered by the company, and that sales are made only to approved credit risks.

SHIPPING OR DELIVERY ADVICES:

6. Are these advices listed in detail showing customers' names and quantities?

   This listing may consist of shipping department copies of sales orders, delivery receipts, completion reports, meter reading reports, entries in a shipping or delivery register, waybills, or manifests.

7. Are such advices under numerical control?

8. Is the listing compared in detail with:
   (a) Sales orders?
   (b) Sales invoices?

9. Are unmatched advices reviewed periodically?

   Internal accounting control over sales and accounts receivable requires that open (unmatched) shipping advices be investigated. The delivery of merchandise represented by an unmatched shipping advice may indicate an unrecorded receivable or sales invoice which has not been properly processed. A delay in matching shipping advices to invoices often results in unreliable inventory accounts.

Processing Sales Invoices or Other Media for Recording Sales or Operating Revenue:

10. Are sales invoices compared with:

    (a) Sales orders?

    (b) Shipping or delivery advices, or service or completion reports?

11. Are sales invoices or other media recording sales or operating revenue checked for:

    (a) Prices (rates) and other terms?

    (b) Extensions?

    (c) Discounts?

    (d) Footings?

    > *When the media are represented by invoices, prices and terms may be checked against approved sales orders or price lists. Counter sales slip prices may also be checked. Meter constants indicated in route books may be checked against meter listing cards. When the media consist of register or adding machine tapes or summarized sales reports, such tests may not be feasible. Frequently cash sales are recorded directly from cash receipts.*

12. Is there a procedure (if so, describe) for investigating and correcting differences disclosed by the comparison and checking indicated in Questions 10 and 11 above?

13. Are processed sales invoices or other media for recording sales or operating revenue listed in detail, showing name and amount?

    > *This listing may be made in a sales journal, a sales invoice register, a cash receipts record, or may consist of duplicate copies of invoices or sales slips.*

14. Are processed sales invoices or other media for recording sales or operating revenue under numerical control?

15. Do the detailed schedules from which periodic summary entries are prepared provide for the inclusion of all sales?

    > *When sales information flows from many sources, procedures should be followed that account for all sources. Such sources might include a number of departments, cash registers, sales books, route books, vending machines, and deferred credit accounts sales offices, and procedures might consist of accounting for prenumbered order forms or sales slips, accounting for*

units sold, accounting for elapsed numbers on numbering devices, comparing number of machines in use with fixed asset records, comparing number of reporting persons with an authorized list, and comparing amounts recorded with like amounts for similar prior periods.

16. Are the periodic totals of recorded sales reconciled with receipts from cash sales plus charges to accounts receivable and transfers from deferred credit accounts?

17. When the recording media show quantities, are the periodic totals reconciled with inventory changes, metered amounts, hours worked, or other unit data?

> *These reconciliations are necessary to assure the accurate recording of sales. When sales are recorded only in dollars, and perpetual inventory records are not maintained, comparison with inventory changes is often made through gross profit markups.*

18. If statistical data are maintained, are they reconciled with recorded sales?

> *Sales analyses, classifying sales by territory, product, or salesmen, may be maintained by the accounting, sales, or other department. These analyses may be used as an additional check on recorded sales.*

ACCOUNTS RECEIVABLE:

19. Are the following entries in the individual accounts posted from original media received direct from the department or person originating them?

    (a) Charges for invoices?
    (b) Credits for sales returns and allowances?
    (c) Credits for remittances?
    (d) Debits for items charged back by banks?
    (e) Other debits or credits such as properly approved journal entries?

> *When mail collections and posting of detail accounts are in large volume, many companies use one of the following as a posting medium:*
>
> *(1) Remittance advices, which may be prepared on receipt of the payment or may be a section of the original invoice returned by the customer with the payment.*
> *(2) Copy of the deposit slip, with details of source added.*
> *(3) Customers' checks.*

> *The direct flow of posting information to the accounts receivable department expedites the accurate posting of debits and credits to the individual accounts.*

20. Is a reconciliation of the total of customers' ledgers with the general ledger control:

   (a) Prepared periodically?

   (b) Reviewed by a responsible person?

   > *When branch offices maintain the details of accounts receivable, the reconciliation procedure should include reconcilement of detailed accounts to branch controls as well as reconcilement of branch controls to general ledger controls.*

21. Are statements of accounts regularly sent to *all* customers?

   > *Periodic statements provide opportunities for debtors to report differences.*
   >
   > *If it is not the practice to send statements regularly to all customers, objectives might be partially attained by other means, for example:*
   >
   > *(a) Statements might be mailed only to customers with delinquent balances.*
   >
   > *(b) A delinquent notice to an instalment or budget account customer when payments are not received as due is a form of statement to the customer.*
   >
   > *(c) Bills from public utilities and other companies furnishing services may serve the dual purpose of invoice and statement.*

22. Are credit memoranda for returned merchandise, price adjustments, special discounts, and damage claims:

   (a) Under numerical control?

   (b) Issued promptly on receipt of proper authorization?

   (c) Recorded promptly when issued?

   (d) Approved by a responsible person?

   > *Undue delay in the recording of these credits may result in a substantial overstatement of accounts receivable.*

23. Are aging schedules:

   (a) Prepared periodically?

   (b) Reviewed by a responsible person?

   > *The review should include consideration of the amount of allowance to be provided for doubtful accounts.*

24. Is approval of a responsible person required for:

   (a) Payment of customer credit balances?

    (b) Write-off of uncollectible amounts?

25. Are accounts receivable that have been written off:
    (a) Under accounting control?
    (b) Reviewed periodically by an informed person?

    Frequently these accounts are transferred to a bad debt ledger under memorandum control.

PART II—INTERNAL CHECK

SALES ORDERS:

1. Is the detailed listing of sales orders, including any sales commitments, prepared by persons independent of:
    (a) Shipping or delivery functions?
    (b) Billing functions?
    (c) Cash receipts functions?

    If the original listing is prepared by persons independent of the above functions, the possibility of excluding delivered, shipped, or completed items from the list will be minimized. The listing may be represented by copies of the orders. The billing function referred to in (b) is that of originating charges to customers through invoices or other documents.

2. Do persons independent of those who prepare sales orders:
    (a) Insert order numbers?
    (b) Account for the sequence of numbers?

    These procedures tend to prevent the issuance of unauthorized sales orders that, through collusion, might be utilized to effect unauthorized deliveries of goods. Order numbers may be inserted by the printer or by other independent persons.

3. Is the list of orders compared with shipping advices or completion reports and invoices or other documents originating charges to customers by persons independent of:
    (a) Shipping or delivery of goods or services to customers?
    (b) Billing functions?
    (c) Cash receipts functions?

    The billing function referred to in (b) is that of originating charges to customers through invoices or other documents.

4. Are sales personnel independent of:
    (a) Cash receipts functions?

(b) Shipping or delivery functions?

(c) Billing functions?

> *The separation of the sales function from receipt of cash, charges to customers, and delivery of goods or performance of services is the most effective means of minimizing opportunities for fraud.*

5. Are sales orders approved for propriety and credit risk by persons independent of:

   (a) Persons making the sales?

   (b) Company personnel who prepare orders?

6. Are the following classes of sales cleared and recorded in the same way as sales to customers:

   (a) Sales to employees?

   (b) Scrap and waste sales?

   (c) Sales of equipment?

   > *While these sales may be only intermittent and rarely large in dollar amount, their susceptibility to manipulation requires that they be subjected to the same procedures as sales to customers.*

SHIPPING OR DELIVERY ADVICES OR COMPLETION REPORTS:

7. Is the detailed listing of shipping or delivery advices prepared by persons independent of:

   (a) Sales functions?

   (b) Processing of sales invoices or other media for recording sales or operating revenue?

8. Do persons independent of persons who prepare shipping or delivery advices:

   (a) Insert shipping or delivery report numbers?

   (b) Account for sequence of numbers?

9. Is the comparison of the list of shipping or delivery advices, or retained copies of shipping or delivery advices, with sales orders and sales invoices made by persons independent of:

   (a) Sales functions?

   (b) Shipping or delivery functions?

10. Is shipping or delivery personnel independent of:

    (a) Processing of sales invoices or other media for recording sales or operating revenue?

    (b) Cash receipts functions?

    (c) Sales functions?

PROCESSING SALES INVOICES OR OTHER MEDIA FOR RECORDING SALES OR
OPERATING REVENUE:

11. Are sales invoices or other media for recording sales or operating
     revenue compared with sales orders and shipping or delivery ad-
     vices by persons independent of:

     (a) Sales functions?
     (b) Shipping or delivery functions?

12. Are the investigation and correction of differences disclosed by the
     comparison indicated in Question 11 above carried out by persons
     independent of:

     (a) Sales functions?
     (b) Shipping or delivery functions?
     (c) Processing of sales invoices or other media for recording sales
          or operating revenue?

13. When it is possible to check prices and other terms and mathematics
     in media for recording sales, is this checking done by persons inde-
     pendent of the persons who prepared the media?

14. Is the detailed listing of processed sales invoices or other media for
     recording sales or operating revenue prepared by persons inde-
     pendent of:

     (a) Sales functions?
     (b) Shipping or delivery functions?
     (c) Cash receipts functions?
     (d) Posting of general ledger accounts?

15. When media for recording sales are summarized after prices and
     other terms and mathematics have been checked, is the checking
     done by persons independent of:

     (a) Cash receipts functions?
     (b) Accounts receivable functions?

          *When sales are prelisted (e.g., in sales registers or a summary
          of sales tickets) or amounts of sales invoices are listed before
          invoice data are checked, the checking operation may be per-
          formed by anyone other than the person who made the list.
          When sales are not prelisted, the independence noted above will
          minimize the opportunities for fraud.*

16. Are the summary sales entries and underlying detailed schedules
     checked periodically by persons independent of:

     (a) Sales functions?
     (b) Cash receipts functions?
     (c) Accounts receivable functions?

17. Are total sales reconciled with receipts from cash sales plus charges to accounts receivable and transfers from deferred credit accounts by persons independent of:
    (a) Sales functions?
    (b) Processing of sales invoices or other media for recording sales or operating revenue?
    (c) Cash receipts functions?

18. When the detailed posting media show quantities, are the periodic summarizations of quantities reconciled with inventory changes, metered amounts or hours worked, by persons independent of:
    (a) Sales functions?
    (b) Perpetual inventory, meter record, or record of hours worked functions?
    (c) Physical inventory functions?

19. Are recorded sales reconciled with sales statistical data by persons independent of:
    (a) Sales functions?
    (b) Processing of sales invoices or other media for recording sales or operating revenue?

20. Is the recording of sales under mechanical or numerical control?
    Internal check of the recording of sales is enhanced if the recording media are under mechanical control (locked cash registers or autographic sales registers) or under numerical control (prenumbered sales invoices or tickets). Independent persons controlling the keys should read cash registers, and independent persons should account for invoice or ticket numbers.

21. Are the employees who post the individual accounts independent of:
    (a) Posting general ledger control?
    (b) Cash functions?

22. Are the reconciliations of the total of individual accounts with the control account prepared or checked periodically by a person independent of the accounts receivable personnel and those who post general ledger controls?
    This practice facilitates the disclosure of irregularities that might otherwise go undetected.

23. Do persons independent of accounts receivable personnel, those who prepare the detailed listing of receipts in support of the cash book entry, and credit department personnel periodically:
    (a) Check customers' statements to accounts?
    (b) Attach request that statement be examined and differences, if any, be reported to the independent personnel?

    (c) Control statements until they are mailed?

    (d) Receive reported differences direct?

    (e) Investigate reported differences?

24. Do only persons with the independence indicated in Question 23 above:

    (a) Number credit memoranda?

    (b) Account for credit memorandum numbers?

    (c) Approve credit memoranda for returned merchandise, special discounts, and damage claims?

    (d) Approve the payment of customer credit balances?

    (e) Approve the write-off of uncollectible accounts?

25. Do persons with the independence indicated in Question 23 above periodically prepare or check aging schedules?

26. Do persons independent of cash receipts functions:

    (a) Maintain records for written-off accounts receivable?

    (b) Periodically review written-off accounts receivable?

NOTES RECEIVABLE

INTRODUCTION

Notes receivable are formal evidence of amounts due from debtors and may be acquired as the result of sales of goods or services, the lending of money to customers, employees, or others, or by purchase. Notes receivable are ordinarily in negotiable form, susceptible of sale or pledge; they may be supported by pledge of collateral. Accounting controls applicable to the various types of notes receivable are substantially similar.

Do notes receivable include notes from:

    (a) Customers?

    (b) Officers and employees?

    (c) Others (specify)?

PART I—INTERNAL ACCOUNTING CONTROL

1. Are notes receivable and their renewals approved prior to acceptance by a responsible designated employee?

2. Are detailed records of notes receivable maintained showing:

    (a) Identification?

    (b) Amount?

    (c) Maturity date?

    (d) Collateral, if any?

The detailed records might be a file of tabulating cards, individual ledger cards, or a written listing, depending on the volume of notes.

3. Is a reconciliation of the total of individual notes with the general ledger control:
    (a) Prepared periodically?
    (b) Reviewed by a responsible employee?

4. Are makers of notes periodically requested to confirm:
    (a) Unpaid balances?
    (b) Maturity dates?
    (c) Collateral pledged?

5. Is a record of discounted notes receivable kept to indicate the contingent liability?

6. Are notes pledged or held for account by independent custodians confirmed periodically?

7. Is a schedule of delinquent notes receivable:
    (a) Prepared periodically?
    (b) Reviewed by a responsible employee?

8. Is approval of a responsible official required for:
    (a) Modification in terms of notes receivable?
    (b) Write-off of uncollectible amounts?

9. Are notes receivable which have been written off:
    (a) Under accounting control?
    (b) Reviewed periodically by a responsible official?

10. Is a designated employee responsible for the custody of:
    (a) Notes receivable?
    (b) Related collateral?

11. Is the custodian of notes receivable:
    (a) Informed of partial reductions in face amounts?
    (b) Required to endorse reductions on the notes?

12. Are notes receivable periodically:
    (a) Inspected?
    (b) Compared with the detailed records?

13. Is collateral held periodically:
    (a) Inspected?
    (b) Compared with the detailed records?
    (c) Evaluated for comparison with the related amount receivable?
    The pledgee has a responsibility for the custody of collateral. Periodic inspection and comparison with the book records

should bring to light errors and omissions. The value of collateral is often a significant factor in determining the reserve for uncollectible amounts.

14. Is collateral released to a debtor only on the approval of a designated official?

> *A clearly defined procedure for the control of collateral is necessary to protect the lender from losses such as those arising from the premature release of collateral or claims by borrowers because of loss or damage to collateral.*

PART II—INTERNAL CHECK

1. Is the custodian of notes receivable and related collateral independent of:
   (a) General ledger functions?
   (b) Keeping detailed notes receivable and collateral records?
   (c) Cash functions?

2. Are the persons who post the detailed notes receivable records independent of:
   (a) General ledger functions?
   (b) Cash functions?
   (c) Voucher functions?

3. Are reconciliations of the total of individual amounts in the detailed records with the control account prepared or checked periodically by a person independent of:
   (a) General ledger functions?
   (b) Keeping detailed records of notes receivable and collateral?
   (c) Custodianship of notes receivable and collateral?

4. Do persons independent of those responsible for custodianship of notes receivable and collateral, posting notes receivable records, preparing the detailed listing in support of the cash book entry, and credit department personnel, confirm accounts by:
   (a) Checking confirmation requests to the detailed record?
   (b) Controlling confirmation requests until they are mailed?
   (c) Receiving reported differences direct?
   (d) Investigating reported differences?

5. Do persons with the independence indicated in Question 4 above:
   (a) Inspect:
       (1) Notes receivable?
       (2) Collateral?

(b) Compare items inspected with the:
  (1) Detailed records of notes receivable?
  (2) Detailed records of collateral?
(c) Obtain confirmation of notes receivable pledged or held by independent custodians?
(d) Periodically prepare or check:
  (1) Listing of delinquent notes?
  (2) Evaluation of collateral?

6. Do only persons with the independence indicated in Question 4 above:
  (a) Approve changes in terms of notes receivable?
  (b) Authorize release of collateral?
  (c) Approve write-off of uncollectible amounts?

7. Is the custodian of notes receivable informed of partial reductions in face amounts of notes receivable by persons independent of those maintaining detailed records of notes receivable?

8. Is it necessary for more than one person to be present to obtain physical access to the notes receivable and collateral?

INVENTORIES

INTRODUCTION

1. Do inventories include:
  (a) Raw materials?
  (b) Purchased parts?
  (c) Purchased finished stock?
  (d) Supplies?
  (e) Work in process?
  (f) Manufactured finished stock?

2. Is accounting for inventories based on:
  (a) Perpetual inventory records?
  (b) Periodic physical inventories only?
  (c) Apportionment of accumulated long-term contract costs?

PART I—INTERNAL ACCOUNTING CONTROL

PHYSICAL INVENTORIES:

1. Are all classes of inventory physically inventoried at least once a year?

2. Are physical inventory procedures:
  (a) Determined by a responsible employee?
  (b) Supervised by a responsible employee?

3. Do written instructions for physical inventories include instructions relating to the following:
    (a) Good physical arrangement of stock?
    (b) Identification and description of stock by persons familiar with it?
    (c) Methods of determining quantities?
    (d) Verification of individual counts?
    (e) Identification to be left on stock to indicate items counted?
    (f) Control of inventory tags or sheets?
    (g) Cutoff of receipts and deliveries?
    (h) Segregation and description of slow-moving, obsolete, and damaged items?
    (i) Merchandise on hand not the property of the client?

4. Are the original physical inventory records, such as tags, cards, and tally sheets, under numerical control?

5. Are the following clerical operations of the physical inventory summarization checked:
    (a) Summarization of quantities?
    (b) Unit conversions?
    (c) Prices used?
    (d) Extensions?
    (e) Additions?

6. Is there written approval by a responsible employee of all adjustments to inventory control accounts?

7. Have procedures been provided for periodic reporting by responsible employees of the following:
    (a) Slow-moving items?
    (b) Obsolete items?
    (c) Overstocks?
    (d) Damaged items?

8. Do responsible employees review prices used in stating inventory on hand at the close of an accounting period?

9. Is merchandise on hand that is not the property of the client, such as customers' merchandise and consignments-in, physically segregated or properly identified?

10. Do responsible company personnel periodically confirm the following classes of inventory:
    (a) Consignments-in?
    (b) Inventory in the hands of processors and suppliers?
    (c) Inventory in warehouses?
    (d) Returnable containers in hands of customers?

11. Does control over the accumulation of scrap include procedures for determining and recording quantities available for sale?

PERPETUAL INVENTORY RECORDS:

12. Are detailed perpetual inventory records maintained for:
    - (a) Raw materials:
        - (1) Quantities?
        - (2) Dollar amounts?
    - (b) Purchased parts:
        - (1) Quantities?
        - (2) Dollar amounts?
    - (c) Supplies:
        - (1) Quantities?
        - (2) Dollar amounts?
    - (d) Work in process:
        - (1) Quantities?
        - (2) Dollar amounts?
    - (e) Finished stock:
        - (1) Quantities?
        - (2) Dollar amounts?
    - (f) Consignments-out:
        - (1) Quantities?
        - (2) Dollar amounts?
    - (g) Inventory in hands of suppliers and processors:
        - (1) Quantities?
        - (2) Dollar amounts?
    - (h) Inventory in warehouses:
        - (1) Quantities?
        - (2) Dollar amounts?
    - (i) Consignments-in:
        - (1) Quantities?
        - (2) Dollar amounts?
    - (j) Returnable containers in hands of customers:
        - (1) Quantities?
        - (2) Dollar amounts?
    - (k) Items charged off but physically on hand, such as expense supplies, small tools, and obsolete stock?

13. Are perpetual inventory records adjusted to physical inventory quantities at least once a year?

14. Are perpetual inventory dollar amounts computed and compared periodically with general ledger control accounts?

15. Is there a procedure for investigating and correcting significant differences between:

    (a) Physical and perpetual inventory quantities?

    (b) Dollar amounts in perpetual inventory records and the controlling accounts?

16. Does a responsible employee:

    (a) Review the reconciliations referred to in Questions 13 and 14 above?

    (b) Approve in writing adjustments indicated by the procedure called for in Question 15 above?

RECEIPT OF INVENTORIES:

17. Does receiving personnel:

    (a) Verify quantity and quality of material?

    (b) Prepare formal receiving reports?

18. Are names of vendors, descriptions of materials, and quantities listed in detail?

> *The listing may be in the form of a materials received book, a copy of the receiving report or purchase order, or a copy of a receipt issued. When necessary, receiving reports should be supplemented by inspection reports.*

19. Are receiving reports under numerical control?

COST OF PROCESSING OR MANUFACTURING:

20. Does the cost system provide for obtaining unit or job order costs for:

    (a) Work in process?

    (b) Finished goods?

21. Is the cost system tied in with the general ledger?

22. Are overhead rates:

    (a) Reviewed periodically by designated employees?

    (b) Adjusted to reflect current experience?

23. Are separate control accounts maintained for:

    (a) Inventory costs applicable to work in process?

    (b) Inventory costs applicable to finished goods?

    (c) Manufacturing expenses (overhead)?

    (d) Manufacturing expenses absorbed in production?

    (e) Variance accounts (when standard costs are used) for:

        (1) Raw materials?

        (2) Direct labor?

        (3) Overhead?

(f) Physical and price adjustments?

(g) Provision for, or write-off of, obsolete or slow-moving inventories?

(h) Provision for interdepartment, interplant, or interdivision profit in inventory?

(i) Direct charges to cost of goods sold, such as engineering expense, development and experimental costs, and royalties?

Such accounting controls provide desirable segregation of the various elements of cost of processing or manufacturing.

24. If a standard cost system is in effect:

(a) Are standards revised currently to reflect changes in production costs?

(b) Are reports prepared that explain to management differences between standard and actual costs?

Even when standard costs are not tied in with the general ledger, comparisons may be made with predetermined unit standards.

USAGE OF INVENTORIES:

Quantities consumed or capitalized:

25. Are approved requisitions or equivalent documents required for all materials issued from stockrooms?

26. Are material requisitions signed by persons to whom the material is issued?

27. Are interdepartmental movements of materials evidenced by work orders, requisitions, or reports?

28. Are quantities used summarized periodically?

These procedures are important safeguards against the unauthorized delivery of materials and assist in the accurate recording and distribution of their cost.

Quantities shipped or delivered to customers:

29. Are shipments authorized by shipping advices, copies of sales orders, or material releases, such as stock requisitions and packing slips?

30. Are shipping advice forms under numerical control?

31. Are acknowledgments of receipt obtained from the carrier or other recipient?

32. Are copies of shipping advices filed in the shipping department in chronological order?

This information assists in establishing the inventory cutoff at physical inventory dates and in tracing shipments.

33. Are established shipping procedures followed for the delivery of:
    (a) Materials returned to suppliers?
    (b) Sales to employees?
    (c) Scrap and waste sales?
    (d) Sales of equipment?
    (e) No-charge shipments?

34. Are quantities shipped summarized periodically?

35. Are quantities transferred from finished goods inventories to cost of sales correlated or reconciled periodically with quantities charged to customers?

> *This comparison provides evidence that inventories have been reduced for all units sold.*

PRICING OF INVENTORY USAGE (CONSUMED OR SHIPPED):

36. Is the total dollar amount of inventory consumed or shipped obtained by:
    (a) Multiplying quantities by unit prices?
    (b) Dollar inventory difference (opening inventory plus purchases and manufacturing cost, if any, less closing inventory)?
    (c) Percentage allocations of accumulated long-term contract costs?

> *When perpetual inventory records are maintained only in quantities or when dollar amount perpetual inventory records are not tied in with general ledger accounts, unit prices may be based on prices of units in the opening physical inventory adjusted to estimated current cost.*
>
> *Allocations of long-term contract costs may be based on engineers' estimates of percentage of completion or on partial delivery of product.*

37. If a single ledger account is maintained for cost of goods sold:
    (a) Is an analysis of the details comprising the account maintained?
    (b) Is this analysis tied in with the changes in the finished goods inventory account?

38. Is gross profit on sales determinable by:
    (a) Product?
    (b) Selling department?

39. Is a breakdown by products maintained for the following elements of cost:
    (a) Raw materials (purchases)?
    (b) Direct labor?
    (c) Manufacturing expenses (overhead)?

The determination of gross profit by products or department requires product or departmental breakdowns of inventories, purchases, and sales. When cost of goods sold is determined under the retail inventory method, complete statistical data of mark-ons and markdowns should be maintained.

Computations and reviews of gross profits and of the relationship of elements of cost to sales are desirable and provide a measure of control when perpetual inventory records are maintained for quantities only or when cost of goods sold is determined by dollar difference in inventories.

PART II—INTERNAL CHECK

PHYSICAL INVENTORIES:

1. Do persons independent of custodianship of inventory and maintenance of the perpetual inventory records:

    (a) Make physical counts of inventories?
    (b) Check physical counts of inventories?
    (c) Determine physical inventory procedures?
    (d) Supervise the taking of physical inventories?
    (e) Prepare written instructions for physical inventory taking?
    (f) Maintain numerical control over original physical inventory records?
    (g) Approve all adjustments to inventory and controlling accounts?
    (h) Confirm inventory quantities held by outsiders if not counted?

PERPETUAL INVENTORY RECORDS:

2. Do persons independent of the custodianship of physical inventories maintain perpetual inventory records?

3. Do persons independent of the custodianship of inventory and the maintenance of the perpetual inventory records:

    (a) Compare perpetual inventory records with physical inventory counts?
    (b) Compute and compare physical inventory dollar amounts with general ledger control accounts?
    (c) Investigate and correct significant differences between:
        (1) Physical and perpetual inventories?
        (2) Perpetual inventory records and controlling accounts?
    (d) Approve all adjustments to perpetual inventory records and related general ledger control accounts?

RECEIPT OF INVENTORIES:

4. Are receiving reports:
   (a) Prenumbered by the printer?
   (b) Accounted for by persons independent of the:
       (1) Custodianship of inventory?
       (2) Maintenance of perpetual inventory records?

USAGE OF INVENTORIES:

5. Are shipping advices:
   (a) Prenumbered by the printer?
   (b) Accounted for by persons independent of the:
       (1) Custodianship of inventory?
       (2) Maintenance of perpetual inventory records?
6. Are quantities transferred from finished goods inventories to cost of sales correlated or reconciled periodically with quantities charged to customers by persons independent of:
   (a) The custodianship of physical inventories?
   (b) The maintenance of perpetual inventory records?
   (c) Accounts receivable functions?

PROPERTY, PLANT, AND EQUIPMENT, AND MAINTENANCE

INTRODUCTION

This section is intended to cover all tangible assets that (1) are to be used in the conduct of business, (2) are not intended to be sold in the ordinary course of business, and (3) have a service life in excess of one year. It also refers to equipment and facilities used by the client but owned by others and to maintenance expenditures that often are subjected to the same accounting controls.

PART I—INTERNAL ACCOUNTING CONTROL

1. Are detailed property records maintained in support of the general ledger control account?
2. Are such records balanced at least annually with the general ledger control account?
3. Are formal requests for authority to disburse funds required for:
   (a) Additions to or replacement of fixed assets?
   (b) Disposal of fixed assets?

      (c) Maintenance or repair of fixed assets?

      (d) Expenditures in excess of amounts originally approved?

4. Does the request for authority to disburse funds for the above purposes include:

      (a) Reason for the expenditure?

      (b) Estimated cost?

      (c) Detail plant or expense accounts to be charged or credited?

      (d) Description, proposed disposition, and estimated original cost of plant displaced?

5. Is formal approval of such request required by:

      (a) Board of Directors?

      (b) Other designated person?

6. Are actual expenditures approved by:

      (a) Board of Directors?

      (b) Other designated person?

7. Does the company have written statement of principles to be followed in:

      (a) Distinguishing between fixed asset additions, renewals, replacements, and maintenance expenditures?

      (b) Providing for depreciation and amortization of assets acquired and disposing of accumulated allowances for assets retired or otherwise disposed of?

8. For costs of work covered by requisitions:

      (a) Are such costs accumulated and recorded by work order number?

      (b) Are such work orders numerically controlled?

      (c) Are actual completed costs:

           (1) Compared periodically with original estimates?

           (2) Reviewed by a designated employee?

9. Are expenditures for construction or installation utilizing client's employees controlled by the same procedures as those controlling operating expenditures through payrolls and vouchers?

      These expenditures should be subject to procedures prescribed for payrolls and voucher payments to insure adequate internal accounting control over these items.

10. Are inventories of property that is reasonably subject to actual count:

      (a) Taken periodically?

      (b) Compared with detailed plant records?

11. For property not inventoried:

      (a) Are accounting records of units compared periodically with similar data kept independently such as engineering records and blueprints?

(b) Are engineering records and blueprints periodically checked against physical plant?

12. Are adjustments to plant records to agree with physical inventories and comparisons with engineering records:

(a) Made promptly?

(b) Approved by a responsible official?

13. Are detailed records maintained for:

(a) Assets fully depreciated?

(b) Equipment and facilities used by client but owned by others?

14. Are such items (Question 13) periodically inventoried and compared to the detailed records?

15. Are expenditures for equipment and facilities for the account of others, such as the U. S. Government:

(a) Reviewed by a responsible employee for compliance with provisions of the contract with the ultimate purchaser?

(b) Subject to the accounting controls outlined in Question 7?

16. Are assets leased or loaned to others physically inspected periodically?

PREPAID EXPENSES AND DEFERRED CHARGES

INTRODUCTION

Prepaid expenses and deferred charges may include insurance, taxes, advertising, supplies, salaries, commissions, rent, debt discount, and experimental and development expenses.

PART I—INTERNAL ACCOUNTING CONTROL

1. Does the company maintain appropriate subsidiary records, controlled by general ledger accounts, for prepaid expenses and deferred charges?

Appropriate subsidiary records may include an insurance register, tax register or due date file, supplies inventory records, and experimental and development expense cost sheets.

2. Are subsidiary records balanced periodically with general ledger controls?

3. Are write-offs (periodic charges to expenses) reviewed and approved by a responsible person?

4. Are procedures established for periodic review of prepaid expenses and deferred charges to determine that they are proper charges to future accounting periods?

5. Are major supplies inventories subject to the same internal accounting control and internal check as regular inventory items?

INTANGIBLE ASSETS

INTRODUCTION

Intangible assets most frequently encountered are patents, copyrights, trade-marks, brand and trade names, franchises, royalty and license agreements, lists of customers, and goodwill.

PART I—INTERNAL ACCOUNTING CONTROL

1. Are general ledger accounts for intangibles supported by detailed records?

2. If the intangibles are amortizable, do the detailed records indicate:
   (a) The basis for amortization?
   (b) The cost and accumulated amortization?

3. Are the detailed records balanced periodically with the general ledger control accounts?

4. Do the detailed records include intangibles that have a zero book value —those which are fully amortized or were charged to expense on acquisition?

5. Are schedules of intangible assets, indicating their cost and basis of amortization:
   (a) Prepared periodically?
   (b) Reviewed by a responsible official?

NOTES PAYABLE AND LONG-TERM LIABILITIES

INTRODUCTION

Among the items comprising notes payable and long-term liabilities are notes, acceptances, debentures, bonds, mortgages, receivers' certificates, and equipment trust certificates. When such liabilities are incurred, signed documents are usually issued describing the terms and conditions under which the liabilities will be liquidated.

1. Does the company have outstanding bonds, notes, debentures, or other written evidences of indebtedness?

2. If so, does it employ an independent:
   (a) Trustee?
   (b) Transfer agent?
   (c) Interest paying agent?

PART I—INTERNAL ACCOUNTING CONTROL

1. Is the borrowing of funds formally authorized by the Board of Directors or other management group, such as Board of Trustees or Executive Committee?

   Authority for the borrowing of funds may also be specified in the charter, by-laws, or partnership agreement.

2. Do the authorizations specify:
   (a) The officers empowered to negotiate loans?
   (b) The maximum commitments such officers may make?
   (c) Collateral which may be pledged to secure loans?
   (d) That, when required, permission has been obtained from regulatory commissions having jurisdiction?

3. Bonds, notes, or other evidences of indebtedness:
   (a) Are they executed in the corporate name of the company?
   (b) Are they prenumbered?
   (c) If prenumbered, are the numbers accounted for?
   (d) Are unsigned instruments in the custody of a responsible employee or a transfer agent?

4. Is a copy of the borrowing instrument or a digest of its terms sent directly to the accounting department by the person executing the borrowing?

5. Are the terms of borrowing compared with the authorizations (Question 2)?

6. Are detailed records maintained of notes payable and long-term liabilities?

7. Are reconciliations of the detailed records with general ledger control accounts:
   (a) Made periodically?
   (b) Reviewed by a responsible official?

8. When an independent transfer agent or registrar is employed, are reports:
   (a) Received periodically from the transfer agent?
   (b) Received periodically from the registrar?
   (c) When received, reconciled with general ledger control accounts?

PART II—INTERNAL CHECK

1. When borrowings are not formally authorized by the Board of Directors or other management group, does company procedure require the signatures of two officials to validate the borrowing instrument?
2. If two signatures are required, are the signers independent of each other?
3. Are persons who make entries in the detailed records independent of cash functions?
4. Are reconciliations of the detailed records, or of reports of a transfer agent or registrar, with general ledger controls checked periodically by persons other than those who:
   (a) Post the general ledger control accounts?
   (b) Maintain the detailed records?
5. Are paid bonds and notes:
   (a) Returned to an employee other than the one who maintains the detailed records?
   (b) Examined for endorsements?
   (c) Effectively canceled?
   (d) Retained in the company files?
6. Are unissued bonds and notes in the custody of persons independent of:
   (a) Cash functions?
   (b) General ledger functions?
   (c) The maintenance of detailed records of bonds and notes?
7. Do persons with the independence listed in Question 6 above record and account for sequence of numbers of bonds and notes?

PURCHASES AND ACCOUNTS PAYABLE

INTRODUCTION

Does internal accounting control of purchases begin with:
   (a) Purchase orders?
   (b) Receiving reports?

(c) Vendors' invoices that are:
  (1) Recorded at time of receipt of the invoice?
  (2) Recorded at time of vouchering or payment?

Internal accounting control of purchases of goods and services may begin with control over purchase orders or a book record of purchases made, with a record of receipt of goods or services (receiving reports), with a record of invoices received, or with the entry of audited vouchers in a voucher register. The method of doing business and the volume of transactions will indicate the point at which accounting controls should be applied. Questions in this section are designed to disclose such controls when they are present. When internal accounting control is not based on control of these documents or recording, "no" answers do not necessarily indicate weaknesses.

Since internal accounting control of the recording of liabilities arising from the purchases of services of employees (payrolls), as contrasted with outside services, differs materially from that recited above, a separate part of this section is devoted to that subject.

PART I—INTERNAL ACCOUNTING CONTROL

PURCHASE ORDERS:
  1. Are purchase orders, including any firm commitments, listed in detail showing vendors' names, quantities, and prices?

> *Purchase requisitions, retained copies of purchase orders, or listings in purchase books or elsewhere provide a means of controlling both the disposition of purchase orders and the recording of purchases by the use of detailed listings to check against subsequent steps in completing transactions.*

  2. Are such orders under numerical control?
  3. Is the listing or are the retained copies of purchase orders compared in detail with:
  (a) Receiving or completion reports?
  (b) Vendors' invoices or other documents originating credits to vendors?

> *This comparison discloses whether the purchase orders have been suitably executed.*

  4. Are open purchase orders or commitments reviewed periodically for:
  (a) Delivery period?
  (b) Terms of commitments related to current needs and prices?

> *When goods or services, for which commitments have been made in contracts or purchase orders, are to be received over*

long periods of time or are significant in amount, open orders or commitments should be reviewed to determine whether there is a commitment to receive goods or services at prices in excess of current or estimated future market, or in excess of requirements.

5. Are purchase orders and changes therein subject to approval, before commitments are made, by a responsible official?

> *This procedure is necessary to assure that commitments are made only upon terms and conditions acceptable to the company and for products and services useful to the company, and that purchases are made only from vendors approved by the company.*

RECEIVING REPORTS:

6. Are receiving reports listed in detail, showing vendors' names and quantities?

> *This listing may consist of a materials received book, copies of receiving reports or purchase orders, or copies of receipts issued. When necessary, receiving reports should be supplemented by inspection reports.*

7. Are such reports under numerical control?

8. Is the listing compared in detail with:

    (a) Purchase orders?

    (b) Vendors' invoices or other documents originating credits to vendors?

9. Are unmatched receiving reports reviewed periodically?

> *Internal accounting control over accounts payable requires that open (unmatched) receiving reports be investigated. The receipt of merchandise represented by an unmatched receiving report may indicate an unrecorded liability or the payment of an invoice which has not been properly processed. A delay in matching receiving reports to invoices often results in unreliable inventory accounts.*

VENDORS' INVOICES:

10. Are all copies of invoices received, except the original, stamped to indicate clearly that they are duplicates?

11. On receipt of vendors' invoices is a detailed listing made showing:

    (a) Vendor's name?

    (b) Amount of invoice?

    (c) Disposition of invoice?

Control over accounts payable may be established at the time vendors' invoices are received by recording invoices in a register or by maintaining an invoice file. Frequently the amounts of such invoices are entered in the accounts as "Unaudited Vouchers."

12. Are such invoices under numerical control?

13. Are unprocessed invoices reviewed periodically?

PROCESSING INVOICES AND SUBSTITUTE DOCUMENTS:

14. Is the information in the invoice or substitute document compared with:

    (a) The purchase order or other authorizing medium?

    (b) The receiving report or other evidence of receipt?

    Certain purchases of goods or services, such as rents, royalties, retainers for professional or other services, payrolls, and fund reimbursements, may not involve preparation of formal purchase orders or receiving reports or receipt of invoices. When these documents are absent, the liability should be substantiated through other documents, such as authorizations to pay or a report of purchases made, or through authorized signatures. When an invoice is not received, substitute documents, such as requests for fund reimbursement or for issuance of checks, tax returns, or payrolls, are usually prepared internally.

15. Are invoices or substitute documents checked mathematically for:

    (a) Extensions?

    (b) Discounts?

    (c) Footings?

16. Is a designated employee assigned the responsibility for investigating and correcting differences disclosed by the comparison and checking indicated in Questions 14 and 15 above?

17. Do invoices, substitute documents, or appropriate attachments indicate that the following work has been performed:

    (a) Comparison with purchase orders?

    (b) Comparison with receiving reports?

    (c) Verification of extensions, discounts, and footings?

    (d) Investigation and correction of differences?

18. Does a responsible person indicate on the invoice, substitute document, or attachments his:

    (a) Approval of the accounting distribution of invoices?

    (b) Approval of the invoices for payment?

19. Are debit memoranda for returned merchandise:
    (a) Under numerical control?
    (b) Issued promptly on receipt of proper authorization?
    (c) Recorded promptly when issued?
    (d) Approved by a responsible person?

    Undue delay in the recording of these debits may result in a substantial overstatement of accounts payable or overpayments to vendors.

20. Are processed invoices (vouchers) listed in detail showing names and amounts?

    This listing may be made in a purchase journal, a voucher register, or in a cash disbursement record.

21. Are processed invoices (vouchers) under numerical control?

22. Is the total of unpaid items in the voucher register reconciled periodically with the general ledger accounts payable control?

    The unpaid items may be indicated in various ways; frequently, paid items are identified by insertion of dates of payment or check numbers.

23. Does a responsible employee approve adjustments indicated by comparison of monthly statements with recorded liabilities or by correspondence from vendors?

PAYROLLS:

The preparation of payrolls involves the gathering of information concerning (a) employees to be paid, (b) their rates of pay, (c) the time, production, or sales they are to be paid for, (d) deductions to be made, and (e) account classifications. It also involves the use of this information in calculations of gross earnings, deductions, and net pay, and of related amounts to be recorded in the accounts.

Are payrolls:
  (a) Prepared on the basis of:
      (1) Hours worked?
      (2) Piecework?
      (3) Commissions on sales?
      (4) Fixed salaries?
      (5) Overtime?
  (b) Disbursed:
      (1) By check?
      (2) In currency?

FOR THE INVESTIGATION OF INTERNAL ACCOUNTING CONTROLS AND IN-
TERNAL CHECKS APPLICABLE TO THE DISBURSEMENT OF PAY CHECKS OR
PAY ENVELOPES, SEE CASH DISBURSEMENTS SECTION. FOR PURPOSES OF
THIS INVESTIGATION, BEAR IN MIND THAT VOUCHER AND PAYROLL, AND
CREDITOR AND EMPLOYEE ARE SYNONYMOUS.

24. Are written authorizations required for all:
   (a) Employees added to the payroll?
   (b) Changes in rates of pay?
   (c) Employees taken off the payroll?
   (d) Payroll deductions?

25. Are hours on time records checked against job time tickets or other
    reports of time charges?

   > *Time may be recorded on clock cards, job, or other reports.
   > Basic time records are sometimes further supported by job
   > tickets or foremen's reports of employees' time.*

26. Are quantities produced according to piecework tickets checked
    against:
   (a) Production schedules?
   (b) Actual production?

27. Are sales subject to salesmen's commissions checked or reconciled
    with recorded sales?

28. Are clerical operations in the preparation of payrolls checked, includ-
    ing:
   (a) Extensions and footings of time clock cards, or other time
       records?
   (b) Summarization of piecework tickets?
   (c) Summarization of sales subject to salesmen's commissions?
   (d) Rates of pay used?
   (e) Calculation of gross earnings, including overtime?
   (f) Calculations of deductions from gross earnings?
   (g) Calculation of net pay?
   (h) Preparation of individual pay checks or envelopes?
   (i) Accounting distribution of payroll items?

29. Are net amounts of pay shown by individual payroll checks or en-
    velopes totaled?

   > *For the purpose of payroll payments made in currency, this
   > total may be derived by denominating the payroll, i.e., in cal-
   > culating the aggregate numbers of pennies, nickels, dimes, etc.,
   > and ones, fives, tens, etc., required to make up the various net
   > amounts of pay.*

30. Is the total derived from individual checks or envelopes compared with:
    (a) Total net payroll?
    (b) Amount of the check covering the payroll?
31. Is a payroll clearing account used in maintaining accounting control over payroll charges?

    Gross payroll charges are often debited to a clearing account during the month and distributed to other accounts at the end of the month.

PART II—INTERNAL CHECK

PURCHASE ORDERS:

1. Is the detailed listing of purchase orders, including any firm commitments, prepared by persons independent of:
    (a) Receiving functions?
    (b) Processing of invoices?
    (c) Cash disbursements functions?

    If the original listing is prepared by persons independent of the above duties, the possibility of excluding purchased goods or services from the list will be minimized. The listing may be represented by retained copies of purchase orders. The invoice function referred to is that of originating credits to vendors through invoices or other documents.

2. Do persons independent of persons who prepare purchase orders:
    (a) Insert purchase order numbers?
    (b) Account for the sequence of numbers?

    These procedures tend to prevent the issuance of unauthorized purchase orders to effect acquisition of goods by an employee. Order numbers may be inserted by a printer or other independent person.

3. Are purchase order personnel independent of:
    (a) Processing of invoices?
    (b) Cash disbursements functions?
    (c) Receiving functions?

4. Are individual purchases or purchase orders approved for propriety of prices, terms, quantities, and vendors by supervisory persons other than persons who:
    (a) Make the purchases?
    (b) Prepare purchase orders?

5. Are the following classes of purchases cleared and recorded in the same way as purchases in the ordinary course of business :

   (a) Purchases for employees?
   (b) Purchases from employees?
   (c) Purchases of equipment?
   (d) Purchases of goods shipped direct to processors or customers?

   While these purchases may be only intermittent, their susceptibility to manipulation requires that they receive the same treatment as all other purchases.

RECEIVING REPORTS :

6. Is the detailed listing of receiving reports prepared by persons independent of :

   (a) Purchasing functions?
   (b) Processing of invoices?
   (c) Cash disbursements functions?

7. Do persons independent of persons who prepare receiving reports :

   (a) Insert receiving report numbers?
   (b) Account for the sequence of numbers?

8. Is the list of receiving reports, or retained copies of receiving reports compared with purchase orders and vendors' invoices or other documents originating credits to vendors by persons independent of :

   (a) Purchasing functions?
   (b) Receiving functions?

9. Is receiving personnel independent of :

   (a) Processing of invoices?
   (b) Cash disbursements functions?
   (c) Purchasing functions?

VENDORS' INVOICES :

10. Is the detailed listing of vendors' invoices prepared by persons independent of :

    (a) Receiving functions?
    (b) Purchasing functions?

11. Do persons independent of those who list vendors' invoices account for the sequence of numbers assigned to invoices?

PROCESSING INVOICES AND SUBSTITUTE DOCUMENTS :

12. Are invoices or substitute documents compared with purchase orders or receiving reports by persons independent of :

    (a) Purchasing functions?
    (b) Receiving functions?

13. Are the investigation and correction of differences disclosed by the comparison indicated in Question 12 above carried out by persons independent of :
    (a) Purchasing functions?
    (b) Receiving functions?
    (c) Processing of invoices or substitute documents?

14. Do persons with the independence indicated in Question 13 above and independent of cash disbursements functions :
    (a) Approve accounting distribution of invoices?
    (b) Approve invoices for payment?

15. Do persons with the independence indicated in Question 13 above:
    (a) Number debit memoranda?
    (b) Account for the sequence of debit memorandum numbers?
    (c) Approve debit memoranda for returned merchandise and damage claims?

16. Is the detailed listing of processed invoices (vouchers) prepared by persons independent of :
    (a) Purchasing functions?
    (b) Receiving functions?
    (c) Cash disbursements functions?
    (d) Posting of general ledger accounts?

17. Are unpaid items in the voucher register compared with the general ledger control by an employee independent of those who:
    (a) Record cash disbursements?
    (b) Process invoices or substitute documents?

18. Does a person independent of the processing and entering of invoices or substitute documents :
    (a) Reconcile vendors' statements with reported liabilities?
    (b) Approve adjustments of recorded liabilities?

PAYROLLS:

19. Are individual employment records maintained by persons independent of those who:
    (a) Authorize payroll changes?
    (b) Prepare payrolls?
    (c) Distribute payroll payments?

20. Do persons with the independence indicated above periodically compare payrolls with employment records for:
    (a) Name?
    (b) Rate?
    (c) Authorizations for deductions?

21. Do persons with the independence indicated in Question 19 above periodically compare:

    (a) Hours worked with payroll hours?

    (b) Quantities produced with production paid for?

    (c) Sales bases with commissions paid?

ACCRUED LIABILITIES

INTRODUCTION

Included in this category are the following:

Taxes, wages, commissions, coupons, vacation pay, interest, royalties, legal and professional fees, rework product service and guaranty, and policy reserves of insurance companies.

PART I—INTERNAL ACCOUNTING CONTROL

1. Are detailed records of accrued liabilities:

    (a) Maintained?

    (b) Reconciled periodically with the general ledger control accounts?

2. Have specific responsible employees been assigned the duty of reviewing accrual accounts by:

    (a) Periodically reviewing current entries?

    (b) Periodically reviewing balances?

    (c) Checking contracts, agreements, and other documents and sources to determine whether additional accruals should be provided?

       Tax calendars, tickler files, and other devices are frequently employed.

3. Are charges against accrual accounts arising from sources other than cash disbursements approved by designated persons?

4. Are disbursements of cash which are charged against accrual accounts subjected to the regular routines covering the payment of vouchers?

PART II—INTERNAL CHECK

1. Are the persons who maintain detailed records of accrued liabilities independent of:

    (a) Cash functions?

(b) Voucher functions?

(c) General ledger functions?

2. Are reconciliations of balances in the detailed records of accrued liabilities with general ledger controls prepared or checked periodically by persons independent of :

(a) General ledger functions?

(b) Those who maintain detailed records?

3. Do persons with the independence indicated in Question 1 and other than those who maintain detailed records :

(a) Approve charges in the accrued liability accounts that arise from sources other than cash disbursements?

(b) Approve credits in the accrued liability accounts that arise from sources other than cash receipts or charges to customers?

(c) Periodically review entries in the accrued liability accounts?

(d) Periodically review balances in the accrued liability accounts?

(e) Check contracts, agreements, and other documents and sources to determine whether accruals should be provided?

DEFERRED CREDITS

INTRODUCTION

Does the company:

(a) Bill or collect in advance for services to be rendered partially or wholly in future accounting periods?

The obligation to perform future services may arise in connection with subscriptions to periodicals, maintenance and service contracts, tickets sold by transportation or amusement companies, rents, or utilities service billed in advance.

(b) Defer to a future accounting period the gross profit on incomplete construction contracts or on the uncollected portion of instalment sales?

(c) Have unamortized premium on bonds sold?

(d) Have other types of deferred credits (describe)?

PART I—INTERNAL ACCOUNTING CONTROL

1. Are detailed records of deferred credits :

(a) Maintained?

(b) Reconciled periodically with the general ledger control account?

2. Have specific responsible employees been assigned the duty of reviewing deferred credit accounts by:

    (a) Periodically reviewing current entries?

    (b) Periodically reviewing balances?

    (c) Checking sales contracts, agreements, and other documents and sources to determine whether deferred credits are involved?

3. Are charges against deferred credit accounts other than regular transfers to income approved by designated persons?

4. Are disbursements of cash which are charged against deferred credit accounts subjected to the regular routines covering the payment of vouchers?

PART II—INTERNAL CHECK

1. Are the persons who maintain detailed records of deferred credits independent of:

    (a) General ledger functions?

    (b) Cash functions?

    (c) Voucher functions?

2. Are reconciliations of balances in the detailed records of deferred credits with general ledger controls prepared or checked periodically by persons independent of:

    (a) General ledger functions?

    (b) Those who maintain detailed records?

3. Do persons with the independence indicated in Question 1 and other than those who maintain detailed records approve the following entries in deferred credit accounts:

    (a) Charges that arise from sources other than cash disbursements?

    (b) Credits that arise from sources other than cash receipts or charges to customers?

4. Do persons with the independence indicated in Question 3:

    (a) Periodically review entries in the deferred credit accounts?

    (b) Periodically review balances in the deferred credit accounts?

    (c) Check sales contracts, agreements, and other documents and sources to determine whether deferred credits are involved?

CAPITAL STOCK

PART I—INTERNAL ACCOUNTING CONTROL

1. Does the company employ for each class of stock an independent:
   (a) Transfer agent?
   (b) Registrar?
   (c) Dividend paying agent?

CLASSES OF STOCK SERVICED BY INDEPENDENT AGENTS:

2. Are reports of the number of shares of stock outstanding:
   (a) Received periodically from the transfer agent?
   (b) Received periodically from the registrar?
   (c) When received, reconciled with general ledger control accounts?

CLASSES OF STOCK NOT SERVICED BY INDEPENDENT AGENTS:

3. Blank certificates:
   (a) Are they and the related stubs prenumbered?
   (b) Are the numbers accounted for?
   (c) Are they in the custody of a responsible employee?

4. Are the officers who may sign stock certificates designated by the Board of Directors?

5. Are stock certificates to be issued accompanied by the certificates that they are to replace when presented for:
   (a) Signature?
   (b) Countersignature?

6. Is a stockholders' ledger for each class of stock:
   (a) Maintained?
   (b) Reconciled periodically with the general ledger control account?
   (c) Reconciled periodically with the stock certificate book?

7. Are dividend checks:
   (a) Drawn on a bank account used only for that purpose?
   (b) Compared with stockholders' ledger before mailing?
   (c) Reconciled in total with the liability computed on the basis of the general ledger stock account?
   (d) If unclaimed, redeposited in the company's regular bank account and credited to an appropriate liability account?

8. Is a designated employee responsible for attaching proper tax stamps to canceled certificates or stubs?

PART II—INTERNAL CHECK

CLASSES OF STOCK NOT SERVICED BY INDEPENDENT AGENTS:

1. Does company procedure require the signatures of two officials to validate stock certificates?

2. If two signatures are required, are the signers independent of each other?

3. Is the reconciliation of the stockholders' ledger or reports of the transfer agent or registrar with the general ledger control account and with the stock certificate book prepared or checked periodically by a person independent of:
   (a) Cash functions?
   (b) Those who maintain the stockholders' ledger?
   (c) General ledger functions?
   (d) Those who maintain the stock certificate book?

4. Are unused certificates or certificate books examined periodically by someone other than the custodian for possible unauthorized extractions?

5. Are surrendered certificates:
   (a) Returned to an employee other than the one who maintains the detailed record?
   (b) Examined for proper endorsement?
   (c) Effectively canceled?
   (d) Reattached to the related stubs?

6. Are the following functions performed by different persons:
   (a) Stock:
       (1) Custodianship of blank certificates and maintenance of the stock certificate book?
       (2) Signing or countersigning of certificates?
       (3) Maintenance of stockholders' ledger?
       (4) Recording and accounting for sequence of numbers?
   (b) Dividends:
       (1) Preparation and recording of checks?
       (2) Signing and mailing of checks?
       (3) Bank reconciliations?

TREASURY STOCK CERTIFICATES:

7. Are treasury stock certificates:
   (a) Registered in company's name?
   (b) Physically segregated from other certificates?

REVENUE OTHER THAN FROM SALES AND OPERATIONS

INTRODUCTION

Does client derive revenue from:

(a) Interest?
(b) Dividends?
(c) Dividends from subsidiaries or affiliates?
(d) Rents?
(e) Royalties?
(f) Sales of assets acquired for investment?
(g) Casual sales of fixed assets?
(h) Receipt of contributions?
(i) Levying taxes?

> *The kind of business in which the enterprise is engaged determines whether revenue of the types listed above is merely incidental (other) income or, as with investment companies and charitable organizations, the principal source of income.*

PART I—INTERNAL ACCOUNTING CONTROL

1. Are receivable accounts provided for:

    (a) Dividends on investments?
    (b) Interest on investments and notes receivable?
    (c) Rents on properties owned or leased?
    (d) Royalties on patents and copyrights?
    (e) Pledges of future contributions?
    (f) Legacies and bequests?
    (g) Taxes levied?

    > *More effective accounting control may result if accrual accounts are provided for expected revenue.*

2. Are budgets prepared for expected revenue from:

    (a) Interest?
    (b) Dividends?
    (c) Rents?
    (d) Royalties?
    (e) Contributions?
    (f) Income from taxation?

3. Are schedules comparing actual revenue with budgeted figures:

    (a) Prepared periodically?

    (b) Reviewed by a responsible employee?

4. Is interest and dividend income checked:

    (a) By computation?

    (b) By reference to a published investment service (dividends and contingent interest)?

5. Are receipts of income from investments posted to the detailed investment record?

> *Such posting provides an earnings history for each asset and facilitates review to determine that all income receivable has been received. When investment income accrues regularly and accrual accounts are used (frequently for interest and rents), these objectives may be accomplished negatively, i.e., posting only income accrued but not received to the detailed records.*

6. Are deductions, such as agents' commissions and dividend taxes withheld from revenue before receipt by client:

    (a) Checked mathematically?

    (b) Charged to an expense account?

    (c) Approved by a responsible employee?

7. Are claims in support of disbursements for dividends or interest on securities registered in the client's name but owned by others:

    (a) Obtained?

    (b) Approved by a responsible employee?

8. Sales of investments or fixed assets:

    (a) Are the terms of sale checked to the documents authorizing the sale (resolution of directors or approved disposal request)?

    (b) Does a responsible employee review the computations of profits and losses?

9. Does a responsible employee approve the accounting for receipts of dividends from affiliates, dividends in arrears, interest in default, dividends in kind, and payments by mortgagors?

> *Such items are frequently partially or entirely a return of capital. The approval of the accounting is frequently embodied in an approved amortization table indicating the apportionment between principal and income.*

10. Are schedules of delinquent items:

    (a) Prepared periodically?

    (b) Reviewed by a responsible employee?

11. Is approval of a designated official required for:
    (a) Writing off (or dropping) delinquent pledges of contributions?
    (b) Compromising penalties or interest on delinquent items?

12. Are schedules of all investments showing income received, if any:
    (a) Prepared periodically?
    (b) Reviewed by a responsible official?

13. Are statements of income, the amount of which depends on the operations of persons not controlled by the client, such as royalties and percentage rentals:
    (a) Received periodically from the licensee or tenant?
    (b) Reviewed by an employee who is qualified to estimate potential earnings under such agreements?
    (c) Checked periodically to records of the licensee or tenant?

14. Are copies of wills and related inventory listings obtained in support of amounts and terms of legacies and bequests?

15. Contributions, legacies, and bequests:
    (a) Are they acknowledged?
    (b) Are official receipts issued?
    (c) Are detailed lists of contributions published?

16. Before being issued, are acknowledgments or official receipts checked to entries in the accounting records?

PART II—INTERNAL CHECK

1. Are the persons who check the computation of dividend and interest income independent of those who:
    (a) Have custody of the securities?
    (b) Handle cash receipts?

2. Do persons other than the persons who actually receive contributions:
    (a) Check acknowledgments or official receipts to entries in the accounts?
    (b) Send out the acknowledgments or official receipts?
    (c) Approve the write-off of delinquent pledges?

INDEX

A

I